CW01187387

WELSH INTERNATIONAL MATCHES

1881 – 2000

WELSH INTERNATIONAL MATCHES
1881 – 2000

HOWARD EVANS

Mainstream Publishing
EDINBURGH AND LONDON

Copyright © Howard Evans, 1999
All rights reserved
The moral right of the author has been asserted

First published in Great Britain in 1999 by
MAINSTREAM PUBLISHING COMPANY (EDINBURGH) LTD
7 Albany Street
Edinburgh EH1 3UG

ISBN 1 84018 215 6

No part of this book may be reproduced or transmitted in any form or by any means without written permission from the publisher, except by a reviewer who wishes to quote brief passages in connection with a review written for insertion in a magazine, newspaper or broadcast

A catalogue record for this book is available from the British Library

Typeset in Garamond
Printed and bound in Great Britain by Butler and Tanner

CONTENTS

Acknowledgements	7
Foreword by Ieuan Evans	9
Introduction	10
Points-scoring System	12
FIVE NATIONS	13
England	14
France	64
Ireland	97
Scotland	144
OTHER INTERNATIONAL MATCHES	189
Australia	190
New Zealand	201
South Africa	212
Canada	220
Fiji	222
Italy	224
USA	227
Argentina	231
France – Non Championship	234
Namibia	236
Romania	238
Tonga	240
Western Samoa	242

Zimbabwe	244
Barbarians	246
Japan	248
NZ Maoris	249
NZ Army	250
WORLD CUP	251
1987	252
1991	256
1995	258
1999	262
Statistics	267
Welsh International Players	284

ACKNOWLEDGEMENTS

The author and Rugby Vision Ltd gratefully acknowledge several written and photographic sources in the preparation of this book. Numerous volumes have been written on various aspects of Welsh rugby over the years and these have been invaluable in updating and rewriting Welsh rugby records. We thank them all.

We are also indebted to Ieuan Evans for his contribution at the beginning of the publication and wish him well during his retirement and parenthood.

For the photographs, we are indebted to the *Western Mail* and the library staff, as well as the Huw Evans Photographic Agency in Cardiff. Tim Auty, as usual, was not only a tremendous source of information, but helped by supplying us with a few 'lost' photographs; thanks also to Josie Rowles of Hills Welsh Press.

Lastly, but by no means least, a personal thanks to researcher Owen Davies and, of course, the author, Howard Evans. There is little in Welsh rugby which escapes his notice, whether it be the triumphs and tribulations of Division 4 West or those of the international stage. He can tell you the precise rugby records from Waunarlwydd to Waikato, but don't ask him for directions to either!

The reward for a lifelong devotion to rugby records and statistics is this publication.

Martyn Williams
Editor, Rugby Vision Ltd

FOREWORD

1999 was a momentous one for Wales, though I regard it with mixed feelings. Announcing my retirement from a game which has been such a huge part of my life was an understandable wrench. It does, however, allow me in my old age to wallow in memories, both good and bad.

For my own country of Wales, it is almost a new beginning. The fourth Rugby World Cup was hosted by us, and we saw to it that such a prestigious event had a worthy stage – the new Millennium Stadium, Cardiff Arms Park. To the challenge of welcoming the world of rugby to Wales, we responded with a red carpet which extended to all six continents.It is my sincere hope that those who visited Wales fully realised what the game of rugby means to us, and has meant to us over the years. It has been an integral part of our culture, society and recent history.

Not all of us are convinced by the 'William Webb Ellis having a fine disregard' theory about the game's invention. The game of 'Cnapan' in the seventeenth century, a mad tussle for a huge ball between two Pembrokeshire coastal villages, sounds far more plausible. Myth? Legend? Perhaps, but so much of Welsh rugby history is shrouded in legendary mist.

At least my first meeting with Welsh legends was a reality. My baptism as a spectator in the Arms Park was as an eight-year-old where I witnessed that game between the 1973 Barbarians and New Zealand. What impression do you imagine it left on me to watch Phil Bennett, Gareth Edwards, Tommy David, J.P.R., John Dawes, Derek Quinnell and John Bevan in those famous black-and-white hoops? It was profound.

But legends are not confined to those household names of the '70s. The game in Wales, and of Wales, has been played for 118 years. A period of great games, great names, huge success and, of course, major disappointments. Some of the bar tales may well have been embellished over the years, but then that is part of rugby folklore. Those which are not disputed are rugby records, even if some of them do cause disruptive debates. Some rugby players will tell you that they are not aware of records, which may be true.

As for me, wearing the cherished red jersey (though these days there are a variety of colours available through most major outlets!) in front of the unwavering and unstinting support of the Welsh public has been a hugely humbling and immensely rewarding experience – all this sometimes with, and in front of, heroes present and past.

To represent your country in whatever sport is the ultimate experience, but it's even better when you happen to be a Welshman and a rugby player. I have had the privilege of leading my country on to the field of dreams, a memory recorded here in this book and embedded even more vividly in my mind. So I am indebted to the author Howard Evans, his researcher Owen Davies, Rugby Vision Ltd and Mainstream Publishing for putting matters right in this invaluable publication. It's a must for all retired players like myself!

Cyhoeddiad i ddechrau a setlo dadleuon yw hwn. Fe fydd e'n feibl poblogaidd i chwaraewyr, newyddiadurwyr a disgyblion o'r bêl hir-gron a cwmni da i lyfrgell y campau yng Nghymru.

Ieuan Evans

INTRODUCTION

Rugby has always fascinated me, particularly the history of rugby football, both union and league. This was partly due to having an uncle who played both codes at international level and a father who was determined that I should follow in his footsteps to Cardiff High School. One of the biggest thrills has been to visit former players, pre- and post-war, and listen to their stories – stories you can't read in any book. It was especially enjoyable to be in the company of men such as Harry Bowcott, Sid Hinam, Albert Fear, Walter Vickery and Wickham Powell but, most of all, my hero Wilfred Wooller. I have been privileged to meet post-war players such as Bleddyn Williams, Jack Matthews, Clem Thomas, Ken Jones, Ossie Williams, Paul Thorburn, Barry John, Ieuan Evans, Phil Bennett, Rupert Moon, John Dawes, Chico Hopkins, Tony Copsey, Mike Rayer and Allan Martin – wonderful players and, more importantly, they are rugby men through and through. To all the 975 players who played in the 487 matches and totalled 7,545 appearances in the red (occasionally green) jersey – thanks. I just wish I had been good enough! I, personally, would split the matches into the following eight eras:

The Early Years 1881–99

Though Scotland played England in 1871, the story of international rugby for Wales started in 1881 against England, with matches against Scotland and Ireland to follow in the following two years. The first tourists, the New Zealand Native team, arrived in 1888. 1893 saw the first Triple Crown success, and in 1899 a record crowd of 40,000 attended the Cardiff Arms Park.

   Played 46   Won 16   Drawn 3   Lost 27

The Golden Era 1900–14

The story continues through to the start of the First World War. Wales won the Triple Crown on six occasions, achieved three Grand Slams and defeated the first All Blacks by 3–0 in 1905. Australia were also beaten, but there were two losses to South Africa. The era ended with the 'roughest ever' game in Belfast.

   Played 56   Won 43   Drawn 1   Lost 12

Depths and Heights 1919–39

Defeat by the New Zealand Army side resumed international rugby for Wales after a four-year gap for the First World War. In the era between the two World Wars, the Triple Crown was won on five occasions – but not once by Wales. The invincible All Blacks of 1924 swept through Britain, as did the New South Wales Waratahs. Wales managed to halt the slide by winning at Twickenham in 1933 and defeating the third All Blacks two years later.

   Played 77   Won 35   Drawn   Lost 36

Exciting Welsh Backs 1947–69

An exhilarating period, full of magical players, it began with high spirits after the Second World War, when 'rugger' was very much the name of the game.
   Wales gained the Triple Crown and Grand Slam in 1950 and 1952, though the former was

dampened by the Llandow Air Crash. In 1953, New Zealand were defeated for a third time and a year later, international rugby ended in Swansea. Mud and rain was often the order of the day in Cardiff.

In 1964, Wales made her first major tour and played a Test in South Africa. The Triple Crown was won twice in the late 1960s, but the second of those was quickly soured by two defeats in New Zealand.

Played 104   Won 55   Drawn 9   Lost 40

Up and Under Here We Go 1970–1987

The '70s was the era of the Pontypool front row, 'J.P.R.', Gareth, Gerald, Barry, Phil and many other great players. Youngsters were thrilled by these unpaid heroes. It was also the time of Max Boyce, the 'Outside Half Factory' and 'The Green, Green Grass of Home'. The decade brought three Grand Slams and five Triple Crowns. A world-record crowd of 104,000 saw Wales lose at Murrayfield in 1975, and defeats were suffered again to South Africa and New Zealand even though Andy Haden 'dived' at the Arms Park in 1978. The '80s began with Paul Ringer taking an 'early bath' against England. New faces emerged such as Holmes, Norster, Ieuan, Jonathan and Paul Thorburn – who landed a 'howitzer' at the Arms Park against Scotland.

Played 86   Won 51   Drawn 4   Lost 31

A Global Game 1987–95

Wales achieved a creditable third place in the inaugural World Cup of 1987 but failed to pass the group stage in both the 1991 and 1995 tournaments. In other matches, New Zealand (twice) and Australia both inflicted 50 point-plus defeats, though Wales did manage to crush Portugal by 102–11 in Lisbon.

Played 70   Won 32   Drawn 1   Lost 37

The Professional Era Begins 1995–98.

On 27 August 1995, the game of rugby union was changed forever by a Welshman. Vernon Pugh, QC, Chairman of the International Rugby Board, declared, 'Rugby will become an open game.' Players for the first time could legitimately receive payment for playing. Despite the return south of rugby league defectors Gibbs, Young, Bateman and Jonathan Davies, professionalism did little to alter the continual decline by Wales. Kevin Bowring coached for 29 of these matches, but resigned after a 51–0 demolition by France at Wembley, where Wales played while the new Millennium Stadium home was being constructed. Further humiliation, this time inflicted by South Africa in Pretoria, marked the lowest point to date at 96–13.

Played 32   Won 16   Drawn 0   Lost 16

A Corner Turned? 1998–99

At long last there came a revival in the spirit and fortunes of Welsh rugby, mostly brought about by the installation of a Kiwi – Graham Henry, the former Auckland coach. He did not impose mass sackings of players, but he did introduce fellow countrymen Shane Howarth and Brett Sinkinson to the side. Many in Wales had not wanted a new stadium, but its opening on 26 June 1999 represented a new dawn that would hopefully culminate in winning the World Cup final of 2003.

Played 16   Won 11   Drawn 0   Lost 5

POINTS-SCORING SYSTEM

Until the 1890–91 season, there was no universally accepted system of points values, so none were awarded. International matches were decided by scoring more goals than the opponent, that is, by kicking conversions after scoring tries, by drop-kicking a goal or by kicking a goal from a mark. A goal of any description was deemed to be worth three tries.

In 1890–91, however, the Four Home Unions' International Board agreed to introduce a scoring system whereby a try was worth one point; a conversion of the try, or a penalty, was worth two points; a drop goal and a goal from a mark was worth three points.

Although the laws of rugby union have frequently changed, the points system for internationals has been relatively stable since the first four seasons of experimentation.

SEASON	POINTS SYSTEM CHANGES			
1890–91	T: 1 point	C: 2 points	P: 2 points	DG & goal from mark: 3 points
1891–92	T: 2 points	C: 3 points		
1892–93			P: 3 points	DG & goal from mark: 4 points
1893–94	T: 3 points	C: 2 points		
1905–06				Goal from mark: 3 points
1948–49				DG: 3 points
1971–72	T: 4 points			
1992–93	T: 5 points			

Scoring: T=try C=conversion P=penalty goal DG=drop goal.
(*Welsh début +captain)

FIVE NATIONS

This section includes all matches played against England, France, Ireland and Scotland except the World Cup matches against England in 1987 and Ireland in 1987 and 1995, which are included in the World Cup chapter. France joined the Championship in 1910, though they were to drop out from 1931 to 1939 due to accusations of professionalism. The matches against England in 1881 and Ireland in 1882 were played before the Championship became official. The non-championship matches against France in 1991, 1996 and 1999 are not featured in this chapter.

ENGLAND

England v Wales

Richardson's Field, Blackheath. 19 February 1881
(No points were awarded until 1891)

England won by 7 goals, 6 tries, 1 drop goal to nil

Though it is recognised as the first international match played by Wales, the match took place three weeks before the WRU (Welsh Rugby Union) was formed. It was hardly a representative Welsh team. It was chosen by Richard Mullock, first honorary secretary, treasurer and referee, and it became known as 'Mullock's private team'. It was skippered by the Australian-born James Bevan, who had played for Cambridge in four varsity matches and later became the father of 13 children. Strangely, ten of the Welsh side were never to appear again with the exception, among others, of Charles Newman, who won a Cambridge Blue in 1882 and went on to gain ten caps. Edward Treharne, a teenager, was believed to have been still a schoolboy at Cowbridge Grammar School. Wing Richard Summers said: 'We played in ordinary, light walking boots with a bar of leather across the sole to help us swerve. Jerseys fitted high at the neck with serge blue knickers fastened below the knee with four or five buttons. We changed at The Princess of Wales public house nearby.' The left-foot kicking of Lennard Stokes confused Wales with Harry Vassall, a late selection, scoring three tries on his début; George Burton, a forward, scored four. England had only two new caps in what was their 18th international match.

The beginnings: Wales pictured in their very first match – against England at Blackheath on 19 February 1881. *Back row*: W.D. Phillips, G.F. Harding, H. Mullock (Hon. Sec.), F.S. Purdon, G. Darbishire, E. Treharne, R.G.D. Williams. *Seated*: T.A. Rees, E. Peake, A.J. Bevan (capt.), B.E. Girling, B.B. Mann. *Front row*: L. Watkins, C.H. Newman, E.J. Lewis, R.H.B. Summers. (© *Western Mail & Echo*)

England T.W. Fry (Queen's House); +L. Stokes (Blackheath), R. Hunt (Preston Grasshoppers/Manchester); H.H. Taylor (Blackheath), H.T. Twynam (Richmond); H.Vassall, A.Budd, G.W. Burton (Blackheath), C.W.L. Fernandes (Leeds), E.T. Gurdon, C. Gurdon (Richmond), W. Hewitt (Queen's House), C.P. Wilson (Marlborough Nomads), H.C. Rowley (Manchester), H. Fowler (Walthamstow).
T: George Burton 4, Harry Vassall 3, Bob Hunt, Henry Taylor, 'Jimmy' Budd, Charles Fernandes, Campbell Rowley, Henry Twynam.
C: Lennard Stokes 6, Hunt.
DG: Hunt.

Wales *C.H. Newman (Cambridge U/Newport), *R.H.B. Summers (Haverfordwest); *+J.A. Bevan (Cambridge U), *E. Peake (Oxford U/Chepstow), *L. Watkins (Oxford U/Llandaff), *E.J. Lewis (Cambridge U/Llandovery); *R.D.G.Williams (Cambridge U/ Newport), *T.A. Rees (Oxford U/Llandovery), *F.T. Purdon, *G.F. Harding (Newport), *B.E. Girling, *B.B. Mann, *W.D. Phillips (Cardiff), *G. Darbishire (Bangor), *E. Treharne (Pontypridd).
Referee: Arthur G. Guillemard (England) – RFU President.

Wales v England

St Helen's, Swansea. 16 December 1882

England won by 2 goals, 4 tries to nil

Once again England proved too strong in what was accepted as the first championship match to be played and also the first home match for Wales. Despite having a Welsh referee in control, England won comfortably and Australian Gregory Wade, the first of many overseas players to appear for England, scored three tries on his début. He would not have played if a forward, Philip Newton, had not withdrawn. Blackheath forward Harry Vassall wanted his clubmate Wade selected. The Australian played 8 matches, all ending in victories for England. A barrister and politician, he later became premier of New South Wales. Try-scorer Robert Henderson was later knighted.

Wales +C.P. Lewis (Llandovery), *D.H. Bowen (Llanelli); W.B. Norton, J.A. Clare (Cardiff), *D.Gwynn (Swansea); C.H. Newman (Newport), E. Treharne (Pontypridd); *T.H. Judson (Llanelli), F.T. Purdon, G.L.B. Morris (Swansea), T.J.S. Clapp (Nantyglo),*A. Cattell (Llanelli), G.F. Harding, R. Gould, T.B. Jones (Newport).

England A.S. Taylor (Blackheath); C.G. Wade, A.M. Evanson (Richmond), W.N. Bolton (Blackheath); Alan Rotherham (Richmond); J.H. Payne (Broughton); +E.T. Gurdon (Richmond); H.G. Fuller (Bath), W.M. Tatham (Oxford U), R.S. Kindersley (Exeter), G.T. Thomson (Halifax), C.S. Wooldridge, R.S.F. Henderson, G. Standing, H. Vassall (Blackheath).
T: Gregory Wade 3, George Thomson, Robert Henderson, Wilf Bolton.
C: Arthur Evanson 2.
Referee: D. Herbert (Wales).

England v Wales

St John's Ground, Cardigan Fields, Leeds. 5 January 1884

England won by 1 goal, 2 tries to 1 goal

Only 2,000 spectators were present as Wales lost again, but they scored for the first time against England when three-quarter Charles Allen, the son of the manager of the *Manchester Guardian*, went over. William Gwynn followed his younger brother David to win a cap but they never appeared together in an international match. William went on to become secretary of the WRU and was an International Board representative. Welsh pole vault champion Charles Taylor played on the wing and in 1915 he became the first Welsh international to be killed in the First World War, when he was struck by gunfire on board HMS *Tiger* at the Battle of the Dogger Bank. On a very wet day, England's best score came when Ireland-born 'Baby' Bolton ran 75 yards to send Alan Rotherham over.

England H.B. Tristram (Durham); W.N. Bolton (Blackheath), C.E. Chapman (Cambridge U), C.G. Wade; Alan Rotherham, H.T. Twynam (Richmond); +E.T. Gurdon; C. Gurdon (Richmond), H.G. Fuller (Bath), C.J.B. Marriott, C.S. Wooldridge, R.S.F. Henderson (Blackheath), W.M. Tatham, E.L. Strong (Oxford U), J.T. Hunt (Preston Grasshoppers/Manchester).
T: Gregory Wade, Alan Rotherham, Henry Twynam.
C: Wilf Bolton.

Wales C.P. Lewis (Llandovery); *C.P. Allen (Beaumaris/Oxford U), W.B. Norton (Cardiff), *C.G. Taylor (Ruabon/Blackheath); +C.H. Newman (Newport); *W.H. Gwynn (Swansea); W.D. Phillips, *J.S. Smith, *H.J. Simpson (Cardiff), T.J.S. Clapp, R. Gould, H.S. Lyne (Newport), G.L.B. Morris, *F.G. Andrews (Swansea), *F.L. Margrave (Llanelli).
T: Charles Allen.

C: Charles Lewis.
Referee: J.A. Gardner (Scotland).

Wales v England

St Helen's, Swansea. 3 January 1885

England won by 1 goal, 4 tries to 1 goal, 1 try.

Tiny Martyn Jordan, nicknamed 'Shorty', was not only one of the smallest men to play for Wales, but he was also the first to score two tries in a match. He may have played against Wales for Ireland the previous year – nobody was ever sure! Among the débutants was Jordan's club colleague, 20-year-old Arthur Gould. Surprisingly picked as a full-back, it was as a centre that he will be remembered. Newport supplied seven of the side, including Arthur's brother, Robert. The referee was the former Wales captain Charles Lewis, who only two matches previously had skippered his country from full-back. He had been elected as a WRU vice-president before being capped and was later Mayor of Llandovery on two occasions.

Wales *A.J. Gould; *H.M. Jordan (Newport), F.E. Hancock (Cardiff), C.G. Taylor (Ruabon/Blackheath); +C.H. Newman (Newport), W.H. Gwynn (Swansea); R. Gould, T.J.S. Clapp, H.S. Lyne, T.B. Jones (Newport), S.J. Goldsworthy, *E.S. Richards (Swansea), J.S. Smith, *L.C. Thomas (Cardiff), *E.M. Rowland (Lampeter).
T: Martyn Jordan 2.
C: Arthur Gould.

England H.B. Tristram (Durham); J.J. Hawcridge (Bradford), A.E. Stoddart (Blackheath), C.G. Wade (Richmond); Alan Rotherham (Richmond); J.H. Payne (Broughton); +E.T. Gurdon (Richmond), R.S. Kindersley (Exeter), E.D. Court, R.S.F. Henderson (Blackheath), H.J. Ryalls (New Brighton), F. Moss (Broughton), A.T. Kemble (Liverpool), G. Harrison (Hull), A. Teggin (Broughton).
T: Gregory Wade, Dick Kindersley, Henry Ryalls, Alf Teggin, Joe Hawcridge.
C: John Payne.
Referee: Charles P. Lewis (Wales).

England v Wales

Rectory Field, Blackheath. 2 January 1886

England won by 2 tries, 1 goal from mark to 1 goal.

The highlight for Wales was an excellent try by Bill Stadden who was initially included as a reserve. He proved the star of the Welsh backs, as his side distinguished themselves with fine tackling and strong forward play. Billy Douglas, the Cardiff captain in 1886–87, made his début. He later refereed international matches and joined the International Board. Andrew Stoddart thrilled the 6,000 crowd when he landed a goal from halfway after Charles Elliot had claimed a mark. At that time, the marker did not necessarily have to kick. Stoddart's kick was the first of its kind in internationals and he was to captain England at cricket and rugby.

England A.S. Taylor (Blackheath); C.G. Wade (Richmond), R. Robertshaw (Bradford), A.E. Stoddart (Blackheath); Alan Rotherham (Richmond), F. Bonsor (Bradford); +C.J.B. Marriott, G.L. Jeffery, R.E. Inglis, P.F. Hancock (Blackheath), C. Gurdon, W.G. Clibborn (Richmond), E. Wilkinson (Bradford), F. Moss (Broughton), C.H. Elliot (Sunderland).
T: Gregory Wade, Edgar Wilkinson.
Goal from mark: Andrew Stoddart.

Wales D.H. Bowen (Llanelli); C.G. Taylor (Ruabon/Blackheath), A.J. Gould (Newport), *W.M. Douglas (Cardiff); +C.H. Newman (Newport), W.J. Stadden (Cardiff); A.F. Hill, *D.H. Lewis, *G.A. Young (Cardiff), *W.A. Bowen, D. Morgan (Swansea), E.P. Alexander (Cambridge U), R. Gould (Newport), W.H. Thomas (Llandovery/Cambridge U), *E. Roberts (Llanelli).
T: Bill Stadden.
C: Charles Taylor.
Referee: D. Frank Moore (Ireland).

Wales v England

Stradey Park, Llanelli. 8 January 1887

Draw. No score.

The match was eventually played on the Llanelli cricket ground adjoining the east end of Stradey Park as the rugby pitch was semi-frozen. England had annoyed spectators by refusing to play on the rugby pitch and many lost good seats as a result. Despite the falling snow it was a surprisingly good game, despite ending scoreless. It was the last as captain for Rev. Charlie Newman, who moved to a parish near Gateshead. Arthur Gould showed why he was called 'Monkey' as a boy, when he climbed up a post to replace a crossbar.

Wales D.H. Bowen (Llanelli); C.G. Taylor (Ruabon/Blackheath), A.J. Gould (Newport), W.M. Douglas (Cardiff); +C.H. Newman (Newport), *O.J. Evans (Cardiff); E.P. Alexander (Cambridge U), W.H. Thomas

(Llandovery/Cambridge U), D. Morgan, W.A. Bowen (Swansea), *A.F. Bland, *A.J. Hybart (Cardiff), T.J.S. Clapp, R. Gould, *T.W. Lockwood (Newport).

England S. Roberts (Swinton); J. Le Fleming (Blackheath), R. Robertshaw (Bradford), R.E. Lockwood (Dewsbury); +Alan Rotherham (Richmond), F. Bonsor (Bradford); W.G. Clibborn; J.H. Dewhurst (Richmond), N. Spurling, G.L. Jeffery, C.R. Cleveland (Blackheath), H.C. Baker (Clifton), E. Wilkinson, J.L. Hickson (Bradford), R.L. Seddon (Broughton).
Referee: G. Rowland Hill (England).

England v Wales

Crown Flatt, Dewsbury. 15 February 1890

Wales won by 1 try to nil.

This was a famous day in Welsh rugby history, as England were beaten for the first time and the move for the try that won the match was to be outlawed 16 years later. The vital score came from Bill Stadden. He was, in fact, the only local player in either team, as he was a butcher in Dewsbury. He scored two minutes into the second half when he appeared to be gearing up for a long throw into a line-out near the England line. As the forwards backed off, Stadden bounced the ball, regathered himself, and was over. He never appeared again for Wales and committed suicide in Dewsbury at the age of 45 in 1906. Wales fielded only eight forwards to the English nine and won, mainly because, despite the slush, Billy Bancroft was brilliant at full-back. Wales had no new caps while England fielded eight newcomers.

England W.G. Mitchell (Richmond); P.H. Morrison (Cambridge U), J. Valentine (Swinton), +A.E. Stoddart (Blackheath); J. Wright (Bradford), F.H. Fox (Marlborough Nomads); A. Robinson, P.F. Hancock, F. Evershed, R.T.D. Budworth (Blackheath), J.H. Dewhurst (Richmond), S.M.J. Woods (Wellington), J.H. Rogers (Moseley), J.L. Hickson (Bradford), F. Lowrie (Batley).

Wales W.J. Bancroft (Swansea); D.P.M. Lloyd (Llanelli), +A.J. Gould (Newport), R.M. Garrett (Penarth), D. Gwynn (Swansea); C.J. Thomas (Newport), W.J. Stadden; W.E.O. Williams, A.F. Bland, D.W. Evans (Cardiff), J. Hannan (Newport), W.H. Thomas (London Welsh), S. Thomas (Llanelli), W.A. Bowen, J. Meredith (Swansea).
T: Bill Stadden.
Referee: R.D. Rainie (Scotland).

Wales 3 England 7

Rodney Parade, Newport. 3 January 1891
(New points system introduced – see p.12)

England won by 3 tries, 2 cons, 1 try to 1 try, 1 con.

Billy Bowen led Wales in the 12th of his 13 appearances. Clubmate Billy Bancroft had a bad day and the England forwards paved the way for two début tries by Percy Christopherson, one converted. During the interval, lemons and grapes were served. Welsh wing, Tom Pearson, also on his début, responded to score a second-half try. England settled the game with a try by Richard Budworth, who was educated at Christ College, Brecon, and later appeared for London Welsh. In the Welsh pack was Harry Packer, who went on to manage the 1924 British team in South Africa.

Wales W.J. Bancroft (Swansea); *T.W. Pearson, C.S. Arthur (Cardiff), D. Gwynn (Swansea), D.P.M. Lloyd (Llanelli); C.J. Thomas (Newport), H.M. Inglebew (Newport); +W.A. Bowen, W. Rice Evans (Swansea), J. Hannan, *H. Packer (Newport), *P. Bennett (Cardiff Harlequins), *E.V. Pegge (Neath), R.L. Thomas (London Welsh), D.W. Evans (Cardiff).
T: Tom Pearson.
C: Billy Bancroft.

England W.G. Mitchell (Richmond); R.E. Lockwood (Dewsbury), +F.H.R. Alderson (Hartlepool Rvs), P. Christopherson (Blackheath); J. Berry (Tyldesley), W.R.M. Leake (Harlequins); S.M.J. Woods (Wellington), E.G.H. North, R.T.D. Budworth (Blackheath), W.E. Bromet (Tadcaster), J.Toothill, J. Richards (Bradford), T. Kent (Salford), D. Jowett (Heckmondwicke), R.P. Wilson (Liverpool OB).
T: Percy Christopherson 2, Richard Budworth.
C: Fred Alderson 2.
Referee: R.D. Rainie (Scotland).

England 17 Wales 0

Rectory Field, Blackheath. 2 January 1892
(Points system amended – see p.12)

England won by 4 tries, 3 cons to nil.

The absence of the James brothers at half-back led to Penarth scrum-half George Rowles joining clubmate Dickie Garrett in the side. Although his half-back partner, Percy 'Sparrow' Phillips lasted for another five matches, Rowles failed to survive the defeat. England went on to win the Triple Crown without having a point scored against them, though this scoreline slightly flattered them. A crowd of 10,000 watched England score two tries by half-time (one converted) and then two more tries, both of which were converted. In the pack Frank Mills and Arthur Boucher went on to gain 13 caps each and Wallace Watts, one of six Newport players, appeared in 12 matches.

England W.B. Thomson (Blackheath); R.E. Lockwood (Heckmondwicke), +F.H.R. Alderson (Hartlepool Rvs), G.C. Hubbard (Blackheath); C. Emmott, A. Briggs (Bradford); F. Evershed, A. Allport (Blackheath), W. Yiend (Hartlepool Rvs), W.E. Bromet (Tadcaster), W. Nichol (Brighouse Rgs), J. Toothill (Bradford), T. Kent (Salford), J. Pyke (St Helen's Rec), E. Bullough (Wigan).
T: William Nichol, George Hubbard, Fred Alderson, Frank Evershed.
C: Dicky Lockwood 2, Alderson.

Wales W.J. Bancroft (Swansea); R.M. Garrett (Penarth), +A.J. Gould (Newport), W.M. McCutcheon (Swansea), T.W. Pearson (Cardiff); *H.P. Phillips (Newport), *G.A. Rowles (Penarth); R.L. Thomas, C.B. Nicholl (Llanelli), *F.M. Mills, J.T. Deacon (Swansea), T.C. Graham, *A.W. Boucher, *W.H. Watts, J. Hannan (Newport).
Referee: Matthew C. McEwan (Scotland).

Wales 12 England 11

Arms Park, Cardiff. 7 January 1893
(Points system amended – see p.12)

Wales won by 3 tries, 1 con, 1 pen to 4 tries, 1 con.

This was the first Triple Crown-winning season for Wales and it began in fairytale fashion when the players were carried shoulder-high out of the ground after defeating England. The game was almost called off due to a bitter frost, but a Cardiff-committee man, Bill Shepherd, suggested that 'devils' be brought in. Devils was the name given to portable fires used by watchmen on street works. Tons of coal were therefore burned on the pitch, night and day, and blackened patches were left on the grass. Fred Lohden and Howard Marshall gave England the lead with tries, the latter converted by Andrew Stoddart; then Marshall, who was making his début, scored again before Wales replied when Arthur Gould ran splendidly from halfway to score between the posts and Billy Bancroft converted. This was followed by Norman Biggs's try for Wales but Bancroft's kick failed. The magnificent Marshall went in for his hat-trick try and an 11–7 lead. Incredibly, England never

selected him again and he missed a blue at Cambridge through injury. He also toured with the British team in South Africa without playing in a Test. Wales were further hampered when centre Conway Rees broke his collar bone, but Gould's second try cut England's lead to 11–9 and, near the end, Wales were awarded a penalty some 30 yards out and near the touch line. Bancroft refused his skipper's plea for a placed goal and wanted to drop kick. Eventually, Gould threw the ball down in anger. The full-back drop kicked the penalty and shouted to Gould that he had been successful before the ball had even cleared the posts. Many in the crowd thought Wales had lost or drawn, but Bancroft had known the new scoring values and gave Wales the win by way of his drop kick. In any event, WRU secretary and former player, W.H. Gwynn, shouted: 'We've won!'

Wales W.J. Bancroft (Swansea); N.W. Biggs (Cardiff), +A.J. Gould (Newport), J. Conway Rees (Llanelli), W.M. McCutcheon (Swansea); H.P. Phillips, *F.C. Parfitt (Newport); T.C. Graham, J. Hannan, W.H. Watts, H.T. Day, A.W. Boucher (Newport), A.F. Hill (Cardiff), C.B. Nicholl (Llanelli), M. Mills (Swansea).
T: Arthur Gould 2, Norman Biggs.
C: Billy Bancroft.
Pen: Bancroft.

England E. Field (Middlesex W); R.E. Lockwood (Dewsbury), F.H.R. Alderson (Hartlepool Rvs), +A.E. Stoddart; H. Marshall, R.F. de Winton (Blackheath); S.M.J. Woods (Wellington), F. Evershed, F.C. Lohden, P. Maud (Blackheath), J. Toothill (Bradford), T. Broadley (Bingley), H. Bradshaw (Bramley), W.E. Bromet (Tadcaster), J.H. Greenwell (Rockcliff).
T: Howard Marshall 3, Fred Lohden.
C: Andrew Stoddart.
Referee: David S. Morton (Scotland).

England 24 Wales 3

Upper Park, Birkenhead Park. 6 January 1894
(Points system amended – see p.12)

England won by 4 tries, 4 cons, 1 goal from mark to 1 try.

The Newport halves Percy Phillips and Fred Parfitt had enough of the ball but the Welsh backs were disappointing as a whole, with Gould playing badly. England skipper Richard Lockwood lived up to his nickname of 'Little Marvel'. He scored a try and three conversions, but a year later he switched to Wakefield Trinity Rugby League club. The other England wing, Fred Firth, made his début and later proved a popular league player with Halifax.

England J.F. Byrne (Moseley); F. Firth (Halifax), S. Morfitt (West Hartlepool), C.A. Hooper (Middlesex W), +W.E. Lockwood (Dewsbury); C.M. Wells (Harlequins), E.W. Taylor (Rockcliff); J. Toothill (Bradford), H. Bradshaw (Bramley), T. Broadley (Bingley), H. Speed (Castleford), W.E. Tucker, A. Allport (Blackheath), J. Hall (North Durham), F. Soane (Bath).
T: Sam Morfitt, Richard Lockwood, Harry Bradshaw, Edward Taylor.
C: Lockwood 3, Taylor.
Goal from mark: Taylor.

Wales W.J. Bancroft; W.M. McCutcheon (Swansea), +A.J. Gould (Newport), J. Conway Rees (Llanelli), N.W. Biggs (Cardiff); H.P. Phillips, F.C. Parfitt (Newport); F.M. Mills (Swansea), A.F. Hill (Cardiff), D.J. Daniel, C.B. Nicholl (Llanelli), W.H. Watts, A.W. Boucher, T.C. Graham, J. Hannan (Newport).
T: Fred Parfitt.
Referee: J. Aikman Smith (Scotland).

Wales 6   England 14

St Helen's, Swansea. 5 January 1895.

England won by 4 tries, 1 con to 2 tries.

Though England had ten newcomers in the side, they proved far too strong for Wales. In the home pack, débutants Tom Jackson and William Elsey, who scored a try, were never selected again. A crowd of around 18,000 saw Tom Pearson kick on for Elsey to score and, though England levelled, Tom Graham scored the second Welsh try before England finished strongly with three further touchdowns. The Rev. Fred Leslie-Jones, who was educated at Hereford Cathedral School, marked his England début with a try.

Wales W.J. Bancroft (Swansea); T.W. Pearson (Cardiff), *O. Badger (Llanelli), +A.J. Gould, W.L. Thomas (Newport); *S.H. Biggs (Cardiff), *B. Davies (Llanelli); T.C. Graham, A.W. Boucher, W.H. Watts, J. Hannan (Newport), *T.H. Jackson (Swansea), C.B. Nicholl (Llanelli), *W.J. Elsey, F.M. Mills (Cardiff).
T: William Elsey, Tom Graham.

England H. Ward (Bradford); J.H.C. Fegan, W.B. Thomson (Blackheath), F.A. Leslie-Jones (Richmond), E.M. Baker; R.H.B. Cattell (Moseley), E.W. Taylor (Rockcliff); +S.M.J. Woods (Wellington), G.M. Carey, F. Mitchell, W.E. Tucker, H.W. Finlinson (Blackheath), F.O. Poole (Oxford U), C. Thomas (Barnstaple), W.E. Bromet (Richmond).
T: W.B. Thomson, Fred Leslie-Jones, Godfrey Carey, Sam Woods
C: Frank Mitchell.
Referee: J. Aikman Smith (Scotland).

England 25   Wales 0

Rectory Field, Blackheath. 4 January 1896

England won by 7 tries, 2 cons to nil.

England scored seven tries in this huge beating. Wales, however, lost centre Owen Badger after only 15 minutes when he broke his collar bone tackling opposite centre James Valentine, as he ran to send Sam Morfitt over. It was 17–0 at the interval when Arthur Boucher came out to Badger's place. Oddly, both Badger and Valentine joined Swinton Rugby League in 1896, Badger for a £75 down payment and £2.10s. a week. Valentine was killed by lightning eight years later. Sam Morfitt also turned to league in 1897.

England S. Houghton (Runcorn); S. Morfitt (West Hartlepool), J. Valentine (Swinton), E.M. Baker (Moseley), E.F. Fookes (Sowerby Bridge); R.H.B. Cattell (Blackheath), +E.W. Taylor (Rockcliff); G.M. Carey, F. Mitchell, L.F. Giblin (Blackheath), W. Whiteley (Bramley), A. Starks, J.W. Ward, J. Rhodes (Castleford), J. Pinch (Lancaster).
T: Sam Morfitt 2, Richard Cattell 2, Ernest Fookes 2, Frank Mitchell.
C: Jim Valentine, Edward Taylor.

Wales W.J. Bancroft (Swansea); *F.H. Dauncey, +A.J. Gould (Newport), O. Badger, *C.A. Bowen; B. Davies, D. Morgan (Llanelli); H. Packer, W.H. Watts, A.W. Boucher (Newport), A.M. Jenkin (Swansea), E.E. George, F.M. Mills (Cardiff), C.B. Nicholl (Llanelli), *S.H. Ramsay (Treorchy).
Referee: D. Graham Findlay (Scotland).

Wales 11   England 0

Rodney Parade, Newport. 9 January 1897

Wales won by 3 tries, 1 con to nil.

There were no matches for Wales against Ireland and Scotland in 1897, since those countries refused to play, accusing Wales of 'professionalising' Arthur Gould. Newport admirers had contributed to a testimonial fund that not only had the Union's support, but WRU president, Sir John Llewellyn, later presented Gould with the deeds of his house.

The Union flatly denied committing any act of professionalism, but fortunately for them Gould decided to retire. He had packed up before the season began, but his club asked him to stay as captain and, when he did, Wales also picked him as captain. Tom Pearson and Arthur Boucher scored first-half tries on a wet surface after the stronger Welsh forwards had taken charge. There then came a début try by tinplate worker Dan Jones, who never appeared for Wales again. Wales introduced the rugged, so-called 'Rhondda type' forwards with Dick Hellings the most effective of these.

Wales W.J. Bancroft (Swansea); C.A. Bowen (Llanelli), E.G. Nicholls (Cardiff), +A.J. Gould, T.W. Pearson (Newport); S.H. Biggs (Cardiff), *Dan Jones (Aberavon); H. Packer, A.W. Boucher (Newport), W. Morris, J. Evans (Llanelli), *R. Hellings (Llwynypia), *F.H. Cornish (Cardiff), D. Evans, *J. Rapps (Penygraig).
T: Tom Pearson, Arthur Boucher, Dan Jones.
C: Billy Bancroft.

England J.F. Byrne (Moseley); E.F. Fookes (Sowerby Bridge), T. Fletcher (Seaton), E.M. Baker, F.A. Byrne (Moseley); C.M. Wells (Harlequins), +E.W. Taylor (Rockcliff); F. Jacob (Cambridge U), R.H. Mangles, W. Ashford, F.M. Stout (Richmond), P.J. Ebdon (Wellington), J.H. Barron (Bingley), R.F. Oakes (Hartlepool Rvs), W.B. Stoddart (Liverpool).
Referee: Joseph T. Magee (Ireland).

England 14 Wales 7

Rectory Field, Blackheath. 2 April 1898

England won by 4 tries, 1 con to 1 try, 1 drop goal.

Viv Huzzey put Wales back into the match after brothers Frank and Percy Stout had scored tries for England. The 21-year-old wing scored a try and then dropped a four-point goal to give Wales a 7–6 lead at the interval. England came back to score two further tries by New Zealander Ernest Fookes. Fookes later switched to rugby league, but returned to union in New Zealand and was selected for the 1905 tour to Britain. He could not travel, however. Referee Joe Magee had played international rugby only two years before with the British team in South Africa.

England +J.F. Byrne (Moseley); E.F. Fookes (Sowerby Bridge), P. Royds (Blackheath), W.L. Bunting, P.W. Stout (Richmond); R.O'H. Livesay (Blackheath), Arthur Rotherham (Richmond); W. Ashford (Exeter), R.F. Oakes (Hartlepool Rvs), F. Jacob, H.W. Dudgeon, F.M. Stout (Richmond), J. Davidson (Aspatria), J.F. Shaw (RNEC Devon), H.E. Ramsden (Bingley).
T: Ernest Fookes 2, Frank Stout, Percy Stout.
C: Fred Byrne.

Wales +W.J. Bancroft (Swansea); H.V.P. Huzzey, E.G. Nicholls, W. Jones (Cardiff), T.W. Pearson (Newport); J.E. Elliot, S.H. Biggs; T. Dobson, F.H. Cornish (Cardiff), W.H. Alexander, R. Hellings (Llwynypia), D.J. Daniel (Llanelli), H. Davies (Swansea), J.G. Boots (Newport), D. Evans (Penygraig).
T: Viv Huzzey.
DG: Huzzey.
Referee: Joseph T. Magee (Ireland).

Wales 26 England 3

St Helen's, Swansea. 7 January 1899.

Wales won by 6 tries, 4 cons to 1 try.

A 25,000 crowd saw Wales win in splendid form, with an astonishing début for Tonypandy-born Willie Llewellyn, just six days after his 21st birthday. He scored four tries in the match from left wing, no player having previously scored more than two for Wales in a match. All six tries came from the wingers, with Bancroft goaling four. The team included another six newcomers, including the outstanding forward Jehoida Hodges and Reg 'Rabbit' Skrimshire, whose best matches were played with the 1903 British team in South Africa where he later played for Western Province. The James brothers were paired after a seven-year absence, but somehow the Welsh selectors never really appreciated them and neither played for Wales again. David James turned professional six weeks later.

Wales +W.J. Bancroft (Swansea); H.V.P. Huzzey, E.G. Nicholls (Cardiff), *R.T. Skrimshire (Newport), *W.M. Llewellyn (Llwynypia); E. James, D. James (Swansea); *J. Blake, T. Dobson (Cardiff), W.H. Alexander (Llwynypia), *F.G. Scrine (Swansea), *A.B. Brice (Aberavon), D.J. Daniel (Llanelli), *J.J. Hodges (Newport), *W.J. Parker (Swansea).
T: Willie Llewellyn 4, Viv Huzzey 2.
C: Billy Bancroft 4.

England H.T. Gamlin (Devonport Albion); R. Forrest (Wellington), P.W. Stout (Richmond), P.M.R. Royds (Blackheath), G.C. Robinson (Percy Park); R.O'H. Livesay (Blackheath), +Arthur Rotherham (Richmond); H.W. Dudgeon, F. Jacob, J. Daniell (Richmond),

C.H. Harper (Exeter), W. Mortimer (Marlborough Nomads), G.R. Gibson (Northern), J. Davidson (Aspatria), R.F. Oakes (Hartlepool Rvs).
T: George Robinson.
Referee: A.J. Turnbull (Scotland).

England 3 Wales 13

Kingsholm, Gloucester. 6 January 1900

Wales won by 2 tries, 2 cons, 1 pen to 1 try.

This day at Kingsholm marked the beginning of a fabulous run of success for Wales. They were to win the Triple Crown six times before the First World War. One of the débutants was Billy Trew, who was on the wing but was more at home as outside-half or centre. He scored 11 tries in 29 appearances. Trew scored a début try while the other try came from Dick Hellings, from Llwynypia, but born in Tiverton. He played almost the whole match with a fractured forearm. Dan Rees, George Davies and Louis Phillips formed a new midfield trio that worked surprisingly well. The England skipper Alf Cattell was reported to have complained that one of the Welsh forwards had called him a pig!

England H.T. Gamlin (Devonport Albion); S.F. Cooper, G. Gordon-Smith (Blackheath), A.T. Brettargh (Liverpool OB), E.T. Nicholson (Birkenhead Park); +R.H.B. Cattell (Moseley), G.H. Marsden (Morley); F.J. Bell, R.W. Bell (Northern), W. Cobby (Hull), A. Cockerham (Bradford Olicana), J.W. Jarman (Bristol), S. Reynolds (Richmond), C.T. Scott (Blackheath), J. Baxter (Birkenhead Park).
T: Elliot Nicholson.

Wales +W.J. Bancroft (Swansea); W.M. Llewellyn (Llwynypia), *D. Rees, *G.Davies, *W.J. Trew (Swansea); *L.A. Phillips, G.L. Lloyd (Newport); R. Hellings (Llwynypia), A.B. Brice (Aberavon), W.H. Millar (Mountain Ash), *W.H. Williams (Pontymister), *R. 'Bob' Thomas (Swansea), J.G. Boots, J.J. Hodges (Newport), J. Blake (Cardiff).
T: Billy Trew, Dick Hellings.
C: Billy Bancroft 2.
P: Bancroft.
Referee: A.J. Turnbull (Scotland).

Wales 13 England 0

Arms Park, Cardiff. 5 January 1901

Wales won by 3 tries, 2 cons to nil.

Wales were adjudged to have played poorly, yet they were convincing winners. Tiny John 'Bala' Jones played in his only international. Three years earlier, the WRU had declared him a professional following his move to Devonport, but later reinstated him. His opposite number, 'Katie' Walton, was also appearing in his first international match. Jones had happened to be in the Queens Hotel when scrum-half Louis Phillips appeared there prior to the match. Phillips said that he could not play as 'he could not do justice to himself', thus the selectors turned to the 5'5" Jones. The *South Wales Times* called the match: 'Far below standard. For the closing ten minutes, however, the game was as exciting and as fast as could be wished.'

Wales +W.J. Bancroft (Swansea); W.M. Llewellyn (Llwynypia), E.G. Nicholls (Cardiff), G. Davies, W.J. Trew (Swansea); G.L. Lloyd (Newport), *J. 'Bala' Jones (Aberavon); R. Hellings (Llwynypia), A.B. Brice (Aberavon), W.H. Millar (Mountain Ash), J.G. Boots, J.J. Hodges (Newport), J. Blake (Cardiff), R. Thomas (Swansea), W.H. Williams (Pontymister).
T: Gwyn Nicholls, 'Buller' Williams, Jehoida Hodges.
C: Billy Bancroft 2.

England J.W. Sagar (Cambridge U); E.W. Elliot (Sunderland), +J.T. Taylor (Castleford), E.J. Vivyan (Devonport Albion), C. Smith (Gloucester); E.J. Walton (Castleford), R.O. Schwarz (Richmond); H. Alexander (Birkenhead Park), A.F.C. Luxmore (Richmond), C.T. Scott (Blackheath), N.C. Fletcher (OMT's), D. Graham (Aspatria), C.O.P. Gibson (Northern), E.W. Roberts (RNC Dartmouth), A. O'Neill (Torquay).
Referee: A.J. Turnbull (Scotland).

England 8 Wales 9

Rectory Field, Blackheath. 11 January 1902

Wales won by 2 tries, 1 pen to 2 tries, 1 con.

After being behind at the interval, Wales rallied in the mist and light drizzle of the second half of a tremendously exciting match, in which Gwyn Nicholls skippered for the first time. Strand Jones, who was only selected by a 6–5 committee vote against Bert Winfield, marked his début by creating a try for Rhys Gabe, who was knocked out as he scored. Jones went further by drop-kicking the winning goal that was to decide the championship, when Bernard Oughtred was tricked offside by the wily Dicky Owen when the score was 8–6 to England. Oughtred was one of two English players who contracted typhoid fever during the trip to Dublin in 1903, but he recovered. The other, Reg Forrest, died two months after the match, as did an England committee man. Wales débutants included Teddy Morgan and 'Boxer' Harding, both of whom toured Down Under with the 1904 British team.

England H.T. Gamlin (Devonport Albion); P.L. Nicholas (Exeter), J.E. Raphael (OMT's), J.T. Taylor (Castleford), S.F. Coopper (Blackheath); P.D. Kendall (Birkenhead Park), B. Oughtred (Hartlepool Rvs); +H. Alexander (Birkenhead Park), D.D. Dobson (Newton Abbot), L.R. Tosswill (Exeter), S.G. Williams (Devonport Albion), T.H. Willocks (Plymouth), J. Jewitt (Hartlepool Rvs), G. Fraser (Richmond), J.J. Robinson (Headingley).
T: Denys Dobson, John Robinson.
C: Harry Alexander.

Wales *J. 'Strand' Jones (Llanelli); W.M. Llewellyn (Llwynypia), +E.G. Nicholls (Newport), R.T. Gabe (Llanelli), *E. Morgan (London Welsh); R.H. Jones, R.M. Owen (Swansea); A.B. Brice (Aberavon), J.J. Hodges, J.G. Boots (Newport), *W. Joseph (Swansea), *D. Jones (Treherbert), *W.T. Osborne (Mountain Ash), *A.F. Harding (Cardiff), *N. Walters (Llanelli).
T: Rhys Gabe, Will Osborne.
P: Strand Jones.
Referee: Rupert W. Jeffares (Ireland).

Wales 21   England 5

St Helen's, Swansea. 10 January 1903

Wales won by 5 tries, 3 cons to 1 try, 1 con.

The match belonged to Newport forward Jehoida Hodges, who switched to wing after just 25 minutes when skipper Tom Pearson fell to a heavy tackle from Bert 'Octopus' Gamlin, the England full-back. By half-time, Hodges had crossed the England line three times in a remarkable display and Wales were 21–0 in front and uncatchable. Pearson had to be lured from retirement to skipper the side, since Gwyn Nicholls was injured, and the captain opened the scoring. It was Pearson's first cap for five years and proved to be his last. Dicky Owen, Hodges, Hodges again (from a Rhys Gabe run) and Hodges with a third (from a Strand Jones move) all crossed the England line with a late reply when Denys 'David' Dobson went over. The intrepid Dobson had played for London Welsh and was the first British tourist to be sent off (1904). His hand-off was rated as 'a bit weak' after he was killed by a rhinoceros in Nyassaland at the age of 36! George Travers from Pill Harriers made his début as a hooker and Fred Jowett made his only appearance on the wing, turning professional two years later.

Wales J. 'Strand' Jones (Llanelli); *W.F. Jowett, D. Rees (Swansea), R.T. Gabe (Llanelli), +T.W. Pearson; G.L. Lloyd (Newport), R.M. Owen (Swansea); J.G. Boots, J.J. Hodges (Newport), A.B. Brice (Aberavon), W. Joseph (Swansea), A.F. Harding (Cardiff/London Welsh), D. Jones (Treherbert), W.T. Osborne (Mountain Ash), *G. Travers (Pill Harriers).
T: Jehoida Hodges 3, Tom Pearson, Dicky Owen.
C: Strand Jones 3.

England H.T. Gamlin (Devonport Albion); J.H. Miles (Leicester), J.T. Taylor (Castleford), R.H. Spooner (Liverpool), T. Simpson (Rockcliff); F.C. Hulme (Birkenhead Park), +B. Oughtred (Hartlepool Rvs); R. Bradley, J. Duthie (West Hartlepool), D.D. Dobson (Newton Abbot), G. Fraser (Richmond), R.F.A. Hobbs (Blackheath), P.F. Hardwick (Percy Park), R.D. Wood (Liverpool OB), V.H. Cartwright (Nottingham).
T: Denys Dobson.
C: Jim Taylor.
Referee: Robin Welsh (Scotland).

England 14   Wales 14

Welford Rd, Leicester. 9 January 1904

Draw. England: 3 tries, 1 con, 1 pen. Wales: 2 tries, 2 cons, 1 goal from mark.

Full-back Bert Winfield kicked a magnificent goal from a mark made just inside the English half by forward Will Joseph, a cousin of Dicky Owen, and the game was drawn, though England appeared to be the luckier side. Wales scored two superb tries through their wings, while England, who led 6–0 at the interval, crossed three times despite the fact that wing Edgar Elliot (who scored twice) was considered 'too slow' and never picked again. Wales were unhappy with referee Crawford Findlay after he disallowed a match-winning effort by Teddy Morgan. Owen, who'd been heavily penalised for 'crooked feeds' to the scrum, eventually asked England's Walter Butcher to do the honours. It was an exciting match: Elliott Vivyan missed five goal kicks for England and Scotland-born Treorchy forward Sam Ramsay appeared after an eight-year absence.

England H.T. Gamlin; E.J. Vivyan (Devonport Albion), A.T. Brettargh (Liverpool OB), E.W. Dillon (Blackheath), E.W. Elliot (Sunderland); P.S. Hancock (Richmond), W.V. Butcher (Bristol); C.J. Newbold, B.A. Hill (Blackheath), G.H. Keeton (Richmond), P.F. Hardwick (Percy Park), V.H. Cartwright (Nottingham), N. Moore (Bristol), J.G. Milton (Bedford GS), +F.M. Stout (Richmond).
T: Edgar Elliot 2, A.T. Brettargh.
C: Frank Stout.
P: Herbert Gamlin.

Wales H.B. Winfield (Cardiff); W.M. Llewellyn (Newport), +E.G. Nicholls, R.T. Gabe (Cardiff), E. Morgan (London Welsh); R.H. Jones, R.M. Owen (Swansea); A.F. Harding (London Welsh), J.G. Boots, J.J. Hodges (Newport), A.B. Brice (Aberavon), *D.J. Thomas, W. Joseph (Swansea),*J.W. Evans (Blaina), S.H. Ramsay (Treorchy).
T: Willie Llewellyn, Teddy Morgan.
C: Bert Winfield 2.
Goal from Mark: Winfield.
Referee: J. Crawford Findlay (Scotland).

Wales 25 England 0

Arms Park, Cardiff. 14 January 1905

Wales won by 7 tries, 2 cons to nil.

A centre, George Davies, was at full-back and played a big part in the astonishing seven-try thrashing handed out by Wales. Wing-forward Harry Watkins ran half the length of the field for his try. Despite it being ten months since they last played, Wales had no new faces – Willie Llewellyn again skippered the side. He was captain on five occasions and victorious in four of those matches. A 30,000 crowd saw Wales give England débutant, full-back Sam Irvin, a nightmare. He was never capped again and switched to Oldham Rugby League club soon afterwards.

Wales G. Davies (Swansea); +W.M. Llewellyn (Newport), D. Rees (Swansea), R.T. Gabe (Cardiff), E. Morgan (London Welsh); R.H. Jones, R.M. Owen; W. Joseph (Swansea), G. Travers (Pill Harriers), W. O'Neil (Cardiff), A.F. Harding (London Welsh), D. Jones (Treherbert), J.J. Hodges, C.M. 'Charlie' Pritchard (Newport), H.W. Watkins (Llanelli).
T: Teddy Morgan 2, Willie Llewellyn, Harry Watkins, Dick Jones, Rhys Gabe, Arthur Harding.
C: George Davies 2.

England S.H. Irvin (Devonport Albion); F.H. Palmer (Richmond), J.E. Raphael (OMT's), E.W. Dillon, S.F. Coopper (Blackheath); W.V. Burcher (Bristol), F.C. Hulme (Birkenhead Park); +F.M. Stout (Richmond), J.L. Mathias (Bristol), V.H. Cartwright (Nottingham), B.A. Hill, W.T.C. Cave, C.J. Newbold, W.L.Y. Rogers (Blackheath), T.A. Gibson (Northern).
Referee: C. Lefevre (Ireland).

England 3 Wales 16

Richmond. 13 January 1906.

Wales won by 4 tries, 2 cons to 1 try.

Cliff Pritchard played the 'rover' role to confuse England and débutant Hop Maddock (wrongly called Maddocks) scored the first of his six tries in six matches. Thirteen of the side which had defeated New Zealand took to the field and proved their worth as 'World Champions' with a splendid display. England played Edward Jackett at full-back who, besides being a nude artist's model, was also cycling champion of Britain. He played in the 1908 Olympic match against Australia and provincial rugby in South Africa. He even appeared for Transvaal against Britain.

England E.J. Jackett (Falmouth); A.E. Hind (Leicester), J.A. Raphael (OMT's), H.E. Shewring (Bristol), A. Hudson (Gloucester); R.A. Jago (Devonport Albion), D.R. Gent (Gloucester); +V.H. Cartwright, H.A. Hodges (Nottingham), C.E.L. Hammond (Harlequins), A.L. Kewney (Rockcliff), T.S. Kelly (Exeter), W.A. Mills, G.E. Dobbs (Devonport Albion), E.W. Roberts (RNC, Dartmouth).
T: Arthur Hudson.

Wales H.B. Winfield (Cardiff); *H.T. Maddock (London Welsh), +E.G. Nicholls, R.T. Gabe (Cardiff), E. Morgan (London Welsh); C.C. 'Cliff' Pritchard (Pontypool)-rover back, P.F. Bush (Cardiff), R.M. Owen; W. Joseph (Swansea), G. Travers (Pill Harriers), H.W. Watkins (Llanelli), A.F. Harding (London Welsh), D. Jones (Aberdare), J.J. Hodges, C.M. 'Charlie' Pritchard (Newport).
T: Charlie Pritchard, Jehoida Hodges, Hop Maddock, Teddy Morgan.
C: Bert Winfield 2.
Referee: A. Jardine (Scotland).

Wales 22 England 0

St Helen's, Swansea. 12 January 1907

Wales won by 6 tries, 2 cons to nil.

One month after losing to South Africa, Wales

responded with an excellent win despite having five newcomers in the side. Reg Gibbs was again used as an extra back and, with Rhys Gabe and Billy Trew on either side of him, they set the wings up for four of the six tries. Strangely, it was a small crowd who saw local boy Dicky Owen lead Wales for the first time. His team ran in three tries in either half of the match.

Wales *D. 'Bailey' Davies (Llanelli); J.L. Williams, R.T. Gabe (Cardiff), *J.H. Evans (Pontypool), H.T. Maddock (London Welsh); R.A. Gibbs (Cardiff)-rover back, W.J. Trew, +R.M. Owen (Swansea); G. Travers (Pill Harriers), W. O'Neil, *J.A. Brown (Cardiff), T.H. Evans, *J. Watts (Llanelli), C.M. 'Charlie' Pritchard, *W.H. Dowell (Newport).
T: Johnnie Williams 2, Hop Maddock 2, Reg Gibbs, Jack Brown.
C: Gibbs 2.

England E.J. Jackett (Falmouth); S.F. Coopper (Blackheath), J.G.G. Birkett (Harlequins), H.E. Shewring, F.S. Scott (Bristol); A.D. Stoop (Harlequins), R. Jago (Devonport Albion); +B.A. Hill, F.J.V. Hopley (Blackheath), C.H. Shaw (Moseley), L.A.N. Slocock (Liverpool), W.A. Mills (Devonport Albion), T.S. Kelly (Exeter), W.M. Nanson (Carlisle), J. Green (Skipton).
Referee: John I. Gillespie (Scotland).

England 18 Wales 28

Ashton Gate, Bristol. 18 January 1908.

Wales won by 5 tries, 3 cons, 1 pen, 1 drop goal to 4 tries, 3 cons.

This was the match which few spectators saw, since thick fog covered much of the Bristol City soccer pitch. It did, however, attract 25,000 spectators – much more than saw Llanelli beat Ebbw Vale there in the 1998 Welsh Cup final. Wales won 5-4 on tries. Percy Bush was the star once again, this time with new cap Tommy Vile as his partner. It was often said of Bush that, on his day, he had no superior. Geoffrey 'Khaki' Roberts, who kicked a conversion for England, became a prosecutor at the Nuremburg Trials for the Second World War. Forward Bob Dibble was later to join the All-International side turned out by the Newport club.

England A.E. Wood (Gloucester); D. Lambert, J.G.G. Birkett (Harlequins), W.N. Lapage (Utd Servs), A. Hudson (Gloucester); J. Peters (Plymouth), R.H. Williamson (Oxford U); R. Gilbert, W. Mills (Devonport Albion), F. Boylen, H. Havelock (Hartlepool Rvs), L.A.N. Slocock (Liverpool), C.E.L. Hammond, G.D. Roberts (Harlequins), R. Dibble (Bridgwater Albion).
T: John Birkett 2, Walter Lapage, Rupert Williamson.
C: Alan Wood 2, Geoffrey Roberts.

Wales H.B. Winfield; J.L. Williams, R.T. Gabe (Cardiff), W.J. Trew (Swansea), R.A. Gibbs; P.F. Bush (Cardiff), *T.H. Vile (Newport); A.J. Webb (Abertillery), G. Travers (Pill Harriers), W. O'Neil, J.A. Brown (Cardiff), J. Watts (Llanelli), C.M. 'Charlie' Pritchard (Newport), W.H. Dowell (Pontypool), +A.F. Harding (London Welsh).
T: Rhys Gabe 2, Percy Bush, Billy Trew, Reg Gibbs.
C: Bert Winfield 2, Bush.
P: Winfield.
DG: Bush.
Referee: J.T. Tulloch (Scotland).

Wales 8 England 0

Arms Park, Cardiff. 16 January 1909.

Wales won by 2 tries, 1 con to nil.

After a gap of 25 years, the name Bancroft was once again the first on the sheet for Wales. Jack, eight years younger than his brother Billy, was picked at full-back because Bert Winfield had withdrawn. He was to score 88 points in 18 matches, but achieved only two conversions in five matches against England. Referee John Dallas returned to the Arms Park for the first time since controlling the New Zealand Test of 1905. Only 25,000 saw Wales gain their fifth consecutive win over England, but the Welsh pack, in which Jake Blackmore won his only cap, had to give best to England. Scotland had refused to play England, accusing them of infringing the amateur laws when they supported expenses for touring countries. When they did eventually meet, former Wales skipper Gwyn Nicholls was the referee.

Wales *J. Bancroft (Swansea); J.L. Williams (Cardiff), J.P. 'Jack' Jones (Newport), +W.J. Trew, P. Hopkins; R.H. Jones, R.M. Owen (Swansea); T.H. Evans (Llanelli), G. Travers (Pill Harriers), P.D. Waller (Newport), J.A. Brown (Cardiff), A.J. Webb, *J.H. Blackmore (Abertillery), G. Hayward, W.I. Morgan (Swansea).
T: Phil Hopkins, Johnnie Williams.
C: Jack Bancroft.

England E.J. Jackett (Leicester); B.B. Bennetts (Penzance), E.W. Assinder (Old Edwardians), F.N. Tarr (Leicester), E.R. Mobbs

(Northampton); J. Davey (Redruth), T.G. Wedge (St Ives); +R. Dibble (Bridgwater), A.L. Kewney (Leicester), J.G. Cooper (Moseley), A.D.W. Morris (Utd Servs), W. Johns (Gloucester), E.D. Ibbitson (Headingley), F.G. Handford (Manchester), H. Archer (Guy's Hosp.).
Referee: John D. Dallas (Scotland).

England 11 Wales 6

Twickenham. 15 January 1910.

England won by 2 tries, 1 con, 1 pen to 2 tries.

Wales were stunned by an England score after only 75 seconds at the new Twickenham ground. Adrian Stoop fielded Ben Gronow's kick-off and ran until, just as he was tackled, he passed to wing Ronnie Poulton who cross-kicked for Henry Berry. Dai Gent, Barney Solomon and John Birkett all handled and set off Fred Chapman to dive over for the first try at the ground, handing-off Billy Trew on the way. Both Chapman and Solomon scored on their débuts, but Welsh critics had given England little hope and outside-half Dick Jones was dropped after this game and was not selected again. Joe Pugsley and Henry Jarman had come into the pack, the latter dying 'a hero's death' some time later by throwing himself in front of a runaway coal truck that was hurtling towards a group of children.

England W.R. Johnston (Bristol); F.E. Chapman (Westoe), B. Solomon (Redruth), J.G.G. Birkett, R.W. Poulton; +A.D. Stoop (Harlequins), D.R. Gent (Gloucester); E.L. Chambers (Bedford), W. Johns, H. Berry (Gloucester), L. Haigh (Manchester), H.J.S. Morton, C.H. Pillman (Blackheath), D.F. Smith (Richmond), L.E. Barrington-Ward (Edinburgh U).
T: Fred Chapman, Barney Solomon.
C: Chapman.
P: Chapman.

Wales J. Bancroft (Swansea); R.A. Gibbs (Cardiff), J.P. 'Jack' Jones (Newport), +W.J. Trew, P. Hopkins; R.H. Jones, R.M. Owen (Swansea); A.J. Webb (Abertillery), *J. Pugsley (Cardiff), T.H. Evans (Llanelli), B. Gronow (Bridgend), C.M. 'Charlie' Pritchard, *H. Jarman (Newport), D.J. Thomas, W.I. Morgan (Swansea).
T: Reg Gibbs, Jim Webb.
Referee: John D. Dallas (Scotland).

Wales 15 England 11

St Helen's, Swansea. 21 January 1911

Wales won by 4 tries, 1 pen to 3 tries, 1 con.

Only England came close to halting Wales in 1911 as the home side held on to a 12–11 lead for dear life, before big Joe Pugsley added a fourth unconverted try. Two Newport clubmen – Bob Dibble and Stan Williams – played for England. Williams, born in Rogerstone, had previously been a Welsh reserve, while two further Newport men – Fred Birt and Percy Coldrick – made their Welsh débuts along with Bill Perry, who was not to appear again. Wing Alan Roberts, who scored a try on his début for England, became a captain in the Welsh Regt and died in Anglesey.

Wales J. Bancroft (Swansea); J.L. Williams, W. Spiller (Cardiff), *F.W. Birt (Newport), R.A. Gibbs (Cardiff); +W.J. Trew, R.M. Owen (Swansea); A.J. Webb (Abertillery), J. Pugsley (Cardiff), *A.P. Coldrick (Newport), H. Jarman (Pontypool), *W.J. Perry (Neath), T.H. Evans (Llanelli), D.J. Thomas, W.I. Morgan (Swansea).
T: Reg Gibbs, Ivor Morgan, Billy Spiller, Joe Pugsley.
P: Fred Birt.

England S.H. Williams (Newport); A.D. Roberts (Northern), J.A. Scholfield (Preston Grasshoppers), +J.G.G. Birkett, D. Lambert (Harlequins); A.D. Stoop (Harlequins), A.L.H. Gotley (Blackheath); A.L. Kewney (Leicester), J.A. King (Headingley), R. Dibble (Bridgwater), W.E. Mann, N.A. Wodehouse (Utd Servs), L. Haigh (Manchester), L.G. Brown, C.H. Pillman (Blackheath).
T: Alan Roberts, Alf Kewney, John Scholfield.
C: Douglas Lambert.
Referee: John I. Gillespie (Scotland).

England 8 Wales 0

Twickenham. 20 January 1912

England won by 2 tries, 1 con to nil.

Dicky Owen won his 34th and penultimate cap to set a British record, having surpassed the 33 caps of Billy Bancroft. It was the defending of Billy's younger brother Jack that helped keep the game scoreless until the last quarter, in front of a capacity crowd which included the Prince of Wales. Some of the great three-quarters had now gone, as had the Welsh monopoly on the Triple Crown. Of the five new caps, Howell

Davies and Len Trump were shortly to turn professional.

England W.R. Johnston (Bristol); F.E. Chapman (Westoe), R.W. Poulton, J.G.G. Birkett, H. Brougham; A.D. Stoop (Harlequins), J.A. Pym (Blackheath); +R. Dibble (Newport), N.A. Wodehouse, A.H. MacIlwaine (Utd Servs), J.A. King, J.H. Eddison (Headingley), R.C. Stafford (Bedford), D. Holland (Devonport Albion), C.H. Pillman (Blackheath).
T: Henry Brougham, John Pym.
C: Frank Chapman.

Wales J. Bancroft (Swansea); *D.E.G. Davies, W. Spiller (Cardiff), F.W. Birt (Newport), J.P. 'Jack' Jones (Pontypool); *J.M.C. Lewis (Cardiff), +R.M. Owen (Swansea); A.J. Webb (Abertillery), *H.J. Davies, *G. Stephens (Neath), R. Thomas (Pontypool), A.P. Coldrick, *L.C. Trump, *H. Uzzell (Newport), D.J. Thomas (Swansea).
Referee: J.T. Tulloch (Scotland).

Wales 0 England 12

Arms Park, Cardiff. 18 January 1913

England won by 2 tries, 1 con, 1 drop goal to nil.

England gained their first win at the Arms Park, thanks largely to Pembroke-born outside-half W.J.A. 'Willie' Davies, who had made his début in England's loss to South Africa, but went on to play 21 further games with 20 wins and a draw. He sent wing Vince Coates to score England's first try at Cardiff for 20 years, with the magnificent loose forward 'Cherry' Pillman crossing for a second. This was the last occasion that Wales failed to score in two successive matches.

Wales R.F. Williams (Cardiff); R.C.S. Plummer, F.W. Birt (Newport), W.J. Spiller (Cardiff), W.P. Geen (Newport); H.W. Thomas (Swansea), +T.H. Vile (Newport); G. Stephens, F.L. Perrett (Neath), B.G. Hollingdale (Swansea), W.H. Wetter, P.L. Jones (Newport), R. Thomas, F. Andrews (Pontypool), J.L. Morgan (Llanelli).

England W.R. Johnston (Bristol); V.H.M. Coates (Bath), F.E. Steinthal (Ilkley), R.W. Poulton (Harlequins), C.N. Lowe (Blackheath); W.J.A. Davies (Utd Servs), W.I. Cheesman (OMT's); +N.A. Wodehouse (Utd Servs), J.A. King (Headingley), L.G. Brown (Blackheath), J.A.S. Ritson (Northern), S. Smart (Gloucester), G. Ward (Leicester), J.E. Greenwood (Cambridge U), C.H. Pillman (Blackheath).
T: Vince Coates, Charles Pillman.
C: John Greenwood.
DG: Ronnie Poulton.
Referee: S.H. Crawford (Ireland).

England 10 Wales 9

Twickenham. 17 January 1914

England won by 2 tries, 2 cons to 1 try, 1 con, 1 drop goal.

Wales missed out on the championship and the Triple Crown with this one-point defeat. Wing George Hirst dropped an amazing goal, but England led 5–4 until new centre Willie Watts crossed and Jack Bancroft converted. Wing Howell Lewis was robbed of a try by a bad bounce but then Watts dropped the ball and the speedy 'Cherry' Pillman was on hand to score – Fred Chapman's conversion won the match for England. Of the new caps, David Watts died in 1916 and Jack 'Bedwellty' Jones later switched to rugby league.

England W.R. Johnston (Bristol); C.N. Lowe (Blackheath), +R.W. Poulton (Harlequins), J.H.D. Watson (Blackheath), F.E. Chapman (West Hartlepool); F.M. Taylor, G.W. Wood (Leicester); J.E. Greenwood, A.F. Maynard (Cambridge U), S. Smart (Gloucester), A.G. Bull (Northampton), J. Brunton (North Durham), G. Ward (Leicester), L.G. Brown, C.H. Pillman (Blackheath).
T: Len Brown, Charles Pillman.
C: Fred Chapman 2.

Wales J. Bancroft; H. Lewis (Swansea), *W.H. Evans (Llwynypia), *W.J. Watts (Llanelli), G.L. Hirst (Newport); J.M.C. Lewis (Cardiff), R.A. Lloyd (Pontypool); Rev. J. Alban Davies (Llanelli), *D. Watts (Maesteg), *J. 'Bedwellty' Jones (Abertillery), T.J. Lloyd (Neath), P.L. Jones (Pontypool), T. Williams, *E. Morgan (Swansea), H. Uzzell (Newport).
T: Willie Watts.
C: Jack Bancroft.
DG: George Hirst.
Referee: James R.C. Greenlees (Scotland).

Wales 19 England 5

St Helen's, Swansea. 17 January 1920

Wales won by 2 tries, 1 con, 1 pen, 2 drop goals to 1 try, 1 con.

Harry Uzzell, the 37-year-old pre-war cap, was selected to lead Wales in what will be forever classed as Jerry Shea's Match. Shea scored four different ways, supplying 16 points for Wales and sending Cardiff club captain Wickham Powell over for the other try. Powell believed England had made a big mistake in selection. One hour before the match, W.M. Lowry, who was given his cap a day earlier, was photographed in the side, but then it rained and the English selectors decided to bring in Harry Day instead. Day opened the scoring with a converted try, but Wales, 5–3 down at half-time, hit back. Shea was often accused of being too selfish by team-mates and spectators, but he was a brilliant individual footballer on his day. He never struck a partnership with the legendary Llanelli centre Albert Jenkins but, on this day, Shea and full-back Joe Rees were carried off in triumph by some of the large crowd. Shea, Powell and George Oliver, the Welsh amateur heavyweight boxing champion, were soon to turn to rugby league.

Wales *J. Rees (Swansea); *W.J. Powell (Cardiff), J. Shea (Newport), *A.E. Jenkins, *B.S. Evans (Llanelli); *B. Beynon (Swansea), J.J. Wetter (Newport); *J.L. Williams (Blaina), +H. Uzzell, J.J. Whitfield (Newport), *S. Morris (Cross Keys), *G. Oliver (Pontypool), E.T. Parker (Swansea), J. Jones (Aberavon), *C.W. Jones (Bridgend).
T: Jerry Shea, Wickham Powell.
C: Shea.
P: Shea.
DG: Shea 2.

England B.S. Cumberlege (Blackheath); H.L.V. Day (Leicester), E.D.G. Hammett (Newport), J.A. Krige (Guy's Hosp.), C.N. Lowe; H. Coverdale (Blackheath), C.A. Kershaw (Utd Servs); G. Holford, S. Smart (Gloucester), J.R. Morgan (Hawick), W.H.G. Wright (Plymouth), L.P.B. Merriam, F.W. Mellish (Blackheath), W.W. Wakefield (Harlequins), +J.E. Greenwood (Cambridge U).
T: Harold Day.
C: Harold Day.
Referee: J.T. Tulloch (Scotland).

England 18 Wales 3

Twickenham. 15 January 1921

England won by 4 tries, 3 cons, 1 drop goal to 1 try.

England's outstanding half-back partnership of the Pembroke-born Willie Davies and Cecil Kershaw took control as the English pack completely outplayed their opponents. Wales centre Jack Jones fractured a collar bone but stayed on; new fly-half 'Codger' Johnson badly hurt his arm and skipper Jack Wetter displaced a knee cartilage after only 20 minutes. England led 12–0 after 15 minutes before two second-half Alistair Smallwood tries and a début try by Johnny Ring squeezed between them. Pontypool-born Reg Edwards of Newport made his England début with clubmate Reg Hammett in the centre. Wales had seven new caps, including Wilf Hodder, Johnny Ring and Ben Edwards, all of whom turned to rugby league.

England B.S. Cumberlege (Blackheath); A.M. Smallwood (Leicester), E. Myers (Bradford), E.D.G. Hammett (Newport), C.N. Lowe (Blackheath); +W.J.A. Davies, C.A. Kershaw (Utd Servs); R. Edwards (Newport), E.R. Gardner (Devonport Servs), L.G. Brown, F.W. Mellish (Blackheath), T. Woods (Navy), A.F. Blakiston (Northampton), W.W. Wakefield (Harlequins), A.T. Voyce (Gloucester).
T: Alistair Smallwood 2, Cecil Kershaw, Cyril Lowe.
C: Ernie Hammett.
DG: Willie Davies.

Wales J. Rees (Swansea); *J. Ring (Aberavon), J.P. 'Jack' Jones (Pontypool), J. Shea (Newport), *T.A.W. Johnson (Cardiff); +J.J. Wetter (Newport), F.C. Reeves (Cross Keys); *S.L. Attewell, J.J. Whitfield (Newport), E.T. Parker (Swansea), *S. Winmill (Cross Keys), *D. Edwards (Glynneath), *W. Hodder (Pontypool), *M.D. Jones (Cardiff), D.E. Morgan (Llanelli).
T: Johnny Ring.
Referee: J.C. Sturrock (Scotland).

Wales 28 England 6

Arms Park, Cardiff. 21 January 1922

Wales won by 8 tries, 2 cons to 2 tries.

Wales crossed for eight tries, with five coming in the first half and all five Swansea players scoring – four with tries. Joe Rees added two conversions. Wing forwards and débutants Dai Hiddlestone and Tom 'Cooking' Jones revelled in the sea of Cardiff mud, with the former scoring a try as did other newcomers Bobby Delahay, Frank Palmer, Islwyn Evans and Cliff Richards. Police officers Tom Jones and Will Cummins joined the pack: Jones later moved to Leeds RL club, while Cummins was a previous winner of the Welsh middleweight boxing title. Hiddlestone was a remarkable player who won his first cap at the age of 31 and was only 5'8" tall. His grandson, Terry Price, played for Wales 43 years later. England captain Len Brown ended his 12-year run in international rugby which had begun with a defeat at Swansea in 1911. Born in Australia, he won the Military Cross in the First World War and was to assist in founding the Australian RFU in 1949. For the first time in a Championship match, players of both sides wore numbers.

Wales J. Rees (Swansea); *W.C. Richards (Pontypool), B.S. Evans (Llanelli), *H.I. Evans, *F.C. Palmer; W.E. Bowen (Swansea), *W.J. Delahay (Bridgend); +E.T. Parker (Swansea), J.J. Whitfield, *T. Jones (Newport), S. Morris (Cross Keys), T. Roberts (Risca), *Rev. J.G. Stephens (Llanelli), *W. Cummins (Treorchy), *D.D. Hiddlestone (Neath).
T: Jack Whitfield, Billy Bowen, Dai Hiddlestone, Bobby Delahay, Frank Palmer, Cliff Richards, Tom Parker, Islwyn Evans.
C: Joe Rees 2.

England B.S. Cumberlege (Blackheath); H.L.V. Day (Leicester), E. Myers (Bradford), E.D.G. Hammett, C.N. Lowe (Blackheath); V.G. Davies (Harlequins), C.A. Kershaw (Utd Servs); +L.G. Brown (Blackheath), J.S. Tucker (Bristol), E.R. Gardner (Devonport Servs), R. Edwards (Newport), G.S. Conway (Rugby), A.F. Blakiston (Northampton), W.W. Wakefield (Harlequins), A.T. Voyce (Gloucester).
T: Cyril Lowe, Harold Day.
Referee: James M. Tennent (Scotland).

England 7 Wales 3

Twickenham. 20 January 1923

England won by 1 try, 1 drop goal to 1 try.

This was the fastest-ever recorded international try to date: after forward Wavell Wakefield had kicked off, another of the home pack, Leo Price, scored only ten seconds later. As in 1910, England scored directly from the kick-off. The wind blew the ball back to the hands of Price after he missed with a drop at goal, but he followed up so fast that he defeated the Welsh defence, who thought the ball would go dead. The time of scoring was eventually beaten in 1999, when Scotland's John Leslie touched down in eight seconds against Wales at Murrayfield. Wales equalised in ten minutes, as Tom Johnson kicked ahead and gathered to put débutant Gwilym Michael over. England won with another remarkable score as Len Corbett threw a pass between his legs to Alistair Smallwood and the wing dropped a 45-yard goal. Wales had injuries galore – David Davies suffered a gash under his eye that needed stitches; Ambrose Baker had bruised ribs; Joe Thompson lost three teeth and Johnson was laid out by a kick on the head. England went on to win a sixth Triple Crown, while Thompson turned to rugby league just three weeks later and played 25 times for Great Britain. Débutants included Arthur Cornish and Rowe Harding and it was the only international match controlled by John Scott, who had scored against Wales in 1911.

England F. Gilbert (Devonport Servs); C.N. Lowe (Blackheath), L.J. Corbett (Bristol), E. Myers (Bradford), A.M. Smallwood (Leicester); +W.J.A. Davies, C.A. Kershaw (Utd Servs); E.R. Gardner (Devonport Servs), R. Edwards (Newport), W.E.G. Luddington (Devonport Servs), R. Cove-Smith (OMT's), W.W. Wakefield (Cambridge U), H.L. Price (Leicester), G.S. Conway (Rugby), A.T. Voyce (Gloucester).
T: Leo Price.
DG: Alistair Smallwood.

Wales J. Rees (Swansea); T.A.W. Johnson, *R.A. Cornish (Cardiff), A.E. Jenkins (Llanelli), *W.R. Harding (Swansea); +J.M.C. Lewis (Cardiff), W.J. Delahay (Bridgend); E.T. Parker (Swansea), T. Roberts (Newport), *D.G. Davies (Cardiff), *S.G. Thomas (Llanelli), A. Baker (Neath), S. Morris, *J.F. Thompson (Cross Keys), *G.M. Michael (Swansea).
T: Gwilym Michael.
Referee: John M.B. Scott (Scotland)

Wales 9 England 17

St Helen's, Swansea. 19 January 1924

England won by 5 tries, 1 con to 3 tries.

England gained their first win at Swansea since 1895, and went on to win the Triple Crown. Wales took the lead on a heavy pitch with a Tom Jones try, but England went 14–3 in front at which point Tom Voyce broke a rib. Nevertheless, the tough Gloucester man played on and though two tries pulled Wales back to 14–9, the 35,000 crowd witnessed a home loss. There was a début for Llanelli forward Ivor Jones, who was outstanding for the 1930 British team in New Zealand and who, in 1968–69, became WRU president. Centre David 'Hunt' Davies wore a reinforced boot after having had part of a foot shot off in the First World War. New caps Edward Watkins and 'Candy' Evans later switched to rugby league.

Wales +J. Rees (Swansea); T.A.W. Johnson, R.A. Cornish (Cardiff), *D.H. 'Hunt' Davies (Aberavon), B.M.G. Thomas (St Bart's Hosp.); *A.D. Owen (Swansea), *E. Watkins (Neath); S. Morris (Cross Keys), *I. Thomas (Bryncethin), *C.H. Pugh (Maesteg), *A. 'Candy' Evans (Pontypool), *J.I.T. Morris (Swansea), T. Jones (Newport), *I.E. Jones (Llanelli), *W.J. Ould (Cardiff).
T: Tom Johnson, Albert Owen, Tom Jones.

England B.S. Chantrill (Bristol); H.C. Catcheside (Percy Park), L.J. Corbett (Bristol), H.M. Locke (Birkenhead Park), H.P. Jacob (Oxford U); E. Myers (Bradford), A.T. Young (Cambridge U); W.E.G. Luddington (Devonport Servs), A. Robson (Northern), R. Edwards (Newport), +W.W. Wakefield (Leicester), R. Cove-Smith (OMT's), A.F. Blakiston (Liverpool), G.S. Conway (Rugby), A.T. Voyce (Gloucester).
T: Carston Catcheside 2, Eddie Myers, Herbert Jacob, Harold Locke.
C: Geoff Conway.
Referee: Alex W. Angus (Scotland).

England 12 Wales 6

Twickenham. 17 January 1925

England won by 3 tries, 1 pen to 2 tries.

The Prince of Wales was among the 40,000 spectators who witnessed Wales fail again in Twickenham. Wing Dicky Hamilton-Wickes was the England match-winner as he scored one try and made another for outside-half Harry Kittermaster, while wing-forward Tommy Voyce finished off a length-of-the-field move. 'Codger' Johnson was switched to full-back and not only played well in that position, but skippered Wales for the first and last time. The seven new caps included four from Aberavon: of those, Will James and Evan Williams joined Leeds RL and Bryn Phillips went to Huddersfield.

England J.W. Brough (Silloth); R.H. Hamilton-Wickes (Harlequins), H.M. Locke (Birkenhead Park), L.J. Corbett (Bristol), J.C. Gibbs (Harlequins); H.J. Kittermaster (Oxford U), E.J. Massey (Leicester); W.E.G. Luddington (Devonport Servs), J.S. Tucker (Bristol), R. Armstrong (Northern), R. Cove-Smith (OMT's), +W.W. Wakefield (Harlequins), H.G. Periton (Waterloo), A.F. Blakiston (Liverpool), A.T. Voyce (Gloucester).
T: Harry Kittermaster, Tommy Voyce, Dicky Hamilton-Wickes.
P: Bob Armstrong.

Wales +T.A.W. Johnson (Cardiff); *W.P. James, *Evan Williams (Aberavon), R.A. Cornish (Cardiff), *C.R. Thomas (Bridgend); *W.J. Hopkins (Aberavon), W.J. Delahay (Cardiff); S. Morris (Cross Keys), C. Williams (Llanelli), *B. Phillips (Aberavon), C.H. Pugh (Maesteg), *E.I. Richards (Cardiff), J.H. Gore (Blaina), D.S. Parker (Swansea), *W.I. Jones (Llanelli).
T: Cyril Thomas, Will James.
Referee: A.A. Lawrie (Scotland).

Wales 3 England 3

Arms Park, Cardiff. 16 January 1926

Draw. 1 try each.

Making the last of his seven appearances against Wales, Wavell Wakefield, later Lord Wakefield, scored a brilliant solo try on the frosty pitch which was responded to in the final quarter of the game by an unconverted try from débutant wing George Andrews. However, Wales were denied a winning try by Bobby Delahay as he picked the ball from an England heel and darted over, only for another scrum to be awarded. Tom Hopkins and Dai Jones were the only non-policemen in the pack, while the side included seven new caps, of whom Jones, Andrews and David Jenkins eventually switched to rugby league.

Wales *D.B. Evans (Swansea); *G.E. Andrews, A. Stock (Newport), R.A. Cornish (Cardiff), +W.R. Harding (Swansea); *R. 'Bobby' Jones (Northampton), W.J. Delahay (Cardiff); *T.W. Lewis (Cardiff), *J.H. John (Swansea), *D.L. Jones (Newport), R.C. Herrera (Cross Keys), S. Hinam (Cardiff), *T. Hopkins (Swansea), *D.M. Jenkins (Treorchy), B. Phillips (Aberavon).
T: George Andrews.

England H.C. Catcheside (Percy Park); H.C. Burton, A.R. Aslett (Richmond), T.E.S. Francis (Blackheath), R.H. Hamilton-Wickes; H.J. Kittermaster, J.R.B. Worton (Harlequins); A. Robson (Northern), J.S. Tucker (Bristol), E. Stanbury (Plymouth Albion), R.J. Hanvey (Aspatria), W.G.E. Luddington (Devonport Servs), H.G. Periton (Waterloo), +W.W. Wakefield (Harlequins), A.T. Voyce (Gloucester).
T: Wavell Wakefield.
Referee: W.H. Acton (Ireland).

England 11 Wales 9

Twickenham. 15 January 1927.

England won by 1 try, 1 con, 1 pen, 1 goal from mark to 2 tries, 1 pen.

Bad luck continued to dog Wales at Twickenham as Dai Jones retired in the opening quarter with a fractured shoulder, but Wales would still have won had not 'Monkey' Sellar ankle-tapped John Roberts near the end. Both Sellar and Roberts were making their débuts at the age of 20. Wales had recovered from a

Len Corbett goal from a mark, thanks to tries by Rowe Harding and George Andrews, to lead 6–3, only for England to go in front (11–6) at half-time. Ossie Male's penalty goal was the only score of the second half, though in another effort later on, he just missed. Bernard Turnbull was the new captain and Watcyn Thomas made the first of his 14 appearances for Wales in the pack. Billy Williams became the only player to be capped from Crumlin but, after playing the season out, he moved to Salford RL and was not given his cap. His family received it in 1975, two years after he died. Outside-half Henri Laird became England's youngest cap at 18 years 134 days.

England K.A. Sellar (Navy); R.H. Hamilton-Wickes (Harlequins), +L.J. Corbett (Bristol), H.M. Locke (Birkenhead Park), J.C. Gibbs; H.C.C. Laird, J.R.B. Worton (Harlequins); R. Cove-Smith (OMT's), J.S. Tucker (Bristol), E. Stanbury (Plymouth Albion), G.S. Conway (Hartlepool Rvs), K.J. Stark (Old Alleynians), H.G. Periton (Waterloo), T. Coulson (Coventry), J. Hanley (Plymouth Albion).
T: Len Corbett.
C: Erb Stanbury.
P: Stanbury.
Goal from mark: Corbett.

Wales B.O. Male (Cardiff); G.E. Andrews (Newport), +B.R. Turnbull, *J. Roberts (Cardiff), W.R. Harding (Swansea); W.H. Lewis, W.C. Powell (London Welsh); T.W. Lewis (Cardiff), J.H. John (Swansea), D. Jones (Newport), S.D. Lawrence (Bridgend), R.C. Herrera, *H.T. Phillips (Newport), *W.A. Williams (Crumlin), *W.G. Thomas (Llanelli).
T: George Andrews, Rowe Harding.
P: Ossie Male.
Referee: R.L. Scott (Scotland).

Wales 8 England 10

St Helen's, Swansea. 21 January 1928

England won by 2 tries, 2 cons to 2 tries, 1 con.

After the fire brigade had pumped water off the ground, Wales took command at forward but still lost the match. England scored two converted tries in the opening 20 minutes, but Wales clawed back with tries by John Bartlett and Dai John, the latter converted. After that, only great defensive play by 'Monkey' Sellar in particular saved England. The Llanelli half-backs Dai and Arthur John were not related.

Wales T.E. Rees; J.D. Bartlett (London Welsh), J. Roberts, B.R. Turnbull (Cardiff), +W.R. Harding (Swansea); Dai E. John, D. Arthur John (Llanelli); F.A. Bowdler (Cross Keys), *Cecil C. Pritchard (Pontypool), H.T. Phillips (Newport), E.M. Jenkins (Aberavon), *A. Skym, T. Iorwerth Jones (Llanelli), T.H. Hollingdale (Neath), I.E. Jones (Llanelli).
T: John Bartlett, Dai John.
C: Ivor Jones.

England K.A. Sellar (Utd Servs); W.J. Taylor, C.D. Aarvold (Blackheath), J.V. Richardson (Birkenhead Park), Sir T.G. Devitt (Blackheath); H.C.C. Laird (Harlequins), A.T. Young (Blackheath); E. Stanbury (Plymouth Albion), J.S. Tucker (Bristol), T. Coulson (Coventry), K.J. Stark (Old Alleynians), +R. Cove-Smith (OMT's), J. Hanley (Plymouth Albion), D. Turquand-Young (Richmond), T.N. Lawson (Workington).
T: Bill Taylor, Colin Laird.
C: Vere Richardson 2.
Referee: R.W. Harland (Ireland).

England 8 Wales 3

Twickenham. 19 January 1929

England won by 2 tries, 1 con to 1 try.

The Prince of Wales was among the 58,000 crowd which saw flanker Harry Wilkinson score a try in each half of his début to give England a deserved victory. Another newcomer, Jack Morley, then scored for Wales and Wick Powell had a drop goal disallowed. Jack Bassett from Penarth made a superb début at full-back, while Bill Roberts joined his elder brother John in the backs. Dick Jones was the brother of the 1926 cap, Robert Jones. Both Morley and the Neath collier Harold Jones later joined Wigan RL.

England T.W. Brown (Bristol); R.W. Smeddle (Durham), C.D. Aarvold (Blackheath), G.M. Sladen (Utd Servs), G.S. Wilson (Tyldesley); H.C.C. Laird (Harlequins), H. Whitley (Northern); E. Stanbury (Plymouth Albion), J.S. Tucker (Bristol), R.T. Foulds (Waterloo), +R. Cove-Smith (OMT's), J.W.R. Swayne (Bridgwater), H.G. Periton (Waterloo), R.H. Sparks (Plymouth Albion), H. Wilkinson (Halifax).
T: Harry Wilkinson 2.
C: Guy Wilson.

Wales *J.A. Bassett (Penarth); E.G. Davies, J. Roberts (Cardiff), W.G. Morgan (Swansea), *J.C. Morley (Newport); *W. Roberts (Cardiff), W.C. Powell (London Welsh); D.R. Jenkins (Swansea), Cecil C. Pritchard (Pontypool), F.A. Bowdler (Cross Keys), T. Arthur, *H.J. Jones

A quartet of Cardiff players. Brothers Bill and John Roberts and Harry Bowcott were all capped for Wales in 1929, but Harry's brother, Jackie, (far right) just missed out on a cap at scrum-half. They were all products of Cardiff High School.

(Neath), *R. 'Dick' Jones (London Welsh), W.G. Thomas (Swansea), +I.E. Jones (Llanelli).
T: Jack Morley.
Referee: R.W. Harland (Ireland).

Wales 3 England 11

Arms Park, Cardiff. 18 January 1930

England won by 2 tries, 1 con, 1 pen to 1 try.

Sam Tucker was flown in from Bristol at lunchtime on the day of the match as a replacement for Henry Rew of Exeter and he performed so well that two matches later he was skippering England! Wing James Reeve struck before and after the interval, with débutant Tommy Jones-Davies, the London Welsh club captain, replying in a match watched by a near 60,000 crowd with the gates locked. Wing Arthur Hickman gained one further cap in 1933 before switching to league, while 'Ocker' Thomas went in 1931. Both Thomas and scrum-half David Roberts never won another cap.

Wales J.A. Bassett (Penarth); J.C. Morley (Newport), +H.M. Bowcott (Cardiff), *T.E. Jones-Davies (London Welsh), *A. Hickman (Neath); F.L. Williams (Cardiff), *D.E.A. Roberts (Oxford U); T. Arthur (Neath), F.A. Bowdler (Cross Keys), A. Skym (Cardiff), D.S. Parker (Swansea), E.M. Jenkins (Aberavon), *W.T. Thomas (Abertillery), T.H. Hollingdale (Neath), I.E. Jones (Llanelli).
T: Tommy Jones-Davies.

England J.G. Askew (Cambridge U); A.L. Novis (Blackheath), F.W.S. Malir (Otley), M. Robson (Oxford U), J.S.R. Reeve (Harlequins); R.S. Spong, W.H. Sobey (Old Millhillians); D.A. Kendrew (Woodford), J.S. Tucker (Bristol), A.H. Bateson (Otley), J.W. Forrest (Utd Servs), B.H. Black, W.E. Tucker (Blackheath), P.D. Howard (Old Millhillians), +H.G. Periton (Waterloo).
T: Jimmy Reeve 2.
C: Brian Black.
P: Black.
Referee: Rupert W. Jeffares (Ireland).

England 11 Wales 11

Twickenham. 17 January 1931.

Draw. England – 1 try, 1 con, 2 pens. Wales – 2 tries, 1 con, 1 goal from mark.

Once again Wales were denied a first win at Twickenham, though with three minutes remaining it appeared likely as they were leading by 11–8. Forward Brian Black, however, who helped Britain win the World Bobsleigh title six years later, placed his second penalty of the match. Wick Powell's goal from a mark, surprisingly not charged by England, opened the scoring. Then, at 6–3 to Wales, Don Burland gathered a Welsh throw to cross the line and level the scores. His conversion attempt was signalled wide by 65-year-old Welsh touch-judge Harry Packer, but the referee over-ruled and at the interval the scoreboard was amended. A Jack Morley try and a Jack Bassett conversion took Wales ahead, only for the 'Twickenham bogy' to strike again.

England L.L. Bedford (Headingley); J.S.R. Reeve (Harlequins), D.W. Burland (Bristol), M.A. McCanlis (Gloucester), C.D. Aarvold (Headingley); T.J.M. Barrington (Bristol), E.B. Pope (Blackheath); H. Rew (Exeter), +J.S. Tucker (Bristol), M.S. Bonaventura, B.H. Black (Blackheath), J.W. Forrest (Utd Servs), D.H. Swayne (Oxford U), P.D. Howard (Old Mill Lillians), R.F. Davey (Leytonstone).
T: Don Burland.
C: Burland.
P: Brian Black 2.

Wales +J.A. Bassett (Penarth); J.C. Morley (Newport), E.C. Davey (Swansea), T.E. Jones-Davies (London Welsh), R.W. Boon; H.M. Bowcott (Cardiff), W.C. Powell (London Welsh); A. Skym (Cardiff), H.C. Day (Newport), *T.B. Day (Swansea), T. Arthur (Neath), E.M. Jenkins (Aberavon), A.W. Lemon (Neath), W.G. Thomas (Swansea), N.H. Fender (Cardiff).

T: Jack Morley, Tommy Jones-Davies.
C: Jack Bassett.
Goal from mark: Wick Powell.
Referee: Dr James R. Wheeler (Ireland).

Wales 12 England 5

St Helen's, Swansea. 16 January 1932

Wales won by 1 try, 1 con, 1 pen, 1 drop goal to 1 try, 1 con.

The Prince of Wales was among a disappointingly small crowd of 30,000 who saw Ronnie Boon drop a goal while standing just underneath the crossbar. That followed an earlier try by the Welsh wing who was to repeat this performance a year later. England were 12 points down before opening their account, but Wales kept the brilliant outside-half, Roger Spong, in check.

Wales +J.A. Bassett (Penarth); J.C. Morley (Newport), E.C. Davey (Swansea), F.L. Williams, R.W. Boon (Cardiff); A.R. Ralph (Newport), W.C. Powell (London Welsh); T.B. Day (Swansea), F.A. Bowdler (Cross Keys), A. Skym (Cardiff), E.M. Jenkins (Aberavon), D.J. Thomas, W. Davies, W.G Thomas (Swansea), A.W. Lemon (Neath).

T: Ronnie Boon.
C: Jack Bassett.
P: Bassett.
DG: Boon.

England R.J. Barr (Leicester); C.C. Tanner (Gloucester), R.A. Gerrard (Bath), J.A. Tallent, +C.D. Aarvold (Blackheath); R.S. Spong, W.H. Sobey (Old Millhillians); G.G. Gregory (Bristol), D.J. Norman (Leicester), N.L. Evans (RNEC, Devonport), R.G.S. Hobbs (Richmond), C.S.H. Webb (Devonport Servs), L.E. Saxby (Gloucester), E. Coley (Northampton), J.McD. Hodgson (Northern).
T: Charlie Webb.
C: Bobby Barr.
Referee: F.J.C. Moffat (Scotland).

England 3 Wales 7

Twickenham. 21 January 1933

Wales won by 1 try, 1 drop goal to 1 try.

This will always be remembered as Ronnie Boon's match. It was the day that the 'Twickenham Bogy' was lifted at last. Wales had waited 23 years for it and this first success was watched by a record championship-

Wales gained their first-ever win at Twickenham on 21 January 1933 – wing Ronnie Boon of Cardiff scored all his side's seven points. *Back row*: Bryn Evans, V.G.J. Jenkins, W. Wooller, I. Isaac, T. Arthur, D. Thomas, W.J. Llewellyn (touch-judge). *Seated*: A.H. Jones, R.B. Jones, R.W. Boon, Watcyn Thomas (capt.), Claude Davey, Edgar Jones, A. Skym. *Front row*: H.M. Bowcott, M.J. Turnbull. (© *Western Mail & Echo*)

Ronald Winston (Ronnie) Boon – the match-winner at Twickenham in 1933. He later emigrated to New Zealand in 1995 and died in Waipukurah three years later at the age of 89. (© Huw Evans)

match crowd of 64,000 which included the Prince of Wales. England led 3–0 at half-time with a try by fly-half Walter Elliot but, within a minute of the second half starting, centre Ron Gerrard soccer-kicked straight to the hands of Boon who, in his usual cheeky manner, dropped a goal with three men outside him for a possible try! At 4–3, it was Boon who clinched the win as Maurice Turnbull sent the ball along the line for Claude Davey to feed the Cardiff wing, who then raced round to the posts for a try. The Welsh touch-judge flagged the Viv Jenkins conversion kick as over, but referee Tom Bell ruled that the effort was wide. It did not matter. Watcyn Thomas was captain for the first time. His side contained seven new caps, including three magnificent backs who were all to play cricket for Glamorgan; Viv Jenkins, the 20-year-old Wilfred Wooller and Maurice Turnbull, who won an England cricket cap. Turnbull was shot dead in Normandy in 1944. It was said that Wooller's tackle on the flying Elliot was alone worth the admission fee! Harry Bowcott and Claude Davey were the 'old hands' who controlled splendidly and Iorrie Isaacs, who joined Leeds seven months afterwards, made a fine start, despite the first-turning up, first-packing down rule for forwards arriving at a scrum. Welsh-speaking, Pontarddulais-born Arthur Vaughan-Jones played in the England pack. It was a false dawn however, as the Welsh selectors made mistake after mistake for subsequent matches.

England T.W. Brown (Bristol); L.A. Booth (Headingley), D.W. Burland (Bristol), R.A. Gerrard (Bath), +C.D. Aarvold (Blackheath); W. Elliot (Utd Servs), A. Key (Old Cranleighans); N.L. Evans (Navy), G.G. Gregory (Bristol), R.J. Longland (Northampton), C.S.H. Webb (Devonport Servs), A.D.S. Roncorni (Richmond), A. Vaughan-Jones (Army), B.H. Black (Blackheath), R. Bolton (Wakefield).
T: Water Elliot.

Wales *V.G. Jenkins (Bridgend); R.W. Boon (Cardiff), E.C. Davey (Swansea), *W. Wooller (Rydal School/Colwyn Bay), *A.H. Jones (Cardiff); H.M. Bowcott (London Welsh), *M.J.L. Turnbull (Cardiff); E.L. Jones, *B. Evans (Llanelli), A. Skym (Cardiff), *R.B. Jones (Anglesey/Cambridge U), D.J. Thomas (Swansea), T. Arthur (Neath), +W.G. Thomas (Swansea), *I. Isaacs (Cardiff).
T: Ronnie Boon.
DG: Boon.
Referee: Tom Bell (Ireland).

Wales 0   England 9

Arms Park, Cardiff. 20 January 1934

England won by 3 tries to nil.

How could you expect to win with 13 new caps and 15 changes in the team? The answer was simple – you couldn't. And Wales were lucky to come second, as England gained revenge for their loss twelve months earlier. The new faces included skipper John Evans, who was to die in the Second World War. He was one of five in the side who did not appear again. Bryn Howell, Glyn Prosser and Gomer Hughes all 'went north' but the match did introduce Cliff Jones at outside-half and Arthur Rees in the pack. A new north stand was opened, with over 50,000 spectators present to see England wing Graham Meikle emulate his elder brother Stephen by scoring a début try. He added a second after the interval with Tim Warr also having scored in his first appearance. Wales failed to score against England for the first time in 21 years and England went on to win the Triple Crown.

Wales *B. Howell (Llanelli); *B.T.V. Cowey (Newport/Welch Regt), E.C. Davey, *J. Idwal Rees (Swansea), *G.R. Rees-Jones (London Welsh); *C.W. Jones (Porth/Cambridge U), *D.D. Evans (Barry/Cheshire); *K.W.J. Jones (Monmouth/London Welsh), +*J.R. Evans (Newport), *W.H. Truman (Llanelli), *G. Hughes (Penarth), D.J. Thomas (Swansea), *I.G. Prosser (Neath), *C.R. Davies (RAF/ London Welsh), *A.M. Rees (London Welsh).

England H.G. Owen-Smith; A.L. Warr, P. Cranmer (Oxford U), R.A. Gerrard (Bath), G.W.C. Meikle (Waterloo); W. Elliot (Utd Servs), +B.C. Gadney (Leicester); R.J. Longland (Northampton), G.G. Gregory (Bristol), H. Rew (Exeter), J.C. Wright (Met Police), J. Dicks (Northampton), J.McD. Hodgson (Northern), P.C. Hordern (Gloucester), H.A. Fry (Liverpool).
T: Graham Meikle 2, Tim Warr.
Referee: Frank W. Haslett (Ireland).

England 3 Wales 3

Twickenham. 19 January 1935

Draw. England – 1 pen. Wales – 1 try.

A crowd of 72,000 saw a scoreless first-half before Cliff Jones made the break which saw Wilfred Wooller crash over for a Welsh try. Wales faded as Edgar Jones suffered a cracked rib but played on bravely. England left the equalising points late but, they eventually came by way of a penalty, kicked by new cap Harold Boughton after the Welsh back-row were adjudged offside at a scrum. Cross Keys forward Con Murphy played in all three championship matches before turning professional in the summer.

England H. Boughton (Gloucester); L.A. Booth (Headingley), P. Cranmer (Oxford U), J. Heaton (Liverpool U), R. Leyland (Waterloo); P.L. Candler (Cambridge U), J.L. Giles (Coventry); R.J. Longland (Northampton), E.S. Nicholson, +D.A. Kendrew (Leicester), A.J. Clarke (Coventry), J. Dicks (Northampton), A.G. Cridlan (Blackheath), D.T. Kemp (Blackheath), W.H. Weston (Northampton).
P: Harold Boughton.

Wales V.G.J. Jenkins (Bridgend); B.T.V. Cowey (Newport/Welsh Regt), +E.C. Davey (Swansea), W. Wooller (Cambridge U), A. Bassett (Aberavon); C.W. Jones (Cambridge U), W.C. Powell (Northampton); E.L. Jones (Llanelli), *C.D. Murphy (Cross Keys), T.B. Day, D.J. Thomas (Swansea), W.H. Truman (Llanelli), A.M. Rees (Cambridge U), J. Lang (Llanelli), A. Skym (Cardiff).
T: Wilf Wooller.
Referee: Frank W. Haslett (Ireland).

Two years after winning at Twickenham, Wales were held 3–3 at rugby's headquarters. Claude Davey led the side which included two exciting young backs, the brilliant Cliff Jones (front, right) and Wilfred Wooller (fourth from the left, back row). Wooller scored the only try of the match.

Wales 0 England 0

St Helen's, Swansea. 18 January 1936

Draw. No score.

Both countries had beaten New Zealand and both had a superb set of backs, but it was a stalemate. Thirty years later at Twickenham there was a similar match when brilliant backs cancelled each other out. England had a magnificent full-back in 'Tuppy' Owen-Smith, the South African Test cricketer. On the wing was the Russian-born Prince Alexander Obolensky, who had twice run through New Zealand, but 'Obbo' never scored another Test try and died in a plane crash in 1940. New cap Harold Thomas had made his Neath debut at 16. In 1937 he transferred to Salford RL.

Wales V.G.J. Jenkins (London Welsh); G.R. Rees-Jones (Oxford U), +J. Idwal Rees (Swansea), W. Wooller (Cambridge U), *B.E.W. McCall (Welsh Regt/Newport); C.W. Jones (Cambridge U), H. Tanner (Swansea); T.J. Rees (Newport), B. Evans (Llanelli), T.G. Williams (Cross Keys), *H.W. Thomas (Neath), *G.M. Williams (Aberavon), A.M. Rees (London Welsh), J. Lang (Llanelli), *E.C. Long (Swansea).

England H.G. Owen-Smith (St Mary's Hosp.); Prince A. Obolensky (Oxford U), R.A. Gerrard (Bath), P. Cranmer (Richmond), H.S. Sever (Sale); P.L. Candler (St Bart's Hosp.), +B.C. Gadney; D.A. Kendrew, E.S. Nicholson (Leicester), R.J. Longland (Northampton), C.S.H. Webb (Devonport Servs), A.J. Clarke (Coventry), W.H. Weston (Northampton), P.E. Dunkley, E.A. Hamilton-Hill (Harlequins).
Referee: Frank W. Haslett (Ireland).

England 4 Wales 3

Twickenham. 16 January 1937

England won by 1 drop goal to 1 try.

England wing Hal Sever drop-kicked an amazing 40-yard goal to win the match after a Viv Jenkins kick for touch had rebounded off Robin Prescott's shoulder into the wing's hands. Wales scored before half-time, when débutant Bill Clement slipped a return pass as he was tackled to Wilfred Wooller, who burst over. The 65,000 crowd witnessed a poor match in which the heavier England pack dominated. Clement later became a splendid secretary of the WRU; Emrys Evans switched to league in 1939 while David Thomas, who joined his younger brother Harold in the pack, made his only appearance.

Cliff Jones OBE, the former outside-half and captain of Wales, with a grog of himself presented to him by his local Pontyclun RFC during his term of office as president of the Welsh Rugby Union in 1981. He played 13 times between 1934 and 1938.
(© *Western Mail & Echo*)

England +H.G. Owen-Smith (St Mary's Hosp.); A.G. Butler (Harlequins), P.L. Candler (St Bart's Hosp.), P. Cranmer (Richmond), H.S. Sever (Sale); T.A. Kemp (St Mary's Hosp.), J.L. Giles (Coventry); R.E. Prescott (Harlequins), H.B. Toft (Waterloo), R.J. Longland (Northampton), T.F. Huskisson (OMT's), A. Wheatley (Coventry), D.A. Campbell (Cambridge U), D.L.K. Milman (Bedford), W.H. Weston (Northampton).
DG: Hal Sever.

Wales V.G.J. Jenkins (London Welsh); *W.H. Clement (Llanelli), W. Wooller (Cardiff), +E.C. Davey (London Welsh), J. Idwal Rees; W.T.H. Davies, H. Tanner (Swansea); T.J. Rees (Newport), B. Evans, *E. Evans (Llanelli), *D.L. Thomas, H.W. Thomas (Neath), A.M. Rees (London Welsh), J. Lang, E.C. Long (Swansea).

T: Wilf Wooller.
Referee: R.A. Beattie (Scotland).

Wales 14 England 8

Arms Park, Cardiff. 15 January 1938.

Wales won by 2 tries, 1 con, 2 pens to 2 tries, 1 con.

Walter Vickery from Aberavon followed his father's footsteps into international rugby: George Vickery, also of Aberavon, had been an England cap four years before Walter was born. New cap Allen McCarley put Wales ahead and two Viv Jenkins penalty shots made it 9–3 at half-time, though several stoppages were made with injuries to home players. A try by Idwal Rees – converted by Jenkins – took Wales clear before Hal Sever scored for England and Hubert Freakes converted. Cliff Jones and Haydn Tanner were once again in fine form at half-back.

Wales V.G.J. Jenkins (London Welsh); W.H. Clement (Llanelli), J. Idwal Rees (Swansea), E.C. Davey (London Welsh), A. Bassett; +C.W. Jones (Cardiff), H. Tanner (Swansea); H.T. Rees (Cardiff), W. Travers (Newport), *M.E. Morgan (Swansea), *F.L. Morgan (Llanelli), E.V. Watkins (Cardiff), A.M. Rees (London Welsh), *W.E. Vickery (Aberavon), *A. McCarley (Neath).
T: Allen McCarley, Idwal Rees.
C: Viv Jenkins.
P: Jenkins 2.

England H.D. Freakes (Harlequins); E.J. Unwin (Rosslyn Park), +P. Cranmer (Moseley), B.E. Nicholson (Harlequins), H.S. Sever (Sale); P.L. Candler (St Bart's Hosp.), B.C. Gadney (Headingley); R.J. Longland (Northampton), H.B. Toft (Waterloo), H.F. Wheatley, A. Wheatley (Coventry), T.F. Huskisson (OMT's), W.H. Weston (Northampton), D.L.K. Milman (Bedford), R. Bolton (Harlequins).
T: Peter Cranmer, Hal Sever.
C: Hubert Freakes.
Referee: R.A. Beattie (Scotland).

England 3 Wales 0

Twickenham. 21 January 1939

Draw. England won by 1 try to nil.

A full house at Twickenham saw England gain a deserved win, though they had to wait until 15 minutes into the second half, when Richmond prop Derek Teden just beat Wilfred Wooller to the ball after a kick over the line. Walter Vickery went off with an injury to his right knee and, when he came back, he had a chance to score. 'But my knee slowed me down and I was pushed out at the corner. If I had not had the knock, I think I would have got there,' he said. Viv Jenkins announced his retirement from international rugby after the match. It was to be the only international played by three of the new caps, of whom Idwal Davies and Syd Williams turned professional that year. Major John Ford became a prisoner of war for four years, while try-scorer Teden was killed in action the following year.

England H.D. Freakes (Oxford U); R.H. Guest (Liverpool U), J. Heaton (Waterloo), G.E. Hancock (Birkenhead Park), R.S.L. Carr (Old Cranleighans); G.A. Walker (RAF), P. Cooke (Richmond); R.E. Prescott (Harlequins), +H.B. Toft (Waterloo), D.E. Teden (Richmond), T.F. Huskisson (OMTs), H.F. Wheatley (Coventry), J.T.W. Berry (Leicester), R.M. Marshall (Oxford U), J.K. Watkins (Utd Servs).
T: Derek Teden.

Wales V.G.J. Jenkins (London Welsh); *F.J.V. Ford (Welch Regt), *D. Idwal Davies (Swansea/London Welsh), +W. Wooller (Cardiff), *S.A. Williams (Aberavon); W.T.H. Davies, H. Tanner; M.E. Morgan (Swansea), W. Travers (Newport), *W.E.N. Davis, E.V. Watkins (Cardiff), F.L. Morgan (Llanelli), A.R. Taylor (Cross Keys), W.E. Vickery (Aberavon), *C. Challinor (Neath).
Referee: James C.H. Ireland (Scotland).

Wales 6 England 9

Arms Park, Cardiff. 18 January 1947

England won by 1 try, 1 con, 1 drop goal to 2 tries.

A total of 27 new caps were on view – only Haydn Tanner, Howard Davies and England's Dickie Guest remained from the 1939 season – for this first official international match after the war. Ken Jones and Rees Stephens were among the débutants for Wales and Bleddyn Williams appeared at outside-half but he looked uncomfortable and never played for Wales in that role again. Centre Keith Scott retired after 15 minutes and Micky Steele-Bodger came out of the pack. Nevertheless the Welsh eight failed to take control and Don White scored the opening try. Wales regained the lead at 6–5 with Rees Stephens before the interval, and Gwyn Evans scored tries only for England to win with a drop-goal by Nim Hall. A wartime land-mine ensured that the upper deck of the north stand was out of action and, with no loudspeakers, programme changes were announced by a man carrying a board around the outside of the

Wales lined up at Cardiff for the first match after the Second World War, but lost 9–6 to England. On 1999 scoring values, however, they would have drawn 10–10! *Back row*: R.A. Beattie (referee), G. Bevan, D. Jones, S. Williams, G. Evans, J.R.G. Stephens, G. Parsons, R.E. Blakemore, O. Williams, I. Jones (touch-judge). *Seated*: C.H. Davies, L. Williams, J. Matthews, H. Tanner (capt.), B.L. Williams, K.J. Jones, W.B. Cleaver.

pitch. Of the new caps, only Reg Blakemore and George Parsons were to 'go north'. Ken Jones, the Olympic sprint medallist of 1948, was on the wing but the selectors chose Cardiff fly-half Billy Cleaver and centre Bleddyn Williams out of place.

Wales C.H. Davies (Llanelli); *K.J. Jones (Newport), *J. Matthews, *W.B. Cleaver (Cardiff), *W. Les T. Williams (Llanelli); *B.L. Williams, +H. Tanner (Cardiff); *D.C.J. Jones (Swansea), *R.E. Blakemore (Newport), *G.W. Bevan, *S. Williams (Llanelli), *G.W. Parsons (Newport), *O. Williams (Llanelli), *J.R.G. Stephens (Neath), *G. Evans (Cardiff).
T: Rees Stephens, Gwyn Evans.

England A. Gray (Otley); R.H. Guest (Waterloo), N.O. Bennett, E.K. Scott (St Mary's Hosp.), D.W. Swarbrick (Oxford U); N.M. Hall (St Mary's Hosp.), W.K.T. Moore (Devonport Servs); G.A. Kelly (Bedford), A.P. Henderson (Cambridge U), H.W. Walker (Coventry), +J.S. Mycock (Sale), S.V. Perry, M.R. Steele-Bodger (Cambridge U), B.H. Travers (Oxford U), D.F. White (Northampton).
T: Don White.
C: Arthur Gray.
DG: Nim Hall.
Referee: R.A. Beattie (Scotland).

England 3 Wales 3

Twickenham. 17 January 1948

Draw. England – 1 pen. Wales – 1 try.

Cardiff supplied a record ten players in the Welsh side, as Frank Trott came in at full-back and Jack Matthews was played out of position on the wing. South African Syd Newman, a POW at Tobruk, had his international career ended with a cracked wrist, with the Australian 'Jyka' Travers coming out of the pack. Newman had landed a penalty and also produced a try-saving tackle on Matthews. The equalising try came from Ken Jones in the second half after Bleddyn Williams and Haydn Tanner had begun the move. Neath prop Les Anthony had a brief union career and turned to Oldham RL seven months later.

England S.C. Newman (Oxford U); R.H. Guest (Waterloo), N.O. Bennett (Utd Servs), E.K. Scott (Redruth), D.W. Swarbrick (Oxford U); +T.A. Kemp (Richmond), R.J.P. Madge (Exeter); H.W. Walker (Coventry), J.H. Keeling (Guy's Hosp.), G.A. Kelly (Bedford), S.V. Perry (Cambridge U), H.F. Luya (Headingley), B.H. Travers (Oxford U), D.B. Vaughan (Devonport Servs), M.R. Steele-Bodger (Edinburgh U).
P: Sid Newman.

Wales *R.F. Trott (Cardiff); K.J. Jones (Newport), W.B. Cleaver, B.L. Williams, J. Matthews (Cardiff); G. Davies (Pontypridd), +H. Tanner (Cardiff); *L. Anthony (Neath), D.M. James, C. Davies, W.E. Tamplin (Cardiff), *W. Des Jones, O. Williams (Llanelli), L. Manfield, G. Evans (Cardiff).
T: Ken Jones.
Referee: R.A. Beattie (Scotland).

Wales 9 England 3

Arms Park, Cardiff. 15 January 1949

(Points system ammended – see p.12)

Wales won by 3 tries to 1 drop goal.

Outside-half Glyn Davies twice made a break and wing Les Williams twice got around the Olympic athlete Jack Gregory to take the pass and score. The next day, Williams signed forms and by the following Saturday he appeared for Hunslet Rugby League club. Nim Hall dropped a goal – now worth only three points – to level the scores at 3–3. Two years earlier at Cardiff his drop shot had counted as four points. Wales, wearing white shorts for the first time, took the lead with a début try from Alun Meredith, after a John Gwilliam burst, and Williams completed the scoring. Gregory had run with Ken Jones in Britain's Olympic silver-medal relay team of 1948. Newbridge forwards Don Hayward and Ray Cale came in, though they later switched to league, while 'Bunner' Travers, the 1938 British Isles hooker, returned after a ten-year absence. England forwards Ted Horsfall and Vic Roberts had spells with Cardiff and Swansea respectively.

Wales R.F. Trott (Cardiff); K.J. Jones (Newport), J. Matthews, B.L. Williams, W. Les T. Williams (Cardiff); G. Davies (Pontypridd/Cambridge U), +H. Tanner (Cardiff); *E.O. Coleman, W. Travers (Newport), D.C.J. Jones (Swansea), *Don J. Hayward (Newbridge), *A. Meredith (Devonport Servs), *W.R. Cale (Newbridge), J.A. Gwilliam (Cambridge U), G. Evans (Cardiff).
T: Les Williams 2, Alun Meredith.

England W.B. Holmes (Cambridge U); J.A. Gregory (Blackheath), L.B. Cannell, C.B. van Ryneveld (Oxford U), T. Danby (Harlequins); +N.M. Hall (Huddersfield), G. Rimmer (Waterloo); T.W. Price (Cheltenham), A.P. Henderson (Edinburgh Wands), M.J. Berridge (Northampton), H.F. Luya (Headingley), G.R.D'A. Hosking (Devonport Servs), E.L. Horsfall (Harlequins), B. Braithwaite-Exley (Headingley), V.G. Roberts (Penryn).
DG: Nim Hall.
Referee: Noel H. Lambert (Ireland).

England 5 Wales 11

Twickenham. 21 January 1950

Wales won by 2 tries, 1 con, 1 pen to 1 try, 1 con.

A massive crowd of 75,500 watched the first Welsh win at Twickenham since 1933 even though the gates were closed an hour before kick-off, with thousands locked outside. Wales lost chosen captain Bleddyn Williams and lock Rees Stephens with injury. In came Trevor Brewer, as the backs shuffled, and Roy John, one of the finest line-out experts the game has known and no mean runner. Rex Willis, the 'tough as teak' scrum-half from Llandaff, former England war-time cap John Robins and police officer Dai Davies began their international careers. More importantly, John Gwilliam took over as leader for the first of 13 such occasions. The new star was Lewis Jones who made his début at the age of 18 years and nine months, and who sadly went on to transfer with great success to Leeds Rugby League club. England scored first, when wing John Smith just beat the diving full-back to the corner and Murray Hofmeyr placed the goal. Jones was soon in full flow, however, and ran when everyone (especially his own team) expected him to kick. Just before half-time he fielded a kick on halfway to run diagonally across field and straighten. Once Malcolm Thomas and Bob Evans had linked, prop Cliff Davies was over for an amazing try. A senior international in the stand had shouted 'Kick, you fool!' when he saw Jones take off. In the second half, he kicked a penalty and converted a Ray Cale try after Billy Cleaver had kicked ahead. Wales had won at Twickenham for only the second time in 15 matches over 40 years.

England M.B. Hofmeyr (Oxford U); J.V. Smith (Cambridge U), B. Boobbyer, L.B. Cannell, I.J. Botting (Oxford U); +I. Preece (Coventry), G. Rimmer (Waterloo); J.MacG.K. Kendall-Carpenter (Oxford U), E. Evans (Sale), W.A. Holmes (Nuneaton), G.R.D'A. Hosking (Devonport Servs), H.A. Jones (Barnstaple), H.D. Small (Oxford U), D.B. Vaughan (Headingley), J.J. Cain (Waterloo).
T: John Smith.
C: Murray Hofmeyr.

Wales *B.L. Jones (Devonport Servs); K.J. Jones, M.C. Thomas (Newport), J. Matthews (Cardiff), *T.J. Brewer (Newport); W.B. Cleaver, *W.R. Willis (Cardiff); *J.D. Robins (Birkenhead Park), *D.M. Davies (Somerset Police), C. Davies (Cardiff), Don J. Hayward

(Newbridge), *E.R. John (Neath), W.R. Cale (Pontypool), +J.A. Gwilliam (Edinburgh Wands), R.T. Evans (Newport).
T: Cliff Davies, Ray Cale.
C: Lewis Jones.
P: Lewis Jones.
Referee: Noel H. Lambert (Ireland).

Wales 23   England 5

St Helen's, Swansea. 20 January 1951

Wales won by 5 tries, 4 cons to 1 try, 1 con.

Wales had eleven Lions from the 1950 tour and England included nine new caps. As a result, it was a crushing Welsh win before a 50,000 crowd. Cardiff-born John Kendall-Carpenter, selected as captain, was a late England withdrawal and after leading 8–0 at half-time, Wales scored three more tries that included a 60-yard run by Lewis Jones for the second try by Malcolm Thomas. The only new cap for Wales was the popular Danny Kaye-lookalike, Peter Evans. The win was a false dawn though, and 14 days later their dreams were rudely disturbed.

Wales G. Williams (Llanelli); K.J. Jones (Newport), J. Matthews (Cardiff), B.L. Jones, M.C. Thomas (Devonport Servs); G. Davies (Cambridge U), W.R. Willis (Cardiff); J.D. Robins (Birkenhead Park), D.M. Davies (Somerset Police), C. Davies (Cardiff), E.R. John (Neath), Don J. Hayward (Newbridge), R.T. Evans (Newport), +J.A. Gwilliam (Edinburgh Wands), *P.D. Evans (Llanelli).
T: Jack Matthews 2, Malcolm Thomas 2, Ken Jones.
C: Lewis Jones 4.

England E.N. Hewitt (Coventry); C.G. Woodruff (Harlequins), L.F.L. Oakley (Bedford), B. Boobbyer (Oxford U), V.R. Tindall (Liverpool U); I. Preece (Coventry), G. Rimmer (Waterloo); R.V. Stirling (Leicester), T.H. Smith (Northampton), W.A. Holmes (Nuneaton), D.T. Wilkins (Roundhay), J.T. Bartlett (Waterloo), G.C. Rittson-Thomas (Oxford U), P.B.C. Moore (Blackheath), +V.G. Roberts (Penryn).
T: George Rittson-Thomas.
C: Edwin Hewitt.
Referee: Capt M.J. Dowling (Ireland).

England 6   Wales 8

Twickenham. 19 January 1952

Wales won by 2 tries, 1 con to 2 tries.

Wales lost Bleddyn Williams on the morning of the match with flu and, though Jack Matthews was called up and changed, it was Alun Thomas who ran out on the pitch. England led 6–0, and with Lewis Jones limping on the wing and Len Blyth pulled out of the pack to cover him after only 15 minutes, it looked odds on an English win. But Wales did score, when Cliff Morgan made a break that saw Ken Jones finish like the Olympic sprinter that he was. Wales held on at 5–6 and, in the second half, with Roy John dominating the line-out, Wales produced a match-winning move. Lewis Jones hobbled into an attack and made the extra man for Ken Jones to swerve around Bill Hook for the winning try.

England W.G. Hook (Gloucester); J.E. Woodward (Wasps), A.E. Agar (Harlequins), L.B. Cannell (St Mary's Hosp.), C.E. Winn (Rosslyn Park); +N.M. Hall (Richmond), G. Rimmer (Waterloo); E.E. Woodgate (Paignton), E. Evans (Sale), R.V. Stirling (Leicester), J.R.C. Matthews (Harlequins), D.T. Wilkins (Utd Servs), A.O. Lewis (Bath), J.MacG.K. Kendall-Carpenter (Penzance), D.F. White (Northampton).
T: Albert Agar, Ted Woodward.

Wales G. Williams (Llanelli); K.J. Jones, M.C. Thomas (Newport), *A.G. Thomas (Cardiff), B.L. Jones (Llanelli); C.I. Morgan, W.R. Willis (Cardiff); W.O.G. Williams (Swansea), D.M. Davies (Somerset Police), Don J. Hayward (Newbridge), E.R. John, J.R.G. Stephens (Neath), A. Forward (Pontypool), +J.A. Gwilliam (Edinburgh Wands), L.G. Blyth (Swansea).
T: Ken Jones 2.
C: Malcolm Thomas.
Referee: Noel H. Lambert (Ireland).

Wales 3   England 8

Arms Park, Cardiff. 17 January 1953

England won by 1 try, 1 con, 1 pen to 1 pen.

This was to be the only cap won by Newport's brilliant little fly-half Roy Burnett. Cliff Morgan had been dropped from the side as his club partner Rex Willis had fractured his shoulder. The selectors therefore chose the Newport partners, Burnett and

Billy Williams, but it was a disappointing game for them. Ken Jones found Reg Bazley a real handful on the wing and, usually immaculate, he also spilled a Malcolm Thomas pass right on the English line. The 19-year-old Terry Davies had a tough début, but did land one superb penalty goal. England took the lead when Martin Regan made the running for centre Lew Cannell to go over before the interval and Ted Woodward kicked a long-range goal in the second half. Among the débutants was the Cardiff forward Sid Judd, who became a superb player for club and country, only to die of leukemia at the age of 30.

Wales *T.J. Davies (Swansea); K.J. Jones, M.C. Thomas (Newport), B.L. Williams, *G.M. Griffiths (Cardiff); *R. Burnett, W.A.Williams (Newport); J.D. Robins (Bradford), *G.T. Beckingham (Cardiff), W.O.G. Williams (Swansea), E.R. John, J.R.G. Stephens (Neath), *S. Judd (Cardiff), +J.A. Gwilliam (Gloucester), *W.D. Johnson (Swansea).
P: Terry Davies.

England +N.M. Hall (Richmond); J.E. Woodward (Wasps), A.E. Agar (Harlequins), L.B. Cannell (St Mary's Hosp.), R.C. Bazley (Waterloo); M. Regan (Liverpool), P.W. Sykes (Wasps); W.A. Holmes (Nuneaton), N.A. Labuschagne (Harlequins), R.V. Stirling (Leicester), S.J. Adkins (Coventry), D.T. Wilkins (Navy), A.O. Lewis, J.MacG.K. Kendall-Carpenter (Bath), D.F. White (Northampton).
T: Lew Cannell.
C: Nim Hall.
P: Ted Woodward.
Referee: Capt M.J. Dowling (Ireland).

England 9 Wales 6

Twickenham. 16 January 1954

England won by 3 tries to 1 try, 1 pen.

After Alun Thomas had failed to find touch in the last minute, England swept the ball out for wing Chris Winn to score and gain their first win over Wales at Twickenham since 1939. Wales had battled bravely to save the match, leading by a Gwyn Rowlands try, before Gerwyn Williams dislocated a shoulder while trying to stop Ted Woodward from equalising. Rowlands switched to full-back and, after Woodward had scored again, Cliff Morgan had to play at scrum-half while Rex Willis sought repairs. Wales still came back with a Rowlands penalty, but just failed to hold out. For the third successive time at Twickenham, centre Bleddyn Williams withdrew. On this occasion, his replacement was a student, Glyn John, who was 'bought' back from rugby league by repaying a signing-on fee of £400 to Leigh, having been only 17 when he signed. England went on to win the Triple Crown for the first time since the war.

England I. King (Harrogate); J.E. Woodward (Wasps), J.P. Quinn (New Brighton), J. Butterfield (Northampton), C.E. Winn (Rosslyn Park); M. Regan (Liverpool), G. Rimmer (Waterloo); +R.V. Stirling (Wasps), E. Evans (Sale), D.L. Sanders (Harlequins), P.D. Young (Dublin Wands), P.G. Yarranton (Wasps), A.R. Higgins (Liverpool), J.MacG.K. Kendall-Carpenter (Bath), D.S. Wilson (Metropolitan Police).
T: Ted Woodward 2, Chris Winn.

Wales G. Williams (London Welsh); K.J. Jones (Newport), A.G. Thomas (Cardiff), *D.G. John (St Luke's Coll/Aberavon), G. Rowlands; C.I. Morgan, W.R. Willis (Cardiff); W.O.G.Williams (Swansea), D.M. Davies (Somerset Police), C.C. Meredith, E.R. John (Neath), J.A. Gwilliam (Gloucester), S. Judd (Cardiff), +J.R.G. Stephens (Neath), R.C.C. Thomas (Swansea).
T: Gwyn Rowlands.
P: Rowlands.
Referee: Capt M.J. Dowling (Ireland).

Wales 3 England 0

Arms Park, Cardiff. 22 January 1955

Wales won by 1 pen to nil.

This was the first of several unmemorable matches at home to England in deplorable conditions. The match was postponed for a week due to snow, and when it was played, heavy rain followed by mist made for little or no rugby. Garfield Owen (Newport), who was due to make his début, cut his knee on brambles at the Glamorgan Wanderers ground in a training session. In came another new cap, Arthur Edwards, who kicked the only points after 10 minutes, when England were caught offside under their own posts. Glyn 'Shorty' Davies made a belated first appearance, while Bleddyn Williams, one of the greatest Welsh centres, was unhappy in the clinging mud, played poorly and finally retired at the end of the season.

Wales *A.B. Edwards (London Welsh); K.J. Jones (Newport), +B.L. Williams, *G.T. Wells (Cardiff), T.J. Brewer (London Welsh); C.I. Morgan, W.R. Willis (Cardiff); W.O.G. Williams (Swansea), B.V. Meredith (Newport), C.C. Meredith, J.R.G. Stephens (Neath), R.J. Robins (Pontypridd), *N.G. Davies (London Welsh), S. Judd (Cardiff), B.A. Sparks (Neath).
P: Arthur Edwards.

England +N.M. Hall (Richmond); J.E. Woodward (Wasps), J. Butterfield (Northampton), W.P.C. Davies (Harlequins), R.C. Bazley (Waterloo); D.G.S. Baker (OMTs), J.E.Williams (Old Millhillians); G.W. Hastings (Gloucester), N.A. Labuschagne (Guy's Hosp.), D.St.G. Hazell (Leicester), P.D. Young (Dublin Wands), J.H. Hancock (Newport), R. Higgins (Liverpool), P.J. Taylor (Northampton), P.H. Ryan (Richmond).
Referee: Ossie B. Glasgow (Ireland).

England 3   Wales 8

Twickenham. 21 January 1956

Wales won by 2 tries, 1 con to 1 pen.

Despite all the talent on view, this match was often a stalemate, very similar to the meeting at Swansea in 1936. The British Lions half-backs, Cliff Morgan and Dickie Jeeps, along with the brilliant centre pairing of Jeff Butterfield and Phil Davies, were present, as were the outstanding Oxford University pair of Onllwyn Brace and England cricketer Mike Smith. For this match the pairings split up. The English centres realised that Morgan was the main danger and continually cut him off from his own three-quarters. Cardiff reserve, 'Cowboy' Davies, was the only second-half scorer, with a try after a run from his own half that ended with him sliding over on his stomach. It was created when Brian Sparks charged down Smith's drop-goal attempt at the other end. The ten new English caps included Peter Jackson, Peter Robbins and the lock pairing of Roddy Marques and John Currie.

England D.F. Allison; P.B. Jackson (Coventry), J. Butterfield (Northampton), W.P.C. Davies (Harlequins), P.H.Thompson (Headingley); M.J.K. Smith (Oxford U/Hinckley), R.E.G. Jeeps (Northampton); D.L. Sanders (Harlequins), +E. Evans (Sale), C.R. Jacobs (Northampton), R.W.D. Marques (Cambridge U), J.D. Currie (Oxford U), V.G. Roberts (Penryn), A. Ashcroft (Waterloo), P.G.D. Robbins (Coventry).
P: Fenwick Allison.

Wales G.D. Owen; K.J. Jones, *H.P. Morgan, M.C.Thomas (Newport), *C.L. Davies; +C.I. Morgan (Cardiff), *D.O. Brace (Newport); W.O.G. Williams (Swansea), B.V. Meredith (Newport), C.C. Meredith (Neath), R.H. Williams (Llanelli), R.J. Robins (Pontypridd), B.A. Sparks (Neath), L.H. Jenkins (Newport), R.C.C. Thomas (Swansea).
T: Russell Robins, Lynn Davies.
C: Garfield Owen.
Referee: R. Mitchell (Ireland).

Wales 0   England 3

Arms Park, Cardiff. 19 January 1957

England won by 1 pen to nil.

Once again a penalty goal that was the only score of a Wales–England match at Cardiff, but this time England were the victors. The score came in the first half, when England wing Peter Thompson threw to a lineout on the South-Stand side. To the amazement of the majority of players and spectators, the referee ran across to the posts having spotted that débutant wing Keith Maddocks was in an offside position. It gave England full-back Fenwick Allison a penalty shot from point-blank range. Despite the loss of the strong wing-forward Reg Higgins with an arm injury, England headed towards their twelfth Triple Crown. Ken Jones was dropped after a run of 43 consecutive matches, while Terry Davies, now with Llanelli, returned after four years. Maddocks, a fine winger with St Luke's College and Neath, was never given another chance.

Wales T.J. Davies; *W.G. Howells (Llanelli), G.M. Griffiths (Cardiff), +M.C. Thomas (Newport), *K. Maddocks (Neath); C.I. Morgan (Cardiff), D.O. Brace (Newport); T.R. Prosser (Pontypool), B.V. Meredith (London Welsh), C.C. Meredith, J.R.G. Stephens (Neath), R.H. Williams (Llanelli), *R. O'Connor (Aberavon), R.J. Robins (Pontypridd), R.C.C. Thomas (Swansea).

England D.F. Allison; P.B. Jackson (Coventry), J. Butterfield (Northampton), L.B. Cannell (St Mary's Hosp.), P.H. Thompson (Headingley); R.M. Bartlett (Harlequins), R.E.G. Jeeps; C.R. Jacobs (Northampton), +E. Evans (Sale), G.W. Hastings (Gloucester), R.W.D. Marques (Cambridge U), J.D. Currie (Oxford U), R. Higgins (Liverpool), A. Ashcroft (Waterloo), P.G.D. Robbins (Oxford U).
P: Fenwick Allison.
Referee: A.I. 'Sandy' Dickie (Scotland).

England 3   Wales 3

Twickenham. 18 January 1958

Draw. England - 1 try. Wales - 1 pen.

Only an amazing display of defensive kicking by Cliff Morgan kept a strong England side at bay, after a 45-yard penalty goal from Terry Davies had given Wales an interval lead. It seemed only a matter of time before England scored. It was not until the 52nd minute that

Cardiff mud, as seen in 1959 after Wales defeated England by 5–0. Skipper Clem Thomas leads his men off, followed by Cliff Ashton, Ray Prosser, Bryn Meredith, Malcolm Price and Haydn Davies. The only try was scored by 20-year-old newcomer, Dewi Bebb. (© *Western Mail & Echo*)

Jeff Butterfield made the break for Peter Robbins to send left-wing Peter Thompson over. It was the first try by England against Wales since 1954 and it appeared to be the start of an avalanche of English scoring. However, it was not to be and Davies went close to putting Wales back in front, with a long penalty into the wind that hit a post. The Welsh team played without the Prince of Wales's feathers on their jerseys, as the red trial jerseys which had been used by the Probables in the final Welsh trial were sent mistakenly from Cardiff. New cap Haydn Morgan was a real 'Red Devil' as he had just finished serving in the Army's Airborne Division. That night after the match, a party of Welshmen returned to the ground and cut down one of the crossbars. A Mr Fred Mathias of Manorbier wrote a letter of apology to the RFU. Astonishingly, a London newspaper 'broke' the same story as an exclusive 39 years later, thinking that Mr Mathias had never previously owned up to the theft!

England D.F. Allison; P.B. Jackson (Coventry), J. Butterfield (Northampton), W.P.C. Davies (Harlequins), P.H. Thompson (Headingley); J.P. Horrocks-Taylor (Halifax), R.E.G. Jeeps (Northampton); G.W. Hastings (Gloucester), +E. Evans (Sale), C.R. Jacobs (Northampton), R.W.D. Marques, J.D. Currie (Harlequins), R.E. Syrett (Wasps), A. Ashcroft (Waterloo), P.G.D. Robbins (Coventry).
T: Peter Thompson.

Wales T.J. Davies (Llanelli); J.E. Collins (Aberavon), M.C. Thomas (Newport), C.A.H. Davies (Llanelli), G.T. Wells; C.I. Morgan, L.H. Williams (Cardiff); T.R. Prosser (Pontypool), B.V. Meredith (Newport), D.B. Devereux (Neath), R.H. Williams (Llanelli), W.R. Evans (Cardiff), +R.C.C. Thomas, J. Faull (Swansea), *H.J. Morgan (Abertillery).
P: Terry Davies.
Referee: R.C. Williams (Ireand)

Wales 5 England 0

Arms Park, Cardiff. 17 January 1959

Wales won by 1 try, 1 con to nil.

This was Dewi Bebb's match. The popular left-wing from Bangor was playing in only his sixth first-class match in Wales, but marked his début with a try typical of the opportunism he always displayed. After 30 minutes of play in the usual January quagmire at the Arms Park, he threw in to a lineout, took the return from Rhys Williams and swerved past Peter Jackson and Jim Hetherington to score for Terry Davies and convert with a fine kick. Spectators carried him off shoulder-high at the end of the match. New laws saw conversions without a placer; tap penalties being taken; and the ball could now be picked up after a tackle without first using the foot. Débutants included the speedy centre Malcolm Price, who was a British Lion later in the year and turned professional in 1962.

Wales T.J. Davies (Llanelli); J.E. Collins, *H.J. Davies (Aberavon), *M.J. Price (Pontypool), *D.I.E. Bebb (Swansea); *C. Ashton (Aberavon), L.H. Williams (Cardiff); T.R. Prosser (Pontypool), B.V. Meredith (Newport), *D.R. Main (London Welsh), *I.R. Ford (Newport), R.H. Williams (Llanelli), +R.C.C. Thomas, J. Faull (Swansea), *J. Leleu (London Welsh).
T: Dewi Bebb.
C: Terry Davies.

England J.G.G. Hetherington (Northampton); P.B. Jackson (Coventry), M.S. Phillips (Oxford U), +J. Butterfield (Northampton), P.H. Thompson (Headingley); A.B.W. Risman (Manchester U), S.R. Smith (Richmond); L.H. Webb (Bedford), J.A.S. Wackett (Rosslyn Park), G.J. Bendon (Wasps), J.D. Currie, R.W.D. Marques (Harlequins), R. Higgins (Liverpool), B.J. Wightman (Moseley), A.J. Herbert (Wasps).
Referee: R.C. Williams (Ireland).

England 14 Wales 6

Twickenham. 16 January 1960

England won by 2 tries, 1 con, 2 pens to 2 pens.

England fielded seven new caps and Wales five. One of the new boys, Richard Sharp, who replaced the injured Bev Risman, gave Wales a first-half runaround. He continually swerved past the speedy Haydn Morgan and made two tries for new left-wing Jim Roberts. Derek Morgan, the Newbridge-born number 8, also made a notable first appearance for England. It was the first time Rhys Williams skippered Wales, but it proved to be his last international match. Scrum-half Colin Evans was also not selected again and he became a rugby league player later in the year.

England D. Rutherford (Percy Park); J.R.C. Young (Harlequins), M.S. Phillips (Oxford U), M.P. Weston (Richmond), J.E. Roberts (Old Millhillians); R.A.W. Sharp (Oxford U), +R.E.G. Jeeps (Northampton); P.T. Wright (Blackheath), S.A.M. Hodgson (Durham City), C.R. Jacobs (Northampton), R.W.D. Marques, J.D. Currie (Harlequins), R.E. Syrett (Wasps), W.G.D. Morgan (Medicals), P.G.D. Robbins (Moseley).
T: Jim Roberts 2.
C: Don Rutherford.
P: Rutherford 2.

Wales T.J. Davies (Llanelli); J.E. Collins (Aberavon), M.J. Price (Pontypool), *G.W. Lewis (Richmond), D.I.E. Bebb (Swansea); C. Ashton (Aberavon), *C. Evans; T.R. Prosser (Pontypool), B.V. Meredith (Newport), *L.J. Cunningham (Aberavon), *G.W. Payne (Pontypridd), +R.H. Williams (Llanelli), *B.R. Cresswell (Newport), J. Faull (Swansea), H.J. Morgan (Abertillery).
P: Terry Davies 2.
Referee: Jack A.S. Taylor (Scotland).

Wales 6 England 3

Arms Park, Cardiff. 21 January 1961

Wales won by 2 tries to 1 try.

Dewi Bebb scored two tries from magnificent flowing moves and had a third disallowed in this fine match. It was splendid running and passing in midfield by Ken Richards, Cyril Davies and Meirion Roberts that set Bebb up for the corner at the Westgate-Street end. No better finisher ever played on the wing for Wales. Unfortunately, a Welsh foot in touch on the other side of the field prevented a Bebb hat-trick and a bigger tragedy occured when centre Davies left the field with a knee injury that was to finish his career. England responded with another good wing try being scored by British international sprinter John Young in the second half, when wing forward Haydn Morgan was acting as an emergency centre.

Wales +T.J. Davies (Llanelli); *P.M. Rees (Newport), C.A.H. Davies, H.M. Roberts (Cardiff), D.I.E. Bebb (Swansea); K.H.L. Richards (Bridgend), A. O'Connor; *P.E.J. Morgan (Aberavon), B.V. Meredith (Newport), K.D. Jones, D.J.E. Harris (Cardiff), W.R. Evans (Bridgend), G.D. Davidge (Newport), D. Nash (Ebbw Vale), H.J. Morgan (Abertillery).
T: Dewi Bebb 2.

England M.N. Gavins (Leicester); J.R.C. Young (Harlequins), M.S. Phillips (Fylde), M.P. Weston

(Richmond), J. Roberts (Old Millhillians); A.B.W. Risman (Loughborough Coll), +R.E.G. Jeeps (Northampton); T.P. Wright (Blackheath), S.A.M. Hodgson (Durham City), C.R. Jacobs (Northampton), R.W.D. Marques (Harlequins), R.J. French (St Helens), L.I. Rimmer (Bath), W.G.D. Morgan (Medicals), P.G.D. Robbins (Moseley).
T: John Young.
Referee: Kevin D Kelleher (Ireland).

England 0 Wales 0

Twickenham. 20 January 1962

Draw. No score.

Neither side deserved to score in a negative encounter, with the 'Twickenham Twirl' in evidence. A crowd of 72,000 saw new full-back Kel Coslett, aged 20 years and six days, having five chances to break the deadlock: he missed with each shot at goal. Another newcomer, Glamorgan cricketer Alan Rees at outside-half, failed with four drop goal attempts. Later that year, both Coslett and Rees turned to rugby league.

England J.G. Willcox (Oxford U); A.M. Underwood (Northampton), M.R. Wade (Cambridge U), M.P. Weston (Richmond), J. Roberts (Sale); R.A.W. Sharp (Oxford U), +R.E.G. Jeeps (Northampton); P.E. Judd (Coventry), S.A.M. Hodgson (Durham City), T.P. Wright (Blackheath), V.S.J. Harding (Sale), J.D. Currie (Bristol), R.E. Syrett (Wasps), P.J. Taylor (Northampton), D.P. Rogers (Bedford).

Wales *T.K. Coslett (Aberavon); *D.R.R. Morgan, *D.K. Jones (Llanelli), M.J. Price (Pontypool), D.I.E. Bebb (Swansea); *A.H.M. Rees (Maesteg), +L.H. Williams (Cardiff); L.J. Cunningham (Aberavon), B.V. Meredith (Newport), K.D. Jones (Cardiff), W.R. Evans (Bridgend), B. Price (Newport), R.H. Davies (London Welsh), A.E.I. Pask, H.J. Morgan (Abertillery).
Referee: Jack A.S. Taylor (Scotland).

Wales 6 England 13

Arms Park, Cardiff. 19 January 1963

England won by 2 tries, 2 cons, 1 drop goal to 1 try, 1 pen.

England skated over the icy conditions to gain their only win in Wales from 16 matches between 1959 and 1989. It was fully deserved, even with six new caps in the pack. A superb try by Malcolm Phillips, after interpassing with 'Peter Pan' (alias Peter Jackson) and John Owen's converted try after the interval, took England to 10–0. It was 13–3 before débutant Dai Hayward fell over the line in the final minute. It was the first try by Wales in five matches. Wales fielded six new caps including skipper Clive Rowlands and the exciting David Watkins at half-back. Rowlands was to lead Wales in 14 consecutive games, but the pair were never suited, as Watkins needed the ball in front of him as his club partner Bobby Prosser had always supplied.

Wales G.T.R. Hodgson (Neath); D.R.R. Morgan, D.K. Jones, D.B. Davies (Llanelli), D.I.E. Bebb (Swansea); *D. Watkins (Newport), +*D.C.T. Rowlands (Pontypool); K.D. Jones (Cardiff), N.R. Gale (Llanelli), *D. Williams (Ebbw Vale), *B.E. Thomas (Neath), B. Price (Newport), A.E.I. Pask (Abertillery), *R.C.B. Michaelson (Aberavon), *Dai J. Hayward (Cardiff).
T: Dai Hayward.
P: Grahame Hodgson.

England J.G. Willcox (Oxford U); P.B. Jackson (Coventry), M.S. Phillips (Fylde), M.P. Weston (Durham City), J. Roberts (Sale); +R.A.W. Sharp (Wasps), S.J.S. Clarke (Cambridge U); B.A. Dovey (Rosslyn Park), J.D. Thorne (Bristol), N.J. Drake-Lee (Cambridge U), A.M. Davis (Torquay Ath), J.E. Owen (Coventry), D.C. Manley (Exeter), B.J. Wightman (Coventry), D.P. Rogers (Bedford).
T: Malcolm Phillips, John Owen.
C: Richard Sharp 2.
DG: Sharp.
Referee: Kevin D. Kelleher (Ireland).

England 6 Wales 6

Twickenham. 18 January 1964

Draw. England – 2 tries. Wales – 2 tries.

England scored two tries in the opening ten minutes, but Wales – or rather, Dewi Bebb – managed to scramble a draw. Bebb scored the first Welsh try at Twickenham for eight years and then scored the only points of the second half when Ken Jones gave him a sniff of the corner, which was all the wing needed. Full-back Grahame Hodgson missed both conversion attempts and also failed with a good chance to win the match, with a penalty goal from dead in front of the England posts. The 21-year-old John Mantle was relatively unknown, but a year later he started to hit the high spots of rugby league, where he played for many years.

England +J.G. Willcox (Harlequins); M.S. Phillips (Fylde), M.P. Weston (Durham City), R.D. Sangwin (Hull & East Riding), J.M. Ranson (Rosslyn Park); J.P. Horrocks-Taylor (Middlesbrough), S.J.S. Clarke (Cambridge U); C.R. Jacobs (Northampton), S.A.M. Hodgson (Durham City), N.J. Drake-Lee (Cambridge U), A.M. Davis (Torquay Ath), R.E. Rowell (Leicester), P.J. Ford (Gloucester), D.G. Perry, D.P. Rogers (Bedford).
T: John Ranson, David Perry.

Wales G.T.R. Hodgson (Neath); *D.S. Weaver (Swansea), D.K. Jones (Llanelli), *K. Bradshaw (Bridgend), D.I.E. Bebb (Swansea); D. Watkins (Newport), +D.C.T. Rowlands (Pontypool); D. Williams (Ebbw Vale), N.R. Gale (Llanelli), L.J. Cunningham (Aberavon), B. Price (Newport), B.E. Thomas (Neath), *J.T. Mantle (Newport), A.E.I. Pask (Abertillery), A. Thomas (Newport).
T: Dewi Bebb 2.
Referee: Kevin D. Kelleher (Ireland).

Wales 14 England 3

Arms Park, Cardiff. 16 January 1965.

Wales won by 3 tries, 1 con, 1 drop goal to 1 pen.

Wales had recently beaten Fiji 28–22 in a sunny match at Cardiff when caps were not awarded. It had introduced the 19-year-old Terry Price to the Test arena and now he won his first cap on a cold, wet and miserable January day, when good rugby was almost impossible. Wales won the match up front and though a David Watkins drop goal was the only score of the first half, they then produced three tries to convincingly beat an English side that contained seven new caps, including the whole of their three-quarter line. Prop Ron Waldron gained his first cap after a three-year wait, having being picked against Ireland in 1962, only for the match to be postponed. Brian Thomas was later accused of biting England centre Geoff Frankcom and was dropped from the side to play Scotland.

Wales *T.G. Price (Llanelli); S.J. Watkins, J. Uzzell (Newport), S.J. Dawes (London Welsh), D.I.E. Bebb (Swansea); D. Watkins (Newport), +D.C.T. Rowlands (Pontypool); D. Williams (Ebbw Vale), N.R. Gale (Llanelli), *R.G. Waldron (Neath), B. Price (Newport), B.E. Thomas (Neath), G.J. Prothero (Bridgend), A.E.I. Pask, H.J. Morgan (Abertillery).
T: Stuart Watkins 2, Haydn Morgan.
C: Terry Price.
DG: David Watkins.

England D. Rutherford (Gloucester); E.L. Rudd (Oxford U), D.W.A. Rosser, G.P. Frankcom (Cambridge U), C.P. Simpson (Harlequins); T.J. Brophy (Liverpool), J.E. Williams (Sale); A.L. Horton (Blackheath), S.B. Richards (Richmond), N.J. Drake-Lee, R.E. Rowell (Leicester), J.E. Owen (Coventry), N.A. Silk (Harlequins), +D.G. Perry, D.P. Rogers (Bedford).
P: Don Rutherford.
Referee: Kevin D. Kelleher (Ireland).

England 6 Wales 11

Twickenham. 15 January 1966.

Wales won by 1 try, 1 con, 2 pens to 1 try, 1 pen.

New skipper Alun Pask took the honours, along with full-back Terry Price. Clive Rowlands was relegated to reserve and replaced by a third Abertillery player, Allan Lewis, who had partnered David Watkins at youth level. Price kicked splendidly, but injury kept him out for the remainder of the season. Wales led 6–3 in the second half, when Ken Jones put in one of his mazy runs that ended with Pask leaping over in the corner. As Winston McCarthy would say, 'A try. A winning try!'

England D. Rutherford (Gloucester); E.L. Rudd (Liverpool), T.G. Arthur, D.W.A. Rosser (Wasps), K.F. Savage (Northampton); T.J. Brophy (Liverpool), Jeremy Spencer (Harlequins); P.E. Judd (Coventry), J.V. Pullin (Bristol), D.L. Powell (Northampton), C.M. Payne (Harlequins), A.M. Davis (Devonport Servs), R.B. Taylor (Northampton), D.G. Perry, +D.P. Rogers (Bedford).
T: David Perry.
P: Don Rutherford.

Wales T.G. Price (Llanelli); S.J. Watkins (Newport), D.K. Jones (Cardiff), K. Bradshaw, *L. Davies (Bridgend); D. Watkins (Newport), *R. Allan Lewis (Abertillery); D. Williams (Ebbw Vale), N.R. Gale (Llanelli), *D.J. Lloyd (Bridgend), B. Price (Newport), B.E. Thomas (Neath), G.J. Prothero (Bridgend), +A.E.I. Pask, H.J. Morgan (Abertillery).
T: Alun Pask.
C: Terry Price.
P: Terry Price 2.
Referee: R.W. Gilliland (Ireland).

Keith Jarrett was the hero after his sensational début shattered England at the Arms Park in 1967. At the age of 18, he scored a try, five conversions and two penalties that destroyed England in a 34–21 win.
(© *Western Mail & Echo*)

Wales 34 England 21

Arms Park, Cardiff. 15 April 1967

Wales won by 5 tries, 5 cons, 2 pens, 1 drop goal to 3 tries, 4 pens.

Quite simply, this was the Jarrett match. Winning his first cap at the age of 18 years and 11 months, Keith Jarrett not only scored 19 points to equal Jack Bancroft's effort in 1910, but also scored a try that almost brought the house down. And yet few would ever have selected him at full-back again and, thankfully, the Welsh selectors agreed. Normally a centre, he was selected as the last line of defence and his club, Newport, were asked to try him there against Newbridge. So bad was he, however, that David Watkins, the Newport and Wales skipper, brought him back to centre at half-time! Few recalled later that England had closed to 19–15 behind, when Watkins waved Jarrett deeper and deeper in defence. The skipper was correct, for when Colin McFadyean kicked deeply, and well, into the Welsh half, it would have carried over a normally positioned full-back. Instead, Jarrett ran into it at pace and away past several astonished defenders to touch down in the north-east corner, just when it appeared that he was about to run out of the gates! He proceeded to place the conversion from the touchline and TV commentator Bill McLaren said: 'This laddie can do no wrong.' And he was right. Everything had gone right for Jarrett: his first goal kick struck a post before going over and six more followed, as did four other good tries by Wales and three by England, including two by lock John Barton. Not that these mattered. It was Jarrett's day and a début out of the storybooks, while for Wales it was their biggest win since the 49–14 beating of France 57 years earlier.

Wales *K.S. Jarrett; S.J. Watkins (Newport), W.H. Raybould (London Welsh), T.G.R. Davies (Cardiff), D.I.E. Bebb (Swansea); +D. Watkins (Newport), G.O. Edwards (Cardiff); D. Williams (Ebbw Vale), N.R. Gale (Llanelli), D.J. Lloyd (Bridgend), B. Price (Newport), G.T. 'Billy' Mainwaring (Aberavon), R.E. Jones (Coventry), W.D. Morris (Neath), J. Taylor (London Welsh).
T: Gerald Davies 2, Keith Jarrett, Dai Morris, Dewi Bebb.
C: Jarrett 5.
P: Jarrett 2.
DG: Billy Raybould.

England R.W. Hosen (Bristol); K.F. Savage (Northampton), R.D. Hearn (Bedford), C.W. McFadyean (Moseley), R.E. Webb (Coventry); J.F. Finlan (Moseley), R.D.A. Pickering (Bradford); M.J. Coulman (Moseley), S.B. Richards (Richmond), +P.E. Judd, J. Barton (Coventry), D.E.J. Watt (Bristol), R.B. Taylor (Northampton), D.M. Rollitt (Bristol), D.P. Rogers (Bedford).
T: John Barton 2, Keith Savage.
P: Roger Hosen 4.
Referee: Doug C.J. McMahon (Scotland).

England 11 Wales 11

Twickenham. 20 January 1968

Draw. England – 2 tries, 1 con, 1 pen. Wales – 2 tries, 1 con, 1 drop goal.

Not for the first time was an England fly-half accused of kicking too much. On this occasion it was John Finlan, whose pack provided him with enough ball to win the match. Wales had to live off scraps and when Keith Jarrett's penalty effort missed, England skipper Colin McFadyean knocked on in front of his posts and Gareth Edwards scored his first international try from the resulting scrum. England held a 11–3 lead when another knock-on, this time by Bob Hiller from another missed Jarrett penalty, resulted in Bobby Wanbon driving over from the scrum. Jarrett's conversion was followed by a Barry John drop goal that levelled the scores. Wales never picked the tough

Bridgend forward, Boyo James, again and his clubmate Wanbon turned to rugby league with the feeling that he, too, was to be ditched after one match. Wales had brought in David Nash of Ebbw Vale, the former international forward, as their first national coach.

England R.B. Hiller (Harlequins); D.H. Prout (Northampton), +C.W. McFadyean (Moseley), R.H. Lloyd (Harlequins), K.F. Savage (Northampton); J.F. Finlan (Moseley), B.W. Redwood (Bristol); B.W. Keen (Newcastle U), J.V. Pullin (Bristol), M.J. Coulman (Moseley), M.J. Parsons, P.J. Larter (Northampton), P.J. Bell (Blackheath), D.J. Gay (Bath), B.R. West (Northampton).
T: Colin McFadyean, Bill Redwood.
C: Bob Hiller.
P: Hiller.

Wales P.J. Wheeler (Aberavon); S.J. Watkins, K.S. Jarrett (Newport), T.G.R. Davies, W. Keri Jones; B. John, G.O. Edwards (Cardiff); D. Williams (Ebbw Vale), +N.R. Gale (Llanelli), *J. 'Boyo' James (Bridgend), M.L. Wiltshire, G.T. 'Billy' Mainwaring (Aberavon), W.D. Morris (Neath), *R. Wanbon (Aberavon), *A.J. Gray (London Welsh).
T: Gareth Edwards, Bobby Wanbon.
C: Keith Jarrett.
DG: Barry John.
Referee: D.P. 'Paddy' D'Arcy (Ireland).

Wales 30 England 9

Arms Park, Cardiff. 12 April 1969

Wales won by 5 tries, 3 cons, 2 pens, 1 drop goal to 3 pens.

Left-wing Maurice Richards equalled the Welsh record of four tries in a match set by Willie Llewellyn (1899) and Reggie Gibbs (1908). It helped take Wales to their eleventh Triple Crown and fifteenth outright championship. The Richards tries almost overshadowed one of the greatest-ever tries scored by a Welshman in an international match – a piece of Barry John magic with a zig-zag run and an astonishing change of pace. Of all his wonderful scores, only the try for the Lions against NZ Universities could rank with this one. Gareth Edwards was back as captain, with Delme Thomas

The Welsh 1969 Triple-Crown winners. Wing Maurice Richards scored four tries in the 30–9 defeat of England to secure the Crown for the 11th time, as well as winning the 15th outright championship for Wales. *Back row*: D.P. D'Arcy (referee), S.J. Watkins, W.D. Thomas, T.M. Davies, B.E. Thomas, D. Williams, W.D. Morris, D.J. Lloyd, F.B. Stephens (touch-judge). *Middle row*: D.C.T. Rowlands (coach), J.P.R. Williams, J. Young, G.O. Edwards (capt.), K.S. Jarrett, M.C.R. Richards. *Front row*: S.J. Dawes, J. Taylor, B. John. (© *Western Mail & Echo*)

Welsh half-backs Barry John and Gareth Edwards are carried from the Arms Park pitch in triumph. John was at his best in the defeat of England and scored one of the greatest-ever tries by a Welsh player.
(© *Western Mail & Echo*)

replacing the injured Brian Price at lock. The change mattered not and though England led 3–0 and were level, they were overwhelmed in the second spell after the first Richards try at half-time. Richards produced three further tries, Keith Jarrett kept scoring and John added a left-foot drop-shot. Keith Jarrett, in fact, finished with 31 points in four matches – a Welsh record for the championship. After the match, Edwards led the toast to the British and European champions, but the All Blacks were waiting for them in just seven weeks' time.

Wales J.P.R. Williams (London Welsh); S.J. Watkins, K.S. Jarrett (Newport), S.J. Dawes (London Welsh), M.C.R. Richards; B. John, +G.O. Edwards (Cardiff); D. Williams (Ebbw Vale), J. Young, D.J. Lloyd (Bridgend), W.D. Thomas (Llanelli), B.E. Thomas, W.D. Morris (Neath), T.M. Davies, J. Taylor (London Welsh).
T: Maurice Richards 4, Barry John.
C: Keith Jarrett 3.
P: Jarrett 2.
DG: John.

England R.B. Hiller (Harlequins); K.C. Plummer (Bristol), J.S. Spencer (Headingley), D.J. Duckham, R.E. Webb (Coventry); J.F. Finlan (Moseley), T.C. Wintle (Northampton); K.E. Fairbrother (Coventry), J.V. Pullin (Bristol), D.L. Powell, P.J. Larter (Northampton), N.E. Horton (Moseley), R.B. Taylor (Northampton), D.M. Rollitt (Bristol), +D.P. Rogers (Bedford).
P: Bob Hiller 3.
Referee: D.P. 'Paddy' D'Arcy (Ireland).

England 13 Wales 17

Twickenham. 28 February 1970

Wales won by 4 tries, 1 con, 1 drop goal to 2 tries, 2 cons, 1 pen.

This was another Wales comeback and another case of a try-scorer winning his only cap. This time it was Ray 'Chico' Hopkins and he played just 20 minutes after skipper Gareth Edwards had retired owing to injury. Wales, losing 6–13, looked beaten. Referee Robert Calmet had also retired after breaking a bone in his left leg when colliding with players. On came 'Johnny' Johnson, the England touch-judge, himself a respected international referee. John Novak, who had begun a club match in the morning, was rushed in as a late replacement for Keith Fielding and not only set up the opening try scored in the opposite corner by David Duckham, but had soon scored himself to make it 13–3 at half-time. Barry John did score a try, but the game changed when 'Chico' appeared. He immediately sent 'J.P.R.' over on the blind-side before scoring the vital fourth try himself after collecting from a lineout. Williams coolly placed the conversion to put Wales ahead and John rubbed it in as he nonchalantly flicked over a long drop-shot to close a memorable match. It was the first time that Wales had scored four tries at Twickenham and Williams became only the third Welsh full-back to score a try.

England +R.B. Hiller; M.J. Novak (Harlequins), J.S. Spencer (Headingley), D.J. Duckham (Coventry), P.M. Hale (Moseley); I.R. Shackleton (Harrogate), N.C. Starmer-Smith (Harlequins); C.B. Stevens (Penzance-Newlyn), J.V. Pullin (Bristol), K.E. Fairbrother (Coventry), A.M. Davis (Harlequins), P.J. Larter (Northampton), A.L. Bucknall (Richmond), B.R. West, R.B. Taylor (Northampton).
T: David Duckham, John Novak.
C: Bob Hiller 2.
P: Hiller.

Wales J.P.R. Williams (London Welsh); S.J. Watkins (Cardiff), W.H. Raybould (Newport), S.J. Dawes (London Welsh), I. Hall (Aberavon); B. John, +G.O. Edwards (Cardiff); D.B. Llewelyn (Newport), J. Young (Harrogate), D. Williams (Ebbw Vale), W.D. Thomas (Llanelli), T.G. Evans (London Welsh), W.D. Morris (Neath), T.M. Davies (London Welsh), D. Hughes (Newbridge). Rep: *R. Hopkins (Maesteg) for Edwards.
T: Mervyn Davies, Barry John, J.P.R. Williams, Ray Hopkins.
C: J.P.R. Williams.

DG: John.
Referee: Robert Calmet (France), replaced by R.F. 'Johnny' Johnson (England).

Wales 22 England 6

Arms Park, Cardiff. 16 January 1971

Wales won by 3 tries, 2 cons, 1 pen, 2 drop goals to 1 try, 1 pen.

England went down to defeat at Cardiff as usual, but their selectors were badly at fault in picking eight new caps in the side. Wales were almost out of sight after 40 minutes with tries by right-wing Gerald Davies, left-wing John Bevan and then Davies again. Barry John had opened the scoring with a drop-goal and finished the match with a similar effort. He had now landed six in four matches against England. Newcomer Bevan followed in the Maurice Richards mould and was a difficult man to oppose. He eventually transferred to Warrington RL in 1973, where he gained a great reputation for the way in which he slammed the ball down over the opposition try-line with his left hand. He has since returned to work for the WRU. It was the first full international match played at the Arms Park as the national stadium; the Cardiff club moving next door.

Wales J.P.R. Williams; T.G.R. Davies, +S.J. Dawes (London Welsh), A.J.L. Lewis (Ebbw Vale), *J.C. Bevan; B. John, G.O. Edwards (Cardiff); D. Williams (Ebbw Vale), J. Young (Harrogate), D.B. Llewelyn, W.D. Thomas (Llanelli), *M.G. Roberts (London Welsh), W.D. Morris (Neath), T.M. Davies, J. Taylor (London Welsh).
T: Gerald Davies 2, John Bevan.
C: John Taylor 2.
P: J.P.R. Williams.
DG: Barry John 2.

England P.A. Rossborough (Coventry); J.P.A.G. Janion (Bedford), C.S. Wardlow (Northampton), J.S. Spencer (Headingley), D.J. Duckham (Coventry), I.D. Wright (Northampton), J.J. Page (Bedford); D.L. Powell (Northampton), J.V. Pullin (Bristol), K.E. Fairbrother, B.F. Ninnes (Coventry), P.J. Larter (Northampton), +A.L. Bucknall (Richmond), R.C. Hannaford (Bristol), A. Neary (Broughton Park).
T: Charlie Hannaford.
P: Peter Rossborough.
Referee: D.P. 'Paddy' D'Arcy (Ireland).

England 3 Wales 12

Twickenham. 15 January 1972
(Points system amended – see p.12)

Wales won by 1 try, 1 con, 2 pens to 1 pen.

England picked six new caps in their side to meet a very experienced Welsh team, in which only the classy centre Roy Bergiers was a newcomer. Mobile prop John Lloyd was the skipper, but the cast was much the same for Wales, who nevertheless struggled to get into a high gear. There has probably never been a bigger contrast in goal-kickers than Bob Hiller and Barry John. They both did it their way and though Hiller opened the score, the clever Welsh outside-half had put two over by half-time. As so often against England, it was full-back J.P.R. Williams who put the icing on the cake. While England expected a John drop-goal, Gareth Edwards fed Williams on the blind-side and he was unstoppable. It was the first four-point try scored by Wales.

England +R.B. Hiller (Harlequins); J.P.A.G. Janion (Bedford), M.C. Beese (Liverpool), D.J. Duckham (Coventry), K.J. Fielding (Moseley); A.G.B. Old (Middlesbrough), J.G. Webster (Moseley); C.B. Stevens (Penzance-Newlyn), J.V. Pullin (Bristol), M.A. Burton, A. Brinn (Gloucester), C.W. Ralston (Richmond), P.J. Dixon (Harlequins), A.G. Ripley (Rosslyn Park), A. Neary (Broughton Park).
P: Bob Hiller.

Wales J.P.R. Williams; T.G.R. Davies (London Welsh), *R.T.E. Bergiers (Cardiff Coll of Ed/Llanelli), A.J.L. Lewis (Ebbw Vale), J.C. Bevan (Cardiff/Cardiff Coll of Ed); B. John, G.O. Edwards (Cardiff); +D.J. Lloyd (Bridgend), J. Young (RAF), D.B. Llewelyn, W.D. Thomas (Llanelli), T.G. Evans (London Welsh), W.D. Morris (Neath), T.M. Davies, J. Taylor (London Welsh).
T: J.P.R. Williams.
C: Barry John.
P: John 2.
Referee: Jake Young (Scotland).

Wales 25 England 9

Arms Park, Cardiff. 20 January 1973

Wales won by 5 tries, 1 con, 1 pen to 2 pens, 1 drop goal.

Wales won easily enough with a 5–0 try-count, though England could look to a turning point coming when Peter Warfield left the field with concussion. His replacement, Geoff Evans, was waiting to take his place. Wales were leading by 4–3 and, as Evans waited, he saw Gerald Davies speed over for the second try of the match. A Gareth Edwards try just before the interval took it to 12–6 and injury time tries by skipper Arthur Lewis and then John Bevan, with his second, rubbed it in.

Wales J.P.R. Williams; T.G.R. Davies (London Welsh), R.T.E. Bergiers (Llanelli), +A.J.L. Lewis (Ebbw Vale), J.C. Bevan (Cardiff); P. Bennett (Llanelli), G.O. Edwards (Cardiff); D.J. Lloyd (Bridgend), J. Young (London Welsh/RAF), G. Shaw (Neath), W.D. Thomas, D.L. Quinnell (Llanelli), W.D. Morris (Neath), T.M. Davies (Swansea), J. Taylor (London Welsh).
T: John Bevan 2, Gerald Davies, Gareth Edwards, Arthur Lewis.
C: Phil Bennett.
P: John Taylor.

England S.A. Doble (Moseley); A.J. Morley (Bristol), P.J. Warfield (Durham U/Rosslyn Park), P.S. Preece, D.J. Duckham; A.R. Cowman (Coventry), J.G. Webster (Moseley); C.B. Stevens (Penzance-Newlyn), +J.V. Pullin (Bristol), F.E. Cotton (Loughborough Coll), P.J. Larter (Northampton), C.W. Ralston (Richmond), J.A. Watkins (Gloucester), A.G. Ripley (Rosslyn Park), A. Neary (Broughton Park).
Rep: G.W. Evans (Coventry) for Warfield.
P: Sam Doble 2.
DG: Dick Cowman.
Referee: Georges Domercq (France).

England 16 Wales 12

Twickenham. 16 March 1974.

England won by 2 tries, 1 con, 2 pens to 1 try, 1 con, 2 pens.

Max Boyce was inspired to sing of 'Blind Irish Referees' after John West had disallowed a try-scoring effort by J.J.Williams in the 69th minute. It was the key to the whole match and helped England defeat Wales at Twickenham for the first time since 1960. Wales led 9–7 at the interval and may well have won the match if the 'try' had been given. Williams dived behind the goal-line with England defenders David Duckham and Peter Squires, but the referee, yards behind, ruled against Wales. Gareth Edwards made his 35th consecutive appearance to be the most-capped Welsh scrum-half, outpassing Dicky Owen. The only new cap was Roger Blyth, who played because J.P.R.Williams had just undergone a cartilage operation. Roger's father, Len, had been capped three times in 1951–52. It was a match which started controversially when the Welsh national anthem was not played.

England W.H. Hare (Notts); P.J. Squires (Harrogate), K. Smith (Roundhay), G.W. Evans, D.J. Duckham (Coventry); A.G.B. Old (Leicester), J.G. Webster (Moseley); C.B. Stevens (Penzance-Newlyn), +J.V. Pullin (Bristol), M.A. Burton (Gloucester), C.W. Ralston (Richmond), R.M. Uttley, P.J. Dixon (Gosforth), A.G. Ripley (Rosslyn Park), A. Neary (Broughton Park).
T: David Duckham, Andy Ripley.
C: Alan Old.
P: Old 2.

Wales *W.R. Blyth (Swansea); T.G.R. Davies (London Welsh), R.T.E. Bergiers (Llanelli), A.A.J. Finlayson (Cardiff), J.J. Williams; P. Bennett (Llanelli), +G.O. Edwards (Cardiff); G. Shaw (Neath), R.W. Windsor (Pontypool), P.D. Llewellyn (Swansea), I.R. Robinson (Cardiff), W.D. Thomas (Llanelli), W.D. Morris (Neath), T.M. Davies (Swansea), T.J. Cobner (Pontypool).
Rep: G.A.D. Wheel (Swansea) for Robinson.
T: Mervyn Davies.
C: Phil Bennett.
P: Bennett 2.
Referee: John R. West (Ireland).

Wales 20 England 4

Arms Park, Cardiff. 15 February 1975

Wales won by 3 tries, 1 con, 2 pens to 1 try.

It was all too easy early on as Wales tore England apart. Allan Martin had landed two penalty goals, and first J.J.Williams and then Gerald Davies scored tries to make it 16–0 at the interval. The game then died until six minutes from time, when Nigel Horton scored for England. It woke Wales up and Steve Fenwick ended a fine move with the third Welsh try. Wales lost Geoff Wheel with a shoulder injury, while England's Jan Webster (cut knee) and Peter Wheeler (neck) were both replaced.

Wales J.P.R. Williams (London Welsh); T.G.R. Davies (Cardiff), S.P. Fenwick (Bridgend), R.W.R. Gravell, J.J. Williams (Llanelli); J.D. Bevan (Aberavon), G.O. Edwards (Cardiff); A.G. Faulkner, R.W. Windsor, G. Price (Pontypool), G.A.D. Wheel (Swansea), A.J. Martin (Aberavon), T.P. Evans, +T.M. Davies (Swansea), T.J. Cobner (Pontypool). Rep: D.L. Quinnell (Llanelli) for Wheel.
T: J.J. Williams, Gerald Davies, Steve Fenwick.

C: Allan Martin.
P: Martin 2.

England A.M. Jorden (Bedford); P.J. Squires (Harrogate), K. Smith (Roundhay), P.S. Preece, D.J. Duckham (Coventry); M.J. Cooper, J.G. Webster (Moseley); C.B. Stevens (Penzance-Newlyn), P.J. Wheeler (Leicester), +F.E. Cotton (Coventry), N.E. Horton (Moseley), C.W. Ralston (Richmond), J.A. Watkins (Gloucester), R.M. Uttley (Gosforth), A. Neary (Broughton Park). Reps: S.J. Smith (Sale) for Webster; J.V. Pullin (Bristol) for Wheeler.
T: Nigel Horton.
Referee: Allan M. Hosie (Scotland).

England 9 Wales 21

Twickenham. 17 January 1976

Wales won by 3 tries, 3 cons, 1 pen to 3 pens.

Wales ran up their highest winning margin at Twickenham, as the running and tackling of J.P.R. Williams frightened friend and foe alike. On the day, he passed Billy Bancroft's 33 appearances to become the most-capped Welsh full-back, scored two of the three Welsh tries and halted any English threats to the Welsh line. Later, he received seven stitches to his right cheek. As he said: 'The Williams blood has been spilt around many battlegrounds of the world!' Inevitably, Gareth Edwards scored the opening try. England heeled the ball, but Edwards beat a startled Mike Lampkowski to it. Just before the interval, J.J. Williams raced down the left-wing and threw the ball inside to 'J.P.R.', who charged over. England lost Yorkshire county cricketer, Peter Squires, with a broken arm, but Alistair Hignell, also a county cricketer, kept his side in the hunt with his third successful penalty. It prompted 'J.P.R.' into action again and he took a switch pass from Phil Bennett to defeat the defence for his second try. Steve Fenwick converted to seal a good win. Bennett had originally been dropped and relegated to third choice. But since both John Bevan and David Richards were injured, Bennett was recalled. The complete Swansea back row was selected, with Mark Keyworth playing for England against his clubmates Trevor Evans and Mervyn Davies.

England A.J. Hignell (Cambridge U); P.J. Squires (Harrogate), A.W. Maxwell (Headingley), D.A. Cooke (Harlequins), D.J. Duckham (Coventry); M.J. Cooper, M.S. Lampkowski (Moseley); M.A. Burton (Gloucester), P.J. Wheeler (Leicester), F.E. Cotton (Sale), W.B. Beaumont (Fylde), R.M. Wilkinson (Bedford), M. Keyworth (Swansea), A.G. Ripley (Rosslyn Park), +A. Neary (Broughton Park). Rep: P.S. Preece (Coventry) for Squires.
P: Alastair Hignell 3.

Wales J.P.R. Williams (London Welsh); T.G.R. Davies (Cardiff), R.W.R. Gravell (Llanelli), S.P. Fenwick (Bridgend), J.J. Williams; P. Bennett (Llanelli), G.O. Edwards (Cardiff); A.G. Faulkner, R.W. Windsor, G. Price (Pontypool), G.A.D. Wheel (Swansea), A.J. Martin (Aberavon), T.P. Evans, +T.M. Davies (Swansea), T.J. Cobner (Pontypool).
T: J.P.R. Williams 2, Gareth Edwards.
C: Steve Fenwick 3.
P: Allan Martin.
Referee: Georges Domercq (France).

Wales 14 England 9

Arms Park, Cardiff. 5 March 1977

Wales won by 2 tries, 2 pens to 3 pens.

As usual, Wales were slow to start and were soon 6–0 down. Then, after a Gareth Edwards try and a Steve Fenwick penalty, they fell back against Alastair Hignell's third successful kick. But, also as usual, the saviour against England was J.P.R. Williams, who followed a second Fenwick penalty with a match-winning try. Centre David Burcher opened a gap for the full-back to dummy a pass to Gerald Davies and leave the defence flat-footed.

Wales J.P.R. Williams (Bridgend); T.G.R. Davies (Cardiff), S.P. Fenwick (Bridgend), D.H. Burcher (Newport), J.J. Williams; +P. Bennett (Llanelli), G.O. Edwards (Cardiff); *C. Williams (Aberavon), R.W. Windsor, G. Price (Pontypool), G.A.D. Wheel (Swansea), A.J. Martin (Aberavon), R.C. Burgess (Ebbw Vale), D.L. Quinnell (Llanelli), T.J. Cobner (Pontypool).
T: Gareth Edwards, J.P.R. Williams.
P: Steve Fenwick 2.

England A.J. Hignell (Cambridge U); P.J. Squires (Harrogate), B.J. Corless (Moseley), C.P. Kent (Rosslyn Park), M.A.C. Slemen (Liverpool); M.J. Cooper (Moseley), M. Young (Gosforth); F.E. Cotton (Sale), P.J. Wheeler, R.J. Cowling (Leicester), W.B. Beaumont (Fylde), N.E. Horton (Moseley), P.J. Dixon, +R.M. Uttley (Gosforth), M. Rafter (Bristol).
P: Alastair Hignell 3.
Referee: David I.H. Burnett (Ireland).

The team of song: the choir of 1978 prepare to cut a record. *Left to right*: John Dawes, Derek Quinnell, Paul Ringer, J.J. Williams, Barry John, Charlie Faulkner, Phil Bennett, Gareth Edwards, Bobby Windsor, Mervyn Davies, Gerald Davies, J.P.R. Williams, John Taylor and Graham Price. (© Huw Evans)

England 6 Wales 9

Twickenham. 4 February 1978
Wales won by 3 pens to 2 pens.

Rarely did it rain so hard for a Twickenham match and no tries resulted – Wales won by three Phil Bennett goals in four attempts against two Alastair Hignell successes in seven attempts. Gareth Edwards won his 50th cap and was probably the game's best performer. Bennett's winning goal came after 72 minutes, when new cap Rob Mordell was adjudged to have handled in a ruck. The Rosslyn Park player was not selected again and turned to rugby league in protest. The Welsh squad had been guests of Prime Minster James Callaghan at 10 Downing Street two months earlier, following their remarkable run in the '70s.

England A.J. Hignell (Cambridge U); P.J. Squires (Harrogate), B.J. Corless (Moseley), P.W. Dodge (Leicester), M.A.C. Slemen (Liverpool); J.P. Horton (Bath), M. Young (Gosforth); B.G. Nelmes (Cardiff), P.J. Wheeler (Leicester), M.A. Burton (Gloucester), +W.B. Beaumont (Fylde), N.E. Horton (Toulouse), M. Rafter (Bristol), J.P. Scott, R.J. Mordell (Rosslyn Park).
P: Alastair Hignell 2.

Wales J.P.R. Williams (Bridgend); T.G.R. Davies (Cardiff), R.W.R. Gravell (Llanelli), S.P. Fenwick (Bridgend), J.J. Williams; +P. Bennett (Llanelli), G.O. Edwards (Cardiff); A.G. Faulkner, R.W. Windsor, G. Price (Pontypool), G.A.D. Wheel (Swansea), A.J. Martin (Aberavon), J. Squire (Newport), D.L. Quinnell (Llanelli), T.J. Cobner (Pontypool).
P: Phil Bennett 3.
Referee: Norman R. Sanson (Scotland).

Wales 27 England 3

Arms Park, Cardiff. 17 March 1979

Wales won by 5 tries, 2 cons, 1 drop goal to 1 pen.

This was a humiliating defeat for England, who were crushed in the last twenty minutes as Wales advanced from 7–3 to 27–3. It was the biggest win by Wales against England since 1905 and came after many had fancied the visitors to win. As France had come from behind on the same day to defeat Scotland by 21–17, it meant the fourth championship in five years for Wales – their 21st in all. The Triple Crown was won for the fourth successive season. David Richards scored the only first-half try and, early in the second spell, J.P.R. Williams retired to have stitches in a gashed calf. He was replaced by Clive Griffiths who was to move to St Helen's RL in the summer. The 33-year-old Mike Roberts had his moment of glory by running all of one yard for the second Welsh try. That opened the floodgates with Paul Ringer and then Elgan Rees scoring, the latter after Griffiths had made the running. Griffiths was just defeated for the touchdown by Rees. Steve Fenwick's final conversion took him to 38 points for the season.

Wales +J.P.R. Williams (Bridgend); H.E. Rees (Neath), D.S. Richards (Swansea), S.P. Fenwick (Bridgend), J.J. Williams (Llanelli); W.G. Davies, T.D. Holmes (Cardiff); S.J. Richardson (Aberavon), *A.J. Phillips (Cardiff), G. Price (Pontypool), M.G. Roberts (London Welsh), A.J. Martin (Aberavon), J. Squire (Pontypool), D.L. Quinnell, P. Ringer (Llanelli). Rep: *C.R. Griffiths (Llanelli) for (J.P.R.)Williams.
T: David Richards, Mike Roberts, Paul Ringer, Elgan Rees.
C: Steve Fenwick, Allan Martin.
DG: Gareth Davies.

England A.J. Hignell (Bristol); P.J. Squires (Harrogate), R.M. Cardus (Roundhay), P.W. Dodge (Leicester), M.A.C. Slemen (Liverpool); W.N. Bennett (London Welsh), P. Kingston (Gloucester); G.S. Pearce (Northampton), P.J. Wheeler (Leicester), C.E. Smart (Newport), +W.B. Beaumont (Fylde), N.E. Horton (Toulouse), M. Rafter (Bristol), J.P. Scott (Cardiff), A. Neary (Broughton Park).
P: Neil Bennett.
Referee: J-P. Bonnet (France).

England 9 Wales 8

Twickenham. 16 February 1980

England won by 3 pens to 2 tries.

The Paul Ringer affair: the Welsh flanker had to be rated as unlucky to have been sent off for a tackle on England outside-half John Horton. It was really the 14 minutes leading up to it, however, which annoyed referee David Burnett with John Scott particularly aggressive on his clubmate Terry Holmes. It was a case of the next one walking. As Ringer walked away, 'Dusty' Hare kicked the first points, but skipper Jeff Squire went over from a scrum to put Wales in front. Another Hare penalty came, only for Wales to score a fine try as speedy hooker Alan Phillips raced away to put Elgan Rees in at the corner. It was 8–6 to Wales and into injury time when Hare fired over the winner. Ringer was suspended for eight weeks and was never allowed to forget it. Two Welsh supporters, delayed by a forged-ticket scare, mentioned at the interval that the Welsh back row had done little work. One said, 'And that Ringer. I haven't seen him yet!'

England W.H. Hare (Leicester); J. Carleton (Orrell), C.R. Woodward, P.W. Dodge (Leicester), M.A.C. Slemen (Liverpool); J.P. Horton (Bath), S.J. Smith (Sale); P.J. Blakeway (Gloucester), P.J. Wheeler (Leicester), F.E. Cotton (Sale), M.J. Colclough (Angouleme), +W.B. Beaumont (Fylde), R.M. Uttley (Wasps), J.P. Scott (Cardiff), A. Neary (Broughton Park). Rep: M. Rafter (Bristol) for Uttley.
P: 'Dusty' Hare 3.

Wales W.R. Blyth (Swansea); H.E. Rees (Neath), D.S. Richards (Swansea), S.P. Fenwick (Bridgend), L. Keen (Aberavon); W.G. Davies, T.D. Holmes (Cardiff); C. Williams (Swansea), A.J. Phillips (Cardiff), G. Price (Pontypool), G.A.D. Wheel (Swansea), A.J. Martin (Aberavon), +J. Squire, E.T. Butler (Pontypool), P. Ringer (Llanelli).
Sent off: Paul Ringer.
T: Jeff Squire, Elgan Rees.
Referee: David I.H. Burnett (Ireland).

Wales 21 England 19

Arms Park, Cardiff. 17 January 1981

Wales won by 1 try, 1 con, 4 pens, 1 drop goal to 1 try, 5 pens.

If they could not win away, at least Wales could win their championship matches at home. It was full of kicking and just one try to either side – the Welsh score came first as Rhodri Lewis helped send Clive Davis over the English line. England full-back 'Dusty' Hare kept scoring and included a good try at the Westgate-Street end after Paul Dodge had paved the way. It was 12–10 to Wales at half-time, but they were 18–19 behind in injury time, when Clive Woodward, the English coach in the 1990s, was lured offside. Steve Fenwick kicked the winning goal. This was the record-breaking 54th cap for Welsh full-back J.P.R. Williams.

Wales J.P.R. Williams (Bridgend); R.A. Ackerman (Newport), D.S. Richards (Swansea), +S.P. Fenwick (Bridgend), *D.L. Nicholas (Llanelli); W.G. Davies (Cardiff), D.B. Williams (Swansea); *I. Stephens (Bridgend), A.J. Phillips (Cardiff), G. Price (Pontypool), G.A.D. Wheel (Swansea), C.E. Davis (Newbridge), J. Squire (Pontypool), Gareth P. Williams (Bridgend), *J.R. Lewis (SG Inst/Cardiff).
T: Clive Davis.
C: Steve Fenwick.
P: Fenwick 4.
DG: Gareth Davies.

England W.H. Hare (Leicester); J. Carleton (Orrell), C.R. Woodward, P.W. Dodge (Leicester), M.A.C. Slemen (Liverpool); J.P. Horton (Bath), S.J. Smith (Sale); P.J. Blakeway (Gloucester), P.J.

Wheeler (Leicester), F.E. Cotton (Sale), +W.B. Beaumont (Fylde), M.J. Colclough (Angouleme), M. Rafter (Bristol), J.P. Scott (Cardiff), D.H. Cooke (Harlequins). Rep: A. Sheppard (Bristol) for Cotton.
T: 'Dusty' Hare.
P: Hare 5.
Referee: J. Brian Anderson (Scotland).

England 17 Wales 7

Twickenham. 6 March 1982

England won by 2 tries, 3 pens to 1 try, 1 drop goal.

If Wales had any chance of winning, it disappeared when Terry Holmes left the field with an injured shoulder after 46 minutes. By then, England had scored tries from left-wing Mike Slemen after a Steve Smith opening, and then right-wing John Carleton, who picked up at scrum-half and found no defender at home to stop him. The only score of the second half was when 'Dusty' Hare placed his third goal. Graham Price won his 37th cap to become the most-capped prop for Wales.

England W.H. Hare (Leicester); J. Carleton (Orrell), C.R. Woodward, P.W. Dodge (Leicester), M.A.C. Slemen (Liverpool); L. Cusworth (Leicester), +S.J. Smith (Sale); C.E. Smart (Newport), P.J. Wheeler (Leicester), P.J. Blakeway (Gloucester), S.J. Bainbridge (Gosforth), M.J. Colclough (Angouleme), N.C. Jeavons (Moseley), J.P. Scott (Cardiff), P.J. Winterbottom (Headingley).
T: John Carleton, Mike Slemen.
P: 'Dusty' Hare 3.

Wales G. Evans (Maesteg); R.A. Ackerman (Newport), R.W.R. Gravell (Llanelli), A.J. Donovan (Swansea), C.F.W. Rees (London Welsh); +W.G. Davies, T.D. Holmes (Cardiff); I. Stephens (Bridgend), A.J. Phillips (Cardiff), G. Price (Pontypool), R.D. Moriarty (Swansea), S. Sutton (Pontypool), R.C. Burgess (Ebbw Vale), J. Squire (Pontypool), J.R. Lewis (Cardiff). Rep: Gerald Williams (Bridgend) for Holmes.
T: Rhodri Lewis.
DG: Gareth Davies.
Referee: François Palmade (France).

Wales 13 England 13

Arms Park, Cardiff. 5 February 1983

Draw. 1 try, 2 pens, 1 drop goal each.

A slight improvement in performance enabled Wales to achieve a draw, though England had to be saved by a 'Dusty' Hare penalty after John Carleton had begun the scoring for them with a try from Hare's pass. Among the new Welsh faces was the talented Mark Ring, while England had Tony Swift, Colin Smart and John Scott who were all playing club rugby in Wales.

Wales *M.A. Wyatt (Swansea); H.E. Rees (Neath), *M.G. Ring (Cardiff), D.S. Richards (Swansea), C.F.W. Rees (London Welsh); *M. Dacey (Swansea), T.D. Holmes (Cardiff); C. Williams (Swansea), *W.J. James (Aberavon), G. Price (Pontypool), R.L. Norster (Cardiff), R.D. Moriarty (Swansea), J. Squire, +E.T. Butler (Pontypool), *D.F. Pickering (Llanelli).
T: Jeff Squire.
P: Mark Wyatt 2.
DG: Malcolm Dacey.

England W.H. Hare (Leicester); J. Carleton (Orrell), P.W. Dodge (Leicester), G.H. Davies (Coventry), A.H. Swift (Swansea); L. Cusworth (Leicester), +S.J. Smith (Sale); G.S. Pearce (Northampton), S.G.F. Mills (Gloucester), C.E. Smart (Newport), S.B. Boyle (Gloucester), S.J. Bainbridge (Gosforth), N.C. Jeavons (Moseley), J.P. Scott (Cardiff), P.J. Winterbottom (Headingley).
T: John Carleton.
P: 'Dusty' Hare 2.
DG: Les Cusworth.
Referee: John R. West (Ireland).

England 15 Wales 24

Twickenham. 17 March 1984

Wales won by 1 try, 1 con, 4 pens, 2 drop goals to 5 pens.

Scotland were defeating France by 21–12 at Murrayfield to win the title and this match was for minor places only. With Wales leading 18–15, outside-half Malcolm Dacey dropped two goals to ensure victory. Terry Holmes was at last fit to return and his task was made easier by the forward play of Robert Norster and Richard Moriarty in particular. At 9–9, the game's only try came when Bleddyn Bowen broke and Eddie Butler linked to send Adrian Hadley over. The last of five goals by Howell Davies gave him a Welsh record of 39 championship points in a season.

England W.H. Hare (Leicester); J. Carleton (Orrell), B. Barley (Wakefield), C.R. Woodward, R. Underwood; L. Cusworth, N.G. Youngs (Leicester); P.A.G. Rendall (Wasps), +P.J. Wheeler (Leicester), P.J. Blakeway (Gloucester), M.J. Colclough (Wasps), S. Bainbridge (Gosforth), A.F. Dun (Wasps), J.P. Scott

(Cardiff), P.J. Winterbottom (Headingley).
P: 'Dusty' Hare 5.

Wales H. Davies; M.H. Titley (Bridgend), R.A. Ackerman (London Welsh), B. Bowen (South Wales Police), A.M. Hadley (Cardiff); M. Dacey (Swansea), T.D. Holmes (Cardiff); I. Stephens (Bridgend), +M.J. Watkins (Newport), I.H. Eidman, R.L. Norster (Cardiff), S.J. Perkins (Pontypool), R.D. Moriarty (Swansea), E.T. Butler (Pontypool), D.F. Pickering (Llanelli).
T: Adrian Hadley.
C: Howell Davies.
P: Davies 4.
DG: Malcolm Dacey 2.
Referee: J. Brian Anderson (Scotland).

Wales 24 England 15

Arms Park, Cardiff. 20 April 1985

Wales won by 2 tries, 2 cons, 3 pens, 1 drop goal to 1 try, 1 con, 2 pens, 1 drop goal.

England succeeded in stopping Terry Holmes only to find he now had a fast, elusive partner in débutant Jonathan Davies, whose brother-in-law Phil was a new face in the pack. England led 15–12 before full-back Chris Martin made a hash of a high ball and Jonathan Davies pounced to add a try to his earlier drop goal. The try was the first by a Welsh fly-half on his début since Dicky Ralph achieved it against France in 1931. The pack took a hand with Bob Norster excelling at the lineout and David Pickering sending Gareth Roberts in for the final try.

Wales P.H. Thorburn (Neath); P.I. Lewis (Llanelli), R.A. Ackerman (London Welsh), *K. Hopkins (Swansea), A.M. Hadley (Cardiff); *J. Davies (Neath), +T.D. Holmes; J. Whitefoot (Cardiff), W.J. James (Aberavon), S. Evans (Swansea), R.L. Norster (Cardiff), S.J. Perkins (Pontypool), G.J. Roberts (Cardiff), *P.T. Davies, D.F. Pickering (Llanelli).
T: Jonathan Davies, Gareth Roberts.
C: Paul Thorburn 2.
P: Thorburn 3.
DG: Jonathan Davies.

England C.R. Martin (Bath); S.T. Smith (Wasps), K.G. Simms (Liverpool), +P.W. Dodge, R. Underwood (Leicester); C.R. Andrew (Notts), N.D. Melville (Wasps); A. Sheppard (Bristol), S.E. Brain (Coventry), G.S. Pearce (Northampton), J. Orwin (Gloucester), W.A. Dooley (Preston Grasshoppers), J.P. Hall (Bath), R. Hesford (Bristol), D.H. Cooke (Harlequins).
T: Simon T. Smith.
C: Rob Andrew.
P: Andrew 2.
DG: Andrew.
Referee: François Palmade (France).

A début try for Jonathan Davies against England in 1985 comes after Wales centre Rob Ackerman and England full-back Chris Martin had missed the ball. (© Huw Evans)

England 21 Wales 18

Twickenham. 18 January 1986
England won by 6 pens, 1 drop goal to 1 try, 1 con, 3 pens, 1 drop goal.

Only one try was scored and that by the losers. A fine run by Jonathan Davies put centre Bleddyn Bowen over to give Wales the lead by 18–15 but Rob Andrew struck back. Having already kicked all of England's points with five penalty goals, he placed a sixth to level the scores. Then, in injury time, he sent over a left-footed drop goal to win the match. One Swansea player – lock Maurice Colclough – was instrumental in England dominating the lineout, while scrum-half Robert Jones started out on an illustrious international career: son-in-law of former captain and coach, Clive Rowlands, he was soon to have the same clever kicking style. The other débutants were John Devereux, later capped for Great Britain at rugby league, and David 'Muddy' Waters, who had originally been selected in 1985, but the match against France was postponed.

England G.H. Davies; S.T. Smith (Wasps), S.J. Halliday (Bath), J.L.B. Salmon (Harlequins), R. Underwood (Leicester/RAF); C.R. Andrew (Notts), +N.D. Melville; P.A.G. Rendall (Wasps), S.E. Brain (Coventry), G.S. Pearce (Northampton), W.A. Dooley (Preston Grasshoppers), M.J. Colclough (Swansea), J.P. Hall (Bath), G.L. Robbins (Coventry), P.J. Winterbottom (Headingley).
P: Rob Andrew 6.
DG: Andrew.

Wales P.H. Thorburn (Neath); P.I. Lewis (Llanelli), *J.A. Devereux (Bridgend/ SG Inst), B. Bowen (South Wales Police), A.M. Hadley (Cardiff); J. Davies (Neath), *R.N. Jones (Swansea); J. Whitefoot (Cardiff), W.J. James (Aberavon), I.H. Eidman (Cardiff), *D.R. Waters (Newport), S.J. Perkins, M.A. Brown (Pontypool), P.T. Davies, +D.F. Pickering (Llanelli).
T: Bleddyn Bowen.
C: Paul Thorburn.
P: Thorburn 3.
DG: Jonathan Davies.
Referee: R.J. 'Bob' Fordham (Australia).

Wales 19 England 12

Arms Park, Cardiff. 7 March 1987

Wales won by 1 try, 5 pens to 4 pens.

A nasty beginning led to Phil Davies being flattened by England lock Wade Dooley in the sixth minute. Referee Ray Megson appeared to be out of his depth in his first full international match and, though he warned Dooley, it was obvious that the police officer should have 'gone for the early bath'. England later dropped Dooley, Richard Hill, Graham Dawe and Gareth Chilcott against Scotland for disciplinary reasons. The Welsh locks Steve Sutton and Bob Norster had clashed at club level, but Norster's breaking his partner's nose was purely accidental. Prop Stuart Evans surged over in the second half for the only try of the match.

Wales M.A. Wyatt (Swansea); G.M.C. Webbe (Bridgend), K. Hopkins (Swansea), J.A. Devereux (Bridgend/SG Inst), I.C. Evans (Llanelli); J. Davies (Neath), R.N. Jones (Swansea); J. Whitefoot (Cardiff), W.J. James (Aberavon), S. Evans (Neath), S. Sutton (South Wales Police), R.L. Norster (Cardiff), W.P. Moriarty (Swansea), P.T. Davies, +D.F. Pickering (Llanelli).
Rep: *R.G. Collins (South Wales Police) for (P.T.)Davies.
T: Stuart Evans.
P: Mark Wyatt 5.

England W.H.M. Rose (Harlequins); M.E. Harrison (Wakefield), K.G. Simms (Wasps), J.L.B. Salmon (Harlequins), R. Underwood (Leicester); C.R. Andrew (Wasps), +R.J. Hill; G.J. Chilcott, R.G.R. Dawe (Bath), G.S. Pearce (Northampton), W.A. Dooley, S. Bainbridge (Fylde), G.W. Rees (Notts), J.P. Hall (Bath), P.J. Winterbottom (Headingley).
P: Marcus Rose 4.
Referee: Ray J. Megson (Scotland).

(NB: RWC 1987 Wales v England)

England 3 Wales 11

Twickenham. 6 February 1988

Wales won by 2 tries, 1 drop goal to 1 pen.

Four outside-halves – Bleddyn Bowen, Mark Ring, Tony Clement and Jonathan Davies – lined up for Wales. The combination succeeded to the extent of winning and scoring two superb tries. A scoreless first half had seen hooker Kevin Phillips retire from the field with injury. Wing Adrian Hadley then struck twice, with the first coming as a result of superb interpassing with Ring. The second was even better, with Davies and Ring beginning the move which saw Hadley score from Bowen's pass. Davies added a drop goal before England managed a late penalty goal.

The explosive start to the 1987 England–Wales battle as Wade Dooley and Bob Norster square up. Steve Sutton and Stuart Evans prepare to give aid. England later dropped Dooley and three other players for disciplinary reasons. (© Huw Evans)

England J.M. Webb (Bristol); +M.E. Harrison (Wakefield), W.D.C. Carling (Durham U/Harlequins), K.G. Simms (Wasps), R. Underwood; L. Cusworth (Leicester), N.D. Melville; P.A.G. Rendall (Wasps), B.C. Moore (Notts), J.A. Probyn (Wasps), J. Orwin (Bedford), W.A. Dooley (Fylde), M.G. Skinner (Harlequins), D. Richards (Leicester), P.J. Winterbottom (Headingley).
P: Jon Webb.

Wales A. Clement (Swansea); I.C. Evans (Llanelli), M.G. Ring (Pontypool), +B. Bowen (South Wales Police), A.M. Hadley (Cardiff); J. Davies (Llanelli), R.N. Jones (Swansea); S.T. Jones (Pontypool), K.H. Phillips (Neath), D. Young (Swansea), *P.S. May (Llanelli), R.L. Norster (Cardiff), R.D. Phillips (Neath), W.P. Moriarty (Swansea), R.G. Collins (South Wales Police). Rep: *I.J. Watkins (Ebbw Vale) for (K.H.) Phillips.
T: Adrian Hadley 2.
DG: Jonathan Davies.
Referee: Stephen R. Hilditch (Ireland).

Wales 12 England 9

Arms Park, Cardiff. 18 March 1989

Wales won by 1 try, 1 con, 2 pens to 2 pens, 1 drop goal.

Once again England flopped in Cardiff when a victory would have given them the championship; it went to France instead. Bob Norster won lineout ball and Robert Jones used the box kick continually. England led at 9–6 only for Wales to score the game's only try as Rory Underwood's pass back to Jon Webb went astray and Mike Hall was given a disputed touchdown as he slid in the pouring rain. England included Will Carling, whose father Bill had played for Cardiff; Mike Teague, who had played for Cardiff, and the Crickhowell-born Dewi Morris. Wales included the North Walian Arthur Emyr on the left-wing.

Wales +P.H. Thorburn (Neath); I.C. Evans (Llanelli), M.R. Hall (Bridgend), D.W. Evans (Cardiff/Oxford U), *A. Emyr (Swansea); P.

Turner (Newbridge), R.N. Jones (Swansea); M. Griffiths (Bridgend), I.J. Watkins (Ebbw Vale), L. Delaney, P.T. Davies (Llanelli), R.L. Norster (Cardiff), G. Jones (Llanelli), M.A. Jones (Neath), D.J. Bryant (Bridgend).
T: Mike Hall.
C: Paul Thorburn.
P: Thorburn 2.

England J.M. Webb (Bristol); R. Underwood (Leicester/RAF), +W.D.C. Carling (Harlequins), S.J. Halliday (Bath), C. Oti; C.R. Andrew (Wasps), C.D. Morris (Liverpool-St Helen's); P.A.G. Rendall (Wasps), B.C. Moore (Notts), G.J. Chilcott (Bath), P.J. Ackford (Harlequins), W.A. Dooley (Preston Grasshoppers), M.C. Teague (Gloucester), D. Richards (Leicester), R.A. Robinson (Bath).
Rep: G.W. Rees (Notts) for Teague.
P: Rob Andrew 2.
DG: Andrew.
Referee: Kerry V.J. Fitzgerald (Australia).

England 34   Wales 6

Twickenham. 17 February 1990

England won by 4 tries, 3 cons, 4 pens to 1 try, 1 con.

Wales had played pluckily in their last two matches against New Zealand and France, but there was little to recommend their efforts. Brian Moore showed his contempt of Welsh efforts after Will Carling had scored the opening try and Rory Underwood followed shortly after with the second. The Air Force-flier ran in another from 80 yards and Richard Hill added a fourth before Phil Davies scored a good try to open the Welsh account. The manner and size of the defeat was embarrassing and coach John Ryan resigned.

England S.D. Hodgkinson (Notts); R. Underwood (Leicester/RAF), J.C. Guscott (Bath), +W.D.C. Carling (Harlequins), S.J. Halliday (Bath); C.R. Andrew (Wasps), R.J. Hill (Bath); P.A.G. Rendall (Wasps), B.C. Moore (Notts), J.A. Probyn (Wasps), P.J. Ackford (Harlequins), W.A. Dooley (Preston Grasshoppers), M.G. Skinner (Harlequins), M.C. Teague (Gloucester), P.J. Winterbottom (Harlequins).
T: Rory Underwood 2, Will Carling, Richard Hill.
C: Simon Hodgkinson 3.
P: Hodgkinson 4.

Wales P.H. Thorburn (Neath); M.H. Titley (Swansea), M.G. Ring, M.R. Hall (Cardiff), A. Emyr (Swansea); D.W. Evans (Cardiff), +R.N. Jones (Swansea); M. Griffiths (Cardiff), K.H. Phillips (Neath), L. Delaney (Llanelli), A.G. Allen (Newbridge), G.O. Llewellyn (Neath), P.T. Davies (Llanelli), M.A. Jones (Neath), R.G. Collins (Cardiff).
T: Phil Davies.
C: Paul Thorburn.
Referee: David Leslie (Scotland).

Wales 6   England 25

Arms Park, Cardiff. 19 January 1991

England won by 1 try, 7 pens to 2 pens.

England were expected to beat Wales at Cardiff for the first time since 1963. They did, but made terribly hard work of it – just one try was scored among the 31 points. The oddity was that England had no comment to make on their victory. Their players wanted to be paid to speak and since they were not, there was little rejoicing. Simon Hodgkinson kicked a world-record seven penalty goals and Mike Teague drove over from a scrum. Wales gave débuts to Neil Jenkins, aged 19, and Scott Gibbs, who was just days short of his 20th birthday. The hard-working Newport flankers, Alun Carter and Glenn George, were brought in, only to be dumped after the Murrayfield defeat.

Wales +P.H. Thorburn (Neath); I.C. Evans (Llanelli), M.G. Ring (Cardiff), *I.S. Gibbs (Neath), S.P. Ford (Cardiff); *N.R. Jenkins (Pontypridd), R.N. Jones (Swansea); Brian R. Williams, K.H. Phillips (Neath), P. Knight (Pontypridd), Glyn D. Llewellyn, Gareth O. Llewellyn (Neath), *A.J. Carter (Newport), P. Arnold (Swansea), *G.M. George (Newport).   Rep: C.J. Bridges (Neath) for Jones.
P: Paul Thorburn, Neil Jenkins.

England S.D. Hodgkinson (Notts); N.J. Heslop (Orrell), +W.D.C. Carling (Harlequins), J.C. Guscott (Bath), R. Underwood (Leicester/RAF); C.R. Andrew (Wasps), R.J. Hill (Bath); J. Leonard, B.C. Moore (Notts), J.A. Probyn (Wasps), P.J. Ackford (Harlequins), W.A. Dooley (Preston Grasshoppers), M.C. Teague (Gloucester), D. Richards (Leicester), P.J. Winterbottom (Harlequins).
T: Mike Teague.
P: Simon Hodgkinson 7.
Referee: Ray J. Megson (Scotland).

England 24   Wales 0

Twickenham. 7 March 1992

England won by 3 tries, 3 cons, 2 pens to nil.

Wales may have taken some big hidings, but they

always managed to score. This was not a massive beating, but for the first time in 22 years there were no points for Wales. For England it was a second successive Grand Slam which was always on the cards after a first-minute try by skipper Will Carling. The last touchdown was performed by Wade Dooley to the delight of his colleagues, as it was his 50th appearance.

England J.M. Webb (Bath); S.J. Halliday (Harlequins), J.C. Guscott (Bath), +W.D.C. Carling (Harlequins), R. Underwood (Leicester/RAF); C.R. Andrew (Toulouse), C.D. Morris (Orrell); J. Leonard, B.C. Moore (Harlequins), J.A. Probyn (Wasps), M.C. Bayfield (Northampton), W.A. Dooley (Preston Grasshoppers), M.G. Skinner (Harlequins), D. Richards (Leicester), P.J. Winterbottom (Harlequins).
Rep: N.J. Heslop (Orrell) for Carling.
T: Will Carling, Mick Skinner, Wade Dooley.
C: Jon Webb 3.
P: Webb 2.

Wales A. Clement (Swansea); +I.C. Evans (Llanelli), N.R. Jenkins (Pontypridd), I.S. Gibbs (Swansea), M.R. Hall (Cardiff); C.J. Stephens (Llanelli), R.N. Jones (Swansea); M. Griffiths (Cardiff), G.R. Jenkins (Swansea), L. Delaney (Llanelli), G.O. Llewellyn (Neath), A.H. Copsey (Llanelli), M.S. Morris (Neath), S. Davies, R.E. Webster (Swansea). Rep: M.A. Rayer (Cardiff) for Clement.
Referee: Ray J. Megson (Scotland).

Wales 10 England 9

Arms Park, Cardiff. 6 February 1993

Wales won by 1 try, 1 con, 1 pen to 2 pens, 1 drop goal.

Wales were the underdogs and for many it was just a question of how many points England would score. Maybe England thought the same, as they led 9–3, until Emyr Lewis kicked ahead. It appeared to be a wasted kick for Rory Underwood had it covered, but Ieuan Evans had followed along the touchline at speed. As Underwood dallied, he did not see that Evans was flying up behind him and was amazed to see him kick the ball on and leave full-back Jonathan Webb standing to race over the line at great pace and dive on the ball for a famous try. Neil Jenkins converted from halfway out and Wales led 10–9 with the second half still to come. England claimed that scrum-half Dewi Morris had scored a try, but it was disallowed and Webb hit a post with a penalty effort. However, Wales resisted with full-back Michael Rayer outstanding as the last line of defence, and the Princess of Wales, at last, was able to witness a win for Wales.

Wales M.A. Rayer (Cardiff); +I.C. Evans (Llanelli), M.R. Hall (Cardiff), I.S. Gibbs (Swansea), W.T. Proctor (Llanelli); N.R. Jenkins (Pontypridd), R.N. Jones (Swansea); *R.L. Evans (Llanelli), *N. Meek (Pontypool), H. Williams-Jones (South Wales Police), G.O. Llewellyn (Neath), A.H. Copsey, E.W. Lewis (Llanelli), S. Davies, R.E. Webster (Swansea).
T: Ieuan Evans.

The Arms Park scoreboard on 6 February 1993, following Neil Jenkins's conversion of a great Ieuan Evans try. Wales won 10–9 despite having started as very much the underdogs. (© Huw Evans)

C: Neil Jenkins.
P: Jenkins.

England J.M. Webb (Bath); I.G. Hunter (Northampton), +W.D.C. Carling (Harlequins), J.C. Guscott (Bath), R. Underwood (Leicester/RAF); C.R. Andrew (Wasps), C.D. Morris (Orrell); J. Leonard, B.C. Moore (Harlequins), J.A. Probyn (Wasps), M.C. Bayfield (Northampton), W.A. Dooley (Preston Grasshoppers), M.C. Teague (Moseley), B.B. Clarke (Bath), P.J. Winterbottom (Harlequins). Rep: P.R. de Glanville (Bath) for Hunter.
P: Jon Webb 2.
DG: Jeremy Guscott.
Referee: Joël Dumé (France).

England 15 Wales 8

Twickenham. 19 March 1994.

England won by 2 tries, 1 con, 1 pen to 1 try, 1 pen.

In an odd ending to the afternoon, Wales captain Ieuan Evans received the Five Nations trophy from Her Majesty the Queen, despite the fact that his side had been beaten by England minutes earlier. It was the first outright win for Wales since 1979, but it was only because of the new aggregate match points system. England had needed to score 16 points more than Wales, but Nigel Walker's try was the clinching score. It came from a clever Phil Davies pass after a burst by Ricky Evans. England had been the better side but lacked a 'killer punch' and Wales hung on doggedly after being 15–3 down. This was their 100th meeting: Wales led 48–40; 12 matches were drawn.

England I.G. Hunter (Northampton); T. Underwood (Leicester), P.R. de Glanville (Bath), +W.D.C. Carling (Harlequins), R. Underwood (Leicester/RAF); C.R. Andrew (Wasps), C.D. Morris (Orrell); J. Leonard, B.C. Moore (Harlequins), V.E. Ubogu (Bath), M.O. Johnson (Leicester), N.C. Redman (Bath), T.A.K. Rodber (Northampton), D. Richards (Leicester), B.B. Clarke (Bath). Rep: M.J. Catt (Bath) for Andrew.
T: Rory Underwood, Tim Rodber.
C: Rob Andrew.
P: Andrew.

Wales M.A. Rayer (Cardiff); +I.C. Evans (Llanelli), M.R. Hall (Cardiff), N.G. Davies (Llanelli), N.K. Walker (Cardiff); N.R. Jenkins (Pontypridd), R.H.StJ.B. Moon; R.L. Evans (Llanelli), G.R. Jenkins (Swansea), J.D. Davies (Neath), P.T. Davies (Llanelli), G.O. Llewellyn (Neath), E.W. Lewis, L.S. Quinnell, M.A. Perego (Llanelli). Rep: A.H. Copsey (Llanelli) for Lewis.
T: Nigel Walker.
P: Neil Jenkins.
Referee: Jim M. Fleming (Scotland).

Wales 9 England 23

Arms Park, Cardiff. 18 February 1995

England won by 3 tries, 1 con, 2 pens to 3 pens.

With Ricky Evans out injured, Wales lost their other experienced prop John Davies who was dismissed after an hour's play for allegedly kicking England forward Ben Clarke at a ruck. Davies disputed it, but Clarke was to have no sympathy for the accused. This led to Hemi Taylor being told to come off. He limped in a strategic move to bring on a prop – Hugh Williams-Jones – and that was allowed by the referee. Davies was banned for 60 days. Victor Ubogu scored the only try of the opening half as England led 13–6. At that point, Rory Underwood took great delight in scoring his first try for England at Cardiff. He was doubly delighted just before the final whistle. It was the 50th appearance by scrum-half Robert Jones.

Wales A. Clement (Swansea); +I.C. Evans (Llanelli), M. Taylor (Pontypool), N.G. Davies (Llanelli), N.K. Walker (Cardiff); N.R. Jenkins (Pontypridd), R.N. Jones (Swansea); M. Griffiths (Cardiff), G.R. Jenkins (Swansea), J.D. Davies (Neath), D. Jones (Cardiff), G.O. Llewellyn (Neath), H.T. Taylor, E.W. Lewis (Cardiff), R.G. Collins (Pontypridd). Reps: M.J. Back (Bridgend) for Clement; R.H.StJ.B. Moon (Llanelli) for Walker; H. Williams-Jones (Llanelli) for Taylor.
Sent off: John Davies.
P: Neil Jenkins 3.

England M.J. Catt (Bath); T. Underwood (Leicester), +W.D.C. Carling (Harlequins), J.C. Guscott (Bath), R. Underwood (Leicester/RAF); C.R. Andrew (Wasps), K.P.P. Bracken (Bristol); J. Leonard, B.C. Moore (Harlequins), V.E. Ubogu (Bath), M.O. Johnson (Leicester), M.C. Bayfield, T.A.K. Rodber (Northampton), D. Richards (Leicester), B.B. Clarke (Bath).
T: Rory Underwood 2, Victor Ubogu.
C: Rob Andrew.
P: Andrew 2.
Referee: Didier Méné (France).

England 21 Wales 15

Twickenham. 3 February 1996

England won by 2 tries, 1 con, 3 pens to 2 tries, 1 con, 1 pen.

Robert Howley's selection had appeared overdue and coach Kevin Bowring was well satisfied with his new scrum-half who scored a second-half try. The side played with new adventure but a crucial error was made by full-back Justin Thomas whose kick was charged down by Jeremy Guscott for the Bath centre to score. Hemi Taylor finished off a fine move for the opening try of the match with Rory Underwood responding with his 49th and final international try – second only to David Campese of Australia.

England M.J. Catt; J.M. Sleightholme (Bath), +W.D.C. Carling (Harlequins), J.C. Guscott (Bath), R. Underwood (Leicester/RAF); P.J. Grayson, M.J.S. Dawson (Northampton); G.C. Rowntree (Leicester), M.P. Regan (Bristol), J. Leonard (Harlequins), M.O. Johnson (Leicester), M.C. Bayfield (Northampton), T.A.K. Rodber (Northampton/Army), B.B. Clarke (Bath), L.B.N. Dallaglio (Wasps). Rep: P.R. de Glanville (Bath) for Carling.
T: Rory Underwood, Jeremy Guscott.
C: Paul Grayson.
P: Grayson 3.

Wales W.J.L. Thomas; I.C. Evans (Llanelli), L.B. Davies (Neath), N.G. Davies, W.T. Proctor (Llanelli); A.C. Thomas (Bristol), *R. Howley (Bridgend); A.L.P. Lewis, +J.M. Humphreys (Cardiff), J.D. Davies, G.O. Llewellyn (Neath), D. Jones, E.W. Lewis, H.T. Taylor (Cardiff), R.G. Jones (Llanelli). Reps: G.R. Jenkins (Swansea) for Humphreys; S.M. Williams (Neath) for R.G. Jones and E.W. Lewis (both as temp).
T: Hemi Taylor, Robert Howley.
C: Arwel Thomas.
P: Arwel Thomas.
Referee: Ken W. McCartney (Scotland).

Wales 13 England 34

Arms Park, Cardiff. 15 March 1997

England won by 4 tries, 4 cons, 2 pens to 1 try, 1 con, 2 pens.

It was farewell day in Cardiff: goodbye to the old Arms Park. Goodbye also to the international careers of Jonathan Davies, Will Carling and Rob Andrew. It was just an ordinary match with England 6–3 ahead after 40 minutes, when Jerry Guscott came on and brought some flair with him. Despite playing as a wing, he showed exactly what England had been missing all season. In a cruel twist of fate, Neil Jenkins, playing for the 50th time and again out of place as a full-back, fractured his arm in the opening minutes and left the field after a quarter of an hour. He had been denied the pivot role when Arwel Thomas withdrew, and Jonathan Davies was given his last run-out. Tactical changes were now allowed and among the many comings and goings, Rob Andrew was given the final eight minutes by coach Jack Rowell, presumably as a reward for long service. Wales were badly mauled, though Robert Howley did, at least, score the final international try in the stadium. Demolition work was done by the English pack and the contractors took over at the ground two months later.

Wales N.R. Jenkins (Pontypridd); S.D. Hill (Cardiff), A.G. Bateman (Richmond), N.G. Davies (Llanelli), G. Thomas (Bridgend); J. Davies, R. Howley (Cardiff); C.D. Loader (Swansea), +J.M. Humphreys, D. Young (Cardiff), G.O. Llewellyn (Harlequins), M.J. Voyle (Llanelli), S.M. Williams (Neath), L.S. Quinnell (Richmond), K.P. Jones (Ebbw Vale). Reps: W.T. Proctor (Llanelli) for Jenkins; S.C. John (Llanelli) for Loader; J.C. Quinnell (Richmond) for Voyle; D.L.M. McIntosh (Pontypridd) for Jones.
T: Robert Howley.
C: Jonathan Davies.
P: Jonathan Davies 2.

England T.R.G. Stimpson (Newcastle); J.M. Sleightholme (Bath), W.D.C. Carling (Harlequins), +P.R. de Glanville (Bath), T. Underwood (Newcastle); M.J. Catt (Bath), A.S. Healey; G.C. Rowntree (Leicester), M.P. Regan (Bristol), J. Leonard (Harlequins), M.O. Johnson (Leicester), S.D. Shaw (Bristol), B.B. Clarke (Richmond), T.A.K. Rodber (Northampton/Army), R.A. Hill (Saracens). Reps: J.C. Guscott (Bath) for Sleightholme; C.R. Andrew (Newcastle) for Catt; D.J. Garforth (Leicester) for Rowntree; P.B.T. Greening (Gloucester) for Regan; C.M.A. Sheasby (Wasps) for Clarke.
T: Tim Stimpson, Richard Hill, Phil de Glanville, Tony Underwood.
C: Mike Catt 4.
P: Catt 2.
Referee: Joël Dumé (France).

Robert Howley scores the final international try at the old Arms Park in 1997. England were worthy winners by 34–13. (© Huw Evans)

England 60 Wales 26

Twickenham. 21 February 1998.

England won by 8 tries, 7 cons, 2 pens to 4 tries, 3 cons.

Wales scored four good tries but were still given a terrible hiding by England which amounted to the highest score by any side in the Five-Nations history and the biggest points aggregate in a match. Nigel Walker's international career came to an end just three minutes into the match. After 17 appearances and 12 tries he suffered a dislocation of his right shoulder. Despite his loss, Wales led 12–6 after almost half an hour's play thanks to two splendid tries by Allan Bateman but, in seven disastrous minutes, England scored 21 points including a try by David Rees which should not have been allowed as 'crossing' had taken place. England went over the Welsh line eight times with Paul Grayson booting 20 points, en route to 66 in the championship. A bemused Neil Jenkins later stated that he never wanted to play at full-back again.

England M.B. Perry (Bath); D.L. Rees (Sale), W.J.H. Greenwood (Leicester), J.C. Guscott (Bath), A.S. Healey (Leicester); P.J. Grayson (Northampton), K.P.P. Bracken (Saracens); J. Leonard (Harlequins), R. Cockerill (Leicester), P.J. Vickery (Gloucester), M.O. Johnson (Leicester), G.S. Archer (Newcastle), +L.B.N. Dallaglio (Wasps), R.A. Hill (Saracens), N.A. Back (Leicester). Reps: P.R. de Glanville (Bath) for Greenwood; M.J. Catt (Bath) for Grayson; M.J.S. Dawson (Northampton) for Bracken; D.J. Garforth (Leicester) for Vickery; D.J. Grewcock (Saracens) for Johnson; A.J. Diprose (Saracens) for Hill.
T: David Rees 2, Austin Healey, Neil Back, Lawrence Dallaglio, Will Greenwood, Kyran Bracken, Matt Dawson.
C: Paul Grayson 7.
P: Grayson 2.

Wales N.R. Jenkins (Pontypridd); G. Thomas (Cardiff), A.G. Bateman (Richmond), I.S. Gibbs (Swansea), N.K. Walker (Cardiff); A.C. Thomas (Swansea), +R. Howley; A.L.P. Lewis (Cardiff), B.H. Williams (Richmond), D. Young (Cardiff), G.O. Llewellyn (Harlequins), M.J. Voyle (Llanelli), C.L. Charvis (Swansea), L.S. Quinnell (Richmond), M.E. Williams (Pontypridd). Reps: L.B. Davies (Cardiff) for Bateman; W.T. Proctor (Llanelli) for Walker; L. Mustoe (Cardiff) for Lewis; J.M. Humphreys (Cardiff) for (B.H.) Williams; *C. Stephens (Bridgend) for Voyle; R.C. Appleyard (Swansea) for Quinnell.
T: Allan Bateman 2, Scott Gibbs, Gareth Thomas.
C: Neil Jenkins 3.
Referee: Colin J. Hawke (New Zealand).

Scott Gibbs about to beat England full-back Matt Perry and score the vital try against England at Wembley in 1999. The try in injury-time was converted by Neil Jenkins to give Wales victory by 32–31. (© Huw Evans)

Wales 32 England 31

Wembley, London. 11 April 1999

Wales won by 2 tries, 2 cons, 6 pens to 3 tries, 2 cons, 4 pens.

A storming, even dancing, run by centre Scott Gibbs in the 82nd minute brought Wales to within a point of England's total. It all rested on the Neil Jenkins conversion. The Pontypridd player had already landed seven out of seven and he made no mistake from halfway out to give Wales an unexpected success. England should have wrapped the match up earlier, but partly through their own arrogance and partly through the new belief in Welsh hearts (instilled by Graham Henry), the men in red stuck it out. England scored three first-half tries and led 25–15 until Jenkins put over his sixth penalty right on the half-time whistle. A Shane Howarth try and a Jenkins conversion levelled it, but Jonny Wilkinson fired over two penalty goals to put England ahead again at 31–25. England attacked in injury time only for Tim Rodber to be penalised for a big hit on Colin Charvis. Wales came downfield for man-of-the-match Chris Wyatt to win a lineout and Gibbs to produce his moment of Welsh wizardry. The attendance of 78,883 represented the biggest-ever for a 'home' Wales international. Tom Jones and Max Boyce led the pre-match singing. Team manager David Pickering called Henry 'The man with the Midas touch'. Henry gave his estimate of Neil Jenkins, saying, 'He is the best goalkicker I have ever worked with. And I've worked with Grant Fox.'

Wales S.P. Howarth (Manchester-Sale); G. Thomas (Cardiff), M. Taylor, I.S. Gibbs (Swansea), D.R. James; N.R. Jenkins (Pontypridd), +R. Howley (Cardiff); P.J.D. Rogers (London Irish), G.R. Jenkins, B.R. Evans (Swansea) J.C. Quinnell (Richmond), C.P. Wyatt (Llanelli), C.L. Charvis (Swansea), L.S. Quinnell (Llanelli), B.D. Sinkinson (Neath). Reps: N.J. Walne (Richmond) for Thomas; A.L.P. Lewis (Cardiff) for Rogers; D. Young (Cardiff) for Evans.
T: Shane Howarth, Scott Gibbs.
C: Neil Jenkins 2.
P: Neil Jenkins 6.

England M.B. Perry (Bath); D. Luger (Harlequins), J.P. Wilkinson (Newcastle), B-J. Mather, S.M. Hanley (Manchester-Sale); M.J. Catt (Bath), M.J.S. Dawson (Northampton); J. Leonard (Harlequins), R. Cockerill, D.J. Garforth, M.O. Johnson (Leicester), T.A.K. Rodber (Northampton), R.A. Hill (Saracens), +L.B.N. Dallaglio (Wasps), N.A. Back (Leicester). Rep: V.E. Ubogu (Bath) for Garforth.
T: Dan Luger, Steve Hanley, Richard Hill.
C: Jonny Wilkinson 2.
P: Wilkinson 4.
Referee: Andre Watson (South Africa).

FRANCE

Wales 36 France 4

Arms Park, Cardiff. 2 March 1908

Wales won by 9 tries, 3 cons, 1 pen to 1 drop goal.

The first meeting between the two countries saw Wales score nine tries with Reg Gibbs equalling the record of four set by Willie Llewellyn in 1899 against England. He missed a fifth when a French defender tripped him up with a dive after the wing had crossed the goal-line and was attempting to go under the posts. It was the last international played by Teddy Morgan whose brother Bill was capped two years later. Teddy will forever be remembered for his try that beat the All Blacks; he almost averaged a try a match in his 16 appearances.

Wales H.B. Winfield; R.A. Gibbs (Cardiff), W.J. Trew (Swansea), R.T. Gabe (Cardiff), +E. Morgan (London Welsh); R.H. Jones, R.M. Owen (Swansea); A.J. Webb (Abertillery), G. Travers (Pill Harriers), E.J. Thomas (Mountain Ash), W. O'Neil, J.A. Brown (Cardiff), J. Watts (Llanelli), G. Hayward (Swansea), W.H. Dowell (Pontypool).
T: Reg Gibbs 4, Billy Trew 2, Teddy Morgan 2, Dick Jones.
C: Bert Winfield 2, Gibbs.
P: Winfield.

France H. Martin (Stade Bordelais); C. Vareilles (Stade Français), G. Lane (Racing Club), M. Leuvielle (Stade Bordelais), E. Lesieur (Stade Français); J. Mayssonnie (Stade Toulousain), A. Hubert (ASF); +M. Communeau, A. Duval (Stade Français), P. Mauriat (Lyons), R. de Malmann, A. Branlat, P. Guillemin (Racing Club), R. Duffourcq, A. Masse (Stade Bordelais).
DG: Charles Vareilles.
Referee: W. Williams (England).

France 5 Wales 47

Stade Colombes, Paris. 23 February 1909

Wales won by 11 tries, 7 cons to 1 try, 1 con.

This was just too easy: Wales ran in eleven tries in this Tuesday match, with only England of the home countries having previously ventured to Paris. The Welsh three-quarters ran riot with ten tries including hat-tricks by Billy Trew and Melville Baker, the latter in only his second international match. Steelworker Jim Watts added the other try from a pack which included newcomers Rees Thomas and Tom Lloyd.

France E. de Jouvencel; E. Lesieur, R. Sagot (Stade Français), T. Varvier, G. Lane (Racing Club); A. Hubert (ASF), A. Theuriet (SCUF); P Dupré, G. Borchard, R. de Malmann (Racing Club), G. Fourcade (Bordeaux Etudiants), P. Mauriat (Lyons), A. Masse (Stade Bordelais), G. Icard, +M. Communeau (Stade Français).
T: R. Sagot.
C: Paul Mauriat.

Wales J. Bancroft (Swansea); A.M. Baker, J.P. 'Jack' Jones (Newport), +W.J. Trew (Swansea), J.L. Williams (Cardiff); R.H. Jones, R.M. Owen (Swansea); A.J. Webb (Abertillery), *T.J. Lloyd (Neath), *R. Thomas (Pontypool), P.D. Waller, E. Thomas (Newport), T.H. Evans, J. Watts (Llanelli), W.I. Morgan (Swansea).
T: Billy Trew 3, Melville Baker 3, Johnnie Williams 2, Jack Jones 2, Jim Watts.
C: Jack Bancroft 6, Trew.
Referee: W. Williams (England).

Wales 49 France 14

St Helen's, Swansea. 1 January 1910

Wales won by 10 tries, 8 cons, 1 pen to 2 tries, 1 con, 2 pens.

This is the only match ever played by Wales on a New Year's Day and a win was never in doubt. French captain Gaston Lane was only on a winning side once in his 16 appearances. Only about 4,000 watched in heavy rain as Wales gained an eleventh consecutive victory, while Jack Bancroft set an individual scoring record of 19 points. This was the first match ever played by France in the international championship. It was of this era that a leading rugby writer, E.H.D. Sewell, wrote: 'What grand stuff the best Welsh rugger has been and still is. So nimble, so able, so instructed, so disciplined, so cute, so thinking. The best Welsh teams are made up of physically fit men who play sound rugger with activity, alike of brain and body, in every phase. I never saw an unfit Welsh side.' Two tries came from the splendid loose forward Ivor Morgan, of whom Sewell said: 'I never saw a more effective Welsh wing forward.'

Wales J. Bancroft (Swansea); H.T. Maddock (London Welsh), J.P. 'Jack' Jones (Newport), +W.J. Trew (Swansea), R.A. Gibbs (Cardiff); R.H. Jones, R.M. Owen (Swansea); T.H. Evans (Llanelli), *J.J.Pullman (Neath), A.J. Webb (Abertillery), C.M. 'Charlie' Pritchard, E. Thomas, P.D. Waller (Newport), *B. Gronow (Bridgend), W.I. Morgan (Swansea).
T: Reg Gibbs 3, Ivor Morgan 2, Hop Maddock 2, Billy Trew, Jack Jones, Ben Gronow.
C: Jack Bancroft 8.
P: Jack Bancroft.

France J. Menrath (SCUF); M. Bruneau (Stade Bordelais), G. Houblain (SCUF), M. Burgun, +G. Lane (Racing Club); C. Martin (Lyon), J. Maysonnie (Stade Toulousain); P. Mauriat (Lyon), A. Masse, M. Hourdebaigt (Stade Bordelais), P. Guillemin (Racing Club), I. Lafitte, G. Thevenot, M. Boudreau, J. Anduran (SCUF).
T: R. Laffitte, Paul Mauriat.
C: J. Menrath.
P: Menrath 2.
Referee: W. Williams (England).

France 0 Wales 15

Parc des Princes, Paris. 28 February 1911

Wales won by 3 tries, 3 cons to nil.

Wing Johnnie Williams was given the captaincy as he could speak French. He was to die in France at Mametz Wood during the battle of the Somme five years later, while captain in the Welsh Regiment. Again it was a case of – 'If it's Paris, it must be a Tuesday!' Wales scored all their points in the second-half rain, including a try by Williams – the last of his 17 for Wales.

France T. Varvier; P. Failliot (Racing Club), J. Dedet (Stade Français), C. du Souich (SCUF), G. Lane (Racing Club); A. Theuriet (SCUF), +A. Duval (Stade Français); P. Mauriat, J. Bavozet (Lyons), G. Duffour (Stade Tarbais), P. Guillemin (Racing Club), P. Mounicq (Stade Toulousain), J. Cadenat (SCUF), F. Forgues (Aviron Bayonnais), M. Legrain (Stade Français).

Wales J. Bancroft (Swansea); R.A. Gibbs, W. Spiller, L.M. Dyke, +J.L. Williams (Cardiff); W.J. Trew, R.M. Owen (Swansea); A.J. Webb (Abertillery), J. Pugsley (Cardiff), G. Travers (Newport), T.H. Evans (Llanelli), J. Birch (Neath), R. Thomas (Pontypool), D.J. Thomas, W.I. Morgan (Swansea).
T: Ivor Morgan, Johnnie Williams, Dicky Owen.
C: Jack Bancroft 3.
Referee: W. Williams (England).

Wales 14 France 8

Rodney Parade, Newport. 25 March 1912

Wales won by 4 tries, 1 con to 2 tries, 1 con.

This time the sides met on a Monday afternoon. Once again, Dicky Owen and Billy Trew opted to play for their club and also missing was Jack Bancroft at full-back. The little-known Harold 'Drummer' Thomas came in for his only cap. France sprang into a shock 8–6 half-time lead, beating the Welsh forwards in the Rodney Parade mud, but Wales recovered to add two more tries in the second half and complete a 13th successive home win.

Wales *H. Thomas (Llanelli); R.C.S. Plummer (Newport), J.P. Jones (Pontypool), W. Spiller, D.E.G. Davies (Cardiff); W.J. Martin, +T.H. Vile (Newport); G. Stephens (Neath), J.A. Merry (Pill Harriers), H. Hiams (Swansea), F.J. Hawkins (Pontypridd), W.J. Jenkins (Cardiff), A.P. Coldrick, L.C. Trump, H. Uzzell (Newport).
T: Ewan Davies 2, Reg Plummer, Jack Jones.
C: Harold Thomas.

France F. Dutour (Stade Toulousain); E. Lesieur (Stade Français), +G. Lane (Racing Club), J. Sentilles (Stade Tarbais), J. Dufau (Biarritz); L. Larribeau (Perigeux), G. Charpentier (Stade Français); F. Forgues (Aviron Bayonnais), M. Communeau (Stade Français), M. Monniot (Racing Club), J. Pascarel (Toulouse OEC), A. Forestier, J. Cadenat (SCUF), P. Thil (Stade Nantais), M. Boyau (Stade Bordelais).
T: Emile Lesieur, Léon Larribeau.
C: Maurice Boyau.
Referee: Arthur Owen Jones (England).

France 8 Wales 11

Parc des Princes, Paris. 27 February 1913

Wales won by 3 tries, 1 con to 1 goal, 1 try.

A month earlier referee John Baxter of England had to be escorted off after the match with Scotland in Paris, so extra police were present to prevent any pitch invasion. This time it was a Thursday match and Wales were now finding the French a tougher proposition as each season went by. Wales led 8–0:

tries were scored by the Rev. Alban Davies and fellow forward Tom Williams, but France levelled the scores at 8–8, before outside-half Clem Lewis scored the winning try. Glyn Gething and Mark Lewis won their only caps, with Lewis having replaced the injured Billy Geen. Skipper Billy Trew never played for Wales again.

France J. Semmartin (SCUF); G. André (Racing Club), A. Francquenelle (SC Vaugirard), P. Jaureguy (Stade Toulousain), P. Failliot (Racing Club); C. Bioussa, P. Struxiano (Stade Toulousain); F. Forgues (Aviron Bayonnais), P. Thil (Stade Nantais), M. Boyau, +M. Leuvielle (Stade Bordelais), P. Mauriat, G. Favre (Lyon), J. Podevin (Stade Français), M. Communeau (SF Beauvais).
T: Pierre Failliot, Georges Andre.
C: Philippe Struxiano.

Wales *G.I. Gething (Neath); *M. Lewis (Llwynypia), J.P. 'Jack' Jones (Pontypool), +W.J. Trew, H. Lewis (Swansea), J.M.C. Lewis (Cardiff), R.A. Lloyd (Pontypool); Rev. J. Alban Davies, T. Williams (Swansea), F.L. Perrett, T.J. Lloyd, G. Stephens (Neath), R. Richards (Aberavon), P.L. Jones, H. Uzzell (Newport).
T: Alban Davies, Tom Williams, Clem Lewis.
C: Clem Lewis.
Referee: John H. Miles (England).

Wales 31 France 0

St Helen's, Swansea. 2 March 1914

Wales won by 7 tries, 5 cons to nil.

The Rev. Alban Davies led Wales to a big win thanks to seven tries scored in this Monday afternoon match. Jack Wetter was in fine form in the centre and Wales were too strong at forward.

Wales J. Bancroft (Swansea); G.L. Hirst, J.J. Wetter (Newport), W.H. Evans (Llwynypia), I.T. Davies (Llanelli); J.M.C. Lewis (Cardiff), R.A. Lloyd (Pontypool); +Rev. J. Alban Davies (Llanelli), D. Watts (Maesteg), J.'Bedwellty' Jones (Abertillery), T.J. Lloyd (Neath), P.L. Jones (Pontypool), T. Williams, E. Morgan (Swansea), H. Uzzell (Newport).
T: Jack Wetter 2, Harry Uzzell 2, George Hirst, William Evans, Alban Davies.
C: Jack Bancroft 5.

France J. Caujolle (Stade Tarbais); G. André (Racing Club), J. Lacoste (Stade Tarbais), A. Besset (SCUF), G. Pierrot (Section Paloise); E. Poydebasque, A. Hedembaigt (Aviron Bayonnais); +M. Leuvielle, M. Legrain, J.C. de Beyssac (Stade Bordelais), R. Faure (Stade Tarbais), R. Desvouges (Stade Français), J. Arnal (Racing Club), P. Lavaud (AS Carcassonnaise), A.Lubin-Lebrère (Stade Toulousain).
Referee: John F.H. Miles (England).

Wing Wickham Powell crosses the halfway line for a try in the 6–5 win over France in Paris, 1920. Nearest to him is French wing Adolphe Jaureguy who tackled Powell just as he reached the goal-line.

France 5 Wales 6

Stade Colombes, Paris. 17 February 1920

Wales won by 2 tries to 1 try, 1 con.

Wick Powell's speed, later to win Powderhall sprints, took him over after a long run for the winning try as his friend Adolphe Jaureguy tackled him. His shirt bore the white of the goalline, but Powell said: 'If I had another 20 yards to go I would still have made it.' French captain Philippe Struxiano claimed he had scored in the corner after gathering his own throw-in, but a Welsh touch-judge raised his flag to indicate a foot in touch. The referee decided that in any case, it should have been a Welsh throw-in. Soon afterwards, referee Craven put the ball in the scrum himself as play had now become 'too keen'. Scrum-half Fred Reeves became the second Cross Keys player in the side as Jack Wetter switched to fly-half; Jerry Shea refused to play and instead earned money as a professional boxer.

France T. Cambre (Oloron); A. Jaureguy (Racing Club), R. Lavigne (Dax), R. Crabos, A. Chilo (Racing Club); E. Billac (Aviron Bayonnais), +P. Struxiano; M. Biraben, P. Pons, A. Lubin-

Lebrère (Stade Toulousain), A. Cassayet (Tarbes), R. Thierry (Racing Club), J. Laurent (Aviron Bayonnais), R. Marchand (Stade Poitevin), G. Constant (Perpignan).
T: Adolphe Jaureguy.
C: Philippe Struxiano.

Wales J. Rees (Swansea); W.J. Powell (Cardiff), J.P. 'Jack' Jones (Pontypool), A.E. Jenkins, B. Williams (Llanelli); J.J. Wetter (Newport), *F.C. Reeves (Cross Keys); J.L. Williams (Blaina), S. Morris (Cross Keys), W.G.H. Morris (Abertillery), +H. Uzzell, J.J. Whitfield (Newport), G. Oliver (Pontypool), *R. Huxtable (Swansea), C.W. Jones (Bridgend).
T: Bryn Williams, Wickham Powell.
Referee: Col. W.S.D. Craven (England).

Wales 12 France 4

Arms Park, Cardiff. 26 February 1921

Wales won by 2 tries, 2 pens to 1 drop goal.

French skipper Rene Crabos was instrumental in establishing a long association between the Nantes and Cardiff clubs which began in this match. On this occasion however, his pack could not supply their backs with enough ball to threaten Wales. The First World War pilot René Lasserre, who was later capped in the backs, played in the French pack and dropped a goal. Ossie Male, then of Cross Keys and later of Cardiff, was a last-minute deputy for Joe Rees. Of the other new caps, Graham Davies lived until the age of 91, but scrum-half Tudor Williams died when only 23, when he was electrocuted at Blaencaegurwen Colliery.

Wales *B.O. Male (Cross Keys); T.A.W. Johnson (Cardiff), *H.G. Davies, A.E. Jenkins (Llanelli), B.M.G. Thomas (St Bart's Hosp./Ogmore Vale); W.E. Bowen, *T. Williams (Swansea); S.L. Attewell (Newport), T. Roberts (Risca), J.L. Williams (Blaina), S. Winmill (Cross Keys), +E.T. Parker (Swansea), W. Hodder (Pontypool), J. Jones (Aberavon), D.E. Morgan (Llanelli).
T: Jack Williams, Wilf Hodder.
P: Albert Jenkins 2.

France J. Clement (Racing Club); R. Got (Perpignan), +R. Crabos, F. Borde, J. Lobies (Racing Club); E. Billac (Aviron Bayonnais), R. Piteu (Section Paloise); R. Lasserre (Aviron Bayonnais), A. Vaquer (Perpignan), J. Larrieu (Stade Tarbais), A. Cassayet (Tarbes), P. Moureu, J. Coscoll (Beziers), M. Biraben (Dax), P. Pons (Stade Toulousain).

DG: René Lasserre.
Referee: Sir P.M.R. Royds (England).

France 3 Wales 11

Stade Colombes, Paris. 23 March 1922

Wales won by 3 tries, 1 con to 1 try.

Wales won the match and thus took the championship after the selectors had made a late decision to omit backs Frank Palmer and Harold Davies (Newport) and bring back Islwyn Evans and Cliff Richards, who had been dropped. The ground was hard after snow and frost and the interval was reached with no score. Skipper René Crabos said: 'We were beaten by better players all round.'
(NB: John Stephens later claimed that he scored the try credited to Bill Cummins.)

France J. Clement (Racing Club); A. Jaureguy, F. Borde (Stade Toulousain), +R. Crabos (Racing Club), R. Got (Perpignan); E. Billac (Aviron Bayonnais), R. Piteu (Section Paloise); R. Lasserre (Cognac), F. Vaquer (Perpignan), J. Boubee (Biarritz), P. Moureu (Beziers), A. Cassayet (Tarbes), A. Lubin-Lebrère (Stade Toulousain), A. Gonnet (Albi), E. Soulie (CASG).
T: Adolphe Jaureguy.

Wales T.F. Samuel (Mountain Ash); W.C. Richards (Pontypool), A.E. Jenkins (Llanelli), H.I. Evans (Swansea), B.S. Evans (Llanelli); W.E. Bowen (Swansea), W.J. Delahay (Bridgend); +E.T. Parker (Swansea), J.J. Whitfield, T. Jones (Newport), S. Morris (Cross Keys), T. Roberts (Risca), Rev. J.G. Stephens (Llanelli), W. Cummins (Treorchy), D.D. Hiddlestone (Neath).
T: Bill Cummins, Jack Whitfield, Islwyn Evans.
C: Albert Jenkins.
Referee: R.W. Harland (Ireland).

Wales 16 France 8

St Helen's, Swansea. 24 February 1923

Wales won by 3 tries, 2 cons, 1 pen to 2 tries, 1 con.

Wales marked the official opening of the new St Helen's grandstand with a win, albeit an unconvincing one. Exchanges became heated and the referee had to call up the French secretary to give a warning to his side. The 31-year-old Mapson Williams played his only game for Wales; the 20-year-old Dai John and Dan Pascoe, who later joined Leeds RL, were also new faces.

Wales J. Rees (Swansea); T.A.W. Johnson (Cardiff), B.M.G. Thomas (St Bart's Hosp.), A.E. Jenkins (Llanelli), W.R. Harding (Swansea); *Dai E. John (Llanelli), W.J. Delahay (Bridgend); +E.T. Parker, G.M. Michael (Swansea), A. Baker (Neath), S.G. Thomas (Llanelli), S. Morris (Cross Keys), J.L. Jenkins (Aberavon), *M.T. Williams (Newport), *D. Pascoe (Bridgend).
T: Rowe Harding, Melbourne Thomas, Ambrose Baker.
C: Albert Jenkins 2.
P: Joe Rees.

France J. Clement (Valence); M. Lalande, H. Behoteguy (Racing Club), A. Ramis (Perpignan), A. Jaureguy (Stade Toulousain); C. Lacazedieu (Dax), C. Dupont (Lourdes); J. Bayard, J. Larrieu (Stade Toulousain), L. Beguet (Racing Club), P. Moureu (Beziers), A. Cassayet (Tarbes), +R. Lasserre (Cognac), J. Castets (Toulon), J. Etcheberry (Rochefort).
T: Max Lalande, René Lasserre.
C: Louis Beguet.
Referee: J.B. McGowan (Ireland).

France 6 Wales 10

Stade Colombes, Paris. 27 March 1924

Wales won by 2 tries, 1 drop goal to 2 tries.

Amazing scenes on the train going from South Wales to Paddington saw the WRU suspend and send home full-back Ossie Male, stating that he had violated the rule of playing within the week before an international by playing for the Cardiff club at Birkenhead Park. Mel Rosser was switched to full-back and Joe Jones won his only cap before going to rugby league. It was the only Welsh win of a season in which they conceded 18 tries. It was played on a Thursday in icy conditions and Adolphe Jaureguy and another player needed medical treatment for frostbite. Ernie Finch and Arnold Rickards scored début tries but Rickards was never selected again.

France E. Bonnes (Narbonnais); R. Got (Perpignan), A. Behoteguy (Aviron Bayonnais), A. Dupouy (Bordelais), A. Jaureguy; H. Galau (Stade Toulousain), C. Dupont (Rouen); A. Bioussa, M.F. Lubin-Lebrère, J. Bayard (Stade Toulousain), E. Piquiral (Racing Club), F. Clauzel, P. Moureu (Beziers), +A. Cassayet (Narbonnais), J. Etcheberry (Rochefort).
T: Andre Behoteguy, Marcel Lubin-Lebrère.

Wales M.A. Rosser (Penarth); *E. Finch (Llanelli), *A. Stock (Newport), *Joe Jones, +W.R. Harding (Swansea); V.M. Griffiths (Newport), E. Watkins (Neath); D.S. Parker (Swansea), G.F. Hathway (Newport), S. Morris (Cross Keys), *A.R. Rickards (Cardiff), R.J. Randall (Aberavon), J.H. Gore (Blaina), C.H. Pugh (Maesteg), A. 'Candy' Evans (Pontypool).
T: Ernie Finch, Arnold Rickards.
DG: Vince Griffiths.
Referee: R.A. Roberts (England).

Wales 11 France 5

Arms Park, Cardiff. 28 February 1925

Wales won by 3 tries, 1 con to 1 try, 1 con

Both this poor-standard match and the 1925 season as a whole would be best forgotten in Welsh rugby history. Arthur Cornish became the fifth captain in five games, even though three previous skippers were still in the side. The French outside-half was 20-year-old Yves du Manoir, who was to die in a plane crash three years later.

Wales T.A.W. Johnson (Cardiff); E. Finch, H.G. Davies (Llanelli), +R.A. Cornish (Cardiff), W.R. Harding (Swansea); Eddie Williams (Neath), W.J. Delahay (Cardiff); S. Morris, R.C. Herrera (Cross Keys), D.S. Parker (Swansea), E.I. Richards (Cardiff), W.I. Jones, *W. Lewis (Llanelli), B. Phillips (Aberavon), *G.E. Beynon (Swansea).
T: Ernie Finch 2, Bobby Delahay.
C: Dai Parker.

France J. Ducousso (Stade Tarbais); J. Halet (Strasbourg), M. de Laborderie (Racing Club), C. Magnanou (Bayonne), A. Bringeon (Biarritz); Y. du Manoir (Racing Club), +R. Piteu (Toulouse Olympic); A. Maury (Stade Toulousain), C. Marcet (Albi), A. Montade (Perpignan), R. Levasseur (Stade Français), A. Laurent, E. Barthe (Biarritz), F. Clauzel (Beziers), A. Cassayet (Narbonne).
T: Marcel de Laborderie.
C: Jean Ducousso.
Referee: R.W. Harland (Ireland).

France 5 Wales 7

Stade Colombes, Paris. 5 April 1926

Wales won by 1 try, 1 drop goal to 1 try, 1 con.

France led 5–0 and gave fair warning that a win was not far away for them, but Emlyn Watkins and Arthur Cornish, both in their final international match, scored the Welsh points in the second half. Windsor Lewis missed the match through injury and

Billy Delahay became the 13th player to captain Wales in a spell of 16 matches.

France L. Destarac (Stade Tarbais); M. Besson (CASG, Paris), M. Baillette (Perpignan), R. Graciet (Stade Bordelais), +A. Jaureguy (Stade Français); V. Graule (Perpignan), H. Lafont; A. Cassayet (Narbonne); E. Ribère, A. Montade, J. Sayrou (Perpignan), G. Gerintes (CASG, Paris), E. Piquiral, C.A. Gonnet (Albi), A. Laurent (Biarritz).
T: Gilbert Gerintes.
C: Charles-Albert Gonnet.

Wales T.E. Rees (Army); E. Finch (Llanelli), +W.J. Delahay, R.A. Cornish (Cardiff), W.R. Harding (Swansea); R. 'Bobby' Jones (Northampton), W.C. Powell (London Welsh); D. Jones (Newport), J.H. John (Swansea), S.D. Lawrence (Bridgend), S. Hinam (Cardiff), R.C. Herrera (Cross Keys), T. Hopkins (Swansea), D.M. Jenkins (Treorchy), Emlyn Watkins (Blaina).
T: Emlyn Watkins.
DG: Arthur Cornish.
Referee: R.W. Harland (Ireland).

Wales 25 France 7

St Helen's, Swansea. 26 February 1927

Wales won by 7 tries, 2 cons to 1 try, 1 drop goal.

The two débutants Guy Morgan and Jim 'Ocker' Burns had splendid matches, as Wales topped 20 points for the first time since 1922. It was played in the rain, though this did not stop the Welsh backs scoring six of the seven tries. French forward Aimé Cassayet, who had played in the 1924 Olympics and had been a prisoner of war, played his 31st and last match. He fell ill and died on 26 May.

Wales B.O. Male (Cardiff); G.E. Andrews (Newport), *W.G. Morgan (Cambridge U), J. Roberts (Cardiff), W.R. Harding (Swansea); W.H. Lewis, +W.C. Powell (London Welsh); H.T. Phillips (Newport), J.H. John (Swansea), *J.J. Burns (Cardiff), T. Arthur (Neath), E.M. Jenkins (Aberavon), W.A. Williams (Crumlin), W.G. Thomas, I.E. Jones (Llanelli).
T: Rowe Harding 2, John Roberts 2, Watcyn Thomas, George Andrews, Guy Morgan.
C: Ossie Male 2.

France L. Destarac (Stade Tarbais); R. Houdet (Stade Français), M. Baillette (Quillan), V. Graule (Perpignan), F. Raymond (Toulouse); A. Verger (Stade Français), P. Carbonne (Perpignan); +E. Piquiral (Lyons), E. Ribère (Quillan), A. Prévost, R. Bousquet (Albi), A. Cassayet (Narbonne), J. Etcheberry (Vienne), R. Hutin (CASG, Paris), C.A. Gonnet (Racing Club).
T: Alfred Prévost.
DG: Andre Verger.
Referee: W.H. Jackson (England).

France 8 Wales 3

Stade Colombes, Paris. 9 April 1928

France won by 2 tries, 1 con to 1 try.

France gained their first-ever victory over Wales after 15 losses, having already defeated the other home countries in previous years. It was a feat they had almost accomplished two years earlier and was fully deserved as Wales hit the depths. Forward André Camel broke his shoulder early in this Easter Monday match and for a while France played two short. Wing Robert Houdet scored both the French tries and some reports credited him with a conversion. Wales retained the pack after the loss to Ireland, but made six changes, one positional, in the backs, including Gwyn Davies on the wing, who moved to Wigan RL in 1930.

France L. Pellissier (Racing Club); +A. Jaureguy (Stade Français), A. Behoteguy, H. Behoteguy (Cognac), R. Houdet; A. Verger (Stade Français), C. Dupont (Stade Bordelais); A. Camel (Stade Toulousain), R. Majerus (Stade Français), H. Lacaze (Perigeux), F. Camicas (Stade Tarbais), J. Sayrou (Perpignan), A. Bioussa (Stade Toulousain), J. Galia, E. Ribère (Quillan).
T: Robert Houdet 2.
C: André Behoteguy.

Wales +B.O. Male; *E.G. Davies, B.R. Turnbull (Cardiff), W.R. Jones (Swansea), J. Roberts (Cardiff); W.H. Lewis (Maesteg), W.C. Powell (London Welsh); F.A. Bowdler (Cross Keys), Cecil C. Pritchard (Pontypool), H.T. Phillips (Newport), E.M. Jenkins (Aberavon), A. Skym, T. Iorwerth Jones (Llanelli), T.H. Hollingdale (Neath), I.E. Jones (Llanelli).
T: Wick Powell.
Referee: R.W. Harland (Ireland).

Wales 8 France 3

Arms Park, Cardiff. 25 February 1929

Wales won by 2 tries, 1 con to 1 try.

France did a superb job of keeping the Welsh backs in check, but the Welsh pack contributed both tries. Visiting forwards André and Marcel Camel became the first twins to appear in an international match and much later prompted the question: 'When did A Camel score at the Arms Park?' Full-back Louis Magnol was shouldered off by some of the 45,000 crowd after giving a fine performance in wet conditions.

Wales J.A. Bassett (Penarth); J. Roberts, H.M. Bowcott (Cardiff), +W.G. Morgan (Swansea), J.C. Morley (Newport); F.L. Williams (Cardiff), W.C. Powell (London Welsh); R.J. Barrell (Cardiff), Cecil C. Pritchard (Pontypool), T. Arthur (Neath), F.A. Bowdler (Cross Keys), E.M. Jenkins (Aberavon), D.S. Parker (Swansea), H. Peacock (Newport), I.E. Jones (Llanelli).
T: Tom Arthur, Bob Barrell.
C: Dai Parker.

France L. Magnol (Toulouse); A. Domec (Carcassonne), +A. Behoteguy (Cognac), G. Gérald (Racing Club), C. Dulaurens (Toulouse); C. Magnanou (Bayonne), L. Serin (Beziers); A. Bioussa (Toulouse), J. Auge (Dax), M. Camel (Toulouse), H. Lacaze (Perigeux), F. Camicas (Tarbes), A. Camel (Toulouse), R. Bousquet (Toulon), J. Sayrou (Perpignan).
T: André Camel.
Referee: H.E.B. Wilkins (England).

France 0 Wales 11

Stade Colombes, Paris. 21 April 1930

Wales won by 1 try, 2 drop goals to nil.

It was another Easter Monday match in Paris which this time resulted in one of the biggest punch-ups since 'The Terrible Eight' had played against Ireland before the First World War. As France had beaten Scotland and Ireland, a win would have given them their first-ever championship. They fought hard enough for hooker Hubert Day to need his lip stitched, but Wales were not slow to hit back. The 21-year-old Claude Davey was an ideal centre for such a match, while the other new caps, Tommy Scourfield and Edgar Jones, both later moved to rugby league. Skipper Guy Morgan made his final appearance, having never led a losing Welsh side.

France M. Piquemal (Tarbes); J. Taillantou (Selection Paloise), G. Gérald (Racing Club), A. Behoteguy (Cognac), R. Samatan (Agen); C. Magnanou (Bayonne), L. Serin (Beziers); J. Choy (Narbonne), A. Ambert (Toulouse), R. Bousquet (Albi), R. Majerus (Stade Français), A. Camel (Toulouse), +E. Ribère, J. Galia (Quillan), A. Bioussa (Toulouse).

Wales *T.B. Scourfield (Torquay); E. Howie Jones (Neath), +W.G. Morgan, *E.C. Davey (Swansea), R.W. Boon; F.L. Williams (Cardiff), W.C. Powell (London Welsh); *E.L. Jones (Llanelli), H.C. Day (Newport), A. Skym (Cardiff), T. Arthur (Neath), E.M. Jenkins (Aberavon), A.W Lemon (Neath), H. Peacock (Newport), N.H. Fender (Cardiff).
T: Archie Skym.
DG: Guy Morgan, Wick Powell.
Referee: D. Hellewell (England).

Wales 35 France 3

St Helen's, Swansea. 28 February 1931

Wales won by 7 tries, 5 cons, 1 drop goal to 1 try.

Despite a Swansea snowstorm, Wales gained their largest win since the First World War, but it was to be 16 years before the countries were to meet again in a full international match. France lost centre Pierre Clement with a dislocated shoulder early in the match. Wales used Tom Day as a hooker in place of the suspended Hubert Day of Newport (the pair were not related!). New caps David James and Dicky Ralph both later joined Leeds RL.

Wales +J.A. Bassett (Penarth); J.C. Morley (Newport), E.C. Davey (Swansea), F.L. Williams, R.W. Boon (Cardiff); *A.R. Ralph (Newport), W.C. Powell (London Welsh); A. Skym (Cardiff), T.B. Day (Swansea), *D.R. James (Treorchy), T. Arthur (Neath), E M. Jenkins (Aberavon), A.W. Lemon (Neath), *J. Lang (Llanelli), N.H. Fender (Cardiff).
T: Raymond Ralph 2, Claude Davey, Norman Fender, Jim Lang, Frank Williams, Tom Arthur.
C: Jack Bassett 5.
DG: Wick Powell.

France M. Savy (Clermont-Ferrand); R. Samatan, P. Clement (Agen), M. Vigerie (Toulon), L. Angras (Agen); L. Servole (Toulouse), L. Serin (Beziers); J. Duhau, R. Scohy (Bordeaux), M. Rodrigo (Mauleon), P. Barrere (Toulon), C. Petit (Nancy), E. Camo, J. Galia (Villeneuve), +E. Ribère (Quillan).
T: Charles Petit.
Referee: R.W. Harland (Ireland).

France 0 Wales 3

Stade Colombes, Paris. 22 March 1947

Wales won by 1 pen to nil.

Wales found France a tough team to defeat in the first

meeting of the countries since 1931 and it took a penalty goal from big Bill Tamplin just before half-time to settle the contest. The superb Cardiff prop, Cliff Davies, had his little finger bitten to the bone by one of the French front row and Wales had problems with the massive locks, Albert Moga and Robert Soro. Billy Cleaver switched to outside-half and replaced the injured Glyn Davies, with wing Les Williams moving inside. The game is remembered for forward George Parsons being told to get off the train en route to London and return to Wales because the Welsh selectors had heard rumours that he was negotiating with rugby league scouts. Though Parsons maintained his innocence, he was virtually forced to go to league ten months later and was a great success there.

France A. Alvarez (Tyrosse); E. Pebeyre (Brive), +L. Junquas (Bayonne), M. Sorondo (Montauban), J. Lassegue (Toulouse); M. Terreau (Bourg), Y. Bergougnan (Toulouse); J. Prin-Clary (Brive), M. Jol (Biarritz), E. Buzy (Lourdes), A. Moga (Begles), R. Soro (Romans), J. Matheu (Castres), G. Basquet (Agen), J. Prat (Lourdes).

Wales C.H. Davies (Llanelli); K.J. Jones (Newport), B.L. Williams (Cardiff), W. Les T. Williams, *P. Rees (Llanelli); W.B. Cleaver, +H. Tanner (Cardiff); D.C.J. Jones (Swansea), W. Gore (Newbridge), C. Davies, W.E. Tamplin (Cardiff), S. Williams (Llanelli), *R.T. Evans (Newport), J.R.G. Stephens (Neath), G. Evans (Cardiff).
P: Bill Tamplin.
Referee: Alan S. Bean (England).

Wales 3 France 11

St Helen's, Swansea. 21 February 1948

France won by 3 tries, 1 con to 1 pen.

France gained their first victory in Wales, but it was like the pre-war days at Swansea when the crowd rioted with bottles and fruit thrown at the French players. In freezing cold conditions, Bill Tamplin hurled one spectator off the field but the crowd chaired the popular wing Michel Pomathios off the pitch. He was later to become the first French player to appear for the Barbarians. Maurice Terreau made two spectacular interceptions, scoring from one and sending Pomathios over from the other.

Wales R.F. Trott (Cardiff); K.J. Jones (Newport), B.L. Williams, W.B. Cleaver, J. Matthews (Cardiff); G. Davies (Pontypridd), +H. Tanner (Cardiff); L. Anthony (Neath), D.M. James, C. Davies, W.E. Tamplin (Cardiff), S. Williams, O. Williams (Llanelli), L. Manfield, G. Evans (Cardiff).
P: Ossie Williams.

France A. Alvarez (Tyrosse); M. Pomathios (Agen), M. Terreau (Bourg), +L. Junquas (Bayonne), J. Lassegue (Toulouse); L. Bordenave (Toulon), Y. Bergougnan (Toulouse); E. Buzy (Lourdes), L. Martin (Pau), L. Caron (Castres), R. Soro (Romans), A. Moga (Begles), J. Matheu (Castres), G. Basquet (Agen), J. Prat (Lourdes).
T: Guy Basquet, Maurice Terreau, Michel Pomathios.
C: André Alvarez.
Referee: Alan S. Bean (England).

France 5 Wales 3

Stade Colombes, Paris. 26 March 1949

France won by 1 try, 1 con to 1 try.

After beating England, Wales had fallen away so badly that they ended with the Wooden Spoon and were outplayed by France. However, Frank Trott in particular performed wonders in defence to prevent France adding to their one try and conversion. This was the last match for the pre-war players, Haydn Tanner and 'Bunner' Travers. The injured Bleddyn Williams was replaced by Jack Matthews, with Malcolm Thomas and Clem Thomas among the new faces. The latter said afterwards that he was too inexperienced, and was cast aside until 1952. Despite French pressure, Wales led by a Ken Jones try at half-time after Malcolm Thomas had cross-kicked. Jean Lassegue, 'The French Buffalo', eventually scored the try that André Alvarez converted to win the match.

France N. Baudry (Montferrand); M. Pomathios (Lyon), P. Dizabo (Tyrosse), H. Dutrain, J. Lassegue (Toulouse); A. Alvarez (Tyrosse), G. Dufau (Racing Club); E. Buzy (Lourdes), M. Jol (Biarritz), L. Caron (Lyons), A. Moga (Begles), R. Soro (Romans), J. Matheu (Castres), +G. Basquet (Agen), J. Prat (Lourdes).
T: Jean Lassegue.
C: André Alvarez.

Wales R.F. Trott (Cardiff); K.J. Jones, *M.C. Thomas (Newport), J. Matthews (Cardiff), *W.C. Major (Maesteg); G. Davies (Pontypridd/Cambridge U), +H. Tanner; C. Davies (Cardiff), W. Travers (Newport), D.C.J. Jones (Swansea), Don J. Hayward (Newbridge), J.A. Gwilliam (Cambridge U), *P. Stone (Llanelli), J.R.G. Stephens (Neath), *R.C.C. Thomas (Swansea).
T: Ken Jones.
Referee: Noel H. Lambert (Ireland).

The 1950 Triple Crown winners pictured here on the Arms Park cricket ground. Only Ray Cale and Gerwyn Williams were left behind on the British Isles tour to New Zealand and Australia at the end of the season. *Back row*: I. Jones (touch-judge), W.R. Willis, D. Hayward, E.R. John, R.T. Evans, M.C. Thomas, J.D. Robins, M.J. Dowling (referee). *Seated*: W.R. Cale, C. Davies, J. Matthews, J.A. Gwilliam (capt.), W.B. Cleaver, K.J. Jones, D.M. Davies. *Front row*: G. Williams, B.L. Jones. (© *Western Mail & Echo*)

Wales 21   France 0

Arms Park, Cardiff. 25 March 1950

Wales won by 4 tries, 3 cons, 1 pen to nil.

The Llandow aircrash overshadowed this one-sided match and the Last Post was played by buglers for a minute's silence. Wales led at half-time by a Jack Matthews interception try converted by Lewis Jones, but France lost Jean Prat with a knee injury and Wales then cut loose. The win gave Wales the championship outright for the first time since 1936 and they had won all four games in a season for the first time since 1911.

Wales G. Williams (London Welsh); K.J. Jones (Newport), J. Matthews (Cardiff), B.L. Jones, M.C. Thomas (Devonport Servs); W.B. Cleaver, W.R. Willis (Cardiff); J.D. Robins (Birkenhead Park), D.M. Davies (Somerset Police), C. Davies (Cardiff), Don J. Hayward (Newbridge), E.R. John (Neath), W.R. Cale (Pontypool), +J.A. Gwilliam (Edinburgh Wands), R.T. Evans (Newport).
T: Ken Jones 2, Roy John, Jack Matthews.
C: Lewis Jones 3.
P: Lewis Jones.

France G. Brun (Vienne); M. Siman (Castres), P. Lauga (Vichy), J. Merquey (Toulon), M. Pomathios (Lyons); F. Fournet (Montferrand), G. Dufau (Racing Club); R. Ferrien (Tarbes), P. Pascalin (Stade Montois), R. Bienes (Cognac), P. Aristouy (Pau), F. Bonnus (Toulon), J. Matheu (Castres), +G. Basquet (Agen), J. Prat (Lourdes).
Referee: Capt. M.J. Dowling (Ireland).

France 8   Wales 3

Stade Colombes, Paris. 7 April 1951

France won by 1 try, 1 con, 1 pen to 1 try.

Jack Matthews led Wales for the only occasion as John Gwilliam was dropped. Billy 'Stoker' Williams came in at prop for Cliff Davies and Cardiff flyer Haydn Morris appeared on the left-wing. Wales led at half-time but France were good value for their win, with a 20-year-old Lucien Mias at the heart of a strong French pack.

France R. Arcalis (Brive); A. Porthault (Racing Club), G. Brun (Vienne), G. Belletante (Nantes), M. Pomathios (Lyons); A.J. Alvarez

(Tyrosse), G. Dufau (Racing Club); R. Bernard (Bergerac), P. Pascalin (Mont de Marsan), P. Bertrand (Bourg), L. Mias (Mazamet), H. Foures (Toulouse), R. Bienes (Cognac), +G. Basquet (Agen), J. Prat (Lourdes).
T: André Alvarez.
C: Jean Prat.
P: Alvarez.

Wales G. Williams (Llanelli); K.J. Jones, M.C. Thomas (Newport), +J. Matthews, *H.T. Morris; C.I. Morgan, W.R. Willis (Cardiff); *W.O.G. Williams (Swansea), D.M. Davies (Somerset Police), J.D. Robins (Birkenhead Park), Don J. Hayward (Newbridge), E.R. John (Neath), R.T. Evans (Newport), J.R.G. Stephens (Neath), P.D. Evans (Llanelli).
T: Ken Jones.
Referee: Capt. M.J. Dowling (Ireland).

Wales 9 France 5

St Helen's, Swansea. 22 March 1952

Wales won by 2 pens, 1 drop goal to 1 try, 1 con.

This was a quiet end to the season, but the Grand Slam was nevertheless achieved. Cliff Morgan dropped out with injury, so the versatile Alun Thomas was called on to play in his favoured position on his old club ground. Another local favourite, Horace Phillips, gained his only cap in what was also the last appearance by Lewis Jones. The popular Michel Pomathios scored the French try and he next met his marker (Phillips) at St Helen's some 44 years later.

Wales G. Williams (Llanelli); K.J. Jones, M.C. Thomas (Newport), B.L. Jones (Llanelli), *D.H. Phillips (Swansea); A.G. Thomas (Cardiff), W.A. Williams (Newport); W.O.G. Williams (Swansea), D.M. Davies (Somerset Police), Don J. Hayward (Newbridge), E.R. John, R.G. Stephens (Neath), A. Forward (Pontypool), +J.A. Gwilliam (Edinburgh Wands), R.C.C. Thomas (Swansea).
P: Lewis Jones 2.
DG: Alun Thomas.

France G. Brun (Vienne); M. Pomathios (Lyons), J. Mauran (Castres), M. Prat (Lourdes), J. Collombier (St Junien); J. Carabignac (Agen), G. Dufau (Racing Club); R. Bienes (Cognac), P. Labadie (Bayonne), R. Brejassou (Pau), B. Chevallier (Montferrand), L. Mias (Mazamet), J.R. Bourdeu (Lourdes), +G. Basquet (Agen), J. Prat (Lourdes).
T: Michel Pomathios.
C: Jean Prat.
Referee: A.W.C. Austin (Scotland).

France 3 Wales 6

Stade Colombes, Paris. 28 March 1953

Wales won by 2 tries to 1 pen.

The superbly fit Gareth Griffiths played a key role, as he had against Ireland two weeks earlier. He scored a first-half try and then added a second, after gathering a cross-kick from the lively Clem Thomas in the second half. Prop Pierre Bertrand's late penalty goal failed to save France from defeat.

France M. Vannier (Racing Club); M. Pomathios (Lyons), M. Galy (Perpignan), G. Brun (Vienne), L. Roge (Beziers); L. Bidart (La Rochelle), G. Dufau (Racing Club); P. Bertrand (Bourg), J. Arieta (Stade Français), R. Brejassou (Tarbes), L. Mias (Mazamet), B. Chevallier (Montferrand), H. Domec (Lourdes), M. Celaya (Biarritz), +J. Prat (Lourdes).
P: Pierre Bertrand.

Wales T.J. Davies (Swansea); K.J. Jones (Newport), A.G. Thomas, +B.L. Williams, G.M. Griffiths; C.I. Morgan (Cardiff), T. Lloyd (Maesteg); W.O.G. Williams (Swansea), D.M. Davies (Somerset Police), J.D. Robins (Bradford), E.R. John, J.R.G. Stephens (Neath), S. Judd (Cardiff), J.A. Gwilliam (Gloucester), R.C.C. Thomas (Swansea)
T: Gareth Griffiths 2.
Referee: Ossie B. Glasgow (Ireland).

Wales 19 France 13

Arms Park, Cardiff. 27 March 1954

Wales won by 2 tries, 2 cons, 3 pens to 2 tries, 2 cons, 1 pen.

Wales only just beat off a spirited French effort that saw the immaculate Viv Evans outkick Jean Prat. Gareth Griffiths scored the opening converted try, but centre Roger Martine crossed and it was 5–5 at the break. At that point, an Evans penalty and conversion of a Billy Williams try put Wales ahead again and although Robert Baulon's try and Prat's conversion closed it to 13–10, it was further Evans kicks that settled it. Rex Willis led Wales after Rees Stephens had withdrawn with injury and Glyn John came in at outside-half for the injured Cliff Morgan. A new cap was flanker Len Davies, whose younger brother Terry was capped the previous year. His career was all too brief as he died three years later at the age of 26.

Wales V. Evans (Neath); K.J. Jones (Newport), A.G. Thomas, G.M. Griffiths, G. Rowlands (Cardiff); D.G. John (St Luke's Coll/Aberavon), +W.R. Willis (Cardiff); W.O.G.Williams (Swansea), B.V. Meredith (Newport), C.C. Meredith (Neath), R.J. Robins (Pontypridd), R.H. Williams, *L.M. Davies (Llanelli), S. Judd (Cardiff), R.C.C. Thomas (Swansea).
T: Gareth Griffiths, Billy Williams.
C: Viv Evans 2.
P: Evans 3.

France H. Claverie (Lourdes); A. Boniface (Stade Montois), M. Prat, R. Martine (Lourdes), F. Cazenave (Stade Montois); A. Labazuy (Lourdes), G. Dufau (Racing Club); A. Domenech (Vichy), P. Labadie (Bayonne), R. Bienes (Cognac), L. Mias (Mazamet), B. Chevallier (Montferrand), +J. Prat (Lourdes), R. Baulon (Vienne), H. Domec (Lourdes).
T: Roger Martine, Robert Baulon.
C: Jean Prat 2.
P: Jean Prat.
Referee: A.I. 'Sandy' Dickie (Scotland).

France 11 Wales 16

Stade Colombes, Paris. 26 March 1955

Wales won by 2 tries, 2 cons, 2 pens to 1 try, 1 con, 1 pen, 1 drop goal.

Wales played superbly, once again to prevent France from winning the championship outright for the first time. The Welsh pack-leader Rees Stephens was in outstanding form and though wing-forwards Clem Thomas and Len Davies withdrew, their replacements Brian Sparks and new cap Derek Williams had fine matches to enable Wales to share the championship. Owen kicked two huge penalties and Alun Thomas scored an opportunist try in the first half. Then wing Haydn Morris leapt like a gazelle to gather an Alun Thomas cross-kick, for a try that took Wales clear at 16–6. It was the first time that a Paris match was all-ticket and it brought a record crowd of 62,000. The match saw the last championship appearances by Welsh scrum-half Rex Willis and Jean Prat, nicknamed 'Monsieur Rugby' by his Lourdes colleagues.

France M. Vannier (Racing Club); H. Rancoulé, M. Prat, R. Martine (Lourdes), J. Lepatey (Mazamet); A. Haget (Paris U), G. Dufau (Racing Club); R. Brejassou (Tarbes), P. Labadie (Bayonne), A. Domenech (Vichy), B. Chevallier (Montferrand), M. Celaya (Biarritz), +J. Prat (Lourdes), R. Baulon (Vienne), H. Domec (Lourdes).
T: Robert Baulon.
C: Michel Vannier.
P: Vannier.
DG: Maurice Prat.

Wales G.D. Owen; K.J. Jones (Newport), A.G. Thomas (Llanelli), G.M. Griffiths, H.T. Morris (Cardiff); C.I. Morgan (Bective Rangers), W.R. Willis (Cardiff); W.O.G. Williams (Swansea), B.V. Meredith (Newport), C.C. Meredith (Neath), R.J. Robins (Pontypridd), R.H. Williams (Llanelli), B.A. Sparks, +J.R.G. Stephens (Neath), *C.D. Williams (Cardiff).
T: Alun Thomas, Haydn Morris.
C: Garfield Owen 2.
P: Owen 2.
Referee: Ossie B. Glasgow (Ireland).

Wales 5 France 3

Arms Park, Cardiff. 24 March 1956

Wales won by 1 try, 1 con to 1 try.

France appeared to be cruelly robbed of victory when Derek Williams was adjudged to have touched the ball down fairly, though to many eyes he appeared to be far past the dead-ball line at the River End of the ground. The conversion by Garfield Owen gave Wales the championship outright. France had taken the lead when 'Jackie' Bouquet's kick ahead was gathered by René Baulon, who returned to Bouquet near the goal-line. Ken Jones gained a record-breaking 43rd cap and Rex 'Tarzan' Richards, a high-diver and later a film stuntman, won his only cap.

Wales G.D. Owen; K.J. Jones, H.P. Morgan, M.C. Thomas (Newport), G. Rowlands; +C.I. Morgan (Cardiff), D.O. Brace (Newport); *R.C. Richards (Cross Keys), B.V. Meredith (Newport), T.R. Prosser (Pontypool), L.H. Jenkins (Newport), J.R.G. Stephens, C.D. Williams (Neath), R.J. Robins (Pontypridd), *G.K. Whitson (Newport).
T: Derek Williams.
C: Garfield Owen.

France M. Vannier (Racing Club); J. Dupuy (Tarbes), M. Prat (Lourdes), A. Boniface (Stade Montois), L. Roge (Beziers); J. Bouquet (Vienne), +G. Dufau (Racing Club); A. Domenech (Brive), R. Vigier (Montferrand), R. Bienes (Cognac), B. Chevallier (Montferrand), M. Celaya (Biarritz), R. Baulon (Bayonne), J. Barthe, H.Domec (Lourdes).
T: Jacques Bouquet.
Referee: Dr Peter F. Cooper (England).

France 13 Wales 19

Stade Colombes, Paris. 23 March 1957

Wales won by 4 tries, 2 cons, 1 pen to 3 tries, 2 cons.

The Pontypool front-row of later years were no doubt told by their coach Ray Prosser that he had also been able to score tries. The one he scored in this match was vital, as Wales were leading 14–8 midway through the second half when he put the issue beyond doubt. Wales had been rocked by a Maurice Prat try, scored after he was first to react when Christian Darrouy's drop-shot had rebounded off a post. But it was the front-row who took matters in hand, with the brilliant Bryn Meredith and then Prosser scoring tries. France played well, but Cliff Morgan and Graham Powell in particular excelled for Wales, as did skipper Rees Stephens, in his final appearance.

France M. Vannier (Racing Club); C. Darrouy, A. Boniface (Stade Montois), M. Prat (Lourdes), J. Dupuy (Stade Tarbais); J. Bouquet (Vienne), G. Dufau (Racing Club); A. Domenech (Brive), R. Vigier (Montferrand), A. Sanac (Perpignan), +M. Celaya (Biarritz), M. Hoche (Paris U), F. Moncla (Racing Club), J. Barthe (Lourdes), J. Carrere (Vichy).
T: Jean Dupuy, Maurice Prat, André Sanac.
C: Jacques Bouquet 2.

Wales T.J. Davies; H. Ray Williams (Llanelli), G. Powell (Ebbw Vale), G.T. Wells (Cardiff), W.G. Howells (Llanelli); C.I. Morgan, L.H. Williams (Cardiff); T.R. Prosser (Pontypool), B.V. Meredith (London Welsh), C.H. Morgan, R.H. Williams (Llanelli), +J.R.G. Stephens (Neath), R.J. Robins (Pontypridd), J. Faull (Swansea), R.H. Davies (London Welsh).
T: Ray Prosser, Geoff Howells, John Faull, Bryn Meredith.
C: Terry Davies 2.
P: Terry Davies.
Referee: Dr Peter F. Cooper (England).

Wales 6 France 16

Arms Park, Cardiff. 29 March 1958.

France won by 2 tries, 2 cons, 2 drop goals to 1 try, 1 pen.

Unbeaten Wales suddenly found a changing world of rugby as France, who were to win a summer series in South Africa, achieved their first-ever success at Cardiff. Pierre Danos, Alfred Rocques, Jean Barthe and Lucien Mias were outstanding and France could well have won by a larger margin. Michel Vannier dropped a goal in either half and though John Collins pegged the gap to 8–6 during the second half, Wales never looked like winning. A 60,000 crowd saw Cliff Morgan end his international career by being tightly marked and he failed to hit it off with Carwyn James, who had been selected at centre.

Wales T.J. Davies (Llanelli); C.R. Roberts (Neath), M.C. Thomas (Newport), C.R. James (Llanelli), J.E. Collins (Aberavon); C.I. Morgan, L.H. Williams (Cardiff); T.R. Prosser (Pontypool), G.T. Beckingham, J.D. Evans (Cardiff), R.H. Williams (Llanelli), W.R. Evans (Cardiff), +R.C.C. Thomas, J. Faull (Swansea), H.J. Morgan (Abertillery).
T: John Collins.
P: Terry Davies.

France M. Vannier (Racing Club); H. Rancoulé, M. Prat, R. Martine, P. Tarricq; A. Labazuy (Lourdes), P. Danos (Beziers); A. Roques (Cahors), R. Vigier (Montferrand), A. Quaglio, L. Mias (Mazamet), +M. Celaya (Biarritz), M. Crauste (Racing Club), J. Barthe, H. Domec (Lourdes).
T: Pierre Danos, Pierre Tarricq.
C: Antoine Labazuy 2.
DG: Michel Vannier 2.
Referee: A.I. 'Sandy' Dickie (Scotland).

France 11 Wales 3

Stade Colombes, Paris. 4 April 1959

France won by 2 tries, 1 con, 1 pen to 1 pen.

France became outright champions for the first time and one of their greatest captains, Lucien Mias, was carried off on the shoulders of his teammates in front of a sell-out crowd of 55,000. It was a triumph for teamwork and the back-row of Michel Crauste, Jean Barthe and François Moncla was outstanding. Malcolm Thomas ended his international career by appearing at outside-half, having already played at centre and wing. His clubmate Billy Watkins won his only cap at scrum-half and for the first time in 66 matches since 1936, there was not a Cardiff man in the team. Terry Davies kicked Wales ahead, but after Antoine Labazuy had levelled, a try in either half of the match by Moncla gave France the title.

France P. Lacaze; H. Rancoulé (Lourdes), J. Bouquet (Vienne), A. Marquesuzaa (Racing Club), J. Dupuy (Tarbes); A. Labazuy (Lourdes), P. Danos (Beziers); A. Quaglio (Mazamet), R. Vigier (Montferrand), A. Roques, B. Mommejat (Cahors), +L. Mias (Mazamet), M. Crauste

(Racing Club), J. Barthe (Lourdes), F. Moncla (Racing Club).
T: François Moncla 2.
C: Antoine Labazuy.
P: Labazuy.

Wales T.J. Davies (Llanelli); J.E. Collins (Aberavon), *R.J. Hurrell (Newport), M.J. Price (Pontypool), D.I.E. Bebb (Swansea); M.C. Thomas, *W.R. Watkins (Newport); T.R. Prosser (Pontypool), B.V. Meredith (Newport), D.R. Main (London Welsh), R.H. Williams (Llanelli), D.J.E. Harris (Pontypridd), +R.C.C. Thomas (Swansea), *G.D. Davidge (Newport), H.J. Morgan (Abertillery).
P: Terry Davies.
Referee: Dr Norman McNeill Parkes (England).

Wales 8 France 16

Arms Park, Cardiff. 26 March 1960

France won by 4 tries, 2 cons to 1 try, 1 con, 1 pen.

France were far too good for Wales – the score flattered the Welsh. Outplayed up front, Wales conceded four tries to a French side, with six changes from the side that had drawn 3–3 with England. New centre Guy Boniface was an immediate success and Pierre Lacroix was like a well-trained dog at the heels of his pack. The Swansea fly-half Bryan Richards had a miserable début and was not selected again. There was a dispute as to who scored the Welsh try, but the referee ruled that Brian Jones did not ground the ball and awarded the score to his clubmate Brian Cresswell.

Wales N.H. Morgan (Newport); F.G. Coles, M.J. Price (Pontypool), B.J. Jones (Newport), D.I.E. Bebb (Swansea); *T.B. Richards (Swansea), D.O. Brace (Llanelli); T.R. Prosser (Pontypool), +B.V. Meredith (Newport), L.J. Cunningham (Aberavon), J. Faull (Swansea), D.J.E. Harris (Cardiff), B.R. Cresswell, G.D. Davidge (Newport), J. Leleu (Swansea).
T: Brian Cresswell.
C: Norman Morgan.
P: Morgan.

France M. Vannier (Racing Club); S. Mericq (Agen), G. Boniface (Mont de Marsan), J. Bouquet (Vienne), J. Dupuy (Tarbes); P. Albaladejo (Dax), P. Lacroix (Mont de Marsan); A. Domenech (Brive), J. de Gregorio (Grenoble), A. Roques (Cahors), J.-P. Saux (Pau), H. Larrue (Carmaux), +F. Moncla (Pau), M. Celaya (Bordeaux), M. Crauste (Lourdes).
T: Michel Celaya, Serge Mericq, Pierre Lacroix, Jean Dupuy.
C: Michel Vannier, Pierre Albaladejo.
Referee: Dr Norman McNeill Parkes (England).

France 8 Wales 6

Stade Colombes, Paris. 25 March 1961

France won by 2 tries, 1 con to 2 tries.

Wales did surprisingly well, with débutant Alun Pask equalising before the interval and Dewi Bebb putting Wales ahead at 6–3 in the second half. Centre Guy Boniface scored an equalising try that Michel Vannier converted to give France a deserved win. Sadly, the talented Boniface was to die at the age of 30 in a car crash. Haydn Mainwaring, who had been at full-back in the Barbarians win over South Africa, was wrongly cast as a centre in his only appearance.

France M. Vannier (Chalon); H. Rancoulé (Toulon), J. Bouquet (Vienne), G. Boniface (Mont de Marsan), G. Mauduy (Perigueux); P. Albaladejo (Dax), P. Lacroix (Agen); A. Domenech (Brive), J. de Gregorio (Grenoble), A. Roques (Cahors), G. Bouguyon (Grenoble), J.-P. Saux, +F. Moncla (Pau), M. Celaya (Bordeaux), M. Crauste (Lourdes).
T: Guy Boniface, Jean-Pierre Saux.
C: Michel Vannier.

Wales T.J. Davies (Llanelli); J.E. Collins (Aberavon), H.M. Roberts (Cardiff), *H.J. Mainwaring, D.I.E. Bebb (Swansea), K.H.L. Richards (Bridgend); +L.H. Williams (Cardiff); T.R. Prosser (Pontypool), *W.J. Thomas (Cardiff), P.E.J. Morgan (Aberavon), W.R. Evans (Bridgend), B. Price (Newport), *A.E.I. Pask (Abertillery), D. Nash (Ebbw Vale), H.J. Morgan (Abertillery).
T: Alun Pask, Dewi Bebb.
Referee: Dr Norman McNeill Parkes (England).

Wales 3 France 0

Arms Park, Cardiff. 24 March 1962

Wales won by 1 pen to nil.

The match with Ireland was set for 10 March and later 28 April, but was postponed until the next season due to an outbreak of smallpox in South Wales which proved disastrous for Neath prop Ron Waldron. Picked to play against Ireland because Kingsley Jones was still injured, he was omitted against France as Jones was now fit. Keith Rowlands made a dramatic entry to top rugby at lock, while David Nash was a shock choice as his partner; Brian Price and Roddy

Evans were dropped. Wales failed to score a try all season, but Kel Coslett at last landed a penalty in the first half. The match was saved by a brilliant Alun Pask tackle on French wing Henri Rancoulé.

Wales T.K. Coslett (Aberavon); D.R.R. Morgan, D.K. Jones (Llanelli), H.M. Roberts (Cardiff), D.I.E. Bebb (Swansea); A.H.M. Rees (Maesteg), A. O'Connor; L.J. Cunningham (Aberavon), +B.V. Meredith (Newport), K.D. Jones, *K.A. Rowlands (Cardiff), D. Nash (Ebbw Vale), G.D. Davidge (Newport), A.E.I. Pask, H.J. Morgan (Abertillery).
P: Kel Coslett.

France C. Lacaze (Lourdes); H. Rancoulé (Tarbes), A. Boniface (Mont de Marsan), J. Bouquet (Vienne), J. Dupuy (Tarbes); P. Albaladejo (Dax), +P. Lacroix (Agen); A. Domenech (Brive), J. de Gregorio (Grenoble), A. Roques (Cahors), B. Mommejat (Albi), J.-P. Saux (Pau), R. Gensanne (Beziers), H. Romero (Montauban), M. Crauste (Lourdes).
Referee: Kevin D. Kelleher (Ireland).

France 5 Wales 3

Stade Colombes, Paris. 23 March 1963

France won by 1 try, 1 con to 1 pen.

Despite a good effort, Wales lost a match where again the weather was cold and the crowd small. Wales led from an early Grahame Hodgson penalty, but a superb Guy Boniface try, aided by his bother André, was close enough to the posts for Pierre Albaladejo to kick the winning conversion.

France C. Lacaze (Angoulême); C. Darrouy, G. Boniface, A. Boniface (Mont de Marsan), J. Dupuy (Tarbes); P. Albaladejo (Dax), +P. Lacroix (Agen); F. Mas (Beziers), J. de Gregorio (Grenoble), A. Domenech, R. Fite (Brive), B.Mommejat (Albi), M. Lira (La Voulte), J. Fabre (Toulouse), M. Crauste (Lourdes).
T: Guy Boniface.
C: Pierre Albaladejo.

Wales G.T.R. Hodgson (Neath); D.R.R. Morgan, D.K. Jones (Llanelli), R. Evans (Bridgend), D.I.E. Bebb (Swansea); D. Watkins (Newport), +D.C.T. Rowlands (Pontypool); D. Williams (Ebbw Vale), W.J. Thomas, *C.H. Norris (Cardiff), B. Price (Newport), B.E. Thomas (Neath), G. Jones (Ebbw Vale), A.E.I. Pask, H.J. Morgan (Abertillery).
P: Grahame Hodgson.
Referee: Peter G. Brook (England).

Wales 11 France 11

Arms Park, Cardiff. 21 March 1964

Draw. 1 try, 1 con, 2 pens each.

While Scotland were defeating England at Murrayfield, Wales earned a share of the championship by snatching a draw late in the match when wing Stuart Watkins scored in the corner for Keith Bradshaw to equalise with a superb touchline kick. France had led 11–3 at the interval with Wales playing poorly and Bradshaw being outkicked by Pierre Albaladejo.

Wales G.T.R. Hodgson (Neath); S.J. Watkins (Newport), S.J. Dawes (London Welsh), K. Bradshaw (Bridgend), D.I.E. Bebb (Swansea); D. Watkins (Newport), +D.C.T. Rowlands (Pontypool); D. Williams (Ebbw Vale), N.R. Gale (Llanelli), L.J. Cunningham (Aberavon), B. Price (Newport), B.E. Thomas (Neath), G.J. Prothero (Bridgend), A.E.I. Pask (Abertillery), Dai J. Hayward (Cardiff).
T: Stuart Watkins.
C: Keith Bradshaw.
P: Bradshaw 2.

France P. Dedieu (Beziers); J. Gachassin (Lourdes), J. Pique (Pau), A. Boniface, C. Darrouy (Mont de Marsan); P. Albaladejo, J.-C. Lasserre (Dax); J.-C. Berejnoi (Tulle), Y. Menthiller (Romans), A. Gruarin, A. Herrero (Toulon), B. Dauga (Mont de Marsan), M. Sitjar (Agen), M. Lira (La Voulte), +M. Crauste (Lourdes).
T: Michel Crauste.
C: Pierre Albaladejo.
P: Albaladejo 2.
Referee: H.B. Laidlaw (Scotland).

France 22 Wales 13

Stade Colombes, Paris. 27 March 1965

France won by 4 tries, 2 cons, 1 pen, 1 drop goal to 3 tries, 2 cons.

Though they were now the champions and Triple Crown holders, Wales conceded four tries in an hour and were 22 points down before they woke up. Referee Gilliland had left the field with a leg injury in the first half and the popular Frenchman, Bernard Marie, who had controlled the splendid Wales XV–Fiji match in 1964, left his duties as a touch-judge to take over. Wales gradually came back, with John Dawes, Dewi Bebb and finally Stuart Watkins scoring tries, but it was too late to save the game. It

The Welsh 1965 Triple-Crown winners. Scores of 14–3, 14–12 and 14–8 were good enough, but defeat came later in Paris. *Back row*: W.K.M. Jones (touch-judge), N.R. Gale, S.J. Watkins, K.A. Rowlands, B. Price, D. Williams, G.J. Prothero, P.G. Brook (referee). *Seated*: T. Price, A.E.I. Pask, D.C.T. Rowlands (capt.), R. Waldron, J. Uzzell. *Front row*: S.J. Dawes, H.J. Morgan, D.I. Bebb, D. Watkins. (© Western Mail & Echo)

was the last appearance by Clive Rowlands, whose 14 consecutive appearances had all been as captain.

France P. Dedieu (Beziers); J. Pique (Pau), G. Boniface, A. Boniface (Mont de Marsan), A. Campaes; J. Gachassin (Lourdes), J.-C. Lasserre (Dax); A. Gruarin (Toulon), J.M. Cabanier (Montauban), J.-C. Berejnoi (Tulle), B. Dauga (Mont de Marsan), W. Spanghero (Narbonne), J.-J. Rupert (Tyrosse), A. Herrero (Toulon), +M. Crauste (Lourdes).
T: Guy Boniface 2, André Herrero 2.
C: Paul Dedieu 2.
P: Dedieu.
DG: Jean-Claude Lasserre.

Wales T.G. Price (Llanelli); S.J. Watkins, J. Uzzell (Newport), S.J. Dawes (London Welsh), D.I.E. Bebb (Swansea); D. Watkins (Newport), +D.C.T. Rowlands (Pontypool); D. Williams (Ebbw Vale), N.R. Gale (Llanelli), R.G. Waldron (Neath), B. Price (Newport), K.A. Rowlands (Cardiff), G.J. Prothero (Bridgend), A.E.I. Pask, H.J. Morgan (Abertillery).
T: John Dawes, Stuart Watkins, Dewi Bebb.
C: Terry Price 2.
Referee: R.W. Gilliland (Ireland) replaced by Bernard Marie (France) after 32 mins.

Wales 9 France 8

Arms Park, Cardiff. 26 March 1966

Wales won by 1 try, 2 pens to 2 tries, 1 con.

One of the most outstanding individual efforts ever seen at Cardiff Arms Park won the match for Wales, just as France, leading 8–6, appeared sure to score again. They attacked at the Westgate-Street end with Jean Gachassin throwing a long pass towards wing Christian Darrouy. At this point the great opportunist Stuart Watkins streaked in, and he intercepted the pass and set off for the French line some 75 yards away. On half-way Claude Lacaze came to him, but the tall, gangling Newport man pushed him off and strode on and over the French line at the Taff End of the ground. The drama had not finished, as Bill Morris was penalised for throwing the ball deliberately into touch. Lacaze took the penalty after which the wind blew the ball down. He sent a good-looking kick that seemed over until a late gust of wind blew it past a Welsh post. Wales had retained the championship for the first time in 57 years. They delayed the naming of the pack until match-day, when it was discovered that Brian Thomas and Denzil Williams had been dropped to bring in Morris and Howard Norris.

Wales G.T.R. Hodgson (Neath); S.J. Watkins (Newport), D.K. Jones (Cardiff), K. Bradshaw (Bridgend), D.I.E. Bebb (Swansea); D. Watkins (Newport), R. Allan Lewis (Abertillery); C.H. Norris (Cardiff), N.R. Gale (Llanelli), D.J. Lloyd (Bridgend), B. Price, W.J. Morris (Newport), G.J. Prothero (Bridgend), +A.E.I. Pask, H.J. Morgan (Abertillery).
T: Stuart Watkins.
P: Keith Bradshaw 2.

France C. Lacaze (Angoulème); B. Duprat (Bayonne), G. Boniface, A. Boniface, C. Darrouy (Mont de Marsan); J. Gachassin (Lourdes), L. Camberabero (La Voulte); A. Gruarin (Toulon), J.-M. Cabanier (Montauban), J.-C. Berejnoi (Tulle), W. Spanghero (Narbonne), B. Dauga (Mont de Marsan), J.-J. Rupert (Tyrosse), A. Herrero (Toulon), +M. Crauste (Lourdes).
T: Bernard Duprat, Jean-Joseph Rupert.
C: Claude Lacaze.
Referee: Kevin D. Kelleher (Ireland).

France 20 Wales 14

Stade Colombes, Paris. 1 April 1967

France won by 3 tries, 1 con, 1 pen, 2 drop goals to 1 try, 1 con, 2 pens, 1 drop goal.

A new era was about to start with the introduction of the 19-year-old scrum-half Gareth Edwards, a student at Cardiff Training College. Dai 'The Shadow' Morris, often seen at the shoulder of Edwards, was another new face who was to remain for some years. This match, however, belonged to the tiny French outside-half Guy Camberabero who scored 14 points and, when his penalty shot hit a Welsh post, centre Claude Dourthe followed up to gain the touchdown. Terry Price ended his union career by missing six of his nine goal attempts and by July had joined Bradford Northern Rugby League club for £10,000. Opinion on his ability was still divided in Wales, but he went on to represent Great Britain at the other code.

France J. Gachassin; M. Arnaudet (Lourdes), C. Dourthe (Dax), J.-P. Lux (Tyrosse), +C. Darrouy (Mont de Marsan); G. Camberabero, L. Camberabero (La Voulte); A. Gruarin (Toulon), J.-M. Cabanier (Montauban), J.-C. Berejnoi (Tulle), E. Cester (Toulouse), J. Fort, M. Sitjar (Agen), B. Dauga (Mont de Marsan), C. Carrere (Toulon).
T: Guy Camberabero, Benoît Dauga, Claude Dourthe.
C: Guy Camberabero.
P: Guy Camberabero.
DG: Guy Camberabero 2.

Wales T.G. Price (London Welsh); S.J. Watkins (Newport), W.H. Raybould (London Welsh), T.G.R. Davies (Cardiff), D.I.E. Bebb (Swansea); +D. Watkins (Newport), *G.O. Edwards (Cardiff); D. Williams (Ebbw Vale), B.I. Rees (London Welsh), D.J. Lloyd (Bridgend), B. Price (Newport), G.T. 'Billy' Mainwaring (Aberavon), *R.E. Jones (Coventry), *W.D. Morris (Neath), J. Taylor (London Welsh).
T: Dewi Bebb.
C: Terry Price.
P: Terry Price 2.
DG: David Watkins.
Referee: D.P. 'Paddy' D'Arcy (Ireland)

Wales 9 France 14

Arms Park, Cardiff. 23 March 1968

France won by 2 tries, 1 con, 1 pen, 1 drop goal to 1 try, 2 pens.

It had taken 58 years, but France at last completed four victories in the Five Nations Tournament, though the defeat was the last suffered by Wales at Cardiff in a championship match until 1982. Once again it was mud and wind at the Arms Park, with Wales 9–3 up at half-time before France, inspired by skipper Christian Carrere, scored two tries for a deserved win. The Welsh scrum suffered after a rib injury early in the match to John O'Shea, who battled on bravely.

Wales D. Rees (Swansea); W. Keri Jones (Cardiff), S.J. Dawes, W.H. Raybould (London Welsh), M.C.R. Richards; B. John, +G.O. Edwards (Cardiff); D.J. Lloyd, J. Young (Bridgend), J.P. O'Shea (Cardiff), W.D. Thomas (Llanelli), M.L. Wiltshire (Aberavon), W.D. Morris (Neath), R.E. Jones (Coventry), J. Taylor (London Welsh).
T: Keri Jones.
P: Doug Rees 2.

France C. Lacaze (Angoulème); J.M. Bonal (Toulouse), J. Maso (Perpignan), C. Dourthe (Dax), A. Campaes (Lourdes); G. Camberabero, L. Camberabero; J.-C. Noble (La Voulte), M. Yachvili (Tulle), M. Lasserre, A. Plantefol (Agen), E. Cester (Toulouse), W. Spanghero (Narbonne), M. Greffe (Grenoble), +C. Carrere (Toulon).
T: Lilian Camberabero, Christian Carrere.
C: Guy Camberabero.

P: Guy Camberabero.
DG: Guy Camberabero.
Referee: H.B. Laidlaw (Scotland).

France 8 Wales 8

Stade Colombes, Paris. 22 March 1969

Draw. France – 1 try, 1 con, 1 pen. Wales – 2 tries, 1 con.

France had lost to Scotland, Ireland and England and were down 0–8 to an unchanged Wales team by the interval. Gareth Edwards had produced a try full of strength and speed and then he placed a kick in Clive Rowlands fashion for Maurice Richards to score and Keith Jarrett convert. France, however, had not read the script and came back with Pierre Villepreux placing a penalty and then kicking high into the Welsh half. Wing André Campaes was the quickest to it and roared under the posts for Villepreux to kick a deserved equalising conversion. Just before the final whistle, Gerald Davies retired with a badly injured elbow and on came the talented Phil Bennett to make history as the first-ever Welsh replacement, even though he never touched the ball.

France P. Villepreux (Toulouse); B. Moraitis (Toulon), C. Dourthe (Dax), J. Trillo (Begles), A. Campaes (Lourdes); J. Maso, G. Sutra (Narbonne); J. Iracabal (Bayonne), R. Benesis (Narbonne), J.-L. Azarete (Dax), A. Plantefol (Agen), E. Cester (Toulouse), J.-P. Biemouret (Agen), +W. Spanghero, G. Viard (Narbonne).
T: André Campaes.
C: Pierre Villepreux.
P: Villepreux.

Wales J.P.R. Williams (London Welsh); S.J. Watkins, K.S. Jarrett (Newport), T.G.R. Davies, M.C.R. Richards; B. John, G.O. Edwards (Cardiff); D. Williams (Ebbw Vale), J. Young, D.J. Lloyd (Bridgend), +B. Price (Newport), B.E. Thomas, W.D. Morris (Neath), T.M. Davies, J. Taylor (London Welsh). Rep: *P. Bennett (Llanelli) for T.G.R. Davies.
T: Gareth Edwards, Maurice Richards.
C: Keith Jarrett.
Referee: R.P. Burrell (Scotland).

Wales 11 France 6

Arms Park, Cardiff. 4 April 1970

Wales won by 1 try, 1 con, 2 pens to 2 tries.

Wales made sure of at least a share in the championship, but France were to rout England in the Paris sunshine two weeks later to draw level. Barry John withdrew giving Phil Bennett an opportunity in his true position, and seven changes included four débutants. Of those, the Llanelli pair of Roy Mathias and Stuart Gallacher did not play again. Gallacher 'went north' at the end of the season, while Mathias followed in 1972. Wales led 6–3 at half-time before Gallacher intercepted and sent Dai Morris over under the posts. France produced a second try, but too late to win the match. This was the first time Phil Bennett partnered Gareth Edwards at half-back for Wales.

Wales J.P.R. Williams; *J.L.Shanklin, +S.J. Dawes (London Welsh), *A.J.L. Lewis (Ebbw Vale), *R. Mathias; P. Bennett (Llanelli), G.O. Edwards (Cardiff); D.J. Lloyd (Bridgend), J. Young (Harrogate), D.B. Llewelyn (Newport), W.D. Thomas, *I.S. Gallacher (Llanelli), W.D. Morris (Neath), T.M. Davies, J. Taylor (London Welsh). Rep: W.H. Raybould (Newport) for Shanklin.
T: Dai Morris.
C: J.P.R.Williams.
P: J.P.R.Williams 2.

France P. Villepreux (Toulouse); J. Cantoni (Beziers), A. Marot (Brive), J.-P. Lux (Tyrosse), J.-M. Bonal (Toulouse); L. Paries (Biarritz), M. Puget (Brive); J. Iracabal (Bayonne), R. Benesis (Narbonne), J.-L. Azarete, J.-P. Bastiat (Dax), E. Cester (Toulouse Olympic), J.-P. Biemouret (Agen), B. Dauga (Mont de Marsan), +C. Carrere (Toulon).
T: Jacques Cantoni, Jean-Marie Bonal.
Referee: Kevin D. Kelleher (Ireland).

France 5 Wales 9

Stade Colombes, Paris. 27 March 1971

Wales won by 2 tries, 1 pen to 1 try, 1 con.

After the Triple Crown came the championship and a Grand Slam, the latter being gained for the first time since 1952. It was the first win for Wales in Paris for 14 years, but France did not make it easy. In fact, the home side took the lead with a Benoît Dauga try converted by Pierre Villepreux, and Barry John had to retire temporarily with a bloodied nose, after stopping another Dauga charge for the line. France were set to score again as wing Roger Bougarel threw the ball inside, but it was J.P.R. Williams who nipped in to catch it ten yards from his own goalline. Away he stormed on a 70-yard run, before going inwards to draw the cover and find Gareth Edwards racing up the left-wing outside him. John's kick missed and France were still in front at the interval. John soon placed a penalty to put Wales in front and then he produced a gem of a try as he took an Edwards pass on the blind-side and glided past the defence, after Jeff Young had taken the heel against the head. It was tense and exciting, and a good French team made Wales work all the way to success.

France P. Villepreux; R. Bourgarel (Toulouse), J.-P. Lux (Tyrosse), R. Bertranne (Bagneres), J. Cantoni (Beziers); J.-L. Berot (Toulouse), M. Barrau (Beaumont); J. Iracabal (Bayonne), R. Benesis (Narbonne), M. Lasserre (Agen), C. Spanghero, W. Spanghero (Narbonne), J.-P. Biemouret (Agen), B. Dauga (Mont de Marsan), +C. Carrere (Toulon).
T: Benoît Dauga.
C: Pierre Villepreux.

Wales J.P.R. Williams; T.G.R. Davies, +S.J. Dawes (London Welsh), A.J.L. Lewis (Ebbw Vale), J.C. Bevan; B. John, G.O. Edwards (Cardiff); D. Williams (Ebbw Vale), J. Young (Harrogate), D.B. Llewelyn, W.D. Thomas (Llanelli), M.G. Roberts (London Welsh), W.D. Morris (Neath), T.M. Davies, J. Taylor (London Welsh).
T: Gareth Edwards, Barry John.
P: John.
Referee: Jake Young (Scotland).

Wales 20 France 6

Arms Park, Cardiff. 25 March 1972

Wales won by 2 tries, 4 pens to 2 pens.

A good win and a sad farewell to the 'The King', Barry John, who departed from international rugby at the age of 27 years and two months. He brought great delight not only to rugby football followers but to sportsmen and women all over the world. He signed off in his quiet, undemonstrative way and went into Welsh history alongside the likes of Percy Bush, Cliff Jones and Cliff Morgan. John stroked over three majestic kicks before Pierre Villepreux kicked an enormous goal with a huge crack, like a bullet out of a cannon. Surely he could not repeat it from 60 yards? Yet the splendid French full-back did just that; John kicked a further effortless goal from long range in the second half. That kick took him to Welsh records of 90 points in a career and 35 points for a season, the latter despite not playing against Ireland. Smart tries by wings Gerald Davies and John Bevan made it a good victory and Davies prevented his opposite number Jean Sillières from scoring, with an amazing tackle that rolled the Frenchman out of play. Derek Quinnell, who was already a British Lion, won his first cap as replacement for the injured Mervyn Davies in the last seconds of injury time. Wales were unbeaten champions, even though the Grand Slam and Triple Crown were not up for grabs as neither Wales, nor Scotland, had travelled to Dublin.

Wales J.P.R. Williams; T.G.R. Davies (London Welsh), R.T.E. Bergiers (Llanelli/Cardiff Coll of Ed), A.J.L. Lewis (Ebbw Vale), J.C. Bevan (Cardiff/Cardiff Coll of Ed); B. John, G.O. Edwards (Cardiff); +D.J. Lloyd (Bridgend), J. Young (RAF), D.B. Llewelyn, W.D. Thomas (Llanelli), T.G. Evans (London Welsh), W.D. Morris (Neath), T.M. Davies, J. Taylor (London Welsh). Rep: *D.L. Quinnell (Llanelli) for T.M. Davies.
T: Gerald Davies, John Bevan.
P: Barry John 4.

France +P. Villepreux (Toulouse); B. Duprat (Bayonne), J. Maso (Narbonne), J.-P. Lux (Dax), J. Sillières (Tarbes); J.-L. Berot (Toulouse), M. Barrau (Beaumont); J. Iracabal (Bayonne), R. Benesis (Agen), J.-L. Azarete (St Jean de Luz), A. Esteve (Beziers), C. Spanghero (Narbonne), J.-C. Skrela (Toulouse), B. Dauga (Mont de Marsan), J.-P. Biemouret (Agen).
P: Pierre Villepreux 2.
Referee: Mike H. Titcomb (England).

France 12 Wales 3

Parc des Princes, Paris. 24 March 1973

France won by 3 pens, 1 drop goal to 1 drop goal.

It was goodbye to Stade Colombes and a return to a revamped Parc des Princes, as France made ten changes from the side that sank at Twickenham. The changes worked largely because of the kicking skills of Jean-Pierre Romeu who won the match with a drop-shot and three penalty goals, while Phil Bennett had an off-day and landed just one drop goal. It was to be two home wins for all the five countries and it meant that the championship was shared between all five of them. Arthur Lewis retired from the field during the interval with a shoulder injury which meant moving Jim Shanklin to centre and introducing another John Williams on the left-wing. He was soon to be christened 'J.J.' to distinguish him from his namesake at full-back. This was the 300th match played by Wales.

France J.-M. Aguirre (Bagneres); J.-F. Philipponneau (Montferrand), C.F. Badin (Cholon), J. Maso (Narbonne), J. Cantoni (Beziers); J.-P. Romeu, M. Pebeyre (Montferrand); J. Iracabal (Bayonne), R. Benesis (Agen), J.-L. Azarete (St Jean de Luz), E. Cester (Valence), +W. Spanghero (Narbonne), J.-C. Skrela (Toulouse),

French scrum-half Jacques ('Napoleon') Fouroux tries to find a way through the Welsh defence at Cardiff in 1974. Defenders are Mervyn Davies and Walter Williams. (© Huw Evans)

O. Saisset (Beziers), J.-P. Biemouret (Agen).
P: Jean-Pierre Romeu 3.
DG: Romeu.

Wales J.P.R. Williams; T.G.R. Davies (London Welsh), R.T.E. Bergiers (Llanelli), A.J.L. Lewis (Ebbw Vale), J.L. Shanklin (London Welsh); P. Bennett (Llanelli), +G.O. Edwards (Cardiff); P.D. Llewellyn (Swansea), J. Young (London Welsh/RAF), G. Shaw (Neath), W.D. Thomas (Llanelli), M.G. Roberts (London Welsh), *T.P. David (Llanelli), T.M. Davies (Swansea), J. Taylor (London Welsh). Rep: *J.J. Williams (Llanelli) for Lewis.
DG: Phil Bennett.
Referee: D.P. 'Paddy' D'Arcy (Ireland).

Wales 16 France 16

Arms Park, Cardiff. 16 February 1974

Draw. 1 try, 3 pens, 1 drop goal each.

Many spectators thought that Phil Bennett would have been better not playing and listening to the doctor's advice. He was suffering from flu, but decided to appear nevertheless. It was not his best performance, though his 70th minute penalty would have won the match if it had not been for a late drop goal by Jean-Pierre Romeu. It was the first time Wales had played two successive drawn matches as they had drawn 9–9 in Dublin two weeks earlier. The sides were also locked at the interval, 13–13. The Welsh try was from a kick and chase – a speciality of J.J. Williams. France gained their try with a clever move by their midfield trio, which saw centre Jean-Pierre Lux dive over. One rather disinterested spectator was a Cardiff Youth player who was acting as a ball-boy near the spot where Lux scored. It was Terry Holmes, soon to be playing there himself!

Wales J.P.R. Williams; T.G.R. Davies (London Welsh), I. Hall (Aberavon), A.A.J. Finlayson (Cardiff), J.J. Williams; P. Bennett (Llanelli), +G.O. Edwards (Cardiff); G. Shaw (Neath), R.W. Windsor (Pontypool), W.P.J. Williams (Neath), *I.R. Robinson (Cardiff), D.L. Quinnell (Llanelli), W.D. Morris (Neath), T.M. Davies (Swansea), J. Taylor (London Welsh).
T: J.J. Williams.
P: Phil Bennett 3.
DG: Gareth Edwards.

France J.-M. Aguirre; R. Bertranne (Bagneres), J. Pecune (Tarbes), J.-P. Lux (Dax), A. Dubertrand; J.-P. Romeu (Montferrand), J. Fouroux (La Voulte); J. Iracabal (Bayonne), R. Benesis (Agen), A. Vaquerin, A. Esteve (Beziers), +E. Cester (Valence), J.-C. Skrela (Toulouse), C. Spanghero (Narbonne), V. Boffelli (Aurillac).
T: Jean-Pierre Lux.
P: Jean-Pierre Romeu 3.
DG: Romeu.
Referee: Norman R. Sanson (Scotland).

France 10 Wales 25

Parc des Princes, Paris. 18 January 1975

Wales won by 5 tries, 1 con, 1 pen to 1 try, 2 pens.

Six new caps took the field for Wales, including Pontypool props 'Charlie' Faulkner and Graham Price who joined Bobby Windsor in the infamous front row. Out went Phil Bennett, cruelly dropped, and in came John Bevan. Price was remarkably young for a prop at 23 years of age, but Faulkner, a judo black-belt, kept his age a mystery though he was reputed to be 'around 34'. Centre Steve Fenwick opened his international career with a try after Gareth Edwards had missed with a drop-kick and tries by Terry Cobner and Gerald Davies took Wales to 17–7 at the break. Edwards produced one of his specials in the second half after which came the try that sealed one of the best wins by Wales for many years. France were attacking when the ball fell loose and was hacked upfield. With the speedy J.J.Williams the favourite to score, the ball fell clear to Graham Price who had run some 75 yards backing up. He fell, as much from exhaustion as from scoring, and registered an astonishing fifth try for Wales. It was a great win and a fine start for the new captain, Mervyn Davies. Wales were not to win again in Paris until 1999.

France M. Taffary; J.-F. Gourdon (Racing Club), C. Dourthe (Dax), R. Bertranne (Bagneres), J.-P. Lux (Dax); J-P. Romeu (Montferrand), +J. Fouroux (La Voulte); J.-L. Azarete (St Jean de Luz), A. Paco, A. Vaquerin, A. Esteve, G. Senal, O. Saisset (Beziers), J.-P. Bastiat (Dax), V. Boffelli (Aurillac). Rep: J. Cantoni (Beziers) for Gourdon; J.-C. Skrela (Toulouse) for Saisset.
T: Jean-François Gourdon.
P: Michel Taffary 2.

Wales J.P.R. Williams (London Welsh); T.G.R. Davies (Cardiff), *S.P. Fenwick (Bridgend), *R.W.R. Gravell, J.J. Williams (Llanelli); *J.D. Bevan (Aberavon), G.O. Edwards (Cardiff); *A.G. Faulkner, R.W. Windsor, *G. Price (Pontypool), G.A.D. Wheel (Swansea), A.J. Martin (Aberavon), *T.P. Evans, +T.M. Davies (Swansea), T.J. Cobner (Pontypool).
T: Steve Fenwick, Terry Cobner, Gerald Davies, Gareth Edwards, Graham Price.
C: Fenwick.
P: Fenwick.
Referee: Ken A. Pattinson (England).

Wales 19 France 13

Arms Park, Cardiff. 6 March 1976

Wales won by 1 try, 5 pens to 2 tries, 1 con, 1 pen.

Wales had to survive a grandstand finish by France who threw everything at the home side, but they held on at the Taff End of the ground and finally extended the lead with a late Steve Fenwick penalty. France started quickest – Jean-François Gourdon scored a try after five minutes. Wales fought back and led 13–6 with three penalties and a J.J.Williams try. It was 13–9 at the interval, but prop Graham Price suffered an eye injury and Cardiff police detective Mike Knill gained his first and only cap. A Fenwick penalty stretched the lead only for slippery Jean-Luc Averous to defeat J.P.R's tackle and score. One more French try would do it and it seemed certain that right-wing Gourdon was in on the North-Stand side, only for the mighty Welsh fullback to hit him into touch with a shoulder-charge that saw J.P.R. raise his fist in triumph. And so Wales made the Grand Slam for the 7th time and they took the championship with it. Phil Bennett, despite an injured leg, ended with 38 points in the season for a new Welsh best; Gareth Edwards won his 45th cap to surpass Ken Jones, and the aggregate of 102 points by Wales was the highest-ever in the Five-Nations tournament. It was to be the last game played by Mervyn Davies for Wales. He appeared in 38 matches and also made two tours with the Lions. In this match he hurt a leg early on, but worse was to follow: he was carried from the club ground next door during the Welsh Cup semi-final tie between Swansea and Pontypool just 22 days later after suffering a brain haemorrhage.

Wales J.P.R. Williams (London Welsh); T.G.R. Davies (Cardiff), R.W.R. Gravell (Llanelli), S.P. Fenwick (Bridgend), J.J. Williams; P. Bennett (Llanelli), G.O. Edwards (Cardiff); A.G. Faulkner, R.W. Windsor, G. Price (Pontypool), G.A.D. Wheel (Swansea), A.J. Martin (Aberavon), T.P. Evans, +T.M. Davies (Swansea), T.P. David (Pontypridd). Rep: *F.M.D. Knill (Cardiff) for Price.
T: J.J.Williams.
P: Phil Bennett 2, Steve Fenwick 2, Allan Martin.

France M. Droitecourt (Montferrand); J.-F. Gourdon (Racing Club), R. Bertranne (Bagneres), J. Pecune (Tarbes), J.-L. Averous (La Voulte); J.-P. Romeu (Montferrand), +J. Fouroux (La Voulte); R. Paparemborde (Pau), A. Paco (Beziers), G. Cholley (Castres), J.-F. Imbernon (Perpignan), M. Palmie (Beziers), J.-C. Skrela (Toulouse), J.-P. Bastiat (Dax), J.-P. Rives (Toulouse). Rep: J-M. Aguirre (Bagneres) for Droitecourt.
T: Jean-François Gourdon, Jean-Luc Averous.
C: Jean-Pierre Romeu.
P: Romeu.
Referee: John R. West (Ireland).

France 16 Wales 9

Parc des Princes, Paris. 5 February 1977

France won by 2 tries, 1 con, 2 pens to 3 pens.

It was the year of 'Napoleon', alias scrum-half and captain Jacques Fouroux, whose army included warriors such as Jean-Pierre Rives and Jean-Claude Skrela in front of him. Wales never really looked like winning, even if Windsor Davies and company were present to record the popular television drama 'Grand Slam'. Wales did lead 6–3 at half-time, by which time they had lost Gerald Davies, concussed by a heavy tackle from the burly Jean-Pierre Bastiat. Skrela's try put France ahead and right-wing Dominique Harize was worked clear for another good score. France were looking towards their second Grand Slam and they were to achieve it eventually without conceding a try in their four matches.

France J.-M. Aguirre (Bagneres); D. Harize (Toulouse), R. Bertranne (Bagneres), F. Sangali (Narbonne), J.-L. Averous (La Voulte); J.-P. Romeu (Montferrand), +J. Fouroux (Auch); R. Paparemborde (Pau), A. Paco (Beziers), G. Cholley (Castres), J.-F. Imbernon (Perpignan), M. Palmie (Beziers), J.-C. Skrela (Toulouse), J.-P. Bastiat (Dax), J-P. Rives (Toulouse).
T: Jean-Claude Skrela, Dominique Harize.
C: Jean-Pierre Romeu.
P: Romeu 2.

Wales J.P.R. Williams (Bridgend); T.G.R. Davies (Cardiff), S.F. Fenwick (Bridgend), D.H. Burcher (Newport), J.J. Williams; +P. Bennett (Llanelli), G.O. Edwards (Cardiff); G. Shaw (Neath), R.W. Windsor, G. Price (Pontypool), D.L. Quinnell (Llanelli), A.J. Martin (Aberavon), R.C. Burgess (Ebbw Vale), J. Squire (Newport), T.J.Cobner (Pontypool). Rep: *G.L. Evans (Newport) for Davies.

P: Steve Fenwick 3.
Referee: Allan M. Hosie (Scotland).

Wales 16 France 7

Arms Park, Cardiff. 18 March 1978

Wales won by 2 tries, 1 con, 2 drop goals to 1 try, 1 drop goal.

It was learned after the match that both skipper Phil Bennett and his partner Gareth Edwards had decided to retire from international rugby. They both played splendidly, as they did on the vast majority of occasions when they appeared. It was hard to think of better players in their position throughout the history of Welsh, and indeed world, rugby. Bennett led Wales to their 15th championship and 8th Grand Slam. Personally, he took his aggregate of points to 166 – a new best for Northern Hemisphere players, ahead of the 158 scored by Ireland's Tom Kiernan. Coach John Dawes said, 'This team deserves to be recognised as one of the greatest of all time.' France led 7–0 before Wales opened their account when Bennett side-stepped the cover for a corner try he also converted. In 36 minutes, Edwards dropped a good goal and two minutes before the break Wales struck again. Edwards gave out to J.J.Williams, who lobbed the ball inside as he was pushed out of play. The skipper was backing up and with a little leap he was over for his second try. The only score of the second half was a drop goal by Steve Fenwick in the dying moments.

Wales J.P.R.Williams (Bridgend); J.J. Williams, R.W.R. Gravell (Llanelli), S.P. Fenwick (Bridgend), G.L. Evans (Newport); +P. Bennett (Llanelli), G.O. Edwards (Cardiff); A.G. Faulkner, R.W. Windsor, G. Price (Pontypool), G.A.D. Wheel (Swansea), A.J. Martin (Aberavon), J. Squire (Newport), D.L. Quinnell (Llanelli), T.J. Cobner (Pontypool).
T: Phil Bennett 2.
C: Bennett.
DG: Gareth Edwards, Steve Fenwick.

France J.-M. Aguirre (Bagneres); D. Bustaffa (Carcassonne), R. Bertranne (Bagneres), C. Belascain (Bayonne), G. Noves (Toulouse); B. Vivies (Agen), J. Gallion (Toulon); R. Paparemborde (Pau), A. Paco (Beziers), G. Cholley (Castres), F. Haget (Biarritz), M. Palmie (Beziers), J.-C. Skrela (Toulouse), +J.-P. Bastiat (Dax), J.-P. Rives (Toulouse).
T: Jean-Claude Skrela,
DG: Bernard Vivies.
Referee: Alan Welsby (England).

Farewell Benny: Phil Bennett scores his last try for Wales in 1978 – his 2nd against France. Defenders Jean-Michel Aguirre, Jerome Gallion (tackling) and Bernard Vivies fail to halt him. (© Huw Evans)

Skipper Phil Bennett breaks the French cover for his first try in the 1978 win and left-wing Gareth Evans leads the celebrations. Bennett scored 166 points for Wales during his 29 appearances. (© Huw Evans)

Phil Bennett kicks for touch after receiving from Gareth Edwards (on the ground) while Derek Quinnell and Jeff Squire watch in admiration.
(© Huw Evans)

France 14 Wales 13

Parc des Princes, Paris. 17 February 1979

France won by 2 tries, 2 pens to 1 try, 3 pens.

Two Swansea players received their first caps; outside-half David Richards was called up as a centre and Barry Clegg replaced his injured clubmate, Geoff Wheel. France brought back Arnaud Vaquerin, who was to lose his life in an unusual fashion – playing Russian roulette! Tries in the first half came from Jean-François Gourdon, with a run inside J.J. Williams and then Terry Holmes, with a typical, crashing effort. At 10–10, Gourdon proved the match-winner with his second try after Jerome Gallion had made the running. It was a deserved French win and ended Wales's Grand Slam hopes.

France J.-M. Aguirre; J.-F. Gourdon, R. Bertranne (Bagneres), C. Belascain (Bayonne), G. Noves (Toulouse); A. Caussade (Lourdes), J. Gallion (Toulon); R. Paparemborde (Pau), A. Paco, A. Vacquerin (Beziers), F. Haget (Biarritz), A. Maleig (Oloron), J.-L. Joinel (Brive), A. Guilbert (Toulon), +J.-P. Rives (Toulouse).
T: Jean-Francois Gourdon 2.
P: Jean-Michel Aguirre 2.

Wales +J.P.R. Williams (Bridgend); H.E. Rees (Neath), *D.S. Richards (Swansea), S.P. Fenwick (Bridgend), J.J. Williams (Llanelli); W.G. Davies, T.D. Holmes (Cardiff); A.G. Faulkner, R.W. Windsor, G. Price (Pontypool), A.J. Martin (Aberavon), *B.G. Clegg (Swansea), J. Squire (Pontypool), D.L. Quinnell, P. Ringer (Llanelli).
T: Terry Holmes.
P: Steve Fenwick 3.
Referee: David I.H. Burnett (Ireland).

Wales 18 France 9

Arms Park, Cardiff. 19 January 1980

Wales won by 4 tries, 1 con to 1 try, 1 con, 1 drop goal.

Four tries, eighteen points and it could have been more. Wales were off to a magnificent start in the new season under their new coach and former skipper John Lloyd. New skipper Jeff Squire and his pack were in control and, after a first-half try by Elgan Rees, whose impetus carried him over as he was tackled, Wales never looked back. Terry Holmes forced his way through, and though Daniel Bustaffa replied with a good run that let in Jean-François

Marchal, it was Wales who had the last say. Gareth Davies was in the move twice that led to David Richards scoring and Graham Price added try number four from an Allan Martin pass.

Wales W.R. Blyth (Swansea); H.E. Rees (Neath), D.S. Richards (Swansea), S.P. Fenwick (Bridgend), *L. Keen (Aberavon); W.G. Davies, T.D. Holmes (Cardiff); C. Williams (Swansea), A.J. Phillips (Cardiff), G. Price (Pontypool), G.A.D. Wheel (Swansea), A.J. Martin (Aberavon), +J. Squire, *E.T. Butler (Pontypool), P. Ringer (Llanelli).
T: Elgan Rees, Terry Holmes, David Richards, Graham Price.
C: Gareth Davies.

France J.-M. Aguirre (Bagneres); D. Bustaffa (Carcassonne), R. Bertranne (Bagneres), D. Codorniou (Narbonne), F. Costes (Montferrand); A. Caussade (Lourdes), J. Gallion (Toulon); R. Paparemborde (Pau), A. Paco (Beziers), P. Salas (Narbonne), F. Haget (Biarritz), J.-F. Marchal (Lourdes), J.-L. Joinel (Brive), A. Maleig (Oloron), +J.-P. Rives (Toulouse).
T: Jean-François Marchal.
C: Alain Caussade.
DG: Caussade.
Referee: Allan M. Hosie (Scotland).

France 19 Wales 15

Parc des Princes, Paris. 7 March 1981

France won by 1 try, 5 pens to 1 try, 1 con, 3 pens.

France gained the championship and Grand Slam but Wales made them work hard for their success. Not only were the visitors level at 9–9 after 40 minutes' play, but a glorious try by David Richards, converted by Gwyn Evans, meant that Wales were in front by 15–9. It could not last, however, as Jean-Pierre Rives whipped up his team to a last big effort. Full-back Serge Gabernet scored a try which went unconverted and first Guy Laporte and then Gabernet placed goals to seal the match. While victory away was not easy to come by, Cardiff Arms Park remained very much a Welsh fortress. One long occupant, WRU secretary and former international wing Bill Clement, retired. His outstanding service to the cause for Wales brought him the deserved award of an OBE.

France S. Gabernet (Toulouse); S. Blanco (Biarritz), R. Bertranne (Bagneres), D. Codorniou (Narbonne), L. Pardo (Bayonne); G. Laporte (Graulhet), P. Berbezier (Lourdes); R. Paparemborde (Pau), P. Dintrans (Tarbes), P. Dospital (Bayonne), J.-F. Imbernon (Perpignan), D. Revallier (Graulhet), P. Lacans (Beziers), J.-L. Joinel (Brive), +J.-P. Rives (Toulouse). Rep: P. Mesny (Grenoble) for Bertranne.
T: Serge Gabernet.
P: Guy Laporte 3, Gabernet 2.

Wales G. Evans (Maesteg); C.F.W. Rees (London Welsh), R.W.R. Gravell (Llanelli), D.S. Richards (Swansea), D.L. Nicholas (Llanelli); P.G. Pearce, Gerald Williams; I. Stephens (Bridgend), A.J. Phillips (Cardiff), G. Price (Pontypool), G.A.D. Wheel (Swansea), A.J. Martin (Aberavon), R.C. Burgess (Ebbw Vale), +J. Squire (Pontypool), J.R. Lewis (SG Inst/Cardiff).
T: David Richards.
C: Gwyn Evans.
P: Evans 3.
Referee: Alan Welsby (England).

Wales 22 France 12

Arms Park, Cardiff. 6 February 1982

Wales won by 1 try, 6 pens to 1 try, 1 con, 2 pens.

If Wales had seen David Burnett as the villain after he had sent Paul Ringer off at Twickenham, then now he was very much 'better', as he penalised France continually. Full-back Gwyn Evans landed six penalty goals to equal the world record achieved by both Don Clarke 23 years before and by outside-half Gerald Bosch of South Africa in 1975. It all helped Evans become the fastest scorer of 50 points for Wales. He had taken just six matches. Marc Sallefranque kicked the opener from his own half and Wales only got in front during the second half. At 12–12, Jeff Squire sent to Ray Gravell who reversed with Rob Ackerman, who in turn gave Terry Holmes a slight opening – and he took it with frightening strength, taking several tacklers with him. A young Serge Blanco, born in Venezuela, scored his first points against Wales. Years later they were fed up with the sight of him!

Wales G. Evans (Maesteg); R.A. Ackerman (Newport), D.S. Richards (Swansea), R.W.R. Gravell (Llanelli), C.F.W. Rees (London Welsh); +W.G. Davies, T.D. Holmes (Cardiff); I. Stephens (Bridgend), A.J. Phillips (Cardiff), G. Price (Pontypool), R.D. Moriarty (Swansea), *S. Sutton (Pontypool), R.C. Burgess (Ebbw Vale), J. Squire (Pontypool), J.R. Lewis (Cardiff).
T: Terry Holmes.
P: Gwyn Evans 6.

France M. Sallefranque (Dax); S. Blanco (Biarritz), P. Perrier, C. Belascain, L. Pardo (Bayonne); J.-P. Lescarboura (Dax), G. Martinez (Toulouse); M.

Cardiff scrum-half Terry Holmes on the burst against France in 1982. Hooker Pierre Dintrans is too late to hold him. A double British Lion, Holmes was to be re-instated as an amateur in November 1991 at the age of 34. (© Huw Evans)

Cremaschi (Lourdes), P. Dintrans (Tarbes), R. Parparemborde (Pau), A. Lorieux (Grenoble), D. Revallier (Graulhet), P. Lacans (Beziers), L. Rodriguez (Mont de Marsan), +J.-P. Rives (Toulouse).
T: Serge Blanco.
C: Marc Sallefranque.
P: Sallefranque, Guy Martinez.
Referee: David I.H. Burnett (Ireland).

France 16 Wales 9

Parc des Princes, Paris. 19 March 1983

France won by 1 try, 3 pens, 1 drop goal to 1 try, 1 con, 1 pen.

Ireland defeated England by 25–15 to join France at the top of the championship, but Wales could have won outright if they had beaten France. The New Zealand referee found the niggling hard to stop, though an inspired Terry Holmes helped Wales lead 9–6 after an hour. Mark Wyatt broke a collar bone, however, and Gwyn Evans dropped back to allow police officer Richie Donovan his only appearance. When wing Patrick Esteve scored, he joined Carston Catcheside (England) and 'Johnny' Wallace (Scotland), as the only players to score in all four matches in a championship season.

France S. Blanco (Biarritz); P. Sella (Agen), C. Belascain (Bayonne), D. Codorniou, P. Esteve (Narbonne); D. Camberabero (La Voulte), G. Martinez (Toulouse); P. Dospital (Bayonne), P. Dintrans (Tarbes), R. Parparemborde (Pau), J.-F. Imbernon (Perpignan), J. Condom (Boucou), D. Erbani (Agen), J.-L. Joinel (Brive), +J.-P. Rives (Racing Club).
T: Patrick Esteve.
P: Serge Blanco 3.
DG: Didier Camberabero.

Wales M.A. Wyatt (Swansea); H.E. Rees (Neath), G. Evans (Maesteg), R.A. Ackerman, C.F.W. Rees (London Welsh); M. Dacey (Swansea), T.D. Holmes (Cardiff); S.T. Jones (Pontypool), W.J. James (Aberavon), G. Price (Pontypool), R.L. Norster (Cardiff), S.J. Perkins, J. Squire, +E.T. Butler (Pontypool), D.F. Pickering (Llanelli). Rep: *R.E. Donovan (South Wales Police) for Wyatt.
T: Jeff Squire.
C: Mark Wyatt.
P: Gwyn Evans.
Referee: Tom F. Doocey (New Zealand).

Terry Holmes has just scored the only Welsh try in a 1982 win over France and number 8 forward Jeff Squire is delighted. Holmes scored 9 tries for Wales and 123 for Cardiff before turning to Rugby League.
(© Huw Evans)

Wales 16 France 21

Arms Park, Cardiff. 18 February 1984

France won by 1 try, 1 con, 4 pens, 1 drop goal to 2 tries, 1 con, 2 pens.

Missed kicks cost Wales the match and France were able to win at Cardiff for the first time since 1968. A Howell Davies try and conversion closed the gap to two points before Jean-Patrick Lescarboura landed his sixth successful shot at goal. It had been 21 years since Wales lost both home championship games, having also been defeated by Scotland in Cardiff.

Wales H. Davies; M.H. Titley (Bridgend), R.A. Ackerman (London Welsh), B. Bowen (South Wales Police), A.M. Hadley (Cardiff); M. Dacey (Swansea), M.H.J. Douglas (Llanelli); I. Stephens (Bridgend), +M.J. Watkins (Newport), I.H. Eidman, R.L. Norster (Cardiff), S.J. Perkins (Pontypool), R.D. Moriarty (Swansea), E.T. Butler (Pontypool), D.F. Pickering (Llanelli).
T: Eddie Butler, Howell Davies.
C: Davies.
P: Davies 2.

France S. Blanco (Biarritz); P. Lagisquet (Bayonne), P. Sella (Agen), D. Codorniou, P. Esteve (Narbonne); J.-P. Lescarboura (Dax), J. Gallion (Toulon); M. Cremaschi (Lourdes), P. Dintrans (Tarbes), D. Dubroca (Agen), A. Lorieux (Grenoble), J. Condom (Boucau), D. Erbani (Agen), J.-L. Joinel (Brive), +J.-P. Rives (Racing Club).
T: Philippe Sella.
C: Jean-Patrick Lescarboura.
P: Lescarboura 4.
DG: Lescarboura.
Referee: R.G. 'Dick' Byres (Australia).

France 14 Wales 3

Parc des Princes, Paris. 30 March 1985

France won by 2 tries, 2 pens to 1 pen.

While Ireland were beating England to take the championship, Wales were finding Serge Blanco their biggest stumbling block in Paris. The French full-back had a hand in both of his side's tries, while the Welsh points came from the boot of débutant Paul Thorburn. Another newcomer was the huge prop Stuart Evans who was to switch to rugby league with St Helen's and much later carried out a long-running argument to return to union.

France S. Blanco (Biarritz); E. Bonneval (Toulouse), P. Sella (Agen), D. Codorniou, P. Esteve (Narbonne); J.-P. Lescarboura (Dax), J. Gallion (Toulon); P. Dospital (Bayonne), +P. Dintrans (Tarbes), J.-P. Garuet (Lourdes), J.-C. Orso (Nice), J. Condom (Boucau), J. Gratton (Agen), J.-L. Joinel (Brive), L. Rodriguez (Mont de Marsan). Rep: D. Erbani (Agen) for Rodriguez.
T: Patrick Esteve, Jerome Gallion.
P: Jean-Patrick Lescarboura 2.

Wales *P.H. Thorburn (Neath); P.I. Lewis (Llanelli), R.A. Ackerman (London Welsh), M.G. Ring, A.M. Hadley; W.G. Davies, +T.D. Holmes; J. Whitefoot (Cardiff), W.J. James (Aberavon), *S. Evans (Swansea), R.L. Norster (Cardiff), S.J. Perkins (Pontypool), M.S. Morris (South Wales Police), R.D. Moriarty (Swansea), D.F. Pickering (Llanelli). Rep: *G.J. Roberts (Cardiff) for Moriarty.
P: Paul Thorburn.
Referee: Steve Strydom (South Africa).

Wales 15 France 23

Arms Park, Cardiff. 1 March 1986

France won by 4 tries, 2 cons, 1 drop goal to 5 pens.

A poor Welsh defence leaked four tries on an unhappy St David's Day afternoon. Only the kicking of Paul Thorburn kept Wales in contention. He scored 15 points and reached 80 in seven games. While the French backs scored the points, their forwards were just as impressive.

Wales P.H. Thorburn (Neath); M.H. Titley (Swansea), J.A. Devereux (Bridgend/SG Inst), B. Bowen (South Wales Police), A.M. Hadley (Cardiff); J. Davies (Neath), R.N. Jones (Swansea); J. Whitefoot (Cardiff), W.J. James (Aberavon), I.H. Eidman (Cardiff), D.R. Waters (Newport), S.J. Perkins (Pontypool), W.P. Moriarty (Swansea), P.T. Davies, +D.F. Pickering (Llanelli).
P: Paul Thorburn 5.

France S. Blanco (Biarritz); J.-B. Lafond (Racing Club), P. Sella (Agen), D. Charvet, E. Bonneval (Toulouse); G. Laporte (Graulhet), P. Berbezier (Agen); P. Marocco (Montferrand), +D. Dubroca (Agen), J.-P. Garuet (Lourdes), F. Haget (Biarritz), J. Condom (Boucau), D. Erbani (Agen), J.-L. Joinel (Brive), E. Champ (Toulon).
T: Jean-Baptiste Lafond 2, Serge Blanco, Philippe Sella.
C: Guy Laporte 2.
DG: Laporte.
Referee: J. Brian Anderson (Scotland).

France 16 Wales 9

Parc des Princes, Paris. 7 February 1987

France won by 2 tries, 1 con, 2 pens to 3 pens.

Though Wales defended well, they never seriously troubled France and had the misfortune of losing their main source of points – Paul Thorburn. The Neath full-back broke his collar bone and missed the remainder of the international season. Bob Norster was his side's best performer and both new caps, Ieuan Evans and Kevin Phillips, were later to skipper their country. Wales had selected centre Roger Bidgood (Newport) to play against Ireland on 17 January, but the weather forced a postponement, and John Devereux was called up to play against France.

France S. Blanco (Biarritz); P. Berot, P. Sella (Agen), D. Charvet, E. Bonneval (Toulouse); F. Mesnel (Racing Club), P. Berbezier (Agen); P. Ondarts (Biarritz), +D. Dubroca (Agen), J.-P. Garuet (Lourdes), A. Lorieux (Aix-les-Bains), J. Condom (Biarritz), D. Erbani (Agen), L. Rodriguez (Montferrand), E. Champ (Toulon).
T: Eric Bonneval, Frank Mesnel.
C: Philippe Berot.
P: Berot 2.

Wales P.H. Thorburn (Neath); G.M.C. Webbe (Bridgend), K. Hopkins (Swansea), J.A. Devereux (Bridgend/SG Inst), *I.C.Evans (Llanelli); J. Davies (Neath), R.N. Jones (Swansea); J. Whitefoot (Cardiff), *K.H. Phillips, S. Evans (Neath), S. Sutton (South Wales Police), R.L. Norster (Cardiff), W.P. Moriarty (Swansea), P.T. Davies, +D.F. Pickering (Llanelli). Rep: M. Dacey (Swansea) for Thorburn.
P: Paul Thorburn 3.
Referee: Colin J. High (England).

Wales 9 France 10

Arms Park, Cardiff. 19 March 1988

France won by 1 try, 2 pens to 1 try, 1 con, 1 pen.

France had lost to Scotland and needed to win in Cardiff to share the championship with Wales. A famous journalist, O.L. Owen, had once said 'Cardiff stood for mud and misery.' On this day the mud and rain were of no help to Wales. France deserved to lead 10–3, as Wales made more mistakes. The try, from a kick-and-chase by Ieuan Evans, was too late. Evans pulled a hamstring in the effort and was replaced by Glen Webbe. The worst news was that a tour of New Zealand was soon to follow!

Wales P.H. Thorburn (Neath); I.C. Evans (Llanelli), M.G. Ring (Pontypool), +B. Bowen (South Wales Police), A.M. Hadley (Cardiff); J. Davies (Llanelli), R.N. Jones (Swansea); S.T. Jones (Pontypool), I.J. Watkins (Ebbw Vale), D. Young (Swansea), P.S. May (Llanelli), R.L. Norster (Cardiff), R.D. Phillips (Neath), W.P. Moriarty (Swansea), R.G. Collins (South Wales Police). Rep: G.M.C. Webbe (Bridgend) for Evans.
T: Ieuan Evans.
C: Paul Thorburn.
P: Thorburn.

France S. Blanco (Biarritz); J.-B. Lafond (Racing Club), P. Sella (Agen), M. Andrieu (Nîmes), P. Lagisquet (Bayonne); J.-P. Lescarboura (Dax), P. Berbezier (Agen); L. Armary (Lourdes), +D.

Dubroca (Agen), P. Ondarts (Biarritz), A. Lorieux (Aix-les-Bains), J. Condom (Biarritz), M. Cecillon (Bourgoin), L. Rodriguez (Dax), A. Carminati (Beziers).
T: Jean-Patrick Lescarboura.
P: Jean-Baptiste Lafond 2.
Referee: Fred A. Howard (England).

France 31 Wales 12

Parc des Princes, Paris. 18 February 1989

France won by 4 tries, 3 cons, 2 pens, 1 drop goal to 4 pens.

Wales never gave in – Robert Norster and Mike Griffiths played superbly – but Serge Blanco was a class act and France were much the better side. A try never looked likely to come, while France scored four and only Paul Thorburn kept Wales on the board.

France S. Blanco (Biarritz); J.-B. Lafond (Racing Club), P. Sella (Agen), M. Andrieu (Nîmes), P. Lagisquet (Bayonne); F. Mesnel (Racing Club), +P. Berbezier (Agen); L. Armary, P. Dintrans (Tarbes), P. Ondarts, J. Condom (Biarritz), A. Lorieux (Aix-le-Bains), D. Erbani (Agen), A. Carminati (Beziers), E. Champ (Toulon).
T: Serge Blanco 2, Pierre Berbezier, Philippe Dintrans.
C: Jean-Baptiste Lafond 3.
P: Lafond 2.
DG: Franck Mesnel.

Wales +P.H. Thorburn (Neath); I.C. Evans (Llanelli), M.R. Hall (Bridgend), *D.W. Evans (Cardiff/Oxford U), C. Davies (Llanelli); P. Turner (Newbridge), R.N. Jones (Swansea); M. Griffiths (Bridgend), I.J. Watkins (Ebbw Vale), L. Delaney, P.T. Davies (Llanelli), R.L. Norster (Cardiff), G. Jones (Llanelli), M.A. Jones (Neath), D.J. Bryant (Bridgend).
P: Paul Thorburn 4.
Referee: Jim M. Fleming (Scotland).

Wales 19 France 29

Arms Park, Cardiff. 20 January 1990

France won by 5 tries, 3 cons, 1 pen to 1 try, 4 pens, 1 drop goal.

Despite having lock-forward Kevin Moseley sent off after 35 minutes of the first half for stamping on wing Marc Andrieu, Wales competed remarkably well and only two late tries extended the winning margin. The action by Moseley was senseless; the punishment of a 33-week ban was just as nonsensical. Phil Davies moved into Moseley's place to partner newcomer Andy Allen.

Wales P.H. Thorburn (Neath); M.H. Titley (Swansea), M.G. Ring, M.R. Hall (Cardiff), A. Emyr (Swansea); D.W. Evans (Cardiff), +R.N. Jones (Swansea); M. Griffiths (Cardiff), K.H. Phillips (Neath), D. Young (Cardiff), *A.G. Allen (Newbridge), K. Moseley (Pontypool), P.T. Davies (Llanelli), M.A. Jones (Neath), G. Jones (Llanelli).   Rep: H. Williams-Jones (South Wales Police) for Griffiths.
Sent off: Kevin Moseley.
T: Mark Titley.
P: Paul Thorburn 4.
DG: David Evans.

France J.-B. Lafond (Racing Club); M. Andrieu (Nîmes), P. Sella (Agen), D. Charvet (Toulouse), P. Lagisquet (Bayonne); D. Camberabero (Beziers), +P. Berbezier (Agen); P. Ondarts (Biarritz), L. Armary, J.-P. Garuet (Lourdes), T. Devergie (Nîmes), D. Erbani (Agen), L. Rodriguez, O. Roumat (Dax), E. Champ (Toulon).
T: Jean-Baptiste Lafond, Philippe Sella, Didier Camberabero, Patrice Lagisquet, Laurent Rodriguez.
C: Camberabero 3.
P: Camberabero.
Referee: Fred A. Howard (England).

France 36 Wales 3

Parc des Princes, Paris. 2 March 1991

France won by 6 tries, 3 cons, 2 pens to 1 pen.

Ireland and Wales shared the Wooden Spoon after Wales were outclassed in Paris. It was 0–0 for less than two minutes, as France swept down the field to a mighty roar and Serge Blanco kicked ahead, regathered and swept majestically in for the try. For the first time, Wales conceded more than 100 points in the championship season and their misery, which had begun with Blanco, also ended with him. His magnificent touchline conversion brought an end to his championship career and registered France's eighth consecutive win against Wales. The Neath formula was not working and only big-hearted Phil Davies came out of the match with credit. This was the 400th match played by Wales.

France +S. Blanco (Biarritz); J.-B. Lafond (Racing Club), P. Sella (Agen), F. Mesnel (Racing Club), P. Saint-André (Montferrand); D. Camberabero (Beziers), P. Berbezier; G. Lascube (Agen), P. Marocco (Montferrand), P. Ondarts (Biarritz), J.-F. Gourragne (Beziers), O. Roumat (Dax), X.

Diana, Princess of Wales, and skipper Ieuan Evans share a joke in 1992, but lock Tony Copsey has his mind on the French opposition. (© Huw Evans)

Blond, C. Deslandes, L. Cabannes (Racing Club). Rep: T. Lacroix (Dax) for Sella.
T: Serge Blanco, Philippe Saint-André, Franck Mesnel, Olivier Roumat, Philippe Sella, Jean-Baptiste Lafond.
C: Didier Camberabero 2, Blanco.
P: Camberabero 2.

Wales +P.H. Thorburn (Neath); I.C. Evans (Llanelli), M.G. Ring (Cardiff), I.S. Gibbs (Neath), A. Emyr (Swansea); N.R. Jenkins (Pontypridd), C.J. Bridges (Neath); M. Griffiths (Cardiff), K.H. Phillips, J.D. Davies, Glyn D. Llewellyn (Neath), P. Arnold (Swansea), E.W. Lewis, P.T. Davies (Llanelli), M.S. Morris (Neath).
P: Paul Thorburn.
Referee: Kerry V.J. Fitzgerald (Australia).

Wales 9 France 12

Arms Park, Cardiff. 1 February 1992

France won by 1 try, 1 con, 1 pen, 1 drop goal to 3 pens.

France improved rapidly when Olivier Roumat came on for the supposedly injured Christophe Mougeot. Certainly, Roumat took charge of the lineout and France just managed to win a scrappy match. It was not a good start for the attending Diana, Princess of Wales, and her sons, Prince Harry and Prince William. However, they were to prove very popular with Ieuan Evans and his team.

Wales A. Clement (Swansea); +I.C. Evans (Llanelli), N.R. Jenkins (Pontypridd), I.S. Gibbs (Swansea), M.R. Hall (Cardiff); C.J. Stephens (Llanelli), R.N. Jones (Swansea); M. Griffiths (Cardiff), G.R. Jenkins (Swansea), L. Delaney (Llanelli), G.O. Llewellyn (Neath), A.H. Copsey, E.W. Lewis (Llanelli), S. Davies,

R.E. Webster (Swansea).
P: Neil Jenkins 3.

France J.-B. Lafond (Racing Club); P. Saint-André (Montferrand), +P. Sella (Agen), F. Mesnel (Racing Club), S. Viars; A. Penaud (Brive), F. Galthie (Colomiers); G. Lascube (Agen), V. Moscato, P. Gimbert (Begles), J.-M. Cadieu (Toulouse), C. Mougeot (Begles), J.-F. Tordo (Nice), M. Cecillon (Bourgoin), L. Cabannes (Racing Club). Rep: O. Roumat (Dax) for Mougeot.
T: Philippe Saint-André.
C: Jean-Baptiste Lafond.
P: Sebastian Viars.
DG: Alain Penaud.
Referee: Owen E. Doyle (Ireland).

France 26 Wales 10

Parc des Princes, Paris. 20 March 1993

France won by 3 tries, 1 con, 3 pens to 1 try, 1 con, 1 pen.

With Ireland defeating England in Dublin, the Five-Nations Trophy went to France and the Wooden Spoon to Wales, despite having beaten England in the season's opener. It was the 12th successive win for France over Wales for which they had to thank flanker Philippe Benetton in particular. He scored twice and assisted in the other French try. Newcomers Rupert Moon and Andrew Lamerton were two of the eight Llanelli players on view and began well. Moon had previously played under coach Alan Davies for England's A team. The try by left-wing Nigel Walker, scrambling over in the right corner, was the first by Wales in Paris since Jeff Squire scored in 1983.

France J.-B. Lafond (Begles); P. Saint-André (Montferrand), P. Sella (Agen), T. Lacroix (Dax), P. Hontas (Biarritz); F. Mesnel (Racing Club), A. Hueber (Toulon); L. Armary (Lourdes), +J.-F. Tordo (Nice), L. Seigne (Merignac), A. Benazzi (Agen), O. Roumat (Dax), P. Benetton (Agen), M. Cecillon (Bourgoin), L. Cabannes (Racing Club).
T: Philippe Benetton 2, Jean-Baptiste Lafond.
C: Lafond.
P: Thierry Lacroix 3.

Wales A. Clement (Swansea); +I.C. Evans (Llanelli), I.S. Gibbs (Swansea), N.G. Davies (Llanelli), N.K. Walker (Cardiff); N.R. Jenkins (Pontypridd), *R.H.St J.B. Moon; R.L. Evans, *A.E. Lamerton (Llanelli), H. Williams-Jones (South Wales Police), G.O. Llewellyn (Neath), P.T. Davies, M.A. Perego, E.W. Lewis (Llanelli),

Scrum-halves with over fifty caps apiece: Robert Jones and Gareth Edwards take the field in Paris prior to the 1993 international. (© Huw Evans)

R.E. Webster (Swansea). Reps: J.D. Davies (Neath) for (R.L.)Evans; P. Arnold (Swansea) for Perego.
T: Nigel Walker.
C: Neil Jenkins.
P: Jenkins.
Referee: Owen E. Doyle (Ireland).

Wales 24 France 15

Arms Park, Cardiff. 19 February 1994

Wales won by 2 tries, 1 con, 4 pens to 2 tries, 1 con 1 pen.

Scott Quinnell was nine years of age when Wales had last defeated France. That was 1982 in Cardiff and it was the Llanelli lad who had a big hand in this magnificent Welsh win. His opening try was scored from a lineout, and had a great similarity to the one scored by his father against Scotland in 1978. France were down by 17–3, but two tries and a conversion closed the gap to two points. Then Quinnell worked the ball to Nigel Walker who showed a sprinter's pace in just defeating a diving Philippe Sella to score in the south-east corner of the pitch. With Ieuan Evans injured, Gareth Llewellyn proved, not for the first time, that he played better when he was the leader.

Wales M.A. Rayer; S.D. Hill, M.R. Hall (Cardiff), A. Clement (Swansea), N.K. Walker (Cardiff); N.R. Jenkins (Pontypridd), R.H.St J.B. Moon; R.L. Evans (Llanelli), G.R. Jenkins (Swansea), J.D.

A great Welsh try – the try which helped Wales gain a surprise win by 24–15 at Cardiff – is coming up as Scott Quinnell roars past France in 1994. Mark Perego is in support but Quinnell does not need it.
(© Huw Evans)

Davies (Neath), P.T. Davies (Llanelli), +G.O. Llewellyn (Neath), E.W. Lewis, L.S. Quinnell, M.A. Perego (Llanelli).
T: Scott Quinnell, Nigel Walker.
C: Neil Jenkins.
P: Neil Jenkins 4.

France J.-L. Sadourny (Colomiers); E. Ntamack (Toulouse), P. Sella (Agen), T. Lacroix (Dax), P. Saint-André (Montferrand); A. Penaud (Brive), F. Galthie (Colomiers); L. Armary (Lourdes), J.-M. Gonzalez (Bayonne), P. Gallart (Beziers), O. Merle (Grenoble), +O. Roumat (Dax), P. Benetton (Agen), M. Cecillon (Bourgoin), A. Benazzi (Agen).
T: Olivier Roumat, Philippe Sella.
C: Thierry Lacroix.
P: Lacroix.
Referee: Lindsay L. McLachlan (New Zealand).

France 21 Wales 9

Parc des Princes, Paris. 21 January 1995

France won by 2 tries, 1 con, 3 pens to 3 pens.

No tries again for Wales in Paris, as was so often the case, though Wales put up a brave performance despite numerous players being out of action with injury. Prop Ricky Evans joined the list after Olivier Merle butted him to the ground. As he fell, the Llanelli fireman broke his ankle and for the next four years was to fight a legal battle against the French lock-forward. The Princess of Wales was among the spectators to see Neil Jenkins contribute all the Welsh points. His partner was Robert Jones, recalled for his 49th cap.

France J.-L. Sadourny (Colomiers); E. Ntamack (Toulouse), P. Sella (Agen), T. Lacroix (Dax), +P.

Saint-André (Montferrand); C. Deylaud (Toulouse), G. Accoceberry (Begles); L. Benezech (Racing Club), J.-M. Gonzalez (Bayonne), C. Califano (Toulouse), O. Merle (Montferrand), O. Roumat (Dax), A. Benazzi, P. Benetton (Agen), L. Cabannes (Racing Club).
T: Emile Ntamack, Philippe Saint-André.
C: Thierry Lacroix.
P: Lacroix 3.

Wales A. Clement (Swansea); S.D. Hill, M.R. Hall (Cardiff), M. Taylor (Pontypool), N.K. Walker (Cardiff); N.R. Jenkins (Pontypridd), R.N. Jones (Swansea); R.L. Evans (Llanelli), G.R. Jenkins (Swansea), J.D. Davies (Neath), D. Jones (Cardiff), +G.O. Llewellyn (Neath), S. Davies (Swansea), P.T. Davies (Llanelli), R.G. Collins (Pontypridd). Reps: *M.J. Back (Bridgend) for Hill; M. Griffiths (Cardiff) for Evans.
P: Neil Jenkins 3.
Referee: J. John M Pearson (England).

Wales 16 France 15

Arms Park, Cardiff. 16 March 1996

Wales won by 1 try, 1 con, 3 pens to 2 tries, 1 con, 1 pen.

For the second time in three seasons France floundered in Cardiff, just when they were favourites to win. Indeed, victory would have given France the title and Wales would have gained the Wooden Spoon. It did not happen, partly because Robert Howley scurried round the blind-side for an early try and also because Neil Jenkins was back in the side. The Pontypridd player, who was seen as villain one day and hero the next, was most certainly the latter when he placed a penalty seven minutes from time.

Wales W.J.L. Thomas; I.C. Evans (Llanelli), L.B. Davies (Neath), N.G. Davies (Llanelli), G. Thomas (Bridgend); N.R. Jenkins (Pontypridd), R. Howley (Bridgend); C.D. Loader (Swansea), +J.M. Humphreys (Cardiff), J.D. Davies, G.O. Llewellyn (Neath), D. Jones, E.W. Lewis, H.T. Taylor (Cardiff), R.G. Jones (Llanelli).
T: Robert Howley.
C: Neil Jenkins.
P: Jenkins 3.

France J.-L. Sadourny (Colomiers); E. Ntamack (Toulouse), S. Glas (Bourgoin), O. Campan (Agen), +P. Saint-André (Montferrand); T. Castaignede (Toulouse), G. Accoceberry (Begles); C. Califano (Toulouse), J.-M. Gonzalez (Bayonne), F. Tournaire (Narbonne), A. Benazzi (Agen), O. Roumat (Dax), R. Castel, S. Dispagne (Toulouse), L. Cabannes (Racing Club). Reps: F. Galthie (Colomiers) for Accoceberry; R. Ibanez (Dax) for Castel; O. Brouzet (Grenoble) for Dispagne.
T: Thomas Castaignede, Emile Ntamack.
C: Castaignede.
P: Castaignede.
Referee: Brian W. Stirling (Ireland).

France 27 Wales 22

Parc des Princes, Paris. 15 February 1997

France won by 4 tries, 2 cons, 1 pen to 3 tries, 2 cons, 1 pen.

Considering France in 1947 were 19–1 down in terms of matches won, they now recorded their 15th win in their last 17 clashes with Wales. Yet Wales played with a lot of spirit, and some skill, in scoring three tries against a team en route to a Grand Slam. Coach Kevin Bowring persisted with an ill-at-ease Neil Jenkins in the full-back role and he was at fault when Laurent Leflamand scored the final French try. Allan Bateman ran splendidly and Gareth Llewellyn leapt to great heights, but the Welsh fightback was just short.

France J.-L. Sadourny (Colomiers); L. Leflamand (Bourgoin), R. Dourthe (Dax), S. Glas (Bourgoin), D. Venditti; C. Lamaison, P. Carbonneau (Brive); C. Califano (Toulouse), M. Dal Maso (Agen), J.-L. Jordana (Toulouse), O. Merle (Montferrand), H. Miorin (Toulouse), +A. Benazzi (Agen), F. Pelous (Dax), R. Castel (Beziers). Reps: D. Aucagne (Pau) for Dourthe; O. Magne (Dax) for Miorin.
T: Laurent Leflamand 2, Olivier Merle, David Venditti.
C: Richard Dourthe, David Aucagne.
P: Aucagne.

Wales N.R. Jenkins (Pontypridd); I.C. Evans (Llanelli), A.G. Bateman (Richmond), I.S. Gibbs (Swansea), G. Thomas (Bridgend); A.C. Thomas (Swansea), R. Howley (Cardiff); C.D. Loader (Swansea), +J.M. Humphreys, D. Young (Cardiff), G.O. Llewellyn (Harlequins), M.A. Rowley (Pontypridd), S.M. Williams (Neath), L.S. Quinnell (Richmond), C.L. Charvis (Swansea). Rep: Jonathan Davies (Cardiff) for (I.C.) Evans.
T: Gareth Thomas, Allan Bateman, Robert Howley.
C: Neil Jenkins 2.
P: Jenkins.
Referee: Peter Marshall (Australia).

Wales 0   France 51

Wembley, London. 5 April 1998

France won by 7 tries, 5 cons, 2 pens to nil.

In 1951, a Scotland supporter came away from Murrayfield after watching South Africa win 44–0 and said 'We were lucky to get nil.' Well, Wales deserved nil. It was boringly one-sided and should have been awarded an 'RSC' (referee stopped contest). 'Outclassed' was putting it mildly, with coach Kevin Bowring determined not to take Neil Jenkins off, despite the fact that the outside-half was being given the run-around by Thomas Castaignede. The little fellow was an old type of Welsh pivot and the darling of the French supporters. By the finish, he was the darling of most neutrals as well. It was the biggest margin in a Five-Nations match and the first time that Wales had failed to score in their 73 meetings with France. Many years ago heads would have rolled. Bowring's eventually did, while Stuart Davies was forced to retire with a spinal injury. The whole Swansea back-row had been picked and each of them was shown a yellow card in separate incidents. France became bored of scoring tries during the second half, and even kicked a penalty goal before giving all seven replacements a run-out. Skipper Raphael Ibánez then took the Five-Nations title, his side already having achieved the Grand Slam.

Wales K.A. Morgan (Pontypridd); W.T. Proctor, N. Boobyer (Llanelli), L.B. Davies, G. Thomas (Cardiff); N.R. Jenkins (Pontypridd), +R. Howley; A.L.P. Lewis (Cardiff), G.R. Jenkins (Swansea), D. Young (Cardiff), Andrew P. Moore (Swansea), M.J. Voyle (Llanelli), R.C. Appleyard, S. Davies, C.L. Charvis (Swansea). Reps: D.R. James (Pontypridd) for Boobyer; L. Mustoe (Cardiff) for Lewis; J.M. Humphreys (Cardiff) for (G.R.)Jenkins; K.P. Jones (Ebbw Vale) for Appleyard.

France J.-L. Sadourny (Colomiers); P. Bernat-Salles (Pau), C. Lamaison (Brive), S. Glas (Bourgoin), X. Garbajosa (Toulouse); T. Castaignede (Castres), P. Carbonneau (Brive); C. Califano (Toulouse), +R. Ibánez (Dax), F. Tournaire (Toulouse), O. Brouzet (Begles-Bordeaux), F. Pelous (Toulouse), M. Lievremont (Stade Français), T. Lievremont (Perpignan), O. Magne (Brive). Reps: J.-M. Aue (Castres) for Lamaison; D. Aucagne (Pau) for Castaignede; F. Galthie (Colomiers) for Carbonneau; C. Soulette (Beziers) for Califano; M. Dal Maso (Agen) for Ibánez; T. Cleda (Pau) for Brouzet; P. Benetton (Agen) for (T.)Lievremont.
T: Jean-Luc Sadourny 2, Xavier Garbajosa 2, Stéphane Glas, Thomas Lievremont, Fabien Galthie.
C: Christophe Lamaison 5.
P: Lamaison 2.
Referee: Peter Marshall (Australia).

France 33   Wales 34

Stade de France, Paris. 6 March 1999

Wales won by 3 tries, 2 cons, 5 pens to 4 tries, 2 cons, 3 pens.

Wales had won dramatically in Paris in 1975, but since then they had lost 12 out of 12 there. It was seemingly impossible to win, especially after losing to Scotland and Ireland. Well, the impossible happened! In truth, France were poor and Wales were improving steadily. The crowd of 80,500 was the largest to watch a rugby match in France. They saw Neil Jenkins kicking superbly and Colin Charvis score a sixth-minute try, but France were 18–16 in front after 31 minutes. Then Dafydd James and Craig Quinnell tries took Wales in for the break as 28–18 leaders. It was 28–28 before Jenkins kicked his fourth penalty. France hit back and Thomas Castaignede went over in the corner. His conversion attempt failed, but France led 33–31 with eight minutes remaining. Five minutes from time, Jenkins kicked another penalty. Castaignede had one last chance, but his effort failed and Wales, despite conceding three tries to full-back Emile Ntamack, had won. England-born Peter Rogers, who had played in South African provincial matches, and New Zealander Brett Sinkinson, were new caps brought in by coach Graham Henry.

France E. Ntamack (Toulouse); P. Bernat-Salles (Biarritz), R. Dourthe, F. Comba, T. Lombard (Stade Français); T. Casstaignede (Castres), P. Carbonneau (Brive); C. Califano (Toulouse), +R. Ibánez (Perpignan), F. Tournaire (Toulouse), O. Brouzet (Begles-Bordeaux), F. Pelous (Toulouse), P. Benetton (Agen), T. Lievremont (Perpignan), M. Raynaud (Narbonne). Reps: D. Aucagne (Pau) for Dourthe; X. Garbajosa (Toulouse) for Bernat-Salles; S. Marconnet (Stade Français) for Tournaire; R. Castel (Beziers) for Benetton.
T: Emile Ntamack 3, Thomas Castaignede.
C: Castaignede 2.
P: Castaignede 3.

Wales S.P. Howarth (Manchester-Sale); M.F.D. Robinson, M. Taylor, I.S. Gibbs (Swansea), D.R. James; N.R. Jenkins (Pontypridd), +R. Howley (Cardiff); *P.J.D. Rogers (London

Irish), G.R. Jenkins, B.R. Evans (Swansea), J.C. Quinnell (Richmond), C.P. Wyatt (Llanelli), C.L. Charvis (Swansea), L.S. Quinnell (Llanelli), *B.D. Sinkinson (Neath). Reps: G. Thomas (Cardiff) for Robinson; D.S. Llewellyn (Ebbw Vale) for Howley; A.L.P. Lewis (Cardiff) for Rogers.

T: Colin Charvis, Craig Quinnell, Dafydd James.
C: Neil Jenkins 2.
P: Neil Jenkins 5
Referee: Jim M. Fleming (Scotland).

IRELAND

Ireland v Wales

Lansdowne Road, Dublin. 28 January 1882
(No points were awarded until 1891 – see p.12)

Wales won by 4 tries, 2 cons to nil

Wales had lost by a goal to a try against the North of England and then defeated the Midland Counties by three goals and three tries to nil, both at Newport, within 12 days of this first meeting with Ireland. Bill Evans of Rhymney scored five of the six tries against the Midland Counties and won his first cap in the backs. The Ireland team was classed as 'makeshift', with two players actually walking off and two leaving with injuries while arguments persisted with Welsh referee Richard Mullock, the WRU secretary. Robert, the first of the three Gould brothers to play for Wales, made his début but unlike Arthur and Bert, he appeared in the pack. Another new face was Hugh Vincent from Trinity College, Dublin, who was later knighted in 1924. Forward Tom Jones (known as Baker-Jones) had the honour of scoring the first international try for Wales. He lived to the age of 96 and saw his son Paul capped in 1921. Charles Newman was at scrum-half after playing at full-back in the England match of 1881.

Ireland R.E. McLean; J.R. Atkinson, St G. McCarthy (Dublin U), W.W. Fletcher (Kingstown); G.C. Bent, E.H. Greene (Dublin U); +A.J. Forrest, F. Kennedy, W.A. Wallis, J.M. Kennedy (Wanderers), H.B. Morfell, A.J. Downing (Dublin U), F.S. Heuston, E. McCarthy (Kingstown), R.G. Thompson (QCC).

Wales *+C.P. Lewis (Llandovery); *S.S. Clark (Neath), W.B. Norton (Cardiff), *W.F. Evans (Oxford U/Rhymney), G.F. Harding (Newport); C.H. Newman, *R.H. Bridie (Newport); F.T. Purdon, *T. Baker Jones, *R. Gould (Newport), *T.J.S. Clapp (Nantyglo), *T. Williams (Pontypridd/Cardiff), W.D. Phillips (Cardiff), *G.L.B. Morris (Swansea), *H.C. Vincent (Bangor).
T: Baker Jones, Tom Clapp, Bill Evans, James Bridie.
C: Charles Lewis 2.
Referee: W.J. Goulding (Ireland).

Wales v Ireland

Arms Park, Cardiff. 12 April 1884

Wales won by 2 tries, 1 drop goal to nil

Confusion surrounded the make up of the Ireland team, and to this day it is considered that ten of the supposed side never played again, but R.O.N. Hall may have been O'Halloran and a player named Eames appeared in some reports. Also in the Ireland side were two Welsh players. Some say that Frank Purdon of Newport and Swansea, already capped four times by Wales, played but others believe it was Henry Purdon of North of Ireland or even J. McDaniel of Newport, whose relatives later confirmed his appearance. McDaniel was never credited with a cap, however. The other Welshman in Irish colours was either little Martyn Jordan, who later won three caps for Wales, or his brother Charles, a forward who was also with Newport. In any event, Irish records name 15 players of whom several never left Ireland. 'Buller' Stadden was a late replacement who played well and dropped the first goal for Wales in international rugby.

Wales *T.M. Barlow (Cardiff); C.G. Taylor (Ruabon/Blackheath), *F.E. Hancock, W.B. Norton (Cardiff); *W.J. Stadden (Cardiff), W.H. Gwynn (Swansea); T.J.S. Clapp, R. Gould, H.S. Lyne (Newport), *S.J. Goldsworthy (Swansea), *J.T. Hinton, +H.J. Simpson, W.D. Phillips, J.S. Smith (Cardiff), *W.R. Roderick (Llanelli).
T: Tom Clapp, William Norton.
DG: Bill Stadden.

Ireland (This is the team listed as playing. No record exists of the exact lineup.) R.W. Morrow (QCB); E.H. Green (Dublin U), J. Pedlow (Bessbrook), R.G. Warren (Lansdowne), H.F. Spunner (Wanderers); A.J. Hamilton, H.G. Cooke (Lansdowne); +D.F. Moore, F.W. Moore, J.M. Kennedy, W.S. Collis, J. Fitzgerald (Wanderers), R.O.N. Hall, L. Moyers, W.E. Johnstone (Dublin U).
Referee: G. Rowland Hill (England).

Wales v Ireland

Birkenhead Park. 12 March 1887

Wales won by 1 try, 1 drop goal to 3 tries.

This match was played in England at Birkenhead Park to reduce travelling expenses for Ireland. In modern times the score would have been 15–8 to Ireland, who outscored Wales 3–1 on tries but lost to Gould's early drop goal. The Irish then woke up and crossed for their tries with some reports giving all three to Bob Montgomery, while others credited one to Max Carpendale. In any event Irish hurdling champion Danny Rambaut missed all the conversion kicks, when one success would have given his side victory.

Wales S.S. Clark (Neath); C.G. Taylor (Ruabon/Blackheath), A.J. Gould (Newport), G.E. Bowen (Swansea); *J.G. Lewis (Llanelli), W.J. Stadden (Cardiff); A.F. Bland, W.E.O. Williams (Cardiff), E.P. Alexander (Cambridge U), +T.J.S. Clapp, T.W. Lockwood (Newport), W.A. Bowen, D. Morgan, *W.H. Towers (Swansea), E. Roberts (Llanelli).
T: D. Morgan.
DG: Arthur Gould.

Ireland D.B. Walkington (NIFC); M.J. Carpendale (Monkstown), D.F. Rambaut (Dublin U), R. Montgomery (QCB); +R.G. Warren, P.J. O'Connor (Lansdowne); E.J. Walsh, V.C. le Fanu (Lansdowne), J. Chambers, T. Taggart (Dublin U), H.J. Neill (NIFC), J. Johnston, W. Davison (Belfast Albion), R. Stevenson (Lisburn), J.S. Dick (QCC).
T: Bob Montgomery 3.
Referee: J.A. Gardner (Scotland).

Ireland v Wales

Lansdowne Road, Dublin. 3 March 1888.

Ireland won by 1 goal, 1 try, 1 drop goal to nil.

Wales suffered a disappointing loss in Dublin and Ireland pipped Scotland by virtue of try-count to win a championship that England again declined to play in. Wales were badly hit by injuries and seasickness from crossing a stormy Irish Sea. This was reflected in the performance, as they rarely troubled the home side. Skipper Tom Clapp played his 14th and last international match before emigrating to the United States. He was the most-capped Welsh player until Arthur Gould overtook him in 1892.

Ireland D.B. Walkington (NIFC); M.J. Carpendale (Monkstown), D.F. Rambaut, C.R. Tillie (Dublin U); R.G. Warren (Lansdowne), J.H. McLaughlin (Derry); +H.J. Neil (NIFC), E.W. Stoker, F.O. Stoker (Wanderers), W.G. Rutherford (Tipperary), T. Shanahan (Lansdowne), C.M. Moore (Dublin U), J. Moffatt, R.H. Mayne (Belfast Albion), W. Ekin (QCB).
T: Bob Warren, Tom Shanahan.
C: Dan Rambaut.
DG: Max Carpendale.

Wales E.J. Roberts (Llanelli); T.J.P. Jenkins (London Welsh), G.E. Bowen (Swansea), *C.S. Arthur; O.J. Evans (Cardiff), *C.J. Thomas (Newport); +T.J.S. Clapp, R.W. Powell (Newport); A.F. Hill, Q.D. Kedzlie, A.F. Bland (Cardiff), W.H. Thomas (Llandovery), W.H. Howell, T. Williams, J. Meredith (Swansea).
Referee: G. Rowland Hill (England).

Wales v Ireland

St Helen's, Swansea. 2 March 1889

Ireland won by 2 tries to nil.

Débutants Alaster McDonnell and John Cotton scored their only tries in international rugby and indeed Cotton never appeared again. The International Board had met in Swansea and their chairman was Andrew Don Wauchope. The Scot was so versatile that he went on to referee the match in the afternoon. Arthur Gould led Wales for the first time with Dr Abel Christmas Davies winning his only cap outside the great Newport centre.

Wales E.J. Roberts (Llanelli); *A.C. Davies (London Welsh), +A.J. Gould (Newport), *T. Morgan (Llanelli), N.W. Biggs (Cardiff); C.J. Thomas (Newport), *G. Griffiths (Llanelli); W.A. Bowen, D. Morgan (Swansea), S.H. Nicholls, D.W. Evans (Cardiff), C.T. Harding, J. Hannan (Newport), R.L. Thomas (London Welsh), D. Griffiths (Llanelli).

Ireland L.J. Holmes (Lisburn); R.A. Yeates, R. Dunlop (Dublin U), R. Pedlow (Bessbrook); +R.G. Warren (Lansdowne), A.C. McDonnell (Dublin U); V.C. le Fanu, J.S. Jameson (Lansdowne), E.G. Forrest, J. Cotton (Wanderers), J. Waites (Bective), H.W. Andrews, J.N. Lytle (NIFC), R. Stevenson (Lisburn), H.A. Richey (Dublin U).
T: Alaster McDonnell, John Cotton.
Referee: Andrew R. Don Wauchope (Scotland).

Ireland v Wales

Lansdowne Road, Dublin. 1 March 1890

Draw. 1 goal each.

Charlie 'Moose' Thomas, a boilermaker in Newport, scored his only try in nine matches for Wales and Billy Bancroft kicked an equalising conversion. One of the four other Newport players in the side was debutant Tom Graham, a minister of religion who was born in England. The other newcomer was solicitor Hugh Ingledew who had failed to win a blue at Oxford University. He was later instrumental in securing the Arms Park from the Bute family's estate. After the St David's Day match, eight Irish players were arrested for riotous behaviour along with one from Wales. Their names remain unknown but they did receive fines later.

Ireland D.B. Walkington (NIFC); R. Dunlop, R.W. Johnston (Dublin U), T. Edwards; +R.G. Warren (Lansdowne), A.C. McDonnell (Dublin U); J. Moffatt, H.T. Galbraith (Belfast Albion), J. Waites, J.H. O'Conor (Bective), R. Stevenson (Lisburn), J. Roche (Wanderers), W.J.N. Davis (Bessbrook), E.F. Doran (Lansdowne), L.C. Nash (QCC).
T: Bob Dunlop.
C: J. Roche.

Wales W.J. Bancroft (Swansea); R.M. Garrett (Penarth), +A.J. Gould, G. Thomas (Newport); D. Gwynn (Swansea), C.J. Thomas (Newport); *H.M. Ingledew, A.F. Hill, D.W. Evans, A.F. Bland (Cardiff), J. Hannan, *T.C. Graham (Newport), W.A. Bowen (Swansea), W.H. Thomas, R.L. Thomas (London Welsh).
T: Charles Thomas.
C: Billy Bancroft.
Referee: F.W. Burnand (England).

Wales 6   Ireland 4

Stradey Park, Llanelli. 7 March 1891

Wales won by 1 try, 1 con, 1 drop goal to 1 try, 1 drop goal.

This match, unlike the one against England in 1887, was played on the actual Stradey Park rugby pitch. It decided bottom place in the championship. With five Llanelli players selected, temporary stands were erected to cater for the attendance of around 10,000. The brilliant James brothers, David and Evan, were at last partnered at half-back. It was a first cap for David James – he and his brother continually switched in the half-back positions. Though they were seemingly years before their time in trickery, neither brother ever scored for Wales. However, Ireland's players were told: 'Go for the James's. Never mind whether the varmints have got the ball or not. By the time you reach them, one of them's sure to have it!' The Samuel brothers were débutants in the pack, and it was David Samuel who scored the Welsh try. Ireland extrovert full-back Dolway Walkington wore a monocle, which he stored in his shorts whenever he made a tackle.

Wales W.J. Bancroft (Swansea); R.M. Garrett (Penarth), C.J. Thomas (Newport), D.P.M. Lloyd (Llanelli), T.W. Pearson (Cardiff); *D. James, E. James (Swansea); +W.H. Thomas, R.L. Thomas, S. Thomas, *C.B. Nicholl (Llanelli), T.C. Graham (Newport), *J. Samuel, *D. Samuel, J.T. Deacon (Swansea).
T: David Samuel.
C: Billy Bancroft.
DG: Bancroft.

Ireland D.B. Walkington; R. Dunlop, S. Lee (NIFC), H.G. Wells; E.D. Cameron (Bective), R. Pedlow (Bessbrook); +R. Stevenson (Lisburn), J. Roche, F.O. Stoker (Wanderers), J.S. Jameson (Lansdowne), L.C. Nash, R.D. Stokes (QCC), T. Fogarty (Garryowen), C.V. Rooke (Dublin U), W.J.N. Davis (Bessbrook).
T: Sam Lee.
DG: Dolway Walkington.
Referee: A. Rowsell (England).

Ireland 9   Wales 0

Lansdowne Road, Dublin. 5 March 1892

Ireland won by 3 tries, 1 con to nil.

Ned Walsh, the Irish hurdles and all-round athletics champion, became the first forward to score two tries in a Test for Ireland as the home pack dominated. Arthur and Bob Gould had appeared five times together for Wales, and now Arthur was joined by a younger brother, Bert, who appeared on three occasions before moving to South Africa, where he died of pneumonia at the age of 43. Four other Newport players were present, including Harry Day, whose nephew, Harry Phillips, appeared in the 1920s.

Ireland T. Peel (Limerick); T. Edwards (Lansdowne), S. Lee (NIFC), R. Montgomery (QCB); T. Thornhill (Wanderers), F.E. Davies (Lansdowne); +V.C. le Fanu, E.J. Walsh, J.S. Jameson (Lansdowne), C.V. Rooke (Dublin U), A.K. Wallis, J. Roche (Wanderers), J.H. O'Conor (Bective), R. Stevenson (Lisburn), T.J. Johnston (QCB).

T: Ned Walsh 2, Fred Davies.
C: J. Roche.

Wales W.J. Bancroft (Swansea); *G.H. Gould, +A.J. Gould (Newport), *F.E. Nicholls (Cardiff Harlequins), N.W. Biggs (Cardiff); E. James, D. James (Swansea); W.H. Watts, J. Hannan, *H.T. Day, A.W. Boucher (Newport), P. Bennett (Cardiff Harlequins), C.B. Nicholl (Llanelli), J.T. Deacon, F.M. Mills (Swansea).
Referee: E.B. Holmes (England).

Wales 2 Ireland 0

Stradey Park, Llanelli. 11 March 1893

Wales won by 1 try to nil.

Bert Gould played his third and final match for Wales, but during the first half he scored the try which won the Triple Crown for the first time. The try came after clever play by his brother Arthur and another clubmate, Percy Phillips. Ireland appeared confused by the four three-quarter system used by Wales and their full-back, Willis Sparrow, a minister from Kilkenny, was simply unable to hold Gould as he dived for the line.

Wales W.J. Bancroft (Swansea); N.W. Biggs (Cardiff), +A.J. Gould, G.H. Gould (Newport), W.M. McCutcheon (Swansea); H.P. Phillips, F.C. Parfitt (Newport); T.C. Graham, W.H. Watts, J. Hannan, A.W. Boucher (Newport), D. Samuel, F.M. Mills (Swansea), A.F. Hill (Cardiff), C.B. Nicholl (Llanelli).
T: G.H. (Bert) Gould.

Ireland W. Sparrow (Dublin U); R. Dunlop, +S. Lee, W. Gardiner (NIFC); F.E. Davies (Lansdowne), W.S. Browne (Dublin U); R. Stevenson (Lisburn), C.V. Rooke, H. Lindsay, A.D. Clinch, B. O'Brien (Dublin U), A.K. Wallis, E.G. Forrest, R. Johnston, R.W. Hamilton (Wanderers).
Referee: W.H. Humphreys (England).

Ireland 3 Wales 0

Ballinafeigh, Belfast. 10 March 1894

Ireland won by 1 pen to nil.

This gave Ireland their first Triple Crown, but the pitch was so muddy that the match became known as the 'Ballinafeigh Bog match'. Wales appeared the better side with the forwards winning a monopoly of the ball – only for the marauding home players to tackle the Welsh backs out of the match. An all-Cardiff three-quarter line included new cap John Elliot, whose son-in-law, Bill Roberts, was capped in 1929. The only score came after ten minutes' play when one of the Lytle brothers, John, landed his only successful international penalty in what was his last appearance.

Ireland P.J. Grant (Bective); R. Dunlop, S. Lee (NIFC), L.H. Gwynn (Dublin U), W. Gardiner (NIFC); B. Tuke (Bective), W.S. Browne (Dublin U); +E.G. Forrest, T.J. Crean (Wanderers), C.V. Rooke, H. Lindsay (Dublin U), J.H. O'Conor (Bective), A.T.W. Bond (Derry), John Lytle, James Lytle (NIFC).
P: John Lytle.

Wales W.J. Bancroft (Swansea); N.W. Biggs, D. Fitzgerald, *J.E. Elliot, T.W. Pearson; R.B. Sweet-Escott (Cardiff), F.C. Parfitt (Newport); +A.F. Hill (Cardiff), J. Hannan, W.H. Watts, H.T. Day (Newport), F.M. Mills (Swansea), D.J. Daniel, *D.W. Nicholl (Llanelli), *F.O. Hutchinson (Neath).
Referee: R.D. Rainie (Scotland).

Wales 5 Ireland 3

Arms Park, Cardiff. 16 March 1895

Wales won by 1 try, 1 con to 1 try.

Two great players scored the tries in this match: Tom Pearson's effort was the winner as Billy Bancroft converted it, while Ireland's try was scored by the immortal Tommy Crean. Crean later won the Victoria Cross in 1901, having led a bayonet charge against the Boers. Severely wounded, Crean lived to serve with honour in the First World War and later became a Harley Street doctor. Pearson survived the First World War as a lieutenant-colonel in the Royal Field Artillery. This was one of a surprisingly small tally of four tries he scored for Wales. He ran from inside his own 25 to the Irish line after splendid passing from centres Arthur Gould and Owen Badger.

Wales W.J. Bancroft (Swansea); T.W. Pearson (Cardiff), O. Badger (Llanelli), +A.J. Gould, W.L. Thomas (Newport); *D. Morgan (Llanelli), R.B. Sweet-Escott (Cardiff); A.W. Boucher, W.H. Watts, J. Hannan, H. Packer (Newport), F.M. Mills (Cardiff), C.B. Nicholl (Llanelli), E.E. George (Pontypridd), *A.M. Jenkin (Swansea).
T: Tom Pearson.
C: Billy Bancroft.

Ireland J. Fulton; W. Gardiner, S. Lee (NIFC), T.H. Stevenson (Belfast Albion), A.P. Gwynn (Dublin U); L.M. Magee, M.G. Delaney (Bective); C.V. Rooke (Monkstown), T.J. Crean, +E.G. Forrest, A.D. Clinch (Wanderers), James Lytle, A. Brunker (Lansdowne), H.C. McCoull (Belfast Albion), E.H. McIlwaine (NIFC).
T: Tommy Crean.
Referee: E.B. Holmes (England).

Ireland 8 Wales 4

Lansdowne Road, Dublin. 14 March 1896.

Ireland won by 2 tries, 1 con to 1 drop goal.

Gould and Nicholls were joined in the backs by the tricky Newport half-back Llewellyn Lloyd, but Ireland gained the Triple Crown with this victory in what was the last meeting in Dublin for 14 years. Lloyd, aged 19, stood just 5ft 6ins high and faced the feared Irish breakaway Charles Rooke. He survived, and both Nicholls and Lloyd's clubmate, Gould, sang the praises of the little genius. The great Tommy Crean scored one of Ireland's tries in his last appearance for them, and another forward, James Lytle, also crossed the Welsh line.

Ireland G.H. McAllan (RHS Dungannon); T.H. Stevenson (Belfast Albion), W. Gardiner, +S. Lee (NIFC), L.Q. Bulger (Lansdowne); L.M. Magee (Bective), G.G. Allen (Derry); C.V. Rooke (Monkstown), T.J. Crean, A.D. Clinch (Wanderers), J. Sealy (Dublin Wdrs), H. Lindsay (Armagh), W.G. Byron, James H. Lytle (NIFC), J.H. O'Conor (Bective).
T: Tommy Crean, James Lytle.
C: Larry Bulger.

Wales W.J. Bancroft (Swansea); C.A. Bowen (Llanelli), E.G. Nicholls (Cardiff), +A.J. Gould, F.H. Dauncey; *G.L. Lloyd, F.C. Parfitt; H. Packer, A.W. Boucher (Newport), J. Evans, W. Morris, C.B. Nicholl (Llanelli), D. Evans (Penygraig), F.O. Hutchinson (Neath), *W.H. Millar (Mountain Ash).
DG: Arthur Gould.
Referee: E.B. Holmes (England).

Ireland 3 Wales 11

Limerick. 19 March 1898

Wales won by 2 tries, 1 con, 1 pen to 1 pen.

Though Scotland still refused to play Wales, Ireland did and England reluctantly gave way late in the season. Billy Bancroft was captain for the first time and two of the seven débutants, Viv Huzzey and Tom Dobson, both from Cardiff, scored tries. Huzzey, a noted athlete, scored four tries in five appearances before joining Oldham at rugby league and later becoming the first rugby international to be capped at baseball. Newport's George Boots was another newcomer, as was a coal trimmer, Joe Booth of Pontymister, who surprisingly was not selected again.

Ireland J. Fulton (NIFC); F. Purser (Dublin U), F.F. Smethwick (Monkstown), +W. Gardiner (NIFC), L.Q. Bulger (Lansdowne); L.M. Magee (Bective), A. Barr (Methodist Coll, Belfast); W.G. Byron, J.E. McIlwaine (NIFC), J.G. Franks (Dublin U), M. Ryan, J. Ryan (Rockwell Coll), T. Little (Bective), H. Lindsay (Armagh), T. McCarthy (Cork).
P: Larry Bulger.

Wales +W.J. Bancroft (Swansea); T.W. Pearson (Newport), E.G. Nicholls, *W. Jones, *H.V.P. Huzzey; J.E. Elliot, S.H. Biggs (Cardiff); R. Hellings, *W.H. Alexander (Llwynypia), D.J. Daniel (Llanelli), *H.Davies (Swansea), *J.G. Boots (Newport), *T. Dobson, F.H. Cornish (Cardiff), *J. Booth (Pontymister).
T: Tom Dobson, Viv Huzzey.
C: Billy Bancroft.
P: Bancroft.
Referee: A.J. Turnbull (Scotland).

Wales 0 Ireland 3

Arms Park, Cardiff. 18 March 1899

Ireland won by 1 try to nil.

Brothers Micky and John Ryan, both farmers, gave Billy Bancroft a severe shaking by throwing him into the crowd and fracturing his ribs. He departed and Aberavon policeman Bobby Brice was moved to the backs. Wales, one short in the pack, almost won when Gwyn Nicholls sent Reg Skrimshire away – only for Ireland skipper Louis Magee to bring off a fine tackle almost on the line. The huge record crowd of 40,000 burst over the rails, which gave way, and Micky Ryan later said that Wales appeared to have had 1,000 full-backs. The famous *Newport Argus* writer, W.J.T. Collins, known as 'Dromio', had to watch the match from the roof of the nearby County Club. The game was halted while the pitch was cleared and the interval lasted for 17 minutes with two further stoppages in the second half. The police appeared reluctant to sort matters out. Ireland scored the only points with a try by wing Gerry Doran in the first half.

Wales +W.J. Bancroft (Swansea); H.V.P. Huzzey, E.G. Nicholls (Cardiff), R.T. Skrimshire

(Newport), W.M. Llewellyn (Llwynypia); S.H. Biggs (Cardiff), G.L. Lloyd (Newport); W.H. Alexander, R. Hellings (Llwynypia), J. Blake, F.H. Cornish (Cardiff), D.J. Daniel (Llanelli), J.G. Boots, J.J. Hodges (Newport), A.B. Brice (Aberavon).

Ireland P. O'Brien (Monkstown); G.P. Doran (Lansdowne), G. Harman (Dublin U), C. Reid (NIFC), E.F. Campbell (Monkstown); +L.M. Magee (Bective), G.G. Allen (Derry); W.G. Byron, J.E. McIlwaine (NIFC), C.C.H. Moriarty (Monkstown), M. Ryan, J. Ryan (Rockwell Coll), J. Sealy, A.W.D. Meares (Dublin U), T. Little (Bective).
T: Gerry Doran.
Referee: A.J. Turnbull (Scotland).

Ireland 0 Wales 3

Balmoral, Belfast. 17 March 1900

Wales won by 1 try to nil.

Wales gained a second Triple Crown by reversing the scoreline of the previous year in Cardiff. Try-scorer George Davies, a Llandeilo stonemason, did not know he had scored as he was knocked unconscious. He never scored another try for Wales, but his final match for Llanelli brought him six tries and three drop goals! Wales opted for scrums in place of lineouts, but it was from the latter that Gwyn Nicholls broke through and gave Davies his chance, though he paid the penalty for his efforts with a kick in the mouth.

Ireland J. Fulton (NIFC); E.F. Campbell (Monkstown), B.R. Doran (Lansdowne), J.B. Allison (QCB), I.G. Davidson (North of Ireland); +L.M. Magee (Bective), J.H. Ferris (QCB); T. Little (Bective), M. Ryan, J. Ryan (Rockwell Coll), A.W.D. Meares, P.C. Nicholson, T.A. Harvey (Dublin U), C.E. Allen (Derry), S.T. Irwin (QCB).

Wales +W.J. Bancroft (Swansea); W.M. Llewellyn (Llwynypia), E.G. Nicholls (Cardiff), G. Davies, W.J. Trew (Swansea); S.H. Biggs (Cardiff), L.A. Phillips (Newport); R. Hellings (Llwynypia), J. Blake (Cardiff), J.J. Hodges, J.G. Boots (Newport), A.B. Brice (Aberavon), W.H. Williams (Pontymister), R. Thomas (Swansea), W.H. Millar (Mountain Ash).
T: George Davies.
Referee: A.J. Turnbull (Scotland).

Wales 10 Ireland 9

St Helen's, Swansea. 16 March 1901

Wales won by 2 tries, 2 cons to 3 tries.

The four new Welsh caps included Rhys Gabe and Dicky Owen, who went on to win 59 caps between them, but the hero was forward Billy Alexander who scored his only points for Wales in what was his last appearance. His cap is now in the South Wales Police clubroom at Bridgend. The Ireland captain Louis Magee called out for younger men as fit as the players to referee matches, being particularly annoyed with one of Alexander's two tries. It was Billy Bancroft's last Test, but he had a poor match and Ireland were rated the better side – they lost mainly because their conversion attempts were all difficult. Ireland's try-scorer Arthur Freear later played for Aberavon and Swansea before turning professional.

Wales +W.J. Bancroft (Swansea); W.M. Llewellyn (Llwynypia/London Welsh), E.G. Nicholls (Cardiff), G. Davies (Swansea), *R.T. Gabe (Llanelli/London Welsh); *R.H. Jones, *R.M. Owen (Swansea); A.B. Brice (Aberavon), W.H. Millar (Mountain Ash), F.G. Scrine, H. Davies (Swansea), J.G. Boots (Newport), J. Blake (Cardiff), W.H. Alexander, *R. 'Bob' Jones (Llwynypia).
T: Billy Alexander 2.
C: Billy Bancroft 2.

Ireland C.A. Boyd (Wanderers); A.E. Freear, B.R. Doran (Lansdowne), J.B. Allison (QCB), I.G. Davidson (NIFC); +L.M. Magee (Bective), J.H. Ferris (QCB); M. Ryan, J. Ryan (Rockwell Coll), C.E. Allen (Derry), F. Gardiner (NIFC), T.A. Harvey (Dublin U), P. Healey (Limerick), J.J. Coffey (Lansdowne), S.T. Irwin (QCB).
T: Jack Ryan, Arthur Freear, Ian Davidson.
Referee: George H. Harnett (England).

Ireland 0 Wales 15

Lansdowne Road, Dublin. 8 March 1902

Wales won by 3 tries, 1 con, 1 drop goal to nil.

Wales secured the Triple Crown largely because they conjured up three second-half tries after a scoreless first half played against a strong wind. Gwyn Nicholls dropped a smart left-foot goal from broken play and Willie Llewellyn added a try before Llewellyn Lloyd crossed for Alf Brice to kick his only goal for Wales. The final try fell fittingly to skipper Nicholls and Wales had gained a memorable victory.

Ireland J. Fulton (NIFC); G.P. Doran, B.R. Doran (Lansdowne), J.B. Allison (QCB), I.G. Davidson (NIFC); +L.M. Magee (Bective), H.H. Gorley (Wanderers); F. Gardiner (NIFC), J.J. Coffey (Lansdowne), A. Tedford (Malone), S.T. Irwin (QCB), T.A. Harvey (Dublin U), P. Healey (Limerick), J.C. Pringle (RIEC/NIFC), G.T. Hamlet (Old Wesley).

Wales J. 'Strand' Jones (Llanelli); W.M. Llewellyn (Llwynypia), +E.G. Nicholls (Newport), R.T. Gabe, E. Morgan (London Welsh); G.L. Lloyd (Newport), R.M. Owen (Swansea); A.B. Brice (Aberavon), W. Joseph (Swansea), J.J. Hodges, J.G. Boots (Newport), A.F. Harding (Cardiff), W.T. Osborne (Mountain Ash), H. Jones (Penygraig), D. Jones (Treherbert).
T: Gwyn Nicholls, Willie Llewellyn, Llewellyn Lloyd.
C: Alfred Brice.
DG: Nicholls.
Referee: J. Crawford Findlay (Scotland).

Wales 18 Ireland 0

Arms Park, Cardiff. 14 March 1903

Wales won by 6 tries to nil.

How Wales ran in six tries, five by their three-quarters despite losing forward George Boots, on a sea of mud, is hard to believe. Boots broke his collar bone after five minutes, but played on until half-time. Wingers Teddy Morgan and Willie Llewellyn accounted for two apiece with superb handling skills coming from their midfield trio. A year later, five of the Irish pack were to be more prepared for their opponents but this day belonged to Wales with full-back Bert Winfield outstanding on his début.

Wales *H.B. Winfield (Cardiff); W.M. Llewellyn (London Welsh), +E.G. Nicholls (Cardiff), R.T. Gabe (Llanelli), E. Morgan (London Welsh); G.L. Lloyd (Newport), R.M. Owen (Swansea); A.B. Brice (Aberavon), J.G. Boots, J.J. Hodges (Newport), G. Travers (Pill Harriers), D. Jones (Treherbert), W. Joseph (Swansea), A.F. Harding (Cardiff/London Welsh), W.T. Osborne (Mountain Ash).
T: Willie Llewellyn 2, Teddy Morgan 2, Rhys Gabe, Alfred Brice.

Ireland J. Fulton (NIFC); G. Bradshaw (Belfast Collegians), C. Reid (NIFC), J.C. Parke (Dublin U), G.P. Doran (Lansdowne); L.M. Magee (Bective), +H.H. Corley (Dublin U); J.J. Coffey (Lansdowne), P. Healey (Garryowen), G. Hamlet (Old Wesley), F. Gardiner (NIFC), C.E. Allen (Derry), T.A. Harvey (Monkstown), A. Tedford (Malone), Joseph Wallace (Wanderers).
Referee: P. Coles (England).

Ireland 14 Wales 12

Balmoral, Belfast. 12 March 1904

Ireland won by 4 tries, 1 con to 4 tries.

Big Alf Tedford played the game of his life, as Wales, once again, had trouble with referee Crawford Findlay – Alf Brice was later suspended for eight months after giving the official some verbal abuse. Findlay would not award a possible winning try by Dickie Jones and was said by 'Dromio' of *Rugby Recollections* to have: 'Blindness to Irish faults and harshness to Wales.' Even that writer agreed that it balanced the 1901 match when Ireland were 'robbed'. A Tedford try was equalised by Teddy Morgan, but Joseph Wallace put Ireland back in front at the interval, later moving to wing when Campbell Robb was injured. Wales scored a fine try by Rhys Gabe and Cliff Pritchard put them ahead, with Morgan then scoring his second before Harry Thrift pulled one back. Despite being a forward short, the Irish pack worked the ball out to Wallace whose cross-kick was missed by Bert Winfield, with Tedford crossing for Jim Parke to kick the only goal of the match.

Ireland M.F. Landers (Cork Const); H. Thrift, J.C. Parke (Dublin U), G.A.D. Harvey (Wanderers), C.G. Robb (QCB); L.M. Magee (Bective), F.A. Kennedy (Wanderers); +C.E. Allen (Derry), A. Tedford, R.W. Edwards (Malone), H.J. Knox (Dublin U), F. Gardiner (NIFC), H.J. Millar (Monkstown), G. Hamlet (Old Wesley), Joseph Wallace (Wanderers).
T: Alf Tedford 2, Joseph Wallace, Harry Thrift.
C: Cecil Parke.

Wales H.B. Winfield (Cardiff); +W.M. Llewellyn, C.C. 'Cliff' Pritchard (Newport), R.T. Gabe (Cardiff), E. Morgan (London Welsh); R.H. Jones, R.M. Owen (Swansea); A.B. Brice (Aberavon), W. O'Neil (Cardiff), E. Thomas, *C.M. 'Charlie' Pritchard (Newport), H.W. Watkins (Llanelli), A.F. Harding (London Welsh), *T.S. Bevan (Swansea), *H. Jones (Neath).
T: Teddy Morgan 2, Rhys Gabe, Cliff Pritchard.
Referee: J. Crawford Findlay (Scotland).

The 1905 Triple-Crown winning Welsh team. *Back row*: A.J. Davies (touch-judge), W. Neill, D. Jones, A.F. Harding, H.W. Watkins, G. Travers, W. Joseph, W. Williams (referee). *Middle row*: J.F. Williams, J.J. Hodges, R.T. Gabe, W.M. Llewellyn (capt.), E.G. Nicholls, E.T. Morgan. *Front row*: R.M. Owen, G. Davies, W. Jones. *Circled*: D. Rees, W.J. Trew, R. Jones, C.M. Pritchard. (© *Western Mail & Echo*)

Wales 10 Ireland 3

St Helen's, Swansea. 11 March 1905

Wales won by 2 tries, 2 cons to 1 try.

The Triple Crown went to the winners in what was reported to be a strong, hard yet sporting match. Ireland, though playing against a strong wind, led by a try from outside-half Tom Robinson, but Wales struck twice before the interval. Cardiff's Gwyn Nicholls and new cap Windham Jones had replaced the injured Swansea pair of Dan Rees and Billy Trew and it was Jones, on his only appearance, who scored the first Welsh try and then created one for wing Teddy Morgan. George Davies converted them both. Jones later ran the line for Wales and he donated his international cap to the Mountain Ash club. It was said that skipper Willie Llewellyn ordered that safety tactics be employed after Wales had scored the second try and the tackling of Nicholls and Rhys Gabe in the centre halted their opponents.

Wales G. Davies (Swansea); +W.M. Llewellyn (Newport), E.G. Nicholls, R.T. Gabe (Cardiff), E. Morgan (London Welsh); *A. Windham Jones (Mountain Ash), R.M. Owen; W. Joseph (Swansea), G. Travers (Pill Harriers), W. O'Neil (Cardiff), A.F. Harding, *J.F. Williams (London Welsh), J.J. Hodges (Newport), D. Jones (Treherbert), H.W. Watkins (Llanelli).
T: Windham Jones, Teddy Morgan.
C: George Davies 2.

Ireland M.F. Landers (Cork Const); H. Thrift, J.C. Parke (Dublin U), B. Maclear (Monkstown), J.E. Moffatt (Old Wesley); T.H. Robinson, E.D. Caddell (Dublin U); +C.E. Allen (Derry), J.J. Coffey (Lansdowne), G. Hamlet (Old Wesley), H.G. Wilson, A. Tedford (Malone), H.J. Knox (Dublin U), H.J. Millar (Monkstown), Joseph Wallace (Wanderers).
T: Tom Robinson.
Referee: W. Williams (England).

Ireland 11 Wales 6

Balmoral, Belfast. 10 March 1906

Ireland won by 3 tries, 1 con to 2 tries.

A run of six consecutive victories over two years ended with defeat to the Irish again in Belfast. The loss of both Tommy Caddell with a broken leg and half-back partner Brooke Purdon with damaged knee ligaments failed to halt fine Irish play. Joe Wallace and Fred Gardiner reverted out of the Irish pack to the backs, but the six who remained were still able to outplay the eight Welshmen. It was the second time Wallace came out of the pack against Wales and once again he scored a try. Reg Gibbs had a poor match and was switched with wing Hop Maddock late on. With limited chances, the Welsh backs did manage two tries, however.

Ireland G.J. Henebrey (Garryowen); B. Maclear (Monkstown), J.C. Parke, F. Casement, H. Thrift (Dublin U); W.B. Purdon (QCB), E.D. Caddell (Dublin U); F. Gardiner (NIFC), +C.E. Allen (Derry), H.J. Knox, J.J. Coffey (Lansdowne), H.G. Wilson, A. Tedford (Malone), M. White (QCC), Joseph Wallace (Wanderers).
T: Harry Thrift, Joseph Wallace, Basil Maclear.
C: Fred Gardiner.

Wales H.B. Winfield (Cardiff); E. Morgan (London Welsh), +E.G. Nicholls, R.T. Gabe (Cardiff), H.T. Maddock (London Welsh); R.A. Gibbs (Cardiff), R.M. Owen; W. Joseph (Swansea), G. Travers (Pill Harriers), *J.A. Powell, *D. Westacott (Cardiff), J.J. Hodges, C.M. 'Charlie' Pritchard (Newport), *T.H. Evans (Llanelli), A.F. Harding (London Welsh).
T: Teddy Morgan, Rhys Gabe.
Referee: Dr John W. Simpson (Scotland).

Wales 29 Ireland 0

Arms Park, Cardiff. 9 March 1907

Wales won by 6 tries, 2 cons, 1 pen, 1 drop goal to nil.

Cardiff half-backs Percy Bush and Dicky David replaced Swansea's Billy Trew and Dicky Owen to great effect. Bush was the star turn – starting one try from behind his own line – and the highly rated David won the cap that many thought was long overdue, as only the brilliance of Owen had kept him out. It was to be his only appearance, though, and eight months later he joined Wigan for a sum of two hundred pounds. Trew refused to play, as his clubmate Fred Scrine had been suspended by the WRU for improper language to a referee. However, the backs played so well that all six tries came from them – three by Johnnie Williams and one to the new wing, 'Ponty' Jones, who was the first of three brothers to be capped though he was never to appear again. Wales led with tries by Williams and Jones at the interval, then Rhys Gabe went over and Bert Winfield kicked a penalty before Bush beat man after man only for John Brown to be stopped short. Bush was not to be denied and first he dropped a goal, then he created a second try for Williams which was converted. Williams scored his third before Bush swerved away to score behind the posts.

Wales H.B. Winfield (Cardiff); *D.P. 'Ponty' Jones, J.H. Evans (Pontypool), +R.T. Gabe, J.L. Williams; P.F. Bush, *R.J. David (Cardiff); G. Travers (Pill Harriers), W. O'Neil, J.A. Brown (Cardiff), T.H. Evans, J. Watts (Llanelli), W.H. Dowell, C.M. 'Charlie' Pritchard (Newport), A.F. Harding (London Welsh).
T: Johnnie Williams 3, Percy Bush, 'Ponty' Jones, Rhys Gabe.
C: Bert Winfield 2.
P: Winfield.
DG: Bush.

Ireland W.P. Hinton (Old Wesley); B. Maclear (Monkstown), T.J. Greeves (NIFC), J.C. Parke, H. Thrift (Dublin U); F.M. Harvey, T.H. Robinson (Wanderers); +C.E. Allen (Derry), A. Tedford, H.G. Wilson (Malone), J.A. Sweeny (Blackrock Coll), F. Gardiner (NIFC), G. Hamlet (Old Wesley), M. White (QCC), H.J. Knox (Lansdowne).
Referee: F.W. Marsh (England).

Ireland 5 Wales 11

Balmoral, Belfast. 14 March 1908

Wales won by 3 tries, 1 con to 1 try, 1 con.

Superb work by the Welsh backs produced two tries in the last ten minutes to win this match, just when Ireland appeared to have done enough to earn a draw. Centres Billy Trew and Rhys Gabe combined well on both occasions, firstly after outside-half Dick Jones made the opening for swift passing to send wing Reggie Gibbs over, too far out for Bert Winfield to convert. When Llanelli forward Tom Evans won a lineout, it was the fly-half and his centres, Trew and Gabe, who this time worked it left to give Johnnie Williams the chance to make it to the corner flag.

Ireland W.P. Hinton (Old Wesley); C. Thompson (Belfast Collegians), +J.C. Parke (Monkstown),

G.P. Beckett, H. Thrift; H.R. Aston (Dublin U), E.D. Caddell (Wanderers); B.A. Solomons, T.G. Harpur (Dublin U), T. Smyth, A. Tedford, H.G. Wilson (Malone), G. Hamlet (Old Wesley), F. Gardiner (NIFC), J.J. Coffey (Lansdowne).
T: Herbert Aston.
C: Cecil Parke.

Wales +H.B. Winfield; R.A. Gibbs (Cardiff), W.J. Trew (Swansea), R.T. Gabe, J.L. Williams (Cardiff); R.H. Jones, R.M. Owen (Swansea); W. O'Neil (Cardiff), G. Travers (Pill Harriers), W.H. Dowell (Pontypool), J. Watts, T.H. Evans (Llanelli), A.J. Webb (Abertillery), G. Hayward (Swansea), E.J. Thomas (Mountain Ash).
T: Johnnie Williams 2, Reg Gibbs.
C: Bert Winfield.
Referee: John D. Dallas (Scotland).

Wales 18 Ireland 5

St Helen's, Swansea. 13 March 1909

Wales won by 4 tries, 3 cons to 1 try, 1 con.

This victory ensured that Wales became the first country to win the Triple Crown in successive seasons. After a scoreless first half, Wales suddenly pulled clear with three tries in an eight-minute spell. The Irish pack included Oliver Piper, born in Aberavon, and Tom Smyth who later moved to Newport to work and play. Tom was the first of three Smyth brothers to win a cap.

Wales J. Bancroft (Swansea); J.L. Williams (Cardiff), J.P. 'Jack' Jones (Newport), +W.J. Trew, P. Hopkins; R.H. Jones, R.M. Owen (Swansea); A.J. Webb (Abertillery), G. Travers (Pill Harriers), P.D. Waller, E. Thomas (Newport), T.H. Evans, J. Watts (Llanelli), R. Thomas (Pontypool), W.I. Morgan (Swansea).
T: Phil Hopkins, Jack Jones, Jim Watts, Billy Trew.
C: Jack Bancroft 3.

Ireland G.J. Henebrey (Garryowen); H.Thrift (Wanderers), J.C. Parke (Monkstown), T.J. Greeves (NIFC), C. Thompson; G. Pinion (Belfast Collegians), F.M. McCormac (Wanderers); T. Halpin (Garryowen), O.J.S. Piper (Cork Const), M.G. Garry (Bective), +G. Hamlet (Old Wesley), T. Smyth, H.G. Wilson (Malone), B.A. Solomons (Dublin U), J.C. Blackham (QCC).
T: Charles Thompson.
C: Cecil Parke.
Referee: Frank C. Potter-Irwin (England).

Ireland 3 Wales 19

Lansdowne Road, Dublin. 12 March 1910.

Wales won by 5 tries, 1 drop goal to 1 try.

Wing Johnnie Williams registered his second try hat-trick against Ireland and went on to score eight tries in five appearances against them, notching 17 tries in his 17 matches. Louis Dyke, whose brother John had been capped in 1906, scored a début try and four of the six Cardiff players in the side scored the 19 points between them. England won the championship however, with three wins and a 0–0 draw against Ireland at Twickenham.

Ireland W.P. Hinton (Old Wesley); C.T. O'Callaghan (Carlow), A.S. Taylor (QCB), R.K. Lyle (Dublin U), +C. Thompson (Belfast Collegians); A.N. McClinton (NIFC), F.M. McCormac (Dublin Wands); H.G. Wilson, T. Smyth, G. McIldowie (Malone), W.S. Smyth (Belfast Collegians), O.J.S. Piper (Cork Const), B.A. Solomons, J.C. Blackham (Wanderers), T. Halpin (Garryowen).
T: George McIldowie.

Wales J. Bancroft (Swansea); +R.A. Gibbs, *L.M. Dyke, W. Spiller, J.L. Williams; P.F. Bush (Cardiff), T.H. Vile (Newport); A.J. Webb (Abertillery), J. Pugsley (Cardiff), B. Gronow (Bridgend), T.H. Evans (Llanelli), H. Jarman, E. Jenkins (Newport), D.J. Thomas, W.I. Morgan (Swansea).
T: Johnnie Williams 3, Louis Dyke, Reg Gibbs.
DG: Percy Bush.
Referee: John D. Dallas (Scotland).

Wales 16 Ireland 0

Arms Park, Cardiff. 11 March 1911

Wales won by 3 tries, 2 cons, 1 pen to nil.

This was a big match as both sides were attempting to win the Triple Crown: an hour before the kick-off the gates were closed, with mounted police being unable to hold back supporters who entered the ground in all directions. Wales won decisively to take the Triple Crown for the seventh time, thanks mostly to the pack, of whom Tom Evans and Jim Webb scored tries. Coal miner Bill Evans replaced Rees Thomas, who had suffered a family bereavement. Ireland lost full-back William Hinton early on. He later became president of the IRFU.

Wales J. Bancroft (Swansea); R.A. Gibbs, W. Spiller,

L.M. Dyke, J.L. Williams (Cardiff); +W.J. Trew, R.M. Owen (Swansea); A.P. Coldrick (Newport), J. Pugsley (Cardiff), G. Travers (Newport), A.J. Webb (Abertillery), T.H. Evans (Llanelli), *W.G. Evans (Brynmawr), D.J. Thomas, W.I. Morgan (Swansea).
T: Tom Evans, Jim Webb, Reg Gibbs.
C: Jack Bancroft 2.
P: Bancroft.

Ireland W.P. Hinton (Old Wesley); C.T. O'Callaghan (Carlow), A.R. Foster (Derry), A.R.V. Jackson (Wanderers), J.P. Quinn; R.A. Lloyd, H.M. Read (Dublin U); +G.T. Hamlet, C. Adams (Old Wesley), T. Smyth (Malone), H. Moore (QUB), T. Halpin (Garryowen), M.G. Garry (Bective), M.R. Heffernan (Cork Const), S.B. Campbell (Derry).
Referee: Frank C. Potter-Irwin (England).

Ireland 12 Wales 5

Balmoral, Belfast. 9 March 1912

Ireland won by 2 tries, 1 con, 1 drop goal to 1 try, 1 con.

Newport half-backs Walter Martin and Tommy Vile played when the Swansea pair of Billy Trew and Dicky Owen made themselves unavailable. Although Wales, with five new caps in the pack, led by a Willie Davies try and a Jack Bancroft conversion at half-time, they could not hold out afterwards. Davies was later suspended on professionalism grounds and moved to rugby league in 1913, six months after Gus Merry had also 'gone north'. The lightweight Welsh pack was handicapped when Tom Williams broke his left forearm, although he insisted on returning with it bound to play out the last few minutes. Try-scorer Charles Macivor died a year later after being kicked during a practice match.

Ireland W.P. Hinton (Old Wesley); J.P. Quinn (Dublin U), A.R. Foster (Derry), M. Abraham (Bective), C.V. Macivor; +R.A. Lloyd, H.M. Read (Dublin U); G.S. Brown (Monkstown), G.V. Killeen (Garryowen), R. Hemphill (Dublin U), W.J. Beatty (NIFC), H Moore (QUB), S.B. Campbell (Derry), C. Adams (Old Wesley), R.D'A. Patterson (Wanderers).
T: Charles Macivor, G Brown.
C: Dicky Lloyd.
DG: Lloyd.

Wales +J. Bancroft (Swansea); R.C.S. Plummer, F.W. Birt (Newport), Willie A. Davies (Aberavon), *B.R. Lewis (Swansea); *W.J. Martin, T.H. Vile (Newport); G. Stephens (Neath), *J.A. Merry (Pill Harriers), *H. Hiams, *T. Williams (Swansea), L.C. Trump, H. Uzzell (Newport), *F.J. Hawkins (Pontypridd), *W.J. Jenkins (Cardiff).
T: Willie Davies.
C: Jack Bancroft.
Referee: John D. Dallas (Scotland).

Wales 16 Ireland 13

St Helen's, Swansea. 8 March 1913

Wales won by 3 tries, 2 cons, 1 pen to 2 tries, 2 cons, 1 pen.

Wales had to hang on to win this match, until wing Bryn Lewis scored two tries in his final international, one after running from halfway. He was killed in action at Ypres in 1917, while serving as a Major in the Royal Field Artillery. Also killed at Ypres, six months later, was the scorer of an Ireland try, Lewis Stewart, a Major in the Royal Irish Rifles. A late penalty attempt by skipper Dicky Lloyd just failed for Ireland and Wales were thankful to have their kicker, Jack Bancroft, back in action.

Wales J. Bancroft (Swansea); B.R. Lewis (Swansea), W.P. Geen (Newport), +J.P. 'Jack' Jones (Pontypool), H. Lewis (Swansea); J.M.C. Lewis (Cardiff), R.A. Lloyd (Pontypool); Rev. J. Alban Davies (Swansea), F. Andrews (Pontypool), W.J. Jenkins (Cardiff), F.L. Perrett, T.J. Lloyd, G. Stephens (Neath), R. Richards (Aberavon), H. Uzzell (Newport).
T: Bryn Lewis 2, Jack Jones.
C: Jack Bancroft 2.
P: Bancroft.

Ireland A.W.P. Todd; G.H. Wood (Dublin U), A.R.V. Jackson (Wanderers), A.L. Stewart (NIFC), J.P. Quinn; +R.A. Lloyd (Dublin U), S.E. Polden (Clontarf); C. Adams (Old Wesley), J.J. Clune (Blackrock Coll), J.E. Finlay, W. Tyrrell (QCB), G.V. Killeen (Garryowen), G. McConnell (Derry), R.D'A. Patterson (Wanderers), P. O'Connell (Derry).
T: Pat Quinn, Lewis Stewart.
C: Dicky Lloyd 2.
P: Lloyd.
Referee: J.G. Cunningham (Scotland).

Ireland 3 Wales 11

Balmoral, Belfast. 14 March 1914

Wales won by 3 tries, 1 con to 1 try.

Remembered as 'The Roughest Ever', this was the day of the 'Terrible Eight' – the Welsh pack who won the battle against eight very strong opponents. Skipper, the Rev. Alban Davies, stated that he had heard no complaints from the Irish players who had begun the niggling by coming into the Welsh hotel on the previous night. Pack leader Dr William Tyrell told Welsh forward Percy Jones: 'It's you and me for it tomorrow.' Jones, a colliery foreman, smiled and answered: 'I shall be with you, doing the best I can.' Another Welsh forward asked: 'Can anyone join in?' And so they did. Players fought when the ball was not near them and some should have been sent off but Mr Tulloch, the referee, took little notice. It was one of the all-time best punch-ups and Percy Jones said: 'The fun just went on.' But after the match Jones said that Tyrell had told him he was the best Welshman he had ever come across, adding: 'You're the only Welshman who ever beat me.' The pair signed each others menu-cards and in 1951, the president of the Irish RU, now Sir William Tyrell, and retired collier and now hotelier, Percy Jones, sat together during the match at Cardiff that day. Ireland led with skipper Alex Foster's try, but Wales clawed back the lead with Bedwellty Jones scoring an equalising try. Two weeks later he signed for Oldham Rugby League club. Irish captain Dicky Lloyd was photographed before the match with his team, but strained a tendon in the warm-up and Harry Jack was called up for his second cap, playing at scrum-half with Victor McNamara switching to outside-half. Jack's third cap came in 1921 and he later became President of the Fiji Rugby Union. For the first time Wales's pack had remained unchanged throughout the season, but the First World War now intervened and Wales did not play an official match for five years and one month. The Rev. Davies died in Los Angeles at the age of 90, while both Tyrell and Jones lived to the age of 82, dying within six months of each other.

Ireland F.P. Montgomery (QUB); J.T. Brett (Monkstown), M. Abraham (Bective), A.R.V. Jackson (Wanderers), +A.R. Foster (Derry); H.W. Jack, V. McNamara (UCC); W.P. Collopy (Bective), S. Parr (Wanderers), P. O'Connell (Derry), W. Tyrrell (QUB), G.V. Killeen (Garryowen), J.C. Dowse (Monkstown), J. Taylor (Belfast Collegians), J.J. Clune (Blackrock Coll).
T: Alec Foster.

Wales R.F. Williams (Cardiff); G.L. Hirst, J.J. Wetter (Newport), W.H. Evans (Llwynypia), I.T. Davies (Llanelli); J.M.C. Lewis (Cardiff), R.A. Lloyd (Pontypool); +Rev. J. Alban Davies (Llanelli), D. Watts (Maesteg), J. 'Bedwellty' Jones (Abertillery), T.J. Lloyd (Neath), P.L. Jones (Pontypool), T. Williams, E. Morgan (Swansea), H. Uzzell (Newport).
T: Bedwellty Jones, Ivor Davies, Jack Wetter.
C: Clem Lewis.
Referee: J.T. Tulloch (Scotland).

Wales 28 Ireland 4

Arms Park, Cardiff. 13 March 1920

Wales won by 6 tries, 3 cons, 1 drop goal to 1 drop goal.

Wales were back to the form which had defeated England, yet the pitch was so bad that referee Frank Potter-Irwin said the match should not have been played. Skipper Harry Uzzell was the only survivor of the 'Terrible Eight'. Llanelli wing Bryn Williams, wounded in the First World War, scored three tries in his final international appearance. Ireland's captain was Cardiff doctor Tom Wallace and wing Basil McFarland, who was later knighted, scored his only international points with a drop goal.

Wales J. Rees (Swansea); W.J. Powell (Cardiff), J.P. 'Jack' Jones (Pontypool), A.E. Jenkins, B. Williams (Llanelli); J.J. Wetter (Newport), F.C. Reeves (Cross Keys); J.L. Williams (Blaina), S. Morris (Cross Keys), G. Oliver (Pontypool), +H. Uzzell, J.J. Whitfield (Newport), R. Huxtable, E.T. Parker (Swansea), *D.E. Morgan (Llanelli).
T: Bryn Williams 3, Albert Jenkins, Jack Whitfield, Tom Parker.
C: Jenkins 2, Jack Wetter.
DG: Jenkins.

Ireland W.E. Crawford (Lansdowne); J.A.N. Dickson (Dublin U), +T. Wallace (Cardiff), W. Duggan (UCC), B.A.T. McFarland (Derry); W. Cunningham (Lansdowne), A.K. Horan (Blackheath); M.J. Bradley (Dolphin), H.H. Coulter, A.W. Courtney, J.E. Finlay (QUB), R.Y. Crichton (Dublin U), W.D. Doherty (Guy's Hosp.), H.N. Potterton (Wanderers), P.J. Stokes (Garryowen).
DG: Basil McFarland.
Referee: Frank C. Potter-Irwin (England).

FIVE NATIONS — IRELAND

Wales triumphed by 28–4 over Ireland at Cardiff Arms Park on 13 March 1920. Llanelli wing Bryn Williams scored three of the six Welsh tries. *Back row*: T. Schofield (touch-judge), R. Huxtable, S. Morris, J. Williams, E. Morgan, G. Oliver, T. Parker, F.C. Potter-Irwin (referee). *Seated*: A. Jenkins, J. Whitfield, H. Uzzell (capt.), J.P. Jones, W.J. Powell. *Front row*: B. Williams, J. Rees, F. Reeves, J. Wetter.

Ireland 0   Wales 6

Balmoral, Belfast. 12 March 1921

Wales won by 1 try, 1 pen to nil.

Medical student Melbourne Thomas scored the only try by handing off Ireland full-back Ernie Crawford so strongly that Crawford had to have stitches in his jaw. The try and Tommy Johnson's penalty came in the last five minutes of a match that Wales worked hard to win. There were the usual withdrawals for the trip, because of the Troubles in Ireland. This led to the only appearances of policeman Fred Prosser and electrician Archie Brown. The latter, plus another new cap, Ambrose Baker, later moved to rugby league.

Ireland W.E. Crawford (Lansdowne); D.J. Cussen (Dublin U), A.R. Foster (Derry), G.V. Stephenson (QUB), H.S.T. Cormac (Clontarf); W. Cunningham (Lansdowne), H.W. Jack (UCC); J.J. Bermingham (Blackrock Coll), W.P. Collopy (Bective), A.W. Courtney (UCD), +W.D. Doherty (Guy's Hosp.), C.F. Hallaran (Utd Servs), T.A. McClelland (QUB), N.M. Purcell (Lansdowne), J.K.S. Thompson (Dublin U).

Wales J. Rees (Swansea); T.A.W. Johnson (Cardiff), H.G. Davies (Llanelli), *D.H. 'Daph' Davies (Bridgend), B.M.G. Thomas (St Bart's Hosp./Ogmore Vale); J.M.C. Lewis (Cardiff), *A. Brown (Newport); J.L. Williams (Blaina), W.G.H. Morris (Abertillery), S. Winmill (Cross Keys), +E.T. Parker (Swansea), *A. Baker (Neath), T. Roberts (Risca), J. Jones (Aberavon), *F.J. Prosser (Cardiff).

T: Melbourne Thomas.
P: Tom Johnson.
Referee: James M. Tennent (Scotland).

Wales 11   Ireland 5

St Helen's, Swansea. 11 March 1922

Wales won by 3 tries, 1 con to 1 try, 1 con.

Once again it was Tom Parker and his pack who won the day, with Jack Whitfield scoring two tries, but the Welsh backs were sluggish. Islwyn Evans bagged the third try for a side which had remained unchanged

109

after the draw in Edinburgh. It was the eighth cap for Ireland centre George Stephenson and the seventh loss, though it was his first international appearance in Wales. He went on to win 42 caps from 1920 until 1930.

Wales T.F. Samuel (Mountain Ash); F.C. Palmer, H.I. Evans (Swansea), B.S. Evans (Llanelli), W.C. Richards (Pontypool); W.E. Bowen (Swansea), W.J. Delahay (Bridgend); +E.T. Parker (Swansea), J.J. Whitfield, T. Jones (Newport), S. Morris (Cross Keys), T. Roberts (Risca), Rev. J.G. Stephens (Llanelli), W. Cummins (Treorchy), D.D. Hiddlestone (Neath).
T: Jack Whitfield 2, Islwyn Evans.
C: Fred Samuel.

Ireland B.A.T. McFarland (Derry); T.G. Wallis (Wanderers), D.B. Sullivan (UCD), G.V. Stephenson (QUB), H.W.V. Stephenson (Utd Servs); J.R. Wheeler (QUB), J.A. Clarke (Bective); J.C. Gillespie (Dublin U), M.J. Bradley (Dolphin), C.F. Hallaran (Utd Servs), +W.P. Collopy (Bective), S. McVicker, T.A. McClelland (QUB), I. Popham (Cork Const), P. Stokes (Garryowen).
T: Pat Stokes.
C: Tommy Wallis.
Referee: J.C. Sturrock (Scotland).

Ireland 5 Wales 4

Lansdowne Road, Dublin. 10 March 1923

Ireland won by 1 try, 1 con to 1 drop goal.

Several Welsh players refused to travel with the Troubles in Ireland and six new caps were brought in, though none of them ever played again. One of them, Jack Powell, younger brother of Wickham, dropped a left-foot goal, but Wales failed to score a try against Ireland for the first time since 1899. Snipers were found to be operating from a roof near the Welsh team hotel. Bill Radford was to drown tragically in Newport Docks just ten months later, while Tom Collins never received his cap as he signed for Hull RL six months after this match.

Ireland W.E. Crawford (Lansdowne); D.J. Cussen (Dublin U), G.V. Stephenson (QUB), J.B. Gardiner (NIFC), R.O. McClenahan; W.H. Hall (Instonians), W. Cunningham (Lansdowne); M.J. Bradley (Dolphin), R. Collopy, W.P. Collopy (Bective), D.M. Cunningham (NIFC), T.A. McClelland (QUB), +J.K.S. Thompson, R.Y. Crichton, J.D. Clinch (Dublin U).
T: Denis Cussen.
C: Ernie Crawford.

Wales J. Rees; W.R. Harding (Swansea), +A.E. Jenkins (Llanelli), *T. Collins (Mountain Ash), *J. Powell (Cardiff); Dai E. John (Llanelli), W.J. Delahay (Bridgend); *H.S. Davies (Treherbert), S.G. Thomas (Llanelli), A. Baker (Neath), S. Morris (Cross Keys), D. Pascoe (Bridgend), *J.H. Davies (Aberavon), *T.L. Richards (Maesteg), *W.J. Radford (Newport).
DG: Jack Powell.
Referee: James M. Tennent (Scotland).

Wales 10 Ireland 13

Arms Park, Cardiff. 8 March 1924

Ireland won by 3 tries, 2 cons to 2 tries, 1 drop goal.

Tom and Frank Hewitt became the first brothers to score on their débuts in the same match, as Ireland gained their first win over Wales for 25 years. Frank, aged 17, was the youngest man to play for Ireland and still at school, while Tom was four days short of his 19th birthday. A third brother, Victor, was capped 11 years later. The Prince of Wales and Duke of York were among the 35,000 crowd watching in ideal conditions. Welsh captain Jack Wetter was 34 years old. His side might have won but for a superb tackle by Henry Stephenson on Rowe Harding. For the second successive year Wales had lost to the other three home countries. Six more newcomers were in the Welsh lineup, including John Gore, who turned to league, and the one-cap pair, Tommy Evans and Bill Jones, the latter later having '71 Lions coach Carwyn James as a pupil of his at Cefneithin School. Dai Parker was the brother of Tom Parker, who had been capped from 1919 until 1923. That night, 'Candy' Evans went across to Queen Street and won both the semi-final and final of the Welsh Amateur Heavyweight Boxing championship. He was later to turn professional at boxing, rugby and also as a gambler – this last profession ruined him and he committed suicide in 1952.

Wales B.O. Male (Cardiff); W.C. Richards (Pontypool), +J.J. Wetter (Newport), *T.D. Evans, W.R. Harding (Swansea); V.M. Griffiths (Newport), E. Watkins (Neath); *D.S. Parker (Swansea), *G.F. Hathway, J.J. Whitfield (Newport), A. 'Candy' Evans (Pontypool), *R.J. Randall (Aberavon), *W.J. Jones (Llanelli), *J.H. Gore (Blaina), C.H. Pugh (Maesteg).
T: Cliff Richards, Charlie Pugh.
DG: Eddie Watkins.

Ireland +W.E. Crawford (Lansdowne); T. Hewitt,

G.V. Stephenson (QUB), J.B. Gardiner (NIFC), H.W.V. Stephenson (Utd Servs); F.S. Hewitt (Instonians), J.A. Clarke (Bective); C.F. Hallaran (Utd Servs), W.P. Collopy, R. Collopy (Bective), R.Y. Crichton, T.A. McClelland (QUB), J.M. McVicker (Belfast Collegians), W.R.F. Collis (Wanderers), J.D. Clinch (Dublin U).
T: Tom Hewitt, Frank Hewitt, George Stephenson.
C: Ernie Crawford 2.
Referee: J.T. Tulloch (Scotland).

Ireland 19 Wales 3

Ravenhill, Belfast. 14 March 1925

Ireland won by 4 tries, 2 cons, 1 pen to 1 try.

Idris Jones was appointed as the sixth captain in as many matches and was never picked again after this decisive loss. The selectors switched the versatile Bobby Delahay from scrum-half to outside-half. Five more new caps were brought in, of whom Cardiff forwards Syd Hinam and Jim Brown were to turn professional, while one of the six Turnbull brothers who played for Cardiff, Bernard, aged 20, scored a début try. Full-back Nathan Rocyn Jones played in his only international, but became both the president and honorary medical officer of the WRU. Wales had Cross Keys forward Ron Herrera injured early on and he was finally forced to retire from the field.

Ireland +W.E. Crawford (Lansdowne); H.W.V. Stephenson (Utd Servs), T.J. Millin (Dublin U), J.B. Gardiner (NIFC), G.V. Stephenson (QUB); E.O'D. Davy (Lansdowne), M. Sugden (Dublin U); G.R. Beamish (Coleraine), M.J. Bradley (Dolphin), W.F. Browne (Utd Servs), S.J. Cagney (London Irish), R. Collopy (Bective), D.M. Cunningham (NIFC), R. Flood (Dublin U), J.C. McVicker (Belfast Collegians).
T: Terry Millin, George Stephenson, Horsey Browne, Harry Stephenson.
C: George Stephenson 2.
P: George Stephenson.

Wales *D.N. Rocyn Jones (St Mary's Hosp./Newport); W.R. Harding (Swansea), *B.R. Turnbull (Cardiff), D.H. 'Daph' Davies (Bridgend), E. Finch (Llanelli); W.J. Delahay (Cardiff), *D. Arthur John (Llanelli); D.S. Parker (Swansea), +W.I. Jones (Llanelli), S.D. Lawrence (Bridgend), R.C. Herrera (Cross Keys), *J. Brown, *S. Hinam (Cardiff), B. Phillips (Aberavon), G.E. Beynon (Swansea).
T: Bernard Turnbull.
Referee: James W. Baxter (England).

Wales 11 Ireland 8

St Helen's, Swansea. 13 March 1926

Wales won by 3 tries, 1 con to 1 try, 1 con, 1 pen.

This was the first win by Wales over any of the home countries for four years, following ten defeats and a draw. It prevented Ireland winning the Triple Crown. Tom Hewitt's late drop shot failed and many of the 55,000 crowd stormed on to the pitch at the finish in delight and relief. Ireland had led 8–3 at the interval, but the 19-year-old Windsor Lewis, making his début at outside-half with Wick Powell moving to his club position of scrum-half, conjured up two more Welsh tries for the victory. Tommy 'Guardsman' Rees from Pontyclun had a good début at full-back, but was to 'go north' in 1928.

Wales *T.E. Rees (Army); *C.F. Rowlands (Aberavon), R.A. Cornish, W.J. Delahay (Cardiff), +W.R. Harding (Swansea); *W.H. Lewis, W.C. Powell (London Welsh); D. Jones (Newport), J.H. John (Swansea), S.D. Lawrence (Bridgend), S. Hinam (Cardiff), R.C. Herrera (Cross Keys), T. Hopkins (Swansea), D.M. Jenkins (Treorchy), Emlyn Watkins (Blaina).
T: Rowe Harding, Tom Hopkins, Ron Herrera.
C: Tommy Rees.

Ireland +W.E. Crawford (Lansdowne); D.J. Cussen (Dublin U), G.V. Stephenson, T.R. Hewitt, J.H. Gage (QUB); E.O'D. Davy (Lansdowne), M. Sugden (Dublin U); M.J. Bradley (Dolphin), A.M. Buchanan (Dublin U), W.F. Browne (Utd Servs), S.J. Cagney (London Irish), J. McVicker (Belfast Collegians), J.L. Farrell (Bective), C.J. Hanrahan (Dolphin), J.D. Clinch (Wanderers).
T: Charles Hanrahan.
C: George Stephenson.
P: Stephenson.
Referee: Barry S. Cumberlege (England).

Ireland 19 Wales 9

Lansdowne Road, Dublin. 12 March 1927

Ireland won by 4 tries, 2 cons, 1 pen to 1 try, 1 con, 1 drop goal.

Wales took the Wooden Spoon for the fourth time in five seasons despite Ireland losing hooker Allan Buchanan with injury just before half-time. Wick Powell led Wales for the second successive game – the first man to do so since Clem Lewis 19 games back in 1923.

Ireland +W.E. Crawford (Lansdowne); J.H. Gage (QUB), G.V. Stephenson (NIFC), F.S. Hewitt (Instonians), J.B. Ganly (Monkstown); E.O'D. Davy (Lansdowne), M. Sugden (Wanderers); C.J. Hanrahan, M.J. Bradley (Dolphin), T.O. Pike (Lansdowne), A.M. Buchanan (Dublin U), H. McVicker (Richmond), J.L. Farrell (Bective), J. McVicker (Belfast Collegians), W.F. Browne (Army).
T: George Stephenson 2, Jim Ganly 2.
C: Stephenson 2.
P: Stephenson.

Wales B.O. Male (Cardiff); G.E. Andrews (Newport), W.G. Morgan (Cambridge U), J. Roberts (Cardiff), W.R. Harding (Swansea); W.H. Lewis (Maesteg), +W.C. Powell (London Welsh); T. Arthur (Neath), J.H. John (Swansea), J.J. Burns (Cardiff), E.M. Jenkins (Aberavon), H.T. Phillips (Newport), W.A. Williams (Crumlin), W.G. Thomas, Ivor E. Jones (Llanelli).
T: Guy Morgan.
C: Wick Powell.
DG: Windsor Lewis.
Referee: Barry S. Cumberlege (England).

Wales 10 Ireland 13

Arms Park, Cardiff. 10 March 1928

Ireland won by 3 tries, 2 cons to 2 tries, 2 cons.

Llanelli had seven players in the side. However, all four backs, including the great Albert Jenkins, were sacked after this defeat. From a high in Murrayfield, Wales were a great disappointment. Right-wing John Bartlett withdrew with a thigh injury. Ernie Finch was on his way with Llanelli to play at Gloucester, but he was called off the train as it passed through Cardiff – this was the only change from the Scotland match. Outside-half Dai John created a piece of history when he scored a try for the third successive match – a feat never ever again recorded by a Welsh international in that position. His reward was to never be selected again!

Wales B.O. Male (Cardiff); W.C. Powell (London Welsh), J. Roberts (Cardiff), +A.E. Jenkins, E. Finch; Dai E. John, D. Arthur John (Llanelli); H.T. Phillips (Newport), Cecil C. Pritchard (Pontypool), F.A. Bowdler (Cross Keys), E.M. Jenkins (Aberavon), A. Skym, T. Iorwerth Jones (Llanelli), T.H. Hollingdale (Neath), I.E. Jones (Llanelli).
T: Dai John, Albert Jenkins.
C: Ivor Jones 2.

Ireland W.J. Stewart (NIFC); J.E. Arigho (Lansdowne), J.B. Ganly (Monkstown), +G.V. Stephenson, R.M. Byers (NIFC); E.O'D. Davy (Lansdowne), M. Sugden (Wanderers); J. McVicker (Belfast Collegians), C.T. Payne (NIFC), T.O. Pike (Lansdowne), G.R. Beamish (Leicester), J.L. Farrell (Bective), J.P. Mullane (Limerick Bohemians), S.J. Cagney (London Irish), J.D. Clinch (Wanderers).
T: Jack Arigho 2, Jim Ganly.
C: George Stephenson 2.
Referee: T.H.H. Warren (Scotland).

Ireland 5 Wales 5

Ravenhill, Belfast. 9 March 1929

Draw. 1 try, 1 con each.

Scotland gained the title by defeating England a week after this draw, in which Ireland's George Stephenson missed a last-minute penalty shot after 'Lonza' Bowdler had been penalised for off-side. Guy Morgan was to skipper Wales on four occasions, winning the other three. The backs were beginning to have a more solid look about them and the pack was bolstered by the inclusion of Arthur Lemon who played 13 times before joining St Helen's RL in 1933.

Ireland W.J. Stewart; R.M. Byers, +G.V. Stephenson (NIFC), M.P. Crowe, J.E. Arigho; E.O'D. Davy (Lansdowne), M. Sugden (Wanderers); H.C. Browne (Utd Servs), C.T. Payne (NIFC), J.L. Farrell, M. Deering (Bective), C.J. Hanrahan (Dolphin), S.J. Cagney (London Irish), G.R. Beamish (RAF), J.D. Clinch (Wanderers).
T: Eugene Davy.
C: George Stephenson.

Wales J.A. Bassett (Penarth); J. Roberts, H.M. Bowcott (Cardiff), +W.G. Morgan (Swansea), J.C. Morley (Newport); F.L. Williams (Cardiff), W.C. Powell (London Welsh); F.A. Bowdler (Cross Keys), Cecil C. Pritchard (Pontypool), D.S. Parker (Swansea), T. Arthur (Neath), R.J. Barrell (Cardiff), *A.W. Lemon (Neath), H. Peacock (Newport), I.E. Jones (Llanelli).
T: Frank Williams.
C: Dai Parker.
Referee: J. McGill (Scotland).

Wales 12 Ireland 7

St Helen's, Swansea. 8 March 1930

Wales won by 3 tries, 1 pen to 1 pen, 1 drop goal.

A magnificent performance by full-back Jack Bassett

helped Wales gain a hard-fought success. The new skipper was superb as last line of defence, reserving his best tackle for Irish centre Eugene Davy who had opened the score with a 2nd-minute drop goal. Archie Skym put Wales ahead with a brilliant solo try, and then forwards Howie Jones and Harry Peacock dived simultaneously for the only joint try in international history. Ireland led 7–6 at the interval after a Paul Murray penalty before a Jack Bassett penalty put Wales back in front. Another forward try, this time by Tom Arthur, settled it. Ireland captain George Stephenson played in the last of his record 42 appearances. New cap Norman Fender of Cardiff became an outstanding rugby league player and Howie Jones followed his father, Howell, who won a cap in 1904.

Wales +J.A. Bassett (Penarth); J.C. Morley (Newport), T.E. Jones-Davies (London Welsh), W.G. Morgan (Guy's Hosp.), *E. Howie Jones (Swansea); F.L. Williams (Cardiff), W.C. Powell (London Welsh); T. Arthur (Neath), H.C. Day (Newport), E.M. Jenkins (Aberavon), A. Skym (Cardiff), D.J. Thomas (Swansea), A.W. Lemon (Neath), H. Peacock (Newport), *N.H. Fender (Cardiff).
T: Archie Skym, Tom Arthur. **Joint T**: Howie Jones/Harry Peacock.
P: Jack Bassett.

Ireland W.F. Williamson (Dolphin); +G.V. Stephenson (London Hosp.), E.O'D. Davy, M.P. Crowe, J.E. Arigho (Lansdowne); P.F. Murray, M. Sugden (Wanderers); H. O'Neill (QUB), C.J. Hanrahan (Dolphin), C.Y. Payne (NIFC), M.J. Dunne (Lansdowne), J.L. Farrell (Bective), N.F. Murphy (Cork Const), G.R. Beamish (Leicester), J.D. Clinch (Lansdowne).
P: Paul Murray.
DG: Eugene Davy.
Referee: D. Hellewell (England).

Ireland 3 Wales 15

Ravenhill, Belfast. 14 March 1931

Wales won by 3 tries, 1 con, 1 drop goal to 1 try.

The lean years appeared to be ending, as Wales took the championship for the first time since 1922. The win was due to a strong defence, marshalled by Jack Bassett and Claude Davey, as Ireland, even after centre Morgan Crowe retired with concussion, kept charging at the Welsh line. In one move, wing Jack Arigho was tackled by Bassett as he unloaded to Noel Murphy who was hit by Davey. Both Irish players were knocked unconscious! Big Jack Siggins, who was to manage the 1955 British Lions, was the only player to defeat the Welsh tacklers and the Irish line was breached on three occasions – twice by the superb 21-year-old Newport wing Jack Morley.

Ireland D.P. Morris (Bective); E.J. Lightfoot, E.O'D. Davy, M.P. Crowe, J.E. Arigho (Lansdowne); P.F. Murray, +M. Sugden (Wanderers); H.H.C. Withers (NIFC), J. Russell (UCC), J.A.E. Siggins (Belfast Collegians), V.J. Pike (Lansdowne), J.L. Farrell (Bective), N. Murphy (Cork Const), G.R. Beamish (RAF), J.D. Clinch (Wanderers).
T: Jack Siggins.

Wales +J.A. Bassett (Penarth); J.C. Morley (Newport), E.C. Davey (Swansea), F.L. Williams, R.W. Boon (Cardiff); A.R. Ralph (Newport), W.C. Powell (London Welsh); A. Skym (Cardiff), T.B. Day (Swansea), D.R. James (Treorchy), T. Arthur (Neath), E.M. Jenkins (Aberavon), A.W. Lemon (Neath), J. Lang (Llanelli), N.H. Fender (Cardiff).
T: Jack Morley 2, Claude Davey.
C: Jack Bassett.
DG: Raymond Ralph.
Referee: Malcolm A. Allan (Scotland).

Wales 10 Ireland 12

Arms Park, Cardiff. 12 March 1932

Ireland won by 4 tries to 2 tries, 1 drop goal.

Once again the Triple Crown was at stake, but Wales, who had not won it for 21 years, were to be denied by Ireland. It was a sad farewell to international rugby for full-back and captain Jack Bassett. He dropped the ball after Eugene Davy had missed with a drop shot and Ned Lightfoot was left with an easy try. He then allowed Shaun Waide to swerve past him to score the final Irish try after a 90-yard run. Waide had gathered the ball only after Jack Morley had dropped it, when the Newport wing seemed set to score at the other end! Wales still almost drew level when Dicky Ralph jinked over, but Bassett's conversion attempt with the last kick of the match was nowhere near. It was a miserable end to the career of one of the best full-backs ever to play for Wales.

Wales +J.A. Bassett (Penarth); J.C. Morley (Newport), E.C. Davey (Swansea), F.L. Williams, R.W. Boon (Cardiff); A.R. Ralph (Newport), W.C. Powell (London Welsh); A. Skym (Cardiff), F.A. Bowdler (Cross Keys), T.B. Day, D.J. Thomas (Swansea), E.M. Jenkins (Aberavon), W. Davies, W.G. Thomas (Swansea), A.W. Lemon (Neath)
T: Claude Davey, Raymond Ralph.
DG: Ralph.

Ireland E.C. Ridgeway (Wanderers); E.J. Lightfoot, M.P. Crowe (Lansdowne), E.W.F. de Vere Hunt, S.L. Waide (Army); E.O'D. Davy (Lansdowne), P. Murray (Wanderers); J.L. Farrell (Bective), C.J. Hanrahan (Dolphin), V.J. Pike, M.J. Dunne (Lansdowne), J.A.E. Siggins (Belfast Collegians), W.McC. Ross (QUB), +G.R. Beamish (RAF), N. Murphy (Cork Const).
T: MacRoss 2, Ned Lightfoot, Shaun Waide.
Referee: E. Holmes (England).

Ireland 10 Wales 5

Ravenhill, Belfast. 11 March 1933

Ireland won by 1 try, 1 pen, 1 drop goal to 1 try, 1 con.

Another defeat saw Watcyn Thomas disappear forever from the international scene, after disagreeing with the 'Big Five' on pack selection. The one bright spot was a truly magnificent try by outside-half Harry Bowcott, which the immaculate Viv Jenkins converted. The two new caps in the pack, Lewis Rees and Billy Moore, were both soon to switch to rugby league.

Ireland R.H. Pratt (Dublin U); E.J. Lightfoot, M.P. Crowe (Lansdowne), R.J. Barnes (Dublin U), S.L. Waide (NIFC); E.O'D. Davy (Lansdowne), P.F. Murray (Wanderers); M.J. Dunne, V.J. Pike (Lansdowne), H. O'Neill, J. Russell (UCC), J.A.E. Siggins (Belfast Collegians), C.E.StJ. Beamish (NIFC), +G.R. Beamish (Leicester), W. McC. Ross (QUB).
T: Bob Barnes.
P: Jack Siggins.
DG: Eugene Davy.

Wales V.G.J. Jenkins (Bridgend); W. Wooller (Rydal School/Colwyn Bay), F.L. Williams, G. Graham Jones (Cardiff), R.W. Boon (Cardiff); H.M. Bowcott (London Welsh), M.J.L. Turnbull (Cardiff); E.L. Jones (Llanelli), F.A. Bowdler (Cross Keys), A. Skym (Cardiff), *W.J. Moore (Bridgend), R.J. Barrell, *L.M. Rees (Cardiff), +W.G. Thomas (Swansea), A.W. Lemon (Neath).
T: Harry Bowcott.
C: Viv Jenkins.
Referee: Malcolm A. Allan (Scotland).

Wales 13 Ireland 0

St Helen's, Swansea. 10 March 1934

Wales won by 3 tries, 2 cons to nil.

The first-ever try by a Welsh full-back broke 74 minutes of deadlock and opened the door to a Welsh victory. Vivian Jenkins raced over but it was to be 33 years before the feat was repeated – when Keith Jarrett did it against England at Cardiff on his début in 1967. Ireland lost full-back Dan Langan with a broken collar-bone in the closing stages of his only international appearance. The defence cracked as the diligent Albert Fear was on hand for the second try and 'Bunny' Cowey scored the third after superb running by Cliff Jones. Wing Arthur Bassett followed his elder brother Jack into the Wales backs. He joined Halifax RL some five years afterwards.

Wales V.G.J. Jenkins (Bridgend); B.T.V. Cowey (Newport/Welsh Regt), +E.C. Davey, J. Idwal Rees (Swansea), *A. Bassett (Aberavon); C.W. Jones (Cambridge U), W.H. 'Bert' Jones (Llanelli); T.B. Day (Swansea), I. Evans (London Welsh), D.R. Prosser (Neath), G. Hughes (Penarth), W.S. Ward (Cross Keys), I.G. Prosser (Neath), J. Lang (Llanelli), A.G. Fear (Newport).
T: Albert Fear, Bernard Cowey, Viv Jenkins.
C: Jenkins 2.

Ireland D.J. Langan (Clontarf); D. Lane (UCC), N.H. Lambert, A.H. Bailey (Lansdowne), J.J. O'Connor (UCC); J.L. Reid (Richmond), G.J. Morgan (Clontarf); N.F. McGrath (London Irish), V.J. Pike (Aldershot Servs), J. Megaw (Instonians), +J.A.E. Siggins (Belfast Collegians), J. Russell (UCC), C.R. Graves (Wanderers), M.J. Dunne (Lansdowne), C.E.StJ. Beamish (RAF).
Referee: W.A. Burnett (Scotland).

Ireland 9 Wales 3

Ravenhill, Belfast. 9 March 1935

Ireland won by 1 try, 2 pens to 1 pen.

Ireland won the championship for the first time since 1899, despite losing wing Joe O'Connor with a broken collar bone after colliding with Wilfred Wooller early on. The Aberavon captain Tommy James, who scored the only Welsh points with a penalty shot, was capped ten years after his brother Will had played on the wing.

Ireland D.P. Morris (Bective); J.J. O'Connor, A.H. Bailey (UCD), E.C. Ridgeway (Wanderers), J.I. Doyle (Bective); V.A. Hewitt (Instonians), G.J. Morgan (Clontarf); C.E.StJ. Beamish (RAF), C.R. Graves (Wanderers), S. Walker (Instonians), J. Russell (UCC), S.J. Deering (Bective), H.J.M. Sayers (Aldershot Servs), +J.A.E. Siggins (Belfast Collegians), P.J. Lawlor (Bective).

T: Jack Doyle.
P: Jack Siggins, Aidan Bailey.

Wales *T.O. James (Aberavon); G.R. Rees-Jones (Oxford U), +E.C. Davey (Swansea), W. Wooller (Cambridge U), A. Bassett (Aberavon); C.W. Jones (Cambridge U), W.C. Powell (Northampton); T.J. Rees (Newport), C.D. Murphy (Cross Keys), T.B. Day, D.J. Thomas (Swansea), T.G. Williams (Cross Keys), A.M. Rees (Cambridge U), J. Lang (Llanelli), A.G. Fear (Newport).
P: Tommy James.
Referee: Malcolm A. Allan (Scotland).

Wales 3   Ireland 0

Arms Park, Cardiff. 14 March 1936

Wales won by 1 pen to nil.

Westgate Street was overrun by fans who rushed the gates which had been closed two hours before kick-off. Police were overwhelmed so the fire brigade was called from the station just opposite the ground. They hosed the crowd, after having already cleared water off the pitch. The ground capacity was broken and it was probably close to 70,000 who entered, standing all around the touchlines very much as had happened in the 1923 FA Cup final at Wembley. Referee Cyril Gadney had great trouble getting in. 'We've had three referees here already!' said a steward. Ireland were going for their first Triple Crown in 37 years, while for Wales a win would have given them the championship. It was not a great game and a Vivian Jenkins penalty was the only score, coming after 20 minutes when Michael Sayers was penalised for not playing the ball after a tackle. In the closing minutes Victor Hewitt had a chance to win the match with a four-point drop goal, but the wind took the ball outside the posts. The 19-year-old Swansea outside-half, Willie Davies, was chosen at centre after Claude Davey had withdrawn with a leg injury. Davies, the cousin of Haydn Tanner, switched successfully to Bradford Northen RL in 1939.

Wales V.G.J. Jenkins (London Welsh); +J. Idwal Rees, *W.T.H. Davies (Swansea), W. Wooller (Cambridge U), B.E.W. McCall (Welsh Regt/Newport); C.W. Jones (Cambridge U), H. Tanner (Swansea); T.J. Rees (Newport), B. Evans (Llanelli), T.G. Williams (Cross Keys), H.W. Thomas (Neath), G.M. Williams (Aberavon), A.M. Rees (London Welsh), J. Lang (Llanelli), E.C. Long (Swansea).
P: Viv Jenkins.

Ireland G.L. Malcolmson (NIFC); C.V. Boyle (Dublin U), A.H. Bailey, L.B. McMahon (UCD), J.J. O'Connor (UCC); V.A. Hewitt (Instonians), G.J. Morgan (Clontarf); S. Walker (Instonians), C.R. Graves (Wanderers), C.E.St.J. Beamish (NIFC), J. Russell (UCC), S.J. Deering (Bective), H.J.M. Sayers (Lansdowne), +J.A.E. Siggins (Belfast Collegians), R. Alexander (NIFC).
Referee: Cyril H. Gadney (England).

Ireland 5   Wales 3

Ravenhill, Belfast. 3 April 1937

Ireland won by 1 try, 1 con to 1 pen.

This game is always remembered for the men who did not play. The Cardiff pair of full-back Tommy Stone and centre Horace Edwards, along with forward Charles Anderson of Maesteg, were picked to play in place of the injured Viv Jenkins, Claude Davey and Trevor Williams on 13 March. But snow caused a three-week delay and all three had recovered. Stone turned professional, seemingly disgusted. Wales led with a penalty by new cap Walter Legge, but Ireland equalised with a try four minutes after the interval as Wales halted, expecting the whistle. Jack Siggins gathered to send centre Aidan Bailey in to score. Surprisingly, it was forward Sammy Walker who kicked the goal. He skippered the British team on tour a year later. New cap Russell Taylor also made that trip and was top scorer. Ivor Bennett won his cap before joining Warrington RL four months later. He was not granted his cap until 1977.

Ireland G.L. Malcolmson (NIFC); F.G. Moran (Clontarf), L.B. McMahon, A.H. Bailey (UCD), C.V. Boyle (Dublin U); G.E. Cromey (QUB), +G.J. Morgan (Clontarf); E. Ryan (Dolphin), T.S. Corken (Belfast Collegians), S. Walker (Instonians), C.J. Reidy (London Irish), R.B. Mayne (QUB), P.J. Lawlor (Bective), J.A.E. Siggins (Belfast Collegians), R. Alexander (Royal Ulster Const).
T: Aidan Bailey.
C: Sammy Walker.

Wales *W.S.G. Legge (Newport); J. Idwal Rees (Swansea), E.C. Davey (London Welsh), +W. Wooller (Cardiff), W.H. Clement (Llanelli); W.T.H. Davies, H. Tanner (Swansea); T.G. Williams (Cross Keys), W. Travers (Newport), *I. Bennett (Aberavon), H.W. Thomas (Neath), H.T. Rees (Cardiff), *A.R. Taylor (Cross Keys), E.V. Watkins (Cardiff), A.M. Rees (London Welsh).
P: Walter Legge.
Referee: Malcolm A. Allan (Scotland).

Wales defeated Ireland by 11–5 in 1938. It was the last international match played at the St Helen's Ground, Swansea before the Second World War. It was also the last game the mercurial Cliff Jones played for his country. *Back row*: R.A. Cornish (touch-judge), E.C. Davey, W.H. Travers, A.R. Taylor, M.E. Morgan, W. Vickery, W. Wooller, J.C.H. Ireland (referee). *Seated*: F.L. Morgan, J.I. Rees, E. Watkins, C.W. Jones (capt.), H. Rees, A. McCarley, W.H. Clement. *Front row*: H. Tanner, W.G. Legge.

Wales 11   Ireland 5

St Helen's, Swansea. 12 March 1938

Wales won by 2 tries, 1 con, 1 pen to 1 try, 1 con.

Cliff Jones, aged 24, played his last game for Wales. Wales scored two tries and were attacking when a superb tackle by Harry McKibbin on Wilfred Wooller saw the Irish 100-yards champion George Moran tear in past Jones, Bill Clement and Walter Legge and score between the Welsh posts. Ireland lost fly-half George Cromey with concussion. New cap Des Torrens moved up from centre with Des O'Loughlin coming out of the pack.

Wales W.S.G. Legge (Newport); J. Idwal Rees (Swansea), E.C. Davey (London Welsh), W. Wooller (Cardiff), W.H. Clement (Llanelli); +C.W. Jones (Cardiff), H. Tanner; M.E. Morgan (Swansea), W. Travers (Newport), H.T. Rees, E.V. Watkins (Cardiff), F.L. Morgan (Llanelli), A.R. Taylor (Cross Keys), W.E. Vickery (Aberavon), A. McCarley (Swansea).
T: Russell Taylor, Bill Clement.
C: Walter Legge.
P: Wilf Wooller.

Ireland R.G. Craig (QUB); F.G. Moran (Clontarf), H.R. McKibbin (QUB), J.D. Torrens (Bohemians), C.V. Boyle (Dublin U); G.E. Cromey (QUB), G.J. Morgan (Old Belvedere); H. Kennedy (Bradford), C.R.A. Graves (Wanderers), C.E.StJ. Beamish (RAF), D. Tierney (UCC), R.B. Mayne (QUB), D. O'Loughlin (UCC), +S. Walker (Instonians), H.J.M. Sayers (Army).
T: Fred Moran.
C: Harry McKibbin.
Referee: James C.H. Ireland (Scotland).

Ireland 0   Wales 7

Ravenhill, Belfast. 11 March 1939

Wales won by 1 try, 1 drop goal to nil.

Again Wales denied Ireland the Triple Crown, as Willie Davies scored the only points in the last five minutes. He dropped a goal after receiving from his cousin, Haydn Tanner, and then scored a try against the run of

Wales won 6–0 and halted Ireland in their bid to gain the Triple Crown at Swansea in 1947. Newport police officer Bob Evans scored the only try after a classic break from skipper Haydn Tanner. *Back row*: R.A. Cornish (touch-judge), G. Evans, K.J. Jones, W.E. Tamplin, D. Jones, C. Davies, R.T. Evans, S. Williams, J.R.G. Stephens, J.B.G. Whittaker (referee). *Seated*: L. Williams, W. Gore, P. Rees, H. Tanner (capt.), B.L. Williams, C.H. Davies, W.B. Cleaver.

play. The drop goal was to prove the last one worth four points that was scored by Wales. This also proved to be the last Welsh international match before the Second World War, with Scotland and England meeting one week later at Murrayfield. Viv Law and Chris Matthews made their only appearances and took the tally of players capped by Wales to 529 in 179 matches.

Ireland C.J. Murphy (Lansdowne); F.G. Moran (Clontarf), H.R. McKibbin (Instonians), J.D. Torrens (Bohemians), C.V. Boyle (Lansdowne); G.E. Cromey (Belfast Collegians), +G.J. Morgan (Old Belvedere); T.A. Headon (UCD), C. Teehan (UCC), J.G. Ryan (UCD), R.B. Mayne (Malone), D. O'Loughlin (Garryowen), R. Alexander (RUC), J.W.S. Irwin (NIFC), H.J.M. Sayers (Aldershot Servs).

Wales C.H. Davies (Swansea); *C.M. Matthews (Bridgend), M.J. Davies (Oxford U), +W. Wooller (Cardiff), S.A. Williams (Aberavon); W.T.H. Davies, H. Tanner (Swansea); W.E.N. Davis (Cardiff), W. Travers (Newport), *V.J. Law (Newport), Leslie Davies (Swansea), E.R. Price (Weston), E. Evans (Llanelli), L. Manfield (Otley/Mountain Ash), E.C. Long (Swansea).
T: Willie Davies.
DG: Willie Davies.
Referee: James C.H. Ireland (Scotland).

Wales 6 Ireland 0

St Helen's, Swansea. 29 March 1947

Wales won by 1 try, 1 pen to nil.

Wales shared the championship with England, who had lost to Ireland in Dublin. In the Swansea mud, Ireland were again denied the Triple Crown. The winning try was a classic from a typical Haydn Tanner break, which Billy Cleaver carried on right up to fullback Jack Higgins before handing to the vigilant Bob Evans. The match had been postponed from 8 March because of a frozen ground and started late when the Irish team were held up in a traffic jam.

Wales C.H. Davies (Llanelli); K.J. Jones (Newport), B.L. Williams (Cardiff), W. Les T. Williams, P. Rees (Llanelli); W.B. Cleaver, +H. Tanner (Cardiff); D.C.J. Jones (Swansea), W. Gore (Newbridge), C. Davies, W.E. Tamplin (Cardiff), S. Williams (Llanelli), R.T. Evans (Newport), J.R.G. Stephens (Neath), G. Evans (Cardiff).
T: Bob Evans.
P: Bill Tamplin.

Ireland J.A.D. Higgins (Civil Serv); B.R. O'Hanlon (Dolphin), +J.D.E. Monteith (QUB), M.F.

Wales could not prevent Ireland taking the Triple Crown with a 5–0 win at Swansea in 1949 before a crowd of 40,000. It was the last home match for both skipper Haydn Tanner and hooker 'Bunner' Travers. *Back row*: (touch-judge), G. Evans, J.A. Gwilliam, E. Coleman, D. Jones, A. Meredith, W.R. Cale, T.N. Pearce (referee). *Seated*: T. Cook, J. Matthews, W.H. Travers, H. Tanner (capt.), B.L. Williams, J.R.G. Stephens, R.F. Trott. *Front row*: K.J. Jones, W.B. Cleaver.

Lane (UCC), B. Mullan (Clontarf); J.W. Kyle (NIFC), E. Strathdee (QUB); M.R. Neely (Belfast Collegians), K.D. Mullen (Old Belvedere), J.C. Daly (London Irish), C.P. Callan (Lansdowne), E. Keeffe (Sunday's Well), D.J. Hingerty (UCD), R.D. Agar (Malone), J.W. McKay (QUB).
Referee: J.B.G. Whittaker (England).

Ireland 6 Wales 3

Ravenhill, Belfast. 13 March 1948

Ireland won by 2 tries to 1 try.

Prop John Daly was carried off shoulder-high without his jersey, which had been torn to shreds after his try had given Ireland their first Triple Crown since 1899. The prop forward never appeared for Ireland again, as he joined Huddersfield RL later in the year. The brilliant Jackie Kyle orchestrated the win and it was he who sent Barney Mullan over for a try. A typical sidestepping run by Bleddyn Williams brought the scores level, before Daly chased a kick from a lineout after 47 minutes to become a national hero. The brilliant Irish back-row of Jimmy McCarthy, Des O'Brien and Bill McKay destroyed the Welsh back play. O'Brien later became a popular player with Cardiff.

Ireland J.A.D. Higgins (Civil Serv); B.R. O'Hanlon (Dolphin), W.D. McKee (NIFC), P.J. Reid (Garryowen), B. Mullan (Clontarf); J.W. Kyle (NIFC), E. Strathdee (QUB); A.A. McConnell (Belfast Collegians), +K.D. Mullen (Old Belvedere), J.C. Daly (London Irish), C.P. Callan (Lansdowne), J.E. Nelson (Malone), J.W. McKay (QUB), D.J. O'Brien (London Irish), J.S. McCarthy (Dolphin).
T: Barney Mullan, Jack Daly.

Wales R.F. Trott (Cardiff); K.J. Jones (Newport), B.L. Williams, W.B. Cleaver, W. Les T. Williams (Cardiff); G. Davies (Pontypridd), +H. Tanner (Cardiff); E.P. Davies (Aberavon), D.M. James, C. Davies (Cardiff), J.A. Gwilliam (Cambridge U), J.R.G. Stephens (Neath), O. Williams (Llanelli), L. Manfield, G. Evans (Cardiff).
T: Bleddyn Williams.
Referee: Malcolm A. Allan (Scotland).

Wales 0 Ireland 5

St Helen's, Swansea. 12 March 1949

Ireland won by 1 try, 1 con to nil.

Ireland thoroughly deserved to win the Triple Crown

for the second successive year and fourth time in their history. However, Welshmen disputed the winning score, thinking that the flying flanker Jim McCarthy could simply not be fast enough to be onside when he jumped and caught Jackie Kyle's kick from the blindside of a scrum across the field. But he was. It was the first win by Ireland at Swansea since 1889. Cardiff supplied six of the seven backs but Karl Mullen's pack held all the aces.

Wales R.F. Trott (Cardiff); K.J. Jones (Newport), J. Matthews, B.L. Williams, T.J. Cook; W.B. Cleaver, +H. Tanner (Cardiff); E.O. Coleman, W. Travers (Newport), D.C.J. Jones (Swansea), J.A. Gwilliam (Cambridge U), A. Meredith (Devonport Servs), W.R. Cale (Newbridge), J.R.G. Stephens (Neath), G. Evans (Cardiff).

Ireland G.W. Norton (Bective); M.F. Lane (UCC), W.D. McKee (NIFC), N.J. Henderson (QUB), B.R. O'Hanlon (Dolphin); J.W. Kyle, E. Strathdee (QUB); J.T. Clifford (Young Munster), +K.D. Mullen (Old Belvedere), L.J. Griffin (Wanderers), R.D. Agar, J.E. Nelson (Malone), J.W. McKay (QUB), D.J. O'Brien (London Irish), J.S. McCarthy (Dolphin).
T: Jim McCarthy.
C: George Norton.
Referee: Tom N. Pearce (England).

Ireland 3 Wales 6

Ravenhill, Belfast. 11 March 1950

Wales won by 2 tries to 1 pen.

Wales won their first Triple Crown for 39 years, but the winning try came with only three minutes remaining and even then after an anxious wait. Ireland's outside-half Jackie Kyle went to clear from a scrum; Ray Cale came at him and Ray Carroll's bad pass and the Welsh forward arrived together. The ball rolled loose and Billy Cleaver swiftly fed a flying Lewis Jones, who drew full-back George Norton and sent Malcolm Thomas, now on the wing, racing for the corner 15 yards away. Corner-flaggers galore arrived, as Thomas dived for the corner-flag. After agonising seconds, referee Beattie raised his arm and the try was given. It was due to the honesty of Irish touch-judge Ossie Glasgow who signalled that Thomas had not knocked the flag down before grounding the ball. The opening try in the 47th minute by Ken Jones from a Jack Matthews pass was cancelled out by Norton's penalty ten minutes later. Ireland almost scored, when Jimmy McCarthy was beaten to the ball by the watchful Billy Cleaver over the Welsh line. On the following morning, a Tudor V aircraft crashed at Llandow, near Cowbridge, in the Vale of Glamorgan. Eighty Welsh supporters died and only three survived in the worst civil air disaster in history to that time.

Ireland G.W. Norton (Bective); M.F. Lane (UCC), R.J.H. Uprichard (RAF), G.C. Phipps (Rosslyn Park), L. Crowe (Old Belvedere); J.W. Kyle (QUB), R. Carroll (Lansdowne); J.T. Clifford (Young Munster), +K.D. Mullen (Old Belvedere), D. McKibbin (QUB), J.E. Nelson, R.D. Agar (Malone), J.W. McKay (QUB), D.J. O'Brien (London Irish), J.S. McCarthy (Dolphin).
P: George Norton.

Wales *G. Williams (London Welsh); K.J. Jones (Newport), B.L. Jones (Devonport Servs), J. Matthews (Cardiff), M.C. Thomas (Devonport Servs); W.B. Cleaver, W.R. Willis (Cardiff); J.D. Robins (Birkenhead Park), D.M. Davies (Somerset Police), C. Davies (Cardiff), E.R. John (Neath), Don J. Hayward (Newbridge), W.R. Cale (Pontypool), +J.A. Gwilliam (Edinburgh Wands), R.T. Evans (Newport).
T: Ken Jones, Malcolm Thomas.
Referee: R.A. Beattie (Scotland).

Wales 3 Ireland 3

Arms Park, Cardiff. 10 March 1951

Draw. Wales – 1 pen. Ireland – 1 try.

This was the first match played by the brilliant Cliff Morgan who gave great pleasure wherever he appeared. He went on to win 29 caps while the other débutant, second-row forward Ben Edwards, was never selected again. However, 'Big Ben' landed the 45-yard penalty which prevented Ireland winning the Triple Crown. Morgan was thrilled to play against his hero, Jackie Kyle, who scored a brilliant individual try and later produced a superb tackle on Ken Jones. In an odd selection move, lineout star Roy John was picked as a blind-side wing forward. Five Cardiff players were included for Wales with a sixth, Des O'Brien, appearing for Ireland.

Wales G. Williams (Llanelli); K.J. Jones (Newport), J. Matthews, B.L. Williams (Cardiff), M.C. Thomas (Devonport Servs); *C.I. Morgan, W.R. Willis (Cardiff); J.D. Robins (Birkenhead Park), D.M. Davies (Somerset Police), C. Davies (Cardiff), Don J. Hayward (Newbridge), *B.O. Edwards (Newport), E.R. John (Neath), +J.A. Gwilliam (Edinburgh Wands), R.T. Evans (Newport).
P: Ben Edwards.

Ireland A. McMorrow (Garryowen); W.H.J. Millar, N.J. Henderson (QUB), R.R. Chambers (Instonians), M.F. Lane (UCC); J.W. Kyle (QUB), J.A. O'Meara (UCC); D. McKibbin (Instonians), +K.D. Mullen (Old Belvedere), J.H. Smith (QUB), J.R. Brady (CIYMS), J.E. Nelson (Malone), J.W. McKay (QUB), D.J. O'Brien (Cardiff), J.S. McCarthy (Dolphin).
T: Jackie Kyle.
Referee: William C.W. Murdoch (Scotland).

Ireland 3 Wales 14

Lansdowne Road, Dublin. 8 March 1952

Wales won by 3 tries, 1 con, 1 pen to 1 pen.

Wales became Triple Crown winners for the ninth time overall, as the pack took control to win far more easily than in 1950. Clem Thomas was restored after three years in the wilderness and Billy Williams replaced the injured Rex Willis. Wales led by a Lewis Jones penalty before Clem Thomas put Rees Stephens over, and Morgan made a darting run for Ken Jones to score a replica of his first Twickenham try two months earlier. Though John Murphy kicked a second-half penalty, Roy John sold two dummies before putting Clem Thomas over. Lewis Jones converted and the Crown was won once more.

Ireland J.G. Murphy (Dublin U); W.H.J. Millar, N.J. Henderson (QUB), R.R. Chambers (Instonians), G.C. Phipps (Rosslyn Park); J.W. Kyle (QUB), J.A. O'Meara (UCC); T. Clifford (Young Munster), K.D. Mullen (Old Belvedere), J.H. Smith (Belfast Collegians), P.J. Lawlor (Clontarf), A. O'Leary (Cork Const), M. Dargan (Old Belvedere), +D.J. O'Brien (Cardiff), J.S. McCarthy (Dolphin).
P: Gerry Murphy.

Wales G. Williams (Llanelli); K.J. Jones, M.C. Thomas (Newport), A.G. Thomas (Cardiff), B.L. Jones (Llanelli); C.I. Morgan (Cardiff), *W.A. Williams (Newport); W.O.G. Williams (Swansea), D.M. Davies (Somerset Police), Don J. Hayward (Newbridge), E.R. John, J.R.G. Stephens (Neath), A. Forward (Pontypool), +J.A. Gwilliam (Edinburgh Wands), R.C.C. Thomas (Swansea).
T: Clem Thomas, Ken Jones, Rees Stephens.
C: Lewis Jones.
P: Lewis Jones.
Referee: Dr Peter F. Cooper (England).

Wales 5 Ireland 3

St Helen's, Swansea. 14 March 1953

Wales won by 1 try, 1 con to 1 try.

A fine try by the 21-year-old Gareth Griffiths, converted by Terry Davies halfway through the second spell, was just enough to beat an Irish try by teenager Cecil Pedlow on his international début. The Welsh forwards were on top in a tight affair and three of them – Roy John, Rees Stephens and John Gwilliam – helped set up the Griffiths try. Cliff Morgan just took the honours over the man he idolised, Jackie Kyle, and was helped by the gritty Trevor Lloyd who was making his début.

Wales T.J. Davies (Swansea); K.J. Jones (Newport), A.G. Thomas, +B.L. Williams, G.M. Griffiths; C.I. Morgan (Cardiff), *T. Lloyd (Maesteg); W.O.G.Williams (Swansea), D.M. Davies (Somerset Police), J.D. Robins (Bradford), E.R. John, J.R.G. Stephens (Neath), S. Judd (Cardiff), J.A. Gwilliam (Gloucester), R.C.C. Thomas (Swansea).
T: Gareth Griffiths.
C: Terry Davies.

Ireland R.J. Gregg (QUB); S.J. Byrne (Lansdowne), N.J. Henderson (NIFC), A.C. Pedlow (QUB), M.P. Mortell (Bective); +J.W. Kyle (NIFC), J.A. O'Meara (UCC); W.A. O'Neill (UCD), R. Roe (Dublin U), F.E. Anderson (QUB), J.R. Brady (CIYMS), T.E. Reid (Garryowen), G.F. Reidy (Dolphin), J.R. Kavanagh (UCD), W.E. Bell (Belfast Collegians).
T: Seamus Byrne.
Referee: Dr Peter F. Cooper (England).

Ireland 9 Wales 12

Lansdowne Road, Dublin. 13 March 1954

Wales won by 3 pens, 1 drop goal to 1 try, 2 pens.

Débutant centre Denzil Thomas dropped the winning goal in the last minute and was rewarded by never being selected again. Another débutant, Viv Evans, a former POW who was aged 34 years and 183 days, landed three fine goals. Among the other new faces were hooker Bryn Meredith and lock Rhys Williams, both of whom became outstanding Lions tourists. Flanker Brian Sparks was a lively performer who became a rugby league player in 1957. One incident amused non-Irishmen, when Herbert McCracken made his one and only appearance, replacing John O'Meara who had ricked a back muscle reading a newspaper in bed in the team's hotel!

Ireland P.J. Berkery (Lansdowne); M.P. Mortell (Bective), N.J. Henderson (NIFC), R.P. Godfrey (UCD), J.T. Gaston (Dublin U); S. Kelly (Lansdowne), H.L. McCracken (NIFC); J.H. Smith (London Irish), R. Roe (Dublin U), F.E. Anderson (QUB), J.R. Brady (CIYMS), R.H. Thompson (Instonians), G.F. Reidy (Dolphin), J.R. Kavanagh (Wanderers), +J.S. McCarthy (Dolphin).
T: Joe Gaston.
P: Noel Henderson, Seamus Kelly.

Wales *V. Evans (Neath); K.J. Jones (Newport), *J. Denzil Thomas (Llanelli), A.G. Thomas, G.M. Griffiths; C.I. Morgan, W.R. Willis (Cardiff); W.O.G. Williams (Swansea), *B.V. Meredith (Newport), C.C. Meredith, +J.R.G. Stephens (Neath), *R.H. Williams (Llanelli), R.C.C. Thomas (Swansea), *L.H. Jenkins (Newport), *B.A. Sparks (Neath).
P: Viv Evans 3.
DG: Denzil Thomas.
Referee: A.W.C. Austin (Scotland).

Wales 21 Ireland 3

Arms Park, Cardiff. 12 March 1955

Wales won by 4 tries, 3 cons, 1 pen to 1 pen.

It was 3–3 with 15 minutes remaining, but Cliff Morgan was unstoppable and he scored a brilliant solo try appearing to run through the entire Irish pack. Tony O'Reilly, aged 18, won the first of his 29 caps spread over 15 years, but found the much smaller Alun Thomas far too clever on this occasion. Thomas had left Cardiff to join Llanelli and Morgan had been moved by his firm to Ireland, where he had joined Bective Rangers. Welsh full-back Garfield Owen landed four successful kicks on his début. A year later he transferred to Halifax Rugby League club and continued to be an outstanding goalkicker. Cardiff speedster Haydn Morris returned after a four-year gap and scored the last of the four Welsh tries.

Wales *G.D. Owen; K.J. Jones (Newport), A.G. Thomas (Llanelli), G.M. Griffiths, H.T. Morris (Cardiff); C.I. Morgan (Bective Rangers), W.R. Willis (Cardiff); W.O.G. Williams (Swansea), B.V. Meredith (Newport), C.C. Meredith (Neath), R.J. Robins (Pontypridd), R.H. Williams, L.M. Davies (Llanelli), +J.R.G. Stephens (Neath), R.C.C. Thomas (Swansea).
T: Courtenay Meredith, Gareth Griffiths, Cliff Morgan, Haydn Morris.

C: Garfield Owen 3.
P: Owen.

Ireland P.J. Berkery (Lansdowne); A.C. Pedlow (QUB), N.J. Henderson (NIFC), A.J.F. O'Reilly (Old Belvedere), J.T. Gaston (Dublin U); J.W. Kyle (NIFC), S.J. McDermott (London Irish); P.J. O'Donoghue (Bective), R. Roe (Lansdowne), F.E. Anderson (NIFC), M.N. Madden (Sunday's Well), +R.H. Thompson (Instonians), M.J. Cunningham (UCC), G.R.P. Ross (CIYMS), P.J. Kavanagh (Wanderers).
P: Noel Henderson.
Referee: A.I. 'Sandy' Dickie (Scotland).

Ireland 11 Wales 3

Lansdowne Road, Dublin. 10 March 1956

Ireland won by 1 try, 1 con, 1 pen, 1 drop goal to 1 pen.

Ken Jones equalled Irishman George Stephenson's British record of 42 caps. The occasion was marred for him, however, since although Wales led by a penalty from Garfield Owen at half-time, the second spell belonged entirely to Ireland. Jackie Kyle's only drop goal for Ireland throughout his long career pulled his side level and Marney Cunningham's try was the clinching score, though he never played for Ireland again. Wales included seven Newport players and prop Billy 'Stoker' Williams appeared for the last time.

Ireland P.J. Berkery (Lansdowne); S.V.J. Quinlan (Highfield), +N.J. Henderson (NIFC), A.J.F. O'Reilly (Old Belvedere), A.C. Pedlow (QUB); J.W. Kyle (NIFC), J.A. O'Meara (Dolphin); P.J. O'Donoghue (Bective), R. Roe (London Irish), B.G. Wood (Garryowen), R.H. Thompson (Instonians), J.R. Brady (CIYMS), M.J. Cunningham (Cork Const), T. McGrath (Garryowen), J.R. Kavanagh (Wanderers).
T: Marney Cunningham.
C: Cecil Pedlow.
P: Pedlow.
DG: Jackie Kyle.

Wales G.D. Owen; K.J. Jones, H.P. Morgan, M.C. Thomas (Newport), C.L. Davies; +C.I. Morgan (Cardiff), D.O. Brace (Newport); W.O.G. Williams (Swansea), B.V. Meredith (Newport), C.C. Meredith, J.R.G. Stephens (Neath), R.H. Williams (Llanelli), B.A. Sparks (Neath), L.H. Jenkins (Newport), R.C.C. Thomas (Swansea).
P: Garfield Owen.
Referee: A.I. 'Sandy' Dickie (Scotland).

Wales 6 Ireland 5

Arms Park, Cardiff. 9 March 1957

Wales won by 2 pens to 1 try, 1 con.

If it was Cardiff, it had to be mud. A whole sea of it, as usual. It was so bad that Wales were told to change their jerseys at half-time. Ireland had not won at Cardiff for 25 years and they looked likely to end that run when Ronnie Kavanagh's try was converted for a 5–3 lead. A penalty from 25 yards by the immaculate Terry Davies was to foil them. Back-row forward John Faull had played at centre for his club against the All Blacks in 1953–54 and his father had refereed three international matches in the 1930s, including the famous England–New Zealand match which featured the great try by Prince Obolensky.

Wales T.J. Davies (Llanelli); W.G. Howells, *Cyril A.H. Davies (Llanelli), *G. Powell (Ebbw Vale), G.T. Wells; C.I. Morgan, L.H. Williams (Cardiff); T.R. Prosser (Pontypool), B.V. Meredith (London Welsh), *C.H. Morgan, R.H. Williams (Llanelli), +J.R.G. Stephens (Neath), R.J. Robins (Pontypridd), *J. Faull (Swansea), R.H. Davies (London Welsh).
P: Terry Davies 2.

Ireland P.J. Berkery (Lansdowne); R.E. Roche (Galwegians), A.J.F. O'Reilly (Old Belvedere), +N.J. Henderson (NIFC), A.C. Pedlow (QUB); J.W. Kyle (NIFC), A.A. Mulligan (London Irish); J.I. Brennan (CIYMS), R. Roe (London Irish), B.G. Wood, T.E. Reid (Garryowen), J.R. Brady (CIYMS), J.R. Kavanagh (Wanderers), P.J.A. O'Sullivan (Galwegians), H.S. O'Connor (Dublin U).
T: Ronnie Kavanagh.
C: Cecil Pedlow.
Referee: Jack A.S. Taylor (Scotland).

Ireland 6 Wales 9

Lansdowne Road, Dublin. 15 March 1958

Wales won by 3 tries to 1 try, 1 pen.

Injuries forced changes, with three Cardiff players and the lively Cyril Roberts on the right-wing all making débuts. Ireland dropped Jackie Kyle and his replacement, Mick English, made a superb start, helping his side to a 6–0 lead at half-time. His opposite number, Cliff Morgan, appeared to play Ireland on his own at times and was to prove the match-winner once again. The speedy Bryn Meredith pulled back a try before Morgan created one for Roberts, after scrum-half John O'Meara had been forced to retire injured. In the last minutes, Cliff again worked the blindside to send the ever-present Haydn Morgan diving over.

Ireland J.G.M.W. Murphy (London Irish); S. Quinlan (Highfield), +N.J. Henderson (NIFC), A.J.F. O'Reilly (Old Belvedere), A.C. Pedlow (CIYMS); M.A. English (Bohemians), J.A. O'Meara (Dolphin); P.J. O'Donoghue (Bective), A.R. Dawson (Wanderers), B.G.M. Wood (Garryowen), J.B. Stevenson (Instonians), W.A. Mulcahy (UCD), J.A. Donaldson (Belfast Collegians), J.R. Kavanagh (Wanderers), N.A. Murphy (Cork Const).
T: John O'Meara.
P: Noel Henderson.

Wales *A.J. Priday (Cardiff); *C.R. Roberts (Neath), M.C. Thomas (Newport), C.A.H. Davies (Llanelli), *H.C.W. Nicholls; C.I. Morgan, L.H. Williams (Cardiff); T.R. Prosser (Pontypool), B.V. Meredith (Newport), *J.D. Evans (Cardiff), R.H. Williams (Llanelli), W.R. Evans (Cardiff), +R.C.C. Thomas, J. Faull (Swansea), H.J. Morgan (Abertillery).
T: Haydn Morgan, Bryn Meredith, Cyril Roberts.
Referee: Dr Norman McNeill Parkes (England).

Ireland 6 Wales 8

Arms Park, Cardiff. 14 March 1959

Wales won by 2 tries, 1 con to 1 try, 1pen.

Just as in the previous season, Wales were 6–0 down at the interval, but stout defence and a late rally robbed Ireland of a deserved win. The opening kick-off almost brought a sensational try when wing Niall Brophy gathered and fed Noel Murphy, but referee Burrell overruled the touch-judge and stated that Murphy had put a foot over the touch line. Cliff Ashton made one excellent save from Brophy and Wales reduced the arrears when Ashton followed up a John Collins kick to score. Malcolm Thomas and Ashton then opened up the defence to give the speedy Malcolm Price the chance to burst over. Terry Davies landed what proved a winning conversion. Wales introduced a lively 21-year-old lock in Danny Harris who played for Pontypridd, but later joined Cardiff and then Leigh Rugby League club.

Wales T.J. Davies (Llanelli); J.E. Collins (Aberavon), M.C. Thomas (Newport), M.J. Price (Pontypool), D.I.E. Bebb (Swansea); C. Ashton (Aberavon), L.H. Williams (Cardiff); T.R. Prosser (Pontypool), B.V. Meredith (Newport), D.R. Main (London Welsh), R.H. Williams

(Llanelli), *D.J.E. Harris (Pontypridd), +R.C.C. Thomas, J. Faull (Swansea), H.J. Morgan (Abertillery).
T: Cliff Ashton, Malcolm Price.
C: Terry Davies.

Ireland N.J. Henderson (NIFC); A.J.F. O'Reilly (Old Belvedere), J.F. Dooley (Galwegians), D. Hewitt (QUB), N.H. Brophy (UCD); W.J. Hewitt (Instonians), A.A. Mulligan (London Irish); B.G.M. Wood (Garryowen), +A.R. Dawson (Wanderers), S. Millar (Ballymena), W.A. Mulcahy (UCD), M.G. Culliton (Wanderers), N.A. Murphy (Cork Const), P.J.A. O'Sullivan (Galwegians), J.R. Kavanagh (Wanderers).
T: Tony O'Reilly.
P: David Hewitt.
Referee: George Burrell (Scotland).

Ireland 9   Wales 10

Lansdowne Road, Dublin. 12 March 1960

Wales won by 2 tries, 2 cons to 1 try, 2 pens.

Wales were once again largely outplayed by Ireland, but they hung on and, ten minutes from time, Onllwyn Brace, the fourth captain in as many matches, scored in the corner. Nevertheless, Norman Morgan was still able to land the winning conversion. When the captain-elect Bryn Meredith dropped out, Wales brought Norman Gale in as hooker, while centre Brian Jones won a long-overdue cap after having played superbly for the Barbarians in South Africa a year earlier. Ireland had led 6–0 and then Noel Murphy's try increased it to 9–5 before Wales robbed them once again.

Ireland T.J. Kiernan (UCC); W.W. Bornemann (Wanderers), D. Hewitt (QUB), A.C. Pedlow (CIYMS), D.C. Glass (Belfast Collegians); S. Kelly (Lansdowne), +A.A. Mulligan (London Irish); S. Millar (Ballymena), L.G. Butler (Blackrock), B.G.M. Wood (Lansdowne), W.A. Mulcahy (UCD), M.G. Culliton, J.R. Kavanagh (Wanderers), T. McGrath (Garryowen), N.A. Murphy (Cork Const).
T: Noel Murphy.
P: Seamus Kelly 2.

Wales N.H. Morgan (Newport); F.G. Coles, M.J. Price (Pontypool), *B.J. Jones (Newport), D.I.E. Bebb (Swansea), C. Ashton (Aberavon), +D.O. Brace (Llanelli); T.R. Prosser (Pontypool), *N.R. Gale (Swansea), L.J. Cunningham (Aberavon), D.J.E. Harris (Cardiff), G.W. Payne (Pontypridd), B.R. Cresswell, G.D. Davidge,

G.K. Whitson (Newport).
T: Brian Cresswell, Onllwyn Brace.
C: Norman Morgan 2.
Referee: D.A. Brown (England).

Wales 9   Ireland 0

Arms Park, Cardiff. 11 March 1961.

Wales won by 1 try, 2 pens to nil.

A beautiful afternoon, but a very poor match. Only fly-half Ken Richards could escape the jeers of the crowd as he scored all the points with a penalty in either half and finished it off with a solo try. Ireland lost prop Gordon Wood with a cut eye after an hour, and David Hewitt was limping for most of the game. Aberavon centre David Thomas won his only cap at the age of 19, but the other newcomer, Brian Price of Newport, was to stay much longer.

Wales A.J. Priday (Cardiff); P.M. Rees (Newport), *D.L. Thomas (Aberavon), H.M. Roberts (Cardiff), D.I.E. Bebb (Swansea); K.H.L. Richards (Bridgend), +D.O. Brace (Llanelli); T.R. Prosser (Pontypool), B.V. Meredith (Newport), K.D. Jones (Cardiff), W.R. Evans (Bridgend), *B. Price, G.D. Davidge (Newport), D. Nash (Ebbw Vale), H.J. Morgan (Abertillery).
T: Ken Richards.
P: Richards 2.

Ireland T.J. Kiernan (UCC); N.H. Brophy (Blackrock), D. Hewitt (QUB), D.C. Glass (Belfast Collegians), R.J. McCarten (London Irish); M.A.F. English (Bohemians), A.A. Mulligan (London Irish); B.G.M. Wood (Lansdowne), +A.R. Dawson (Wanderers), S. Millar, C.J. Dick (Ballymena), W.A. Mulcahy (UCD), M.G. Culliton, J.R. Kavanagh (Wanderers), N.A. Murphy (Garryowen).
Referee: Doug C.J. McMahon (Scotland).

Ireland 3   Wales 3

Lansdowne Road, Dublin. 17 November 1962

Draw. Ireland – 1 drop goal. Wales – 1 pen.

This match was played eight months late due to an outbreak of smallpox in South Wales. It was a drab affair with little public interest. Flanker John Davies played his only Test before transferring to Leeds RL. While playing for Dewsbury in 1969 he collapsed and died during a match. Bryn Meredith played his 34th and last international – a record for a Welsh forward. Mick English dropped a first-half goal, with

Grahame Hodgson equalising after the interval. Brian Davies won his first cap and received it 12 years before the WRU finally gave his father (Idwal) the cap he had earned in 1939 before turning professional. Lively prop John Warlow was another to switch to rugby league after just one appearance.

Ireland T.J. Kiernan (UCC); W.R. Hunter, A.C. Pedlow (CIYMS), M.K. Flynn (Wanderers), N.H. Brophy (London Irish); M.A.F. English (Lansdowne), J.C. Kelly (UCD); M.P. O'Callaghan (Sunday's Well), A.R. Dawson (Wanderers), P.J. Dwyer (UCD), W.J. McBride (Ballymena), +W.A. Mulcahy (Bective), P.J.A. O'Sullivan (Galwegians), C.J. Dick (Ballymena), M.D. Kiely (Lansdowne).
DG: Mick English.

Wales *G.T.R. Hodgson (Neath); D.R.R. Morgan, D.K. Jones, *D.B. Davies (Llanelli), D.I.E. Bebb (Swansea); C. Ashton, A. O'Connor (Aberavon); *D.J.Warlow (Llanelli), +B.V. Meredith (Newport), L.J. Cunningham (Aberavon), W.R. Evans (Bridgend), K.A. Rowlands (Cardiff), *D. John Davies (Neath), A.E.I. Pask, H.J. Morgan (Abertillery).
P: Grahame Hodgson.
Referee: Jack A.S. Taylor (Scotland).

Wales 6 Ireland 14

Arms Park, Cardiff. 9 March 1963

Ireland won by 1 try, 1 con, 2 pens, 1 drop goal to 1 try, 1 drop goal.

Welsh tactics had seen a loss of interest by their supporters and only 45,000 braved the dreadful weather at Cardiff to witness the first Irish win there for 31 years. It was Ireland's only win of the season and Wales were on their way to their first Wooden Spoon for 14 years. They had also failed to win a home match in a season for the first time since 1937. Wing-forward Graham Jones opened the scoring before Pat Casey equalised and the visitors took an 8–3 lead to half-time. Kicks by Tom Kiernan and Mick English increased it to 14–3, before David Watkins dropped a consolation goal.

Wales G.T.R. Hodgson (Neath); D.R.R. Morgan (Llanelli), R. Evans (Bridgend), H.M. Roberts (Cardiff), W.J.B. Morris (Pontypool); D. Watkins (Newport), +D.C.T. Rowlands (Pontypool); D. Williams (Ebbw Vale), N.R. Gale (Llanelli), K.D. Jones, K.A. Rowlands (Cardiff), B.E. Thomas (Neath), G. Jones (Ebbw Vale), A.E.I. Pask, H.J. Morgan (Abertillery).

T: Graham Jones.
DG: David Watkins.

Ireland T.J. Kiernan (UCC); A.J.F. O'Reilly (Old Belvedere), J.C. Walsh (UCC), P.J.Casey (UCD), N.H. Brophy (Blackrock); M.A.F. English (Lansdowne), J.C. Kelly (UCD); R.J. McLoughlin (Gosforth), A.R. Dawson (Wanderers), S. Millar, W.J. McBride (Ballymena), +W.A. Mulcahy (Bective), M.D. Kiely (Lansdowne), C.J. Dick (Ballymena), E.P. McGuire (UCG).
T: Pat Casey.
C: Tom Kiernan.
P: Kiernan 2.
DG: Mick English.
Referee: A.C. Luff (England).

Ireland 6 Wales 15

Lansdowne Road, Dublin. 7 March 1964

Wales won by 3 tries, 3 cons to 2 pens.

Despite a brilliant individual try by David Watkins, Ireland led 6–5 at half-time and retained that position until ten minutes from time, when new cap John Dawes and wing Stuart Watkins scored tries. Dawes, later to become Wales and British Lions captain and coach, and Peter Rees replaced the injured Ken Jones and Dewi Bebb.

Ireland F.S. Keogh (Bective); P.J. Casey (UCD), M.K. Flynn (Wanderers), J.C. Walsh (UCC), K.J. Houston (QUB); C.M.H. Gibson (NIFC), J.C. Kelly; P.J. Dwyer (UCD), P. Lane (Old Crescent), T.A. Moroney (UCD), M.W. Leahy (UCC), +W.A. Mulcahy (Bective), E.P. McGuire (UCG), M.G. Culliton (Wanderers), N.A. Murphy (Cork Const).
P: Fergus Keogh 2.

Wales G.T.R. Hodgson (Neath); S.J. Watkins (Newport), *S.J. Dawes (London Welsh), K. Bradshaw (Bridgend), P.M. Rees; D. Watkins (Newport), +D.C.T. Rowlands (Pontypool); D. Williams (Ebbw Vale), N.R. Gale (Llanelli), L.J. Cunningham (Aberavon), B. Price (Newport), B.E. Thomas (Neath), G.J. Prothero (Bridgend), A.E.I. Pask (Abertillery), Dai J. Hayward (Cardiff).
T: Stuart Watkins, John Dawes, David Watkins.
C: Keith Bradshaw 3.
Referee: A.C. Luff (England).

Wales 14 Ireland 8

Arms Park, Cardiff. 13 March 1965

Wales won by 2 tries, 1 con, 1 pen, 1 drop goal to 1 try, 1 con, 1 pen.

Wales were attempting to win the Triple Crown for the tenth time but, more importantly, for the first time in thirteen years. Ireland, meanwhile, were looking for their first Crown since 1949. It meant that tickets were hard to come by and tempers on the pitch were often frayed. Tries were scored by David Watkins and Dewi Bebb. Bebb's came with one of his specialities, after a tap back from a lineout. It took Wales to an 8–0 lead and though Ireland closed the gap, Terry Price landed a magnificent 40-yard drop shot. Despite a Kevin Flynn try, Price then landed a pressure kick from the touch-line to ensure victory.

Wales T.G. Price (Llanelli); S.J. Watkins, J. Uzzell (Newport), S.J. Dawes (London Welsh), D.I.E. Bebb (Swansea); D. Watkins (Newport), +D.C.T. Rowlands (Pontypool); D. Williams (Ebbw Vale), N.R. Gale (Llanelli), R.G. Waldron (Neath), B. Price (Newport), K.A. Rowlands (Cardiff), G.J. Prothero (Bridgend), A.E.I. Pask, H.J. Morgan (Abertillery).
T: David Watkins, Dewi Bebb.
C: Terry Price.
P: Terry Price.
DG: Terry Price.

Ireland T.J. Kiernan (Cork Const), D. Hewitt (Instonians), M.K. Flynn (Wanderers), J.C. Walsh, P.J. McGrath (UCC); C.M.H. Gibson (NIFC), R.M. Young (QUB); S. MacHale (Lansdowne), K.W. Kennedy (QUB), +R.J. McLoughlin (Gosforth), W.J. McBride (Ballymena), W.A. Mulcahy (Bective), N.A. Murphy (Cork Const), H. Wall (Dolphin), M.G. Doyle (UCD).
T: Kevin Flynn.
C: Tom Kiernan.
P: Kiernan.
Referee: Peter G. Brook (England).

Ireland 9 Wales 6

Lansdowne Road, Dublin. 12 March 1966

Ireland won by 1 try, 1 pen, 1 drop goal to 1 try, 1 pen.

Ireland had lost to Scotland and France and had drawn with England, but they were now carried from the field in triumph by their supporters after this huge upset. They were leading 6–3 when centre Barrie Bresnihan virtually settled the match by dashing over after an error in the Welsh defence. A late Keith Bradshaw penalty made little difference as Ireland, with Michael Gibson and Tom Kiernan in control, were worthy winners.

Ireland +T.J. Kiernan (Cork Const); A.T.A. Duggan (Lansdowne), F.P.K. Bresnihan (UCD), J.C. Walsh (Sunday's Well), P.J. McGrath (UCC); C.M.H. Gibson (NIFC), R.M. Young (QUB); S. MacHale (Lansdowne), K.W. Kennedy (CIYMS), R.J. McLoughlin (Gosforth), O.C. Waldron (Oxford U), W.J. McBride (Ballymena), N.A. Murphy (Cork Const), R.A. Lamont (Instonians), M.G. Doyle (Cambridge U).
T: 'Barrie' Bresnihan.
P: Mike Gibson.
DG: Gibson.

Wales G.T.R. Hodgson (Neath); S.J. Watkins (Newport), D.K. Jones (Cardiff), K. Bradshaw, L. Davies (Bridgend); D. Watkins (Newport), R. Allan Lewis (Abertillery); D. Williams (Ebbw Vale), N.R. Gale (Llanelli), D.J. Lloyd (Bridgend), B. Price (Newport), B.E. Thomas (Neath), G.J. Prothero (Bridgend), +A.E.I. Pask, H.J. Morgan (Abertillery).
T: Gary Prothero.
P: Keith Bradshaw.
Referee: R.P. Burrell (Scotland).

Wales 0 Ireland 3

Arms Park, Cardiff. 11 March 1967

Ireland won by 1 try to nil.

Alun Pask remained in the side but David Watkins took over the captaincy of a match played in high wind where the only score came after just three minutes' play. Jerry Walsh kicked to the corner and the alert wing Alan Duggan snapped up a try. Watkins threatened to equalise, but the quick-thinking Ken Goodall arrived back to halt him and save the day for Ireland.

Wales G.T.R. Hodgson (Neath); S.J. Watkins (Newport), W.H. Raybould (London Welsh), T.G.R. Davies (Cardiff), D.I.E. Bebb (Swansea); +D. Watkins (Newport), R. Allan Lewis (Abertillery); J.P. O'Shea (Cardiff), B.I. Rees(London Welsh), D.J. Lloyd (Bridgend), B. Price (Newport), G.T. 'Billy' Mainwaring (Aberavon), K.J. Braddock (Newbridge), A.E.I. Pask (Abertillery), J. Taylor (London Welsh).

Ireland T.J. Kiernan (Cork Const); A.T.A. Duggan (Lansdowne), F.P.K. Bresnihan (UCD), J.C. Walsh (Sunday's Well), N.H. Brophy (Blackrock); C.M.H. Gibson (NIFC), R.M. Young (QUB); S. McHale (Lansdowne), K.W. Kennedy (CIYMS), S.A. Hutton (Malone), W.J. McBride (Ballymena), M.G. Molloy (UCG), +N.A. Murphy (Cork Const), K.G. Goodall (Newcastle U), M.G. Doyle (Edinburgh Wands).
T: Alan Duggan.
Referee: Mike H. Titcomb (England).

Ireland 9 Wales 6

Lansdowne Road, Dublin. 9 March 1968

Ireland won by 1 try, 1 pen, 1 drop goal to 1 pen, 1 drop goal.

Referee Mike Titcomb was let off the hook by flanker Mick Doyle's try nine minutes into injury time. The English official had earlier given a Gareth Edwards drop-goal attempt as over, though almost everyone in the ground realised it had missed. Indeed, the Irish players had lined up for the drop-out when Mr Titcomb, who four years later was to control the historic Llanelli–All Blacks encounter, ran to the halfway line. The spectators held up play and booed loudly. However, the official may have balanced matters, as a Welsh player appeared to have touched the earlier drop-goal attempt by Michael Gibson in flight. Gibson's effort had taken Ireland to 6–0, but the Edwards 'score' made it 6–6, before the late Doyle try settled it. John Dawes was the captain but lasted for this game only, though he was to regain it 13 matches later. Débutants were wing Maurice Richards and the South African-born lock Ian Jones. Richards became one of the best Welsh wingers before turning professional in October 1969, while Jones was never selected again.

Ireland +T.J. Kiernan (Cork Const); A.T.A. Duggan (Lansdowne), L.M. Hunter (Civil Serv), F.P.K. Bresnihan (UCD), J.C.M. Moroney (London Irish); C.M.H. Gibson (NIFC), R.M. Young (QUB); P. O'Callaghan (Dolphin), A.M. Brady (Malone), S. Millar, W.J. McBride (Ballymena), M.G. Molloy (UCG), T.J. Doyle (Wanderers), K.G. Goodall (City of Derry), M.G. Doyle (Blackrock).
T: Mick Doyle.
P: Tom Kiernan.
DG: Mike Gibson.

Wales D. Rees (Swansea); W. Keri Jones (Cardiff), +S.J. Dawes, W.H. Raybould (London Welsh), *M.C.R. Richards; B. John, G.O. Edwards; J.P. O'Shea (Cardiff), J. Young, D.J. Lloyd (Bridgend), *I.C. Jones (London Welsh), W.D. Thomas (Llanelli), W.D. Morris (Neath), R.E. Jones (Coventry), J. Taylor (London Welsh).
P: Doug Rees.
DG: Gareth Edwards.
Referee: Mike H. Titcomb (England).

Wales 24 Ireland 11

Arms Park, Cardiff. 8 March 1969

Wales won by 4 tries, 1 con, 1 pen, 1 drop goal to 1 try, 1 con, 2 pens.

Wales won convincingly, after being 6–3 down with 30 minutes played, but the match will long be remembered for an incident in the first 15 minutes of play. Lock and captain, Brian Price, could have become the first Welsh player to be sent off in an international match when he punched Irish flanker Noel Murphy as a maul broke up. It was seen quite clearly by the majority of spectators, thousands watching television, the referee and the Prince of Wales, who was at the match. Referee Doug McMahon did not send Price off. Astonishingly, he merely warned him and penalised Wales. This caused a leading English TV broadcaster to say: 'What must you do to be sent off at rugby union?' It was certainly out of character for the Newport forward, but he was a very lucky man to stay on the field. Ireland skipper Tom Kiernan threatened to take his side off, as Mr McMahon appeared to be losing his grip on the forward battle, but one cool head was still present. Keith Jarrett had a penalty chance, but never indicated to the referee that he was going for goal and, as Ireland retreated, the centre delivered the ball to the prop Denzil Williams, who scampered over for a try which Jarrett duly converted. In the second half, superb running led to three tries and the score sped to 21–6 before Mike Gibson grabbed a consolation try. An Ireland victory would have given them the Triple Crown, but Wales now had the opportunity themselves if they could defeat England, which they did five weeks later. As for Mr McMahon, he never controlled another international match!

Wales J.P.R. Williams (London Welsh); S.J. Watkins, K.S. Jarrett (Newport), T.G.R. Davies, M.C.R. Richards; B. John, G.O. Edwards (Cardiff); D. Williams (Ebbw Vale), J. Young, D.J. Lloyd (Bridgend), +B. Price (Newport), B.E. Thomas, W.D. Morris (Neath), T.M. Davies, J. Taylor (London Welsh).
T: Stuart Watkins, Denzil Wiliams, Dai Morris, John Taylor.
C: Keith Jarrett 3.
P: Jarrett.
DG: Barry John.

Ireland +T.J. Kiernan (Cork Const); A.T.A. Duggan (Lansdowne), F.P.K. Bresnihan (UCD), C.M.H. Gibson (NIFC), J.C.M. Moroney (London Irish); B.J. McGann (Lansdowne), R.M. Young (QUB); P. O'Callaghan (Dolphin), K.W. Kennedy (London Irish), S. Millar, W.J. McBride (Ballymena), M.G. Molloy (London Irish), J.C. Davidson (Dungannon), M.L. Hipwell (Terenure Coll), N.A. Murphy (Cork Const).
T: Mike Gibson.
C: Tom Kiernan.
P: Kiernan 2.
Referee: Doug C.J. McMahon (Scotland).

Ireland 14 Wales 0

Lansdowne Road, Dublin. 14 March 1970

Ireland won by 2 tries, 1 con, 1 pen, 1 drop goal to nil.

Wales had escaped defeat by Scotland and England, but there was no such story at Lansdowne Road, as Ireland scored 14 points in the last 24 minutes to crush hopes of a Welsh Triple Crown. A drop goal then an Alan Duggan try, followed by a penalty took Ireland to 9–0. At that point Wales were really shattered as number 8 forward Ken Goodall gathered a poor kick by John and ran up to J.P.R. Williams, kicked on, and regathered to score. John and Edwards set a record of 16 appearances together at half-back, beating the 15 times that Dick Jones and Dicky Owen played for Wales from 1901–1910. Despite playing badly the pair were retained, but Edwards lost the captaincy to John Dawes.

Ireland +T.J. Kiernan (Cork Const); A.T.A. Duggan (Lansdowne), F.P.K. Bresnihan (London Irish), C.M.H. Gibson (NIFC), W.J. Brown (Malone); B.J McGann (Cork Const), R.M. Young (Belfast Collegians); P. O'Callaghan (Dolphin), K.W. Kennedy (London Irish), S. Millar, W.J. McBride (Ballymena), M.G. Molloy (London Irish), R.A. Lamont (Instonians), K.G. Goodall (City of Derry), J.F. Slattery (UCD).
T: Alan Duggan, Ken Goodall.
C: Tom Kiernan.
P: Kiernan.
DG: Barry McGann.

Wales J.P.R. Williams (London Welsh); S.J. Watkins (Cardiff), S.J. Dawes (London Welsh), W.H. Raybould (Newport), *K. Hughes (Cambridge U/New Dock Stars); B. John, +G.O. Edwards (Cardiff); D.B. Llewelyn (Newport), J. Young (Harrogate), D. Williams (Ebbw Vale), W.D. Thomas (Llanelli), T.G. Evans (London Welsh), W.D. Morris (Neath), T.M. Davies (London Welsh), D. Hughes (Newbridge).
Referee: G.C. 'Larry' Lamb (England).

Wales 23 Ireland 9

Arms Park, Cardiff. 13 March 1971

Wales won by 4 tries, 1 con, 2 pens, 1 drop goal to 3 pens.

It was the Triple Crown for the twelfth time, as the half-back pair Barry John and Gareth Edwards orchestrated a comfortable win. Ireland had led 6–0 before a Gerald Davies try and two kicks by 'King' John saw Wales in front at the break. Edwards then got in on the act with a try, sending in Gerald Davies and then gaining his second. Prop forward Denzil Williams won his 35th cap to pass the previous best by a Welsh forward – hooker Bryn Meredith.

Wales J.P.R. Williams; T.G.R. Davies, +S.J. Dawes (London Welsh), A.J.L. Lewis (Ebbw Vale), J.C. Bevan; B. John, G.O. Edwards (Cardiff); D. Williams (Ebbw Vale), J. Young (Harrogate), D.B. Llewelyn, W.D. Thomas (Llanelli), M.G. Roberts (London Welsh), W.D. Morris (Neath), T.M. Davies, J. Taylor (London Welsh).
T: Gerald Davies 2, Gareth Edwards 2.
C: Barry John.
P: John 2.
DG: John.

Ireland B.J. O'Driscoll (Manchester); A.T.A. Duggan (Lansdowne), F.P.K. Bresnihan (London Irish), +C.M.H. Gibson (NIFC), E.L. Grant (CIYMS); B.J. McGann (Cork Const), R.M. Young (Belfast Collegians); R.J. McLoughlin (Blackrock Coll), K.W. Kennedy (London Irish), J.F. Lynch (St Mary's Coll), W.J. McBride (Ballymena), M.G. Molloy (London Irish), M.L. Hipwell (Terenure Coll), D.J. Hickie (St Mary's Coll), J.F. Slattery (UCD).
P: Mike Gibson 3.
Referee: R.F. 'Johnny' Johnson (England).

Ireland v Wales

Lansdowne Road, Dublin. 11 March 1972

Wales followed Scotland in declining to visit Dublin following the IRA's bomb attack in Aldershot. Ireland refused to switch to a neutral venue, despite threats made in letters from Dublin to the WRU, Welsh clubs and players.

Wales 16 Ireland 12

Arms Park, Cardiff. 10 March 1973

Wales won by 2 tries, 1 con, 2 pens to 1 try, 1 con, 2 pens.

Half-backs Gareth Edwards and Phil Bennett were starting to dominate matches in the way that Edwards and Barry John had done previously. It was true that they and Wales were often slow to start, but the last 40 minutes often saw the Welsh magic flow forth. This time it was only 6–3 at the break, until the pair sent Jim Shanklin over and Edwards then started and finished a move that saw him take an outside pass from Gerald Davies to go across the Irish line. Bennett's conversion from the touch-line took it to 16–6, though Michael Gibson showed his qualities with Ireland's sole try just before full-time.

Wales J.P.R. Williams; T.G.R. Davies (London Welsh), R.T.E. Bergiers (Llanelli), +A.J.L. Lewis (Ebbw Vale), J.L. Shanklin (London Welsh); P. Bennett (Llanelli), G.O. Edwards (Cardiff); *P.D. Llewellyn (Swansea), J. Young (London Welsh/RAF), G. Shaw (Neath), W.D. Thomas (Llanelli), M.G. Roberts (London Welsh), W.D. Morris (Neath), T.M. Davies (Swansea), J. Taylor (London Welsh).
T: Jim Shanklin, Gareth Edwards.
C: Phil Bennett.
P: Bennett 2.

Ireland A.H. Ensor (Wanderers); T.O. Grace (St Mary's Coll), R.A. Milliken (Bangor), C.M.H. Gibson (NIFC), A.W. McMaster (Ballymena); B.J. McGann (Cork Const), J.J. Maloney; J.F. Lynch (St Mary's Coll), K.W. Kennedy (London Irish), R.J. McLoughlin (Blackrock Coll), +W.J. McBride (Ballymena), K.M.A. Mays (UCD), S.A. McKinney (Dungannon), T.A.P. Moore (Highfield), J.F. Slattery (Blackrock Coll).
T: Mike Gibson.
C: Barry McGann.
P: McGann 2.
Referee: T.F.E. Grierson (Scotland).

Ireland 9 Wales 9

Lansdowne Road, Dublin. 2 February 1974.

Draw. Ireland – 3 pens. Wales – 1 try, 1 con, 1 pen.

Ireland certainly had the chances to win the match and, though Tony Ensor kicked three penalty goals, he missed on seven other occasions and Mick Quinn also

The greatest? Phil Bennett in the Stradey Park museum with English and Welsh jerseys. He appeared for Wales from 1969 until 1978 until he retired from international rugby at the age of 29. (© Huw Evans)

failed twice. Wales scored after just six minutes' play, when Phil Bennett switched to the blindside with J.P.R. Williams racing up to send J.J. Williams across for the only try of the match. Bennett's conversion was the only other score of the half; Ensor then kicked Ireland in front at 9–6 before Bennett levelled it.

Ireland A.H. Ensor (Wanderers); V.A. Becker (Lansdowne), C.M.H. Gibson (NIFC), R.A. Milliken (Bangor), P. Lavery (London Irish); M.A.M. Quinn (Lansdowne), J.J. Moloney; J.F. Lynch (St Mary's Coll), K.W. Kennedy (London Irish), R.J. McLoughlin (Blackrock Coll), +W.J. McBride (Ballymena), M.I. Keane (Lansdowne), S.M. Deering (Garryowen), T.A.P. Moore (Highfield), J.F. Slattery (Blackrock Coll).
P: Tony Ensor 3.

Wales J.P.R. Williams; *C.F.W. Rees (London Welsh), I. Hall (Aberavon), *A.A.J. Finlayson (Cardiff), J.J. Williams; P. Bennett (Llanelli), +G.O. Edwards (Cardiff); G. Shaw (Neath), R.W. Windsor (Pontypool), *W.P.J. Williams (Neath), *G.A.D. Wheel (Swansea), A.J.

Martin (Aberavon), W.D. Morris (Neath), T.M. Davies (Swansea), T.J. Cobner (Pontypool).
T: J.J. Williams.
C: Phil Bennett.
P: Bennett.
Referee: Ken A. Pattinson (England).

Wales 32 Ireland 4

Arms Park, Cardiff. 15 March 1975

Wales won by 5 tries, 3 cons, 2 pens to 1 try.

Roy Bergiers and Geoff Wheel came back and, with John Bevan still injured, Phil Bennett was played from the start. It turned out to be his match. Only 9–0 ahead after 40 minutes, Wales then proceeded to run Ireland ragged, as the tries rained on the Taff End of the ground. Bennett, along with Gareth Edwards, conducted the whole show to once more gain the championship title and inflict the biggest championship loss on Ireland for 68 years. The last Welsh try was the most popular, as it was scored by 'Charlie' Faulkner from a Bobby Windsor pass. Even the presence of Mike Gibson on the back of 'Charlie' failed to halt the Pontypool prop. Ireland did respond just before the final whistle as Willie Duggan intercepted a careless Edwards pass to score with ease. It could not hide the fact that this had been Welsh rugby at its best.

Wales J.P.R. Williams (London Welsh); T.G.R. Davies (Cardiff), R.T.E. Bergiers, R.W.R. Gravell, J.J. Williams; P. Bennett (Llanelli), G.O. Edwards (Cardiff); A.G. Faulkner, R.W. Windsor, G. Price (Pontypool), G.A.D. Wheel (Swansea), A.J. Martin (Aberavon), T.P. Evans, +T.M. Davies (Swansea), T.J. Cobner (Pontypool).
T: Gerald Davies, Roy Bergiers, J.J. Williams, Charlie Faulkner, Gareth Edwards.
C: Phil Bennett 3.
P: Bennett 2.

Ireland A.H. Ensor (Wanderers); T.O. Grace (St Mary's Coll), R.A. Milliken (Bangor), C.M.H. Gibson (NIFC), A.W. McMaster (Ballymena); W.McM. McCombe (Bangor), J.J. Moloney (St Mary's Coll); R.J. Clegg (Bangor), K.W. Kennedy (London Irish), R.J. McLoughlin (Blackrock Coll), M.I. Keane (Lansdowne), +W.J. McBride (Ballymena), M.J.A. Sherry (Lansdowne), W.P. Duggan, J.F. Slattery (Blackrock Coll).
T: Willie Duggan.
Referee: J. St Guilheim (France).

One of the most popular Welsh tries: 'Charlie' Faulkner outstrips the Irish defence to score in 1975, followed by Phil Bennett. A black-belt at judo, Faulkner was within ten days of his 38th birthday when he played in his 19th and final match. (© Huw Evans)

Gareth Edwards welcomed as a Druid at the National Eisteddfod. In 1975, he was awarded the MBE for his services to rugby. (© Huw Evans)

Ireland 9 Wales 34

Lansdowne Road, Dublin. 21 February 1976

Wales won by 4 tries, 3 cons, 4 pens to 3 pens.

Wales took the Triple Crown for the 13th time, though it was a far harder match than the scoreline suggested. It was only 10–9 at half-time, with Gerald Davies having scored the only try. Phil Bennett kicked Wales to 16–9 and then came three tries in a five-minute spell. It was started by a second from Davies and followed by Gareth Edwards, who recorded a record-breaking 18th try for Wales and equalled Teddy Morgan's effort of tries in five successive matches. The best was left until last, as Wales were now in full flow and none better than the half-backs, with 'Benny' producing a classic try to resemble the one he scored for the Lions in the 3rd Test of 1974. Ray Gravell charged at the Irish defence, out came the ball and Bennett, in his best hopping-style, was over for a delightful score. He followed with a superb conversion that gave him 19 points in the match and equalled the previous best by Jack Bancroft and Keith Jarrett. Skipper Mervyn Davies became the most-capped Welsh forward, winning his 37th cap to pass Denzil Williams.

Ireland A.H. Ensor (Wanderers); +T.O. Grace (St Mary's Coll), P. Lavery (London Irish), C.M.H. Gibson (NIFC), A.W. McMaster (Ballymena); B.J. McGann (Cork Const), D.M. Canniffe (Lansdowne); P. O'Callaghan (Dolphin), J.L. Cantrell (UCD), P.A. Orr (Old Wesley), M.I. Keane (Lansdowne), R.F. Hakin (CIYMS), S.A. McKinney (Dungannon), W.P. Duggan (Blackrock Coll), S.M. Deering (Garryowen). Rep: L.A. Moloney (Garryowen) for Lavery.
P: Barry McGann 3.

Wales J.P.R. Williams (London Welsh); T.G.R. Davies (Cardiff), R.W.R. Gravell (Llanelli), S.P. Fenwick (Bridgend), J.J. Williams; P. Bennett (Llanelli), G.O. Edwards (Cardiff); A.G. Faulkner, R.W. Windsor, G. Price (Pontypool),

G.A.D. Wheel (Swansea), A.J. Martin (Aberavon), T.P. Evans, +T.M. Davies (Swansea), T.P. David (Pontypridd).
T: Gerald Davies 2, Gareth Edwards, Phil Bennett.
C: Bennett 3.
P: Bennett 3, Allan Martin.
Referee: Norman R. Sanson (Scotland).

Wales 25 Ireland 9

Arms Park, Cardiff. 15 January 1977

Wales won by 3 tries, 2 cons, 2 pens, 1 drop goal to 3 pens.

Wales lock Geoff Wheel and Ireland's number 8 Willie Duggan were dismissed after a punching incident 37 minutes into the first half. They were the first players ever to be sent off in the history of the championship, though it should be noted that referee Norman Sanson was one of the best referees in the Northern Hemisphere at that time. Phil Bennett was the new captain and he must have been worried when Wales slumped to 0–6 after 40 minutes and then 6–9 after an hour. Gerald Davies began the fightback that brought 19 points in the last 20 minutes. It included a try from débutant flanker Clive Burgess. Ireland included 19-year-olds in wing Jimmy Bowen and centre Alistair McKibbin, the latter having had his birthday only two days before the match.

Wales J.P.R. Williams (Bridgend); T.G.R. Davies (Cardiff), S.P. Fenwick (Bridgend), *D.H. Burcher (Newport), J.J. Williams; +P. Bennett (Llanelli), G.O. Edwards (Cardiff); G. Shaw (Neath), R.W. Windsor, G. Price (Pontypool), G.A.D. Wheel (Swansea), A.J. Martin (Aberavon), *R.C. Burgess (Ebbw Vale), *J. Squire (Newport), T.P. Evans (Swansea). Rep: D.L. Quinnell (Llanelli) for Evans.
Sent off: Geoff Wheel.
T: Gerald Davies, J.P.R. Williams, Clive Burgess.
C: Phil Bennett 2.
P: Bennett 2.
DG: Steve Fenwick.

Ireland F. Wilson (CIYMS); +T.O. Grace (St Mary's Coll), A.R. McKibbin (Instonians), J.A. McIlrath (Ballymena), D.StJ. Bowen (Cork Const); C.M.H. Gibson (NIFC), R.J.M. McGrath (Wanderers); T.A.O. Feighery (St Mary's Coll), P.C. Whelan (Garryowen), P.A. Orr (Old Wesley), M.I. Keane (Lansdowne), R.F. Hakin (CIYMS), S.A. McKinney (Dungannon), W.P. Duggan (Blacrock Coll), S.M. Deering (Garryowen). Rep: B.O. Foley (Shannon) for Hakin.
Sent off: Willie Duggan

P: Mike Gibson 3.
Referee: Norman R. Sanson (Scotland).

Ireland 16 Wales 20

Lansdowne Road, Dublin. 4 March 1978

Wales won by 2 tries, 4 pens to 1 try, 3 pens, 1 drop goal.

Victory was required in Dublin to achieve the Triple Crown for the third successive year – a feat never accomplished by any country. Wales did win, but Ireland, as ever, made them fight every inch of the way. Steve Fenwick outkicked Tony Ward by 3–1, to give Wales a 9–3 lead, and then the Bridgend centre scored a try after 30 minutes. Ward responded with a penalty before the interval and a drop goal just afterwards. Then, when J.P.R. Williams muffed a kick, it was John Moloney who dived on it: 13–13 and all to play for! Wales produced a match-winning try, as Bobby Windsor delivered from a maul to Gareth Edwards going left. On it came to Fenwick with Ireland streaming across to cover. The centre lobbed a pass to J.J. Williams who hared for the corner and scored as he was tackled. Fenwick kicked his fourth penalty goal and Wales were home and dry. There was one sour spot. The outstanding Mike Gibson, now selected as a wing and making a world record 64th appearance, was fouled badly and blatantly by J.P.R. Williams. Williams could, and possibly should, have been dismissed and was booed thereafter every time he touched the ball.

Ireland A.H. Ensor (Wanderers); C.M.H. Gibson (NIFC), A.R. McKibbin (London Irish/Instonians), P.P. McNaughton (Greystones), A.C. McLennan (Wanderers); A.J.P. Ward (Garryowen), +J.J. Moloney (St Mary's Coll); E.M.J. Byrne (Blackrock Coll), P.C. Whelan (Garryowen), P.A. Orr (Old Wesley), M.I. Keane (Lansdowne), H.W. Steele (Ballymena), S.A. McKinney (Dungannon), W.P. Duggan, J.F. Slattery (Blackrock Coll).
T: John Moloney.
P: Tony Ward 3.
DG: Ward.

Wales J.P.R. Williams (Bridgend); T.G.R. Davies (Cardiff), R.W.R. Gravell (Llanelli), S.P. Fenwick (Bridgend), J.J. Williams; +P. Bennett (Llanelli), G.O. Edwards (Cardiff); A.G. Faulkner, R.W. Windsor, G. Price (Pontypool), G.A.D. Wheel (Swansea), A.J. Martin (Aberavon), J. Squire (Newport), D.L. Quinnell (Llanelli), T.J. Cobner (Pontypool).
T: Steve Fenwick, J.J. Williams.
P: Fenwick 4.
Referee: Georges Domercq (France).

The Pontypool front row: Graham Price, Bobby Windsor and Charlie Faulkner after their international careers had ended. The fearsome trio also appeared together for the British Lions in New Zealand.
(© Huw Evans)

Wales 24 Ireland 21

Arms Park, Cardiff. 3 February 1979

Wales won by 2 tries, 2 cons, 4 pens to 2 tries, 2 cons, 3 pens.

Deadly kicking by Steve Fenwick and Tony Ward monopolised the match. Ward placed five from six, but Fenwick kept in front with six from seven and became the second Welshman to pass 100 points in international matches. Wales led 21–9 after an hour, first with Allan Martin and then Paul Ringer crossing, the latter after Terry Holmes had harried the defence. By then, Wales had lost Geoff Wheel with a shoulder injury. Ireland scored two late tries to register their highest score against Wales, but Fenwick placed a penalty between those tries to ensure a win in the 50th appearance by J.P.R. Williams.

Wales +J.P.R. Williams (Bridgend); H.E. Rees (Neath), S.P. Fenwick (Bridgend), R.W.R. Gravell, J.J. Williams (Llanelli); W.G. Davies, T.D. Holmes (Cardiff); A.G. Faulkner, R.W. Windsor, G. Price (Pontypool), G.A.D. Wheel (Swansea), A.J. Martin (Aberavon), J. Squire (Pontypool), D.L. Quinnell, P. Ringer (Llanelli). Rep: S.M. Lane (Cardiff) for Wheel.
T: Allan Martin, Paul Ringer.
C: Steve Fenwick 2.
P: Fenwick 4.

Ireland R.M. Spring (Lansdowne); T.J. Kennedy (St Mary's Coll), A.R. McKibbin (London Irish), P.P. McNaughton (Greystones), A.C. McLennan (Wanderers); A.J.P. Ward (Garryowen), C.S. Patterson (Instonians); G.A.J. McLoughlin (Shannon), P.C. Whelan (Garryowen), P.A. Orr (Old Wesley), M.I. Keane (Lansdowne), H.W. Steele (Ballymena), C.C. Tucker (Shannon), M.E. Gibson (Lansdowne), +J.F. Slattery (Blackrock Coll).
T: Freddie McLennan, Colin Patterson.
C: Tony Ward 2.
P: Ward 3.
Referee: Allan M. Hosie (Scotland).

Ireland 21 Wales 7

Lansdowne Road, Dublin. 15 March 1980.

Ireland won by 3 tries, 3 cons, 1 pen to 1 try, 1 pen.

England took the Grand Slam, Triple Crown and championship by winning 30–13 at Murrayfield on the day Wales took a pounding in Dublin. It was the first time Ireland scored three tries against Wales in a match since 1932. Two of the tries came when Welsh kicks were charged down, first when David Richards erred and John O'Driscoll pounced, and then when Peter Morgan muffed it for Irish skipper Ciaran Fitzgerald to score. Roger Blyth's try was too little, too late for Wales.

Ireland R.C. O'Donnell; T.J. Kennedy (St Mary's Coll), D.G. Irwin (QUB), P.P. McNaughton (Greystones), J.J. Moloney (St Mary's Coll); S.O. Campbell (Old Belvedere), C.S. Patterson (Instonians); M.P. Fitzpatrick (Wanderers), C.F. Fitzgerald (St Mary's Coll), P.A. Orr (Old Welsey), M.I. Keane (Lansdowne), B.O. Foley (Shannon), J.B. O'Driscoll (London Irish), D.E. Spring (Dublin U), +J.F. Slattery (Blackrock Coll).
T: David Irwin, John O'Driscoll, Ciaran Fitzgerald.
C: Ollie Campbell 3.
P: Campbell.

Wales W.R. Blyth (Swansea); H.E. Rees (Neath), D.S. Richards (Swansea), S.P. Fenwick (Bridgend), L. Keen (Aberavon); P.J. Morgan (Llanelli), T.D. Holmes (Cardiff); C. Williams (Swansea), A.J. Phillips (Cardiff), G. Price (Pontypool), G.A.D. Wheel (Swansea), A.J. Martin (Aberavon), +J. Squire, E.T. Butler (Pontypool), S.M. Lane (Cardiff).
T: Roger Blyth.
P: Steve Fenwick.
Referee: Laurie M. Prideaux (England).

Wales 9 Ireland 8

Arms Park, Cardiff. 21 February 1981

Wales won by 2 pens, 1 drop goal to 2 tries.

Wales made changes galore, just like the old days. Only the original front row, Rhodri Lewis and Geoff Wheel retained their positions after the loss to Scotland. Clive Burgess was brought back out of the wilderness; the captaincy was back with Jeff Squire and he responded well; and the Bridgend half-backs Gerald Williams and Gary Pearce were a qualified success. Ireland ran riot early on as Tony Ward ripped the home defence apart to create tries for Hugo MacNeill and Fergus Slattery. It was 8–6 to Ireland when Gary Pearce dropped the goal which won the match after 69 minutes of play. Pearce went on to play for Llanelli and much later switched to rugby league.

Wales G. Evans (Maesteg); D.S. Richards (Swansea), R.W.R. Gravell, P.J. Morgan, D.L.Nicholas (Llanelli); *P.G. Pearce, *Gerald Williams; I. Stephens (Bridgend), A.J. Phillips (Cardiff), G. Price (Pontypool), G.A.D. Wheel (Swansea), A.J. Martin (Aberavon), R.C. Burgess (Ebbw Vale), +J. Squire (Pontypool), J.R. Lewis (SG Inst/Cardiff). Rep: A.J. Donovan (Swansea) for Morgan.
P: Gwyn Evans 2.
DG: Gary Pearce.

Ireland H.P. MacNeill (Dublin U); F.P. Quinn (Old Belvedere), D.G. Irwin (QUB), S.O. Campbell (Old Belvedere), A.C. McLennan (Wanderers); A.J.P. Ward (Garryowen), J.C. Robbie (Greystones); M.P. Fitzpatrick (Wanderers), P.C. Whelan (Garryowen), P.A. Orr (Old Wesley), M.I. Keane (Lansdowne), D.E. Spring (Dublin U), J.B. O'Driscoll (London Irish), W.P. Duggan, +J.F. Slattery (Blackrock Coll). Rep: M.E. Gibson (Lansdowne) for Spring.
T: Hugo MacNeill, Fergus Slattery.
Referee: François Palmade (France).

Ireland 20 Wales 12

Lansdowne Road, Dublin. 23 January 1982

Ireland won by 3 tries, 1 con, 2 pens to 1 try, 1 con, 1 pen, 1 drop goal.

In 1981, Gary Pearce dropped the goal which defeated Ireland. This time, as a replacement, his drop-shot was too late because Ireland was already 17–9 ahead. Away victories now looked a thing of the past for Wales as Ireland gained their first win in eight international matches. All the old skill in the Welsh midfield was missing and the home pack gave a rousing display. Indeed, Ireland had to overcome the loss of David Irwin with a broken leg after half an hour, and co-centre Paul Dean at half-time. The Gwyn Evans conversion of a Terry Holmes try put Wales 9–7 ahead at the interval. There was no answer to Ollie Campbell who created all three Irish tries and kicked eight points. The match had been postponed for a week owing to snow.

Ireland H.P. MacNeill (Dublin U); T.M. Ringland, D.G. Irwin (QUB), P.M. Dean (St Mary's Coll), M.C. Finn (Cork Const); S.O. Campbell (Old

Belvedere), R.J.M. McGrath (Wanderers); P.A. Orr (Old Wesley), +C.F. Fitzgerald (St Mary's Coll), G.A.J. McLoughlin (Shannon), M.I. Keane (Lansdowne), D.G. Lenihan (UCC), J.B. O'Driscoll (London Irish), W.P. Duggan, J.F. Slattery (Blackrock Coll). Reps: M.J. Kiernan (Dolphin) for Irwin; J.J. Murphy (Greystones) for Dean.
T: Moss Finn 2, Trevor Ringland.
C: Ollie Campbell.
P: Campbell 2.

Wales G. Evans (Maesteg); R.A. Ackerman (Newport), P.C.T. Daniels (Cardiff), D.S. Richards (Swansea), C.F.W. Rees (London Welsh); +W.G. Davies, T.D. Holmes (Cardiff); I. Stephens (Bridgend), A.J. Phillips (Cardiff), G. Price (Pontypool), R.D. Moriarty, G.A.D. Wheel, M. Davies (Swansea), J. Squire (Pontypool), Gareth P. Williams (Bridgend). Rep: P.G. Pearce (Bridgend) for (W.G.)Davies.
T: Terry Holmes.
C: Gwyn Evans.
P: Evans.
DG: Gary Pearce.
Referee: J.A. Short (Scotland).

Wales 23 Ireland 9

Arms Park, Cardiff. 5 March 1983

Wales won by 3 tries, 1 con, 3 pens to 3 pens.

This was the best performance of the season by Wales. Terry Holmes was the inspiration, opening the way for David Richards to send full-back Mark Wyatt over and then score the next himself. The third try came from Elgan Rees – his sixth in 12 matches. Prop Graham Price was back in the side because of an injury to Ian Eidman.

Wales M.A. Wyatt (Swansea); H.E. Rees (Neath), D.S. Richards (Swansea), R.A. Ackerman, C.F.W. Rees (London Welsh); M. Dacey (Swansea), T.D. Holmes (Cardiff); S.T. Jones (Pontypool), W.J. James (Aberavon), G. Price (Pontypool), R.L. Norster (Cardiff), S.J. Perkins, J. Squire, +E.T. Butler (Pontypool), D.F. Pickering (Llanelli).
T: Mark Wyatt, Terry Holmes, Elgan Rees.
C: Wyatt.
P: Wyatt 3.

Ireland H.P. MacNeill (Oxford U); T.M. Ringland (Ballymena), D.G. Irwin (Instonians), M.J. Kiernan (Dolphin), M.C. Finn (Cork Const); S.O. Campbell (Old Belvedere), R.J.M. McGrath (Wanderers); P.A. Orr (Old Wesley), +C.F. Fitzgerald (St Mary's Coll), G.A.J. McLoughlin (Shannon), D.G. Lenihan (Cork Const), M.I. Keane (Lansdowne), J.B. O'Driscoll (Manchester), W.P. Duggan, J.F. Slattery (Blackrock Coll).
P: Ollie Campbell 2, Hugo MacNeill.
Referee: J.A.F. Trigg (England).

Ireland 9 Wales 18

Lansdowne Road, Dublin. 4 February 1984

Wales won by 1 try, 1 con, 4 pens to 3 pens.

Mike 'Spikey' Watkins became only the second player since the Second World War to skipper Wales on his début. He was always controversial but also a great motivator, and the side responded to him to pull off a fine win. His opposite number, Ciaran Fitzgerald, left after 15 minutes with a cut head and the Welsh pack then held the aces. Leading 12–6, Rob Ackerman produced the decisive score as he sold full-back Hugo MacNeill a dummy and ran in from the halfway line.

Ireland H.P. MacNeill (Blackrock Coll); T.M. Ringland (Ballymena), D.G. Irwin (Instonians), R.J.M. Moroney (Lansdowne), K.D. Crossan (Instonians); S.O. Campbell (Old Belvedere), R.J.M. McGrath (Wanderers); P.A. Orr (Old Wesley), +C.F. Fitzgerald (St Mary's Coll), J.J. McCoy (Dungannon), M.I. Keane (Lansdowne), D.G. Lenihan (Cork Const), J.B. O'Driscoll (London Irish), W.P. Duggan (Blackrock Coll), W.R. Duncan (Malone). Rep: H.T. Harbison (Bective Rangers) for Fitzgerald.
P: Ollie Campbell 3.

Wales H. Davies; M.H. Titley (Bridgend), R.A. Ackerman (London Welsh), B. Bowen (South Wales Police), A.M. Hadley (Cardiff); M. Dacey (Swansea), M.H.J. Douglas (Llanelli); I. Stephens (Bridgend), *+M.J. Watkins (Newport), I.H. Eidman, R.L. Norster (Cardiff), S.J. Perkins (Pontypool), R.D. Moriarty (Swansea), E.T. Butler (Pontypool), D.F. Pickering (Llanelli).
T: Robert Ackerman.
C: Howell Davies.
P: Davies 2, Bleddyn Bowen 2.
Referee: R.G. 'Dick' Byres (Australia).

Wales 9 Ireland 21

Arms Park, Cardiff. 16 March 1985

Ireland won by 2 tries, 2 cons, 3 pens to 1 try, 1 con, 1 drop goal.

If hopes were high after winning at Murrayfield 14 days earlier, they were almost non-existent after this defeat. The front row did well enough, but there it ended. Mark Wyatt had an off-day with his kicking and missed six times, as Ireland won in Cardiff for the first time since 1967. The Irish wings scored tries in either half, with Phil Lewis scoring for Wales after good work from the half-backs.

Wales M.A. Wyatt (Swansea); M.H. Titley (Bridgend), R.A. Ackerman (London Welsh), M.G. Ring (Cardiff), P.I. Lewis (Llanelli); W.G. Davies, +T.D. Holmes; J. Whitefoot (Cardiff), W.J. James (Aberavon), I.H. Eidman, R.L. Norster (Cardiff), S.J. Perkins (Pontypool), M.S. Morris (South Wales Police), R.D. Moriarty (Swansea), D.F. Pickering (Llanelli).
T: Phil Lewis.
C: Mark Wyatt.
DG: Gareth Davies.

Ireland H.P. MacNeill (Blackrock Coll); T.M. Ringland (Ballymena), B.J. Mullin (Dublin U), M.J. Kiernan (Lansdowne), K.D. Crossan (Instonians); P.M. Dean (St Mary's Coll), M.T. Bradley (Cork Const); P.A. Orr (Old Wesley), +C.F. Fitzgerald (St Mary's Coll), J.J. McCoy (Dungannon), D.G. Lenihan (Cork Const), W.A. Anderson (Dungannon), N.J. Carr (Ards), B.J. Spillane (Bohemians), P.M. Matthews (Ards).
T: Trevor Ringland, Keith Crossan.
C: Michael Kiernan 2.
P: Kiernan 3.
Referee: Kerry V.J. Fitzgerald (Australia).

Ireland 12 Wales 19

Lansdowne Road, Dublin. 15 February 1986

Wales won by 2 tries, 1 con, 3 pens to 1 try, 1 con, 2 pens.

By scoring 12 points in a ten-minute burst after half-time, Wales came back from 4–12 to lead 16–12 before a late Paul Thorburn penalty was added to the total. Wing Phil Lewis scored and then Jonathan Davies worked the blindside to link with Lewis, who sent Phil Davies over. While Thorburn produced a faultless display, there was a good début by Paul Moriarty, the younger brother of Richard, who brought fire and strength to the back row. Two years later he was lost to rugby league.

Ireland H.P. MacNeill (London Irish); T.M. Ringland (Ballymena), M.J. Kiernan (Dolphin), B.J. Mullin (Dublin U), M.C. Finn (Cork Const); P.M. Dean (St Mary's Coll), M.T. Bradley (Cork Const); A.P. Kennedy (London Irish), +C.F. Fitzgerald (St Mary's Coll), D.C. Fitzgerald (Lansdowne), J.J. Holland (Wanderers), D.G. Lenihan (Cork Const), N.J. Carr (Ards), B.J. Spillane (Bohemians), R.K. Kearney (Wanderers).
T: Trevor Ringland.
C: Michael Kiernan.
P: Kiernan 2.

Wales P.H. Thorburn (Neath); P.I. Lewis (Llanelli), J.A. Devereux (Bridgend/SG Inst), B. Bowen (South Wales Police), A.M. Hadley (Cardiff); J. Davies (Neath), R.N. Jones (Swansea); J. Whitefoot (Cardiff), W.J. James (Aberavon), I.H. Eidman (Cardiff), D.R. Waters (Newport), S.J. Perkins (Pontypool), *W.P. Moriarty (Swansea), P.T. Davies, +D.F. Pickering (Llanelli).
T: Phil Lewis, Phil Davies.
C: Paul Thorburn.
P: Thorburn 3.
Referee: Fred A. Howard (England).

Wales 11 Ireland 15

Arms Park, Cardiff. 4 April 1987

Ireland won by 2 tries, 2 cons, 1 pen to 2 tries, 1 pen.

While England beat Scotland and Ireland won at Cardiff, France had already secured the Grand Slam in March. Wales finished joint bottom with England and it was the poor goal-kicking of Mark Wyatt which cost them the game. Ieuan Evans scored his first international try in his fourth appearance. There was also a first for Bob Norster, who finished a move started by Jonathan Davies. Indeed, Davies and Norster were the best performers in a poor season for Wales.

Wales M.A. Wyatt (Swansea); I.C. Evans (Llanelli), J.A. Devereux (Bridgend/SG Inst), M.G. Ring, A.M. Hadley (Cardiff); J. Davies (Neath), R.N. Jones (Swansea); J. Whitefoot (Cardiff), +W.J. James (Aberavon), *S.W. Blackmore (Cardiff), S. Sutton (South Wales Police), R.L. Norster (Cardiff), W.P. Moriarty (Swansea), P.T. Davies (Llanelli), R.G. Collins (South Wales Police).
T: Ieuan Evans, Bob Norster.
P: Mark Wyatt.

Scrum-half Robert Jones is closely watched by Jeff Whitefoot, Phil Davies, Bob Norster, Steve Blackmore and Paul Moriarty in this 1987 match against Ireland. (© Huw Evans)

Ireland H.P. MacNeill (London Irish); T.M. Ringland (Ballymena), B.J. Mullin (Oxford U), M.J. Kiernan (Dolphin), K.D. Crossan (Instonians); P.M. Dean (St Mary's Coll), M.T. Bradley (Cork Const); P.A. Orr (Old Wesley), H.T. Harbison (Bective Rangers), D.C. Fitzgerald (Lansdowne), +D.G. Lenihan (Cork Const), W.A. Anderson (Dungannon), N.J. Carr (Ards), B.J. Spillane (Bohemians), P.M. Matthews (Wanderers).
T: Brendan Mullin, Paul Dean.
C: Michael Kiernan 2.
P: Kiernan.
Referee: Guy Maurette (France).

(NB: RWC 1987 Wales v Ireland)

Ireland 9 Wales 12

Lansdowne Road, Dublin. 5 March 1988

Wales won by 1 try, 1 con, 1 pen, 1 drop goal to 1 try, 1 con, 1 pen.

The Triple Crown was gained for the first time since 1979, thanks to a finely judged penalty goal from Paul Thorburn which the Neath full-back reckoned was one of his best pressure kicks. Wales had led with a Jonathan Davies drop goal, but fell 9–3 down and had Bob Norster injured. They hit back for Paul Moriarty to score and Thorburn's conversion brought the scores level. Then, in injury time, Ireland killed the ball at a ruck and Thorburn struck.

Ireland P.P. Danaher (Lansdowne); T.M. Ringland (Ballymena), B.J. Mullin (Blackrock Coll), M.J. Kiernan (Dolphin), K.D. Crossan (Instonians);

P.J. Dean (St Mary's Coll), M.T. Bradley (Cork Const); T.P.J. Clancy (Lansdowne), T.J. Kingston (Dolphin), D.C. Fitzgerald (Lansdowne), +D.G. Lenihan (Cork Const), W.A. Anderson (Dungannon), P.M. Matthews (Wanderers), M.E. Gibson (London Irish), W.D. McBride (Malone).
T: Terry Kingston.
C: Michael Kiernan.
P: Kiernan.

Wales P.H. Thorburn (Neath); I.C. Evans (Llanelli), M.G. Ring (Pontypool), +B. Bowen (South Wales Police), A.M. Hadley (Cardiff); J. Davies (Llanelli), R.N. Jones (Swansea); D.A. Buchanan (Llanelli), I.J. Watkins (Ebbw Vale), D. Young (Swansea), P.S. May (Llanelli), R.L. Norster (Cardiff), R.D. Phillips (Neath), W.P. Moriarty (Swansea), R.G. Collins (South Wales Police).
T: Paul Moriarty.
C: Paul Thorburn.
P: Thorburn.
DG: Jonathan Davies.
Referee: Ray J. Megson (Scotland).

Wales 13 Ireland 19

Arms Park, Cardiff. 4 February 1989

Ireland won by 2 tries, 1 con, 3 pens to 1 try, 3 pens.

If the winning try for Ireland was disputed – when a David Irwin knock-on went unseen and allowed Paul Dean to score – there were few who felt that Wales would have been worthy winners. Rather than the Dean score, the match will be remembered for the try by forward Noel Mannion who snapped up a Bleddyn Bowen kick to run away with David Bryant chasing in vain.

Wales +P.H. Thorburn (Neath); I.C. Evans (Llanelli), J.A. Devereux (Bridgend), N.G. Davies (Llanelli), M.R. Hall (Bridgend); B. Bowen (Swansea), R.N. Jones (Swansea); M. Griffiths (Bridgend), I.J. Watkins (Ebbw Vale), *L. Delaney, P.T. Davies (Llanelli), K. Moseley (Pontypool), R.D. Phillips, M.A. Jones (Neath), D.J. Bryant (Bridgend). Reps: C. Davies (Llanelli) for Devereux; *P. Turner (Newbridge) for Thorburn.
T: Mark Jones.
P: Paul Thorburn 3.

Ireland F.J. Dunlea (Lansdowne); M.J. Kiernan (Dolphin), B.J. Mullin (London Irish), D.G. Irwin, K.D. Crossan (Instonians); P.M. Dean (St Mary's Coll), L.F.P. Aherne; T.P.J. Clancy (Lansdowne), S.J. Smith (Ballymena), J.J. McCoy (Bangor), D.G. Lenihan (Cork Const),

W.A. Anderson (Dungannon), +P.M. Matthews (Wanderers), N.P. Mannion (Corinthians), P.J. O'Hara (Sunday's Well).
T: Noel Mannion, Paul Dean.
C: Michael Kiernan.
P: Kiernan 3.
Referee: Roger C. Quittenton (England).

Ireland 14 Wales 8

Lansdowne Road, Dublin. 24 March 1990

Ireland won by 3 tries, 1 con to 2 tries.

If at first Neath don't succeed, try a few more, was the Waldron doctrine. In came Martyn Morris after a five-year absence, and Alan Edmunds won a cap as a replacement. Wales lost and finished clear Wooden Spoon winners. For the first time, they lost five consecutive games. These were still amateur, or even 'shamateur', days and Steve Ford played despite having had a life ban for taking part in a trial match with Leeds RL club. He won a long fight to have the sentence removed and, after taking the injured Mike Hall's place, he scored a début try. Wales were two tries and ten points behind when Ford scored. Hooker Terry Kingston restored the ten-point gap, though Gareth Llewellyn went over for the second Welsh try. An Ireland try-scorer was outside-half Brian Smith, who had played at scrum-half for Australia against Wales in the 1987 World Cup.

Ireland K. Murphy (Cork Const); K.J. Hooks (Ards), B.J. Mullin (Blackrock Coll), M.J. Kiernan (Dolphin), K.D. Crossan (Instonians); B.A. Smith (Oxford U), M.T. Bradley (Cork Const); J.J. Fitzgerald (Young Munster), T.J. Kingston (Dolphin), D.C. Fitzgerald (Lansdowne), N.P.J. Francis (Blackrock Coll), +D.G. Lenihan (Cork Const), W.D. McBride (Malone), N.P. Mannion (Corinthians), P.T.J. O'Hara (Sunday's Well). Rep: L.F. Aherne (Lansdowne) for Bradley.
T: Brian Smith, Denis McBride, Terry Kingston.
C: Michael Kiernan.

Wales P.H. Thorburn (Neath); *S.P. Ford, M.G. Ring (Cardiff), A.G. Bateman (Neath), A. Emyr (Swansea); D.W. Evans (Cardiff), +R.N. Jones (Swansea); B.R. Williams, K.H. Phillips (Neath), H. Williams-Jones (South Wales Police), A.G. Allen (Newbridge), G.O. Llewellyn, M.S. Morris, M.A. Jones (Neath), R.G. Collins (Cardiff). Reps: A. Clement (Swansea) for Thorburn; *D.A. Edmunds (Neath) for Evans.
T: Steve Ford, Gareth Llewellyn.
Referee: David J. Bishop (New Zealand).

Wales 21 Ireland 21

Arms Park, Cardiff. 16 February 1991

Draw. Wales – 2 tries, 2 cons, 2 pens, 1 drop goal; Ireland – 4 tries, 1 con, 1 drop goal.

Mark Ring jokingly worked out that if he had appeared in every match since his début, he would have broken the Welsh record of caps. The great entertainer made a try which Neil Jenkins touched down, but he gave one away when his kick was charged down and Brendan Mullin went over. Phil Davies had a fine game in the Welsh pack, while Simon Geoghegan was a threat on the Ireland wing. It was an interesting match, but not a great one. It marked the débuts of the excellent prop forward John Davies and Emyr 'Tarw – the Bull' Lewis.

Wales +P.H. Thorburn (Neath); I.C. Evans (Llanelli), M.G. Ring (Cardiff), I.S. Gibbs (Neath), S.P. Ford (Cardiff); N.R. Jenkins (Pontypridd), C.J. Bridges (Neath); M. Griffiths (Cardiff), K.H. Phillips, *J.D. Davies, Glyn D. Llewellyn (Neath), P. Arnold (Swansea), *E.W. Lewis, P.T. Davies (Llanelli), M.S. Morris (Neath).
T: Neil Jenkins, Paul Arnold.
C: Paul Thorburn 2.
P: Thorburn 2.
DG: Neil Jenkins.

Ireland J.E. Staples; S.P. Geoghegan (London Irish), B.J. Mullin (Blackrock Coll), D.M. Curtis (London Irish), D.J. Clarke (Dolphin); B.A. Smith (Leicester), +R. Saunders (London Irish); J.J. Fitzgerald (Young Munster), S.J. Smith (Ballymena), D.C. Fitzgerald (Lansdowne), M.J. Galwey (Shannon), B.J. Rigney (Greystones), P.M. Matthews (Wanderers), B.F. Robinson (Ballymena), G.F. Hamilton (NIFC). Rep: K.J. Murphy (Cork Const) for Staples.
T: Jim Staples, Brendan Mullin, Jack Clarke, Simon Geoghegan.
C: Brian Smith.
DG: Smith.
Referee: David J. Bishop (New Zealand).

Ireland 15 Wales 16

Lansdowne Road, Dublin. 18 January 1992

Wales won by 1 try, 3 pens, 1 drop goal to 1 try, 1 con, 3 pens.

Once more came the question: 'Have Wales turned the corner?' The side worked hard and deserved victory, coming from 6–15 to 12–15, before

Centre Scott Gibbs is about to pass the ball in training for the match against Ireland in Dublin, 1992. He is flanked by forwards Stuart Davies and Richard Webster. (© Huw Evans)

débutant Stuart Davies dived over for the winning try. Wales could have been down to 14 men early on, when English-born débutant Tony Copsey smacked Neil Francis with a haymaker which temporarily put the Irish lock off the field. Fred Howard did not, astonishingly, dismiss Copsey and the Irish, to their credit, did not make a meal out of it. The leadership of Alan Davies, Bob Norster and Ieuan Evans was, at least, putting a bit of pride back in the team. It was their first championship win since England in 1989.

Ireland J.E. Staples (London Irish); R.M. Wallace (Garryowen), D.M. Curtis (London Irish), B.J. Mullin (Blackrock Coll), K.D. Crossan (Instonians); R.P. Keyes (Cork Const), R. Saunders (London Irish); N.J. Popplewell (Greystones), S.J. Smith (Ballymena), D.C. Fitzgerald (De la Salle), N.P.J. Francis (Blackrock Coll), D.G. Lenihan (Cork Const), +P.M. Matthews (Wanderers), B.F. Robinson (Ballymena), M.J. Fitzgibbon (Shannon).
T: Richard Wallace.
C: Ralph Keyes.
P: Keyes 3.

Wales A. Clement (Swansea); +I.C. Evans (Llanelli), I.S. Gibbs (Swansea), N.R. Jenkins (Pontypridd), M.R. Hall (Cardiff); *C.J. Stephens (Llanelli), R.N. Jones (Swansea); M.

Griffiths (Cardiff), G.R. Jenkins (Swansea), L. Delaney (Llanelli), G.O. Llewellyn (Neath), *A.H. Copsey, E.W. Lewis (Llanelli), *S. Davies, R.E. Webster (Swansea).
T: Stuart Davies.
P: Neil Jenkins 3.
DG: Colin Stephens.
Referee: Fred A. Howard (England).

Wales 14 Ireland 19

Arms Park, Cardiff. 6 March 1993

Ireland won by 1 try, 1 con, 3 pens, 1 drop goal to 1 try, 3 pens.

New cap Eric Elwood and Ireland captain Michael Bradley combined well enough to deny Wales their first win over Ireland since 1983. Neil Jenkins missed seven goal attempts out of ten, while Elwood was all confidence. One bright spot was the try by Ieuan Evans, but the other Welsh wing saw little of the ball. He was Nigel Walker, an international athlete in his first senior rugby season. A near-veteran at 29, Walker had been an Olympic Games 110m hurdles semi-finalist in 1984, nine years earlier in Los Angeles.

Wales M.A. Rayer (Cardiff); +I.C. Evans (Llanelli), M.R. Hall (Cardiff), I.S. Gibbs (Swansea), *N.K. Walker (Cardiff); N.R. Jenkins (Pontypridd), R.N. Jones (Swansea); R.L. Evans (Llanelli), N. Meek (Pontypool), H. Williams-Jones (South Wales Police), G.O. Llewellyn (Neath), A.H. Copsey, E.W. Lewis (Llanelli), S. Davies, R.E. Webster (Swansea). Rep: A. Clement (Swansea) for (I.C.) Evans.
T: Ieuan Evans.
P: Neil Jenkins 3.

Ireland C.P. Clarke (Terenure Coll); R.M. Wallace (Garryowen), V.G.J. Cunningham (St Mary's Coll), P.P.A. Danaher (Garryowen), S.P. Geoghegan (London Irish); E.P. Elwood (Lansdowne), +M.T. Bradley (Cork Const); N.J. Popplewell (Greystones), T.J. Kingston (Dolphin), P.M. Clohessy (Young Munster), P.S. Johns (Dungannon), M.J. Galwey (Shannon), P.T.J. O'Hara (Cork Const), B.F. Robinson (London Irish), W.D. McBride (Malone).
T: Brian Robinson.
C: Eric Elwood.
P: Elwood 3.
DG: Ciaran Clarke.
Referee: A.R. 'Sandy' MacNeill (Australia).

Ireland 15 Wales 17

Lansdowne Road, Dublin. 5 February 1994

Wales won by 1 try, 4 pens to 5 pens.

Wales deserved victory, if only for scoring the sole try of the match, but Eric Elwood hit a post with what could have been a match-winning effort for Ireland. The Neil Jenkins try came after a clever pass by his half-back partner, Rupert Moon. It was a tough afternoon for the back division, as Wayne Proctor broke his jaw and both Tony Clement and Nigel Davies pulled up with hamstring injuries. With replacement scrum-half Robert Jones even lined up in the three-quarters, the cry went out for Ieuan Evans to stay on the field, despite a badly injured shoulder. He did, and was one of the nine Llanelli players in the starting lineup. With his 16 points in the match, Neil Jenkins moved to 170 points in 19 matches, thus passing Phil Bennett's total of 166 and moving into second place of scorers for Wales, behind Paul Thorburn.

Ireland C.M.P. O'Shea (Lansdowne); R.M. Wallace (Garryowen), M.C. McCall (Bangor), P.P.A. Danaher (Garryowen), S.P. Geoghegan (London Irish); E.P. Elwood (Lansdowne), +M.T. Bradley (Cork Const); N.J. Popplewell (Greystones), T.J. Kingston (Dolphin), P.M. Clohessy (Young Munster), M.J. Galwey (Shannon), N.P.J. Francis (Old Belvedere), B.F. Robinson (Ballymena), P.S. Johns (Dungannon), W D McBride (Malone).
P: Eric Elwood 5.

Wales A. Clement (Swansea); +I.C. Evans (Llanelli), M.R. Hall (Cardiff), N.G. Davies, W.T. Proctor (Llanelli); N.R. Jenkins (Pontypridd), R.H.StJ.B. Moon; R.L. Evans (Llanelli), G.R. Jenkins (Swansea), J.D. Davies (Neath), P.T. Davies (Llanelli), G.O. Llewellyn (Neath), E.W. Lewis, L.S. Quinnell, M.A. Perego (Llanelli). Reps: M.A. Rayer (Cardiff) for Clement; R.N. Jones (Swansea) for (N.G.)Davies; S.D. Hill (Cardiff) for Proctor.
T: Neil Jenkins.
P: Neil Jenkins 4.
Referee: A.J. 'Tony' Spreadbury (England).

Wales 12 Ireland 16

Arms Park, Cardiff. 18 March 1995

Ireland won by 1 try, 1 con, 2 pens, 1 drop goal to 4 pens.

It was Wooden Spoon time for Wales and, nine days after the loss, it was goodbye to coach Alan Davies, his assistant Gareth Jenkins and team manager Bob Norster, who were said to have tendered their resignations. Ireland pulled off their fifth win in six visits to Cardiff, having drawn the other. Centre Brendan Mullin celebrated his 50th cap with the only try of the match. Richie Collins did Wales a disservice by putting Eric Elwood off the pitch with a strong tackle. On came Paul Burke, who was to partner Robert Jones for the Cardiff club in 1998–99. Burke and Neil Jenkins landed four goal attempts apiece. Wales had scored just one try in the championship which may have been the worst statistic of all. On the same afternoon that Ireland won, England took the championship, Grand Slam and Triple Crown by defeating Scotland at Twickenham. Eight weeks before the World Cup finals were due to start, the WRU turned to Cardiff's coach, Australian Alex Evans, to take control in South Africa. It was almost a repeat of the scenario which had seen Alan Davies move in just before the 1991 World Cup.

Wales M. Back (Bridgend); +I.C. Evans (Llanelli), M.R. Hall (Cardiff), N.G. Davies, W.T. Proctor (Llanelli); N.R. Jenkins (Pontypridd), R.N. Jones (Swansea); M. Griffiths (Cardiff), G.R. Jenkins (Swansea), S.C. John, P.T. Davies (Llanelli), G.O. Llewellyn (Neath), *A. Gibbs (Newbridge), E.W. Lewis (Cardiff), R.G. Collins (Pontypridd).
P: Neil Jenkins 4.

Ireland J.E. Staples (Harlequins); R.M. Wallace (Garryowen), B.J. Mullin (Blackrock Coll), P.P.A. Danaher (Garryowen), S.P. Geoghegan (Bath); E.P. Elwood (Lansdowne), N.A. Hogan (Terenure Coll); N.J. Popplewell (Wasps), +T.J. Kingston (Dolphin), P.M.N. Clohessy (Young Munster), D.A. Tweed (Ballymena), G.M. Fulcher (Cork Const), A.G. Foley (Shannon), P.S. Johns (Dungannon), E.O. Halvey (Shannon). Reps: M.J. Field (Malone) for Geoghegan (temp); P. Burke (Cork Const) for Elwood.
T: Brendan Mullin.
C: Paul Burke.
P: Burke 2.
DG: Burke.
Referee: Ray J. Megson (Scotland).

(NB: RWC 1995 Wales v Ireland)

Ireland 30 Wales 17

Lansdowne Road, Dublin. 2 March 1996.

Ireland won by 4 tries, 2 cons, 2 pens to 2 tries, 2 cons, 1 pen.

This was the 100th meeting of the two countries. Wales remained well ahead 58–36, with six matches drawn. This match showed up the Welsh defence as being extremely brittle and even two fine Ieuan Evans tries could not make up for the four given away. Evans had now scored 27 tries in 60 international matches, but these were the first away from home in the championship. Simon Mason had a superb début for Ireland, but it was left-wing Niall Woods who scored the most important try of the day. He caught a poor kick by Arwel Thomas on the touchline, kicked ahead, regathered and brought the crowd to their feet. It was a giveaway and, hard though Wales and Leigh Davies in particular, tried, there was no way back.

Ireland S.J.P. Mason (Orrell); S.P. Geoghegan (Bath), J.C. Bell (Northampton), M.J. Field (Malone), N.K.P.J. Woods (Blackrock Coll); D.G. Humphreys (London Irish), +N.A. Hogan (Terenure Coll); N.J. Popplewell (Newcastle), A.T.H. Clarke (Northampton), P.S. Wallace (Blackrock Coll), G.M. Fulcher (Cork Const), J.W. Davidson (Dungannon), D.S. Corkery (Cork Const), V.C.P. Costello (St Mary's Coll), W.D. McBride (Malone).
T: Simon Geoghegan, Niall Woods, Gabriel Fulcher, David Corkery.
C: Simon Mason 2.
P: Mason 2.

Wales W.J.L. Thomas; I.C. Evans (Llanelli), L.B. Davies (Neath), N.G. Davies, W.T. Proctor (Llanelli); A.C. Thomas (Bristol), R. Howley (Bridgend); A.L.P. Lewis, +J.M. Humphreys (Cardiff), J.D. Davies, G.O. Llewellyn (Neath), D. Jones, E.W. Lewis, H.T. Taylor (Cardiff), R.G. Jones (Llanelli).
T: Ieuan Evans 2.
C: Arwel Thomas 2.
P: Arwel Thomas.
Referee: Didier Mene (France).

Ieuan Evans scores one of his two tries in Dublin in 1996, despite the tackle of Ireland centre Jonathan Bell. The tries nevertheless failed to save Wales from a 30–17 defeat. (© Huw Evans)

Wales 25   Ireland 26

Arms Park, Cardiff. 1 February 1997

Ireland won by 3 tries, 1 con, 3 pens to 3 tries, 2 cons, 2 pens.

Ireland must have considered playing all their home matches in Cardiff, after their sixth win in seven visits since 1983 (the other being a draw). It all started well for Wales, as superb handling saw the ball flow out to right-wing Ieuan Evans, who was over the Irish line after just 33 seconds. It was the quickest ever by a Welsh player in an international match. Ireland were shaken, but then stirred to action. In ten minutes they were in front, as Eric Elwood's wicked garryowen rebounded off a post to give Jonathan Bell a try in the follow-up. It was soon 20–10 to Ireland and even a second try by Evans and one from Scott Quinnell, failed to halt Ireland.

Wales N.R. Jenkins (Pontypridd); I.C. Evans (Llanelli), G. Thomas (Bridgend), I.S. Gibbs (Swansea), D.R. James (Bridgend); A.C. Thomas (Swansea), R. Howley (Cardiff); C.D. Loader (Swansea), +J.M. Humphreys, D. Young (Cardiff), G.O. Llewellyn (Harlequins), M.A. Rowley (Pontypridd), S.M. Williams (Neath), L.S. Quinnell (Richmond), C.L. Charvis (Swansea). Reps: J.C. Quinnell (Richmond) for Rowley; K.P. Jones (Ebbw Vale) for Charvis.
T: Ieuan Evans 2, Scott Quinnell.
C: Neil Jenkins 2.
P: Jenkins 2.

Ireland +J.E. Staples (Harlequins); D.A. Hickie (St Mary's Coll), J.C. Bell (Northampton), M.J. Field (Malone), D.J. Crotty (Garryowen); E.P. Elwood (Lansdowne), N.A. Hogan (Terenure Coll); N.J. Popplewell, R.P. Nesdale (Newcastle), P.S. Wallace, P.S. Johns (Saracens), J.W. Davidson (London Irish), D.S. Corkery (Bristol), E.R.P. Miller (Leicester), W.D. McBride (Malone). Rep: G.M. Fulcher (London Irish) for Johns.
T: Jonathan Bell, Eric Miller, Dennis Hickie.
C: Eric Elwood.
P: Elwood 3.
Referee: Wayne J. Erickson (Australia).

Ireland 21   Wales 30

Lansdowne Road, Dublin. 21 March 1998

Wales won by 3 tries, 3 cons, 3 pens to 2 tries, 1 con, 3 pens.

This followed a win over Scotland and yet it was all second-division standard, in a season where England

Cardiff Arms Park auction in 1997 as time ran out for the fixtures and fittings at the Arms Park. (© Huw Evans)

and France appeared to be playing in a different league. Wales worked hard for the win and scored some good tries with Neil Jenkins, who was back yet again in the number 10 jersey, scoring 20 points which included a try. The support for Wales in away matches remained as good, if not better, than any of the other countries, and so it was in Dublin. Of the five tries in the match, Ireland scored two early on, but Wales responded with three. Allan Bateman scored before the interval; Kevin Morgan went over for a glorious second try just after the break and then Jenkins capped it after replacement Stuart Davies, who had last appeared in 1995, opened the way from the back of the scrum.

Ireland C.P. Clarke (Terenure Coll); R.M. Wallace (Saracens), K.M. Maggs (Bristol), R.A.J. Henderson (Wasps), D.A. Hickie (St Mary's Coll); E.P. Elwood (Galwegians), C.D. McGuinness (St Mary's Coll); R. Corrigan (Greystones), +K.G.M. Wood (Harlequins), P.S. Wallace, P.S. Johns (Saracens), M.E. O'Kelly (London Irish), D.S. Corkery (Bristol), V.C.P. Costello (St Mary's Coll), A.J. Ward (Ballinahinch). Reps: R.P. Nesdale (Newcastle) for Wood; P.M.N. Clohessy (Young Munster) for (P.S.) Wallace; E.R.P. Miller (Leicester) for Ward.
T: Andrew Ward, Victor Costello.
C: Eric Elwood.
P: Elwood 3.

Wales K.A. Morgan (Pontypridd); W.T. Proctor (Llanelli), A.G. Bateman (Richmond), L.B. Davies, G. Thomas (Cardiff); N.R. Jenkins (Pontypridd), +R. Howley; A.L.P. Lewis (Cardiff), G.R. Jenkins (Swansea), D. Young (Cardiff), Andrew P. Moore (Swansea), M.J. Voyle (Llanelli), R.C. Appleyard, C.L. Charvis (Swansea), K.P. Jones (Ebbw Vale). Reps: J.M. Humphreys (Cardiff) for (G.R.) Jenkins; L. Mustoe (Cardiff) for Young; S. Davies (Swansea) for Jones.
T: Allan Bateman, Kevin Morgan, Neil Jenkins.
C: Neil Jenkins 3.
P: Neil Jenkins 3.
Referee: Ed F. Morrison (England).

Wales 23   Ireland 29

Wembley, London. 20 February 1999

Ireland won by 2 tries, 2 cons, 3 pens, 2 drop goals to 2 tries, 2 cons, 3 pens.

Ireland took their tally to seven wins and a draw in eight away matches against Wales since 1983. Beaten in the lineout and outscrummaged, Wales were down by 16–6 at half-time. It became 26–6, but there was a fightback which brought Wales to 26–23, only for fly-half David Humphreys to drop a second goal and give his side a deserved victory. When Neil Jenkins had a kick charged down, Kevin Maggs virtually strolled over, escorted by several colleagues, while hooker Keith Wood side-stepped Scott Gibbs for the other Irish try. Jenkins kicked his goals, and tries came from Craig Quinnell and Shane Howarth in a 14-minute spell. 'We will go to Paris with nothing to lose,' said Graham Henry. 'Who knows what could happen?' Most Welshmen were pretty sure of what would happen against both France and England. Memories of the 1998 losses were engraved in the minds of Welsh supporters. They were proved wrong!

Wales S.P. Howarth (Manchester-Sale); M.F.D. Robinson, M. Taylor, I.S. Gibbs (Swansea), D.R. James; N.R. Jenkins (Pontypridd), +R. Howley (Cardiff); D.R. Morris (Swansea), B.H. Williams (Richmond), D. Young (Cardiff), J.C. Quinnell (Richmond), C.P. Wyatt (Llanelli), C.L. Charvis (Swansea), L.S. Quinnell (Llanelli), M.E. Williams (Pontypridd). Reps: G.R. Jenkins (Swansea) for (B.H.) Williams; C.T. Anthony (Swansea) for Young; M.J. Voyle (Llanelli) for (M.E.) Williams (temp).
T: Craig Quinnell, Shane Howarth.
C: Neil Jenkins 2.
P: Neil Jenkins 3.

Ireland C.M.P. O'Shea; J.P. Bishop (London Irish), K.M. Maggs (Bath), J.C. Bell (Dungannon), N.K.P.J. Woods (London Irish); D.G. Humphreys (Dungannon), C.D. McGuinness (St Mary's Coll); P.S. Wallace (Saracens), K.G.M. Wood (Harlequins), P.M.N. Clohessy (Young Munster), +P.S. Johns (Saracens), J.W. Davidson (Castres), D. O'Cuinneagain (Manchester-Sale), E.R.P. Miller (Terenure Coll), A.J. Ward (Ballynahinch). Reps: J.M. Fitzpatrick (Dungannon) for Clohessy; M.J. Galwey (Shannon) for Johns; V.C.P. Costello (St Mary's Coll) for Miller.
T: Kevin Maggs, Keith Wood.
C: David Humphreys 2.
P: Humphreys 3.
DG: Humphreys 2.
Referee: Scott Young (Australia).

Cardiff Arms Park demolition in 1997.
(© Huw Evans)

SCOTLAND

Scotland v Wales

Raeburn Place, Edinburgh. 8 January 1883.
(No points were awarded until 1891)

Scotland won by 3 tries, 3 cons to 1 try, 1 con.

Only 4,000 spectators turned up for the Monday match on a bitterly cold day in which Dr John Griffin of Edinburgh University appeared for Wales. Eight years later, he was to referee the first-ever South African Test, in 1891 against the British Isles. Born in Southampton, he had no Welsh connections and was the University's third-team captain. Newspaper reports listed Glasgow-born James Bridie of Greenock Wanderers as playing for Wales, but his appearance is thought to have been prevented by Scotland and it is uncertain whether Griffin or William Norton took his place. Anyway, both eventually appeared.

Scotland D.W. Kidston (Glasgow Acads); W.E. Maclagan (Edinburgh Acads/London Scottish), D.J. MacFarlan (London Scottish); W.S. Brown (Edinburgh Inst FP), A.R. Don Wauchope (Edinburgh Wands); +D.Y. Cassels, J.G. Walker, J. Jamieson, A. Walker (West of Scotland), J.B. Brown, W.A. Walls, J.G. Mowat (Glasgow Acads), C. Reid (Edinburgh Acads), D. Somerville, T. Ainslie (Edinburgh Inst FP).
T: David MacFarlan 2, Andrew Don Wauchope.
C: Bill Maclagan 3.

Wales +C.P. Lewis (Llandovery); C.H. Newman (Newport), W.B. Norton (Cardiff); W.F. Evans (Oxford U/Rhymney), G.F. Harding (Newport); T.H. Judson (Llanelli), T.J.S. Clapp, R. Gould, T.B. Jones, *H.S. Lyne (Newport), F.T. Purdon, G.L.B. Morris (Swansea), A. Cattell (Llanelli), *J.A. Jones (Cardiff), *Dr J. Griffin (Edinburgh U).
T: Tom Judson.
C: Charles Lewis.
Referee: G. Rowland Hill (England).

Wales v Scotland

Rodney Parade, Newport. 12 January 1884

Scotland won by 1 try, 1 drop goal to nil.

Scotland won, but Wales disputed both the Grant Asher drop goal and the Tom Ainslie try, while William Gwynn went over the line but dropped the ball. He must have been forgiven, as he was capped on another three occasions, but was to die in 1897 following a stroke. This was the first time that Wales had not fielded a new cap and was also notable for the fact that the secretaries of the two unions were the touch-judges, while the referee was from Scotland.

Wales C.P. Lewis (Llandovery); C.P. Allen (Beaumaris/Oxford U), W.B. Norton (Cardiff), C.G. Taylor (Ruabon/Blackheath); C.H. Newman (Newport), W.H. Gwynn (Swansea); H.J. Simpson, W.D. Phillips (Cardiff), R. Gould, H.S. Lyne, T.B. Jones, T.J.S. Clapp (Newport), F.L. Margrave (Llanelli), G.L.B. Morris, F.G. Andrews (Swansea).

Scotland J.P. Veitch (Royal HSFP); G.C. Lindsay, D.J. MacFarlan, +W.E. Maclagan (London Scottish); A.R. Don Wauchope, A.G.G. Asher (Edinburgh Wdrs); C. Reid (Edinburgh Acads), T. Ainslie, D. Somerville, R. Maitland (Edinburgh Inst FP), J.B. Brown, W.A. Walls (Glasgow Acads), J. Jamieson (West of Scotland), J. Tod (Watsonians), W.A. Peterkin (Edinburgh U).
T: Tom Ainslie.
DG: Grant Asher.
Referee: James S. McLaren (Scotland).

Scotland v Wales

Hamilton Crescent, Partick. 10 January 1885

Draw. No score.

Wales played their first drawn match. Included in the pack was William Henry Thomas at the age of 18 years and 10 months, who was still believed to have been studying at Llandovery College before going up to Cambridge University. Three years later he became the first Welshman to tour Australia and New Zealand with a British Isles team.

Scotland P.R. Harrower (London Scottish); A.E. Stephen (West of Scotland), +W.E. Maclagan (London Scottish), G. Maitland (Edinburgh Inst FP); A.R. Don Wauchope, A.G.G. Asher (Edinburgh Wdrs); C. Reid (Edinburgh Acads), J. Tod (Watsonians), T. Ainslie, R. Maitland (Edinburgh Inst FP), J. Jamieson, J.G. Mitchell

(West of Scotland), C.W. Berry (Fettesian-Lorettonians), W.A. Peterkin (Edinburgh U), G.H. Robb (Glasgow Acads).

Wales A.J. Gould (Newport); C.G. Taylor (Ruabon/Blackheath), F.E. Hancock (Cardiff), H.M. Jordan; +C.H. Newman (Newport), W.H. Gwynn (Swansea); *E.P. Alexander (Cambridge U), *A.F. Hill, L.C. Thomas (Cardiff), *W.H. Thomas (Llandovery/Cambridge U), S.J. Goldsworthy, *D. Morgan (Swansea), T.J.S. Clapp, R. Gould, T.B. Jones (Newport).
Referee: G. Rowland Hill (England).

Wales v Scotland

Arms Park, Cardiff. 9 January 1886

Scotland won by 3 tries, 2 cons to nil.

Wales made history by becoming the first international team to introduce four three-quarters, but it was later abandoned as Frank Hancock, the Wiveliscombe-born captain, moved full-back Harry Bowen to the pack to even it up at nine each up front, with Arthur Gould moving to the last line of defence. Scotland's half-backs were brothers Pat and 'Bunny' Don Wauchope while brewery director Hancock followed his younger brother 'Baby' Hancock into international rugby. The latter had played for England in the previous match against Wales.

Wales D.H. Bowen (Llanelli); W.M. Douglas, +F.E. Hancock (Cardiff), A.J. Gould (Newport), C.G. Taylor (Ruabon/Blackheath); *A.A. Mathews (Lampeter), W.J. Stadden (Cardiff); A.F. Hill, G.A. Young, D.H. Lewis (Cardiff), T.J.S. Clapp (Newport), W.A. Bowen, D. Morgan (Swansea), W.H. Thomas (Llandovery/Cambridge U), E.P. Alexander (Cambridge U).

Scotland F.J. McIndoe (Glasgow Acads); D.J. MacFarlan (London Scottish), R.H. Morrison (Edinburgh U), W.F. Holms (RIE Coll); A.R. Don Wauchope, P.H. Don Wauchope (Edinburgh Wdrs); +J.B. Brown, W.A. Walls, J. French (Glasgow Acads), C. Reid, T.W. Irvine, A.T. Clay (Edinburgh Acads), J. Tod (Watsonians), C.J.B. Milne, W.M. MacLeod (Fettesian-Lorettonians).
T: Andrew Don Wauchope, Alex Clay, John Tod.
C: William MacLeod 2.
Referee: D. Frank Moore (Ireland).

Scotland v Wales

Raeburn Place, Edinburgh. 26 February 1887

Scotland won by 12 tries, 4 cons to nil.

Scotland ran riot with twelve tries recorded and five of them went to the London-based three-quarter George Lindsay. He was not originally selected, but the match was postponed for a month and David MacFarlan, the first choice, dropped out. Wales lost Cardiff teenager Jem Evans with injury in the second half of his début and also had Billy Douglas injured, and though he bravely stayed on the field, he never appeared for Wales again.

Scotland A.W.C. Cameron (Watsonians); W.E. Maclagan, G.C. Lindsay (London Scottish), A.N. Woodrow (Glasgow Acads); C.E. Orr (West of Scotland), P.H. Don Wauchope (Edinburgh Wdrs); +C. Reid, T.W. Irvine, A.T. Clay, M.C. McEwan (Edinburgh Acads), C.W. Berry (Fettesian-Lorettonians), R.G. McMillan (London Scottish), D.S. Morton (West of Scotland), H.T. Ker, J. French (Glasgow Acads).
T: George Lindsay 5, Patrick Don Wauchope, Charles Orr, Charles Reid, Robert McMillan, Matthew McEwan, Bill Maclagan, David Morton.
C: Charles Berry 2, Alex Woodrow 2.

Wales *H. Hughes (Cardiff); D. Gwynn (Swansea), A.J. Gould (Newport), W.M. Douglas (Cardiff); *G.E. Bowen (Swansea), O.J. Evans (Cardiff); W.A. Bowen, E.S. Richards, D. Morgan (Swansea), A.F. Bland, *W.E.O. Williams (Cardiff), W.H. Thomas (Llandovery/Cambridge U), +R. Gould, T.W. Lockwood, T.J.S. Clapp (Newport).
Referee: Fred I. Currey (England).

Wales v Scotland

Rodney Parade, Newport. 4 February 1888

Wales won by 1 try to nil.

Wales gained their first victory over Scotland through a disputed try scored by débutant wing Tom Jenkins. Known as Pryce-Jenkins, he founded London Welsh and was a medical officer who also became an actor. Scotland claimed that he had put his foot into touch before crossing the line. This was Charles Reid, the Scotland captain's 19th cap, the man who'd made his début against Wales as a 17-year-old Edinburgh Academy schoolboy. Joseph Chambers, later knighted, controlled his first match. He was the IRFU president and played against Wales the previous year.

Wales *E.J. Roberts (Llanelli); G.E. Bowen (Swansea), A.J. Gould (Newport), *T.J.P. Jenkins (London Welsh); O.J. Evans, W.J. Stadden (Cardiff); +T.J.S. Clapp, *R.W. Powell (Newport), W.H. Thomas (Llandovery), A.F. Bland, A.F. Hill, *Q.D. Kedzlie (Cardiff), *J. Meredith, *T. Williams, *W.H. Howell (Swansea).
T: Tom Jenkins.

Scotland H.F.T. Chambers (Edinburgh U); W.E. Maclagan (London Scottish), H.J. Stevenson (Edinburgh Acads), M.M. Duncan (Fettesian-Lorettonians); C.E. Orr (West of Scotland), C.F.P. Fraser (Glasgow U); C.W. Berry (Fettesian-Lorettonians), +C. Reid, A.T. Clay, M.C. McEwan, T.W. Irvine, T.B. White (Edinburgh Acads), A. Duke (Royal HSFP), D.S. Morton (West of Scotland), L.E. Stevenson (Edinburgh U).
Referee: Joseph Chambers (Ireland).

Scotland v Wales

Raeburn Place, Edinburgh. 2 February 1889

Scotland won by 2 tries to nil.

Wales lost in a snow storm, with the game restricted to two half-hour periods. New caps Rosser Evans and Teddy Bishop, both from Llandovery College, never played again for Wales. Frank Hill continued as Wales skipper, while Scotland were led by David Morton, who refereed the Wales–England match in 1893.

Scotland H.F.T. Chambers (Edinburgh U); W.F. Holms, J.H. Marsh (Edinburgh RIE Coll), H.J. Stevenson (Edinburgh Acads); C.E. Orr (West of Scotland), C.F.P. Fraser (Glasgow U); +D.S. Morton, J.D. Boswell, W. Auld (West of Scotland), H.T. Ker (Glasgow Acads), M.C. McEwan, T.B. White (Edinburgh Acads), A. Duke (Royal HSFP), W.A. McDonald (Glasgow U), A. Methuen (London Scottish).
T: Charles Orr, Hugh Ker.

Wales H. Hughes (Cardiff); R.M. Garrett (Penarth), J.E. Webb (Newport), *E.H. Bishop (Swansea), H.M. Jordan (London Welsh/Newport); C.J. Thomas (Newport), *G. Rosser Evans (Cardiff); S.H. Nicholls, +A.F. Hill, W.E.O. Williams, *D.W. Evans (Cardiff), C.T. Harding, J. Hannan (Newport), *R.L. Thomas (London Welsh), W.A. Bowen (Swansea).
Referee: A. McAllister (Ireland).

Wales v Scotland

Arms Park, Cardiff. 1 February 1890

Scotland won by 3 tries, 1 con to 1 try.

Confusion with the scoring system saw Scotland call it 8–2 and Wales 5–1, but there was no universally accepted scoring system in place until the following season. In any event, it was a Scotland win before a record crowd of 10,000 that saw England miss out on playing for Wales! The man was the Newport full-back Tom England, who was injured and thereby opened the door for the début of the immortal W.J. 'Billy' Bancroft who played continually for eleven seasons, thus denying England a chance in the international arena. Some reports gave John Boswell as scoring a try, others Matthew McEwan. However, the first international try in the 'new' scoring system came from Darsie Anderson, who was later an elephant exporter in Siam!

Wales *W.J. Bancroft (Swansea); C.J. Thomas, A.J. Gould (Newport), R.M. Garrett (Penarth), *D.P.M. Lloyd (Llanelli); *Evan James (Swansea), W.J. Stadden; +A.F. Hill, W.E.O. Williams, A.F. Bland (Cardiff), W.A. Bowen, J. Meredith, *W. Rice Evans (Swansea), J. Hannan (Newport), *S. Thomas (Llanelli).
T: Arthur Gould.

Scotland G. MacGregor; +W.E. Maclagan (London Scottish), H.J. Stevenson (Edinburgh Acads), G.R. Wilson (Royal HSFP); C.E. Orr (West of Scotland), D.G. Anderson (London Scottish); W. Auld, J.E. Orr, J.D. Boswell (West of Scotland), R.G. MacMillan, F.W.J. Goodhue (London Scottish), M.C. McEwan (Edinburgh Acads), A. Duke (Royal HSFP), A. Dalgleish (Gala), I. MacIntyre (Edinburgh Wdrs).
T: Darsie Anderson, Matthew McEwan, Bill Maclagan.
C: McEwan.
Referee: A. McAllister (Ireland).

Scotland 15 Wales 0

Raeburn Place, Edinburgh. 7 February 1891

Scotland won by 7 tries, 1 con, 2 drop goals to nil.

Scotland followed this win with others against Ireland and England to take the Triple Crown for the first time. Again it was Bancroft's suspect defence that was a weakness. One of the newcomers in the back division was Billy McCutcheon, who later refereed rugby league Test matches in 1908 and 1909.

Scotland fielded the teenage Neilson brothers, both making their début with William, aged 17, dropping a goal. The score of 15–0 may not seem impressive now, but it included seven tries by the home side.

Scotland H.J. Stevenson (Edinburgh Acads); P.R.A. Clauss (Birkenhead Park), G. MacGregor, W. Neilson (London Scottish); C.E. Orr (West of Scotland), D.G. Anderson (London Scottish); +M.C. McEwan (Edinburgh Acads), G.T. Neilson, J.D. Boswell, J.E. Orr (West of Scotland), F.W.J. Goodhue, R.G. MacMillan (London Scottish), I. MacIntyre (Edinburgh Wdrs), H.T.O. Leggatt (Watsonians), A. Dalgleish (Gala).
T: Paul Clauss 2, Charles Orr, John Orr, John Boswell, Herbert Leggatt, Fred Goodhue.
C: Matthew McEwan,
DG: Henry Stevenson, William Neilson.

Wales W.J. Bancroft (Swansea); R.M. Garrett (Penarth), D. Gwynn (Swansea), G. Thomas (Newport), *W.M. McCutcheon (Swansea); *R.B. Sweet-Escott, H.M. Ingledew (Cardiff); +W.H. Thomas, R.L. Thomas (Llanelli), T.C. Graham (Newport), P. Bennett (Cardiff Harlequins), W.A. Bowen, W. Rice Evans (Swansea), *D.J. Daniel (Llanelli), S.H. Nicholls (Cardiff).
Referee: H.L. Ashmore (England).

Wales 2   Scotland 7

St Helen's, Swansea. 6 February 1892

Scotland won by 2 tries, 1 con to 1 try.

Six Swansea players appeared but neither they nor the home crowd covered themselves with glory in the heavy rain. Referee Jack Hodgson angered the crowd with several of his decisions, and some spectators attacked him. The WRU apologised after both the referee and Arthur Gould were knocked down. James Hannan scored a try, which was to be the only Wales score of the season. Percy Bennett was the first player from Cardiff Harlequins to appear and, in the following match, against New Zealand, F.E. Nicholls became the second and last from that club.

Wales W.J. Bancroft (Swansea); T.W. Pearson (Cardiff), +A.J. Gould (Newport), *J. Conway Rees (Llanelli), W.M. McCutcheon (Swansea); E. James, D. James (Swansea); C.B. Nicholl (Llanelli), W.H. Watts, J. Hannan, T.C. Graham, A.W. Boucher (Newport), F.M. Mills, J.T. Deacon (Swansea), P. Bennett (Cardiff Harlequins).
T: Jim Hannan.

Scotland H.J. Stevenson (Edinburgh Acads); P.R. Clauss (Birkenhead Park), G.T. Campbell, W. Neilson (London Scottish); +C.E. Orr (West of Scotland), D.G. Anderson (London Scottish); F.W.J. Goodhue, R.G. MacMillan (London Scottish), G.T. Neilson, J.N. Millar, J.D. Boswell, J.E. Orr (West of Scotland), A. Dalgleish (Gala), H.T.O. Leggatt (Watsonians), W.R. Gibson (Royal HSFP).
T: John Boswell, George Campbell.
C: Boswell.
Referee: Jack R. Hodgson (England).

Scotland 0   Wales 9

Raeburn Place, Edinburgh. 4 February 1893

Wales won by 3 tries, 1 pen to nil.

Wales won for the first time on Scottish soil. As well as Newport's Gould brothers in the centre, there were also Newport half-backs and five of the club in the pack, though only Bert Gould was among the scorers. After a scoreless first-half, the immaculate Bancroft placed a goal of which some reports stated it was from a mark and some from a penalty – probably drop-kicked. Gould's try was the first by a Welsh player in Scotland and all three Welsh tries came from the three-quarter line.

Scotland A.W.C. Cameron (Watsonians); D. Robertson (Glasgow Acads), G. MacGregor, J.J. Gowans (London Scottish); R.C. Greig (Glasgow Acads), W. Wotherspoon (West of Scotland); A. Dalgleish (Gala), +R.G. MacMillan (London Scottish), H.T.O. Leggatt, W.B. Cownie (Watsonians), G.T. Neilson, H.F. Menzies, J.N. Millar (West of Scotland), W.R. Gibson (Royal HSFP), T.L. Hendry (Clydesdale).

Wales W.J. Bancroft (Swansea); N.W. Biggs (Cardiff), +A.J. Gould, G.H. Gould (Newport), W.M. McCutcheon (Swansea); H.P. Phillips, F.C. Parfitt; H.T. Day, T.C. Graham, J. Hannan, W.H. Watts, A.W. Boucher (Newport), F.M. Mills (Swansea), A.F. Hill (Cardiff), C.B. Nicholl (Llanelli).
T: Bert Gould, Norman Biggs, Billy McCutcheon.
P: Billy Bancroft.
Referee: W.H. Humphreys (England).

Wales 7 Scotland 0

Rodney Parade, Newport. 3 February 1894

(Points system amended – see p.12)

Wales won by 1 try, 1 drop goal to nil.

David Fitzgerald, a centre from the Grangetown area of Cardiff, marked his début with both scores of the match. After one more match, however, he was to transfer to Leigh and later Batley in rugby league. His cap was sold 99 years later for £440. The Newport club was represented by eight players, including new cap William Thomas who later became vicar of Bootle in Cumberland. His cousin and fellow Christ College, Brecon pupil, Richard Budworth, had played twice for England against Wales.

Wales W.J. Bancroft (Swansea); T.W. Pearson, *D. Fitzgerald (Cardiff), +A.J. Gould, *W.L. Thomas; H.P. Phillips, F.C. Parfitt (Newport); F.M. Mills (Swansea), C.B. Nicholl, D.J. Daniel (Llanelli), A.F. Hill (Cardiff), T.C. Graham, H.T. Day, J. Hannan, W.H. Watts (Newport).
T: David Fitzgerald.
DG: Fitzgerald.

Scotland J. Rogerson (Kelvinside Acads); J.J. Gowans, G. MacGregor, G.T. Campbell, H.T.S. Gedge (London Scottish); W. Wotherspoon (West of Scotland), J.W. Simpson (Royal HSFP); W.B. Cownie, H.B. Wright (Watsonians), G.T. Neilson, H.F. Menzies (West of Scotland), A. Dalgleish (Gala), W.M.C. McEwan (Edinburgh Acads), +R.G. MacMillan (London Scottish), W.R. Gibson (Royal HSFP).
Referee: E.B. Holmes (England).

Scotland 5 Wales 4

Raeburn Place, Edinburgh. 26 January 1895

Scotland won by 1 try, 1 con to 1 goal from mark.

Wales were persuaded to play on a badly frozen pitch but only after, at Gould's suggestion, the pitch was shortened by some 15–20 yards. It was a surprisingly good game which was settled when Billy Bancroft gifted Scotland the only try. Though he drop kicked a fine goal from a mark, he allowed wing Jim Gowans to charge a kick down and score. Wales did have their chances and the Cardiff forward Frank Mills had a try disallowed when the ball ended just over the temporary tape, marking the shortened goal-line. For Wales, the speedy Evan Lloyd and Newport forward Tom Pook made their only appearances.

Scotland A.R. Smith; J.J. Gowans, G.T. Campbell, W. Neilson (London Scottish), R. Welsh (Watsonians); J.W. Simpson (Royal HSFP), M. Elliot (Hawick); W.B. Cownie, H.O. Smith (Watsonians), T.M. Scott (Hawick), G.T. Neilson (West of Scotland), +W.R. Gibson (Royal HSFP), W.M.C. McEwan, J.H. Dods (Edinburgh Acads), R.G. MacMillan (London Scottish).
T: Jim Gowans.
C: Allan Smith.

Wales W.J. Bancroft (Swansea); T.W. Pearson (Cardiff), +A.J. Gould (Newport), O. Badger, *E. Lloyd (Llanelli); S.H. Biggs (Cardiff), F.C. Parfitt (Newport); T.C. Graham, A.W. Boucher, J. Hannan, H. Packer, *T.R. Pook (Newport), F.M. Mills (Cardiff), C.B. Nicholl (Llanelli), *E.E. George (Pontypridd).
Goal from mark: Billy Bancroft.
Referee: E.B. Holmes (England).

Wales 6 Scotland 0

Arms Park, Cardiff. 25 January 1896

Wales won by 2 tries to nil.

This match marked the début of the great Gwyn Nicholls in the centre for Wales alongside Arthur Gould. Nicholls, born in Westbury on Severn, went on to play 24 times, but only three of those games were with Gould. Both men were hailed as 'The Prince of Players' during their careers. Llanelli skipper Cliff Bowen scored the first try and Gould the other in the mud of the Arms Park, and the pairing was a success – at least on this occasion.

Wales W.J. Bancroft (Swansea); C.A. Bowen (Llanelli), *E.G. Nicholls (Cardiff), +A.J. Gould, F.H. Dauncey (Newport); S.H. Biggs (Cardiff), F.C. Parfitt (Newport); H. Packer (Newport), *J. Evans, *W. Morris, C.B. Nicholl (Llanelli), *W. Cope (Blackheath), *W. Davies (Cardiff), *D. Evans (Penygraig), F.O. Hutchinson (Neath).
T: Cliff Bowen, Arthur Gould.

Scotland A.R. Smith (London Scottish); T.L. Scott (Langholm), G.T. Campbell (London Scottish), A.B. Timms (Edinburgh Wdrs), R. Welsh (Watsonians); J.W. Simpson (Royal HSFP), D. Patterson (Hawick); +G.T. Neilson, J.H. Couper (West of Scotland), A. Balfour, H.O. Smith (Watsonians), J.H. Dods, W.M.C. McEwan (Edinburgh Acads), M.C. Morrison (Royal HSFP), T.M. Scott (Hawick).
Referee: George H. Harnett (England).

Scotland 21 Wales 10

Inverleith, Edinburgh. 4 March 1899

Scotland won by 3 tries, 2 drop goals, 1 goal from mark to 2 tries, 2 cons.

A frozen Inverleith pitch meant four postponements before the match was eventually played in the snow. Wales led 10–3, with Willie Llewellyn once again a try-scorer, but when Gwyn Nicholls was injured Scotland added two further tries in addition to two dropped goals and a goal from a mark by a forward, new cap William Thomson. Referee Mike Delaney had played against Wales in 1895.

Scotland H. Rottenburg; H.T.S. Gedge, D.B. Monypenny (London Scottish), G.W. Lamond (Kelvinside Acads), T.L. Scott (Langholm); J.W. Simpson (Royal HSFP), R.T. Neilson (West of Scotland); +M.C. Morrison (Royal HSFP), W.M.C. McEwan (Edinburgh Acads), H.O. Smith (Watsonians), G.C. Kerr (Durham City), R.C. Stevenson, A. MacKinnon (London Scottish), J.M. Dykes (Glasgow HSFP), W.J. Thomson (West of Scotland).
T: Henry Gedge, Harry Smith, Douglas Monypenny.
DG: Gedge, George Lamond.
Goal from mark: William Thomson.

Wales +W.J. Bancroft (Swansea); H.V.P. Huzzey, E.G. Nicholls (Cardiff), R.T. Skrimshire (Newport), W.M. Llewellyn (Llwynypia); S.H. Biggs (Cardiff), G.L. Lloyd (Newport); W.H. Alexander, R. Hellings (Llwynypia), W.J. Parker, F.G. Scrine (Swansea), T. Dobson, J. Blake (Cardiff), A.B. Brice (Aberavon), J.J. Hodges (Newport).
T: Llewellyn Lloyd, Willie Llewellyn.
C: Billy Bancroft 2.
Referee: Michael G. Delaney (Ireland).

Wales 12 Scotland 3

St Helen's, Swansea. 27 January 1900
Wales won by 4 tries to 1 try.

Wales proved Arthur Gould wrong and skipper Billy Bancroft correct when he said: 'We will whack them.' Nearly 40,000 spectators saw a good Welsh victory, though Bancroft missed with all four conversion attempts. The injured Dick Hellings was out and in came George Dobson, a coal trimmer, for his only cap. His brother, Tom, had already played on four occasions.

Wales +W.J. Bancroft (Swansea); W.M. Llewellyn (Llwynypia), E.G. Nicholls (Cardiff), G. Davies, W.J. Trew (Swansea); L.A. Phillips, G.L. Lloyd (Newport); A.B. Brice (Aberavon), W.H. Millar (Mountain Ash), J.G. Boots, J.J. Hodges (Newport), J. Blake, *G.A.Dobson (Cardiff), W.H. Williams (Pontymister), R. Thomas (Swansea).
T: Willie Llewellyn 2, Gwyn Nicholls, 'Buller' Williams.

Scotland H. Rottenburg (London Scottish); T.L. Scott (Langholm), A.B. Timms, W.H. Morrison, J.E. Crabbie (Edinburgh Acads); F.H. Fasson (Edinburgh U), J.I. Gillespie (Edinburgh Acads); +M.C. Morrison (Royal HSFP), W.M.C. McEwan (Edinburgh Acads), W.J. Thomson (West of Scotland), J.M. Dykes, F.W. Henderson (London Scottish), G.C. Kerr (Durham City), T.M. Scott (Hawick), D.R. Bedell-Sivright (Edinburgh U).
T: Johnny Dykes.
Referee: A. Hartley (England).

Scotland 18 Wales 8

Inverleith, Edinburgh. 9 February 1901

Scotland won by 4 tries, 3 cons to 2 tries, 1 con.

A run of four consecutive wins was halted, as Scotland ended hopes of a third Triple Crown with a convincing win in front of 10,000 spectators. Half-back Lou Phillips was a passenger after ten minutes with a knee injury and never played for Wales again. Scotland led 18–0 at one stage, in a match which had been put back due to Queen Victoria's death. Two of the tries came from John Gillespie, who was to referee Wales against England in 1907 and 1911.

Scotland A.W. Duncan (Edinburgh U); W.H. Welsh, A.B. Timms, P. Turnbull (Edinburgh Acads), A.N. Fell; F.H. Fasson (Edinburgh U), J.I. Gillespie (Edinburgh Acads); +M.C. Morrison (Royal HSFP), J.M. Dykes (Glasgow HSFP), A.B. Flett, A. Frew, D.R. Bedell-Sivright (Edinburgh U), J. Ross (London Scottish), J.A. Bell (Clydesdale), R.S. Stronach (Glasgow Acads).
T: Johnnie Gillespie 2, Phipps Turnbull, Alfred Fell.
C: Gillespie 2, Andrew Flett.

Wales +W.J. Bancroft (Swansea); W.M. Llewellyn (Llwynypia/London Welsh), E.G. Nicholls (Cardiff), G. Davies, W.J. Trew (Swansea); L.A. Phillips, G.L. Lloyd (Newport); R. Hellings, W.H. Alexander (Llwynypia), A.B. Brice (Aberavon), W.H. Millar (Mountain Ash), J.G. Boots, J.J. Hodges (Newport), H. Davies (Swansea), J. Blake (Cardiff).

T: Llewellyn Lloyd, George Boots.
C: Billy Bancroft.
Referee: Rupert W. Jeffares (Ireland).

Wales 14 Scotland 5

Arms Park, Cardiff. 1 February 1902

Wales won by 4 tries, 1 con to 1 try, 1 con.

Scotland were the Triple Crown holders and had an outstanding pack of forwards which included the Bedell-Sivright brothers. A 40,000 crowd saw Wales more than hold them up front and the backs ran in four tries. Scotland had refused to play if Will Osborne was selected, claiming he had signed professional forms. Osborne signed a statement denying the allegation, but was to join Huddersfield Rugby League club a year later. He did play however, and a Porth boxer, Harry Jones, was brought in to bolster the pack.

Wales J. 'Strand' Jones (Llanelli); W.M. Llewellyn (Llwynypia), +E.G. Nicholls (Newport), R.T. Gabe, E. Morgan (London Welsh); G.L. Lloyd (Newport), R.M. Owen (Swansea); A.B. Brice (Aberavon), J.J. Hodges, J.G. Boots (Newport), W. Joseph (Swansea), D. Jones (Treherbert), A.F. Harding (Cardiff), W.T. Osborne (Mountain Ash), *H. Jones (Penygraig).
T: Willie Llewellyn 2, Rhys Gabe 2.
C: 'Strand' Jones.

Scotland A.W. Duncan; W.H. Welsh, A.B. Timms (Edinburgh U), P. Turnbull (Edinburgh Acads), A.N. Fell; F.H. Fasson (Edinburgh U), J.I. Gillespie (Edinburgh Acads); +M.C. Morrison (Royal HSFP), J.V. Bedell-Sivright, D.R. Bedell-Sivright (Cambridge U), J.R.C. Greenlees (Kelvinside Acads), J. Ross (London Scottish), J.A. Bell (Clydesdale), A.B. Flett (Edinburgh U), W.E. Kyle (Hawick).
T: Willie Welsh.
C: John Gillespie.
Referee: P. Gilliard (England).

Scotland 6 Wales 0

Inverleith, Edinburgh. 7 February 1903

Scotland won by 1 try, 1 pen to nil.

A small crowd in gale-force conditions saw Scotland en route to taking the Triple Crown as their pack drove on relentlessly to the cries of 'Feet, feet!' The press could hardly see out of their box. The pitch was awash and, with a hurricane wind, errors were plentiful. Scotland's Alec Timms, a doctor in Cardiff at a later date, drop-kicked a goal early on and ten minutes from time William Kyle scored after a forward rush. Scotland captain Mark Morrison led the British team to South Africa soon afterwards. Will Osborne was outstanding in the Welsh pack, and wing Willie Arnold, who missed the best Welsh opportunity, was not selected again.

Scotland W.T. Forrest (Hawick); A.N. Fell, A.B. Timms (Edinburgh U), H.J. Orr (London Scottish), J.E. Crabbie (Edinburgh Acads); J. Knox (Kelvinside Acads), E.D. Simson (Edinburgh U); +M.C. Morrison (Royal HSFP), W.E. Kyle (Hawick), D.R. Bedell-Sivright (Cambridge U), A.G. Cairns (Watsonians), W.P. Scott, N. Kennedy (West of Scotland), J.R.C. Greenlees (Kelvinside Acads), L. West (Edinburgh U).
T: William Kyle.
P: Alec Timms.

Wales J. 'Strand' Jones (Llanelli); *W.R. Arnold, R.T. Gabe (Llanelli), D. Rees, W.J. Trew (Swansea); +G.L. Lloyd (Newport), R.M. Owen (Swansea); J.J. Hodges, J.G. Boots (Newport), A.B. Brice (Aberavon), A.F. Harding (Cardiff/London Welsh), W. Joseph (Swansea), D. Jones (Treherbert), W.T. Osborne (Mountain Ash), G. Travers (Pill Harriers).
Referee: A.E. Martelli (Ireland).

Wales 21 Scotland 3

St Helen's, Swansea. 6 February 1904

Wales won by 4 tries, 3 cons, 1 pen to 1 try.

Scotland went on to win the championship, but Wales raced away to a 16–0 lead before their opponents scored. Swansea pair Dickie Jones and Dickie Owen were excellent at half-back and Cliff Pritchard made a good impression in the centre while Bobby Brice scored a storming try. Referee Nicholls of England wore an overcoat and white boots. New faces included Edwin Thomas Maynard who played under the name of Edwin Thomas. Invading spectators were a danger and a Welsh player was said to have shouted, 'Why don't you behave like sportsmen, not bloody dogs!'

Wales H.B. Winfield (Cardiff); +W.M. Llewellyn, *C.C. 'Cliff' Pritchard (Newport), R.T. Gabe (Newport), E. Morgan (London Welsh); R.H. Jones, R.M. Owen (Swansea); A.F. Harding (London Welsh), J.J. Hodges, *E. Thomas (Newport), A.B. Brice (Aberavon), *W. O'Neil (Cardiff), W. Joseph (Swansea), *D.H. Davies (Neath), *H.V. Watkins (Llanelli).

T: Rhys Gabe, Dick Jones, Teddy Morgan, Alfred Brice.
C: Bert Winfield 3.
P: Winfield.

Scotland W.T. Forrest (Hawick); G.E. Crabbie (Edinburgh Acads), H.J. Orr (London Scottish), L.M. MacLeod (Cambridge U), J.S. McDonald (Edinburgh U); A.A. Bissett (RIEC), E.D. Simson (Edinburgh U); +M.C. Morrison (Royal HSFP), W.E. Kyle (Hawick), W.P. Scott, G.O. Turnbull (West of Scotland), D.R. Bedell-Sivright (Cambridge U), A.G. Cairns (Watsonians), E.J. Ross (London Scottish), L.H. Bell (Edinburgh Acads).
T: Hugh Orr.
Referee: F.W. Nicholls (England).

Scotland 3 Wales 6

Inverleith, Edinburgh. 4 February 1905

Wales won by 2 tries to 1 try.

Skipper Willie Llewellyn showed a great example to his battling side by scoring a brace of tries as Wales completed the second leg of the Triple Crown. Billy Trew, replacing clubmate Dicky Jones at fly-half, was the only change from the side that had defeated England. It was the last match played by the efficient Dan Rees at centre. He joined the exodus north to Hull Kingston Rovers in October 1905.

Scotland W.T. Forrest (Hawick); J.E. Crabbie (Edinburgh Acads), L.M. MacLeod (Cambridge U), J.L. Forbes (Watsonians), J.S. McDonald (Edinburgh U); P. Munro (London Scottish), E.D. Simson (Edinburgh U); A.W. Little, W.E. Kyle (Hawick), W.M. Milne, R.S. Stronach (Glasgow Acads), A. Ross (Royal HSFP), H.N. Fletcher (Edinburgh U), +W.P. Scott (West of Scotland), A.G. Cairns (Watsonians).
T: Arthur Little.

Wales G. Davies (Swansea); +W.M. Llewellyn (Newport), D. Rees (Swansea), R.T. Gabe (Cardiff), E. Morgan (London Welsh); W.J. Trew, R.M. Owen; W. Joseph (Swansea), G. Travers (Pill Harriers), W. O'Neil (Cardiff), A.F. Harding (London Welsh), D. Jones (Treherbert), C.M. 'Charlie' Pritchard, J.J. Hodges (Newport), H.W. Watkins (Llanelli).
T: Willie Llewellyn 2.
Referee: G.H.B. Kennedy (Ireland).

Wales 9 Scotland 3

Arms Park, Cardiff. 3 February 1906

Wales won by 3 tries to 1 pen.

The Scotland pack turned on a powerful performance with 'Darkie' Bedell-Sivright always to the fore, but Wales survived and won the match behind the scrum by taking their rare chances. Reggie Gibbs, who played as a rover, was to score 17 tries in 16 matches, but did not touch down on his début. Bedell-Sivright did so for Scotland, but his effort was disallowed as the ball rebounded after hitting the chief constable of Cardiff who was walking around in-goal.

Wales H.B. Winfield (Cardiff); H.T. Maddock (London Welsh), +E.G. Nicholls (Cardiff), C.C. 'Cliff' Pritchard (Pontypool), E. Morgan (London Welsh); *R.A. Gibbs (Cardiff), W.J. Trew (Swansea), R.M. Owen; W. Joseph (Swansea), G. Travers (Pill Harriers), D. Jones (Aberdare), A.F. Harding, J.F. Williams (London Welsh), C.M. 'Charlie' Pritchard, J.J. Hodges (Newport).
T: Cliff Pritchard, Hop Maddock, Jehoida Hodges.

Scotland J.G. Scoular (Cambridge U); W.C. Church, T. Sloan (Glasgow Acads), K.G. MacLeod (Cambridge U), A.L. Purves; P. Munro (London Scottish), E.D. Simson; +L. West (Edinburgh U), W.E. Kyle (Hawick), W.P. Scott (West of Scotland), W.L. Russell (Glasgow Acads), H.G. Monteith (Cambridge U), D.R. Bedell-Sivright (Edinburgh U), A.G. Cairns, J.C. McCallum (Watsonians).
P: Kenneth MacLeod.
Referee: J.W. Allen (Ireland).

Scotland 6 Wales 3

Inverleith, Edinburgh. 2 February 1907

Scotland won by 2 tries to 1 pen.

Scotland selected Duncan MacGregor, the Pontypridd captain, while Wales also wanted him but as a reserve. The player himself, however, whose father was Scottish, opted for the home side and his brother John, also born in Wales, was to follow him into the Scotland side two years later. Bert Winfield kicked Wales ahead with a magnificent effort, but after the interval he left the field with a back injury and Reg Gibbs deputised. Scotland took control to score two tries but Gibbs had a try disallowed when even the home players thought it was a legitimate score.

Scotland T. Sloan (Glasgow Acads); A.L. Purves, M.W. Walter (London Scottish), D.G. McGregor (Pontypridd), K.G. MacLeod (Cambridge U); +L.L. Greig (Utd Servs), E.D. Simson (London Scottish); D.R. Bedell-Sivright (Edinburgh U), H.G. Monteith (Utd Hosp.itals), J.C. McCallum, L.M. Spiers (Watsonians), I.C. Geddes (London Scottish), G.M. Frew (Glasgow HSFP), W.P. Scott (West of Scotland), G.A. Sanderson (Royal HSFP).
T: Alex Purves, Hugh Monteith.

Wales H.B. Winfield; J.L. Williams, R.T. Gabe (Cardiff), J.H. Evans (Pontypool), H.T. Maddock (London Welsh); R.A. Gibbs (Cardiff)-rover back, +W.J. Trew, R.M. Owen (Swansea); *A.J. Webb (Abertillery), G. Travers (Pill Harriers), J. Watts, T.H. Evans (Llanelli), C.M. 'Charlie' Pritchard, W.H. Dowell (Newport), J.A. Brown (Cardiff).
P: Bert Winfield.
Referee: C. Lefevre (Ireland).

Wales 6 Scotland 5

St Helen's, Swansea. 1 February 1908

Wales won by 2 tries to 1 try, 1 con.

Scotland almost spoiled the Welsh Triple Crown hopes as Irvine Geddes was ruled to have wriggled forward while still held after grounding the ball just short of the line in the last minute of play. It was a case of Welsh backs versus Scots forwards, but the tries by three-quarters Billy Trew and Johnnie Williams won it for the home side.

Wales H.B. Winfield; J.L. Williams, R.T. Gabe (Cardiff), W.J. Trew (Swansea), R.A. Gibbs; P.F. Bush (Cardiff), T.H. Vile (Newport); A.J. Webb (Abertillery), +G. Travers (Pill Harriers), W. O'Neil, J.A. Brown (Cardiff), W.H. Dowell (Pontypool), A.F. Harding (London Welsh), J. Watts (Llanelli), *G. Hayward (Swansea).
T: Billy Trew, Johnnie Williams.

Scotland D.G. Schulze; A.L. Purves, M.W. Walter, T. Sloan (London Scottish), H. Martin (Edinburgh Acads); +L.L. Greig (Utd Servs), G. Cunningham (London Scottish); D.R. Bedell-Sivright (Edinburgh U), J.C. McCallum, L.M. Spiers (Watsonians), I.G. Geddes, G.C. Gowlland (London Scottish), J.M.B. Scott (Edinburgh Acads), J.A. Brown (Glasgow Acads), G.M. Frew (Glasgow HSFP).
T: Alex Purves.
C: Ian Geddes.
Referee: W. Williams (England).

Scotland 3 Wales 5

Inverleith, Edinburgh. 6 February 1909

Wales won by 1 try, 1 con to 1 pen.

The long Welsh victory run could have ended if George (later Sir George) Cunningham had placed a late penalty attempt. Jack Bancroft was penalised for not playing the ball, even though he had been knocked unconscious after courageously diving to halt a foot-rush. Just minutes earlier the 18-year-old John Simson seemed clear, but débutant Melville Baker got back to push him over the corner flag. Wales won when Jack Jones, the youngest of the three Pontypool-born brothers to be capped, sent Billy Trew over with a perfect pass for Jack Bancroft to convert.

Scotland D.G. Schulze (London Scottish); H. Martin (Edinburgh Acads), C.M. Gilray (London Scottish), A.W. Angus, T.J. Simson (Watsonians); J.McW. Tennent (West of Scotland), G. Cunningham (London Scottish); +J.M.B. Scott (Edinburgh Acads), W.E. Kyle (Hawick), G.M. Frew (Glasgow HSFP), G.C. Gowlland, J.S. Wilson (London Scottish), J.M. Mackenzie (Edinburgh U), J.C. McCallum (Watsonians), A. Ross (Royal HSFP).
P: George Cunningham.

Wales J. Bancroft (Swansea); *A.M. Baker, J.P. 'Jack' Jones (Newport), +W.J. Trew (Swansea), J.L. Williams (Cardiff); R.H. Jones, R.M. Owen (Swansea); A.J. Webb (Abertillery), G. Travers (Pill Harriers), T.H. Evans, J. Watts (Llanelli), E.J. Thomas (Mountain Ash), P.D. Waller, E. Thomas (Newport), W.I. Morgan (Swansea).
T: Billy Trew.
C: Jack Bancroft.
Referee: Rupert W. Jeffares (Ireland).

Wales 14 Scotland 0

Arms Park, Cardiff. 5 February 1910

Wales won by 4 tries, 1 con to nil.

Police officer Billy Spiller scored a try on his début and eleven years later he became the first man to score a century for Glamorgan in first-class cricket, made against Northamptonshire. Other débutants were Teddy Morgan's brother, Bill, and docker Ernie Jenkins. Scotland lost fly-half Jim Tennent just after half-time, when he was raked. He never played against Wales again but was to referee them on three occasions in the 1920s.

Wales J. Bancroft (Swansea); R.A. Gibbs, *W. Spiller

(Cardiff), +W.J. Trew (Swansea), A.M. Baker (Newport); P.F. Bush, *W.L. Morgan (Cardiff); A.J. Webb (Abertillery), J. Pugsley (Cardiff), B. Gronow (Bridgend), T.H. Evans (Llanelli), H. Jarman, *E. Jenkins (Newport), D.J. Thomas, W.I. Morgan (Swansea).
T: Joe Pugsley, Billy Spiller, Melville Baker, Ivor Morgan.
C: Jack Bancroft.

Scotland D.G. Schulze (London Scottish); W.R. Sutherland (Hawick), J. Pearson, A.W. Angus, J.T. Simson (Watsonians); J.McW. Tennent (West of Scotland), E. Milroy; L.M. Spiers, J.C. McCallum (Watsonians), J.M.B. Scott (Edinburgh Acads), G.C. Gowlland (London Scottish), +G.M. Frew (Glasgow HSFP), W.E. Kyle (Hawick), J.M. Mackenzie (Edinburgh U), C.D. Stuart (West of Scotland).
Referee: G.H.B. Kennedy (England).

Scotland 10 Wales 32

Inverleith, Edinburgh. 4 February 1911

Wales won by 8 tries, 2 cons, 1 drop goal to 2 tries, 1 drop goal.

This win could have been bigger had not Louis Dyke, Billy Spiller and Fred Birt missed six conversions between them. Spiller's drop goal helped Wales lead 7–4 at the interval and the Cardiff three-quarter line accounted for seven of the eight tries. Wing John Macdonald retired injured early in the second half in his only international match for Scotland, while Englishman Jim Birch was controversially brought into the Welsh pack.

Scotland D.G. Schulze (London Scottish); D.M. Grant (Elstow School), F.G. Buchanan (Kelvinside Acads), A.W. Angus (Watsonians), J.M. Macdonald (Edinburgh Wands); +P. Munro (London Scottish), F.L. Osler (Edinburgh U); J.M.B. Scott (Edinburgh Acads), R. Stevenson (St Andrews U), F.H. Turner (Liverpool), R. Fraser (Cambridge U), J.M. MacKenzie, A.R. Ross (Edinburgh U), L. Robertson (London Scottish), C.H. Abercrombie (Utd Servs).
T: Fred Turner, John Scott.
DG: Pat Munro.

Wales F.W. Birt (Newport); R.A. Gibbs, W. Spiller, L.M. Dyke, J.L. Williams (Cardiff); +W.J. Trew, R.M. Owen (Swansea); A.J. Webb (Abertillery), J. Pugsley (Cardiff), G. Travers, A.P. Coldrick (Newport), R. Thomas (Pontypool), D.J. Thomas (Swansea), T.H. Evans (Llanelli), *J. Birch (Neath).
T: Reg Gibbs 3, Billy Spiller 2, Johnnie Williams 2, Rhys Thomas.
C: Louis Dyke 2.
DG: Spiller.
Referee: I.G. Davidson (Ireland).

Wales 21 Scotland 6

St Helen's, Swansea. 3 February 1912

Wales won by 3 tries, 2 cons, 2 drop goals to 2 tries.

Newport wings Reggie Plummer and George Hirst scored début tries, while Billy Trew and Fred Birt dropped goals. Birt dislocated his shoulder in the final minute, before Trew and Dicky Owen were carried off shoulder high to the pavilion in triumph. Owen was never to play again for Wales. Of the newcomers, Plummer was the brother-in-law of Tommy Vile and William Avon Davies had twice played in the winning Devon side in English County championship finals.

Wales J. Bancroft (Swansea); *R.C.S. Plummer, F.W. Birt (Newport), *Willie A. Davies (Aberavon), *G.L. Hirst (Newport); W.J. Trew, +R.M. Owen (Swansea); G. Stephens, H.J. Davies (Neath), A.J. Webb (Abertillery), A.P. Coldrick, H. Uzzell, L.C. Trump (Newport), R. Thomas (Pontypool), W.I. Morgan (Swansea).
T: George Hirst, Ivor Morgan, Reg Plummer.
C: Jack Bancroft 2.
DG: Billy Trew, Fred Birt.

Scotland W.M. Dickson (Blackheath); W.R. Sutherland (Hawick), A.W. Angus, J. Pearson (Watsonians), J.G. Will (OMTs); A.W. Gunn (Royal HSFP), E. Milroy; +J.C. McCallum (Watsonians), L. Robertson, W.D.C.L. Purves (London Scottish), D.D. Howie (Kirkcaldy), J.M.B. Scott, D.M. Bain (Edinburgh Acads), J. Dobson (Glasgow Acads), F.H. Turner (Liverpool).
T: George Will 2.
Referee: Frank C. Potter-Irwin (England).

Scotland 0 Wales 8

Inverleith, Edinburgh. 1 February 1913

Wales won by 2 tries, 1 con to nil.

Numerous scrums made the game boring to watch, but Wales skipper Billy Trew would have been happy to settle for a win by any means in Scotland, especially with five new caps in the side including the amazing Rev. Jenkin Alban Davies in the pack. There was a début try for 'Tuan' Jones who followed his brothers Jack and 'Ponty' into a Wales shirt. Oddly, both 'Tuan' and 'Ponty' scored a try in their only appearances. Rhys Richards and Bobby Lloyd were soon lost to rugby league, particularly sad in the case of the latter, who was often called 'The Hafodyrynys Wonder' and who played for Great Britain at the 13-a-side game.

Scotland W.M. Dickson (Blackheath); W.R. Sutherland (Hawick), R.E. Gordon (Army), A.W. Angus (Watsonians), W.A. Stewart (London Hosp.); J.H. Bruce Lockhart (London Scottish), E. Milroy (Watsonians); L. Robertson (London Scottish), +F.H. Turner (Liverpool), C.M. Usher (Edinburgh Wands), D.D. Howie (Kirkcaldy), C.H. Abercrombie (US Portsmouth), D.M. Bain, J.M.B. Scott (Edinburgh Acads), P.C.B. Blair (Cambridge U).

Wales R.F. Williams (Cardiff); G.L. Hirst (Newport), *J.P. 'Tuan' Jones (Pontypool), +W.J. Trew, *H. Lewis (Swansea); J.M.C. Lewis (Cardiff), *R.A. Lloyd (Pontypool); *Rev. J. Alban Davies (Swansea), *R. Richards (Aberavon), F.L. Perrett, G. Stephens (Neath), W.J. Jenkins (Cardiff), F. Andrews (Pontypool), P.L. Jones, H. Uzzell (Newport).
T: Clem Lewis, Tuan Jones.
C: Lewis.
Referee: S.H. Crawford (Ireland).

Wales 24 Scotland 5

Arms Park, Cardiff. 7 February 1914

Wales won by 3 tries, 2 cons, 1 try, 1 pen, 2 drop goals to 1 try, 1 con.

This match came just five weeks before 'The Roughest Ever', but this too was a pretty tough battle, with the Scotland captain David Bain stating that, 'The dirtier team won'. Bain, who received six stitches to a cut head, was to die just 16 months later. Wales gained a 7th consecutive win over Scotland, with début tries by Ivor Davies and Jack Wetter. The latter went on to play for Wales until 1924, his brother Harry having been capped in 1912 and 1913. Scotland had stolen a 5–0 lead after William Stewart, later to be an 'evens' sprinter for Australia, scored a try, but Wales were in front by 7–5 at the interval.

Wales J. Bancroft (Swansea); G.L. Hirst, *J.J. Wetter (Newport), W.H. Evans (Llwynypia), *I.T. Davies (Llanelli); J.M.C. Lewis (Cardiff), R.A. Lloyd (Pontypool); +Rev. J. Alban Davies (Llanelli), D. Watts (Maesteg), J. 'Bedwellty' Jones (Abertillery), T.J. Lloyd (Neath), P.L. Jones (Pontypool), T. Williams, E. Morgan (Swansea), H. Uzzell (Newport).
T: Ivor Davies, Jack Wetter, George Hirst.
C: Jack Bancroft 2.
P: Bancroft.
DG: Hirst, Clem Lewis.

Scotland W.M. Wallace (London Scottish); J.G. Will (OMTs), W.R. Sutherland (Hawick), R.M. Scobie (London Scottish), W.A. Stewart (London Hosp.); A.T. Sloan (Edinburgh Acads), A.S. Hamilton (Headingley); A.M. Stewart, +D.M. Bain, G.H.H. Maxwell (Edinburgh Acads), A.W. Symington (Cambridge U), A. Wemyss (Gala), A.D. Laing (Royal HSFP), A.R. Ross (Edinburgh U), D.G. Donald (Oxford U).
T: William Stewart.
C: Arthur Laing.
Referee: V. Drennon (Ireland).

Scotland 9 Wales 5

Inverleith, Edinburgh. 7 February 1920

Scotland won by 1 try, 2 pens to 1 try, 1 con.

The day after this defeat, the Welsh team were taken to see the Forth Bridge which was in the process of being built. Jerry Shea was told: 'Take a good look, you will not see it again!' It had been a surprising defeat that cost Wales the Triple Crown on the previous day and Shea was accused, as usual, of selfishness. Wales had won their seven previous games against Scotland and led 5–0, but near the end they were reduced to 13 when forwards Harry Uzzell and Jim Jones left injured. Seven months later Ben Beynon scored a hat-trick for Swansea Town against Norwich City and the WRU withheld his cap as he was then a professional at soccer. New wing Bryn Williams also turned professional that year, but at rugby league. Neil Macpherson, born in Cardiff but playing for Newport, made his Scotland début. Four years later he was banned *sine die* by the SRFU for accepting a gold watch from Newport. At centre for Scotland was the Abertillery doctor Ernest Fahmy.

Scotland G.L. Pattullo (Panmure); G.B. Crole (Edinburgh Acads), +A.W. Angus (Watsonians), E.C. Fahmy (Abertillery/Edinburgh U), E.B. MacKay (Glasgow Acads); A.T. Sloan (Edinburgh Acads), J.A.R. Selby (Watsonians); G.H.H. Maxwell (Edinburgh Acads), A.D. Laing (Royal HSFP), F. Kennedy (Stewart's Coll FP), N.C. Macpherson (Newport), G. Thom (Kirkcaldy), C.M. Usher (London Scottish), D.D. Duncan (Oxford U), R.A. Gallie

'Our Boys' – Four Llanelli players who represented Wales in the 1920 season, pictured here at Stradey Park. Left to right: Bryn Evans, Edgar Morgan, Albert Jenkins and Bryn Williams. Evans and Jenkins made their débuts against England, Williams against Scotland and Morgan against France.

(Glasgow Acads).
T: Allen Sloan.
P: Finlay Kennedy 2.

Wales J. Rees (Swansea); W.J. Powell (Cardiff), J. Shea (Newport), A.E. Jenkins, *B. Williams (Llanelli); B. Beynon (Swansea), J.J. Wetter (Newport); J.L. Williams (Blaina), S. Morris (Cross Keys), +H. Uzzell, J.J. Whitfield (Newport), G. Oliver (Pontypool), E.T. Parker (Swansea), J. Jones (Aberavon), C.W. Jones (Bridgend).
T: Albert Jenkins.
C: Jenkins.
Referee: S.H. Crawford (England).

Wales 8 Scotland 14

St Helen's, Swansea. 5 February 1921

Scotland won by 3 tries, 1 con, 1 pen to 2 drop goals.

Pitch invasions repeatedly stopped play and, as a result, Wales never got started. It was Scotland's first win in Wales since 1892, when the Swansea crowd had also rioted. Wales, 11–0 behind at the interval, hit back with two long-range drop goals by Albert Jenkins, but as the crowd overspilled, play was held up for 12 minutes. Scotland captain 'Jenny' Hume threatened to take his team off. When it restarted, Jenkins was carried off with a twisted knee and Allen Sloan clinched Scotland's victory with a try. The Welsh players appeared to tire themselves out in their efforts to clear the pitch when the crowd spilled out while the Scotland players rested. There was a début by 'Baker' Jones, who was the son of Tom Jones, a pre-1900s cap in the Welsh pack. Two other newcomers, Frankie Evans and Billy Bowen, were soon to join the exodus to rugby league.

Wales J. Rees (Swansea); *F. Evans, A.E. Jenkins (Llanelli), *P.E.R. 'Baker' Jones (Newport), B.M.G. Thomas (St Bart's Hosp./Ogmore Vale); *W.E. Bowen (Swansea), +T.H. Vile (Newport); J.L. Williams (Blaina), S. Winmill (Cross Keys), *T. Roberts (Risca), W. Hodder (Pontypool), S.L. Attewell (Newport), E.T. Parker (Swansea), J. Jones (Aberavon), D.E. Morgan (Llanelli).
DG: Albert Jenkins 2.

Scotland H.H. Forsayth (Oxford U); J.H. Carmichael (Watsonians), A.L. Gracie (Harlequins), A.E. Thomson (Utd Servs), A.T. Sloan (Edinburgh Acads); +J. Hume (Royal HSFP), R.L.H. Donald; J.M. Bannerman (Glasgow HSFP), J.N. Shaw (Edinburgh Acads), J.C.R. Buchanan (Stewart's Coll FP), R.A. Gallie (Glasgow Acads), R.S. Cumming (Aberdeen U), G. Douglas (Jedforest), C.M. Usher (Edinburgh Wands), G.H.H. Maxwell (Edinburgh Acads).
T: Tommy Thomson, Rankin Buchanan, Allen Sloan.
C: George Maxwell.
P: Maxwell.
Referee: James W. Baxter (England).

Scotland 9 Wales 9

Inverleith, Edinburgh. 4 February 1922

Draw. Scotland – 2 tries, 1 pen. Wales – 1 try, 1 con, 1 drop goal.

The two countries have not played another drawn match against each other since this one. Wales were saved by centre Islwyn Evans who scored in every international match he played. On three occasions it was a try, but this time it was a 20-yard drop goal. Fred Samuel, who replaced Joe Rees at full-back, joined Hull RL eight months later.

Scotland H.H. Forsayth (Oxford U); E.H. Liddell (Edinburgh U), A.L. Gracie (Harlequins), R.C. Warren (Glasgow Acads), A. Browning

(Glasgow HSFP); G.P.S. Macpherson (Oxford U), W.E. Bryce (Selkirk); +C.M. Usher (Edinburgh Wands), D.S. Davies (Hawick), J.M. Bannerman (Glasgow HSFP), D.M. Bertram (Watsonians), A. Wemyss (Edinburgh Wands), J.R. Lawrie (Melrose), W.G. Dobson (Heriot's FP), J.C.R. Buchanan (Stewart's Coll FP).
T: Arthur Browning 2.
P: Browning.

Wales *T.F. Samuel (Mountain Ash); F.C. Palmer, H.I. Evans (Swansea), B.S. Evans (Llanelli), W.C. Richards (Pontypool); W.E. Bowen (Swansea), W.J. Delahay (Bridgend); +E.T. Parker (Swansea), J.J. Whitfield, T. Jones (Newport), S. Morris (Cross Keys), T. Roberts (Risca), Rev. J.G. Stephens (Llanelli), W. Cummins (Treorchy), D.D. Hiddlestone (Neath).
T: Billy Bowen.
C: Fred Samuel.
DG: Islwyn Evans.
Referee: R.A. Lloyd (Ireland).

Wales 8 Scotland 11

Arms Park, Cardiff. 3 February 1923

Scotland won by 3 tries, 1 con to 1 try, 1 con, 1 pen.

Archie Gracie received the biggest reception ever given by a Cardiff crowd to a visiting player after his brilliant run, two minutes from time, won the match for Scotland. He was the best player on the field and, though he was injured stopping a foot-rush, he was twice tackled short of the line before racing almost to the dead-ball line to score for Scotland's first win at Cardiff since 1890. A small boy sitting nearby lost some teeth, as Gracie struck him in the mouth by accident – he too came from Scotland! The Harlequins centre, who was also skippering Scotland, was carried shoulder-high by the crowd and said: 'It was the most wonderful crowd I have ever seen in the whole world. Whoever did a good thing was applauded, no matter which side he belonged to.' The renowned journalist, Colonel Trevor, said: 'Let us hope that the great performance of the Cardiff crowd will be appraised as well.' The gates were closed before the match with more than 40,000 inside.

Wales B.O. Male (Pontypool); T.A.W. Johnson, R.A. Cornish (Cardiff), A.E. Jenkins (Llanelli), W.R. Harding (Swansea); +J.M.C. Lewis (Cardiff), W.J. Delahay (Bridgend); A. Baker (Neath), S. Morris (Cross Keys), D.G. Davies (Cardiff), E.T. Parker, G.M. Michael (Swansea), S.G. Thomas (Llanelli), *J.L. Jenkins (Aberavon), T. Roberts (Newport).
T: Clem Lewis.
C: Albert Jenkins.
P: Albert Jenkins.

Scotland D. Drysdale (Heriot's FP); E.H. Liddell (Edinburgh U), +A.L. Gracie (Harlequins), E. McLaren (Royal HSFP), A. Browning (Glasgow HSFP); S.B. McQueen (Waterloo), W.E. Bryce (Selkirk); J.M. Bannerman, L.M. Stuart (Glasgow HSFP), J.C.R. Buchanan (Stewart's Coll, FP), D.S. Davies (Hawick), J.R. Lawrie (Melrose), D.M. Bertram (Watsonians), D.S. Kerr (Heriot's FP), A.K. Stevenson (Glasgow Acads).
T: Eric Liddell, Ludovic Stuart, Archie Gracie.
C: Dan Drysdale.
Referee: James W. Baxter (England).

Scotland 35 Wales 10

Inverleith, Edinburgh. 2 February 1924

Scotland won by 8 tries, 4 cons, 1 pen to 2 tries, 2 cons.

Wales conceded eight tries in one of their worst-ever performances, failing to open their account until they trailed by 35-0. Wing Ian Smith, the 'Flying Scot', scored three of the five touched down by the all-Oxford University three-quarter-line. Thirteen new caps had been blooded in two matches. Jack Evans and Harold Davies became 'one-cap wonders' and new skipper Jack Whitfield was removed for the next match. Evans and Mel Rosser later switched to rugby league.

Scotland D. Drysdale (Heriot's FP); I.S. Smith, G.P.S. Macpherson, G.G. Aitken, A.C. Wallace (Oxford U); H. Waddell (Glasgow Acads), W.E. Bryce (Selkirk); +J.C.R. Buchanan (Stewart's Coll FP), J.M. Bannerman (Glasgow HSFP), D.M. Bertram, A.C. Gillies (Watsonians), K.G.P. Hendrie (Heriot's FP), R.A. Howie (Kirkcaldy), J.R. Lawrie (Leicester), A. Ross (Kilmarnock).
T: Ian Smith 3, Willie Bryce, David Bertram, Johnny Wallace, Herbert Waddell, Phil Macpherson.
C: Dan Drysdale 4.
P: Drysdale.

Wales B.O. Male (Cardiff); *H.J. Davies (Newport), *J.E. Evans (Llanelli), *M.A. Rosser (Penarth), T.A.W. Johnson (Cardiff); *V.M. Griffiths (Newport), E. Watkins (Neath); +J.J. Whitfield (Newport), S. Morris (Cross Keys), J.I.T. Morris (Swansea), T. Jones (Newport), C.H. Pugh (Maesteg), Ivor E. Jones (Llanelli), W.J. Ould

(Cardiff), D.G. Francis (Llanelli).
T: Vince Griffiths, Ivor Jones.
C: Ossie Male 2.
Referee: J.B. McGowan (Ireland).

Wales 14 Scotland 24

St Helen's, Swansea. 7 February 1925

Scotland won by 6 tries, 1 con, 1 drop goal to 3 tries, 1 con, 1 pen.

Wing Ian Smith made it seven tries in two matches against Wales by scoring four of his side's six tries on this occasion. He had also crossed for four tries against France just two weeks before this game. Scotland shot away to lead 21–0, but Alex Gillies and Dan Drysdale missed five conversion kicks between them and saved Wales from a bigger defeat. Wales recovered enough to score their points in the last 15 minutes but the all-Oxford three-quarters were hard to hold with Johnny Wallace, later to skipper the 1927–28 Waratahs, crossing twice for Scotland. Scotland went on to win the Triple Crown. Steve Morris led Wales for the only time and had new caps Ron Herrera and Steve Lawrence, both police officers, with him in the pack.

Wales T.A.W. Johnson (Cardiff); W.P. James, Evan Williams (Aberavon), R.A. Cornish (Cardiff), C.R. Thomas (Bridgend); W.J. Hopkins (Aberavon), W.J. Delahay (Cardiff); C.H. Pugh (Maesteg), +S. Morris, *R.C. Herrera (Cross Keys), B. Phillips (Aberavon), W.I. Jones (Llanelli), D.S. Parker (Swansea), E.I. Richards (Cardiff), *S.D. Lawrence (Bridgend).
T: Willie Hopkins, Idris Jones, Arthur Cornish.
C: Dai Parker.
P: Parker.

Scotland D. Drysdale (Heriot's FP); I.S. Smith, +G.P.S. Macpherson, G.G. Aitken, A.C. Wallace (Oxford U); J.C. Dykes, J.B. Nelson (Glasgow Acads); J.M. Bannerman, J.C.H. Ireland (Glasgow HSFP), D.S. Davies (Hawick), J.R. Paterson (Birkenhead Park), J.W. Scott (Stewart's Coll FP), A.C. Gillies (Watsonians), R.A. Howie (Kirkcaldy), D.J. MacMyn (London Scottish).
T: Ian Smith 4, Johnny Wallace 2.
C: Dan Drysdale.
DG: Drysdale.
Referee: James W. Baxter (England).

Scotland 8 Wales 5

Murrayfield, Edinburgh. 6 February 1926

Scotland won by 1 try, 1 con, 1 pen to 1 try, 1 con.

Wales travelled to Murrayfield for the first time, and the selectors came up with the surprise move of playing scrum-half, Wick Powell, as wing to take on the 'Flying Scotsman', Ian Smith. Bill Everson scored on his only appearance, while another newcomer, Emlyn Watkins, joined Leeds RL seven months later.

Scotland +D. Drysdale (Heriot's FP); I.S. Smith (Edinburgh U), R.M. Kinnear (Heriot's FP), J.C. Dykes, W.M. Simmers; H. Waddell, J.B. Nelson (Glasgow Acads); J.M. Bannerman, J.C.H. Ireland (Glasgow HSFP), A.C. Gillies (Watsonians), D.S. Davies (Hawick), D.J. MacMyn (London Scottish), J.R. Paterson (Birkenhead Park), J.W. Scott (Stewart's Coll FP), G.M. Murray (Glasgow Acads).
T: Herbert Waddell.
C: Dan Drysdale.
P: Alex Gillies.

Wales *W.A. Everson; G.E. Andrews, A. Stock (Newport), +R.A. Cornish (Cardiff), *W.C. Powell (London Welsh); R. 'Bobby' Jones (Northampton), W.J. Delahay (Cardiff); S.D. Lawrence (Bridgend), J.H. John (Swansea), D. Jones (Newport), S. Hinam (Cardiff), R.C. Herrera (Cross Keys), T. Hopkins (Swansea), D.M. Jenkins (Treorchy), *Emlyn Watkins (Blaina).
T: Ron Herrera.
C: Bill Everson.
Referee: D. Hellewell (England).

Wales 0 Scotland 5

Arms Park, Cardiff. 5 February 1927

Scotland won by 1 try, 1 con to nil.

Ossie Male skippered Wales for the first of three occasions, but never in successive matches. The Scottish pack engineered the only try, scored by David Kerr (later President of SRFU) from a foot-rush in the first half. It was Cardiff mud again, as Welsh defender after defender made desperate stops and Tom Arthur suffered injury. Windsor Lewis and Wick Powell were originally chosen at half-back, but Lewis was injured, so the WRU asked Powell to stand down in order to play Billy Delahay and Gwyn Richards. Of the new caps, both Arthur and Ned

Jenkins were police officers and boxers of note; John Bartlett became a Navy chaplain and Richards was to move to rugby league.

Wales +B.O. Male (Cardiff); *J.D. Bartlett (Llanelli/London Welsh), B.R. Turnbull, J. Roberts (Cardiff), W.R. Harding (Swansea); *E.G. Richards, W.J. Delahay; T.W. Lewis (Cardiff), J.H. John (Swansea), H.T. Phillips (Newport), *T. Arthur (Neath), *E.M. Jenkins (Aberavon), W.A. Williams (Crumlin), I.E. Jones, W.G. Thomas (Llanelli).

Scotland D. Drysdale (Heriot's FP); E.G. Taylor (Oxford U), +G.P.S. Macpherson (Edinburgh Acads), J.C. Dykes, W.M. Simmers; H. Waddell, J.B. Nelson (Glasgow Acads); D.S. Kerr (Heriot's FP), J.M. Bannerman (Glasgow HSFP), D.S. Davies (Hawick), J. Graham (Kelso), J.C.H. Ireland (Glasgow HSFP), J.R. Paterson (Birkenhead Park), J.W. Scott (Stewart's Coll, FP), A.C. Gillies (Watsonians).
T: David Kerr.
C: Alex Gillies.
Referee: W.H. Jackson (England).

Scotland 0 Wales 13

Murrayfield, Edinburgh. 4 February 1928

Wales won by 3 tries, 2 cons to nil

Wales gained a first-ever win at Murrayfield, but more importantly it was the first over Scotland since 1914 at Cardiff. Despite playing into the wind and rain, Wales led 13–0 at the break and defended well, with Wick Powell again cast as a wing – one of the three changes from the previous match.

Scotland D. Drysdale (London Scottish); J. Goodfellow (Langholm), G.P.S. Macpherson (Edinburgh Acads), R.F. Kelly (Watsonians), W.M. Simmers (Glasgow Acads); H.D. Greenlees (Leicester), P.S. Douty (London Scottish); W.B. Welsh (Hawick), W.N. Roughead (London Scottish), W.G. Ferguson (Royal HSFP), +J.M. Bannerman (Glasgow HSFP), J. Graham (Kelso), J.R. Paterson (Birkenhead Park), J.W. Scott (Stewart's Coll FP), J.H. Ferguson (Gala).

Wales +B.O. Male (Cardiff); J.D. Bartlett (London Welsh), J. Roberts (Cardiff), A.E. Jenkins (Llanelli), W.C. Powell (London Welsh); Dai E. John, D. Arthur John (Llanelli); F.A. Bowdler (Cross Keys), Cecil C. Pritchard (Pontypool), H.T. Phillips (Newport), E.M. Jenkins (Aberavon), A. Skym, T. Iowerth Jones (Llanelli), T.H. Hollingdale (Neath), I.E. Jones (Llanelli).
T: Albert Jenkins, Dai John, John Roberts.
C: Ossie Male 2.
Referee: R.W. Harland (Ireland).

Wales 14 Scotland 7

St Helen's, Swansea. 2 February 1929

Wales won by 4 tries, 1 con to 1 pen, 1 drop goal.

Cardiff backs Harry Bowcott and Frank Williams and clubmate Bob Barrell in the pack, began their international careers with a win far greater than the scoreline showed. A try-count of 4–0 in favour of Wales showed the difference in sides on the day.

Wales J.A. Bassett (Penarth); J. Roberts, *H.M. Bowcott (Cardiff), +W.G. Morgan (Swansea), J.C. Morley (Newport); *F.L. Williams (Cardiff), W.C. Powell (London Welsh); F.A. Bowdler (Cross Keys), Cecil C. Pritchard (Pontypool), *R.J. Barrell (Cardiff), T. Arthur, H.J. Jones (Neath), *H. Peacock (Newport), A.S. Broughton (Treorchy), I.E. Jones (Llanelli).
T: John Roberts 2, Guy Morgan, Harry Peacock.
C: Ivor Jones.

Scotland T.G. Aitchison; I.S. Smith (Edinburgh U), T.G. Brown (Heriot's FP), J.C. Dykes, W.M. Simmers (Glasgow Acads); A.H. Brown (Heriot's FP), J.B. Nelson (Glasgow Acads); +J.M. Bannerman (Glasgow HSFP), H.S. Mackintosh (West of Scotland), J.A. Beattie (Hawick), W.V. Berkley (London Scottish), R.T. Smith (Kelso), K.M. Wright (London Scottish), J.W. Allan (Melrose), J.R. Paterson (Birkenhead Park).
P: Jimmy Dykes.
DG: Alec Brown.
Referee: D. Hellewell (England).

Scotland 12 Wales 9

Murrayfield, Edinburgh. 1 February 1930

Scotland won by 2 tries, 1 con, 1 drop goal to 1 try, 1 con, 1 drop goal.

Dropped goals were to become the scourge of Wales in Murrayfield as the last-minute effort by fly-half Herbert Waddell set the fashion. Wing Max Simmers was to see his son Brian drop two against Wales in 1965. Wales fell behind to the first of a brace of tries by Simmers, but the lead changed as débutant Graham Jones first scored a try and then dropped a goal. Simmers scored his second try just before the interval and, trailing 8–9, Scotland were awarded a scrum after centre Jones was forced to touch down behind his own line. In the drizzling rain, Waddell popped the winning drop goal over after receiving from James Nelson. Wales skipper Ivor Jones did not play again, but in the 1950s he became a touch-judge on many occasions. Of the new caps, Bert Day later moved to Salford RL, while the elusive Ronnie Boon was to become a hero in 1933 at Twickenham.

Scotland R.C. Warren (Glasgow Acads); I.S. Smith (London Scottish), +G.P.S. Macpherson (Edinburgh Acads), T.M. Hart (Glasgow U), W.M. Simmers; H. Waddell, J.B. Nelson (Glasgow Acads); W.B. Welsh (Hawick), H.S. Mackintosh (West of Scotland), J.A. Beattie, R.A. Foster (Hawick), R.T. Smith (Kelso), W.G. Agnew (Stewart's Coll FP), R. Rowand (Glasgow HSFP), F.H. Waters (London Scottish).
T: Max Simmers 2.
C: Frank Waters.
DG: Herbert Waddell.

Wales J.A. Bassett (Penarth); E.G. Davies, B.R. Turnbull, *G. Graham Jones, *R.W. Boon; F.L. Williams (Cardiff), W.C. Powell (London Welsh); T. Arthur (Neath), *H.C. Day (Newport), A. Skym (Cardiff), E.M. Jenkins (Aberavon), *D.J. Thomas (Swansea), A.W. Lemon (Neath), H. Peacock (Newport), +I.E. Jones (Llanelli).
T: Graham Jones.
C: Ivor Jones.
DG: Graham Jones.
Referee: Dr James R. Wheeler (Ireland).

Wales 13 Scotland 8

Arms Park, Cardiff. 7 February 1931

Wales won by 3 tries, 2 cons to 2 tries, 1 con.

Welsh back-row forward Watcyn Thomas broke his collar bone early in the second half when he collided with a post while scoring a try that Jack Bassett converted to level the score at 8–8. Thomas refused to leave the field and 50,000 watching in fine conditions saw Wales lucky to win, with a late Ronnie Boon try which Bassett again converted. Many people present thought that the pass to Boon was forward and also knocked on, but the referee missed the infringements. The Welsh team played with letters, rather than numbers, on their backs.

Wales +J.A. Bassett (Penarth); J.C. Morley (Newport), E.C. Davey (Swansea), T.E. Jones-Davies (London Welsh), R.W. Boon; H.M. Bowcott (Cardiff), W.C. Powell (London Welsh); A. Skym (Cardiff), H.C. Day (Newport), T.B. Day (Swansea), T. Arthur (Neath), E.M. Jenkins (Aberavon), A.W. Lemon (Neath), W.G. Thomas (Swansea), N.H. Fender (Cardiff).
T: Jack Morley, Watcyn Thomas, Ronnie Boon.
C: Jack Bassett 2.

Scotland R.W. Langrish; I.S. Smith (London Scottish), G.P.S. Macpherson (Edinburgh Acads), W.M. Simmers (Glasgow Acads), G. Wood (Gala); H. Lind (Dunfermline), J.B. Nelson (Glasgow Acads); J.W. Allan (Melrose), +W.N. Roughead (London Scottish), H.S. Mackintosh (West of Scotland), A.W. Walker (Birkenhead Park), J.A. Beattie, W.B. Welsh (Hawick), J.S. Wilson (St Andrews U), D. Crichton-Miller (Gloucester).
T: Donald Crichton-Miller 2.
C: John Allan.
Referee: J.G. Bott (England).

Scotland 0 Wales 6

Murrayfield, Edinburgh. 6 February 1932

Wales won by 1 try, 1 pen to nil.

A big Welsh presence in the huge crowd appeared to inspire the pack in particular, with Arthur Lemon of Neath now showing outstanding form, as he rampaged among the home backs. The lively Ronnie Boon scored a first-half try and skipper Jack Bassett placed a second-half penalty goal.

Scotland T.H.B. Lawther (Old Millhillians); I.S. Smith (London Scottish), +W.M. Simmers (Glasgow Acads), D.StJ. Clair-Ford (Utd Servs), G. Wood (Gala); H. Lind (Dunfermline), W.R. Logan (Edinburgh U); J.W. Allan (Melrose), W.N. Roughead (London Scottish), J.A. Beattie, W.B. Welsh (Hawick), H.S. Mackintosh (West of Scotland), M.S. Stewart (Stewart's Coll FP), J. Graham (Kelso), F.H. Waters (London Scottish).

Wales +J.A. Bassett (Penarth); J.C. Morley (Newport), E.C. Davey (Swansea), F.L. Williams, R.W. Boon (Cardiff); A.R. Ralph (Newport), W.C. Powell (London Welsh); A. Skym (Cardiff), F.A. Bowdler (Cross Keys), T.B. Day, D.J. Thomas (Swansea), E.M. Jenkins (Aberavon), W. Davies, W.G. Thomas (Swansea), A.W. Lemon (Neath).
T: Ronnie Boon.
P: Jack Bassett.
Referee: Tom Bell (Ireland).

Wales 3 Scotland 11

St Helen's, Swansea. 4 February 1933

Scotland won by 2 tries, 1 con, 1 pen to 1 try.

With four changes in the backs, Wales were unrecognisable as the side which had defeated England fourteen days earlier. Three new caps included Swansea skipper Bryn Evans at scrum-half, but both he and full-back Gwyn Bayliss were never selected again. It was a sorry day for Swansea: Ronnie Morris, playing with his half-back club partner Bryn Evans, experienced disaster. Local forward Dai Thomas broke a collar bone and retired at the interval when Scotland led 6–0. That increased to 11–0 before Tom Arthur scored a try for Wales.

Wales *G. Bayliss (Pontypool); A. Hickman (Neath), E.C. Davey (Swansea), W. Wooller (Rydal School/Colwyn Bay), A.H. Jones (Cardiff); *R.R. Morris, *D. Bryn Evans (Swansea); E.L. Jones, B. Evans (Llanelli), A. Skym (Cardiff), R.B. Jones (Anglesey/Cambridge U), D.J. Thomas (Swansea), T. Arthur (Neath), +W.G. Thomas (Swansea), I. Isaacs (Cardiff).
T: Tom Arthur.

Scotland D.I. Brown (Cambridge U); +I.S. Smith (London Scottish), H.D.B. Lorraine (Oxford U), H. Lind (Dunfermline), K.C. Fyfe (Cambridge U); K.L.T. Jackson (Oxford U), W.R. Logan (Edinburgh Wands); J.M. Ritchie (Watsonians), J. McL Henderson (Edinburgh Acads), M.S. Stewart (Stewart's Coll FP), W.B. Welsh, J.A. Beattie (Hawick), J.R. Thom (Watsonians), R. Rowand (Glasgow HSFP), J.A. Waters (Selkirk).
T: Ian Smith, Ken Jackson.
C: Ken Fyfe.
P: Fyfe.
Referee: J.G. Bott (England).

Scotland 6 Wales 13

Murrayfield, Edinburgh. 3 February 1934

Wales won by 3 tries, 2 cons to 1 try, 1 pen.

It was a surprise win for Wales, owing in no small part to the genius of Cliff Jones. His mother later sent débutant flanker Albert Fear a letter thanking the Newport player for 'taking care of my son'. Wales led 5–0 at the interval after an Idwal Rees try and then 'Bunny' Cowey crossed. Scotland then opened their account, only for Claude Davey to send Cowey over for his second try with Viv Jenkins converting. Welsh critic 'Old Stager' wrote: 'The whole Welsh team shared in a great rugby triumph. Those who reside in Edinburgh will not speedily forget the Welsh victory.' Former Scotland forward Jock Wemyss said: 'It was one of the best Welsh packs in recent years. The score in no way exaggerated their all-round superiority.' New caps Bert Jones and Dai Prosser soon switched to rugby league. The brothers, Dai and Glyn Prosser, packed down together in this match and the following one against Ireland.

Scotland K.W. Marshall (Edinburgh Acads); R.W. Shaw (Glasgow HSFP), R.C.S. Dick (Cambridge U), +H. Lind (Dunfermline), J. Park (Royal HSFP); K.L.T. Jackson (Oxford U), W.R. Logan (Edinburgh Wands); W.A. Burnet (West of Scotland), L.B. Lambie (Glasgow HSFP), J.M. Ritchie (Watsonians), J.D. Lowe (Heriot's FP), M.S. Stewart (Stewart's Coll FP), D.A. Thom (London Scottish), J.A. Waters (Selkirk), R. Rowand (Glasgow HSFP).
T: Ross Logan.
P: Jim Ritchie.

Wales V.G.J. Jenkins (Bridgend); B.T.V. Cowey (Newport/Welsh Regt), +E.C. Davey, J. Idwal Rees (Swansea), G.R. Rees-Jones (London Welsh); C.W. Jones (Porth/Cambridge U), *W.H. 'Bert' Jones (Llanelli); T.B. Day (Swansea), *I. Evans (London Welsh), *D.R. Prosser (Neath), G. Hughes (Penarth), *W.S. Ward (Cross Keys), I.G. Prosser (Neath), J. Lang (Llanelli), *A.G. Fear (Newport).
T: Bernard Cowey 2, Idwal Rees.
C: Viv Jenkins 2.
Referee: Harold L.V. Day (England).

Wales 10 Scotland 6

Arms Park, Cardiff. 2 February 1935

Wales won by 2 tries, 1 drop goal to 2 tries.

Cliff Jones had an amazing game even though he was injured and forced to leave the field. Before he went, he scored a brilliant try after a 40-yard run, and he and Claude Davey then paved the way for a try by Wilfred Wooller. Albert Fear came out of the pack and Idwal Rees moved to fly-half, with Fear being denied a try when Wooller turned inside and was tackled. 'He wouldn't give it to a forward, though I was shouting for it,' said Fear. Scotland drew level with tries by David Thom before the interval and Wilson Shaw after it. Wales kept Scotland at bay and full-back Vivian Jenkins won the match with a 40-yard drop goal. NB: Jenkins, who wore 'A' on his back, was listed in the programme as from Dover College and Cliff Jones (letter 'F') from Porth. The famous J. Lot Thorn of Penarth was the Wales touch-judge.

Wales V.G.J. Jenkins (Bridgend); J. Idwal Rees (Swansea), W. Wooller (Cambridge U), +E.C. Davey, A. Bassett (Aberavon); C.W. Jones (Cambridge U), W.C. Powell (Northampton); *T.J. Rees (Newport), C.D. Murphy (Cross Keys), T.B. Day, D.J. Thomas (Swansea), *T.G. Williams (Cross Keys), A.M. Rees (Cambridge U), J. Lang (Llanelli), A.G. Fear (Newport).
T: Cliff Jones, Wilf Wooller.
DG: Viv Jenkins.

Scotland K.W. Marshall (Edinburgh Acads); W.G.S. Johnston (Cambridge U), R.C.S. Dick (Blackheath/Guy's Hosp.), R.W. Shaw (Glasgow HSFP), +K.C. Fyfe (Cambridge U); C.F. Grieve (Oxford U), W.R. Logan (Edinburgh Wands); R.O. Murray (Cambridge U), G.S. Cottington, R.M. Grieve (Kelso), J.A. Beattie (Hawick), W.A. Burnet (West of Scotland), D.A. Thom (London Scottish), J.A. Waters (Selkirk), L.B. Lambie (Glasgow HSFP).
T: David Thom, Wilson Shaw.
Referee: Frank W. Haslett (Ireland).

Scotland 3 Wales 13

Murrayfield, Edinburgh. 1 February 1936

Wales won by 3 tries, 2 cons to 1 try.

Cliff Jones (who wore 'G') again inspired a Welsh win in a colourful match full of thrilling movement. The Cambridge Blue was dazed in a tackle, and although he wandered around the field, he nevertheless made the first try for Wilfred Wooller before scoring the final try himself after receiving from Haydn Tanner and bewildering the Scotland defence.

Scotland K.W. Marshall (Edinburgh Acads); W.C.W. Murdoch (Hillhead HSFP), +R.C.S. Dick (Guy's Hosp.), H.M. Murray (Glasgow U), K.C. Fyfe (Cambridge U); R.W. Shaw (Glasgow HSFP), W.R. Logan (Edinburgh Wands); R.M. Grieve (Kelso), W.A.H. Druitt (London Scottish), J.A. Waters (Selkirk), J.A. Beattie (Hawick), W.A. Burnet (West of Scotland), M.McG. Cooper (Oxford U), P.L. Duff (Glasgow Acads), G.D. Shaw (Gala/Sale).
T: H.M. Murray.

Wales V.G.J. Jenkins (London Welsh); J. Idwal Rees (Swansea), W. Wooller (Cambridge U), +E.C. Davey, B.E.W. McCall (Welsh Regt/Newport); C.W. Jones (Cambridge U), H. Tanner (Swansea); T.J. Rees (Newport), B. Evans (Llanelli), T.G. Williams (Cross Keys), H.W. Thomas (Neath), G.M. Williams (Aberavon), A.M. Rees (London Welsh), J. Lang (Llanelli), E.C. Long (Swansea).
T: Wilf Wooller, Claude Davey, Cliff Jones.
C: Viv Jenkins 2.
Referee: Cyril H. Gadney (England).

Wales 6 Scotland 13

St Helen's, Swansea. 6 February 1937

Scotland won by 3 tries, 2 cons to 2 tries.

Classy Scotland centre Charles Dick, who played with Wilfred Wooller for Cambridge in 1933, scored a try either side of half-time, after Wooller had opened the scoring for Wales. A try by Wilson Shaw, picked as a wing instead of outside-half, kept Scotland in front though Wooller crossed again, but it was too late. The rival captains, Idwal Rees and Ross Logan, were both representing the Edinburgh Wanderers club, who presented the pair with engraved silver cigarette cases. The fine Newport wing, Bill Hopkin, made his only appearance and later turned professional, while his clubmate, 'Bunner' Travers, emulated his father (George) with his superb hooking skills. He toured with the British team to South Africa in 1938 and continued for Wales after the Second World War. NB: The match programme listed Hopkin from Chepstow/Newport. Wooller wore 'C' on his back, while his opposing centre, Dick, wore 11.

Wales T.O. James (Aberavon); *W.H. Hopkin (Newport), +J. Idwal Rees (Swansea/ Edinburgh Wands), W. Wooller (Cardiff), W.H. Clement (Llanelli); R.R. Morris (Swansea/Bristol), H. Tanner (Swansea); T.G. Williams (Cross Keys), *W. Travers, T.J. Rees (Newport), *H.T. Rees (Cardiff), H.W. Thomas (Neath), E.C. Long (Swansea), E.V. Watkins (Cardiff), A.M. Rees (London Welsh).
T: Wilf Wooller 2.

Scotland J.M. Kerr (Heriot's FP); W.G.S. Johnston (Richmond), R.C.S. Dick (Guy's Hosp.), D.J. Macrae (St Andrews U), R.W. Shaw (Glasgow HSFP); W.A. Ross (Hillhead HSFP), +W.R. Logan (Edinburgh Wands); M.M. Henderson (Dunfermline), G.L. Gray (Gala), W.M. Inglis, C.L. Melville (Army), G.B. Horsburgh, W.B. Young (London Scottish), J.A. Waters (Selkirk), G.D. Shaw (Gala/Sale).
T: Charles Dick 2, Wilson Shaw.
C: Duncan Shaw 2.
Referee: Cyril H. Gadney (England).

Scotland 8 Wales 6

Murrayfield, Edinburgh. 5 February 1938

Scotland won by 1 try, 1 con, 1 pen to 2 tries.

Wales led 6–0 at the interval, but had lost Eddie Morgan with a fractured rib after just 12 minutes. With Morgan en route for the local infirmary and Wilfred Wooller also injured, wing-forward Allen McCarley floated between backs and forwards and was on hand twice to score. The first was when he pounced on a fumble by débutant George Roberts after a Cliff Jones cross-kick and then when he intercepted a pass from another newcomer, Tom Dorward, to Wilson Shaw. Wales gallantly tried to hold out, but Scotland's pack surged on for Wilf Crawford to score and convert. It was 6–5 until two minutes from time, when referee Cyril Gadney awarded Scotland a point-blank penalty that Crawford goaled. Mr Gadney said that he awarded the penalty because the Welshman wearing 'J' (Harry Rees) was lying on the ball. Rees said: 'I was lying on the ground with the ball, but Haydn Tanner was lying under me unconscious.'

Scotland G. Roberts (Watsonians); A.H. Drummond (Kelvinside Acads), R.C.S. Dick (Guy's Hosp.), D.J. Macrae (St Andrews U), J.G.S. Forrest (Cambridge U); +R.W. Shaw (Glasgow HSFP), T.F. Dorward (Gala); J.B. Borthwick (Stewart's Coll FP), J.D. Hastie (Melrose), W.M. Inglis (Army), G.B. Horsburgh (London Scottish), A. Roy (Waterloo), W.B. Young (London Scottish), P.L. Duff (Glasgow Acads), W.H. Crawford (Utd Servs).
T: Wilf Crawford.
C: Crawford.
P: Crawford.

Wales V.G.J. Jenkins (London Welsh); W.H. Clement (Llanelli), J. Idwal Rees (Swansea), W. Wooller, A. Bassett; +C.W. Jones (Cardiff), H. Tanner; M.E. Morgan (Swansea), W. Travers (Newport), H.T. Rees, E.V. Watkins (Cardiff), F.L. Morgan (Llanelli), A.M. Rees (London Welsh), W.E. Vickery (Aberavon), A. McCarley (Neath).
T: Allen McCarley 2.
Referee: Cyril H. Gadney (England).

The last home match before the Second World War saw Wales defeat Scotland by 11–3 in Cardiff. Only four players appeared after the war – Howard Davies, Haydn Tanner, 'Bunner' Travers and Les Manfield. *Back row*: A.S. Bean (referee), M.J. Davies, L. Davies, R.E. Price, L. Manfield, E. Watkins, C.H. Davies (touch-judge). *Seated*: E.L. Jones, W.E.N. Davis, E. Long, W. Wooller (capt.), W.H. Travers, S. Williams, E. Evans. *Front row*: W.T.H. Davies, H. Tanner.

Wales 11   Scotland 3

Arms Park, Cardiff. 4 February 1939

Wales won by 2 tries, 1 con, 1 pen to 1 pen.

Wales won despite having Haydn Tanner off the field for a time after injuring a nerve in his left arm. It meant that Eddie Long moved from wing-forward to scrum-half, a role he filled adequately. New wing Elvet Jones had already played in two Tests for the British team in South Africa in 1938. His clubmate, prop Emrys Evans, was selected at wing-forward. Full-back Christmas Howard Davies went on to play for Wales until 1947. A Mickey Davies try and a Wilfred Wooller penalty came before half-time and, though Wilf Crawford reduced the arrears, 'Bunner' Travers scored a clinching try, which Wooller converted.

Wales *C.H. Davies (Swansea); *E.L. Jones (Llanelli), *M.J. Davies (Oxford U), +W. Wooller (Cardiff), S.A. Williams (Aberavon); W.T.H. Davies, H. Tanner; *Leslie Davies (Swansea), W. Travers (Newport), W.E.N. Davis, E.V. Watkins (Cardiff), *E.R. Price (Weston), E. Evans (Llanelli), *L. Manfield (Otley/Mountain Ash), E.C. Long (Swansea).
T: Mickey Davies, Bill Travers.
C: Wilf Wooller.
P: Wooller.

Scotland G. Roberts (Watsonians); J.B. Craig (Heriot's FP), D.J. Macrae (St Andrews U), J.R.S. Innes (Aberdeen U), W.N. Renwick (Edinburgh Wands); +R.W. Shaw (Glasgow HSFP), W.R.C. Brydon (Heriot's FP); G.H. Gallie (Edinburgh Acads), R.W.F. Sampson (London Scottish), W. Purdie (Jedforest), G.B. Horsburgh (London Scottish), A. Roy (Waterloo), W.H. Crawford (Utd Servs), P.L. Duff (Glasgow Acads), W.B. Young (London Scottish).
P: Wilf Crawford.
Referee: Alan S. Bean (England).

Scotland 8   Wales 22

Murrayfield, Edinburgh. 1 February 1947

Wales won by 5 tries, 2 cons, 1 pen to 1 try, 1 con, 1 pen.

Wales ran up their biggest win over Scotland for 33 years but petrol rationing kept the number of Welsh supporters down. The 19-year-old Glyn Davies partnered skipper Haydn Tanner at half-back and helped inspire a second-half rally from 8–6 down. Bill Gore, at hooker, followed his father Jack who was capped 1924–25. Like his father, Bill also moved to rugby league.

Scotland +K.I. Geddes; T.G.H. Jackson (London Scottish), C.W. Drummond (Melrose), C.R. Bruce (Glasgow Acads), D.D. Mackenzie (Edinburgh U); I.J.M. Lumsden (Watsonians), A.W. Black (Edinburgh U); I.C. Henderson (Edinburgh Acads), R.W. Sampson, R. Aitken (London Scottish), D.W. Deas (Heriot's FP), F.H. Coutts (Melrose), J.H. Orr (Edinburgh Police), A.G.M. Watt, W.I.D. Elliot (Edinburgh Acads).
T: Douglas Elliot.
C: Keith Geddes.
P: Geddes.

Wales C.H. Davies (Llanelli); K.J. Jones (Newport), B.L. Williams, W.B. Cleaver (Cardiff), W. Les T. Williams (Llanelli), *G. Davies (Pontypridd), +H. Tanner (Cardiff); *W.J. Evans (Pontypool), *W. Gore (Newbridge), *C. Davies, *W.E. Tamplin (Cardiff), S. Williams, O. Williams (Llanelli), J.R.G. Stephens (Neath), G. Evans (Cardiff).
T: Ken Jones 2, Bleddyn Williams, Billy Cleaver, Les Williams.
C: Bill Tamplin 2.
P: Tamplin.
Referee: Capt. M.J. Dowling (Ireland).

Wales 14   Scotland 0

Arms Park, Cardiff. 7 February 1948

Wales won by 3 tries, 1 con, 1 pen to nil.

Wales scored all the points in the second half when the strong wind was at their backs – it was the three-quarters who accounted for all three tries. The side included ten players from Cardiff, as it had against England a month earlier, though Billy Cleaver was still selected as a centre.

Wales R.F. Trott (Cardiff); K.J. Jones (Newport), B.L. Williams, W.B. Cleaver, J. Matthews (Cardiff); G. Davies (Pontypridd), +H. Tanner (Cardiff); L. Anthony (Neath), D.M. James, C. Davies, W.E. Tamplin (Cardiff), S. Williams, O. Williams (Llanelli), L. Manfield, G. Evans (Cardiff).
T: Bleddyn Williams, Jack Matthews, Ken Jones.
C: Bill Tamplin.
P: Tamplin.

Scotland W.C.W. Murdoch (Hillhead HSFP);

T.G.H. Jackson (London Scottish), +J.R.S. Innes (Aberdeen GSFP), A. Cameron (Glasgow HSFP), D.D. Mackenzie (Edinburgh U); D.P. Hepburn (Woodford), W.D. Allardice (Aberdeen GSFP); L.R. Currie (Dunfermline), G.C. Lyall (Gala), R.M. Bruce (Aberdeen GSFP), J.C. Dawson (Glasgow Acads), W.P. Black (Glasgow HSFP), W.I.D. Elliot (Edinburgh Acads), G.M. Watt (Edinburgh Wands), J.B. Lees (Gala).
Referee: Tom N. Pearce (England).

Scotland 6   Wales 5

Murrayfield, Edinburgh. 5 February 1949

Scotland won by 2 tries to 1 try, 1 con.

Former Wallaby forward, Doug Keller, led a Scotland side which was determined to keep Glyn Davies in check. They succeeded. Laurie Gloag in the first half, and Doug Smith (later to be the 1971 Lions manager) after the interval, scored tries. Wales pulled back with a brilliant side-stepping try by Bleddyn Williams, as Haydn Tanner sent him on the blindside for Frank Trott to convert. Trott's only mistake came when he slipped and allowed Scotland through for their second try.

Scotland I.J.M. Lumsden (Watsonians); T.G.H. Jackson (London Scottish), L.G. Gloag (Cambridge U), D.P. Hepburn (Woodford), D.W.C. Smith (London Scottish); C.R. Bruce (Glasgow Acads), W.D. Allardice (Aberdeen GSFP); J.C. Dawson (Glasgow Acads), J.G. Abercrombie (Edinburgh U), S. Coltman (Hawick), L.R. Currie (Dunfermline), G.A. Wilson (Oxford U), +D.H. Keller (London Scottish), P.W. Kininmonth (Oxford U), W.I.D. Elliot (Edinburgh Acads).
T: Doug Smith, Laurie Gloag.

Wales R.F. Trott (Cardiff); K.J. Jones (Newport), J. Matthews, B.L. Williams, *T.J. Cook (Cardiff); G. Davies (Pontypridd/Cambridge U), +H. Tanner (Cardiff); E.O. Coleman, W. Travers (Newport), D.C.J. Jones (Swansea), J.A. Gwilliam (Cambridge U), A. Meredith (Devonport Servs), W.R. Cale (Newbridge), J.R.G. Stephens (Neath), G. Evans (Cardiff).
T: Bleddyn Williams.
C: Frank Trott.
Referee: Noel H. Lambert (Ireland).

Wales 12   Scotland 0

St Helen's, Swansea. 4 February 1950.

Wales won by 2 tries, 1 pen, 1 drop goal to nil

Playing against the wind in the first half, Wales produced a Malcolm Thomas try after a Jack Matthews burst. A Lewis Jones penalty was followed by a Ken Jones try, before Billy Cleaver ended the scoring with a drop goal. Cleaver later said that he could be booed at Swansea for dropping a goal for Cardiff, but cheered when he did it for Wales.

Wales B.L. Jones (Devonport Servs); K.J. Jones, M.C. Thomas (Newport), J. Matthews (Cardiff), W.C. Major (Maesteg); W.B. Cleaver, W.R. Willis (Cardiff); J.D. Robins (Birkenhead Park), D.M. Davies (Somerset Police), C. Davies (Cardiff), Don J. Hayward (Newbridge), E.R. John (Neath), W.R. Cale (Pontypool), +J.A. Gwilliam (Edinburgh Wands), R.T. Evans (Newport).
T: Malcolm Thomas, Ken Jones.
P: Lewis Jones.
DG: Billy Cleaver.

Scotland G. Burrell (Gala); D.W.C. Smith (Army), R. Macdonald (Edinburgh U), D.A. Sloan (Edinburgh Acads), C.W. Drummond (Melrose); L. Bruce Lockhart (London Scottish), A.W. Black (Edinburgh U); J.C. Dawson (Glasgow Acads), J.G. Abercrombie (Edinburgh U), G.M. Budge (Edinburgh Wands), D.E. Muir (Heriot's FP), R. Gemmill (Glasgow HSFP), +W.I.D. Elliot (Edinburgh Acads), P.W. Kininmonth (Richmond), D.H. Keller (London Scottish).
Referee: Capt. M.J. Dowling (Ireland).

Scotland 19   Wales 0

Murrayfield, Edinburgh. 3 February 1951

Scotland won by 3 tries, 2 cons, 1 pen, 1 drop goal to nil.

An amazing drop goal by back-row forward Peter Kinninmonth turned the match into one hailed by the media as: 'The Murrayfield Massacre.' Wales were favourites to win and Scotland were classed as no-hopers. Then, at 3–0, Scotland's captain caught a stray kick on the touchline and drop-kicked high between the posts for one of the greatest drop goals in international rugby history. It was another Murrayfield nightmare for outside-half Glyn Davies. Both he and Lewis Jones were among those dropped, with the team to meet Ireland having five 'A.N. Other' places in it. The name A. Forward was not ficticious, however, as it was Allen Forward from Pontypool. For Scotland, teenager David Rose and 20-year-olds Robert Gordon and Ian Thomson were outstanding and the full-back was carried off shoulder-high by some of the massive 80,000 crowd.

Scotland I.H.M. Thomson (Heriot's FP); R.A. Gordon (Edinburgh Wands), D.A. Sloan (Edinburgh Acads), D.M. Scott (Langholm), D.M. Rose (Jedforest); A. Cameron (Glasgow HSFP), I.A. Ross (Hillhead HSFP); J.C. Dawson (Glasgow Acads), N.G.R. Mair (Edinburgh U), R.L. Wilson (Gala), R. Gemmill (Glasgow HSFP), H.M. Inglis, W.I.D. Eliot (Edinburgh Acads), +P.W. Kininmonth (Richmond), R.C. Taylor (Kelvinside West).
T: Bob Gordon 2, James Dawson.
C: Hamish Inglis, Ian Thomson.
P: Thomson.
DG: Peter Kininmonth.

Wales G. Williams (Llanelli); K.J. Jones (Newport), J. Matthews (Cardiff), B.L. Jones, M.C. Thomas (Devonport Servs); G. Davies (Cambridge U), W.R. Willis (Cardiff); J.D. Robins (Birkenhead Park), D.M. Davies (Somerset Police), C. Davies (Cardiff), E.R. John (Neath), Don J. Hayward (Newbridge), *A. Forward (Pontypool), +J.A. Gwilliam (Edinburgh Wands), R.T. Evans (Newport).
Referee: Capt. M.J. Dowling (Ireland).

Wales 11 Scotland 0

Arms Park, Cardiff. 2 February 1952

Wales won by 1 try, 1 con, 2 pens to nil.

This was a disappointing game before a new record Welsh crowd of 56,000, in which Wales were depleted when Rex Willis suffered a fractured jaw but refused to leave the field. A penalty was the only score of the second half. Newport players again scored all the points, including another fine Ken Jones try after approach work from Rex Willis and Alun Thomas, who was now playing as a wing.

Wales G. Williams (Llanelli); K.J. Jones, M.C. Thomas (Newport), B.L. Williams, A.G. Thomas; C.I. Morgan, W.R. Willis (Cardiff); W.O.G. Williams (Swansea), D.M. Davies (Somerset Police), Don J. Hayward (Swansea), E.R. John, J.R.G. Stephens (Neath), A. Forward (Pontypool), +J.A. Gwilliam (Edinburgh Wands), L.G. Blyth (Swansea).
T: Ken Jones.

C: Malcolm Thomas.
P: Malcolm Thomas 2.

Scotland I.H.M. Thomson (Heriot's FP); R. Gordon, I.F. Cordial (Edinburgh Wands), J.L. Allan (Melrose), D.M. Scott (London Scottish); N.G. Davidson (Edinburgh U), A.F. Dorward (Gala); J.C. Dawson (Glasgow Acads), N.M. Munnoch (Watsonians), J. Fox (Gala), J. Johnston (Melrose), D.E. Muir (Heriot's FP), +P.W. Kininmonth (Richmond), H.M. Inglis, W.I.D. Elliot (Edinburgh Acads).
Referee: Capt. M J Dowling (Ireland).

Scotland 0 Wales 12

Murrayfield, Edinburgh. 7 February 1953

Wales won by 3 tries, 1 pen to nil.

Bleddyn Williams was never to lead a losing Wales team and this was most certainly his match, as he scored all the second-half points with two excellent tries. Terry Davies had kicked Wales ahead and Ken Jones gathered Cliff Morgan's kick to score a try in the first half. The one blot was when Rex Willis hurt his shoulder just after the interval. Cliff Morgan took over at scrum-half, with Clem Thomas on the wing. Wales kept up the pressure as Gareth Griffiths and Jones worked Williams clear before the skipper produced a briliant solo effort for the final score. Courtenay Meredith and Russell Robins made their debuts and both played splendidly on the Lions tour to South Africa in 1955. Robins lectured at Leeds College of Engineering and joined the local rugby league side there in 1959.

Scotland N.W. Cameron (Glasgow U); R.A. Gordon (Edinburgh Wands), K.J. Dalgleish (Cambridge U), J.L. Allan (Melrose), D.M. Rose (Jedforest); N.G. Davidson (Edinburgh U), +A.F. Dorward (Gala); B.E. Thomson (Oxford U), J. King (Selkirk), R.L. Wilson (Gala), J.H. Henderson (Oxford U), J.J. Hegarty (Hawick), J.V. Valentine (Navy), D.C. Macdonald (Edinburgh U), K.H.D. McMillan (Sale).

Wales T.J. Davies (Swansea); K.J. Jones (Newport), A.G. Thomas, +B.L. Williams, G.M. Griffiths; C.I. Morgan, W.R. Willis (Cardiff); W.O.G. Williams (Swansea), G.T. Beckingham (Cardiff), *C.C. Meredith, E.R. John, J.R.G. Stephens (Neath), S. Judd (Cardiff), *R.J. Robins (Pontypridd), R.C.C. Thomas (Swansea).
T: Bleddyn Williams 2, Ken Jones.
P: Terry Davies.
Referee: Dr Peter F. Cooper (England).

Wales 15 Scotland 3

St Helen's, Swansea. 10 April 1954

Wales won by 4 tries, 1 pen to 1 try.

This was the last international match to be played at Swansea for 43 years. Wales had played their first home international at St Helen's 72 years before. The match was put back from 30 January due to frost. It was a quiet affair, in which the fine Llanelli three-quarter, Ray Williams, scored a début try. He went on to play 450 times for the Scarlets and score 213 tries. Wales scored two tries in each half and led 15–0 before the South African 'Chick' Henderson crossed for Scotland in his final appearance before returning to Natal. Scotland's loss gave them the Wooden Spoon. Ken Jones equalled Dicky Owen's Welsh record of 35 caps and the legendary Billy Bancroft, aged 83, made a presentation to the right-wing who was made captain for the match.

Wales V. Evans (Neath); +K.J. Jones (Newport), G.M. Griffiths, B.L. Williams (Cardiff), *H. Ray Williams (Llanelli); C.I. Morgan, W.R. Willis (Cardiff); W.O.G. Williams (Swansea), B.V. Meredith (Newport), C.C. Meredith (Neath), R.J. Robins (Pontypridd), R.H. Williams, L.M. Davies (Llanelli), S. Judd (Cardiff), R.C.C. Thomas (Swansea).
T: Rhys Williams, Bryn Meredith, Ray Williams, Cliff Morgan.
P: Viv Evans.

Scotland J.C. Marshall; J.S. Swan, M.K. Elgie (London Scottish), D. Cameron (Glasgow HSFP), T.G. Weatherstone (Stewart's Coll FP); G.T. Ross (Watsonians), L.P. MacLachlan (Oxford U); T.P.L. McGlashan (Royal HSFP), R.K.G. MacEwan (Cambridge U), H.F. McLeod (Hawick), E.A.J. Fergusson (Oxford U), J.W.K. Kemp (Glasgow HSFP), +W.I.D. Elliot (Edinburgh Acads), P.W. Kininmonth, J.H. Henderson (Richmond).
T: 'Chick' Henderson.
Referee: Dr Peter F. Cooper (England).

Scotland 14 Wales 8

Murrayfield, Edinburgh. 5 February 1955

Scotland won by 2 tries, 1 con, 1 pen, 1 drop goal to 2 tries, 1 con.

Scotland ended a run of 17 consecutive defeats in thrilling fashion when the classy Arthur Smith, winning the first of 33 caps, scored the try of the season. Losing 3–0 at half-time, Scotland worked the ball to Smith on his own '25' and he beat man after man, kicking on and gathering to score at the corner flag. Again there was a drop goal to haunt Wales, this time from fly-half Jim Docherty, while Cliff Morgan's miserable day ended when he lost the ball between his legs in-goal for scrum-half James Nichol to fall on it and score a début try. This was the last appearance by the excellent Sid Judd, who was obviously ill and only a shadow of his true self.

Scotland +A. Cameron (Glasgow HSFP); A.R. Smith (Cambridge U), M.K. Elgie (London Scottish), R.G. Charters (Hawick), J.S. Swan (London Scottish); J.T. Docherty (Glasgow HSFP), J.A. Nichol (Royal HSFP); H.F. McLeod (Hawick), W.K.L. Relph (Stewart's Coll FP), T. Elliot (Gala), J.W.Y. Kemp (Glasgow HSFP), E.J.S. Michie (Aberdeen U), W.S. Glen (Edinburgh Wands), J.T. Greenwood (Dunfermline), A. Robson (Hawick).
T: Arthur Smith, James Nichol.
C: Kim Elgie.
P: Elgie.
DG: Jim Docherty.

Wales A.B. Edwards (London Welsh); K.J. Jones (Newport), G.T. Wells (Cardiff), A.G. Thomas (Llanelli), T.J. Brewer (London Welsh); C.I. Morgan, +W.R. Willis (Cardiff); W.O.G. Williams (Swansea), B.V. Meredith (Newport), C.C. Meredith (Neath), R.J. Robins (Pontypridd), R.H. Williams (Llanelli), S. Judd (Cardiff), J.R.G. Stephens (Neath), R.C.C. Thomas (Swansea).
T: Trevor Brewer 2.
C: Rees Stephens.
Referee: Capt. M.J. Dowling (Ireland).

Wales 9 Scotland 3

Arms Park, Cardiff. 4 February 1956

Wales won by 3 tries to 1 pen.

Cardiff Arms Park was an incredible sight with braziers all over the pitch in an effort to thaw it out. Open rugby was again almost impossible, but Wales managed three good tries – Onllwyn Brace and Cliff Morgan had their best match together. Harry Morgan's opening try was equalised by a Scotland penalty, but Lynn Davies scored to give Wales the half-time lead. The second half will be remembered solely for Cliff Morgan's try, created by Brace. The new South Stand extension was opened officially and the seating increased by 3,300 to 12,800. There was a début for the popular Ray Prosser at prop for Wales and Tylorstown-born Norman Campbell was at scrum-half for Scotland with Llanelli's Ian MacGregor in the pack.

Wales G.D. Owen; K.J. Jones, H.P. Morgan, M.C. Thomas (Newport), C.L. Davies; +C.I. Morgan (Cardiff), D.O. Brace (Newport); W.O.G. Williams (Swansea), B.V. Meredith (Newport), *T.R. Prosser (Pontypool), R.H. Williams (Llanelli), J.R.G. Stephens, B.A. Sparks (Neath), L.H. Jenkins (Newport), R.C.C.Thomas (Swansea).
T: Lynn Davies, Harry Morgan, Cliff Morgan.

Scotland R.W.T. Chisholm (Melrose); A.R. Smith (Cambridge U), +A. Cameron (Glasgow HSFP), K.R. Macdonald (Stewart's Coll FP), J.S. Swan (Coventry); M.L. Grant (Harlequins), N.M. Campbell (London Scottish); H.F. McLeod (Hawick), R.K.G. MacEwan (London Scottish), T. Elliot (Gala), E.J.S. Michie (Aberdeen GSFP), J.W.Y. Kemp (Glasgow HSFP), I.A.A. MacGregor (Llanelli), J.T. Greenwood (Dunfermline), A. Robson (Hawick).
P: Angus Cameron.
Referee: Leslie M. Boundy (England).

Scotland 9 Wales 6

Murrayfield, Edinburgh. 2 February 1957

Scotland won by 1 try, 1 pen, 1 drop goal to 1 try, 1 pen.

Only one score came in the second half, and it was once more a drop goal that shattered Wales at Murrayfield. Scrum-half Arthur Dorward, whose brother had played against Wales in 1938, caught a misplaced kick from Terry Davies and dropped a 45-yard goal from the touch-line. It was the first time Wales had lost two championship matches in a season since 1937. Wales led 3–0 and then 6–3, but Arthur Smith dashed over after gathering Tom McClung's well-placed kick to the corner just before the interval. Ken Jones played his final match for Wales. He was one of the finest players ever to represent his country, both on track and field. Though remembered for his speed and the tries he scored, he was also an outstanding tackler and coverer. His tries against New Zealand – one for the British Isles in Auckland and the one at the Arms Park – will remain two of the greatest ever scored.

Scotland K.J.F. Scotland (Heriot's FP); A.R. Smith (Cambridge U), E. McKeating (Heriot's FP), K.R. Macdonald (Stewart's Coll FP), J.S. Swan (Coventry); T. McClung (Edinburgh Acads), A.F. Dorward (Gala); H.F. McLeod (Hawick), R.K.G. MacEwan (London Scottish), T. Elliot (Gala), E.J.S. Michie (London Scottish), J.W.Y. Kemp (Glasgow HSFP), I.A.A. MacGregor (Llanelli), +J.T. Greenwood (Perthshire Acads), A. Robson (Hawick).
T: Arthur Smith.
P: Ken Scotland.
DG: Arthur Dorward.

Wales T.J. Davies (Llanelli); K.J. Jones, +M.C. Thomas (Newport), G.M. Griffiths (Cardiff), W.G. Howells (Llanelli); C.I. Morgan, *L.H. Williams (Cardiff); T.R. Prosser (Pontypool), B.V. Meredith (London Welsh), C.C. Meredith, J.R.G. Stephens (Neath), R.H. Williams (Llanelli), *R.H. Davies (Oxford U), R.J. Robins (Pontypridd), B.A. Sparks (Neath).
T: Robin Davies.
P: Terry Davies.
Referee: R.C. Williams (Ireland).

Wales 8 Scotland 3

Arms Park, Cardiff. 1 February 1958

Wales won by 2 tries, 1 con to 1 pen.

It was Cliff Morgan and Terry Davies who made the big difference in the sides. Left-wing Gordon Wells scored a first-half try which Davies converted and, in the second half, right-wing John Collins clinched the win after Scotland skipper Arthur Smith had closed the gap to two points.

Wales T.J. Davies (Llanelli); J.E. Collins (Aberavon), M.C. Thomas (Newport), C.A.H. Davies (Llanelli); G.T. Wells; C.I. Morgan, L.H. Williams (Cardiff); T.R. Prosser (Pontypool), B.V. Meredith (Newport), D.B. Devereux (Neath), R.H. Williams (Llanelli), W.R. Evans (Cardiff), +R.C.C. Thomas, J. Faull (Swansea), H.J. Morgan (Abertillery).
T: Gordon Wells, John Collins.
C: Terry Davies.

Scotland R.W.T. Chisholm (Melrose); +A.R. Smith (Cambridge U), G.D. Stevenson (Hawick), J.T. Docherty (Glasgow HSFP), T.G. Weatherstone (Stewart's Coll FP); G.H. Waddell (Devonport Servs), J.A.T. Rodd (Utd Servs); H.F. McLeod (Hawick), R.K.G. MacEwan (Lansdowne), T. Elliot (Gala), M.W. Swan (Oxford U), J.W.Y. Kemp (Glasgow HSFP), G.K. Smith (Kelso), J.T. Greenwood (Perthshire Acads), A. Robson (Hawick).
P: Arthur Smith.
Referee: Dr Norman McNeill Parkes (England).

Scotland 6 Wales 5

Murrayfield, Edinburgh. 7 February 1959.

Scotland won by 1 try, 1 pen to 1 try, 1 con.

Wales took a fifth-minute lead with a magnificent effort by the 21-year-old RAF centre Malcolm Price. It was not enough, however, as a Ken Scotland penalty and a Norman Bruce try before half-time put Scotland in front, though Cliff Ashton just missed with a drop-shot in the closing minutes.

Scotland K.J.F. Scotland (Cambridge U); A.R. Smith (Gosforth), T. McClung (Edinburgh Acads), G.D. Stevenson (Hawick), T.G. Weatherstone (Stewart's Coll FP); G.H. Waddell (Cambridge U), S. Coughtrie (Edinburgh Acads); H.F. McLeod (Hawick), N.S. Bruce (Blackheath), I.R. Hastie (Kelso), M.W. Swan (London Scottish), J.W.Y. Kemp (Glasgow HSFP), G.K. Smith (Kelso), +J.T. Greenwood (Perthshire Acads), A. Robson (Hawick).
T: Norman Bruce.
P: Ken Scotland.

Wales T.J. Davies (Llanelli); J.E. Collins, H.J. Davies (Aberavon), M.J. Price (Pontypool), D.I.E. Bebb (Swansea); C. Ashton (Aberavon), L.H. Williams (Cardiff); T.R. Prosser (Pontypool), B.V. Meredith (Newport), D.R. Main (London Welsh), I.R. Ford (Newport), R.H. Williams (Llanelli), +R.C.C. Thomas, J. Faull (Swansea), J. Leleu (London Welsh).
T: Malcolm Price.
C: Terry Davies.
Referee: R.C. Wiliams (Ireland).

Wales 8 Scotland 0

Arms Park, Cardiff. 6 February 1960.

Wales won by 1 try, 1 con, 1 pen to nil.

Despite a large Newport presence in the side, Wales were not convincing and scored all their points in the second half. New cap Norman Morgan at full-back kicked two goals with his superb left foot. Wales fielded the complete back row from Newport with Geoff Whitson and Glyn Davidge returning to join Brian Cresswell. Scotland captain Arthur Smith was working at the Ebbw Vale steelworks and playing for the local club.

Wales *N.H. Morgan (Newport); *F.G. Coles, M.J. Price (Pontypool), G.W. Lewis (Richmond), D.I.E. Bebb (Swansea); C. Ashton (Aberavon), D.O. Brace (Llanelli); T.R. Prosser (Pontypool), +B.V. Meredith (Newport), L.J. Cunningham (Aberavon), G.W. Payne (Pontypridd), D.J.E. Harris (Cardiff), B.R. Cresswell, G.D. Davidge, G.K. Whitson (Newport).
T: Dewi Bebb.
C: Norman Morgan.
P: Morgan.

Scotland K.J.F. Scotland (Cambridge U); +A.R. Smith (Ebbw Vale), J.J. McPartlin (Harlequins), I.H.P. Laughland (London Scottish), G.D. Stevenson (Hawick); T. McClung (Edinburgh Acads), J.A.T. Rod (Navy); H.F. McLeod (Hawick), N.S. Bruce (London Scottish), D.M.D. Rollo (Howe of Fife), F.H. ten Bos (Oxford U), J.W.Y. Kemp (Glasgow HSFP), G.K. Smith (Kelso), K.R.F. Bearne (Cambridge U), C.E.B. Stewart (Kelso).
Referee: Kevin D Kelleher (Ireland).

Scotland 3 Wales 0

Murrayfield, Edinburgh. 11 February 1961

Scotland won by 1 try to nil.

There was no joy once again at Murrayfield. It was, inevitably, Arthur Smith who sent Wales to defeat. After 32 minutes he finished a move in which full-back Ken Scotland had joined. Dewi Bebb thought he had equalised only for the referee to rule against it. Bebb had been tackled into touch after a 60-yard run, but his quick throw-in to Meirion Roberts, who then returned the pass, was said not to have gone infield by the required five yards. The only new cap was police officer Gordon Britton, who won his only cap at the age of 21.

Scotland K.J.F. Scotland (London Scottish); +A.R. Smith (Edinburgh Wands), E. McKeating (Heriot's FP), G.D. Stevenson (Hawick), R.H. Thomson; I.H.P. Laughland (London Scottish), A.J. Hastie (Melrose); H.F. McLeod (Hawick), N.S. Bruce (London Scottish), D.M.D. Rollo (Howe of Fife), F.H. ten Bos (London Scottish), M.J. Campbell-Lamerton (Halifax), G.K. Smith (Kelso), J. Douglas (Stewart's Coll FP), K.I. Ross (Boroughmuir FP).
T: Arthur Smith.

Wales +T.J. Davies (Llanelli); P.M.Rees, *G.R. Britton (Newport), H.M. Roberts (Cardiff), D.I.E. Bebb (Swansea); K.H.L. Richards (Bridgend), A. O'Connor; P.E.J. Morgan (Aberavon), B.V. Meredith (Newport), K.D. Jones, D.J.E. Harris (Cardiff), W.R. Evans

(Bridgend), G.D. Davidge (Newport), D. Nash (Ebbw Vale), H.J. Morgan (Abertillery).
Referee: R.C. Williams (Ireland).

Wales 3   Scotland 8

Arms Park, Cardiff. 3 February 1962

Scotland won by 2 tries, 1 con to 1 drop goal.

Scotland flanker Ronnie Glasgow gained his country's first try for 27 years at Cardiff, in what was to be their only win there in 18 matches from 1939 until 1980. Frans ten Bos followed Glasgow to the Welsh line, with Ken Scotland converting the latter before half-time. Wales scored in the final minutes with a drop goal from Alan Rees. Des Greenslade won his only cap, replacing the injured Kingsley Jones at prop.

Wales T.K. Coslett (Aberavon); D.R.R. Morgan, D.K. Jones (Llanelli), H.M. Roberts (Cardiff), D.I.E. Bebb (Swansea); A.H.M. Rees (Maesteg), +L.H. Williams (Cardiff); L.J. Cunningham (Aberavon), B.V. Meredith, *D. Greenslade, B. Price (Newport), W.R. Evans (Bridgend), R.H. Davies (London Welsh), A.E.I. Pask, H.J. Morgan (Abertillery).
DG: Alan Rees.

Scotland K.J.F. Scotland (Leicester); +A.R. Smith (Edinburgh Wands), J.J. McPartlin (Oxford U), I.H.P. Laughland (London Scottish), R.C. Cowan (Selkirk); G.H. Waddell (London Scottish), S. Coughtrie (Edinburgh Acads); H.F. McLeod (Hawick), N.S. Bruce (London Scottish), D.M.D. Rollo (Howe of Fife), F.H. ten Bos (London Scottish), M.J. Campbell-Lamerton (Halifax), R.J.C. Glasgow (Dunfermline), J. Douglas (Stewart's Coll FP), K.I. Ross (Boroughmuir FP).
T: Ron Glasgow, Frans ten Bos.
C: Ken Scotland.
Referee: Dr Norman McNeill Parkes (England).

Scotland 0   Wales 6

Murrayfield, Edinburgh. 2 February 1963

Wales won by 1 pen, 1 drop goal to nil.

A crowd of 60,000 witnessed what was probably the biggest bore in rugby history as Clive Rowlands kicked continuously and 111 lineouts took place. The three-quarters were frozen, and centre Brian Davies hardly touched the ball yet was dropped for the next match. A penalty by Hodgson was followed by an amazing drop goal from Rowlands after receiving from a lineout.

Scotland +K.J.F. Scotland (Heriot's FP); R.H. Thomson, J.A.P. Shackleton (London Scottish), D.M. White (Kelvinside Acads), G.D. Stevenson (Hawick); I.H.P. Laughland (London Scottish), S. Coughtrie (Edinburgh Acads); D.M.D. Rollo (Howe of Fife), N.S. Bruce, A.C.W. Boyle, F.H. ten Bos (London Scottish), M.J. Campbell-Lamerton (Halifax), W.R.A. Watherston (London Scottish), J. Douglas (Stewart's Coll FP), K.I. Ross (Boroughmuir FP).

Wales G.T.R. Hodgson (Neath); D.R.R. Morgan, D.B. Davies (Llanelli), *R. Evans (Bridgend), *W.J.B. Morris (Pontypool); D. Watkins (Newport), +D.C.T. Rowlands (Pontypool); D. Williams (Ebbw Vale), N.R. Gale (Llanelli), K.D. Jones (Cardiff), B. Price (Newport), B.E. Thomas (Neath), *G. Jones (Ebbw Vale), A.E.I. Pask, H.J. Morgan (Abertillery).
P: Grahame Hodgson.
DG: Clive Rowlands.
Referee: R.C. Williams (Ireland).

Wales 11   Scotland 3

Arms Park, Cardiff. 1 February 1964

Wales won by 2 tries, 1 con, 1 pen to 1 try.

Scotland, who had beaten France and drawn with New Zealand, led 3–0 at the interval, but Wales produced a second-half rally. Clive Rowlands and David Watkins combined to put Keith Bradshaw over for a try. The Bridgend centre added a conversion and penalty before lock Brian Thomas plunged over from a lineout.

Wales G.T.R. Hodgson (Neath); *S.J. Watkins (Newport), D.K. Jones (Llanelli), K. Bradshaw (Bridgend), D.I.E. Bebb (Swansea); D. Watkins (Newport), +D.C.T. Rowlands (Pontypool); D. Williams (Ebbw Vale), N.R. Gale (Llanelli), L.J. Cunningham (Aberavon), B. Price (Newport), B.E. Thomas (Neath), *G.J. Prothero (Bridgend), A.E.I. Pask (Abertillery), Dai J. Hayward (Cardiff).
T: Keith Bradshaw, Brian Thomas.
C: Bradshaw.
P: Bradshaw.

Scotland S. Wilson (Oxford U); C. Elliot (Langholm), J.A.P. Shackleton, I.H.P. Laughland, R.H. Thomson (London Scottish); G. Sharp (Stewart's Coll FP), J.A.T. Rodd (London Scottish); D.M.D. Rollo (Howe of Fife), N.S. Bruce (London Scottish), +J.B. Neill (Edinburgh Acads), W.J. Hunter (Hawick), P.C.

Brown (West of Scotland), J.W. Telfer (Melrose), T.O. Grant (Hawick), J.P. Fisher (Royal HSFP).
T: Iain Laughland.
Referee: Peter G. Brook (England).

Scotland 12 Wales 14

Murrayfield, Edinburgh. 6 February 1965

Wales won by 2 tries, 1 con, 2 pens to 2 pens, 2 drop goals.

Wales led 8–6 and 11–9 but were losing 11–12 when hooker Norman Gale crashed over the Scotland line near the end of the match. Hundreds of Welsh fans poured on to the field to mob their team at the final whistle. Once again there were drop goals at Murrayfield, with Brian Simmers notching two despite being dazed and spending some time off the pitch. This time, however, the drop shots were not enough to defeat Wales. A débutant was lock Bill Morris, who was born in Australia, but schooled in Wrexham before joining New Brighton and then Newport.

Scotland S. Wilson (London Scottish); C. Elliot (Langholm), I.H.P. Laughland (London Scottish), B.C. Henderson, D.J. Whyte (Edinburgh Wands); B.M. Simmers (Glasgow Acads), J.A.T. Rodd (London Scottish); D.M.D. Rollo (Howe of Fife), F.A.L. Laidlaw (Melrose), N. Suddon (Hawick), P.K. Stagg (Sale), +M.J. Campbell-Lamerton, J.P. Fisher (London Scottish), J.W. Telfer (Melrose), R.J.C. Glasgow (Dunfermline).
P: Stewart Wilson 2.
DG: Brian Simmers 2.

Wales T.G. Price (Llanelli); S.J. Watkins, J. Uzzell (Newport), S.J. Dawes (London Welsh), D.I.E. Bebb (Swansea); D. Watkins (Newport), +D.C.T. Rowlands (Pontypool); D. Williams (Ebbw Vale), N.R. Gale (Llanelli), R.G. Waldron (Neath), B. Price, *W.J. Morris (Newport), G.J. Prothero (Bridgend), A.E.I. Pask, H.J. Morgan (Abertillery).
T: Stuart Watkins, Norman Gale.
C: Terry Price.
P: Terry Price 2.
Referee: R.W. Gilliland (Ireland).

Wales 8 Scotland 3

Arms Park, Cardiff. 5 February 1966

Wales won by 2 tries, 1 con to 1 pen.

Wales often seemed to waste the genius of Ken Jones. In 1962, he had scored an amazing try for the Lions in a 3–3 draw against South Africa. On this typical Cardiff day of mud and rain, his skill shone out just as brightly and his brace of tries gave Wales victory. David Watkins was also in fine form and Jones was able to run on to the ball at top speed and leave Scotland skipper Stewart Wilson helpless. They sent Wales home, but not dry, though second-row forward Brian Price had battled on with a leg injury that required a mass of bandages.

Wales T.G.R. Hodgson (Neath); S.J. Watkins (Newport), D.K. Jones (Cardiff), K. Bradshaw, L. Davies (Bridgend); D. Watkins (Newport), R. Allan Lewis (Abertillery); D. Williams (Ebbw Vale), N.R. Gale (Llanelli), D.J. Lloyd (Bridgend), B. Price (Newport), B.E. Thomas (Neath), G.J. Prothero (Bridgend), +A.E.I. Pask, H.J. Morgan (Abertillery).
T: Ken Jones 2.
C: Keith Bradshaw.

Scotland +S. Wilson; A.J.W. Hinshelwood, I.H.P. Laughland (London Scottish), B.C. Henderson, D.J. Whyte (Edinburgh Wands); J.W.C. Turner (Gala), A.J. Hastie (Melrose); D.M.D. Rollo (Howe of Fife), F.A.L. Laidlaw (Melrose), J.D. Macdonald, M.J. Campbell-Lamerton (London Scottish), P.K. Stagg (Sale), J.P. Fisher (London Scottish), J.W. Telfer (Melrose), D. Grant (Hawick).
P: Stewart Wilson.
Referee: Mike H. Titcomb (England).

Scotland 11 Wales 5

Murrayfield, Edinburgh. 4 February 1967

Scotland won by 2 tries, 1 con, 1 drop goal to 1 try, 1 con

Wales brought in six new caps after the defeat by Australia. They included the clever Cardiff scrum-half Billy Hullin, who partnered Barry John. But the two runners were given the task of kicking and Welsh tactics were sadly at fault. Both were dropped through no fault of their own and Hullin was never again selected. Scotland's half-backs David Chisholm and Alex Hastie called the tune, playing together for the tenth time without being on the losing side. Wales led 5–0 at half-time after a typical Stuart Watkins opportunist try, but never looked capable of winning. John had received 13 stitches in a knee from a Welsh trial match and later said he should not have played.

Scotland S. Wilson; A.J.W. Hinshelwood (London Scottish), J.W.C. Turner (Gala), B.M. Simmers (Glasgow Acads), D.J. Whyte (Edinburgh

Gareth Edwards tests the Scotland defence to the full, and is watched by an admiring Gerald Davies. The great scrum-half played 53 times for Wales and scored 20 tries. (© Huw Evans)

Wands); D.H. Chisholm, A.J. Hastie (Melrose); J.D. Macdonald (London Scottish), F.A.L. Laidlaw (Melrose), D.M.D. Rollo (Howe of Fife), P.K. Stagg (Sale), W.J. Hunter (Hawick), +J.P. Fisher (London Scottish), J.W. Telfer (Melrose), D. Grant (Hawick).
T: Sandy Hinshelwood, Jim Telfer.
C: Stewart Wilson.
DG: David Chisholm.

Wales T.G. Price (Hendy/Leicester U); S.J. Watkins (Newport), *W.H. Raybould (London Welsh), T.G.R. Davies (Cardiff), D.I.E. Bebb (Swansea); B. John (Llanelli), *W.G. Hullin (Cardiff); *J.P. O'Shea (Cardiff), *B.I. Rees (London Welsh), D.J. Lloyd (Bridgend), B. Price (Newport), *G.T. 'Billy' Mainwaring (Aberavon), K.J. Braddock (Newbridge), +A.E.I. Pask (Abertillery), *J. Taylor (London Welsh).
T: Stuart Watkins.
C: Terry Price.
Referee: Kevin D. Kelleher (Ireland).

Wales 5   Scotland 0

Arms Park, Cardiff. 3 February 1968

Wales won by 1 try, 1 con to nil.

Wales's only victory of the season came from what many considered a forward pass by Keith Jarrett to Gerald Davies after 17 minutes of the first half. Davies handed on to wing Keri Jones who touched down for Jarrett to convert. It was a disappointing game in which Gareth Edwards became the youngest player ever to captain Wales at the age of 20 years and seven months.

Wales *D. Rees (Swansea); S.J. Watkins, K.S. Jarrett (Newport), T.G.R. Davies, W. Keri Jones; B. John, +G.O. Edwards (Cardiff); D.J. Lloyd, *J. Young (Bridgend), J.P. O'Shea (Cardiff), M.L. Wiltshire (Aberavon), W.D. Thomas (Llanelli), W.D. Morris (Neath), R.E. Jones (Coventry), A.J. Gray (London Welsh).
T: Keri Jones.
C: Keith Jarrett.

Scotland S. Wilson; A.J.W. Hinshelwood (London Scottish), J.N.M. Frame (Edinburgh U), J.W.C. Turner (Gala), G.J. Keith (Wasps); D.H. Chisholm, A.J. Hastie (Melrose); A.B. Carmichael (West of Scotland), F.A.L. Laidlaw (Melrose), D.M.D. Rollo (Howe of Fife), P.K. Stagg (Sale), G.W.E. Mitchell (Edinburgh Wands), +J.P. Fisher, A.H.W. Boyle (London Scottish), T.G. Elliot (Langholm).
Referee: G.C. 'Larry' Lamb (England).

Scotland 3 Wales 17

Murrayfield, Edinburgh. 1 February 1969

Wales won by 3 tries, 1 con, 2 pens to 1 pen.

It was the new dawn in Welsh rugby as the class of the 70s began assembling. There was a new coach in the former scrum-half and captain Clive Rowlands; a new full-back in J.P.R.Williams (at that time he was called John) and a new number 8, Mervyn Davies. New rules now allowed kicking the Australian way – direct to touch only from inside the kicker's '25'. Also available was a replacement for an injured player, though few players wished to leave the field early. Wales led by two penalties going into the second half. Then Gareth Edwards and Maurice Richards scored tries before Scotland opened their account. Barry John quickly responded by charging down Colin Telfer's kick, selling a superb dummy, and was over.

Scotland C.F. Blaikie (Heriot's FP); A.J.W. Hinshelwood (London Scottish), J.N.M. Frame (Gala), C.W.W. Rea (West of Scotland), W.D. Jackson (Hawick); C.M. Telfer (Hawick), I.G. McCrae (Gordonians); N. Suddon (Hawick), F.A.L. Laidlaw (Melrose), A.B. Carmichael (West of Scotland), P.K. Stagg (Sale), A.F. McHarg (London Scottish), T.G. Elliot (Langholm), +J.W. Telfer (Melrose), R.J. Arneil (Edinburgh Acads).
P: Colin Blaikie.

Wales *J.P.R. Williams (London Welsh); S.J. Watkins, K.S. Jarrett (Newport), T.G.R. Davies, M.C.R. Richards; B. John, G.O. Edwards (Cardiff); D. Williams (Ebbw Vale), J. Young, D.J. Lloyd (Bridgend), +B. Price (Newport), B.E. Thomas, W.D. Morris (Neath), *T. Mervyn Davies, J. Taylor (London Welsh).
T: Barry John, Gareth Edwards, Maurice Richards.
C: Keith Jarrett.
P: Jarrett 2.
Referee: Kevin D. Kelleher (Ireland).

Wales 18 Scotland 9

Arms Park, Cardiff. 7 February 1970

Wales won by 4 tries, 3 cons to 1 try, 1 pen, 1 drop goal.

Phil Bennett gained his second full cap, this time as a centre where he replaced the injured Billy Raybould. Also into the side came new cap Laurie Daniel on the wing since Gerald Davies was studying hard at Cambridge University. It was Daniel who hauled Wales back from 0–9 just before the interval with a try which he also converted. His reward was never to be picked again! The second half was a different story and Barry Llewelyn, John Dawes and finally Dai Morris scored tries. When Gordon Brown was replaced by Peter Brown it was the first case of one brother coming on for another in Test rugby, while their father was the Scotland trainer.

Wales J.P.R. Williams (London Welsh); *L.T.D. Daniel (Newport), S.J. Dawes (London Welsh), P. Bennett (Llanelli), I. Hall (Aberavon); B. John, +G.O. Edwards (Cardiff); D.B. Llewelyn, V.C. Perrins (Newport), D. Williams (Ebbw Vale), W.D. Thomas (Llanelli), T.G. Evans (London Welsh), W.D. Morris (Neath), T.M. Davies (London Welsh), D. Hughes (Newbridge).
T: Laurie Daniel, Barry Llewelyn, John Dawes, Dai Morris.
C: Gareth Edwards 2, Daniel.

Scotland I.S.G. Smith; M.A. Smith (London Scottish), J.N.M. Frame (Gala), C.W.W. Rea (West of Scotland), A.J.W. Hinshelwood (London Scottish); I. Robertson, R.G. Young (Watsonians); J. McLauchlan (Jordanhill Coll FP), F.A.L. Laidlaw (Melrose), A.B. Carmichael (West of Scotland), P.K. Stagg (Sale), P.C. Brown (Gala), W. Lauder (Neath), +J.W. Telfer (Melrose), R.J. Arneil (Leicester). Rep: G.L. Brown (West of Scotland) for (P.C.) Brown.
T: Ian Robertson.
P: Wilson Lauder.
DG: Robertson.
Referee: D.P. 'Paddy' D'Arcy (Ireland).

Scotland 18 Wales 19

Murrayfield, Edinburgh. 6 February 1971

Wales won by 4 tries, 2 cons, 1 pen to 2 tries, 4 pens.

The bearded English-born-and-bred flanker, John Taylor, will always be remembered for the kick that beat Scotland just two minutes from time. Wales had played well, but Scotland led 18–14, when Delme Thomas won a lineout and Gareth Edwards set his backs running. It went out along the line to Gerald Davies on the right-wing. He tore over, but the Scottish cover cut him off from running around in-goal. The kick was from the right touchline and more natural to the left-footed Taylor, so John Dawes, always a wise leader, made his decision. Amid much nail-biting, the cool Taylor placed a splendid kick over between the posts for a Welsh victory. The match was very exciting throughout, but Scotland skipper Peter Brown will forever rue the kick that hit a post

FIVE NATIONS — SCOTLAND

Wales pictured just before they thrashed Scotland by 35–12 in 1972 at Cardiff. The match featured two tries by Gareth Edwards – the second being one of the finest individual efforts ever seen at the Arms Park. *Back row*: D.C.T. Rowlands (coach), J. Young, R.T.E. Bergiers, D.B.Llewelyn, T.G. Evans, T.M. Davies, W.D. Thomas, J.C. Bevan, W.D. Morris, G.A. Jamieson (referee), (touch-judge). *Seated*: A.J.L. Lewis, J.P.R. Williams, J. Taylor, D.J. Lloyd (capt.), B. John, G.O. Edwards, T.G.R. Davies. (© *Western Mail & Echo*)

from close range after centre Chris Rea's try. Two Brown kicks led against a Barry John drop goal before Taylor sprinted over at the posts. John's conversion took it to 8–6 at the break and then a Gareth Edwards try put Wales on top. Scotland hit back, as Sandy Carmichael plunged over and another Brown penalty gave Scotland the lead at 12–11. Again the lead changed, as John weaved his way right through the defence, but he looked tired as he missed the goal points. Brown struck his fourth penalty to put Scotland back in front at 15–14 and, when the Welsh defence were caught sleeping, Rea weaved clear and over. Brown then missed what should have been a winning kick and Taylor was to make him pay for it. The only Welsh change of the season was on account of Arthur Lewis's pulled hamstring. Ian Hall took his place.

Scotland I.S.G. Smith (London Scottish); W.C.C. Steele (Bedford), J.N.M. Frame (Gala), C.W.W. Rea (Headingley), A.G. Biggar (London Scottish); J.W.C. Turner, D.S. Paterson (Gala); J. McLauchlan (Jordanhill Coll), F.A.L. Laidlaw (Melrose), A.B. Carmichael, G.L. Brown (West of Scotland), A.F. McHarg (London Scottish), R.J. Arneil (Leicester), +P.C. Brown, N.A. MacEwan (Gala).

T: 'Sandy' Carmichael, Chris Rea.
P: Peter Brown 4.

Wales J.P.R. Williams; T.G.R. Davies, +S.J. Dawes (London Welsh), I. Hall (Aberavon), J.C. Bevan; B. John, G.O. Edwards (Cardiff); D. Williams (Ebbw Vale), J. Young (Harrogate), D.B. Llewelyn, W.D. Thomas (Llanelli), M.G. Roberts (London Welsh), W.D. Morris (Neath), T.M. Davies, J. Taylor (London Welsh).

T: John Taylor, Gareth Edwards, Barry John, Gerald Davies.
C: Taylor, John.
P: John.
Referee: Mike H. Titcomb (England).

Wales 35 Scotland 12

Arms Park, Cardiff. 5 February 1972

Wales won by 5 tries, 3 cons, 3 pens to 1 try, 1 con, 2 pens.

It was just another international match for at least 60 minutes. Scotland led 12–10 just after half-time and, even when they were trailing at 12–16, they were well into the Welsh half. Then it happened: one of the greatest individual tries ever seen on the Arms Park. Scrum-half Gareth Edwards, who had already given Wales the lead with a try, came around the blind-side of a scrum on the South-Stand side of the field in his own half. He pushed off flanker Rodger Arneil and was away. The alarm bells were ringing in Scotland's defence as he kicked over full-back Arthur Brown and, though he was under pressure from several defenders and the bounce was not kind, he hacked the ball left-footed to the muddiest, most horrible part of a very dirty pitch. 'It would be a miracle if he scored,' roared the commentary. It was a miracle right enough. Edwards dived into the sea of mud at the Westgate-Street end and came up looking like a different person. Only the face of Lions prop Fran Cotton later in New Zealand ever resembled it. The crowd were wilder than just wild. Spike Milligan suggested that a church should be built on the spot. The screaming went on and on as Edwards trudged back to his own half, a lot slower than he had run in the other direction! The game ceased to matter. It was game, set and match to Wales who ran in further tries by Roy Bergiers and John Taylor, with Barry John adding both conversions and a penalty. Scotland did not add any points. They had been too stunned by Edwards. Scotland lost wing Alastair Biggar with a hamstring injury and J.P.R. Williams was carried off with a fractured jaw that now saw the versatile Phil Bennett in a full-back role. It was Wales's highest score against Scotland and the biggest victory by Wales over anyone for 41 years.

Wales J.P.R. Williams; T.G.R. Davies (London Welsh), R.T.E. Bergiers (Llanelli/Cardiff Coll of Ed), A.J.L. Lewis (Ebbw Vale), J.C. Bevan (Cardiff/Cardiff Coll of Ed); B. John, G.O. Edwards (Cardiff); +D.J. Lloyd (Bridgend), J. Young (RAF), D.B. Llewelyn, W.D. Thomas (Llanelli), T.G. Evans (London Welsh), W.D. Morris (Neath), T.M. Davies, J. Taylor (London Welsh). Rep: P. Bennett (Llanelli) for Williams.
T: Gareth Edwards 2, Gerald Davies, Roy Bergiers, John Taylor.
C: Barry John 3.
P: John 3.

Scotland A.R. Brown (Gala); W.C.C. Steele (RAF), J.N.M. Frame (Gala), J.M. Renwick (Hawick), A.G. Biggar (London Scottish); C.M. Telfer (Hawick), D.S. Paterson (Gala); A.B. Carmichael (West of Scotland), R.L. Clark (Edinburgh Wands), J. McLauchlan (Jordanhill), I.A. Barnes (Hawick), G.L. Brown (West of Scotland), N.A. MacEwan, +P.C. Brown (Gala), R.J. Arneil (Northampton). Rep: L.G. Dick (Loughborough Coll) for Biggar.
T: Bobby Clark.
C: Peter Brown.
P: Peter Brown, Jim Renwick.
Referee: G. Alf Jamieson (Ireland).

Scotland 10 Wales 9

Murrayfield, Edinburgh. 3 February 1973

Scotland won by 2 tries, 1 con to 3 pens.

Scotland gained their first win over Wales for six years, scoring two tries to lead 10–0 and then to hang on as Wales cut the deficit to one point with three successful penalty attempts. Peter Brown dominated at the lineout and the backs took advantage as Colin Telfer dummied his way over. Then Gordon Strachan put Billy Steele across on the blind-side after Roy Bergiers had been forced to carry over his own line.

Scotland A.R. Irvine (Heriot's FP); W.C.C. Steele (Bedford/RAF), I.R. McGeechan (Headingley), I.W. Forsyth (Stewart's FP), D. Shedden (West of Scotland); C.M. Telfer (Hawick), D.W. Morgan (Melville FP); A.B. Carmichael (West of Scotland), R.L. Clark (Edinburgh Wands/Navy), +J. McLauchlan (Jordanhill), A.F. McHarg (London Scottish), P.C. Brown (Gala), J.G. Millican (Edinburgh U), G.M. Strachan (Jordanhill), N.A. MacEwan (Gala).
T: Colin Telfer, Billy Steele.
C: Douglas Morgan.

Wales J.P.R. Williams; T.G.R. Davies (London Welsh), R.T.E. Bergiers (Llanelli), +A.J.L. Lewis (Ebbw Vale), J.C. Bevan (Cardiff); P. Bennett (Llanelli), G.O. Edwards (Cardiff); D.J. Lloyd (Bridgend), J. Young (London Welsh/RAF), G. Shaw (Neath), W.D. Thomas, D.L. Quinnell (Llanelli), W.D. Morris (Neath), T.M. Davies (Swansea), J. Taylor (London Welsh).
P: Phil Bennett 2, John Taylor.
Referee: François Palmade (France).

Wales 6 Scotland 0

Arms Park, Cardiff. 19 January 1974

Wales won by 1 try, 1 con to nil.

Terry Cobner, the only new cap on the Welsh side, had a début to remember. The Pontypool skipper was nine days past his 28th birthday when he scored the only try of the match after 23 minutes, after his clubmate Bobby Windsor took a strike against the head and Gerald Davies received on the South-Stand side at the Westgate-Street end. He evaded two defenders and, when tackled, unloaded to the supporting Cobner, who crossed halfway out and Phil Bennett converted. Scotland's experienced props –

FIVE NATIONS — SCOTLAND

Terry Cobner, on his début, about to score the only try of the match against Scotland at Cardiff in 1974. Gerald Davies (on the ground), Phil Bennett and Dai Morris are the other Welsh players. (© Huw Evans)

Scotland forwards Duncan Madsen and Ian 'Mighty Mouse' McLauchlan cannot prevent another burst from Gareth Edwards in this 1974 match. Wales forwards are Derek Quinnell and Terry Cobner. (© Huw Evans)

'Mighty Mouse' McLauchlan and Sandy Carmichael – gave the Welsh pack problems and no further score resulted.

Wales J.P.R. Williams; T.G.R. Davies, K. Hughes (London Welsh), I. Hall (Aberavon), J.J. Williams; P. Bennett (Llanelli), +G.O. Edwards (Cardiff); G. Shaw (Neath), R.W. Windsor (Pontypool), P.D. Llewellyn (Swansea), D.L. Quinnell (Llanelli), A.J. Martin (Aberavon), W.D. Morris (Neath), T.M. Davies (Swansea), *T.J. Cobner (Pontypool).
T: Terry Cobner.
C: Phil Bennett.

Scotland A.R. Irvine (Heriot's FP); A.D. Gill (Gala), J.M. Renwick (Hawick), I.R. McGeechan (Headingley), L.G. Dick (Jordanhill); C.M. Telfer (Hawick), A.J.M. Lawson (Edinburgh Wands); +J. McLauchlan (Jordanhill), D.F. Madsen (Gosforth), A.B. Carmichael (West of Scotland), A.F. McHarg (London Scottish), G.L. Brown (West of Scotland), W. Lauder (Neath), W.S. Watson (Boroughmuir FP), N.A. MacEwan (Highland).
Referee: R.F. 'Johnny' Johnson (England).

Scotland 12 Wales 10

Murrayfield, Edinburgh. 1 March 1975

Scotland won by 3 pens, 1 drop goal to 1 try, 2 pens.

1 March – St David's Day – appeared to be a good day for Wales to take the third leg of a Grand Slam. The turnstiles were open and the crowd flooded in, estimated to be of around 104,000 in size – a world record. Many more were outside. It forced the SRU to make future matches at Murrayfield all-ticket. Wales had the double blow of losing John Bevan with a dislocated shoulder after 26 minutes and then Steve Fenwick, eleven minutes later, with a fractured cheek bone. On came Phil Bennett and Roger Blyth in their places. Bennett, eager to convince the selectors that he should not have been dropped, proceeded to have a 'howler' and Wales were 12–6 behind in the closing minutes. Then Gerald Davies worked flanker Trevor Evans clear, but he was only able to score near the corner-flag. With memories of the John Taylor kick in similar circumstances on the same ground – though at the opposite end of the pitch – Allan Martin attempted to draw the match. Though, like Taylor, he was a left-footer, it was not to be. Martin made a good effort, but missed, and Wales lost.

Scotland A.R. Irvine (Heriot's FP); W.C.C. Steele (London Scottish), J.M. Renwick (Hawick), D.I. Bell (Watsonians), L.G. Dick (Jordanhill); I.R. McGeechan (Headingley), D.W. Morgan (Stewart's Melville FP); A.B. Carmichael (West of Scotland), D.F. Madsen (Gosforth), +J. McLauchlan (Jordanhill), A.F. McHarg (London Scottish), G.L. Brown (West of Scotland), M.A. Biggar (London Scottish), D.G. Leslie (Dundee HSFP), N.A. MacEwan (Highland).
P: Douglas Morgan 3.
DG: Ian McGeechan.

Wales J.P.R. Williams (London Welsh); T.G.R. Davies (Cardiff), S.P. Fenwick (Bridgend), R.W.R. Gravell, J.J. Williams (Llanelli); J.D. Bevan (Aberavon), G.O. Edwards (Cardiff); A.G. Faulkner, R.W. Windsor, G. Price (Pontypool), M.G. Roberts (London Welsh), A.J. Martin (Aberavon), T.P. Evans, +T.M. Davies (Swansea), T.J. Cobner (Pontypool).
Reps: W.R. Blyth (Swansea) for Fenwick; P. Bennett (Llanelli) for Bevan.
T: Trevor Evans.
P: Steve Fenwick 2.
Referee: John R. West (Ireland).

Wales 28 Scotland 6

Arms Park, Cardiff. 7 February 1976

Wales won by 3 tries, 2 cons, 3 pens, 1 drop goal to 1 try, 1 con.

How a French doctor, almost 50 years of age, could be allowed to referee an international match was beyond belief. Even when he was fit he did not look good enough. It was even worse when he began to limp and still refused to leave the field. The result was a stop-start, frustrating match and Dr Cluny was never put in charge again. Wales opened smartly as Phil Bennett kicked on for J.J. Williams to score, but Scotland responded with a fine try by Andy Irvine. It was 18–6 to Wales after a Steve Fenwick drop goal and they finished off with first Trevor Evans and then Gareth Edwards going in for tries. Bennett's final conversion made him the highest scorer for Wales with 92 points, ahead of the 90 by Barry John, while the Edwards try equalled the Welsh record of 17 set by Ken Jones (1947–57).

Wales J.P.R. Williams (London Welsh); T.G.R. Davies (Cardiff), R.W.R. Gravell (Llanelli), S.P. Fenwick (Bridgend), J.J. Williams; P. Bennett (Llanelli), G.O. Edwards (Cardiff); A.G. Faulkner, R.W. Windsor, G. Price (Pontypool), G.A.D. Wheel (Swansea), A.J. Martin (Aberavon), T.P. Evans, +T.M. Davies (Swansea), T.J. Cobner (Pontypool).
T: J.J. Williams, Trevor Evans, Gareth Edwards.
C: Phil Bennett 2.

Gareth Edwards breaks against Scotland in 1976, with flankers Terry Cobner (6) and Trevor Evans in support. The ineffective referee Dr Andre Cluny of France looks on. (© Huw Evans)

P: Bennett 3.
DG: Steve Fenwick.

Scotland A.R. Irvine (Heriot's FP); W.C.C. Steele (London Scottish/RAF), J.M. Renwick, A.G. Cranston (Hawick), D. Shedden (West of Scotland); I.R. McGeechan (Headingley), D.W. Morgan (Stewart's Melville FP); A.B. Carmichael (West of Scotland), C.D. Fisher (Waterloo), +J. McLauchlan (Jordanhill), A.F. McHarg (London Scottish), G.L. Brown (West of Scotland), M.A. Biggar (London Scottish), G.Y. Mackie (Highland), D.G. Leslie (West of Scotland).
T: Andy Irvine.
C: Douglas Morgan.
Referee: André Cluny (France).

Scotland 9 Wales 18

Murrayfield, Edinburgh. 19 March 1977

Wales won by 2 tries, 2 cons, 2 pens to 1 try, 1 con, 1 drop goal.

A magnificent try, scored by outside-half Phil Bennett, took Wales to their 14th Triple Crown success. It was the try of the season and began deep in the Welsh half on the left flank, weaving across and up the pitch and finishing under the Scottish posts. Scotland were attacking in force as Wales led 12–9 when J.P.R. Williams and Steve Fenwick worked the ball to Gerald Davies who jinked away before linking with Bennett. The outside-half found David Burcher, who sent an inside pass to Fenwick who in turn flicked a one-handed pass back to Bennett. One superb jink from 'Benny' and he sprinted to the posts and collapsed in relief. With the scores level at 3–3 after 40 minutes, Andy Irvine tore over for a superb try which he converted. Back came Wales and J.J. Williams scored for Bennett to land a fine conversion kick and the outside-half placed a penalty on the hour, to give Wales a lead they did not lose.

Scotland A.R. Irvine (Heriot's FP); W.B.B. Gammell (Edinburgh Wands), J.M. Renwick, A.G. Cranston (Hawick), D. Shedden (West of Scotland); +I.R. McGeechan (Headingley), D.W. Morgan (Stewart's Melville FP); A.B. Carmichael (West of Scotland), D.F. Madsen (Gosforth), J. McLauchlan (Jordanhill), I.A. Barnes (Hawick), A.F. McHarg (London Scottish), W.S. Watson (Boroughmuir FP), D.S.M. MacDonald (Oxford U/London Scottish), M.A. Biggar (London Scottish).
T: Andy Irvine.
C: Irvine.
DG: Ian McGeechan.

Wales J.P.R. Williams (Bridgend); T.G.R. Davies (Cardiff), S.P. Fenwick (Bridgend), D.H. Burcher (Newport), J.J. Williams; +P. Bennett (Llanelli), G.O. Edwards (Cardiff); C. Williams (Aberavon), R.W. Windsor, G. Price

177

(Pontypool), G.A.D. Wheel (Swansea), A.J. Martin (Aberavon), R.C. Burgess (Ebbw Vale), D.L. Quinnell (Llanelli), T.J. Cobner (Pontypool).
T: J.J. Williams, Phil Bennett.
C: Bennett 2.
P: Bennett 2.
Referee: Georges Domercq (France).

Wales 22 Scotland 14

Arms Park, Cardiff. 18 February 1978

Wales won by 4 tries, 1 pen, 1 drop goal to 2 tries, 2 pens.

It was freezing cold. Possibly as cold as it had ever been for 20 years in Cardiff. Somehow the players put on a good show, with a 20th try for Gareth Edwards and a 1st for Ray Gravell leaving Wales at 8–7, as Jim Renwick had run in splendidly for Scotland. In the second half, Steve Fenwick crossed and then big Derek Quinnell thundered away along the South-Stand touchline beating off three tacklers to the corner. His son Scott was to repeat the feat against France in 1994, the only difference being that Derek scored at the Taff End and Scott at the Westgate End. A few hours after the match, the worst blizzard for 30 years hit South Wales, cutting Cardiff off from the outside world. Scotland managed to get away by coach to Birmingham to get a flight home, as Rhoose Airport was snowed in.

Wales J.P.R. Williams (Bridgend); T.G.R. Davies (Cardiff), R.W.R. Gravell (Llanelli), S.P. Fenwick (Bridgend), J.J. Williams; +P. Bennett (Llanelli), G.O. Edwards (Cardiff); A.G. Faulkner, R.W. Windsor, G. Price (Pontypool), G.A.D. Wheel (Swansea), A.J. Martin (Aberavon), J. Squire (Newport), D.L. Quinnell (Llanelli), T.J. Cobner (Pontypool).
T: Gareth Edwards, Ray Gravell, Steve Fenwick, Derek Quinnell.
P: Bennett.
DG: Bennett.

Scotland B.H. Hay (Boroughmuir); W.B.B. Gammell (West of Scotland), J.M. Renwick, A.G. Cranston (Hawick), D. Shedden (West of Scotland); I.R. McGeechan (Headingley), +D.W. Morgan (Stewart's Melville FP); N.E.K. Pender, C.T. Deans (Hawick), J. McLauchlan (Jordanhill), A.J. Tomes (Hawick), A.F. McHarg (London Scottish), C.B. Hegarty (Hawick), D.S.M. MacDonald (West of Scotland), M.A. Biggar (London Scottish). Rep: C.G. Hogg (Boroughmuir) for Shedden.
T: Jim Renwick, Alan Tomes.
P: Douglas Morgan 2.
Referee: John R. West (Ireland).

Scotland 13 Wales 19

Murrayfield, Edinburgh. 20 January 1979

Wales won by 2 tries, 1 con, 3 pens to 1 try, 3 pens.

Excellent play by the Welsh pack, particularly the Pontypool front row and the partnership of Geoff Wheel and Allan Martin at lock, laid the foundations for victory. A Scotland win looked to be on the cards when Andy Irvine started and finished a move in the first half and they led 13–6 at the interval. Wales eventually levelled when J.P.R. Williams chipped ahead and new cap Elgan Rees made a wonderful catch and scored in the corner. The Neath wing had already played in a Test for the Lions before winning his Welsh cap, just as Elvet Jones, Derek Quinnell and Delme Thomas had before him. Wales won the match with a try from a scrum wheel which Steve Fenwick converted. The scorer was thought to be Terry Holmes. However, confusion reigns, since Holmes stated on one occasion that he thought Derek Quinnell had the first touch.

Scotland A.R. Irvine (Heriot's FP); K.W. Robertson (Melrose), J.M. Renwick (Hawick), +I.R. McGeechan (Headingley), B.H. Hay (Boroughmuir); J.Y. Rutherford (Selkirk), A.J.M. Lawson (London Scottish); R.F. Cunningham (Gala), C.T. Deans (Hawick), J. McLauchlan (Jordanhill), A.J. Tomes (Hawick), A.F. McHarg, M.A. Biggar (London Scottish), I.K. Lambie (Watsonians), G. Dickson (Gala).
T: Andy Irvine.
P: Irvine 3.

Wales +J.P.R. Williams (Bridgend); *H.E. Rees (Neath), S.P. Fenwick (Bridgend), R.W.R. Gravell, J.J. Williams (Llanelli); W.G. Davies, T.D. Holmes (Cardiff); A.G. Faulkner, R.W. Windsor, G. Price (Pontypool), G.A.D. Wheel (Swansea), A.J. Martin (Aberavon), J. Squire (Pontypool), D.L. Quinnell, P. Ringer (Llanelli).
T: Elgan Rees, Terry Holmes.
C: Steve Fenwick.
P: Fenwick 3.
Referee: François Palmade (France).

Wales 17 Scotland 6

Arms Park, Cardiff. 1 March 1980

Wales won by 3 tries, 1 con, 1 pen to 1 try, 1 con.

Home on St David's Day and it was fortress Arms Park, as Wales pulled off another win in Cardiff. Terry Holmes dominated the match and scored the opening try after taking a return pass from Elgan Rees. New cap Les Keen, the brother-in-law of lock Allan Martin, scored the second and David Richards scored an excellent third. Richards was then at outside-half since Gareth Davies had left the field. Scotland woke up too late with Jim Renwick scoring a magnificent try, started in his own half.

Wales W.R. Blyth (Swansea); H.E. Rees (Neath), D.S. Richards (Swansea), S.P. Fenwick (Bridgend), L. Keen (Aberavon); W.G. Davies, T.D. Holmes (Cardiff); C. Williams (Swansea), A.J. Phillips (Cardiff), G. Price (Pontypool), G.A.D. Wheel (Swansea), A.J. Martin (Aberavon), +J. Squire, E.T. Butler (Pontypool), S.M. Lane (Cardiff). Rep: *P.J. Morgan (Llanelli) for Davies.
T: Terry Holmes, Les Keen, David Richards.
C: Roger Blyth.
P: Steve Fenwick.

Scotland A.R. Irvine (Heriot's FP); K.W. Robertson (Melrose), J.M. Renwick (Hawick), D.I. Johnston (Watsonians), B.H. Hay (Boroughmuir); B.M. Gossman (West of Scotland), R.J. Laidlaw (Jedforest); N.A. Rowan (Boroughmuir), K.G. Lawrie (Gala), J.N. Burnett (Heriot's FP), D. Gray (West of Scotland), A.J. Tomes (Hawick), M.A. Biggar (London Scottish), J.R. Beattie (Glasgow Acads), G. Dickson (Gala). Rep: A.J.M. Lawson (Heriot's FP) for Laidlaw.
T: Jim Renwick.
C: Andy Irvine.
Referee: Laurie M. Prideaux (England).

Scotland 15 Wales 6

Murrayfield, Edinburgh. 7 February 1981

Scotland won by 2 tries, 2 cons, 1 pen to 2 pens.

Scotland ended a particularly bad run with a deserved win against a poor Welsh team. The match hinged on a penalty try awarded to Andy Irvine when Scotland were leading by 9–6. Bruce Hay kicked on and Irvine was clearly going to defeat Gareth Davies in a race for the ball over the Welsh line. Davies deliberately obstructed the flying Scot and David Burnett was quite correct in his decision. It was to be the last penalty try awarded to an individual player in a match involving Wales. After the defeat Wales dropped, among others, J.P.R. Williams, who had won 55 caps, Gareth Davies and Steve Fenwick.

Scotland +A.R. Irvine (Heriot's FP); S. Munro (Ayr), J.M. Renwick (Hawick), K.W. Robertson (Melrose), B.H. Hay (Boroughmuir); J.Y. Rutherford (Selkirk), R.J. Laidlaw (Jedforest); N.A. Rowan (Boroughmuir), C.T. Deans (Hawick), J. Aitken (Gala), A.J. Tomes (Hawick), W. Cuthbertson (Kilmarnock), D.G. Leslie (Gala), J.R. Beattie (Heriot's FP), J.H. Calder (Stewart's-Melville FP).
T: Alan Tomes, Andy Irvine (pen-try).
C: Jim Renwick 2.
P: Renwick.

Wales J.P.R. Williams (Bridgend); R.A. Ackerman (Newport), D.S. Richards (Swansea), +S.P. Fenwick (Bridgend), D.L. Nicholas (Llanelli); W.G. Davies (Cardiff), D.B. Williams (Swansea); I. Stephens (Bridgend), A.J. Phillips (Cardiff), G. Price (Pontypool), G.A.D. Wheel (Swansea), C.E. Davis (Newbridge), J. Squire (Pontypool), Gareth P. Williams (Bridgend), J.R. Lewis (SG Inst/Cardiff). Rep: *G. Evans (Maesteg) for Nicholas.
P: Steve Fenwick 2.
Referee: David I.H. Burnett (Ireland).

Wales 18 Scotland 34

Arms Park, Cardiff. 20 March 1982

Scotland won by 5 tries, 4 cons, 2 drop goals to 1 try, 1 con, 4 pens.

Scotland inflicted the first championship defeat by Wales at Cardiff since 1968 – a run of 27 games without loss. It was also the first win by Scotland at the ground since 1962 and, though Wales led by 3–0, once Scotland scored their opening try it was one-way traffic. Whereas Scotland ran in tries, Wales muddled along with Gareth Davies using the boot far too often. Scotland began with the try of the season. Wing Roger Baird ran from near his own line with his pack roaring in support. Iain Paxton took it on, then Alan Tomes, who was stopped by Clive Rees, but sent on to Jim Calder, to end a magnificent move. A wonderful Jim Renwick try – his third in succession at Cardiff – took it to 13–9 and in the second half, Scotland roared away to 34–9 before Wales scored again. It was the first time that five tries had been scored against Wales at home and also the first time for 45 years that Wales had lost to England, Scotland and Ireland in the same season.

Wales G. Evans (Maesteg); R.A. Ackerman (Newport), R.W.R. Gravell (Llanelli), A.J. Donovan (Swansea), C.F.W. Rees (London Welsh); +W.G. Davies (Cardiff), Gerald Williams (Bridgend); I. Stephens (Bridgend), A.J. Phillips (Cardiff), G. Price (Pontypool), *R.L. Norster (Cardiff), R.D. Moriarty (Swansea), R.C. Burgess (Ebbw Vale), E.T. Butler (Pontypool), J.R. Lewis (Cardiff).
T: Eddie Butler.
C: Gwyn Evans.
P: Evans 4.

Scotland +A.R. Irvine (Heriot's FP); J.A. Pollock (Gosforth), J.M. Renwick (Hawick), D.I. Johnston (Watsonians), G.R.T. Baird (Kelso); J.Y. Rutherford (Selkirk), R.J. Laidlaw (Jedforest); J. Aitken (Gala), C.T. Deans (Hawick), I.G. Milne (Heriot's FP), W. Cuthbertson (Kilmarnock), A.J. Tomes (Hawick), J.H. Calder (Stewart's Melville), I.A.M. Paxton (Selkirk), D.B. White (Gala).
Rep: G. Dickson (Gala) for Paxton.
T: Jim Pollock, Jim Renwick, David Johnston, Jim Calder, Derek White.
C: Andy Irvine 4.
DG: Renwick, John Rutherford.
Referee: J.-P. Bonnet (France).

Scotland 15 Wales 19

Murrayfield, Edinburgh. 19 February 1983

Wales won by 2 tries, 1 con, 3 pens to 1 try, 1 con, 3 pens.

There was much criticism of the Welsh selectors, but thanks mainly to the play of scrum-half Terry Holmes, a win was recorded. Two new props were brought in and Graham Price was dropped. His clubmates John Perkins and Steve 'Staff' Jones joined Eddie Butler in the pack and Jones scored the only try of the opening half. A 9–0 lead was caught back by Scotland, but then Clive Rees made a mazy run to set up right-wing Elgan Rees for the second Welsh try.

Scotland P.W. Dods (Gala); K.W. Robertson (Melrose), J.M. Renwick (Hawick), D.I. Johnston (Watsonians), G.R.T. Baird (Kelso); B.M. Gossman (West of Scotland), +R.J. Laidlaw (Jedforest); J. Aitken (Gala), C.T. Deans (Hawick), I.G. Milne (Heriot's FP), W. Cuthbertson (Harlequins), A.J. Tomes (Hawick), J.H. Calder (Stewart's-Melville FP), J.R. Beattie (Glasgow Acads), D.G. Leslie (Gala).
T: Jim Renwick.
C: Peter Dods.
P: Dods 3.

Wales M.A. Wyatt (Swansea); H.E. Rees (Neath), D.S. Richards (Swansea), R.A. Ackerman, C.F.W. Rees (London Welsh); M. Dacey (Swansea), T.D. Holmes (Cardiff); *S.T. Jones (Pontypool), W.J. James (Aberavon), *I.H. Eidman, R.L. Norster (Cardiff), *S.J. Perkins, J. Squire, +E.T. Butler (Pontypool), D.F. Pickering (Llanelli).
T: 'Staff' Jones, Elgan Rees.
C: Mark Wyatt.
P: Wyatt 3.
Referee: Roger C. Quittenton (England).

Pit prop. Staff Jones at work in the Lady Windsor (no relation to Bobby !!) Colliery at Ynysybwl in March 1988. Jones was a blacksmith's striker, who scored a début try against Scotland in 1983.
(© Huw Evans)

Wales 9 Scotland 15

Arms Park, Cardiff. 21 January 1984

Scotland won by 2 tries, 2 cons, 1 pen to 1 try, 1 con, 1 pen.

A dour Scotland side – led by prop Jim Aitken and with flanker David Leslie outstanding – won again at Cardiff and went on to a Grand Slam. France and Wales, as so often, were to play open rugby, but that did not always pay off. Despite a try by Iain Paxton, Wales pulled ahead at 9–6 when newcomer Howell Davies converted Mark Titley's try from the touchline. It was skipper Aitken who stunned many in the 62,000 crowd by snatching victory for his side.

Wales *H. Davies; M.H. Titley (Bridgend), R.A. Ackerman (London Welsh), B. Bowen (South Wales Police), A.M. Hadley (Cardiff); M. Dacey (Swansea), *M.H.J. Douglas (Llanelli); S.T. Jones (Pontypool), W.J. James (Aberavon), *G.R. Morgan (Newport), R.L. Norster (Cardiff), S.J. Perkins (Pontypool), R.D. Moriarty (Swansea), +E.T. Butler (Pontypool), D.F. Pickering (Llanelli).
T: Mark Titley.
C: Howell Davies.
P: Howell Davies.

Scotland P.W. Dods (Gala); S. Munro (Ayr), D.I. Johnston, A.E. Kennedy (Watsonians), G.R.T. Baird (Kelso); J.Y. Rutherford (Selkirk), R.J. Laidlaw (Jedforest); +J. Aitken (Gala), C.T. Deans (Hawick), I.G. Milne (Heriot's FP), W. Cuthbertson (Harlequins), A.J. Tomes (Hawick), J.H. Calder (Stewart's-Melville FP), I.A.M. Paxton (Selkirk), D.G. Leslie (Gala).
T: Jim Aitken, Iain Paxton.
C: Peter Dods 2.
P: Dods.
Referee: Owen E. Doyle (Ireland).

Scotland 21 Wales 25

Murrayfield, Edinburgh. 2 March 1985

Wales won by 2 tries, 1 con, 4 pens, 1 drop goal to 2 tries, 2 cons, 1 pen, 2 drop goals.

It was March before the season started for Wales, as the games against France and England had fallen foul of the weather. For the fourth year in succession the away team won. This time it was the turn of Wales. Though Gareth Davies dropped a first-minute goal, Scotland led midway through the second half until David Pickering scored two tries. Mark Wyatt placed the final points with a penalty goal.

Scotland P.W. Dods (Gala); P.D. Steven (Heriot's FP), K.T. Murray (Hawick), K.W. Robertson (Melrose), G.R.T. Baird (Kelso); J.Y. Rutherford, I.G. Hunter (Selkirk); G.M. McGuinness (West of Scotland), C.T. Deans (Hawick), I.G. Milne (Harlequins), A.J. Tomes, A.J. Campbell (Hawick), J.H. Calder (Stewart's-Melville FP), I.A.M. Paxton (Selkirk), +D.G. Leslie (Gala). Rep: D.S. Wyllie (Stewart's-Melville FP) for Murray.
T: Iain Paxton 2.
C: Peter Dods 2.
P: Dods.
DG: John Rutherford 2.

Wales M.A. Wyatt (Swansea); M.H. Titley (Bridgend), R.A. Ackerman (London Welsh), M.G. Ring (Cardiff), P.I. Lewis (Llanelli); W.G. Davies, +T.D. Holmes; J. Whitefoot (Cardiff), W.J. James (Aberavon), I.H. Eidman, R.L. Norster (Cardiff), S.J. Perkins (Pontypool), *M.S. Morris (South Wales Police), R.D. Moriarty (Swansea), D.F. Pickering (Llanelli).
T: David Pickering 2.
C: Mark Wyatt.
P: Wyatt 4.
DG: Gareth Davies.
Referee: René Hourquet (France).

Wales 22 Scotland 15

Arms Park, Cardiff. 1 February 1986

Wales won by 1 try, 5 pens, 1 drop goal to 3 tries, 1 pen.

The longest goal ever kicked at the Arms Park was the highlight of the game and also helped Wales to victory, as it was landed by full-back Paul Thorburn when Wales held the slender 16–15 lead. From a distance of 70 yards and 8 inches, Thorburn, with a slight breeze at his back, gave the ball a massive thump. He said later: 'That kick alone almost led to me having an American Football career. I had told David Pickering I would have a go and knew that if I missed it would still leave play in the Scotland half. I probably kicked more important goals, but that was my longest.' A further penalty by Thorburn settled the match and gave him a Welsh record of being the fastest to reach 50 points, his 54 being scored in just five matches. The lead changed hands on six occasions and Scotland outscored Wales by 3–1 on the try-count.

Wales P.H. Thorburn (Neath); P.I. Lewis (Llanelli), J.A. Devereux (Bridgend/SG Inst), B. Bowen (South Wales Police), A.M. Hadley (Cardiff); J.

Davies (Neath), R.N. Jones (Swansea); J. Whitefoot (Cardiff), W.J. James (Aberavon), I.H. Eidman (Cardiff), D.R. Waters (Newport), S.J. Perkins, M.A. Brown (Pontypool), P.T. Davies, +D.F. Pickering (Llanelli).
T: Adrian Hadley.
P: Paul Thorburn 5.
DG: Jonathan Davies.

Scotland A.G. Hastings (Cambridge U/London Scottish); M.D.F. Duncan (West of Scotland), D.I. Johnston, S. Hastings (Watsonians), G.R.T. Baird (Kelso); J.Y. Rutherford (Selkirk), R.J. Laidlaw (Jedforest); D.M.B. Sole (Bath), +C.T. Deans (Hawick), I.G. Milne (Harlequins), A.J. Campbell (Hawick), I.A.M. Paxton (Selkirk), J. Jeffrey (Kelso), J.R. Beattie (Glasgow Acads), J.F. Calder (Stewart's-Melville FP).
T: Matt Duncan, John Jeffrey, Gavin Hastings.
P: Gavin Hastings.
Referee: R.C. 'Bob' Francis (New Zealand).

Scotland 21 Wales 15

Murrayfield, Edinburgh. 21 March 1987

Scotland won by 2 tries, 2 cons, 2 pens, 1 drop goal to 1 try, 1 con, 2 pens, 1 drop goal.

The troubles began for Wales when prop Stuart Evans broke a bone in his foot during a run-out. In came Peter Francis at prop and Wales were struggling in the scrums. The 29-year-old farmer never recovered completely from this match and soon departed the senior scene. Once John Beattie scored a pushover try, the writing was on the wall. Luckily, Gavin Hastings kicked poorly and Wales had the last say when lively new cap, Mark Jones, scored a try. He was later to join the exodus to rugby league.

Scotland A.G. Hastings (Watsonians); M.D.F. Duncan (West of Scotland), K.W. Robertson (Melrose), S. Hastings (Watsonians), I. Tukalo; J.Y. Rutherford (Selkirk), R.J. Laidlaw (Jedforest); D.M.B. Sole (Bath), +C.T. Deans (Hawick), I.G. Milne (Heriot's FP), D.B. White (Gala), I.A.M. Paxton (Selkirk), J. Jeffrey (Kelso), J.R. Beattie (Glasgow Acads), F. Calder (Stewart's-Melville FP).
T: John Beattie, John Jeffrey.
C: Gavin Hastings 2.
P: Gavin Hastings 2.
DG: John Rutherford.

Wales M.A. Wyatt (Swansea); G.M.C. Webbe (Bridgend), K. Hopkins (Swansea), J.A. Devereux (Bridgend/SG Inst), I.C. Evans (Llanelli); J. Davies (Neath), R.N. Jones (Swansea); J. Whitefoot (Cardiff), W.J. James (Aberavon), *P.W. Francis (Maesteg), S. Sutton (South Wales Police), R.L. Norster (Cardiff), W.P. Moriarty (Swansea), *M.A. Jones (Neath), +D.F. Pickering (Llanelli). Rep: A.M. Hadley (Cardiff) for Evans.
T: Mark Jones.
C: Mark Wyatt.
P: Wyatt 2.
DG: Jonathan Davies.
Referee: Keith H. Lawrence (New Zealand).

Wales 25 Scotland 20

Arms Park, Cardiff. 20 February 1988

Wales won by 3 tries, 2 cons, 1 pen, 2 drop goals to 2 tries, 4 pens.

Two magnificent Welsh tries were the highlights of this match. The first came from Jonathan Davies, who grubber-kicked at speed and just defeated Derek White in a race for the ball. If that score typified the Welsh outside-half factory, the score by Ieuan Evans was one of the very best from a wing. The Llanelli flier was given a clever pass by Mark Ring and instead of going for the corner, he cut inside. Defender after defender was caught on the wrong foot and Evans went over by the posts at the Westgate-Street end as he was tackled. Scotland had led 20–10, but Wales closed the gap to 20–19 for the elusive Davies to put them in front with a drop goal and repeat the feat minutes later.

Wales P.H. Thorburn (Neath); I.C. Evans (Llanelli), M.G. Ring (Pontypool), +B. Bowen (South Wales Police), A.M. Hadley (Cardiff); J. Davies (Llanelli), R.N. Jones (Swansea); S.T. Jones (Pontypool), I.J. Watkins (Ebbw Vale), D. Young (Swansea), P.S. May (Llanelli), R.L. Norster (Cardiff), R.D. Phillips (Neath), W.P. Moriarty (Swansea), R.G. Collins (South Wales Police). Rep: J.D. Pugh (Neath) for (S.T.) Jones.
T: Ieuan Evans, Ian Watkins, Jonathan Davies.
C: Paul Thorburn 2.
P: Thorburn.
DG: Jonathan Davies 2.

Scotland A.G. Hastings (Watsonians); M.D.F. Duncan (West of Scotland), A.V. Tait (Kelso), S. Hastings (Watsonians), I. Tukalo (Selkirk); A.B.M. Ker (Kelso), R.J. Laidlaw (Jedforest); D.M.B. Sole (Edinburgh Acads), +G.J. Callander (Kelso), N.A. Rowan (Boroughmuir), A.J. Campbell (Hawick), D.F. Cronin (Bath), J. Jeffrey (Kelso), D.B. White (Gala), F. Calder (Stewart's-Melville FP).
T: Matt Duncan, Finlay Calder.

P: Gavin Hastings 4.
Referee: Yves Bressy (France).

Scotland 23 Wales 7

Murrayfield, Edinburgh. 21 January 1989

Scotland won by 3 tries, 1 con, 2 pens, 1 drop goal to 1 try, 1 pen.

Sean Lineen, son of All Black Terry Lineen, had played club rugby for Pontypool. He now made his Scotland début and fitted in well with Scott Hastings at centre. So good was the start by the home side that they led 19–0 at the interval. Mike Hall did score a good try, but Craig Chalmers responded with Scotland's third.

Scotland P.W. Dods (Gala); M.D.F. Duncan (West of Scotland), S. Hastings (Watsonians), S.R. Lineen (Boroughmuir), I. Tukalo (Selkirk); C.M. Chalmers (Melrose), G. Armstrong (Jedforest); D.M.B. Sole (Edinburgh Acads), K.S. Milne, I.G. Milne (Heriot's FP), C.A. Gray (Notts), D.F. Cronin (Bath), J. Jeffrey (Kelso), D.B. White (Gala), +F. Calder (Stewart's-Melville FP).
T: Gary Armstrong, Derek White, Craig Chalmers.
C: Peter Dods.
P: Dods 2.
DG: Chalmers.

Wales +P.H. Thorburn (Neath); M.R. Hall (Bridgend), N.G. Davies (Llanelli), J.A. Devereux (Bridgend), C. Davies (Llanelli); B. Bowen (Swansea), J.L. Griffiths (Llanelli); M. Griffiths (Bridgend), I.J. Watkins (Ebbw Vale), D. Young (Cardiff), K. Moseley (Pontypool), P.T. Davies (Llanelli), R.D. Phillips, M.A. Jones (Neath), D.J. Bryant (Bridgend). Rep: *H. Williams-Jones (South Wales Police) for Young.
T: Mike Hall.
P: Bleddyn Bowen.
Referee: Jean-Claude Doulcet (France).

Wales 9 Scotland 13

Arms Park, Cardiff. 3 March 1990

Scotland won by 1 try, 3 pens to 1 try, 1 con, 1 pen.

The new national coach was Ron Waldron of Neath. He had the answer to Welsh problems – play Neath forwards, and add a few backs for good luck. It was not, however, the answer as Scotland and Ireland soon showed. In came Allan Bateman, Brian Williams and Mark Perego for their débuts. Bateman was still relatively unknown to Welsh supporters when he turned professional, but when he eventually came back to union, he was a strong and seasoned centre. Paul Thorburn's conversion of a Arthur Emyr try kept Wales within one point, only for Craig Chalmers to extend Scotland's lead with his third penalty effort.

Wales P.H. Thorburn (Neath); M.R. Hall (Cardiff), *A.G. Bateman (Neath), M.G. Ring (Cardiff), A. Emyr (Swansea); D.W. Evans (Cardiff), +R.N. Jones (Swansea); *B.R. Williams, K.H. Phillips, J.D. Pugh (Neath), P.T. Davies (Llanelli), Gareth O. Llewellyn (Neath), *M.A. Perego (Llanelli), M.A. Jones (Neath), R.G. Collins (Cardiff). Rep: A. Clement (Swansea) for Evans.
T: Arthur Emyr.
C: Paul Thorburn.
P: Thorburn.

Scotland A.G. Hastings (London Scottish); A.G. Stanger (Hawick), S. Hastings (Watsonians), S.R.P. Lineen (Boroughmuir), I. Tukalo (Selkirk); C.M. Chalmers (Melrose), G. Armstrong (Jedforest); +D.M.B. Sole (Edinburgh Acads), K.S. Milne (Heriot's FP), A.P. Burnell (London Scottish), C.A. Gray (Notts), D.F. Cronin (Bath), J. Jeffrey (Kelso), D.B. White (London Scottish), F. Calder (Stewart's-Melville FP).
T: Damian Cronin.
P: Craig Chalmers 3.
Referee: René Hourquet (France).

Scotland 32 Wales 12

Murrayfield, Edinburgh. 2 February 1991

Scotland won by 4 tries, 2 cons, 3 pens, 1 drop goal to 1 try, 1 con, 2 pens.

Wales scored a nice try, but did little else right: they now looked a good bet for the Wooden Spoon. Back-row forward Derek White scored the first and last tries for Scotland, while the Welsh consolation came when Scott Gibbs ran well before linking with Alun Carter. Steve Ford finished it off.

Scotland A.G. Hastings (Watsonians); A.G. Stanger (Hawick), S. Hastings (Watsonians), S.R.P. Lineen (Boroughmuir), A. Moore (Edinburgh Acads); C.M. Chalmers (Melrose), G. Armstrong (Jedforest); +D.M.B. Sole, J. Allan (Edinburgh Acads), A.P. Burnell (London Scottish), C.A. Gray (Notts), D.F. Cronin (Bath), J. Jeffrey (Kelso), D.B. White (London Scottish), D.J. Turnbull (Hawick). Rep: K.S. Milne (Heriot's FP) for Allan.
T: Derek White 2, Gary Armstrong, Craig Chalmers.
C: Chalmers, Gavin Hastings.

Centre Roger Bidgood strains in an attempt to make the line as Scotland's Scott Hastings tackles. Mike Hall is the supporting Welsh player in this 1992 match. (© Huw Evans)

P: Gavin Hastings 2, Chalmers.
DG: Chalmers.

Wales +P.H. Thorburn (Neath); I.C. Evans (Llanelli), M.G. Ring (Cardiff), I.S. Gibbs (Neath), S.P. Ford (Cardiff); N.R. Jenkins (Pontypridd), R.N. Jones (Swansea); B.R. Williams, K.H. Phillips (Neath), P. Knight (Pontypridd), Glyn D. Llewellyn, Gareth O. Llewellyn (Neath), A.J. Carter (Newport), P. Arnold (Swansea), G.M. George (Newport). Rep: A. Clement (Swansea) for Thorburn.
T: Steve Ford.
C: Paul Thorburn.
P: Thorburn 2.
Referee: David J. Bishop (New Zealand).

Wales 15 Scotland 12

Arms Park, Cardiff. 21 March 1992

Wales won by 1 try, 1 con, 3 pens to 3 pens, 1 drop goal.

A win was a win, no matter how it was gained. Wales were marginally the better of two ordinary sides. They scored a good try when Hugh Williams-Jones broke through and Richard Webster finished strongly. Scotland had what seemed a good try disallowed, when wing Iwan Tukalo was adjudged to have knocked the ball forward. Centre Roger Bidgood was capped after a five-year wait. He had been picked against Ireland at Cardiff in 1987, but snow had caused a postponement and he was then omitted. 'I watched the match eventually from the crowd,' said Bidgood. 'This time I did not want to listen to the weather forecast.'

Wales A. Clement (Swansea); +I.C. Evans (Llanelli), *R.A. Bidgood (Newport), I.S. Gibbs (Swansea), M.R. Hall (Cardiff); N.R. Jenkins (Pontypridd), R.N. Jones (Swansea); M. Griffiths (Cardiff), G.R. Jenkins (Swansea), H. Williams-Jones (South Wales Police), G.O. Llewellyn (Neath), A.H. Copsey, E.W. Lewis (Llanelli), S. Davies, R.E. Webster (Swansea).
T: Richard Webster.
C: Neil Jenkins.
P: Neil Jenkins 3.

Scotland A.G. Hastings (Watsonians); A.G. Stanger (Hawick), S. Hastings (Watsonians), S.R.P. Lineen (Boroughmuir), I. Tukalo (Selkirk); C.M. Chalmers (Melrose), A.D. Nichol (Dundee HSFP); +D.M.B. Sole (Edinburgh Acads), K.S. Milne (Heriot's FP), A.P. Burnell (London Scottish), N.G.B. Edwards (Harlequins), G.W. Weir (Melrose), D.J. McIvor (Edinburgh Acads), D.B. White (London Scottish), I.R. Smith (Gloucester). Rep: P.M. Jones (Gloucester) for Burnell.
P: Craig Chalmers 2, Gavin Hastings.
DG: Chalmers.
Referee: Marc Desclaux (France).

Scotland 20 Wales 0

Murrayfield, Edinburgh. 20 February 1993

Scotland won by 1 try, 5 pens to nil.

From the heights of beating England at Cardiff to the depths of defeat at Murrayfield. Scotland scored just one try, but nevertheless they were right on top, winning the game up front and letting Gavin Hastings apply the finishing touches. The try came when flanker Derek Turnbull was driven over from a lineout and it helped send coach Alan Davies back to the drawing-board.

Scotland +A.G. Hastings (Watsonians); A.G. Stanger (Hawick), S. Hastings (Watsonians), A.G. Shiel (Melrose), D.A. Stark (Boroughmuir); C.M. Chalmers (Melrose), G. Armstrong (Jedforest); P.H. Wright (Boroughmuir), K.S. Milne (Heriot's FP), A.P. Burnell (London Scottish), A.I. Reed (Bath), D.F. Cronin, I.R. Morrison (London Scottish), G.W. Weir (Melrose), D.J. Turnbull (Hawick).
T: Derek Turnbull.
P: Gavin Hastings 5.

Wales M.A. Rayer (Cardiff); +I.C. Evans (Llanelli),

Lock Tony Copsey is all smiles as he watches scrum-half Robert Jones fire out a pass against Scotland. Wales won the match by 15–12 with Richard Webster scoring the only try. (© WRU Press Office)

M.R. Hall (Cardiff), I.S. Gibbs (Swansea), W.T. Proctor (Llanelli); N.R. Jenkins (Pontypridd), R.N. Jones (Swansea); R.L. Evans (Llanelli), N. Meek (Pontypool), H. Williams-Jones (South Wales Police), G.O. Llewellyn (Neath), A.H. Copsey, E.W. Lewis (Llanelli), S. Davies, R.E. Webster (Swansea).
Referee: Joël Dumé (France).

Wales 29   Scotland 6

Arms Park, Cardiff. 15 January 1994

Wales won by 3 tries, 1 con, 4 pens to 2 pens.

Nobody watching Wales lose to Canada in their previous match would have thought they would be taking the Five Nations Trophy at the end of the season. It all began in the pouring rain at Cardiff. Scotland lost flanker Iain Morrison with a broken leg after 18 minutes and outside-half Craig Chalmers left early in the second half. Wales had led 12–3 at the interval and held back the scoring until the final 25 minutes, in which time they ran in three tries. Two of them were scored by Michael Rayer, who had come on as a replacement for the injured Nigel Walker on the left-wing. Rayer looked far too good a player to leave out. A complete back row from Llanelli was the first from the same club for Wales in the championship since 1960. In all, the Scarlets supplied five forwards and two backs. Hooker Garin Jenkins was warned by the team management as to his future conduct after an incident during the match.

Wales A. Clement (Swansea); +I.C. Evans (Llanelli), M.R. Hall (Cardiff), N.G. Davies (Llanelli), N.K. Walker (Cardiff); N.R. Jenkins (Pontypridd), R.H.St.J.B. Moon; R.L. Evans (Llanelli), G.R. Jenkins (Swansea), J.D. Davies (Neath), P.T. Davies (Llanelli), G.O. Llewellyn (Neath), E.W. Lewis, L.S. Quinnell, M.A. Perego (Llanelli). Rep: M.A. Rayer (Cardiff) for Walker.
T: Mike Rayer 2, Ieuan Evans.
C: Neil Jenkins.
P: Neil Jenkins 4.

Scotland +A.G. Hastings (Watsonians); A.G. Stanger (Hawick), G.P.J. Townsend (Gala), I.C. Jardine, K.M. Logan (Stirling C); C.M. Chalmers (Melrose), A.D. Nichol (Dundee HSFP); P.H. Wright (Boroughmuir), K.S. Milne (Heriot's FP), A.P. Burnell (London Scottish), N.G.B.

Edwards (Northampton), D.S. Munro (Glasgow High-Kelvinside), I.R. Morrison (London Scottish), R.I. Wainwright (Edinburgh Acads), D.J. Turnbull (Hawick). Reps: D.S. Wyllie (Stewart's Melville FP) for Chalmers; G.W. Weir (Melrose) for Morrison.
P: Gavin Hastings 2.
Referee: Patrick Robin (France).

Scotland 26 Wales 13

Murrayfield, Edinburgh. 4 March 1995

Scotland won by 2 tries, 2 cons, 4 pens to 1 try, 1 con, 2 pens.

The match opened with a rare try by Robert Jones in the second minute. It ended with snow in the air and Wales soundly beaten. Neil Jenkins took all his three chances at goal, but Scotland led 20–7 with tries from Eric Peters, after a long run by Kenny Logan, and David Hilton. It was a miserable match for Ieuan Evans to make his 50th appearance.

Scotland +A.G. Hastings (Watsonians); C.A. Joiner (Melrose), G.P.J. Townsend (Gala), S. Hastings (Watsonians), K.M. Logan (Stirling County); C.M. Chalmers, B.W. Redpath (Melrose); D.I.W. Hilton (Bath), K.S. Milne (Heriot's FP), P.H. Wright (Boroughmuir), G.W. Weir (Melrose), S.J. Campbell (Dundee HSFP), I.R. Morrison (London Scottish), E.W. Peters (Bath), R.I. Wainwright (West Hartlepool).
T: Eric Peters, David Hilton.
C: Gavin Hastings 2.
P: Gavin Hastings 4.

Wales M. Back (Bridgend); +I.C. Evans (Llanelli), M.R. Hall (Cardiff), N.G. Davies, W.T. Proctor (Llanelli); N.R. Jenkins (Pontypridd), R.N. Jones (Swansea); M. Griffiths (Cardiff), G.R. Jenkins (Swansea), *S.C. John (Llanelli), D. Jones (Cardiff), G.O. Llewellyn (Neath), H.T. Taylor, E.W. Lewis (Cardiff), R.G. Collins (Pontypridd).
T: Robert Jones.
C: Neil Jenkins.
P: Neil Jenkins 2.
Referee: Steve J.D. Lander (England).

Wales 14 Scotland 16

Arms Park, Cardiff. 17 February 1996

Scotland won by 1 try, 1 con, 3 pens to 1 try, 3 pens.

It was another Five-Nations defeat – and at home – but nevertheless there was a belief that Kevin Bowring was helping Wales turn the corner and play flowing rugby. Unfortunately, Scotland did not agree. At 9–9, Gregor Townsend went over the line under the Welsh posts for a clever try which Michael Dods converted. Wales had one late effort that produced a good try by wing Wayne Proctor. The draw rested on a near-touch conversion attempt by Arwel Thomas. He missed, and Wales were beaten again. It was the 100th meeting of the countries and Wales led 54–44, with two matches having been drawn.

Wales W.J.L. Thomas; I.C. Evans (Llanelli), L.B. Davies (Neath), N.G. Davies, W.T. Proctor (Llanelli); A.C. Thomas (Bristol), R. Howley (Bridgend); A.L.P. Lewis, +J.M. Humphreys (Cardiff), J.D. Davies, G.O. Llewellyn (Neath), D. Jones, E.W. Lewis, H.T. Taylor (Cardiff), R.G. Jones (Llanelli).
T: Wayne Proctor.
P: Arwel Thomas 3.

Scotland R.J.S. Shepherd; C.A. Joiner (Melrose), S. Hastings (Watsonians), I.C. Jardine (Stirling C), M. Dods; G.P.J. Townsend (Northampton), B.W. Redpath (Melrose); D.I.W. Hilton (Bath), K.D. McKenzie (Stirling C), P.H. Wright (Boroughmuir), S.J. Campbell (Dundee HSFP), G.W. Weir (Melrose), +R.I. Wainwright (West Hartlepool), E.W. Peters (Bath), I.R. Smith (Gloucester). Rep: K.M. Logan (Stirling C) for Joiner.
T: Gregor Townsend.
C: Michael Dods.
P: Dods 3.
Referee: Joël Dumé (France).

Scotland 19 Wales 34

Murrayfield, Edinburgh. 18 January 1997

Wales won by 4 tries, 4 cons, 2 pens to 1 try, 1 con, 3 pens, 1 drop goal.

As Jimmy Greaves would say: 'It's a funny old game.' In 1966, Wales played four matches, won the championship and scored 34 points. In this away win, they also scored 34 points. Indeed, they finished the season on 94 points, yet had lost the three remaining matches. And yet again, two points was enough to see them finish third. Confusing! Scotland were winning 16–10 in the second spell when Wales hit a purple patch. Three tries rained in on Scotland in a six-minute spell from Neil Jenkins, Arwel Thomas and finally Ieuan Evans. The mercurial little Thomas almost forgot to dot the ball down as he flew over the dead-ball line. Neil Jenkins equalled the Welsh best for a Five Nations match of 19 points; he became the highest scorer for Wales in the Five Nations and passed 500 points in Test rugby.

Scotland R.J.S. Shepherd (Melrose); A.G. Stanger (Hawick), S. Hastings (Watsonians), G.P.J. Townsend (Northampton), K.M. Logan (Stirling C); C.M. Chalmers (Melrose), G. Armstrong (Newcastle); D.I.W. Hilton (Bath), D.G. Ellis (Currie), M.J. Stewart (Northampton), G.W. Weir (Newcastle), A.I. Reed (Wasps), P. Walton (Newcastle), +R.I. Wainwright (Watsonians), M.I. Wallace (Glasgow High-Kelvinside). Reps: D.A. Stark (Melrose) for Chalmers; D.S. Munro (Glasgow High-Kelvinside) for Reed.
T: Scott Hastings.
C: Rowen Shepherd.
P: Shepherd 3.
DG: Craig Chalmers.

Wales N.R. Jenkins (Pontypridd); I.C. Evans (Llanelli), A.G. Bateman (Richmond), I.S. Gibbs (Swansea), G. Thomas (Bridgend); A.C. Thomas (Swansea), R. Howley (Cardiff); C.D. Loader (Swansea), +J.M. Humphreys, D. Young (Cardiff), G.O. Llewellyn (Harlequins), M.A. Rowley (Pontypridd), S.M. Williams (Neath), L.S. Quinnell (Richmond), C.L. Charvis (Swansea). Reps: Jonathan Davies (Cardiff) for Gibbs; J.C. Quinnell (Richmond) for Rowley; R.G. Jones (Cardiff) for Charvis.
T: Scott Quinnell, Ieuan Evans, Neil Jenkins, Arwel Thomas.
C: Jenkins 4.
P: Jenkins 2.
Referee: H.A. 'Bertie' Smith (Ireland).

Wales 19 Scotland 13

Wembley, London. 7 March 1998

Wales won by 1 try, 1 con, 4 pens to 2 tries, 1 pen.

While Wales were conceding 60 points to England, Scotland had lost 51–16 at home to France. It was therefore a battle of the 'also-rans' and, just before the interval, Wales had not only conceded two tries, but were losing 13–3 and had seen Neil Jenkins, now at fly-half, leave the field with double vision. On came Arwel Thomas to kick four excellent goals and secure the win.

Wales K.A. Morgan (Pontypridd); W.T. Proctor (Llanelli), A.G. Bateman (Richmond), I.S. Gibbs (Swansea), G. Thomas (Cardiff); N.R. Jenkins (Pontypridd), +R. Howley; A.L.P. Lewis (Cardiff), G.R. Jenkins (Swansea), D. Young (Cardiff), Andrew P. Moore (Swansea), M.J. Voyle (Llanelli), R.C. Appleyard, C.L. Charvis (Swansea), K.P. Jones (Ebbw Vale). Reps: A.C. Thomas (Swansea) for (N.R.) Jenkins; J.M. Humphreys (Cardiff) for (G.R.) Jenkins; L.S. Quinnell (Richmond) for Appleyard.
T: Wayne Proctor.
C: Arwel Thomas.
P: Arwel Thomas 3, Neil Jenkins.

Scotland D.J. Lee (London Scottish); A.G. Stanger (Hawick), G.P.J. Townsend (Northampton), A.V. Tait (Newcastle), S.L. Longstaff (Dundee HSFP); C.M. Chalmers (Melrose), +G. Armstrong (Newcastle); D.I.W. Hilton (Bath), G.C. Bulloch (West of Scotland/Glasgow), M.J. Stewart (Northampton), D.F. Cronin (Wasps), G.W. Weir (Newcastle), R.I. Wainwright (Dundee HSFP), E.W. Peters (Bath), A.J. Roxburgh (Kelso). Reps: R.J.S. Shepherd (Melrose) for Lee; G. Graham (Newcastle) for Stewart; S.B. Grimes (Watsonians) for Cronin.
T: Gregor Townsend, Damian Cronin.
P: Craig Chalmers.
Referee: Joël Dumé (France).

Scotland 33 Wales 20

Murrayfield, Edinburgh. 6 February 1999

Scotland won by 4 tries, 2 cons, 3 pens to 2 tries, 2 cons, 2 pens.

Coach Graham Henry had never experienced the Five Nations championship. After the loss, he commented: 'There is nothing like this in the Southern Hemisphere. Scotland were the better team. We were lucky to come second.' Murrayfield spelt disaster, yet again. Scotland coach Jim Telfer decided that new cap Matthew Robinson had to be targeted from the kick-off. Duncan Hodge changed direction, fired it high and, as Shane Howarth and Robinson waited, centre John Leslie jumped in and was away for a try in just eight seconds. John and his brother Martin were the sons of the former New Zealand captain, Andy Leslie. With Hodge missing kicks and Neil Jenkins taking all his chances, Wales were still in the hunt. They were leading 13–8 at the break and later by 20–15, following a Scott Gibbs try. Gregor Townsend had moved from centre to replace the injured Hodge and Alan Tait came on. It was the turning point, and both Townsend and Tait scored. Suddenly Scotland looked unstoppable and Scott Murray went over from a lineout for his side's fourth try.

Scotland G.H. Metcalfe (Glasgow); C.A. Murray (Edinburgh), G.P.J. Townsend (Brive), J.A. Leslie (Glasgow), K.M. Logan (Wasps); D.W. Hodge (Edinburgh), +G. Armstrong (Newcastle); T.J. Smith (Glasgow), G.C. Bulloch (West of Scotland), A.P. Burnell (London Scottish), S. Murray (Bedford), G.W. Weir (Newcastle), P.

Walton (Newcastle), E.W. Peters (Bath), M.D. Leslie (Edinburgh). Reps: A.V. Tait (Edinburgh) for Hodge; D.I.W. Hilton (Bath) for Burnell; S.B. Grimes (Watsonians) for Weir; A.C. Pountney (Northampton) for Walton.
T: John Leslie, Gregor Townsend, Alan Tait, Scott Murray.
C: Kenny Logan 2.
P: Logan 2, Duncan Hodge.

Wales S.P. Howarth (Manchester-Sale); *M.F.D. Robinson (Swansea), A.G. Bateman (Richmond), I.S. Gibbs (Swansea), D.R. James; N.R. Jenkins (Pontypridd), +R. Howley (Cardiff); D.R. Morris (Swansea), J.M. Humphreys (Cardiff), C.T. Anthony (Swansea), I. Gough (Pontypridd), C.P. Wyatt (Llanelli), C.L. Charvis (Swansea), L.S. Quinnell (Llanelli), M.E. Williams (Pontypridd). Reps: B.H. Williams (Richmond) for Humphreys; M.J. Voyle (Llanelli) for Gough.
T: Dafydd James, Scott Gibbs.
C: Neil Jenkins 2.
P: Jenkins 2.
Referee: Ed F. Morrison (England).

OTHER INTERNATIONAL MATCHES

AUSTRALIA

Wales 9 Australia 6

Arms Park, Cardiff. 12 December 1908.

Wales won by 2 tries, 1 pen to 2 tries.

Dr 'Paddy' Moran led the first Australian tourists to Cardiff and played in his only international match, having missed the 9–3 win over England. Though equalling Wales on try-count, they finally lost to a Bert Winfield penalty. Wing Phil Hopkins of Swansea scored a try on his début and was to score again in his next two matches. He was to die in 1966, just a few months before Wales lost to Australia at the Arms Park. George Travers scored his only try in 25 Tests, but Australia equalised with a try by débutant Tom 'Rusty' Richards. In the second half, the multi-talented Hopkins scored and then Winfield struck the important goal before 'Boxer' Russell scored a second Australian try. The tourists went on to win the Olympic gold medal at the White City in London by defeating England, who were represented by the County champions, Cornwall.

Wales H.B. Winfield (Cardiff); *P. Hopkins, +W.J. Trew (Swansea), *J.P. 'Jack' Jones (Newport), J.L. Williams (Cardiff); R.H. Jones, R.M. Owen (Swansea); A.J. Webb (Abertillery), G. Travers (Pill Harriers), *P.D. Waller (Newport), T.H. Evans, J. Watts (Llanelli), G. Hayward, D.J. Thomas, *W.I. Morgan (Swansea).
T: Phil Hopkins, George Travers.
P: Bert Winfield.

Australia P. Carmichael (Queensland); C. Russell, J. Hickey, E. Mandible, D.B. Carroll; W. Prentice, C.H. McKivatt; +Dr H.M. Moran (NSW), T.J. Richards (Queensland), R.R. Craig, P.A. McCue, A.B. Burge, C.A. Hammand, T.S. Griffen, J.E.T. Barnett (NSW).
T: Tom Richards, Charles Russell.
Referee: Gil Evans (England).

Wales 8 NSW 18

Arms Park, Cardiff. 26 November 1927

New South Wales won by 4 tries, 3 cons to 2 tries, 1 con.

The New South Wales 'Waratahs' were led by the former Scotland international Johnny Wallace, but although Wales provided caps, it was to be 59 years before the Australian RU retrospectively granted Test status to this fine team. The tourists won 23 games in Britain and France but lost to Pontypool, Oxford University, South-West France, Scotland and England. Wallace scored two tries in this match, having scored 11 in nine matches for Scotland, three of them against Wales. The Waratahs extended a 5–3 half-time lead to 18–3 before Windsor Lewis crossed for Tommy Rees to convert. Dan Jones, who scored 59 tries for Neath in the following season, gained his only cap when the selected captain, Rowe Harding, withdrew. Leeds RL later captured forwards Iorwerth Jones and David Jenkins. Tom Hollingdale's brother Bert had been capped from 1912–13.

Wales T.E. Rees (Army/London Welsh); E. Finch (Llanelli), J. Roberts (Cardiff), *W.R. Jones (Swansea), *D. Jones (Neath); W.H. Lewis (Maesteg), *C.A. Harris (Aberavon); *F.A. Bowdler (Cross Keys), *D.R. Jenkins (Swansea), *A.S. Broughton (Treorchy), H.T. Phillips (Newport), E.M. Jenkins (Aberavon), *T.H. Hollingdale (Neath), *T. Iorwerth Jones, +I.E. Jones (Llanelli).
T: Ernie Finch, Windsor Lewis.
C: Tommy Rees.

New South Wales A.W. Ross (Sydney U); E.E. Ford (Glebe-Balmain), W.B.J. Sheehan (University), S.C. King (Western Suburbs), +A.C. Wallace (University/Glebe-Balmain); T. Lawton (Western Suburbs), F.W. Meagher (Randwick); H.F. Woods (YMCA), J.G. Blackwood (Eastern Suburbs), B. Judd (Randwick), A.N. Finlay (University), G.P. Storey (Western Suburbs), J.W. Breckenridge, J.A. Ford, A.J. Tancred (Glebe-Balmain).
T: Johnny Wallace 2, Billy Sheehan, Syd King.
C: Tom Lawton 3.
Referee: D. Hellewell (England).

Wales 6 Australia 0

Arms Park, Cardiff. 20 December 1947

Wales won by 2 pens to nil.

Australia had not failed to score in 25 matches on tour. Acting captain Trevor Allan and full-back Brian Piper had five penalty chances but missed, while

'Tamp' (Bill Tamplin) landed two of his three attempts, both from 40 yards. Both scores came in the first half, with Allan giving the first away by deliberately throwing the ball into touch. Skipper Haydn Tanner withdrew with injury and Handel Greville, the reliable Llanelli scrum worker, made his only international appearance. Also making his début was a future skipper, John Gwilliam, in the second row. Cardiff player Billy Cleaver was given the full-back role. Three years later he played at scrum-half against Cardiff for the British Isles team. Cardiff supplied nine players, including pre-war cap Les Manfield; Les Williams had also just joined them, from Llanelli. The super-fit Australians at least prevented Wales scoring a try – a feat they accomplished against all four Home Unions. Included in their back-row was Doug Keller, who was to skipper Scotland against Wales 15 months later.

Wales W.B. Cleaver (Cardiff); K.J. Jones (Newport), B.L. Williams, J. Matthews, W. Les T. Williams (Cardiff); G. Davies (Pontypridd), *H.G. Greville (Llanelli); *E.P. Davies (Aberavon), *D.M. James, C. Davies, +W.E. Tamplin (Cardiff), *J.A. Gwilliam (Cambridge U), O. Williams (Llanelli), L. Manfield, G. Evans (Cardiff).
P: Bill Tamplin 2.

Australia B.J.C. Piper; A.E. Tonkin, +T. Allan, M.L. Howell, J.W.T. MacBride; N.A. Emery, C.T. Burke (NSW); R.E. McMaster (Queensland), K.H. Kearney (NSW), E.H. Davis (Victoria), G.M. Cooke (Queensland), D.F. Kraefft, D.H. Keller, A.J. Buchan, C.J. Windon (NSW).
Referee: Alan S. Bean (England).

Wales 9 Australia 3

Arms Park, Cardiff. 4 January 1958

Wales won by 1 try, 1 pen, 1 drop goal to 1 try.

Carwyn James was called on to play his only full international match as an outside-half and was partnered by fellow Scarlet Wynne Evans. Indeed Llanelli were represented by five backs as well as Rhys Williams in the second row. Cliff Morgan was out with injury and Wales struggled as they went 3–0 down in the first half through a Tony Miller try. Wales began to get on top at forward. A Terry Davies penalty was followed by a try from débutant John Collins in the corner at the Westgate-Street end before James scored his only international points by dropping a neat goal. Australia had a fine pair of half-backs in Arthur Summons and Des Connor, but were generally an unlucky side and lost all five Tests on their tour. As well as winning twelve caps for Australia, Connor also played twelve times for New Zealand. Roddy Evans, the Cambridge Blue, was a powerful new Welsh lock and Don Devereux was lively at prop, though he transferred to Huddersfield RL a month later.

Wales T.J. Davies (Llanelli); *J.E. Collins (Aberavon), G.T. Wells (Cardiff), Cyril A.H. Davies, H. Ray Williams, *C.R. James, T. Wynne Evans (Llanelli); T.R. Prosser (Pontypool), B.V. Meredith (Newport), *D.B. Devereux (Neath), R.H. Williams (Llanelli), *W.R. Evans (Cardiff), R.H. Davies (London Welsh), J. Faull, +R.C.C. Thomas (Swansea).
T: John Collins.
P: Terry Davies.
DG: Carwyn James.

Australia T.G.P. Curley; R. Phelps, J.M. Potts, J.K. Lenehan (NSW), K.J. Donald (Queensland); A.J. Summons (NSW), D.M. Connor (Queensland); N.M. Shehadie, J.V. Brown, +R.A.L. Davidson, A.R. Miller, D.M. Emanuel, J.E. Thornett, N.McL. Hughes, P.T. Fenwicke (NSW).
T: Tony Miller.
Referee: A.I. 'Sandy' Dickie (Scotland).

Wales 11 Australia 14

Arms Park, Cardiff. 3 December 1966

Australia won by 2 tries, 1 con, 1 pen, 1 drop goal to 2 tries, 1 con, 1 pen.

Australian captain John Thornett left himself out as he was not fully fit, and he watched his deputy Kenny Catchpole lead his country to a deserved win over Wales. It was the first Welsh home defeat since being beaten by the 1963 New Zealand side, and the win was gained by a fine running rugby that was also later to destroy England. There were débuts for 20-year-old backs – outside-half Barry John, the genius from Cefneithin, and another West Walian, Gerald Davies, at centre. It seemed a win was on the cards when Haydn Morgan burst clear for an excellent try but Phil Hawthorne equalised with a drop goal. Then Jim Lenehan and Terry Price exchanged penalties before Lenehan ended a superb round of passing with a try to put Australia ahead 9–6 at half-time. Wales looked completely stunned when wing Alan Cardy stormed over in the second half with the brave Hawthorne converting (he had suffered a fractured cheekbone after only 30 minutes). John Dawes scored a late try which Price converted, but by then it was too late to save Wales.

Wales T.G. Price (Llanelli); S.J. Watkins (Newport), S.J. Dawes (London Welsh), *T.G.R. Davies

Barry John in action during his début against Australia in 1966. Norman Gale (on the ground) and Allan Lewis (on the right) await proceedings. John was then playing for Llanelli but later switched to Cardiff and went on to gain 25 caps, before retiring at the age of 27. (© *Western Mail & Echo*)

(Cardiff), D.I.E. Bebb (Swansea); *B. John (Llanelli), R. Allan Lewis (Abertillery); D. Williams (Ebbw Vale), N.R. Gale (Llanelli), D.J. Lloyd (Bridgend), B. Price (Newport), *W.D. Thomas (Llanelli), *K.J. Braddock (Newbridge), +A.E.I. Pask, H.J. Morgan (Abertillery).

T: Haydn Morgan, John Dawes.
C: Terry Price.
P: Terry Price.

Australia J.K. Lenehan; E.S. Boyce (NSW), R.J.P. Marks (Queensland), J.E. Brass, A.M. Cardy; P.F. Hawthorne, +K.W. Catchpole; J.M. Miller, P.G. Johnson, A.R. Miller (NSW), R.G. Teitzel (Queensland), R.J. Heming (NSW), M.P. Purcell (Queensland), J.F. O'Gorman, G.V. Davis (NSW).

T: Jim Lenehan, Alan Cardy.
C: Phil Hawthorne.
P: Lenehan.
DG: Hawthorne.
Referee: Kevin D. Kelleher (Ireland).

Australia 16 Wales 19

Sydney Cricket Ground. 21 June 1969

Wales won by 3 tries, 2 cons, 2 pens to 2 tries, 2 cons, 2 pens.

Australia led 11–0 and the match appeared to be lost, but a Keith Jarrett penalty and a Dai Morris try clawed Wales back. Gerald Davies then produced the first of many thrilling wing tries in his career. It was converted by Jarrett to level the scores. The Newport centre then landed a long penalty and converted a John Taylor try that was made by Davies, at which point Wales led by 19–11. Australia rallied and fullback Arthur McGill crossed in the corner and converted. The Welsh protested, led by Maurice Richards, that McGill had wriggled over. Richards swore at Australian referee Craig Ferguson (though Gareth Edwards maintained it was said in Welsh!) and the official marched to the muddy centre spot for a penalty to the home side. With time up, lock Alan Skinner was surprisingly given the attempt as McGill was adjudged by skipper Greg Davis to be too tired by efforts in scoring. It was to prove an error, as Skinner missed and Wales had won. They also defeated Fiji en route to Britain in a non-cap match, as Dennis Hughes scored three of the six tries in a 31–11 scoreline and J.P.R. Williams dropped a goal. His next drop shot was to win the series for the 1971 Lions.

Australia A.N. McGill; T.R. Forman, P.V. Smith, G.A. Shaw, J.W. Cole; J.P. Ballesty, J.N.B. Hipwell; R.B. Prosser, P. Darveniza, J.R. Roxburgh (NSW), N.P. Reilly (Queensland), A.M.F. Abrahams, H.A. Rose, A.J. Skinner, +G.V. Davis (NSW).
T: Phil Smith, Arthur McGill.

C: McGill 2.
P: McGill 2.

Wales J.P.R. Williams (London Welsh); T.G.R. Davies (Cardiff), K.S. Jarrett (Newport), S.J. Dawes (London Welsh), M.C.R. Richards; B. John, G.O. Edwards (Cardiff); D. Williams (Ebbw Vale), N.R. Gale (Llanelli), D.J. Lloyd (Bridgend), +B. Price (Newport), W.D. Thomas (Llanelli), W.D. Morris (Neath), T.M. Davies, J. Taylor (London Welsh).
T: Dai Morris, Gerald Davies, John Taylor.
C: Keith Jarrett 2.
P: Jarrett 2.
Referee: Craig F. Ferguson (Australia).

Wales 24 Australia 0

Arms Park, Cardiff. 10 November 1973

Wales won by 3 tries, 4 pens to nil.

The short tour by Australia was not a good one. They were not yet a strong force in world rugby and lost to England in their other Test. While in Wales they went down by 19–11 to East Wales at Newport and drew 9–9 at Swansea. Wing Jeff McLean missed four attempts at goal, while Phil Bennett landed four and hit a post with two other penalty shots. All three tries came in the second half, including a début try for Pontypool hooker Bobby Windsor. There was also a first cap for Allan 'Panther' Martin and, during injury time, Gareth Edwards limped off with hamstring trouble for Clive Shell to replace him and win his only cap.

Wales J.P.R. Williams; T.G.R. Davies, K. Hughes (London Welsh), R.T.E. Bergiers, J.J.Williams; P. Bennett (Llanelli), +G.O. Edwards (Cardiff); G. Shaw (Neath), *R.W. Windsor (Pontypool), P.D. Llewellyn (Swansea), D.L. Quinnell (Llanelli), *A.J. Martin (Aberavon), W.D. Morris (Neath), T.M. Davies (Swansea), T.P. David (Llanelli).
Rep: *R.C. Shell (Aberavon) for Edwards.
T: Gerald Davies, Bobby Windsor, Dai Morris.
P: Phil Bennett 4.

Australia R.L. Fairfax; O.G. Stephens (NSW), R.D. L'Estrange (Queensland), G.A. Shaw (NSW), J.J. McLean; G.C. Richardson (Queensland), J.N.B. Hipwell; J.L. Howard (NSW), M.E. Freney (Queensland), R. Graham, G. Fay, S.C. Gregory (NSW), M.R. Cocks, A.A. Shaw (Queensland), +P.D. Sullivan (NSW).
Referee: Ken A. Pattinson (England).

Wales 28 Australia 3

Arms Park, Cardiff. 20 December 1975

Wales won by 4 tries, 3 cons, 1 pen, 1 drop goal to 1 pen.

Australia had already lost to Scotland and later on they also fell to England, though they did beat Ireland. Losses were also recorded against Cardiff, the East Midlands of England and the Barbarians, while Llanelli drew 28–28. It was too good and experienced a Welsh team for the Wallabies to stop, even without Phil Bennett who had suffered a foot injury. John Bevan was selected and played steadily, starting well by sending J.J.Williams in at the corner for the first of the Llanelli player's three tries. This time he was on the right-wing, where he had moved in place of Gerald Davies. Geoff Wheel and Allan Martin cleaned out the tourists at the lineout and Gareth Edwards, supplied with good ball, was the chief executioner. The scrum-half scored one and created the position for 'JJ's' second with a high punt, while the hat-trick try came from the familiar Williams kick-and-chase that thrilled the 50,000 crowd.

Wales J.P.R. Williams (London Welsh); J.J. Williams, R.W.R. Gravell (Llanelli), S.P. Fenwick (Bridgend), C.F.W. Rees (London Welsh); J.D. Bevan (Aberavon), G.O. Edwards (Cardiff); A.G. Faulkner, R.W. Windsor, G. Price (Pontypool), G.A.D. Wheel (Swansea), A.J. Martin (Aberavon), T.P. Evans, +T.M. Davies (Swansea), T.J. Cobner (Pontypool).
T: J.J.Williams 3, Gareth Edwards.
C: Steve Fenwick 2, Allan Martin.
P: Fenwick.
DG: John Bevan.

Australia P.E. McLean; P.G. Batch, R.D. L'Estrange (Queensland), G.A. Shaw, L.E. Monaghan; J.C. Hindmarsh, +J.N.B. Hipwell; R. Graham, P.A. Horton (NSW), J.E.C. Meadows (Victoria), R.A. Smith, G. Fay (NSW), A.A. Shaw (Queensland), G. Cornelson, J.K. Lambie (NSW). Reps: R.G. Hauser (Queensland) for Hipwell; G.K. Pearse (NSW) for Lambie.
P: Paul McLean.
Referee: D.P. 'Paddy' D'Arcy (Ireland).

Australia 18 Wales 8 – 1st Test

Ballymore, Brisbane. 11 June 1978

Australia won by 1 try, 1 con, 4 pens to 2 tries.

No Edwards and no Bennett. And no success either

193

for Wales on a nine-match tour which saw both Tests lost, as well as defeats to Sydney and ACT. Troubles arose on and off the field. Manager Clive Rowlands admitted that there was a disciplinary problem within the team. Australia nominated Bob Burnett as referee. Wales refused him and were told, 'Take it or leave it.' New half-backs Gareth Davies and Brynmor Williams faced a tough task, made all the harder by Paul McLean's five successful kicks in five attempts. Gerald Davies became Wales's most-capped three-quarter in his 45th appearance and scored a first-half try. When Ray Gravell sent Williams over, Wales were only one point behind, but Oxford University student Phil Crowe went over under the posts after a swerving run and McLean converted.

Australia L.E. Monaghan (NSW); P.G. Batch, A.G. Slack (Queensland), M. Knight, P.J. Crowe (NSW); P.E. McLean, R.G. Hauser (Queensland); S.C. Finnane, P.A. Horton (NSW), S.T. Pilecki (Queensland), G. Fay (NSW), D.W. Hillhouse, +A.A. Shaw, M.E. Loane (Queensland), G. Cornelson (NSW).
T: Phil Crowe.
C: Paul McLean.
P: McLean 4.

Wales J.P.R. Williams (Bridgend); T.G.R. Davies (Cardiff), S.P. Fenwick (Bridgend), R.W.R. Gravell, J.J. Williams (Llanelli); *W.G. Davies (Cardiff), *D.B. Williams (Newport); A.G. Faulkner, R.W. Windsor, G.Price (Pontypool), G.A.D. Wheel (Swansea), A.J. Martin (Aberavon), J. Squire (Newport), D.L. Quinnell (Llanelli), +T.J. Cobner (Pontypool). Rep: *S.M. Lane (Cardiff) for Squire.
T: Gerald Davies, Brynmor Williams.
Referee: R.T. 'Bob' Burnett (Australia).

Australia 19 Wales 17 – 2nd Test

The Cricket Ground, Sydney. 17 June 1978

Australia won by 1 try, 3 pens, 2 drop goals to 2 tries, 2 pens, 1 drop goal.

The match erupted after three minutes when Aussie prop Steve Finnane broke Graham Price's jaw with a punch from behind. He was not sent off. Wales had been forced to play J.P.R. Williams as a flanker, but emergency full-back Alun Donovan went off after 36 minutes and replacement Gareth Evans fractured his cheek bone in his first tackle. Evans stayed on, 'J.P.R.' went back to full-back and Wales played one short in the pack with J.J.Williams a limping passenger on the wing. Cardiff's Terry Holmes filled the scrum-half position. Like Brynmor Williams, he marked his début with a try and this took Wales ahead at 10–9, but Mark Loane responded with a similar score and Australia were 19–13 in front until the closing minutes. Then Gerald Davies, who was captaining Wales in what was to be his last game, pounced for a try which Gareth Davies could not convert from the touchline. Australian outside-half Paul McLean played throughout both Tests with a broken thumb, but was a match-winner. Manager Clive Rowlands had a last blast on dirty play at the dinner after the Test. Graham Price was unable to say anything for quite some time.

Australia L.E. Monaghan (NSW); P.G. Batch, A.G. Slack (Queensland), M. Knight, P.J. Crowe (NSW); P.E. McLean, R.G. Hauser (Queensland); S.C. Finnane, P.A. Horton (NSW), S.T. Pilecki (Queensland), G. Fay (NSW), D.W. Hillhouse, +A.A. Shaw, M.E. Loane (Queensland), G. Cornelson (NSW).
T: Mark Loane.
P: Paul McLean 3.
DG: Laurie Monaghan, McLean.

Wales *A.J. Donovan (Swansea); +T.G.R. Davies (Cardiff), R.W.R. Gravell (Llanelli), S.P. Fenwick (Bridgend), J.J. Williams (Llanelli); W.G. Davies, *T.D. Holmes (Cardiff); A.G. Faulkner, R.W. Windsor, G. Price (Pontypool), G.A.D. Wheel (Swansea), A.J. Martin (Aberavon), J.P.R. Williams (Bridgend), *C.E. Davies (Newbridge), S.M. Lane (Cardiff). Reps: G.L. Evans (Newport) for Donovan; *S.J. Richardson (Aberavon) for Price.
T: Terry Holmes, Gerald Davies.
P: Gareth Davies 2.
DG: Gareth Davies.
Referee: R.G. 'Dick' Byres (Australia).

Wales 18 Australia 13

Arms Park, Cardiff. 5 December 1981

Wales won by 1 try, 1 con, 3 pens, 1 drop goal to 2 tries, 1 con, 1 pen.

Australia had beaten Ireland, but fell again at Cardiff before going on to lose to Scotland and England. They suffered losses to the Midlands of England, Bridgend and Munster in other tour matches. This match was a triumph for new cap Richard Moriarty who scored a second-half try that woke Wales up, after falling behind by 6–13. Australian tries had come from centre Andy Slack after Terry Holmes had a mark disallowed, and wing Mitchell Cox after a break on the blind-side by Mark Loane. Losing 12–13, Wales took the lead for the first time when new skipper Gareth Davies

Skipper Gareth Davies, watched by forwards Mark Davies and Jeff Squire, on the burst against Australia in 1981. A prolific scorer, Davies registered 2,753 points for Cardiff in 11 seasons. (© Huw Evans)

dropped a goal and Gwyn Evans finished it off with his third penalty.

Wales G. Evans (Maesteg); R.A. Ackerman (Newport), *P.C.T. Daniels (Cardiff), A.J. Donovan (Swansea), C.F.W. Rees (London Welsh); +W.G. Davies, T.D. Holmes (Cardiff); I. Stephens (Bridgend), A.J. Phillips (Cardiff), G. Price (Pontypool), *R.D. Moriarty, G.A.D. Wheel, *M. Davies (Swansea), J. Squire (Pontypool), G.P. Williams (Bridgend).
T: Richard Moriarty.
C: Gwyn Evans.
P: Evans 3.
DG: Gareth Davies.

Australia R.G. Gould (Queensland); M.H. Cox (NSW), A.G. Slack (Queensland), M.J. Hawker (NSW), B.J. Moon; Paul E. McLean (Queensland), J.N.B. Hipwell (NSW); A.M. D'Arcy, C.M. Carberry (Queensland), D.J. Curran (NSW), +A.A. Shaw, Peter W. McLean (Queensland), G. Cornelson (NSW), M.F. Loane (Queensland), S.P. Poidevin (NSW). Reps: M.C. Martin (NSW) for Hawker; P.A. Cox (NSW) for Hipwell;
T: Mitchell Cox, Andy Slack.
C: Paul McLean.
P: Paul McLean.
Referee: John R. West (Ireland).

Wales 9   Australia 28

Arms Park, Cardiff. 24 November 1984

Australia won by 4 tries, 3 cons, 2 pens to 1 try, 1 con, 1 pen.

Captain Andrew Slack and coach Alan Jones were in control of a superb Australian squad which defeated the four Home Unions and the Barbarians. They did lose, however, to Cardiff by 12–16, Llanelli 16–19, Ulster 13–15 and the South of Scotland 6–9. The biggest embarrassment to Wales came when their scrum was shoved over their own line for Steve Tuynman to gain the touchdown. Outside-half Mark Ella followed that up by taking a senseless pass from Eddie Butler and running over. He went on to score against Scotland and complete a quartet of tries, touching down in all four internationals. Wales brought in David Bishop at scrum-half since Terry Holmes was out with a dislocated shoulder. 'Bish' responded with the final try of the match after a juggling act. It proved to be the only try scored against Australia in the Tests. However, Holmes was to return for the next match and Bishop moved off to rugby league with Hull KR. When he came back with Pontypool over ten years later, he was still a great attraction.

Wales M.A. Wyatt (Swansea); M.H. Titley (Bridgend), R.A. Ackerman (London Welsh), M.G. Ring (Cardiff), *P.I. Lewis (Llanelli); M. Dacey (Swansea), *D.J. Bishop (Pontypool); I. Stephens (Bridgend), +M.J. Watkins (Newport), I.H. Eidman, R.L. Norster (Cardiff), S.J. Perkins (Pontypool), *A.E. Davies (Llanelli), E.T. Butler (Pontypool), D.F. Pickering (Llanelli). Rep: *J. Whitefoot (Cardiff) for Stephens.
T: David Bishop.
C: Mark Wyatt.
P: Wyatt.

Australia R.G. Gould; P.C. Grigg, +A.G. Slack, M.P. Lynagh (Queensland), D.I. Campese; M.G. Ella, N.C. Farr-Jones; E.E. Rodríguez (NSW), T.A. Lawton, A.J. McIntyre (Queensland), S.A. Williams, S.A.G. Cutler (NSW), D. Codey (Queensland), S.N. Tuynman, S.P. Poidevin (NSW).
T: Michael Lynagh, Mark Ella, Tom Lawton, Steve Tuynman.
C: Roger Gould 3.
P: Gould 2.
Referee: Owen E. Doyle (Ireland).

(NB: RWC 1987 Wales v Australia)

Australia 63 Wales 6

Ballymore, Brisbane. 21 July 1991

Australia won by 12 tries, 6 cons, 1 pen to 1 pen, 1 drop goal.

There seemed little sense in going to Australia on tour, when three months later Wales had to play the same opponents in the World Cup. Queensland beat Wales 35–24 and New South Wales ran in 13 tries for a 71–8 thrashing. Internationals Mark Ring and David Bishop were in a Liverpool hotel about to play for Wales at baseball. They hung their heads as they heard the New South Wales score. 'I just can't believe it,' said Ring. Paul Thorburn quit international rugby. Ron Waldron stood down for health reasons. Welsh international rugby was sick and the uproar at the dinner after the Test beating only showed the players in worse light. Not only could they not perform well enough on the pitch, but they were fast becoming a disgrace off it. Prop Mark Davis, aged 20, made his only Test appearance. 'Australia complimented the three of us in the front row. We did not buckle or lose a tight head,' he said. Sadly, he never had another chance.

Australia M.C. Roebuck; D.I. Campese (NSW), J.S. Little, T.J. Horan (Queensland), R.H. Egerton (NSW); M.P. Lynagh (Queensland), +N.C. Farr-Jones; A.J. Daly, P.N. Kearns, E.J.A. McKenzie (NSW), R.J. McCall, J.A. Eales (Queensland), V. Ofahengaue, B.T. Gavin (NSW), J.S. Miller (Queensland). Rep: P.J. Slattery (Queensland) for Farr-Jones.
T: Michael Lynagh 2, Phil Kearns 2, Tim Gavin 2, Willie Ofahengaue, Tim Horan, Marty Roebuck, David Campese, Rob Egerton, Jason Little.
C: Lynagh 6.
P: Lynagh.

Wales +P.H. Thorburn (Neath); I.C. Evans (Llanelli), I.S. Gibbs (Neath), M.R. Hall, S.P. Ford (Cardiff); A. Davies, C.J. Bridges (Neath); *M.E. Davis (Newport), K.H. Phillips (Neath), H. Williams-Jones (South Wales Police), Glyn D. Llewellyn (Neath), P. Arnold (Swansea), E.W. Lewis, P.T. Davies (Llanelli), R.G. Collins (Cardiff). Reps: A. Clement (Swansea) for Thorburn; D.W. Evans (Cardiff) for Ford; Gareth O. Llewellyn (Neath) for (P.T.) Davies.
P: Paul Thorburn.
DG: Adrian Davies.
Referee: Fred A. Howard (England).

(NB: RWC 1991 Wales v Australia)

Wales 6 Australia 23

Arms Park, Cardiff. 21 November 1992

(Points system amended – see p.12)

Australia won by 3 tries, 1 con, 2 pens to 2 pens.

The world champions beat Ireland 42–17 and included wins over Wales B, Neath, Monmouthshire and Wales Students on their 13-match tour. They were defeated by Munster (19–22), Swansea (6–21) and Llanelli (9–13) and when they met Wales they had lost key players – John Eales and Michael Lynagh – with injury. A try was now valued at five points and a capacity crowd hoped that Wales could repeat the performances given by Swansea and Llanelli. However, this was Test rugby and Australia were too strong. Marty Roebuck's kick rebounded off a post for flanker David Wilson to score the first try; lock Rod McCall gained the second and David Campese raced past new cap Wayne Proctor for his 52nd Test try. It was a glorious last try and 'Campo' was given the ovation he deserved after a 60-yard dash. Australian coach Bob Dwyer commented: 'Wales have improved out of

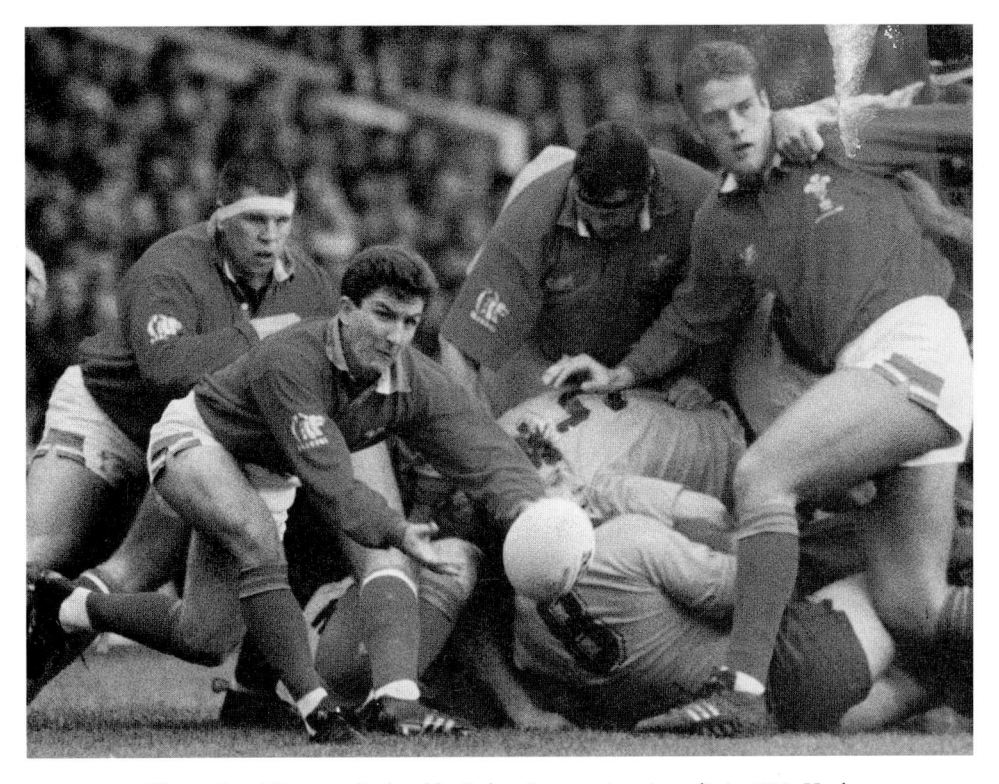

The perfect delivery, as displayed by Robert Jones against Australia in 1992. Hugh Williams-Jones and Gareth Llewellyn are the Welsh forwards. (© Huw Evans)

sight.' Wales team manager Bob Norster praised the lineout work of Gareth Llewellyn and Tony Copsey in particular. He added: 'I feel we have come a long way.'
Wales M.A. Rayer (Cardiff); +I.C. Evans (Llanelli), M.R. Hall (Cardiff), I.S. Gibbs (Swansea), *W.T. Proctor; C.J. Stephens (Llanelli), R.N. Jones (Swansea); M. Griffiths (Cardiff), G.R. Jenkins (Swansea), H. Williams-Jones (South Wales Police), G.O. Llewellyn (Neath), A.H. Copsey, E.W. Lewis (Llanelli), S. Davies, R.E. Webster (Swansea). Rep: A.D. Reynolds (Swansea) for Lewis.
P: Colin Stephens 2.

Australia M.C. Roebuck; D.I. Campese (NSW), J.S. Little, T.J. Horan, P.V. Carozza; P.R. Kahl, P.J. Slattery; D.J. Crowley (Queensland), +P.N. Kearns, E.J.A. McKenzie (NSW), R.J. McCall, G. Morgan (Queensland), V. Ofahengaue, B.T. Gavin (NSW), D.J. Wilson (Queensland). Rep: T. Coker (Queensland) for Wilson.
T: David Wilson, Rod McCall, David Campese.
C: Marty Roebuck.
P: Roebuck 2.
Referee: A.J. 'Tony' Spreadbury (England).

Australia 56 Wales 25 – 1st Test

Ballymore Oval, Brisbane. 8 June 1996

Australia won by 7 tries, 6 cons, 3 pens to 3 tries, 2 cons, 2 pens.

Australia were playing a different game from Wales. This had already been found out when, after defeating Western Australia in the tour opener, Wales lost 30–69 to ACT and 20–27 to New South Wales. Despite having not played a Test match for eleven months, Australia topped the half century and scored seven tries. Centre Joe Roff went in for the first after 55 seconds, but there was no try for David Campese who was playing in his 93rd match, having already scored 63 times. Mike Voyle came on twice as a temporary replacement and won his first cap. Wales had conceded 42 points before scoring their opening try.

Australia M.C. Burke; D.I. Campese (NSW), J.W. Roff (ACT), T.J. Horan (Queensland), A.R. Murdoch (NSW); P.W. Howard, G.M. Gregan (ACT); R.L.L. Harry (NSW), M Caputo, E.J.A.

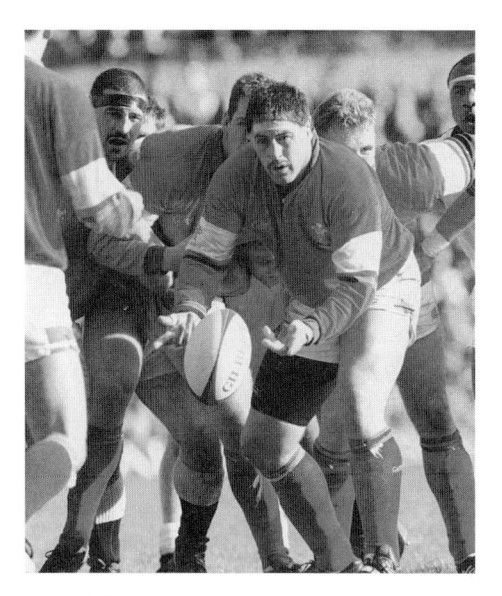

Phil Davies, once the most-capped Welsh forward, but never a Lion. The big-hearted Llanelli man appeared 46 times before taking charge at Leeds RFC.
(© Huw Evans)

Most-capped Welsh hooker of all time, Garin Jenkins, in a sombre pre-international mood. Jenkins led Wales out against Australia in his 50th appearance during the 1999 World Cup.
(© Huw Evans)

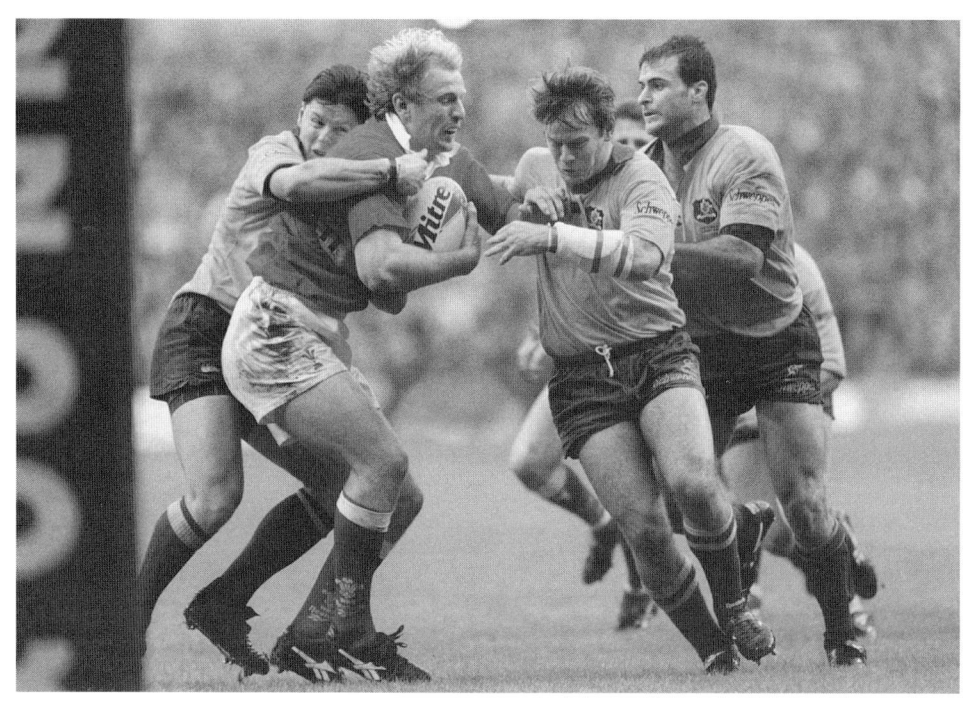

Gareth Thomas takes on three Australian defenders at Cardiff in 1996. The big three-quarter scored 21 tries in 40 matches for Wales. (© Huw Evans)

McKenzie (ACT), G.J. Morgan, +J.A. Eales (Queensland), O.D.A. Finegan (ACT), D.T. Manu (NSW), D.J. Wilson (Queensland). Rep: M.C. Brial (NSW) for Manu.
T: Daniel Manu, Marco Caputo, David Wilson, Alistair Murdoch, Joe Roff, Garrick Morgan, Pat Howard.
C: Matt Burke 6.
P: Burke 3.

Wales W.T. Proctor; I.C. Evans (Llanelli), L.B. Davies (Neath), N.G. Davies (Llanelli), G. Thomas (Bridgend); N.R. Jenkins (Pontypridd), R. Howley (Bridgend); C.D. Loader (Swansea), +J.M. Humphreys, J.D. Davies (Neath), G.O. Llewellyn (Harlequins), D. Jones, H.T. Taylor (Cardiff), S.M. Williams (Neath), R.G. Jones (Llanelli). Reps: L. Mustoe for (J.D.) Davies; *M.J. Voyle (Newport) for (R.G.) Jones and (D.) Jones (both temp).
T: Wayne Proctor, Hemi Taylor, Gareth Llewellyn.
C: Neil Jenkins 2.
P: Jenkins 2.
Referee: Glenn K. Wahlstrom (New Zealand).

Australia 42 Wales 3 – 2nd Test

Sydney Football Ground, Sydney. 22 June 1996

Australia won by 6 tries, 3 cons, 2 pens to 1 pen.

Full-back Matt Burke took his tally to 36 points in two Tests, though Wales played better than the score suggested. Gareth Llewellyn and Derwyn Jones played well at the lineout. Llewellyn won his 47th cap, to pass Phil Davies as the most-capped forward for Wales. Three-quarter Dafydd James, born in Zambia, came on for his début three minutes from full-time. Wales had lost to Australia B 41–51 between Tests and had beaten NSW Country and Victoria.

Australia M.C. Burke; D.I. Campese (NSW), J.W. Roff (ACT), T.J. Horan, B.N. Tune (Queensland); P.W. Howard (ACT), S.J. Payne; R.L.L. Harry (NSW), M. Caputo, E.J.A. McKenzie (ACT), G.J. Morgan, +J.A. Eales (Queensland), O.D.A. Finegan (ACT), M.C. Brial (NSW), D.J. Wilson (Queensland). Reps: S.J. Larkham (ACT) for Burke; M.A. Foley (Queensland) for Caputo; D. Manu (NSW) for Foley; D.J. Crowley (Queensland) for McKenzie.
T: Owen Finegan, Michael Foley, Garrick Morgan, Joe Roff, Tim Horan, Matt Burke.
C: Burke 2, John Eales.
P: Burke 2.

Wales W.T. Proctor; I.C. Evans (Llanelli), G. Thomas (Bridgend), N.G. Davies (Llanelli), S.D. Hill (Cardiff); N.R. Jenkins (Pontypridd), R. Howley (Bridgend); C.D. Loader (Swansea), +J.M. Humphreys, L. Mustoe (Cardiff), G.O. Llewellyn (Neath), D. Jones (Cardiff), A. Gibbs (Newbridge), H.T. Taylor (Cardiff), S.M. Williams (Neath). Reps: *D.R. James (Bridgend) for Davies; A.L.P. Lewis (Cardiff) for Loader (temp).
P: Neil Jenkins.
Referee: Colin J. Hawke (New Zealand).

Wales 19 Australia 28

Arms Park, Cardiff. 1 December 1996

Australia won by 3 tries, 2 cons, 3 pens to 1 try, 1 con, 4 pens.

Jonathan Davies was back from the 'north' after a gap of 67 matches over eight years. Also back from rugby league after missing 61 Tests was prop David Young. Lock forward John Eales led Australia to victory through Italy, Scotland, Ireland and Wales. The last match was against the Barbarians at Twickenham and also brought a win. They scored 91 points in three Tests and continued the trend in this 11th match of the tour. Australia were coasting at 18–9 with the expected big finale to come. It did not, largely because when they were attacking the Wales line, Gareth Thomas suddenly intercepted a George Gregan pass with not one Australian in front of him. Joe Roff, David Campese and Matt Burke led the race, but Thomas arrived at the line first with the crowd on its feet. Jonathan Davies converted and added a penalty and, against the run of play, Wales were in front. Not that it lasted. At the end, everyone stood to applaud David Campese who played his 101st and final Test after scoring 315 points, which included a world record of 64 tries.

Wales W.T. Proctor; I.C. Evans (Llanelli), G. Thomas (Bridgend), I.S. Gibbs (Swansea), D.R. James (Bridgend); J. Davies, R. Howley (Cardiff); C.D. Loader (Swansea), +J.M. Humphreys, D. Young (Cardiff), G.O. Llewellyn (Harlequins), D. Jones, H.T. Taylor (Cardiff), S.M. Williams (Neath), K.P. Jones (Ebbw Vale). Reps: N.R. Jenkins (Pontypridd) for Proctor; J.C. Quinnell (Richmond) for (D.) Jones; *C.L. Charvis (Swansea) for Taylor.
T: Gareth Thomas.
C: Jonathan Davies.
P: Davies 4.

Australia M. Burke; D.I. Campese (NSW), J.S.

Little, +T.J. Horan (Queensland), J.W. Roff; P.W. Howard, G.M. Gregan (ACT); D.J. Crowley, M.A. Foley (Queensland), A.T. Blades, T.B. Gavin (NSW), D. Giffin (ACT), O.D.A. Finegan, M.C. Brial (NSW), D.J. Wilson (Queensland).
T: Matt Burke, Michael Brial (pen try).

C: Burke 2.
P: Burke 3.
Referee: D. Iain Ramage (Scotland).

(NB: RWC 1999 quarter-final Wales v Australia)

NEW ZEALAND

Wales 3 New Zealand 0

Arms Park, Cardiff. 16 December 1905

Wales won by 1 try to nil.

The All Blacks, with a record of 27 victories to no defeats on their tour, met Wales for the first-ever occasion and it could be claimed that the match was between the two best sides in the world at that time. The match went on to form a big part of rugby football folklore and was notable not only for the fact that Wales won but also for the try by Teddy Morgan that was allowed and the 'try' by New Zealand centre Bob Deans that was not. Oddly, though both occurred at almost the same spot on the Arms Park, it is the 'Deans spot' that is remembered in both Welsh and All Black history. Some of the Welsh players admitted that they thought Deans had scored. Equally, some of the All Blacks considered Deans had not. Referee John Dallas ruled no try, but that was only the start of the argument. Mr Dallas was later described in New Zealand rugby history as 'an old man in a long jacket', yet he had played for Scotland in 1903 and at 27 he was four or five years younger than rival captains Nicholls and Gallaher. An hour before the start the gates were closed on a 47,000 crowd, who saw, unusually, that both teams were wearing numbers. Wales scored the only points, ten minutes before half-time. It was a try planned by the 'Little General', Dicky Owen, and had been practised by the backs at a special session – almost unheard of in that era. It was felt that after the Cardiff match, the All Blacks had great regard for Percy Bush as a brilliant side-stepper and Owen therefore plied the ball out continually to Bush, never once passing to Cliff Pritchard, the rover back. Then, from a scrum in the midfield, just inside the New Zealand half, Wales heeled, Bush, Gwyn Nicholls and Willie Llewellyn raced right to act as a decoy and Owen made as if to pass out to Bush. Instead, he sent one of his famous reverse passes towards Cliff Pritchard. It was not his best pass and it fell on the ground, but Pritchard picked it up, swerved and passed to Rhys Gabe, who unloaded outside to Teddy Morgan. The wing rounded Duncan McGregor and darted past George Gillett to score an historic try – the 10th of 14 that he was to score for Wales in 16 matches. The *News Chronicle*'s reporter stated that his hat was hit over his eyes by an excited Welsh journalist just as Morgan was about to score! Dave Gallaher, the New Zealand captain, was often penalised for not putting the ball in straight, and Wales countered the All Blacks' 2-3-2 scrum by keeping a forward waiting on each side of the two New Zealand hookers at the last moment to keep the loose head. New Zealand had their best scoring chance in the second half. Billy Wallace ran up the wing and slipped a pass to Bob Deans. Newspapers of the time say that Deans was brought down by two or three defenders, which seems most likely, because Morgan was named as dashing across from his wing to make the tackle and Gabe also claimed he tackled Deans. 'I thought he had scored,' said Gabe. 'Then I felt him wriggling forward to reach the goal-line. So I pulled him back.' Gallaher said that the better team had won. Gwyn Nicholls commented: 'There really was nothing between the teams. The real difference appeared to be that we took advantage of our only opportunity to score.' The crowd burst on to the pitch and carried Morgan and Bush around the field in triumph. Afterwards it was found that Owen had displaced a cartilage in his chest. 'I was in agony,' he said. 'I would have gone off the field if it had been any other match than this.'

Wales H.B. Winfield (Cardiff); W.M. Llewellyn (Penygraig), +E.G. Nicholls, R.T. Gabe (Cardiff), E. Morgan (London Welsh); C.C. 'Cliff' Pritchard (Pontypool) – rover back, *P.F. Bush (Cardiff), R.M. Owen (Swansea); D. Jones (Aberdare), G. Travers (Pill Harriers), J.J. Hodges, C.M. 'Charlie' Pritchard (Newport), W. Joseph (Swansea), A.F. Harding, J.F. Williams (London Welsh).
T: Teddy Morgan.

New Zealand G.A. Gillett (Canterbury); D. McGregor (Wellington), R.G. Deans (Canterbury), W.J. Wallace (Wellington); H.J. Mynott, J. Hunter (Taranaki), F. Roberts (Wellington); J.J. O'Sullivan (Taranaki), G.A. Tyler (Auckland), S. Casey (Otago), F. Newton (Canterbury), F.T. Glasgow (Taranaki), A. McDonald (Otago), C.E. Seeling, +D. Gallaher (Auckland).
Referee: John D. Dallas (Scotland).

Wales 0 New Zealand 19

St Helen's, Swansea. 29 November 1924

New Zealand won by 4 tries, 2 cons, 1 pen to nil.

New Zealand's 19-year-old full-back George Nepia

The athleticism of the great wing Kenneth Jeffrey Jones was manifest when he played for the British Isles tourists against New Zealand in 1950 – his try in the fourth test in Auckland will never be forgotten. He scored 17 tries in 44 appearances for Wales. (© *Western Mail & Echo*)

played in every game of the tour for the 'Invincibles' and said of this one: 'Revenge is sweet. The score represented a point for every year since 1905.' Welsh captain Jack Wetter refused to accept the ball brought out by 'Jock' Richardson and vice versa, before the referee intervened. The All Blacks then performed their haka, only for Neath forward Dai Hiddlestone to lead the Welsh team in a war-dance of their own. This delighted the 50,000 crowd, who were perched all around the ground. So excited did a hundred or so become that as Nepia dived to make an early save, a balcony on the north side collapsed with the crowd falling on those below. Wales soon realised that they had made a big mistake in selecting Wetter as player and captain at the age of 36 years and 11 months. He was taken off after a collision with Nepia and when he resumed after the interval he limped into the pack and Hiddlestone moved out as the extra back. Wales began well enough, but Nepia and Bert Cooke repelled the forward drives and New Zealand led 11–0 at half-time with a Mark Nicholls conversion and penalty to add to tries by forwards Maurice Brownlie and Bill Irvine. Brownlie scored with two defenders hanging on to him, while Irvine scrambled over from a lineout near the corner flag. In the second half, wing Karl Svensen went over from Jimmy Mill's pass and Irvine scored again after following up his own kick. Nicholls converted the latter. Nepia was to return to Wales 58 years later and met, among others, Wales wing Ernie Finch. English journalist Denzil Batchelor said of Nepia: 'He leapt at the ball like an art critic snatching at a fault of technique by his best friend. He went to work, a fury of shoulders, elbows and thighs storming through the massed ranks of the opposing pack. Eight to one were the odds which exactly suited him.' From the Welsh team, Nepia selected Tommy Johnson as the best player. Of the two new caps, Cliff Williams was to die at the age of 32, while Edwin Williams joined Huddersfield RL in 1925. This was the only international match controlled by Colonel Brunton, who had played against Wales in 1914. He had been awarded the Military Cross in 1916 and was to become RFU president in 1953–54.

Wales T.A.W. Johnson (Cardiff); W.R. Harding (Swansea), A.R. Stock (Newport), A.E. Jenkins, E. Finch (Llanelli); +J.J. Wetter (Newport) – rover back, *E. Williams (Neath), W.J. Delahay (Cardiff); D.S. Parker (Swansea), J.H. Gore (Blaina), M.D. Jones (Cardiff/London Welsh), *C. Williams (Llanelli), S. Morris (Cross Keys), C.H. Pugh (Maesteg), D.D. Hiddlestone (Neath).

New Zealand G. Nepia (Hawke's Bay); J. Steel (West Coast), A.E. Cooke (Auckland), K.S. Svenson; M.F. Nicholls (Wellington), N.P. McGregor (Canterbury), J.J. Mill; W.R. Irvine (Hawke's Bay), Q. Donald (Wairarapa), M.J. Brownlie (Hawke's Bay), R.R. Masters (Canterbury), +J. Richardson (Southland), C.J. Brownlie (Hawke's Bay), L.F. Cupples (Bay of Plenty), J.H.Parker (Canterbury).
T: Bill Irvine 2, Maurice Brownlie, Karl Svenson.
C: Mark Nicholls 2.
DG: Nicholls.
Referee: Col. Joseph S. Brunton (England).

Wales 13 New Zealand 12

Arms Park, Cardiff. 21 December 1935

Wales won by 3 tries, 2 cons to 2 tries, 1 con, 1 drop goal.

This was the match that marked Wilfred Wooller as a centre three-quarter of class, yet he played much of the match as a wing, where the selectors had ridiculously selected him. He was moved by his skipper Claude Davey and Wales went 2–1 up on New Zealand by emulating the 1905 success. The ground had been covered by straw and was bone-hard, but the sun came out at first, before a mist gradually came over the ground. New Zealand led 12–10 with only ten minutes remaining, when a scrum collapsed and débutant hooker Don Tarr was stretchered off with a broken neck. It was later said that referee Cyril Gadney had saved Tarr's life by insisting he was placed face downwards on the stretcher. The All Blacks almost scored direct from Mike Gilbert's long kick-off, when Viv Jenkins slipped up with the All Black pack bearing down on him. No score came until just before half-time, when Joey Sadler sent Jack Griffiths down the blindside and he put wing Nelson Ball in at the corner. Davey had brought Wooller infield and sent Idwal Rees to the wing and now Wales looked smarter, with 18-year-old Haydn Tanner sending out a stream of passes for the elusive Cliff Jones. It had been Tanner and his cousin, Willie Davies, who helped Swansea beat New Zealand earlier in the tour, when All Black skipper Jack Manchester had said: 'Tell them back home that we lost, but not that two schoolboys beat us!' Now Wales were on fire. Jones kicked, Davey chased, gathered and scored, for Jenkins to convert. Soon afterwards, Jones delivered to Wooller, who split the New Zealand centres and kicked over Gilbert. The ball went over

The Welsh team who defeated New Zealand by 13–12 in December, 1935. They finished with 14 men after débutant hooker Dai Tarr broke his neck at a second-half scrum. *Back row*: C.H. Gadney (referee), T.J. Rees, T. Williams, J. Lang, A.M. Rees, E. Watkins, D.J. Tarr, M. Moses (touch-judge). *Seated*: V.G.J. Jenkins, H. Payne, G. Prosser, E.C. Davey (capt.), J.I. Rees, W. Wooller, G. Rees-Jones. *Front row*: C.W. Jones, H. Tanner. (© *Western Mail & Echo*)

both Wooller and Gilbert, but little Geoffrey Rees-Jones was following and he scored. Jenkins converted for a 10–3 lead. New Zealand were not finished, though, as Gilbert collected a stray kick from Jones and calmly dropped a 35-yard goal. 10–7. Gilbert had another shot. Wales dithered and Ball was up to score his fourth and final Test try, with Gilbert's conversion taking New Zealand in front at 12–10. Wales were on the ropes, with Tarr departing for Tommy Rees to take over as hooker. But the seven men hooked it. Tanner passed to Jones, then Wooller received. New Zealand were ready for the pass to Davey and downed him, but the pass never arrived. Wooller was away through the gap and again came up to Gilbert. Again he kicked high and again the ball bounced right back over his head. Wooller recalled: 'I went into the straw. Some said Gilbert had pushed me, but he had not and he too was beaten by the icy ground. As I hit the straw I heard a roar and turned to see Rees-Jones dive over. He was not as quick as me, but he had read my mind and followed up once more. It was a wonderful day and they took defeat like the great sportsmen they were.' New Zealand came once more, but Jenkins was calm and resolute. He gathered, found his touch and it was all over. As well as Tanner and Tarr, Harry Payne and Eddie Watkins also played their first games. Neither Tarr nor Payne played again for Wales, but Payne played in a match with Ray Gravell at the age of 83. Watkins turned professional just before war broke out and much more was to be heard of Tanner.

Wales V.G.J. Jenkins (London Welsh); G.R. Rees-Jones (Oxford U), +E.C. Davey, J. Idwal Rees (Swansea), W. Wooller; C.W. Jones (Cambridge U), *H. Tanner; *H. Payne, *D.J. Tarr (Swansea), T.J. Rees (Newport), T.G. Williams (Cross Keys), *E.V. Watkins (Cardiff), I.G. Prosser (Neath), J. Lang (Llanelli), A.M. Rees (London Welsh).
T: Geoffrey Rees-Jones 2, Claude Davey.
C: Viv Jenkins 2.

New Zealand G.D.M. Gilbert (West Coast); G.F. Hart (Canterbury), N.A. Mitchell (Southland), N. Ball (Wellington); C.J. Oliver (Canterbury), J.L. Griffiths, B.S. Sadler; A. Lambourn (Wellington), W.E. Hadley (Auckland), D. Dalton, S.T. Reid (Hawke's Bay), R.R. King (West Coast), +J.E. Manchester (Canterbury), A. Mahoney (Bush), H.F. McLean (Auckland).
T: Nelson Ball 2.
C: Mike Gilbert.
DG: Gilbert.
Referee: Cyril H. Gadney (England).

Wales 13 New Zealand 8

Arms Park, Cardiff. 19 December 1953

Wales won by 2 tries, 2 cons, 1 pen to 1 try, 1 con, 1 pen.

Wales took a 3–1 lead over New Zealand in international meetings, after looking certain to lose when 8–5 behind and losing the dangerous Gareth Griffiths with a dislocated shoulder. However, New Zealand failed to capitalise, though they came close when Brian Fitzpatrick, whose son Sean later became a great All Black skipper, was held up just short of the line by captain Bleddyn Williams and full-back Gerwyn Williams. Back came Griffiths, and though he played little part, it inspired the Welsh team. The forwards roared downfield and created a position for a Gwyn Rowlands penalty. It was 8–8 and Wales attacked again. The ball fell loose on the South Stand touchline and Clem Thomas gathered and cross-kicked right-footed from the left-wing to the Taff End. The ball bounced splendidly for the flying Ken Jones to race past Bob Scott and Ron Jarden and go over near the posts. It brought the famous comment from the great New Zealand commentator Winston McCarthy, who said: 'It's a try! A winning try.' And so it was, as Rowlands added the conversion points. New Zealand went on to beat England, Scotland and Ireland and lose to France. They had begun the match badly when Scott panicked and the vigilant Sid Judd swooped to score, but an excellent Jarden penalty levelled the scores. Just before the interval, Scott's cross-kick created havoc and the alert number 21 Bill Clark, with his white scrum cap evident, was up to score close enough for Jarden to convert. Judd was surprisingly not an original selection, despite having scored a try in Cardiff's 8–3 win over New Zealand. He played only because Glyn 'Shorty' Davies withdrew with injury, while Clem Thomas was passed fit to play despite being involved in a traffic accident in England on the previous day. It was just as well for Wales that he did appear! The popular wing Dr Gwyn Rowlands made his début, after having scored a superb try for Cardiff against the All Blacks. He had played in English trials as a right-wing, but his great ploy of cross-kicking was wasted as he was picked on the left flank.

Wales G. Williams (London Welsh); K.J. Jones (Newport), G.M. Griffiths, +B.L. Williams, *G. Rowlands; C.I. Morgan, W.R. Willis (Cardiff); W.O.G. Williams (Swansea), D.M. Davies (Somerset Police), C.C. Meredith, E.R. John, J.R.G. Stephens (Neath), S. Judd (Cardiff), J.A. Gwilliam (Gloucester), R.C.C. Thomas (Swansea).

Wales pictured before defeating New Zealand by 13–8 at Cardiff in 1953. A thrilling try by wing Ken Jones proved to be the winner after an astonishing cross-kick by Clem Thomas. *Back row*: Dr P.F. Cooper (referee), R.C.C. Thomas, S. Judd, J.R.G. Stephens, E.R. John, J.A. Gwilliam, C.C. Meredith, I. Jones (touch-judge). *Seated*: W.O. Williams, G.M. Griffiths, B.L. Williams (capt.), K.J. Jones, D.M. Davies. *Front row*: G. Rowlands, W.R. Willis, C.I. Morgan, G. Williams. (© *Western Mail & Echo*)

T: Sid Judd, Ken Jones.
C: Gwyn Rowlands 2.
P: Rowlands.

New Zealand R.W.H. Scott (Auckland); A.E.G. Elsom (Canterbury), J.M. Tanner (Auckland), R.A. Jarden; B.B.J. Fitzpatrick (Wellington), L.S. Haig (Otago), K. Davis (Auckland); K.L. Skinner (Otago), R.C. Hemi, I.J. Clarke (Waikato), R.A. White (Poverty Bay), G.N. Dalzell, +R.C. Stuart (Canterbury), W.A. McCaw (Southland), W.H. Clark (Wellington).
T: Bill Clark.
C: Ron Jarden.
P: Jarden.
Referee: Dr Peter F. Cooper (England).

Wales 0   New Zealand 6

Arms Park, Cardiff. 21 December 1963

New Zealand won by 1 pen, 1 drop goal to nil.

After defeats in 1905, 1935 and 1953, New Zealand came to win and did not worry too much if they failed to score a try. It was their first victory over Wales at Cardiff in a full international match. The margin was far wider than the penalty and drop goal showed, as Wilson Whineray's team played most of the match in the Welsh half. Full-back Don Clarke was already a legend, after having kicked six penalty goals to beat the Lions in the first Test of 1959 and had made his Test début in helping defeat South Africa in 1956. This time he was far from full fitness, but landed a close-range goal for the only points of the first half. The second score was when Bruce Watt dropped a close-range goal, after turning inside Dai Hayward. New Zealand appeared content to sit on their lead and there was little to enthuse over. Clive Rowlands was carried off in the closing minutes after a bone-jerking charge from Colin 'Pinetree' Meads, the huge King Country lock, who was the pick of one of the greatest packs ever to play in Test rugby. John Uzzell was picked at centre, largely because of his drop shot which had defeated the All Blacks at Newport.

Wales G.T.R. Hodgson (Neath); D.R.R. Morgan, D.K. Jones (Llanelli), *J. Uzzell (Newport), D.I.E. Bebb (Swansea); D. Watkins (Newport), +D.C.T. Rowlands (Pontypool); K.D. Jones (Cardiff), N.R. Gale (Llanelli), L.J. Cunningham (Aberavon), B. Price (Newport), B.E. Thomas (Neath), Dai J. Hayward (Cardiff), A.E.I. Pask (Abertillery), *A. Thomas (Newport).

New Zealand D.B. Clarke (Waikato); M.J. Dick, P.F. Little (Auckland), R.W. Caulton (Wellington); D.A. Arnold, B.A. Watt (Canterbury), K.C. Briscoe (Taranaki); K.F. Gray (Wellington), D. Young (Canterbury), +W.J. Whineray (Auckland), A.J. Stewart (Canterbury), C.E. Meads (King Country), W.J. Nathan (Auckland), D.J. Graham (Canterbury), K.R. Tremain (Hawke's Bay).
P: Don Clarke
DG: Bruce Watt.
Referee: R.C. Williams (Ireland).

Wales 6   New Zealand 13

Arms Park, Cardiff. 11 November 1967

New Zealand won by 2 tries, 2 cons, 1 pen to 1 pen, 1 drop goal.

Brian Lochore's All Blacks strode through Europe unbeaten, defeating Wales, England, Scotland and France but being denied an Ireland match due to the outbreak of foot-and-mouth disease. They won this unspectacular Test and were later to be held at 3–3 on the same pitch by an East Wales XV. This match will be remembered for a John Jeffery blunder in his first, and last, international cap. The fine Newport forward caught a Fergie McCormick kick at goal that dropped wide at the Taff End and unwisely threw it backwards, into the hands of Bill Davis, who had just to drop over the Welsh line close to the posts. The conversion took New Zealand to 13–3 and Wales were doomed. The usual Cardiff rain descended and a smart corner try by Bill Birtwistle helped New Zealand to an 8–0 lead at the interval. A Barry John drop goal pegged it back but then the Davis try settled it. After misses by Paul Wheeler and Gareth Edwards, skipper Norman Gale decided to have a shot at goal himself and kicked it. Wales paired John and Edwards for the first time, before which they had their famous 'You throw it and I'll catch it' meeting. Brian Thomas was astonishingly selected as a prop with the sprinter Keri Jones called up on the wing. Jones joined Wigan Rugby League club a year later.

Wales *P.J. Wheeler (Aberavon); S.J. Watkins (Newport), W.H. Raybould (London Welsh), *I. Hall (Aberavon), *W. Keri Jones; B. John, G.O. Edwards (Cardiff); D. Williams (Ebbw Vale), +N.R. Gale (Llanelli), B.E. Thomas (Neath), *M.L. Wiltshire, G.T. 'Billy' Mainwaring (Aberavon), *D. Hughes (Newbridge), *J.J. Jeffery (Newport), J. Taylor (London Welsh).
P: Norman Gale.
DG: Barry John.

New Zealand W.F. McCormick (Canterbury); M.J. Dick (Auckland), I.R. MacRae (Hawke's Bay), W.M. Birtwistle (Waikato); W.L. Davis (Hawke's Bay), E.W. Kirton, C.R. Laidlaw (Otago); K.F. Gray (Wellington), B.E. McLeod (Counties), B.L. Muller (Taranaki), S.C. Strahan (Manawatu), C.E. Meads (King Country), K.R. Tremain (Hawke's Bay), +B.J. Lochore (Wairarapa), G.C. Williams (Wellington).
T: Bill Birtwistle, Bill Davis.
C: Fergie McCormick 2.
P: McCormick.
Referee: Mike H. Titcomb (England).

New Zealand 19   Wales 0 – 1st Test

Lancaster Park Oval, Christchurch. 31 May 1969

New Zealand won by 4 tries, 2 cons, 1 pen to nil.

Three Tests in seven games saw this labelled the 'suicide tour', and with Pat Murphy of New Zealand refereeing both Tests, it was an impossible task. Certainly, it was one that Carwyn James must have noted and two years later many of the Welsh team returned to help his Lions win the Test series. New Zealand had a superb pack and Wales suffered a handicap when hooker Jeff Young had his jaw fractured by a Colin Meads punch in retaliation for jersey-pulling. How Meads stayed on the field was hard to understand. Maybe only Brian Price could work it out! For New Zealand it was their fourth win in seven meetings and the memories of 1905 were finally buried. Wales had chances, but Keith Jarrett missed five shots at goal. The Ken Gray try typified the home pack's power. The big prop shook J.P.R. Williams into the Christchurch mud after scoring, as the full-back had clung despairingly to Gray's ankle.

New Zealand W.F. McCormick (Canterbury); M.J. Dick (Auckland), W.L. Davis (Hawke's Bay), G.S. Thorne (Auckland); I.R. MacRae (Hawke's Bay), E.W. Kirton (Otago), S.M. Going (North Auckland); K.F. Gray (Wellington), B.E. McLeod (Counties), B.L. Muller (Taranaki), C.E. Meads (King Country), A.E. Smith (Taranaki), T.N. Lister (South Canterbury), +B.J. Lochore (Wairarapa), I.A. Kirkpatrick (Poverty Bay).
T: Malcolm Dick, Bruce McLeod, Brian Lochore, Ken Gray.
C: Fergie McCormick 2.
P: McCormick.

Wales J.P.R. Williams (London Welsh); S.J. Watkins, K.S. Jarrett (Newport), T.G.R. Davies, M.C.R.

Richards; B. John, G.O. Edwards (Cardiff); D. Williams (Ebbw Vale), J. Young, D.J. Lloyd (Bridgend), +B. Price (Newport), B.E. Thomas, W.D. Morris (Neath), T.M. Davies, J. Taylor (London Welsh). Rep: N.R. Gale (Llanelli) for Young.
Referee: J. Pat Murphy (New Zealand).

New Zealand 33 Wales 12 – 2nd Test

Eden Park, Auckland. 14 June 1969

New Zealand won by 3 tries, 3 cons, 5 pens, 1 drop goal to 2 tries, 2 pens.

Wales had drawn with Taranaki and beaten both Otago and Wellington and in hindsight, though the score of 33–12 made the match look one-sided, it was only 3–2 on try-count, with both Wales tries being fine efforts and the Maurice Richards score being quite outstanding. Full-back Fergie McCormick set a world record for Test rugby with 24 points that all came from kicks, with a superb drop goal going over from some 55 yards near the touchline. However, referee Pat Murphy, who leapt for joy at one point, only made the case for neutral officials much stronger. He was not popular with the Welsh or British Lions teams! Wales led 6–3, helped by the Richards effort that saw him run for the corner as McCormick and Earle Kirton covered. His only option was to go for the flag, but a sudden change down and then up in gear caused two fine tacklers to pause a fraction and the wing was over inches in front of both men. Keith Jarrett added nine points including a smart try, but there was no doubting the better side won and the defeat was the highest since Scotland had beaten Wales 35–10 at Inverleith in 1924. Lessons were learned and five of the backs returned two years later to haunt New Zealand. It was the first time that Gerald Davies had played on the wing in a Test. The move was a great success, even if Gerald said: 'I saw it as demotion!'

New Zealand W.F. McCormick (Canterbury); M.J. Dick (Auckland), W.L. Davis (Hawke's Bay), G.R. Skudder (Waikato); I.R. MacRae (Hawkes Bay), E.W. Kirton (Otago), S.M. Going (North Auckland); K.F. Gray (Wellington), B.E. McLeod (Counties), A.E. Hopkinson (Canterbury), C.E. Meads (King Country), A.E. Smith (Taranaki), T.N. Lister (South Canterbury), +B.J. Lochore (Canterbury), I.A. Kirkpatrick (Poverty Bay).
T: George Skudder, Ian MacRae, Ian Kirkpatrick.
C: Fergie McCormick 3.
P: McCormick 5.
DG: McCormick.

Wales J.P.R. Williams (London Welsh); T.G.R. Davies (Cardiff), K.S. Jarrett (Newport), S.J. Dawes (London Welsh), M.C.R. Richards; B. John, G.O. Edwards (Cardiff); D. Williams (Ebbw Vale), N.R. Gale (Llanelli), B.E. Thomas (Neath), +B. Price (Newport), W.D. Thomas (Llanelli), W.D. Morris (Neath), T.M. Davies, J. Taylor (London Welsh).
T: Maurice Richards, Keith Jarrett.
P: Jarrett 2.
Referee: J. Pat Murphy (New Zealand).

Wales 16 New Zealand 19

Arms Park, Cardiff. 21 December 1972

New Zealand won by 1 try, 5 pens to 1 try, 4 pens.

This could have been New Zealand prop forward Keith Murdoch's great day, as he scored his side's only try, but in the nearby Angel Hotel hours later came an incident with a security guard that led to the fiery Otago man being sent home in disgrace. Only Murdoch never reached home. He left the plane in Australia to vanish into the outback. Murdoch's try was awarded in much the same circumstances as those in which Welsh full-back J.P.R. Williams had his effort disallowed. It was marginal, but referee 'Johnny' Johnson was a good official who controlled a difficult match well enough. Débutant Joe Karam just outkicked Phil Bennett 5–4 on penalties, but 'Benny' missed with a fifth kick in the final minute from 35 yards. New Zealand led 13–3 at the interval before John Bevan ran 40 yards for a splendid try. It was not a happy match, nor a happy tour. But at least it had been happy enough for all Scarlets supporters at Stradey Park when Llanelli gained a 9–3 win in the second match of the tour. For the All Blacks, their biggest problem was the fitness of their dangerous scrum-half Sid Going, who carried a leg injury throughout the tour. The only new Welsh cap was the Neath prop Glyn Shaw, who eventually turned professional for Widnes in 1977.

Wales J.P.R. Williams; T.G.R. Davies (London Welsh), R.T.E. Bergiers (Llanelli), J.L. Shanklin (London Welsh), J.C. Bevan (Cardiff); P. Bennett (Llanelli), G.O. Edwards (Cardiff); *G. Shaw (Neath), J. Young (London Welsh/RAF), D.B. Llewelyn, +W.D. Thomas, D.L. Quinnell (Llanelli), W.D. Morris (Neath), T.M. Davies (Swansea), J. Taylor (London Welsh).
T: John Bevan.
P: Phil Bennett 4.

New Zealand J.F. Karam (Wellington); B.G. Williams (Auckland), D.A. Hales (Canterbury), R.M. Parkinson (Poverty Bay), G.B. Batty (Wellington); R.E. Burgess

(Manawatu), S.M. Going (North Auckland); J.D. Matheson (Otago), R.W. Norton (Canterbury), K. Murdoch (Otago), P.J. Whiting (Auckland), H.H. MacDonald, A.J. Wyllie (Canterbury), A.R. Sutherland (Marlborough), +I.A. Kirkpatrick (Poverty Bay). Rep: A.I. Scown (Taranaki) for Wyllie.
T: Keith Murdoch.
P: Joe Karam 5.
Referee: R.F. 'Johnny' Johnson (England).

Wales 12 New Zealand 13

Arms Park, Cardiff. 11 November 1978.

New Zealand won by 1 try, 3 pens to 4 pens.

New Zealand rugby had always been held in great esteem throughout the world, not only for their strength in the forwards and general ability, but also for their tackling and support. Those attributes made the All Blacks models for any youngster to follow. The incident which happened near the close of this match, however, brought only shame to a great team. The sad thing was that no New Zealander could bring himself to say so. Lock forwards Andy Haden and Frank Oliver had obviously hatched a plan to win a penalty if things were not going well by diving from the lineout as if they had been pushed. At 12–10 to Wales, this was the case. Both dived. Big fellows, they were. But it was cheating. Many later blamed referee Roger Quittenton. They were entirely wrong. A splendid referee was crucified by the Welsh public. He gave what he saw, which was what looked like a foul by Geoff Wheel. In the press box, former Wales skipper Clem Thomas alone was suspicious. The light was fading and the incident had occurred on the South Stand side at the Taff End. The press were high up on halfway in the North Stand. Clem rushed down to get a look on the TV replay. Yes, he was right. They had dived, but the running stories of the match never mentioned the 'dives', simply because other journalists had not seen them. Andy Haden mimicked the dive on many future occasions. It was not sportsmanlike and both locks should have faced long suspensions. New Zealand replacement Brian McKechnie kicked his third penalty of the match and Wales had lost. The great respect held for skipper Graham Mourie went with it. The game had not lived up to expectations. New Zealand scored the only try, when Stu Wilson outsped the defence to gather Bill Osborne's clever kick ahead. Full-back Clive Currie had his jaw broken after a charge by Steve Fenwick and McKechnie, later an international cricketer, entered the match after only five minutes' play. Wales led 9–0 and then 12–4, but somehow never looked convincing. The new caps in this match were Paul Ringer for Wales and scrum-half Dave Loveridge for New Zealand. Ringer was a vastly underrated flanker, while Loveridge was the best scrum-half of his era.

Wales +J.P.R. Williams (Bridgend); J.J. Williams, R.W.R. Gravell (Llanelli), S.P. Fenwick (Bridgend), C.F.W. Rees (London Welsh); W.G. Davies, T.D. Holmes (Cardiff); A.G. Faulkner, R.W. Windsor, G. Price (Pontypool), G.A.D. Wheel (Swansea), A.J. Martin (Aberavon), J. Squire (Pontypool), D.L. Quinnell (Llanelli), *P. Ringer (Ebbw Vale).
P: Gareth Davies 3, Steve Fenwick.

New Zealand C.J. Currie (Canterbury); S.S. Wilson (Wellington), B.J. Robertson (Counties), W.M. Osborne (Wanganui), B.G. Williams (Auckland); O.D. Bruce (Canterbury), D.S. Loveridge (Taranaki); W.K. Bush (Canterbury), A.G. Dalton (Counties), B.R. Johnstone, A.M. Haden (Auckland), F.J. Oliver (Otago), +G.N.K. Mourie (Taranaki), G.A. Seear (Otago), L.M. Rutledge (Southland). Rep: B.J. McKechnie (Southland) for Currie.
T: Stu Wilson.
P: Brian McKechnie 3.
Referee: Roger C. Quittenton (England).

Wales 3 New Zealand 23

Arms Park, Cardiff. 1 November 1980

New Zealand won by 4 tries, 2 cons, 1 pen to 1 pen.

There was no diving from the All Blacks in the WRU Centenary year and they were back to their own excellent brand of rugby. Welshmen grumbled over the Nicky Allen and Hika Reid tries but generally accepted that it could have been a lot, lot worse. Graham Mourie led by example and his try was a gem, as new cap Rob Ackerman bought a half dummy by the flanker which most of Wales bought every time they watched it on TV. The All Blacks had defeated Cardiff, Llanelli, Swansea and Newport before this Test and though Ackerman and flanker Gareth Williams had good débuts, it was of little use. Allen touched down (or really bounced it down) and after the interval bustling Bernie Fraser and hooker Reid went over. Mourie and his main henchman Dave Loveridge called the tune. Sadly, Nicky Allen, a beautiful footballer, collapsed and died on the field in an Australian club match less than four years later. He was only 26 years old.

Wales J.P.R. Williams (Bridgend); H.E. Rees (Neath), D.S. Richards (Swansea), +S.P. Fenwick (Bridgend), *R.A. Ackerman (Newport); W.G. Davies, T.D. Holmes

Thirteen veterans prepare for a film of a fictitious match against New Zealand. The match ended as a draw when the ball burst on a crossbar! *Back row*: G. Price, D. Hughes, A. Martin, M. Roberts, D. Morris, A. Faulkner. *Seated*: R. Windsor, T.G.R. Davies, P. Bennett (capt.), G.O. Edwards, B. John, J.J. Williams.
(© Huw Evans)

(Cardiff); C. Williams (Swansea), A.J. Phillips (Cardiff), G. Price (Pontypool), D.L. Quinnell (Llanelli), A.J. Martin (Aberavon), J. Squire (Pontypool), *Gareth P. Williams (Bridgend), P. Ringer (Llanelli). Reps: P.J. Morgan (Llanelli) for Rees; E.T. Butler (Pontypool) for Squire.
P: Steve Fenwick.

New Zealand D.L. Rollerson (Manawatu); S.S. Wilson (Wellington), B.J. Robertson (Counties), W.M. Osborne (Wanganui), B.G. Fraser (Wellington); N.H. Allen (Counties), D.S. Loveridge (Taranaki); G.A. Knight (Manawatu), H.R. Reid (Bay of Plenty), R.C. Ketels (Counties), A.M. Haden (Auckland), G. Higginson (Canterbury), +G.N.K. Mourie (Taranaki), M.G. Mexted (Wellington), M.W. Shaw (Manawatu).
T: Graham Mourie, Nicky Allen, Bernie Fraser, Hika Reid.
C: Doug Rollerson 2.
P: Rollerson.
Referee: John R. West (Ireland).

(NB: RWC 1987 semi-final Wales v New Zealand)

New Zealand 52 Wales 3 – 1st Test

Lancaster Park Oval, Christchurch. 28 May 1988

New Zealand won by 10 tries, 6 cons to 1 pen.

Wales have never been at their best on tours, but this was one of their worst. If it had been a boxing contest, the referee would have stopped it long before the end. As it was, the tour ended with a beating from Waikato followed by a hiding in Wellington. Outside the Tests, there was also a loss to North Auckland, a draw and only two victories. In all, 243 points were conceded in eight matches. Robert Norster was the 100th captain of Wales. He would want to forget it, as New Zealand ran in ten tries, with Glen Webbe overrun by the incredible John Kirwan, who touched down four times.

New Zealand J.A. Gallagher (Wellington); J.J. Kirwan, J.T. Stanley (Auckland), W.T. Taylor (Canterbury), T.J. Wright; G.J. Fox (Auckland), I.B. Deans (Canterbury); S.C. McDowell, S.B.T. Fitzpatrick (Auckland), R.W. Loe (Waikato), M.J. Pierce (Wellington), G.W. Whetton, A.J. Whetton (Auckland), +W.T. Shelford (North Harbour), M.N. Jones (Auckland).

A smiling Jonathan Davies, followed by Rowland Phillips and Glen Webbe as they prepare to leave for the tour to New Zealand in 1988. There would soon be little to smile at. (© Huw Evans)

T: John Kirwan 4, Terry Wright 2, Gary Whetton, Bruce Deans, Wayne Shelford, John Gallagher.
C: Grant Fox 6.

Wales A. Clement (Swansea); I.C. Evans (Llanelli), J.A. Devereux (Bridgend), M.G. Ring (Pontypool), G.M.C. Webbe (Bridgend); Jonathan Davies (Llanelli), R.N. Jones (Swansea); S.T. Jones (Pontypool), K.H. Phillips (Neath), D. Young (Swansea), P.S. May (Llanelli), +R.L. Norster (Cardiff), R.D. Phillips (Neath), W.P. Moriarty (Swansea), *D.J. Bryant (Bridgend/SG Inst). Reps: *M.R. Hall (Bridgend/Cambridge U) for Clement; *T.J. Fauvel (Aberavon) for Moriarty.
P: Mark Ring.
Referee: Guy Maurette (France).

New Zealand 54 Wales 9 – 2nd Test

Eden Park, Auckland. 11 June 1988

New Zealand won by 8 tries, 8 cons, 2 pens to 1 try, 1 con, 1 pen.

With tour captain Bleddyn Bowen out with a fractured wrist and his deputy, Bob Norster, suffering from a gashed knee, Wales turned to Jonathan Davies for leadership. The outside-half scored a brilliant try from a move started by Mark Ring and replacement Jonathan Mason on the Wales line, but it was all in vain. Davies played his heart out, only for Wayne Shelford's side to score eight tries and Grant Fox to kick ten goals in a haul of 22 points. The popular Llanelli scrum-half Jonathan Griffiths made his début. As with four others in the side, he later switched to rugby league.

New Zealand J.A. Gallagher (Wellington); J.J. Kirwan, J.T. Stanley (Auckland), W.T. Taylor (Canterbury), T.J. Wright; G.J. Fox (Auckland), I.B. Deans (Canterbury); S.C. McDowell, S.B.T. Fitzpatrick (Auckland), R.W. Loe (Waikato), M.J. Pierce (Wellington), G.W. Whetton, A.J. Whetton (Auckland), +W.T. Shelford (North Harbour), M.N. Jones (Auckland).
T: John Kirwan 2, Terry Wright 2, Bruce Deans, Steve McDowell, Warwick Taylor, Michael Jones.
C: Grant Fox 8.
P: Fox 2.

Wales M.G. Ring (Pontypool); I.C. Evans, *N.G. Davies (Llanelli), J.A. Devereux (Bridgend), M.R. Hall (Bridgend/Cambridge U); +Jonathan Davies, *J.L. Griffiths (Llanelli); S.T. Jones (Pontypool), I.J. Watkins (Ebbw Vale), D. Young (Swansea), P.S. May (Llanelli), *K. Moseley (Pontypool), *G. Jones (Llanelli), R.D. Phillips (Neath), D.J. Bryant (Bridgend/SG Inst). Reps: *J.E. Mason (Pontypridd) for Hall; M.A. Jones (Neath) for Phillips.
T: Jonathan Davies.
C: Mark Ring.
P: Ring.
Referee: Guy Maurette (France).

Wales 9 New Zealand 34

Arms Park, Cardiff. 4 November 1989

New Zealand won by 4 tries, 3 cons, 4 pens to 3 pens.

Wayne Shelford's all-conquering squad played 14 and won 14. They defeated Cardiff, Pontypool, Swansea,

Neath, Llanelli and Newport, and there was some relief that Wales conceded only four tries against them. Times had changed. Now Wales were settling for any score under 50 against New Zealand. Gareth Llewellyn began his international career and Robert Jones captained Wales for the first time. For New Zealand there were try-scoring débuts for Craig Innes and Graeme Bachop. Wales hung on at 6–12 after 40 minutes, and then 6–15 before New Zealand scored three more tries.

Wales P.H. Thorburn (Neath); M.R. Hall (Bridgend), M.G. Ring, D.W. Evans (Cardiff), A. Emyr; A. Clement, +R.N. Jones (Swansea); M. Griffiths (Bridgend), K.H. Phillips (Neath), D. Young (Cardiff), P.T. Davies (Llanelli), *G.O. Llewellyn, *P. Pugh, M.A. Jones (Neath), G. Jones (Llanelli).
P: Paul Thorburn 3.

New Zealand J.A. Gallagher (Wellington); C.R. Innes, J.T. Stanley (Auckland), N.J. Schuster (Wellington), T.J. Wright; G.J. Fox (Auckland), G.T.M. Bachop (Canterbury); S.C. McDowell (Bay of Plenty), S.B.T. Fitzpatrick (Auckland), R.W. Loe (Waikato), G.W. Whetton (Auckland), M.J. Pierce (Wellington), A.T. Earl (Canterbury), +W.T. Shelford (North Harbour), M.R. Brewer (Otago).
T: Craig Innes 2, Graeme Bachop, Terry Wright.
C: Grant Fox 3.
P: Fox 4.
Referee: A.R. 'Sandy' MacNeill (Australia).

(NB: RWC 1995 Wales v New Zealand)

Wales 7 New Zealand 42

Wembley, London. 29 November 1997

New Zealand won by 5 tries, 4 cons, 2 pens, 1 drop goal to 1 try, 1 con.

Matches at Wrexham and Swansea were only a prelude to playing home matches at Wembley as work commenced on the new Millennium Stadium in Cardiff. Because of the venue, it meant that Wales appeared in front of their largest-ever 'home' crowd of 76,000. Sean Fitzpatrick, dogged by injury, led New Zealand on their nine-match tour, in which they defeated Llanelli 81–3 and Wales 'A' 51–8, as well as Ireland and England. Wales were the opposition in game seven, but England were to meet New Zealand again in the final tour match and draw 26–26. Though Fitzpatrick was not fit enough to skipper at Wembley (the honour being handed to Justin Marshall), he did appear for 25 minutes, to win his 92nd and final cap. When Wales won in 1953, they led 3–1 on victories, but now it was 3–14! There was bad luck when Scott Gibbs came off with a badly cut eyebrow after 26 minutes and full-back Christian Cullen swept in for three of the five tries, despite good tackling by Allan Bateman, Leigh Davies and Nigel Walker in particular. Walker twice hauled down the elusive Jeff Wilson, who had scored 24 tries in 34 Tests. Cullen had scored 21 tries in 21 Tests! The match closed with Zinzan Brooke's third Test drop goal being struck in the last moments of his 57th and penultimate Test appearance. Walker's excellent form in defence and attack – he scored the only Welsh try – did him little good. He was dropped by coach Kevin Bowring, which did little for morale.

Wales K.A. Morgan (Pontypridd); G. Thomas (Bridgend), A.G. Bateman (Richmond), I.S. Gibbs (Swansea), N.K. Walker (Cardiff); N.R. Jenkins (Pontypridd), R. Howley (Cardiff); C.D. Loader (Swansea), B.H. Williams (Richmond), D. Young (Cardiff), G.O. Llewellyn (Harlequins), M.J. Voyle (Llanelli), R.C. Appleyard (Swansea), N. Thomas (Bath), +R.G. Jones (Cardiff). Reps: A.C. Thomas (Swansea) for Bateman (temp); L.B. Davies (Cardiff) for Gibbs; J.M. Humphreys (Cardiff) for B.H. Williams; S.M. Williams (Cardiff) for N. Thomas; S.C. John (Cardiff) for Loader.
T: Nigel Walker.
C: Neil Jenkins.

New Zealand C. Cullen (Central Vikings); J.W. Wilson (Otago), F.E. Bunce, W.K. Little (North Harbour), J.T. Lomu (Counties); A.P. Mehrtens, +J.W. Marshall (Canterbury); C.W. Dowd (Auckland), N.J. Hewitt (Southland), O.M. Brown (Auckland), I.D. Jones (North Harbour), R.M. Brooke (Auckland), T.C. Randell (Otago), Z.V. Brooke (Auckland), J.A. Kronfeld (Otago). Reps: S.B.T. Fitzpatrick (Auckland) for Hewitt; M.R. Allen (Manawatu) for Brown; A. Blowers (Auckland) for Randell; S.J. McLeod (Waikato) for Little (temp).
T: Christian Cullen 3, Taine Randell, Justin Marshall.
C: Andrew Mehrtens 4.
P: Mehrtens 2.
DG: Zinzan Brooke.
Referee: Wayne J. Erickson (Australia).

SOUTH AFRICA

Wales 0 South Africa 11

St Helen's, Swansea. 1 December 1906

South Africa won by 3 tries, 1 con to nil.

Despite fielding many of the 'great names' of early Welsh rugby, Wales failed to score against a very formidable Springbok side. It was rated the poorest performance by Wales for ten years and Percy Bush and Dicky Owen were never paired again, but it was up front where Paul Roos and his pack were in complete control. Opposing centres Japie Krige and Gwyn Nicholls were rated the world's best, though Krige took the honours on this occasion, making a try for Bob Loubser, who resisted a magnificent effort by new cap John Dyke to halt him. The Springbok knocked himself out in the dive for the line. Centre 'Boy' de Villiers called the Dyke tackle 'a superhuman effort', whilst tour vice-captain Paddy Carolin did not play, but commented: 'We were a happy band that night.' Defeat was accepted well by the 40,000 crowd, some of whom carried Roos and full-back Arthur Marsberg off shoulder-high from the field. Meanwhile, injured skipper Gwyn Nicholls did not attend the post-match dinner, nor did he play for Wales again. However, wing Johnnie Williams made his début and was later to star in Cardiff's 17–0 win over the Springboks. After he swerved past Marsberg, the full-back was to shake the wing's hand for doing so. Williams went on to score 17 tries in as many matches for Wales. He died during the Battle of the Somme at the age of only 34.

Wales *J.C.M. Dyke (Penarth); E. Morgan (London Welsh), +E.G. Nicholls, R.T. Gabe, *J.L. Williams; P.F. Bush (Cardiff), R.M. Owen; W. Joseph (Swansea), G. Travers (Pill Harriers), D. Jones (Treherbert), A.F. Harding, *J.C. Jenkins, J.F. Williams (London Welsh), C.M. 'Charlie' Pritchard (Newport), *E.J. Thomas (Mountain Ash).

South Africa A.F.W. Marsberg (Griqualand West); S. Joubert, H.A. de Villiers, J.D. Krige, J.A. Loubser; D.C. Jackson (Western Province), F.J. Dobbin (Griqualand West); +P. Roos (Western Province), W.A. Burger (Border), H.J. Daneel, P.A. le Roux, D.J. Brink (Western Province), W.C. Martheze, J.W.E. Raaff (Griqualand West), W.S. Morkel (Transvaal).

T: Steve Joubert, Bob Loubser, 'Klondyke' Raaff.
C: Joubert.
Referee: Arthur Owen Jones (England).

Wales 0 South Africa 3

Arms Park, Cardiff. 14 December 1912

South Africa won by 1 pen to nil.

The Springbok head had already fallen at Newport, with Fred Birt scoring a goal and a drop goal for a 9–3 win for his club. But for Wales, in heavy rain and against a gale-force wind, he failed with a simple penalty, whilst Springbok forward Douglas Morkel landed one from similar range to win the match. It was the first loss at Cardiff since 1899 and the match was decided when Rees Thomas, a Pontypool collier, was penalised for offside, having been forced in front of the ball at a loose scrummage. Wales fielded nine newcomers, with outside-half Horace Wyndham Thomas, who won a Cambridge Blue in the same week, narrowly missing a drop-kick, as did Vile. They would have been worth four points and either one would have won the match. 'We were lucky to win it,' conceded South African captain Billy Millar, who had won the toss and decided to play with the elements. Thomas died four years later in the Battle of the Somme and fellow newcomers Billy Geen and Fred Perrett were also to die in action. Juan Morgan, the only Argentinian to play for Wales, returned home by ship after playing in the next match against England. Rees Stephens, the son of Glyn, was to play for Wales against South Africa on the same ground 39 years later. The Springboks just edged out Llanelli (8–7), Neath (9–3) and Cardiff (7–6) before Swansea followed Newport's example with a 3–0 win, following a try by a former international forward, David Thomas.

Wales *R.F. Williams (Cardiff); *W.P. Geen, F.W. Birt (Newport), W. Spiller (Cardiff), R.C.S. Plummer (Newport); *H.W. Thomas (Swansea/Cambridge U), +T.H. Vile (Newport); G. Stephens, *F.L. Perrett (Neath), *W.H. Wetter, *P.L. Jones (Newport), *F. Andrews, R. Thomas (Pontypool), *B.G. Hollingdale (Swansea), *J.L. Morgan (Llanelli).

South Africa P.G. Morkel; J.A. Stegmann, R.R. Luyt, J. Morkel (Western Province), E.E. McHardy (OFS); F.P. Luyt (Western Province), F.J. Dobbin (Griqualand West); +W.A. Millar, W.H.

Wales 3   South Africa 8

St Helen's, Swansea. 5 December 1931

South Africa won by 2 tries, 1 con to 1 try.

As usual in a Wales–South Africa meeting, the conditions were bad, with pools of water on the pitch. It did not favour the tourists, but Bennie Osler's side adapted magnificently. Making his début in Test rugby was the 20-year-old Danie Craven, who gained the nod at scrum-half from skipper Osler over the experienced Pierre de Villiers. It was Osler who dictated the tactics, with the boot being used freely, as he guided his side, and his new partner in particular, through the match. Wales drew first blood when, after being halted, the slippery wing Ronnie Boon had another go, but this time sent up a kick that eluded Morris Zimmerman. The ball was driven over the line by Swansea wing forward Will Davies, playing in his first international match. That was how it stayed until the second half, when it was Welsh captain and full-back Jack Bassett who held up the relentless Springbok pressure. An Osler kick ahead was followed by Ferdie Bergh, who dribbled it on for George Daneel to just win the touchdown and make it 3–3. Another fine piece of dribbling by the Springbok pack in the watery conditions saw Bergh score what proved to be the winning try and Osler, who took over the kicking from Gerry Brand, converted. Wales refused to quit, however, and it was now the turn of South Africa, who lost only to the Midland Counties at Leicester on this tour, to defend stoutly. They did so, though Jack Morley came close to scoring. (NB: In Britain, the Springbok skipper was often shown as Benny Osler, but he preferred it as Bennie.)

Wales +J.A. Bassett (Penarth); J.C. Morley (Newport), E.C. Davey (Swansea), F.L. Williams, R.W. Boon (Cardiff); A.R. Ralph (Newport), W.C. Powell (London Welsh); T.B. Day (Swansea), F.A. Bowdler (Cross Keys), A. Skym (Cardiff), T. Arthur (Neath), E.M. Jenkins (Aberavon), *W. Davies, W.G. Thomas (Swansea), A.W. Lemon (Neath).
T: Will Davies.

South Africa G.H. Brand; M. Zimerman, B.G. Gray (Western Province), J. White (Border), F.D. Venter (Transvaal); +B.L. Osler (Western Province), D.H. Craven (Stellenbosch U); P.J. Mostert (Western Province), H.G. Kipling (Griqualand West), M.M. 'Boy' Louw (Western Province), W.F. Bergh (South-West Districts), P.J. Nel (Natal), G.M. Daneel (Transvaal), A.J. Macdonald (Western Province), A. van der Merwe (Worcester).
T: George Daneel, Ferdie Bergh.
C: Bennie Osler.
Referee: E. Holmes (England).

Wales 3   South Africa 6

Arms Park, Cardiff. 22 December 1951

South Africa won by 1 try, 1 drop goal to 1 try.

South African full-back Johnny Buchler and wing 'Chum' Ochse must have enjoyed Cardiff Arms Park more than any other ground. Ochse had scored two tries and Buchler had played immaculately against Cardiff and both were again outstanding, though Buchler was helped by some bad kicking by Cliff Morgan. The little Welsh genius had an 'off' day and often sent the ball direct to Buchler, while the bald head of Basie van Wyk was evident in curbing Morgan, along with his brilliant back-row colleagues Hennie Muller and Stephen Fry. Roy John was on top in the lineout and the pack, with lock Don Hayward tried out successfully as a prop, won their share of possession. South Africa struck just before half-time, when Hannes Brewis and Tjol Lategan combined to send Ochse in at the corner just ahead of Ken Jones and Gerwyn Williams. With ten minutes to go, Brewis dropped a fine goal, but in the gathering gloom Wales produced a superb try when John Gwilliam handed direct to Morgan, who passed to Bleddyn Williams. The Cardiff centre called a scissors move and took a return pass from Malcolm Thomas to dive over near the corner at the Taff End of the ground. Bleddyn had previously scored for Cardiff in an 11–9 defeat by South Africa, who won all five Tests and only lost 11–9 to the London Counties at Twickenham.

Wales G. Williams (Llanelli); K.J. Jones, M.C. Thomas (Newport), B.L. Williams (Cardiff), B.L. Jones (Llanelli); C.I. Morgan, W.R. Willis (Cardiff); W.O.G. Williams (Swansea), D.M. Davies (Somerset Police), Don J. Hayward (Newbridge), E.R. John, J.R.G. Stephens (Neath), *L.G. Blyth (Swansea), +J.A. Gwilliam (Edinburgh Wands), A. Forward (Pontypool).
T: Bleddyn Williams.

South Africa J.U. Buchler (Transvaal); P.G. Johnstone (Western Province), R.A.M. van Schoor (Rhodesia), M.T. Lategan, J.K. Ochse (Western

Province); J.D. Brewis, P.A. du Toit (Northern Transvaal); A.O. Geffin (Transvaal), W.H. Delport (Eastern Province), A.C. Koch (Boland), W.H.M. Barnard (Griqualand West), J.A. du Rand (Rhodesia), S.P. Fry (Western Province), +H.S.V. Muller, C.J. van Wyk (Transvaal).
T: Chum Ochse.
DG: Hannes Brewis.
Referee: Noel H. Lambert (Ireland).

Wales 0 South Africa 3

Arms Park, Cardiff. 3 December 1960

South Africa won by 1 pen to nil.

Bad weather had often dogged matches at the Arms Park, but never had it been as bad as the Saturday and Sunday of 3 and 4 December. The wind was so strong and the rain so hard that many supporters reached Westgate Street and turned back on trolley-buses to watch the match on television sets. By the following day, the River Taff had broken its banks and completely flooded the pitch. A Five Nations match would not have taken place, but this was a tour and the Springboks were on a tight schedule. Welsh skipper Terry Davies had won the toss, but decided – unwisely, as it later transpired – to play against the gale. The match was won by a goal kicked by outside-half Keith Oxlee from under the posts, after new cap Tony O'Connor was adjudged not to have put the ball in straight at a scrummage. Oxlee even required the ball to be held for him by Piet Uys in the gale-force wind. Referee Taylor actually asked the captains if they wanted to call it off some 15 minutes from full-time, but Davies wished to carry on. For the powerful Springboks, Doug Hopwood and the one-eyed flanker Martin Pelser gained ground in rugby league style and Lionel Wilson was calm at full-back. Wales once came close to a try, with Danny Harris just being denied in a dive for the corner. Only one match was to be lost on the tour by the South Africans – the final one, by 6–0 to the Barbarians at Cardiff. Six players made their international débuts, with one of them, wing Denis Evans, never selected again. He did, however, become secretary of the WRU. Of the others, David Nash was to become the first official Welsh coach, while Ken Richards turned professional at the end of the season.

Wales +T.J. Davies; *D.P. Evans (Llanelli), C.A.H. Davies, *H.M. Roberts (Cardiff), D.I.E. Bebb (Swansea); *K.H.L. Richards (Bridgend), *A. O'Connor (Aberavon); T.R. Prosser (Pontypool), B.V. Meredith (Newport), *K.D. Jones, D.J.E. Harris (Cardiff), W.R. Evans (Bridgend), G.D. Davidge (Newport), *D. Nash (Ebbw Vale), J. Leleu (Swansea).

South Africa L.G. Wilson; F. du T. Roux (Western Province), A.I. Kirkpatrick (Griqualand West), J.L. Gainsford, J.P. Engelbrecht (Western Province); K. Oxlee (Natal), P. de W. Uys (Northern Transvaal); S.P. Kuhn (Transvaal), R.A. Hill (Rhodesia), P.S. du Toit (Western Province), +A.S. Malan (Transvaal), J.T. Claassen (Western Transvaal), G.H. van Zyl, D.J. Hopwood (Western Province), H.J.M. Pelser (Transvaal).
P: Keith Oxlee.
Referee: Jack A.S. Taylor (Scotland).

South Africa 24 Wales 3

King's Park, Durban. 23 May 1964

South Africa won by 3 tries, 3 cons, 2 pens, 1 drop goal to 1 pen.

Wales undertook their first tour during the SARB's 75th anniversary and fell to their biggest defeat for 40 years. In the heat at Durban, the Springboks ran them off their feet in the final quarter. Not since Inverleith in 1924 had Wales taken such a hammering, though they were level at half-time and Norman Gale won the tight-head count by 6–3. Brian Price jumped well in the lineout, but it was in the loose that the Springbok pack excelled, with Hannes Marais and Doug Hopwood scoring tries before scrum-half Nelie Smith crossed for the final score. Keith Oxlee, who had won the 1960 match at Cardiff, kicked 12 points, and though Wales tackled bravely, they were well beaten. In other tour matches, Wales beat East Africa 26–8, Boland 17–6 and Orange Free State 14–6, but lost 9–22 to Northern Transvaal at Pretoria.

South Africa L.G. Wilson; J.P. Engelbrecht, J.L. Gainsford, D.A. Stewart (Western Province), C.G. Dirksen (Northern Transvaal); K. Oxlee (Natal), C.M. Smith (OFS); J.L. Myburgh (Northern Transvaal), +G.F. Malan, J.F.K. Marais (Western Province), G. Carelse (Eastern Province), A.S. Malan (Transvaal), F.C.H. du Preez (Northern Transvaal), D.J. Hopwood (Western Province), T.P. Bedford (Natal).
T: Hannes Marais, Doug Hopwood, Nelie Smith.
C: Keith Oxlee 3.
P: Oxlee 2.
DG: Lionel Wilson.

Wales G.T.R. Hodgson (Neath); D.K. Jones (Llanelli), S.J. Dawes (London Welsh), K. Bradshaw (Bridgend), D.I.E. Bebb (Swansea); D. Watkins (Newport), +D.C.T. Rowlands (Pontypool); D. Williams (Ebbw Vale), N.R. Gale (Llanelli), L.J. Cunningham (Aberavon), B. Price (Newport), B.E. Thomas (Neath),

A.E.I. Pask (Abertillery), J.T. Mantle (Newport), Dai J. Hayward (Cardiff).
P: Keith Bradshaw.
Referee: Dr G.K. Engelbrecht (South Africa).

Wales 6   South Africa 6

Arms Park, Cardiff. 24 January 1970

Draw. 1 try, 1 pen each.

Anti-apartheid demonstrations disrupted the Springbok tour. Tests against England and Scotland were lost and Ireland held them to a draw, so Wales had a real chance to defeat South Africa for the first time. It was not to be, but there was a dramatic ending to the match. The Arms Park was covered in thick mud, as was so often the case for post-war international matches. It was a day of barbed wire and police, but surprisingly it was one of the few peaceful matches of the tour. The weather was almost a replica of that during the 1960 match and it was again South Africa who adapted better, with their back row of Piet Greyling, Tommy Bedford and Jan Ellis in control.

Henry de Villiers landed a penalty when Barry John was caught offside, and after Gareth Edwards had landed a similar goal, wing Syd Nomis scored from a blind-side move eight minutes into the second half. Time was almost up when Wales scored in dramatic fashion. Phil Bennett – too good to leave out, so selected on the wing – threw infield for John to punt across field. Up came Ian Hall to tackle Nomis and somehow Barry Llewelyn emerged to give Edwards a sniff of the corner-flag. The scrum-half defeated both the clinging mud and a good Hannes Marais tackle to score in the north corner at the Westgate-Street end. Despite the presence of John and Bennett, Edwards was the skipper. He decided to take the conversion kick himself, but he was too exhausted and the conditions helped defeat his effort to win the match.

Wales J.P.R. Williams (London Welsh); P. Bennett (Llanelli), S.J. Dawes (London Welsh), W.H. Raybould (Newport), I. Hall (Aberavon); B. John, +G.O. Edwards (Cardiff); D. Williams (Ebbw Vale), *V.C. Perrins, *D.B. Llewelyn (Newport), W.D. Thomas (Llanelli), *T.G. Evans (London Welsh), W.D. Morris (Neath), T.M. Davies (London Welsh), D. Hughes (Newbridge).
T: Gareth Edwards.
P: Edwards.

South Africa H.O. de Villiers (Western Province); S.H. Nomis (Transvaal), O.A. Roux (Northern Transvaal), J.P. van der Merwe, G.H. Muller; M.J. Lawless (Western Province), +D.J. de Villiers (Boland); J.L. Myburgh (Northern Transvaal), C.H. Cockrell (Western Province), J.F.K. Marais (Eastern Province), F.C.H. du Preez (Northern Transvaal), I.J. de Klerk, P.J.F. Greyling (Transvaal), T.P. Bedford (Natal), J.H. Ellis (South-West Africa).
T: Syd Nomis.
P: Henry de Villiers.
Referee: G.C. 'Larry' Lamb (England).

Wales 12   South Africa 20

Arms Park, Cardiff. 26 November 1994

South Africa won by 3 tries, 1 con, 1 pen to 4 pens.

South Africa won 11 of the 13 matches on their tour of Britain, losing to Scotland A and the Barbarians. In Wales, they defeated Llanelli, Neath, Swansea, Pontypridd and Wales A. Swansea received a 78-7 battering and, with Scotland beaten 34-10 in Murrayfield, the outlook looked black for Wales. With Ieuan Evans out of action, Gareth Llewellyn again won the captaincy and had new cap Derwyn Jones to aid him at the lineout. Jones, at six foot ten, worried the Springboks and gave Llewellyn room. The pair gained Wales a big advantage. Four Neil Jenkins kicks took Wales ahead at 12–10, but South Africa rallied and Chester Williams scored a decisive try. Full-back André Joubert was outstanding and Rudi Straeuli, who had played for Penarth as a teenager, was the pick of the South African pack.

Wales A. Clement (Swansea); W.T. Proctor (Llanelli), M.R. Hall (Cardiff), *M. Taylor (Pontypool), S.D. Hill (Cardiff); N.R. Jenkins (Pontypridd), R.H.StJ.B. Moon; R.L. Evans (Llanelli), G.R. Jenkins (Swansea), J.D. Davies (Neath), *D. Jones (Cardiff), +G.O. Llewellyn (Neath), H.T. Taylor, E.W. Lewis (Cardiff), R.G. Collins (Pontypridd). Rep: R.C. McBryde (Llanelli) for G.R. Jenkins (temp).
P: Neil Jenkins 4.

South Africa A.J. Joubert (Natal); P. Hendriks (Transvaal), P.G. Muller (Natal), J.C. Mulder (Gauteng Lions), C.M. Williams (Western Province); H.P. le Roux (Trasnvaal), J.H. van der Westhuizen (Northern Transvaal); J.P. du Randt (Free State), U.L. Schmidt (Northern Transvaal), T.G. Laubscher (Western Province), M.G. Andrews (Natal), P.J.W. Schutte, +J.F. Pienaar (Transvaal), R.A.W. Straeuli (Transvaal), R.J. Kruger (Northern Transvaal).
T: Rudi Straeuli, André Joubert, Chester Williams.
C: Hennie le Roux.
P: le Roux.
Referee: Didier Méné (France).

The tallest-ever Welsh international player, lock Derwyn Jones, wins a good lineout ball. The big Cardiff forward moved to Bedford and then France.
(© Huw Evans)

South Africa 40 Wales 11

Ellis Park, Johannesburg. 2 September 1995

South Africa won by 5 tries, 3 cons, 3 pens to 1 try, 2 pens.

South Africa made their first appearance since winning the World Cup 70 days earlier. It seemed a senseless two-match trip for Wales and proved to be just that. The defeat by 47–6 to South-East Transvaal at Witbank was one of the biggest-ever disasters for a Wales XV. Alex Evans chose a young squad for what was his last match in charge. An early Mark Bennett try did a lot for confidence, despite Wales having lost lock Derwyn Jones after just five minutes' play. A knockout punch on Jones from behind by Kobus Wiese earned the Springbok a suspension of just 30 days, when a much longer ban should have been in force. Incredibly, referee Joël Dumé did not send Wiese off. He did, however, dismiss hooker Garin Jenkins, playing as a replacement flanker, for punching scrum-half Joost van der Westhuizen. Jenkins was also banned for 30 days. Jonathan Humphreys skippered Wales in his third appearance, all made at Ellis Park. Neil Jenkins went through 400 points for Wales with the first of his penalty goals, achieving this feat in his 37th appearance.

South Africa A.J. Joubert (Natal); J.T. Small (Western Province), J.C. Mulder (Guateng Lions), H.P. le Roux (Transvaal), J. Olivier (Northern Transvaal); J.T. Stransky (Western Province), J.H. van der Westhuizen (Northern Transvaal); I.S. Swart, J. Dalton (Transvaal), M.H. Hurter (Northern Transvaal), J.J. Wiese (Transvaal), M.G. Andrews (Natal), +J.F. Pienaar (Transvaal), G.H. Teichmann (Natal), R.J. Kruger (Northern Transvaal).
T: Kobus Wiese, James Small, Gary Teichmann, Japie Mulder, François Pienaar.
C: Joel Stransky 3.
P: Stransky 3.

Wales *W.J.L. Thomas; I.C. Evans (Llanelli), *G.H. Jones, G. Thomas (Bridgend), S.D. Hill (Cardiff); N.R. Jenkins (Pontypridd), Andy P. Moore (Cardiff); *C.D. Loader (Swansea), +J.M. Humphreys (Cardiff), J.D. Davies (Neath), P. Arnold (Swansea), D. Jones (Cardiff), A. Gibbs (Newbridge), H.T. Taylor, A.M. Bennett (Cardiff). Reps: M. Taylor (Swansea) for G. Thomas; *Andrew P. Moore (Swansea) for D. Jones; G.R. Jenkins (Swansea) for Gibbs.
Sent off: Garin Jenkins.
T: Mark Bennett.
P: Neil Jenkins 2.
Referee: Joël Dumé (France).

Wales 20 South Africa 37

Arms Park, Cardiff. 15 December 1996

South Africa won by 5 tries, 3 cons, 2 pens to 1 try, 5 pens.

Just two weeks after playing Australia, Wales took on the world champions. The Boks had lost twice on a nine-match tour of Argentina and France, but had won all four Test matches. This was the only match played in Britain and such were the demands on international players that South African skipper Gary Teichmann was winning his 14th cap, just 15 months after making his début against Wales in Johannesburg. The New Zealand-born Dale 'Chief' McIntosh was one of two new men in the pack from the Pontypridd club. Normally a number 8, he played on the flank of the scrum. In the centre was Allan Bateman, yet another player back from rugby league.

The score did not really reflect the margin between the sides, though the 5–1 try-count did. Springbok scrum-half Joost van der Westhuizen became the first player to score three tries in a Test against Wales on Welsh territory.

Wales N.R. Jenkins (Pontypridd); I.C. Evans (Llanelli), A.G. Bateman (Richmond), I.S. Gibbs (Swansea), D.R. James (Bridgend); A.C. Thomas (Swansea), R. Howley (Cardiff); C.D. Loader (Swansea), +J.M. Humphreys, D. Young (Cardiff), G.O. Llewellyn (Harlequins), *M.A. Rowley, *D.L.M. McIntosh (Pontypridd), S.M. Williams (Neath), C.L. Charvis (Swansea). Rep: *N. Thomas (Bath) for McIntosh.
T: Arwel Thomas.
P: Neil Jenkins 5.

South Africa A.J. Joubert; J.T. Small (Natal), J.C. Mulder, H.P. le Roux (Transvaal), J. Olivier (Northern Transvaal); H.W. Honiball (Natal), J.H. van der Westhuizen (Northern Transvaal); D. Theron (Griqualand West), J. Dalton (Transvaal), A.C. Garvey (Natal), J.J. Wiese (Transvaal), M.G. Andrews (Natal), R.J. Kruger (Northern Transvaal), +G. Teichmann (Natal), A.G. Venter (OFS). Reps: A.H. Snyman (Northern Transvaal) for Olivier; A. van der Linde (Western Province) for Theron; J.J. Strydom (Transvaal) for Andrews.
T: Joost van der Westhuizen 3, André Joubert, Jacques Olivier.
C: Henry Honiball 2, Joubert.
P: Honiball 2.
Referee: Steve J.D. Lander (England).

South Africa 96 Wales 13

Loftus Versfeld, Pretoria. 27 June 1998

South Africa won by 15 tries, 9 cons, 1 pen to 1 try, 1 con, 2 pens.

Tour skipper Robert Howley missed the Test after being injured against Natal and David Llewellyn was rushed out by plane, to appear for only one minute to replace Paul John. Five other players made their débuts, as Wales were 'lambs to the slaughter' against opponents who searched for a century of points but were denied by a last-second knock-on. Welsh journalist Paul Rees commented, 'Once we were unhappy when we lost by a point; then losing by 20 was a disaster. It soon became a case of hoping New Zealand would not beat us by over 50 points and now we were being thankful that South Africa had only scored 96!' Kingsley Jones was the new captain of Wales, though he did not finish the match. One hero was little Arwel Thomas, who scored a fine try and also added all the goal points. For South Africa, centre-turned-full-back Percy Montgomery scored 31 points and ten players shared the 15 tries. Gary Teichmann, Franco Smith and Robbie Kempson all signed for Newport in 1999. No Cardiff player appeared, for the first time since the game against Ireland in 1989 – 85 matches ago.

South Africa P.C. Montgomery (Western Province); C.S. Terblanche (Boland), A.H. Snyman (Western Province), P.G. Muller (Natal), P. Rossouw (Western Province); P.F. Smith (Gauteng Lions), J.H. van der Westhuizen (Blue Bulls); R.B. Kempson (Natal), J. Dalton (Gauteng Lions), A.C. Garvey (Natal), K. Otto (Blue Bulls), M.G. Andrews (Natal), J. Erasmus (Free State), +G.H. Teichmann (Natal), A.G. Venter (Free State). Reps: McNeil Hendricks (Boland) for Terblanche; H.W. Honiball (Natal) for Muller; W. Swanepoel (Free State) for van der Westhuizen; A.E. Drotske (Free State) for Dalton; A.H. 'Ollie' le Roux (Natal) for Garvey; R.B. Skinstad (Western Province) for Andrews; A.D. Aitken (Western Province) for Teichmann.
T: Pieter Rossouw 3, Stefan Terblanche 2, Percy Montgomery 2, André Venter 2, Franco Smith, Johan Erasmus, Krynauw Otto, McNeil Hendricks, Joost van der Westhuizen, Bobby Skinstad.
C: Montgomery 9.
P: Montgomery.

Wales B.I. Hayward (Ebbw Vale); *G.R. Evans (Llanelli), M. Taylor (Swansea), J. Funnell (Ebbw Vale), D.R. James (Pontypridd); A.C. Thomas (Swansea), P. John; M. Griffiths (Pontypridd), B.H. Williams, J.D. Davies (Richmond), Andrew P. Moore (Swansea), *I. Gough (Newport), N. Thomas (Bath), C.L. Charvis (Swansea), +K.P. Jones (Ebbw Vale). Reps: *D. Williams (Llanelli) for Hayward; *S.M. Jones (Llanelli) for Funnell; *D.S. Llewellyn (Ebbw Vale) for John; G.R. Jenkins (Swansea) for (B.H.) Williams; D.R. Morris (Neath) for Davies; *G. Lewis (Pontypridd) for Charvis; C.P. Wyatt (Llanelli) for (K.P.) Jones.
T: Arwel Thomas.
C: Arwel Thomas.
P: Arwel Thomas 2.
Referee: Paddy D. O'Brien (New Zealand).

Centre Mark Taylor helps to make 13 lucky for Wales! – his try gave Wales their first win over South Africa after 11 defeats and a draw. Full-back Shane Howarth is second from the right in this 1999 encounter at Cardiff. (© Huw Evans)

Wales 20 South Africa 28

Wembley, London. 14 November 1998

South Africa won by 3 tries, 2 cons, 3 pens to 1 try, 5 pens.

Dennis John had urged the WRU to pick a Welshman as coach, but Auckland's Graham Henry was the man chosen to be the 13th (unlucky for some) in charge. Henry's opening match of his five-year contract should have given him nightmares. Since the massacre of Pretoria, the world champions had brushed aside New Zealand (twice), Australia (twice) and England. But this was almost the biggest upset in the history of international rugby, as Wales led 20–17 with three minutes remaining, when Franco Smith placed a penalty over to equalise. Another two minutes elapsed before Joost van der Westhuizen broke to the blind-side and threw a pass that hit Johan Erasmus on the shoulder and bounced kindly for André Venter to score. Even then, eight minutes of injury time were played, with Smith kicking another penalty, as much to waste time as to add to the winning margin. Henry was now King Henry. He had almost achieved the impossible. It was a victory even in defeat. A fine three-quarter move saw Gareth Thomas score the opening points and with Neil Jenkins placing a hat-trick of goals to go over 600 points for Wales it was suddenly 14–0. A cruel penalty try and a typical van der Westhuizen try, both converted, drew the scores level, but South Africa were worried enough to take off Mark Andrews, who was playing in his 50th Test. The long injury time was due to a male streaker – later found to be a South African. 'He should be shot,' said Henry. 'I think we caught South Africa with their pants down.' Springbok coach Nick Mallett had said six months earlier: 'Wales are the worst international side I have seen.' This time he was gracious, stating: 'I take my hat off to them. Today they were superb.' At full-back for Wales was Shane Howarth, who had played four times for New Zealand in 1994 and scored 54 points. He had also played for Auckland during Henry's reign as coach.

Wales *S.P. Howarth (Manchester-Sale); G. Thomas (Cardiff), M. Taylor, I.S. Gibbs (Swansea), D.R. James; N.R. Jenkins (Pontypridd), +R. Howley;

A.L.P. Lewis, J.M. Humphreys (Cardiff), C.T. Anthony (Swansea), J.C. Quinnell (Richmond), C.P. Wyatt (Llanelli), C.L. Charvis (Swansea), L.S. Quinnell (Llanelli), M.E. Williams (Pontypridd). Reps: D.R. Morris (Swansea) for Lewis; *B.R. Evans (Swansea) for Anthony.
T: Gareth Thomas.
P: Neil Jenkins 5.

South Africa P.C. Montgomery (Western Province); C.S. Terblanche (Boland), A.H. Snyman, P.F. Smith (Blue Bulls), P. Rossouw (Western Province); H.W. Honiball (Natal), J.H. van der Westhuizen (Blue Bulls); R.B. Kempson (Natal), J. Dalton (Golden Lions), A.C. Garvey (Natal), K. Otto (Blue Bulls), M.G. Andrews (Natal), J. Erasmus (Free State), +G.H. Teichmann (Natal), A.G. Venter (Free State). Reps: A.H. 'Ollie' le Roux (Natal) for Garvey; R.B. Skinstad (Western Province) for Andrews.
T: Joost van der Westhuizen, André Venter, pen try.
C: Franco Smith 2.
P: Smith 3.
Referee: Stuart Dickinson (Australia).

Wales 29 South Africa 19

The Millennium Stadium, Cardiff. 26 June 1999.

Wales won by 2 tries, 2 cons, 5 pens to 2 tries, 3 pens.

It was lucky 13 for Wales as they registered their first-ever win over South Africa, following twelve defeats and a lone draw that had been achieved in 1970 – there was no doubting that Wales deserved to extend their winning streak to six matches with a remarkable homecoming to Cardiff. The stadium had not been finished and only just over 27,000 spectators viewed the match, although they sounded more like 100,000 as they roared on Henry's Heroes. Despite losing Craig Quinnell with a broken thumb, Wales were only seriously tested in a spell after the interval, as South Africa tightened up matters and produced a try. The visitors were poorly served at half-back despite trying two different combinations and, up front, they were beaten out of sight by the Welsh front row. Brett Sinkinson excelled at open-side flanker and Neil Jenkins hardly put a foot wrong. It was 19–6 at the interval and, though Werner Swanepoel scored a try, it was Jenkins who put Gareth Thomas in for his 19th try in 35 Tests to make victory a certainty, even though Percy Montgomery slipped past Shane Howarth for a late Springbok score.

Wales S.P. Howarth (Manchester-Sale); G. Thomas (Cardiff), M. Taylor (Swansea), A.G. Bateman (Northampton), D.R. James; N.R. Jenkins (Pontypridd), +R. Howley (Cardiff); P.J.D. Rogers (Newport), G.R. Jenkins (Swansea), D. Young, J.C. Quinnell (Cardiff), C.P. Wyatt (Llanelli), C.L. Charvis (Swansea), L.S. Quinnell (Llanelli), B.D. Sinkinson (Neath). Reps: A.L.P. Lewis (Cardiff) for Rogers; J.M. Humphreys (Cardiff) for (G.R.) Jenkins; M.J. Voyle (Llanelli) for (J.C.) Quinnell.
T: Mark Taylor, Gareth Thomas.
C: Neil Jenkins 2.
P: Neil Jenkins 5.

South Africa P.C. Montgomery (Western Province); C.S. Terblanche, P.G. Muller (Natal), J.C. Mulder (Golden Lions), P.W.G. Rossouw; A.J.C. van Straaten (Western Province), W. Swanepoel (Golden Lions); R.B. Kempson (Western Province), A.E. Drotske (Free State), I.J. Visagie, C.S. Boome (Western Province), K. Otto (Blue Bulls), C.P.J. Krige (Western Province), +G.H. Teichmann (Natal), J. Erasmus (Golden Lions). Reps: G.S. Du Toit (Griquas) for van Straaten; D.J.B. von Hoesslin (Griquas) for Swanepoel; A.H. le Roux (Natal) for Kempson; A.G. Venter (Free State) for Boome.
T: Werner Swanepoel, Percy Montgomery.
P: Braam van Straaten 2, Gaffie du Toit.
Referee: Ed Morrison (England).

CANADA

(NB: Wales played Canada in RWC 1987)

Wales 24 Canada 26

Arms Park, Cardiff. 10 November 1993

Canada won by 2 tries, 2 cons, 4 pens to 8 pens.

Tactics were confusing and the communication lines between coach Alan Davies and outside-half Adrian Davies, in particular, went down in the second half. The Cardiff pivot seemed to shrug his shoulders, as if to say: 'What am I supposed to be doing?' Unluckily for Wales, Gareth Rees, who was soon to join Newport, was in splendid form for Canada and knew exactly what was required. Wales were kept in the match by eight Neil Jenkins kicks and even led 24–19 in the dying seconds, before Canada moved the ball across the field for lock Al Charron to appear in a centre position and cross the Welsh line halfway out. At 24–24 and with time up, Rees was left with the tricky conversion to win the match. He never looked like missing it. There was a début by 21-year-old Scott Quinnell, whose father Derek had been capped 23 times for Wales and had toured on three occasions with the British Lions.

The 1995 World Cup captain Mike Hall takes on the Canadian defence at Toronto in 1994. In this match Hall scored two tries in a 33–15 victory.
(© Huw Evans)

Wales A. Clement (Swansea); +I.C. Evans (Llanelli), I.S. Gibbs (Swansea), N.R. Jenkins (Pontypridd), W.T. Proctor (Llanelli); A. Davies (Cardiff), R.H.StJ.B. Moon (Llanelli); M. Griffiths (Cardiff), G.R. Jenkins (Swansea), J.D. Davies (Neath), A.H. Copsey (Llanelli), G.O. Llewellyn (Neath), *L.S. Quinnell, E.W. Lewis, R.L. Jones (Llanelli).
P: Neil Jenkins 8.

Canada M. Williams; R. Toews, S.D. Gray, +I.C. Stuart, D.S. Stewart; G.L. Rees, C.J.C. Tynan; P. Szabo, I. Kennedy, D.C. Jackart, J. Knauer, A.J. Charron, I. Gordon, C. McKenzie, J.R. Hutchinson. Reps: I. Mackay for Tynan (temp); I. Cooper for Knauer.
T: Ian Stuart, Al Charron.
C: Gareth Rees 2.
P: Rees 4.
Referee: Owen E. Doyle (Ireland).

Canada 15 Wales 33

Fletcher's Field, Markham. 11 June 1994.

Wales won by 3 tries, 3 cons, 4 pens to 5 pens.

Two matches were played in Canada, before Wales moved on to the South Seas for three Tests. The opener was a 28–19 win over a Canadian XV at Hamilton, before the match in Toronto three days later. Gareth Rees soon kicked Canada into a 9–0 lead, but Wales hit back with Michael Rayer influential. Mike Hall scored two tries to help gain a 17–15 lead. Ieuan Evans scored his 20th try to equal the Welsh record set by both Gerald Davies and Gareth Edwards. The Welsh skipper seemed to have suffered concussion, but remained on for some time, before Tony Clement replaced him.

Canada D.S. Stewart; R. Toews, S.D. Gray, +I.C. Stuart, D.C. Lougheed; G.L. Rees, J.D. Graf; E.A. Evans, K.F. Svoboda, D.C. Jackart, A.J. Charron, M.B. James, G.I. MacKinnon, C. McKenzie, I. Gordon. Rep: G.D. Ennis for McKenzie.
P: Gareth Rees 5.

Wales M.A. Rayer (Cardiff); +I.C. Evans (Llanelli), M.R. Hall (Cardiff), N.G. Davies, W.T. Proctor (Llanelli); N.R. Jenkins (Pontypridd), R.H.StJ.B. Moon; R.L. Evans (Llanelli), G.R.

Jenkins (Swansea), J.D. Davies (Neath), P.T. Davies (Llanelli), G.O. Llewellyn (Neath), H.T. Taylor (Cardiff), L.S. Quinnell (Llanelli), R.G. Collins (Pontypridd). Rep: A. Clement (Swansea) for I.C. Evans.
T: Mike Hall 2, Ieuan Evans.
C: Neil Jenkins 3.
P: Neil Jenkins 4.
Referee: Ian Rogers (South Africa).

Canada 25 Wales 28

Fletcher's Field, Markham. 19 July 1997

Wales won 3 tries, 2 cons, 3 pens to 3 tries, 2 cons, 1 pen, 1 drop goal.

Coach Kevin Bowring knew that Canada would prove an even tougher test than the USA and after defeating Ontario by 54–10 at Hamilton, the team got down to plotting how to win on Fletcher's Field. However, Canada struck in just 20 seconds, when Bobby Ross, soon to be a Cardiff player, caught a loose kick and dropped a splendid goal from at least 50 yards out on the touchline. Canada, with their squad mostly playing in Britain, led 3–2 on tries and 25–21 on points, with another Cardiff-bound player, John Tait, particularly impressive. Wales had one more try left in the locker, however, and powerful centre Leigh Davies crossed the home line nine minutes from time, for Arwel Thomas to convert. Paul John was the new skipper, Thomas took his tally to 107 points in 13 Tests for Wales and North Walian Steve Moore emulated his younger brother Andrew by winning his first cap.

Canada R.P. Ross; W. Stanley, S. Bryan, D.C. Lougheed, D.S. Stewart; +G.L. Rees, J.D. Graf; E.A. Evans, K. Morgan, R.G.A. Snow, J.N. Tait, M.B. James, A.J. Charron, M. Schmid, J.R. Hutchinson. Reps: R. Bice for Evans; M.E. Cardinal for Morgan.
T: Mike Schmid 2, Bobby Ross.
C: Gareth Rees 2.
P: Rees.
DG: Ross.

Wales K.A. Morgan (Pontypridd); W.T. Proctor (Llanelli), L.B. Davies (Cardiff), G. Thomas (Bridgend), N.K. Walker (Cardiff); A.C. Thomas (Swansea), +P. John (Pontypridd); I.M. Buckett, G.R. Jenkins (Swansea), L. Mustoe (Cardiff), *S.J. Moore (Swansea), M.J. Voyle, A. Gibbs (Llanelli), S.M. Williams (Neath), *R.C. Appleyard (Swansea). Reps: C.T. Anthony (Swansea) for Buckett; N. Thomas (Bath) for Gibbs.
T: Gareth Thomas, Wayne Proctor, Leigh Davies.
C: Arwel Thomas 2.
P: Arwel Thomas 3.
Referee: Santiago Borsani (Argentina).
(NB: Wales have also played Canada in RWC 1987)

Wales 33 Canada 19

The Millennium Stadium, Cardiff. 21 August 1999.

Wales won by 2 tries, 1 con, 7 pens to 1 try, 1 con, 3 pens, 1 drop goal.

This was a very forgettable match in which there was little constructive play, and referee David McHugh did not help matters. Neil Jenkins looked to be well on course to breaking the world international record of nine penalty goals in a match until tries at last came. Dave Lougheed of Leicester gained the first, but then Jenkins supported a Scott Gibbs break and good passing enabled Nick Walne to score the second. The 28 points scored by Jenkins took him past 800 for Wales. Canada included four players who had played for Cardiff – John Tait, Bobby Ross, Dan Baugh and Morgan Williams.

Wales S.P. Howarth (Newport); N.J. Walne, L. Davies (Cardiff), I.S. Gibbs (Swansea), A.G. Bateman (Northampton); N.R. Jenkins, +R. Howley (Cardiff); P.J.D. Rogers (Newport), J.M. Humphreys (Cardiff), B.R. Evans (Swansea), J.C. Quinnell (Cardiff), A.P. Moore (Swansea), G. Lewis (Pontypridd), L.S. Quinnell (Llanelli), M.E. Williams (Cardiff). Reps: S.M. Jones (Llanelli) for Bateman; A.L.P. Lewis (Cardiff) for Humphreys; D. Young (Cardiff) for Evans; G.O. Llewellyn (Harlequins) for (J.C.) Quinnell; C.P. Wyatt (Llanelli) for (L.S.) Quinnell.
T: Neil Jenkins, Nick Walne.
C: Jenkins.
P: Jenkins 7.

Canada D.S. Stewart; W. Stanley, D.C. Lougheed, S. Bryan, C. Smith; +G.L. Rees, M. Williams; R.G.A. Snow, M.E. Cardinal, R. Bice, J.N. Tait, M.B. James, J.R. Hutchinson, A.J. Charron, D.R. Baugh. Reps: R.P. Ross for Rees; J. Thiel for Bice; M. Schmid for Tait; R. Banks for Hutchinson.
T: Dave Lougheed.
C: Gareth Rees.
P: Rees 3.
DG: Rees.
Referee: David.T.M. McHugh (Ireland).

FIJI

Wales 40 Fiji 3

Arms Park, Cardiff. 9 November 1985

Wales won by 7 tries, 3 cons, 2 pens to 1 pen.

Fiji lost five and won five on their short tour, conceding 31 points to both Cardiff and Llanelli but failing by only one point against Ireland. They found Wales far too strong, however, in a match played in heavy rain. The home pack dominated and the Fijian cause was not helped when wing Tuvula left the field after 20 minutes. Terry Holmes also departed with a knee injury.

Wales P.H. Thorburn (Neath); M.H. Titley (Swansea), R.A. Ackerman (London Welsh), B. Bowen (South Wales Police), A.M. Hadley (Cardiff); Jonathan Davies (Neath), +T.D. Holmes; J. Whitefoot (Cardiff), W.J. James (Aberavon), I.H. Eidman, R.L. Norster (Cardiff), S.J. Perkins (Pontypool), Mark Davies (Swansea), P.T. Davies, D.F. Pickering (Llanelli). Rep: R. Giles (Aberavon) for Holmes.
T: Phil Davies 2, Adrian Hadley, Terry Holmes, David Pickering, Mark Titley, Billy James.
C: Paul Thorburn 3.
P: Thorburn 2.

Fiji J. Damu (Auckland); M. Nabati (Suva), S. Laulau (Nadi), T. Cama (Suva), S. Tuvula (Nadi); A. Niuqila (Rewa), P. Nawalu (Suva); P. Volavola (Nadi), E. Rakai, R. Namoro, K. Rakoroi, A. Hughes (Suva), I. Finau (Nadi), +E. Teleni (Suva), P. Gale (Nadi). Rep: J. Kubu (Naitasiri) for Tuvula.
P: Jimi Damu.
Referee: Stephen R. Hilditch (Ireland).

Fiji 15 Wales 22

Buckhurst Park, Suva. 31 May 1986

Wales won by 2 tries, 1 con, 3 pens, 1 drop goal to 2 tries, 2 cons, 1 pen.

Skipper David Pickering's tour ended after this match. He took a hard kick in the head and suffered concussion, with Richard Moriarty taking over the captaincy. In this match he was paired with his brother Paul at lock, while clubmate Malcolm Dacey was switched to the full-back position. Wales led 13–0 and then 13–12, before pulling away to safety.

Fiji J. Kubu; J. Damu, S. Aria, A. Niuqila, S. Tuvula; S. Lovokuro, P. Nawalu; P. Volavoli, E. Rakai, R. Namoro, R. Cavukubu, K. Rakoroi, I. Tawake, +E. Teleni, A. Dere. Rep: R. Naituku for Volavola.
T: Acura Niuqila, Serupepeli Tuvula.
C: Jone Kubu 2.
P: Sirilo Lovokuro.

Wales M. Dacey; M.H. Titley (Swansea), J.A. Devereux (Bridgend/SG Inst), B. Bowen (South Wales Police), A.M. Hadley (Cardiff); J. Davies (Neath), R.N. Jones (Swansea); J. Whitefoot (Cardiff), W.J. James (Aberavon), S. Evans (Neath), R.L. Norster (Cardiff), R.D. Moriarty, W.P. Moriarty (Swansea), P.T. Davies, +D.F. Pickering (Llanelli). Rep: M.A. Brown (Pontypool) for Pickering.
T: Jonathan Davies, Adrian Hadley.
C: Bleddyn Bowen.
P: Malcolm Dacey 3.
DG: Jonathan Davies.
Referee: David J. Bishop (New Zealand).

Fiji 8 Wales 23

National Stadium, Suva. 18 June 1994

Wales won by 2 tries, 2 cons, 3 pens to 1 try, 1 pen.

Changes were made to give all players a chance on the short tour. It brought a complete Llanelli three-quarter line together and skipper Ieuan Evans played his 45th game to pass Ken Jones as the most-capped wing for Wales. Another Scarlet, Phil Davies, came on to equal Graham Price's 41 caps. Michael Rayer scored his fourth Test try, his first from full-back. 'Don't forget,' said team manager Bob Norster, 'these boys have had a long domestic and international season.' Wales led 17–3 at the interval and then 23–3, before the huge Joeli Veitayaki scored. He was later to join Dunvant for two seasons! The Fijians were coached by former All Black wing Bernie Fraser.

Fiji R. Bogisa; J. Vidiri, J. Toloi, E. Nauga, P. Tuidraki; R. Rayasi, J. McLennan; R. Williams, E. Batimala, J. Veitayaki, +I. Tawake, I. Savai, S. Matalulu, A. Moceletu, J. Campbell. Rep: M. Korovou for Campbell.

T: Joeli Veitayaki.
P: Rasolsolo Bogisa.

Wales M.A. Rayer (Cardiff); +I.C. Evans, N. Boobyer, N.G. Davies, W.T. Proctor (Llanelli); A. Davies (Cardiff), R.H.StJ.B. Moon; R.L. Evans (Llanelli), *R.C. McBryde (Swansea), H. Williams-Jones, A.H. Copsey (Llanelli), P. Arnold (Swansea), H.T. Taylor (Cardiff), E.W. Lewis (Llanelli), R.G. Collins (Pontypridd). Rep: P.T. Davies (Llanelli) for Lewis.
T: Mike Rayer, Richie Collins.
C: Adrian Davies 2.
P: Adrian Davies 3.
Referee: Ephraim J. Sklar (Argentina).

Wales 19 Fiji 15

Arms Park, Cardiff. 11 November 1995

Wales won by 2 tries, 3 pens to 2 tries, 1 con, 1 pen.

Kevin Bowring took over as caretaker coach for this match and soon afterwards became the first WRU full-time professional coach. It was a cold day and play was not very exciting, though Neil Jenkins woke spectators up by perfecting a Keith Jarrett-type trick. As the sand bucket was on its way across the pitch, 'Jenks' tapped the ball and dived over unopposed to catch Fiji napping, having not indicated that he was going for the posts. Aled Williams made his second and final appearance, replacing the injured Nigel Davies, with Jenkins moving to centre. The game will be best remembered for Ieuan Evans becoming the most-capped Welsh player, passing J.P.R. Williams by winning his 56th cap. There was also the début of Craig Quinnell as a blind-side flanker. His father, Derek, and elder brother, Scott, had already been capped. Fiji lost six of their nine matches in Wales and Ireland, including those against Neath, Cardiff and Pontypridd, yet it was they, and not Wales, who took the applause at Cardiff. Man of the match in the international was not a Welshman, but Fijian full-back Filipe Rayasi.

Wales W.J.L. Thomas; I.C. Evans (Llanelli), G. Thomas (Bridgend), N.G. Davies, W.T. Proctor (Llanelli); N.R. Jenkins (Pontypridd), Andy P. Moore (Cardiff); C.D. Loader (Swansea), +J.M. Humphreys, *L. Mustoe (Cardiff), Andrew P. Moore (Swansea), D. Jones (Cardiff), *J.C.Quinnell (Llanelli), H.T. Taylor, A.M. Bennett (Cardiff). Reps: D. Aled Williams (Swansea) for Davies; G.R. Jenkins (Swansea) for Humphreys (temp).
T: Neil Jenkins, Andy P. Moore.
P: Neil Jenkins 3.

Fiji F. Rayasi; P. Bale, S.C. Sorovaki, L. Little, M. Bari; J. Waqa, J. Rauluni; +J. Veitayaki, G. Smith, E. Natuivau, E. Katalau, I. Tawake, T. Tamanivalu, D. Rouse, W. Masireva. Rep: R. Bogisa for Waqa.
T: Manasa Bari, Filipe Rayasi.
C: Jonetani Waqa.
P: Waqa.
Referee: Paddy D. O'Brien (New Zealand).

ITALY

(NB: RWC 1995 seeding. October 1994 Wales v Italy)

Wales 31   Italy 26

Arms Park, Cardiff. 16 January 1996

Wales won by 3 tries, 2 cons, 4 pens to 2 tries, 2 cons, 4 pens.

The Arms Park thrilled to the exciting skills of 21-year-old outside-half Arwel Thomas, who was a throw-back to the Welsh artful dodgers of the past. He scored 16 points and Wales led 31–6 at one stage, before inexperience told and the Italian pack began to dominate. The young Wales side included five new caps; one of them, centre Leigh Davies, was a month short of his 20th birthday. Italian try-scorer Julian Gardner had been capped by Australia in 1987–88.

Wales W.J.L. Thomas; I.C. Evans, *M.E. Wintle (Llanelli), *L.B. Davies (Neath), W.T. Proctor (Llanelli); *A.C. Thomas (Bristol), Andy P. Moore (Cardiff); *A.L.P. Lewis, +J.M. Humphreys (Cardiff), J.D. Davies, G.O. Llewellyn (Neath), D. Jones, E.W. Lewis, H.T. Taylor (Cardiff), *R.G. Jones (Llanelli).
T: Ieuan Evans 2, Justin Thomas.
C: Arwel Thomas 2.
P: Arwel Thomas 4.

Italy M. Ravazzolo; P. Vaccari (Calvisano), I. Francescato, T. Visentin (Treviso), F. Roselli (Roma); D. Dominguez (Milan), A. Troncon (Treviso); +Massimo Cuttitta, C. Orlandi, F. Properzi-Curti (Milan), M. Giacheri (Treviso), P.P. Pedroni (Milan), O. Arancio (Catania), J.M. Gardner (Treviso), A. Sgorlon (Lafert San Dona). Reps: M. Bonomi (Milan) for Visentin; G. de Carli (Roma) for Orlandi.
T: Julian Gardner, Franco Properzi-Curti.
C: Diego Dominguez 2.
P: Dominguez 4.
Referee: Gordon Black (Ireland).

Italy 22   Wales 31

Stadio Olimpico, Rome. 5 October 1996

Wales won by 3 tries, 2 cons, 4 pens to 1 try, 1 con, 5 pens.

This match may be remembered for the return of Scott Gibbs, who had left St Helen's Rugby League club and returned to another St Helen's, the home of Swansea RFC. It could also be remembered as the last match for John Davies in Kevin Bowring's reign as coach. In Davies, Wales had probably the best player in his position in world rugby. Mr Bowring, however, appeared to care little. Welsh international rugby was to suffer humiliation without Davies up front. Only a late rally which produced ten points took Wales to victory, with Gibbs instrumental in the second try by Gareth Thomas. Wayne Proctor had been carried off after 50 minutes with concussion. For Italy, the try-scorer was the popular Ivan Francescato, this time playing in his best position as a centre. Sadly, he died less than three years later. Diego Dominguez shaded the kicking duel with Neil Jenkins, winning 17–16.

Italy M. Ravazzolo; P. Vaccari (Calvisano), S. Bordon (Rovigo), I. Francescato, L. Manteri (Treviso); D. Dominguez (Milan), A. Troncon (Treviso); +Massimo Cuttitta, C. Orlandi, F. Properzi-Curti, P.P. Pedroni (Milan), D. Scaglia, A. Sgorlon, C. Checchinato (Treviso), O. Arancio (Milan). Reps: J.A. Pertile (Roma) for Vaccari; A. Castellani (Treviso) for Properzi-Curti; R. Rampazzo (Padova) for Checchinato.
T: Ivan Francescato.
C: Diego Dominguez.
P: Dominguez 5.

Wales W.T. Proctor (Llanelli); S.D. Hill (Cardiff), G. Thomas (Bridgend), I.S. Gibbs (Swansea), D.R. James (Bridgend); N.R. Jenkins (Pontypridd), R. Howley (Cardiff); C.D. Loader (Swansea), +J.M. Humphreys (Cardiff), J.D. Davies (Neath), G.O. Llewellyn (Harlequins), D. Jones, H.T. Taylor (Cardiff), S.M. Williams (Neath), K.P. Jones (Ebbw Vale). Reps: L.B. Davies (Cardiff) for Proctor; M.E. Williams (Pontypridd) for K.P. Jones (temp).

T: Gareth Thomas 2, Dafydd James.
C: Neil Jenkins 2.
P: Jenkins 4.
Referee: Carl Spannenberg (South Africa).

Wales 23 Italy 20

Stradey Park, Llanelli. 7 February 1998

Wales won by 2 tries, 2 cons, 3 pens to 2 tries, 2 cons, 2 pens.

Ieuan Evans came home to Stradey Park to play in his 72nd and final international match. The crowd were disappointed that he could not add to the 33 wonderful tries he had scored for his country, all scored whilst he was a Scarlet. This was his only cap gained from the Bath club. Wales flattered to deceive with a superb Gareth Thomas try run in from halfway, but Italy kept coming back in what was the first international game in Llanelli for 105 years. A serious spinal injury suffered by flanker Gwyn Jones while playing for Cardiff against Swansea in December gave his club colleague Robert Howley the chance to become the 112th captain of Wales.

Wales N.R. Jenkins (Pontypridd); I.C. Evans (Bath), A.G. Bateman (Richmond), I.S. Gibbs (Swansea), G. Thomas (Cardiff); A.C. Thomas (Swansea), +R. Howley; A.L.P. Lewis (Cardiff), B.H. Williams (Richmond), D. Young (Cardiff), G.O. Llewellyn (Harlequins), M.J. Voyle (Llanelli), R.C. Appleyard (Swansea), L.S. Quinnell (Richmond), M.E. Williams (Pontypridd). Reps: J.M. Humphreys (Cardiff) for B.H. Williams; C.L. Charvis (Swansea) for M.E. Williams.
T: Gareth Thomas (pen try).
C: Neil Jenkins 2.
P: Jenkins 3.

Italy C. Pilat (Treviso); P. Vaccari (Calvisano), L. Martin (Padova), A.C. Stoica (Narbonne), Marcello Cuttitta (Milan); D. Dominguez (Stade Français), A. Troncon (Treviso); G. de Carli, C. Orlandi (Milan), A. Castellani (L'Aquila), G. Croci (Milan), V. Cristofoletto (Treviso), +M. Giovanelli (Narbonne), J.M. Gardner, A. Sgorlon (Treviso).
T: Cristian Stoica, Andrea Sgorlon.
C: Diego Dominguez 2.
P: Dominguez 2.
Referee: Steve J.D. Lander (England).

Wing Ieuan Evans steps up the pace: when he retired from international rugby in 1998, he had set a Welsh record of 72 appearances. (© Huw Evans)

Italy 21 Wales 60

Stadio Communale di Monigo, Treviso. 20 March 1999

Wales won by 7 tries, 5 cons, 5 pens to 2 tries, 1 con, 3 pens.

Italy had lost on four previous occasions to Wales, by margins of ten, five, nine and three points respectively. Now the margin rocketed to 39, as the confident new Wales struck hard in Treviso. Neil Jenkins set a Welsh record of 30 points in a match to take his tally to 704 for Wales in 63 Tests. Gareth Thomas became the sixth player to score four tries in a match for Wales. Jenkins had now scored 80 points in four appearances against Italy and Thomas had scored seven tries in his three appearances. With Diego Dominguez taking his tally to 68 in five matches against Wales, his side led 13–8 and were only 16–18 behind at the interval. Then came the flood. Graham Henry commented: 'We must not get carried away.'

Italy J.-A. Pertile; F. Roselli (Roma), A.C. Stoica (Narbonne), L. Martin (Begles-Bordeaux), D.

Dallan (Treviso); D. Dominguez (Stade Français), A. Troncon (Treviso); Massimo Cuttitta (Calvisano), A. Moscardi, F. Properzi-Curti, V. Cristofoletto (Treviso), M. Giacheri (West Hartlepool), +M. Giovanelli (Narbonne), D. Scaglia, A. Sgorlon (Treviso). Reps: M. Baroni (Padua) for Stoica; A. Castellani (L'Aquila) for Properzi-Curti; S. Stocco (Padua) for Cristofoletto; S. Saviozzi (Treviso) for Sgorlon.
T: Luca Martin, Diego Scaglia.
C: Diego Dominguez.
P: Dominguez 3.

Wales S.P. Howarth (Manchester-Sale); G. Thomas (Cardiff), M. Taylor, I.S. Gibbs (Swansea), D.R. James; N.R. Jenkins (Pontypridd), +R. Howley (Cardiff); P.J.D. Rogers (London Irish), G.R. Jenkins, B.R. Evans (Swansea), J.C. Quinnell (Richmond), C.P. Wyatt (Llanelli), C.L. Charvis (Swansea), L.S. Quinnell (Llanelli), B.D. Sinkinson (Neath). Reps: *N.J. Walne (Richmond) for James; N. Boobyer (Llanelli) for Taylor; D.S. Llewellyn (Ebbw Vale) for Howley; B.H. Williams (Richmond) for G.R. Jenkins; M.J. Voyle (Llanelli) for J.C. Quinnell; G. Lewis (Pontypridd) for Charvis; D.R. Morris (Swansea) for Rogers (temp).
T: Gareth Thomas 4, Craig Quinnell, Neil Jenkins, Robert Howley.
C: Neil Jenkins 5.
P: Neil Jenkins 5.
Referee: Rob J. Dickson (Scotland).

USA

Wales 46 USA 0

Arms Park, Cardiff. 7 November 1987

Wales won by 8 tries, 4 cons, 2 pens to nil.

Bleddyn Bowen switched from centre to outside-half and also became the new skipper. It was a good start for him, as Wales led 22–0 at half-time and were never worried by the Eagles. Bowen celebrated with two tries, as did replacement Anthony Clement, aged 19, who scored his in the last quarter of the match. The four new caps included Stuart Russell, who was born in Kenya and was completely unknown in Wales. Rowland Phillips made his début on the blindside. He was to join Warrington RL in 1990, but returned to captain London Welsh and Neath.

Wales P.H. Thorburn (Neath); G.M.C. Webbe (Bridgend), M.G. Ring (Pontypool), K. Hopkins (Swansea), A.M. Hadley (Cardiff); +B. Bowen (South Wales Police), R.N. Jones (Swansea); *J.D. Pugh, K.H. Phillips (Neath), D. Young (Swansea), *S. Russell (London Welsh), R.L. Norster (Cardiff), *R.D. Phillips (Neath), W.P. Moriarty (Swansea), R.G. Collins (South Wales Police). Rep: *A. Clement (Swansea) for Hopkins.
T: Bleddyn Bowen 2, Anthony Clement 2, David Young, Paul Moriarty, Glen Webbe, Bob Norster.
C: Paul Thorburn 4.
P: Thorburn 2.

USA A. Montgomery; W. Jefferson, K. Higgins, C. Doherty, G. Hein; M. Williams, M. Saunders; B. Horwath, P. Johnson, +F. Paoli, K. Swords, R. Zenker, M. Carlson, B. Vizard, J. Peter. Rep: D. Shanagher for Hein.
Referee: Colin J. High (England).

Wales 34 USA 14

Arms Park, Cardiff. 11 January 1997

Wales won by 4 tries, 4 cons, 2 pens to 1 try, 3 pens.

There were 11 British-based players in the United States squad which lost to Neath 15–39 but defeated Pontypridd by 15–13. Several were linked with Welsh clubs. In this Test, Cliff Vogl (Bridgend) and Rob Lumkong (Pontypridd) played, while Jay Wilkerson

A rare sight: the popular lock Bobby Norster makes the line against the United States in this 1987 encounter.
(© Huw Evans)

Scrum-half Robert Jones breaks through against the United States Eagle flanker Mark Carlson in 1987. Forwards Paul Moriarty and Richie Collins are in support. (© Huw Evans)

Bleddyn Bowen, the last Welsh Triple-Crown winning captain, in his 1988 South Wales police uniform on the beat in Cwmavon. Bowen skippered Wales five times in his 24 appearances as centre and outside-half. (© Huw Evans)

Wales captain Gwyn Jones on the charge before his career was shattered by a serious injury while playing for Cardiff against Swansea. He had played 13 times for Wales. (© Huw Evans)

was later with Narberth and Dunvant and Tom Billups with Neath and Pontypridd. Also in the tour party was Ian Stevens, formerly of South Wales Police and Wales Youth and latterly winner of a Wales rugby league cap. Centre Scott Gibbs was the captain because Jonathan Humphreys was suspended. Scott Quinnell was back in harness and the former rugby league contingent was at five when Jonathan Davies came on as a replacement.

Wales W.J.L. Thomas (Cardiff); I.C. Evans (Llanelli), A.G. Bateman (Richmond), +I.S. Gibbs (Swansea), G. Thomas (Bridgend); A.C. Thomas (Swansea), R. Howley (Cardiff); C.D. Loader, G.R. Jenkins (Swansea), D. Young (Cardiff), G.O. Llewellyn (Harlequins), M.A. Rowley (Pontypridd), S.M. Williams (Neath), L.S. Quinnell (Richmond), C.L. Charvis (Swansea). Reps: J. Davies (Cardiff) for Gibbs (temp); P. John (Pontypridd) for Howley; J.C. Quinnell (Richmond) for Rowley; R.G. Jones (Cardiff) for Charvis.
T: Ieuan Evans 2, Scott Gibbs (pen try).
C: Arwel Thomas 4.
P: Arwel Thomas 2.

USA M. Williams; V. Anitoni, R. Tardits, M. Scharrenberg, B. Hightower; M. Alexander, A. Bachelet; R. Lehner, T.W. Billups, B. Le Clerc, C. Vogl, A. Parker, +D. Lyle, R. Lumkong, J. Wilkerson. Reps: C. Morrow for Williams; J. Walker for Wilkerson.
T: Andre Bachelet.
P: Matt Alexander 3.
Referee: Leo Mayne (Ireland).

USA 20 Wales 30 – 1st Test

Wilmington, North Carolina. 5 July 1997

Wales won by 4 tries, 2 cons, 2 pens to 2 tries, 2 cons, 2 pens.

A six-match tour of North America had opened with a 94–3 romp over Southern USA at Charlotte. The squad moved on to the heat of Wilmington on the same day that the Lions were playing the third and final Test of a winning series in South Africa. With no Scott Gibbs, Robert Howley, Neil Jenkins, Ieuan Evans and others, Wales gave a début to 20-year-old full-back Kevin Morgan (the 950th player to play for Wales) and flanker Gwyn Jones took over as captain in his ninth Test. Wales struggled, and after Nigel Walker had scored from an early touch of the ball, he was ignored. Arwel Thomas was at his best, however, and contributed 20 points, including two good tries.

USA C. Morrow; V. Anitoni, T. Takau, M. Scharrenberg, B. Hightower; M. Alexander, A. Bachelet; C. Lippert, T.W. Billups, R. Lehner, D. Hodges, L. Gross, J. Walker, +D. Lyle, J. Wilkerson. Reps: K. Shuman for Morrow; A. Saulala for Scharrenberg; M. McLeod for Wilkerson; S. Allen for Billups (temp).
T: Tomasi Takau, Vaea Anitoni.
C: Matt Alexander 2.
P: Alexander 2.

Wales *K.A. Morgan (Pontypridd); W.T. Proctor (Llanelli), L.B. Davies (Cardiff), G. Thomas (Bridgend), N.K. Walker (Cardiff); A.C. Thomas (Swansea), P. John (Pontypridd); C.D. Loader, G.R. Jenkins (Swansea), L. Mustoe (Cardiff), G.O. Llewellyn (Harlequins), M.J. Voyle, A. Gibbs (Llanelli), S.M. Williams (Neath), +R.G. Jones (Cardiff). Reps: *C.T. Anthony (Swansea) for Loader; N. Thomas (Bath) for Williams.
T: Arwel Thomas 2, Gwyn Jones, Nigel Walker.
C: Arwel Thomas 2.
P: Arwel Thomas 2.
Referee: Ken W. McCartney (Scotland).

USA 23 Wales 28 – 2nd Test

Balboa Park, San Francisco. 12 July 1997

Wales won by 4 tries, 1 con, 2 pens to 2 tries, 2 cons, 3 pens

The tour progressed to San Francisco, where Wales beat a USA Development team by 55–23 and then, thanks again to Arwel Thomas, won the second Test. His try won the match after the USA had drawn level at 23–23. Earlier, Wayne Proctor showed excellent pace in going over for a hat-trick of tries. Skipper Gwyn Jones picked up an injury that saw him depart after 41 minutes and was to keep him out of the Canada Test.

USA C. Morrow; V. Anitoni, T. Takau, M. Scharrenberg, B. Hightower; M. Alexander, A. Bachelet; C. Lippert, T.W. Billups, R. Lehner, L. Gross, D. Hodges, +D. Lyle, J. Walker, J. Wilkerson. Reps: A. Saulala for Takau; M. Sika for Hightower; S. Allen for Billups; M. McLeod for Walker; S. Youngling for Wilkerson.
T: Vaea Anitoni, Jason Walker.
C: Matt Alexander 2.
P: Alexander 3.

Wales K.A. Morgan (Pontypridd); W.T. Proctor (Llanelli), L.B. Davies (Cardiff), G. Thomas (Bridgend), N.K. Walker (Cardiff); A.C. Thomas (Swansea), P. John (Pontypridd); I.M. Buckett (Swansea), R.C. McBryde (Llanelli), L. Mustoe (Cardiff), G.O. Llewellyn (Harlequins), M.J. Voyle, A. Gibbs (Llanelli), N. Thomas (Bath), +R.G. Jones (Cardiff). Reps: C.T. Anthony (Swansea) for Buckett; S.M. Williams (Neath) for Jones.
T: Wayne Proctor 3, Arwel Thomas.
C: Arwel Thomas.
P: Arwel Thomas 2.
Referee: C.B. 'Chuck' Muir (Scotland).

ARGENTINA

Wales 43 Argentina 30

Stradey Park, Llanelli. 21 November 1998

Wales won by 4 tries, 4 cons, 5 pens to 4 tries, 2 cons, 2 pens.

A win was a win, but the match did not go as planned. Wales scored some good tries but were found badly wanting up front, where the strong Argentinian front row gave their opponents a good working-over. Graham Henry's words of caution after the South Africa match needed to be remembered. Wales were nowhere near the full product yet. They did begin well, though. Colin Charvis had not scored in 14 matches but now he went over twice. The first try began deep in Welsh territory, with Scott Gibbs taking up the running over halfway. On it went to Mark Taylor, then inside to Chris Wyatt and Charvis took a further inside pass to dive over. The second came when a charging Gibbs was backed up by Martyn Williams, who found Charvis at his side to burst clear. Argentina, aided by a penalty try, came back to close the gap to one point at 26–25, but Neil Jenkins kept spraying kicks over the bar to finish with 23 points.

Wales S.P. Howarth (Manchester-Sale); G. Thomas (Cardiff), M. Taylor, I.S. Gibbs (Swansea), D.R. James; N.R. Jenkins (Pontypridd), +R. Howley; A.L.P. Lewis, J.M. Humphreys (Cardiff), C.T. Anthony (Swansea), J.C. Quinnell (Richmond), C.P. Wyatt (Llanelli), C.L. Charvis (Swansea), L.S. Quinnell (Llanelli), M.E. Williams (Pontypridd). Reps: M.J. Voyle (Llanelli) for L.S. Quinnell; B.H. Williams (Richmond) for M.E. Williams.
T: Colin Charvis 2, Dafydd James, Mark Taylor.
C: Neil Jenkins 4.
P: Jenkins 5.

Argentina M. Contepomi; I. Corletto, J. Orengo, L. Arbizu, F. Soler; F. Contepomi, A. Pichot; M. Reggiardo, F.E. Mendez, O. Hasan-Jalil, +P.L. Sporleder, A. Allub, M. Durand, P.J. Camerlinckx, M.A. Ruiz. Reps: E. Simone for Orengo; D.L. Albanese for Soler; M. Ledesma for Reggiardo; R.A. Martin for Durand.
T: Agustin Pichot, Luis Sporleder, Felipe Contepomi (pen try).
C: Felipe Contepomi 2.
P: Felipe Contepomi 2.
Referee: Alan Lewis (Ireland).

One of the Gerald Davies specials at the river end on the North-Stand side of the Arms Park. J.P.R. Williams is in support in this non-test match against Argentina. Davies scored 20 tries in 46 appearances for Wales.
(© Huw Evans)

Centre Allan Bateman displays his class to defeat Argentinian defenders at Buenos Aires in 1999. Scott Quinnell is on hand with the scrum-capped Brett Sinkinson at the rear. (© Huw Evans)

Argentina 26 Wales 36 – 1st Test

Ferro Carril Oeste Stadium, Buenos Aires. 5 June 1999

Wales won by 3 tries, 3 cons, 4 pens, 1 drop goal to 2 tries, 2 cons, 4 pens.

Argentina led 23–0, only for Wales to stage an astonishing comeback, aided by their new never-say-die spirit. Hooker Federico Mendez accused Wales of cheating in the scrums, and it was there that the match was won and lost. From 0–23 it became 23–23 then 23–26, and then Shane Howarth produced an equalising drop-goal. Chris Wyatt added a try and the reliable boot of Neil Jenkins took Wales ten points clear.

Argentina D.L. Albanese; O. Bartolucci, E. Simone, L. Arbizu, E. Jurado; G. Quesada, A. Pichot; R. Grau, F.E. Mendez, M. Reggiardo, +P.L. Sporleder, A. Allub, I.F. Lobbe, P.J. Camerlinckx, R.A. Martin. Reps: O. Hasan-Jalil for Grau; G. Longo for Camerlinckx; L. Ostiglia for Allub.
T: Gonzalo Quesada, Octavio Bartolucci.
C: Quesada 2.
P: Quesada 4.

Wales S.P. Howarth (Manchester-Sale); M.F.D. Robinson, M. Taylor (Swansea), A.G. Bateman (Northampton), D.R. James; N.R. Jenkins (Pontypridd), +R. Howley (Cardiff); P.J.D. Rogers (Newport), G.R. Jenkins, B.R. Evans (Swansea), J.C. Quinnell (Cardiff), C.P. Wyatt (Llanelli), C.L. Charvis (Swansea), L.S. Quinnell (Llanelli), B.D. Sinkinson (Neath). Reps: A.L.P. Lewis (Cardiff) for Rogers; D. Young (Cardiff) for Evans.
T: Dafydd James, Brett Sinkinson, Chris Wyatt.
C: Neil Jenkins 3.
P: Neil Jenkins 4.
DG: Shane Howarth.
Referee: Brian Campsall (England).

Argentina 16 Wales 23 – 2nd Test

Ferro Carril Oeste Stadium, Buenos Aires. 12 June 1999

Wales won by 1 try, 5 pens, 1 drop goal to 1 try, 1 con, 3 pens.

Wales achieved a 2–0 series win, though it was not the first by a British team as many suggested, but it was the first for some 60 years. It was achieved by the solid base up front, surprisingly split up by coach Graham Henry in the last quarter of the match. Argentina were unfortunate to again be faced by a

British referee, but they had enough penalty chances to have won the match. Full-back Diego Albanese made a bad error in running out of defence and the alert Allan Bateman sent Garin Jenkins rumbling for the corner for a vital score. The highlight was a massive punch-up in the first half as the packs fought for supremacy.

Argentina D.L. Albanese; O. Bartolucci, J. Orengo, L. Arbizu, G.F. Camardon; F. Contepomi, A. Pichot; R.Grau, F.E. Mendez, M. Reggiardo, +P.L. Sporleder, I.F. Lobbe, R.A. Martin, G. Longo, M.A. Ruiz. Reps: J. Cilley for Contepomi; A. Allub for Lobbe; M. Ledesma for Mendez; L. Ostiglia for Martin; O. Hasan-Jalil for Reggiardo.
T: José Orengo.
C: José Cilley.
P: Felipe Contepomi 3.

Wales S.P. Howarth (Manchester-Sale); G.Thomas (Cardiff), M. Taylor (Swansea), A.G. Bateman (Northampton), D.R. James; N.R. Jenkins (Pontypridd), +R. Howley (Cardiff); P.J.D. Rogers (Newport), G.R. Jenkins, B.R. Evans (Swansea), J.C. Quinnell (Cardiff), C.P. Wyatt (Llanelli), G. Lewis (Pontypridd), L.S. Quinnell (Llanelli), B.D. Sinkinson (Neath). Reps: D. Young (Cardiff) for Evans; J.M. Humphreys (Cardiff) for G.R. Jenkins; A.L.P. Lewis (Cardiff) for Rogers.
T: Garin Jenkins.
P: Neil Jenkins 5.
DG: Neil Jenkins.
Referee: Chris White (England).

(NB: Wales have also played Argentina in RWC 1991 and RWC 1999)

FRANCE – Non Championship

Wales 9 France 22

Arms Park, Cardiff. 4 September 1991

France won by 3 tries, 2 cons, 2 pens to 1 try, 1 con, 1 pen.

It was the first floodlit international to be played in Cardiff and was the first with Alan Davies in charge as coach, albeit a caretaker. Bob Norster was the team manager, but had to be introduced to Davies! The pair worked hard together, though salvaging anything from the coming World Cup appeared out of the question. Davies chose Ieuan Evans as his captain and gave Mark Ring the outside-half role the player wanted so badly. Evans was to be a success, but 'Ringo' was still suffering injury and was not at full pace. Serge Blanco scored a beautiful try and Didier Camberabero played splendidly. Wales worked hard to stay in contention, as supporters looked for a sign of a recovery in this 7th match without a victory.

Wales A. Clement (Swansea); +I.C. Evans (Llanelli), I.S. Gibbs (Neath), M.R. Hall (Cardiff), A. Emyr (Swansea); M.G. Ring (Cardiff), R.N. Jones (Swansea); M. Griffiths (Cardiff), *G.R. Jenkins (Pontypool), L. Delaney (Llanelli), Glyn D. Llewellyn (Neath), K. Moseley (Newport), E.W. Lewis, P.T. Davies (Llanelli), R.G. Collins (Cardiff). Reps: *I. Luc Evans (Llanelli) for (I.C.)Evans; D.W. Evans (Cardiff) for Ring.
T: Richie Collins.
C: Mark Ring.
P: Ring.

France +S. Blanco (Biarritz); J.-B. Lafond (Racing Club), P. Sella (Agen), F. Mesnel (Racing Club), P. Saint-André (Montferrand); D. Camberabero (Beziers), H. Sanz (Narbonne); G. Lascube (Agen), L. Armary (Lourdes), P. Ondarts (Biarritz), T. Devergie (Nimes), O. Roumat (Dax), M. Courtoils (Begles), M. Cecillon (Bourgoin), L. Cabannes (Racing Club). Reps: J.-L. Sadourny (Colomiers) for Blanco; T. Lacroix (Dax) for Sella.
T: Philippe Saint-André, Didier Camberabero, Serge Blanco.
C: Camberabero 2.
P: Camberabero 2.
Referee: Jim M. Fleming (Scotland).

Wales 33 France 40

Arms Park, Cardiff. 25 Sept 1996

France won by 4 tries, 4 cons, 4 pens to 3 tries, 3 cons, 4 pens.

As in 1991, France were the visitors for a non-championship floodlit match. Billed as a friendly, which international matches will never be, France were jolted into action after new hooker Barry Williams opened the scoring in the second minute. Wales were in danger of running away with the match but, after the interval, they only scored two penalty goals while France took over the match.

Wales W.T. Proctor; I.C. Evans (Llanelli), L.B. Davies (Cardiff), +N.G. Davies (Llanelli), G. Thomas (Bridgend); N.R. Jenkins (Pontypridd), R. Howley (Cardiff); C.D. Loader (Swansea), *B.H. Williams, J.D. Davies (Neath), M.J. Voyle (Llanelli), G.O. Llewellyn (Harlequins), K.P. Jones (Ebbw Vale), S.M. Williams (Neath), M.E. Williams (Pontypridd). Reps: A.C. Thomas (Swansea) for Evans; S.D. Hill (Cardiff) for (N.G.)Davies.
T: Barry Williams, Ieuan Evans, Gareth Thomas.
C: Neil Jenkins 3.
P: Jenkins 4.

France J.-L. Sadourny (Colomiers); E. Ntamack (Toulouse), R. Dourthe (Dax), S. Glas (Bourgoin), +P. Saint-André (Montferrand); A. Penaud (Brive), P. Carbonneau (Brive); F. Tournaire (Narbonne), M. de Rougemont (Toulon), J.-L. Jordana (Toulouse), O. Merle (Montferrand), F. Pelous (Dax), P. Benetton, A. Benazzi (Agen), R. Castel (Beziers). Reps: D. Berty (Toulouse) for Saint-André; G. Accoceberry (Begles-Bordeaux) for Carbonneau; T. Lievremont (Perpignan) for Benetton.
T: Stéphane Glas 2, Jean-Luc Sadourny, Abdelatif Benazzi.
C: Richard Dourthe 4.
P: Dourthe 4.
Referee: George Gadjovich (Canada).

Wales 34 France 23

The Millennium Stadium, Cardiff. 28 August 1999.

Wales won by 1 try, 1 con, 9 pens to 2 tries, 2 cons, 3 pens.

It was a good victory over a French side battling for World Cup places and yet, though the spectators appeared to be happy, Wales managed only a good Dafydd James try against two scored by France. By half-time, it was 4–2 to Wales on penalties kicked and, though France led 13–12, four more Neil Jenkins shots in a 15-minute spell raised it to 24–13. Two minutes from time, the 'Ginger Monster' placed a ninth penalty to equal the world record for an international match. France came across as a very ordinary side, beaten up front and using the term 'Friendly Match' afterwards, when full caps were awarded. Xavier Garbajosa returned as a replacement until Clive Norling of the WRU came on to request his dismissal from the pitch. If he had scored, what would have happened? It was the eighth consecutive victory for the new-look Wales.

Wales S.P. Howarth (Newport); G. Thomas (Cardiff), M. Taylor, I.S. Gibbs (Swansea), D.R. James (Llanelli); N.R. Jenkins, +R.Howley (Cardiff); P.J.D. Rogers (Newport), G.R. Jenkins (Swansea), D. Young, J.C. Quinnell (Cardiff), C.P. Wyatt (Llanelli), C.L. Charvis (Swansea), L.S. Quinnell (Llanelli), B.D. Sinkinson (Neath). Rep: M.J. Voyle (Llanelli) for (L.S.) Quinnell.
T: Dafydd James.
C: Neil Jenkins.
P: Neil Jenkins 9.

France U. Mola (Castres); X. Garbajosa (Toulouse), R. Dourthe (Dax), S. Glas (Bourgoin), C. Dominici (Stade Francais); T. Castaignede (Castres), S. Castaignede (Mont de Marsan); C. Califano (Toulouse), +R. Ibanez (Perpignan), P. de Villiers (Stade Francais), A. Benazzi (Agen), F. Pelous (Toulouse), M. Lievremont (Stade Francais), T. Lievremont (Perpignan), O. Magne (Montferrand). Reps: E. Ntamack (Toulouse) for Garbajosa; Garbajosa for Dourthe; D. Auradou (Stade Francais) for Garbajosa; C. Lamaison (Brive) for Glas; P. Mignoni (Toulon) for (S.) Castaignede; M. Dal Maso (Colomiers) for Ibanez; C. Soulette (Toulouse) for Califano; Califano for de Villiers; L. Mallier (Brive) for (T.) Lievremont.
T: Lionel Mallier, Pierre Mignoni.
C: Richard Dourthe, Cristophe Lamaison.
P: Dourthe 2, Lamaison.
Referee: Paul Honiss (New Zealand).

NAMIBIA

Namibia 9 Wales 18 – 1st Test

Windhoek. 2 June 1990

Wales won by 2 tries, 2 cons, 2 pens to 1 try, 1 con, 1 pen.

Wales had to find somewhere to succeed and they found it in Namibia. Six matches, including two Tests, were all won. It was still a Neath set-up, with Kevin Phillips as skipper and both Chris Bridges and Glyn Llewellyn winning caps. Glyn was the elder brother of Gareth, and oddly shared the same birthplace – Bradford-on-Avon – as England skipper Will Carling. Bridges scored a decisive try after Namibia had levelled at 9–9. Mark Ring was lively in attack – but Namibian full-back André Stoop was even livelier. He butted Steve Ford and was sent off by Fred Howard, who was touring with Wales. Rugby league scouts liked the look of Stoop and he was soon on his way to the north of England.

Namibia A. Stoop; +G. Mans, V. du Toit, J. Deysel, B. Swartz; S. McCulley, B. Buitendag; C. Derks, S. Smit, M. Grobler, S. Losper, A. van der Merwe, J. Barnard, T. Oosthuizen, A. Skinner. Sent off: André Stoop.
T: Gerhard Mans.
C: Shaun McCulley.
P: McCulley.

Wales P.H. Thorburn (Neath); S.P. Ford, M.G. Ring (Cardiff), A.G. Bateman (Neath), A. Emyr; A. Clement (Swansea), *C.J. Bridges (Neath); M. Griffiths (Cardiff), +K.H. Phillips (Neath), *P. Knight (Pontypridd), *Glyn D. Llewellyn (Neath), *P. Arnold (Swansea), M.S. Morris, M.A. Jones (Neath), *A.D. Reynolds (Swansea). Rep: *S.A. Parfitt (South Wales Police) for Emyr.
T: Chris Bridges, Paul Thorburn.
C: Thorburn 2.
P: Thorburn 2.
Referee: Fred A. Howard (England).

Namibia 30 Wales 34 – 2nd Test

Windhoek. 9 June 1990

Wales won by 4 tries, 3 cons, 3 pens, 1 drop goal to 3 tries, 3 cons, 3 pens, 1 drop goal.

Steve Ford was in the wars again, as he was taken out and a penalty try granted. The Cardiff wing departed, to be replaced by outside-half Aled Williams, who played out of position. Owain Williams, the former Glamorgan Wanderers forward, marked his only appearance with a try. It was still an unconvincing performance, as 15 points by Paul Thorburn and a long drop-shot by Anthony Clement helped Wales to a 30–15 lead. Then the alarm bells started ringing as Namibia climbed back to 30–21, 30–27 and 30–30. At that point, Arthur Emyr scored to send Wales home unbeaten.

Namibia Jaco Coetzee; +G. Mans, V. du Toit, J. Deysel, B. Swartz; S. McCulley, B. Buitendag; C. Derks, S. Smit, M. Grobler, S. Losper, A. van der Merwe, J. Barnard, T. Oosthuizen, A. Skinner. Rep: Jasper Coetzee for Barnard.
T: Ben Swartz 2, Gerhard Mans.
C: Jaco Coetzee 2, Shaun McCulley.
P: McCulley 2, Jaco Coetzee.
DG: Jaco Coetzee.

Wales P.H. Thorburn (Neath); S.P. Ford, M.G. Ring (Cardiff), A.G. Bateman (Neath), A. Emyr; A. Clement (Swansea), C.J. Bridges (Neath); M. Griffiths (Cardiff), +K.H. Phillips (Neath), P. Knight (Pontypridd), Glyn D. Llewellyn (Neath), P. Arnold (Swansea), *O.L. Williams (Bridgend), M.A. Jones, M.S. Morris (Neath). Reps: *D. Aled Williams (Bridgend) for Ford; A.D. Reynolds (Swansea) for Jones.
T: Arthur Emyr 2, Owain Williams (pen try).
C: Paul Thorburn 3.
P: Thorburn 3.
DG: Anthony Clement.
Referee: Fred A. Howard (England).

Namibia 23 Wales 38

Windhoek. 5 June 1993

Wales won by 5 tries, 2 cons, 3 pens to 2 tries, 2 cons, 3 pens.

A double sending-off had marred the Wales win over Namibia B by 47–10, hooker Robin McBryde of Swansea and the home team's scrum-half Wakkies Husselman the players involved in seperate incidents. Both players were rebuked, but not banned. In this Test, Wales struggled and found themselves 19–20 down midway through the second spell. The lead changed five times in all. Namibian full-back Jaco Coetzee scored 18 points, while Neil Jenkins, restored to outside-half, completed a century of points in this, his 15th Test match. Rupert Moon scored the final try on this short tour.

Namibia J. Coetzee; +G. Mans, H. Snyman, M. Marais, E. Meyer; M. Booysen, B. Buitendag; C. Derks, S. Smith, A. van Wyk, D. Kotze, B. Malgas, J. Barnard, K. Goosen, H. Brink.
T: Jaco Coetzee, Dirk Kotze.
C: Coetzee 2.
P: Coetzee 3.

Wales M.A. Rayer; S.D. Hill (Cardiff), N. Boobyer (Llanelli), R.A. Bidgood (Newport), W.T. Proctor (Llanelli); N.R. Jenkins (Pontypridd), R.H.StJ.B. Moon (Llanelli); M. Griffiths (Cardiff), A.E. Lamerton (Llanelli), H. Williams-Jones (South Wales Police), P.T. Davies (Llanelli), +G.O. Llewellyn (Neath), S. Davies (Swansea), E.W. Lewis, R.L. Jones (Llanelli). Rep: M.A. Perego (Llanelli) for R.L. Jones.
T: Emyr Lewis 2, Simon Hill, Wayne Proctor, Rupert Moon.
C: Neil Jenkins 2.
P: Jenkins 3.
Referee: Ken W. McCartney (Scotland).

ROMANIA

Romania 24 Wales 6

Bucharest. 12 November 1983

Romania won by 4 tries, 1 con, 2 pens to 2 pens.

Despite warnings that this first full international against Romania was going to be difficult, the selectors chose six new caps and Wales were sunk with very little trace. It was one of the worst performances for several years, with the pack thoroughly outplayed and Wales sorely missing Terry Holmes, who had suffered a serious knee injury on the Lions tour of New Zealand.

Romania V. Ion; S. Fuicu, A. Lungu, M. Marghescu, M. Aldea; D. Alexandru, +M. Paraschiv; I. Bucan, M. Munteanu, V. Pascu, G. Dumitru, G. Caragea, F. Murariu, S. Constantin, A. Radulescu.
T: Gheorghe Caragea, Florica Murariu, Marian Aldea, Adrian Lungu.
C: Dumitru Alexandru.
P: Alexandru 2.

Wales G. Evans (Maesteg); *M.H. Titley (Bridgend), R.A. Ackerman (London Welsh), *B. Bowen (South Wales Police), *A.M. Hadley (Cardiff); M. Dacey (Swansea), *R. Giles (Aberavon); S.T. Jones (Pontypool), W.J. James (Aberavon), I.H. Eidman (Cardiff), S.J. Perkins (Pontypool), *T.W. Shaw (Newbridge), *M.A. Brown, +E.T. Butler (Pontypool), D.F. Pickering (Llanelli). Rep: D.S. Richards (Swansea) for Dacey.
P: Gwyn Evans 2.
Referee: Jean-Claude Yche (France).

Wales 9 Romania 15

Arms Park, Cardiff. 10 December 1988

Romania won by 1 try, 1 con, 3 pens to 1 try, 1 con, 1 pen.

It was the double for Romania over Wales. It was, more tragically, the death-knell for Jonathan Davies, who was wrongly singled out as the biggest villain, having captained woeful Wales. A month later he was in the colours of Widnes Rugby League club and was to prove an outstanding performer in that sport. Romania kept it tight and scored a first-half try from a lineout. Wales levelled at 9–9, before Gelu Ignat landed two further penalty goals which brought a slow handclap from the crowd. Paul Thorburn, playing as a replacement wing, reached 170 points, to pass Phil Bennett's tally of 166. Bennett played 29 times, however, whilst this was only the 20th appearance by Thorburn.

Wales A. Clement (Swansea); G.M.C. Webbe, M.R. Hall, J.A. Devereux, *R.S. Diplock (Bridgend); +J. Davies (Llanelli), R.N. Jones (Swansea); M. Griffiths (Bridgend), I.J. Watkins (Ebbw Vale), D. Young (Cardiff), J.D.M. Wakeford (South Wales Police), K. Moseley (Pontypool), D.J. Bryant (Bridgend), P.T. Davies (Llanelli), R.G. Collins (Cardiff). Rep: P.H. Thorburn (Neath) for Webbe.
T: John Devereux.
C: Paul Thorburn.
P: Thorburn.

Romania M. Toader; N. Racean, N. Fulina, A. Lungu, D. Boldor; G. Ignat, D. Neaga; G. Leonte, G. Ion, G. Dumitrescu, S. Ciorascu, H. Dumitras, +F. Murariu, I. Doja, A. Radulescu. Rep: T. Oroian for Dumitras.
T: Gheorghe Ion.
C: Gelu Ignat.
P: Ignat 3.
Referee: Ian M. Bullerwell (England).

(NB: RWC 1995 Euro qualifier v Wales)

Wales 70 Romania 21

Racecourse Ground, Wrexham. 30 August 1997

Wales won by 11 tries, 6 cons, 1 pen to 2 tries, 1 con, 3 pens.

Wrexham's soccer ground was the venue for a near-capacity 11,000 to enjoy rugby in the sun, as Wales ran in 11 tries, with Arwel Thomas notching 23 points. The little Swansea pivot scored two tries, to give him seven in Test rugby, and that represented the most by any Welsh outside-half. If he had converted the final try, he would have set a new Welsh record of points in a match too. As it was, replacement Lee Jarvis completed the scoring in the two minutes he was on the field. Four days earlier, Romania had lost 36–21 to Wales 'A' at Pontypridd.

OTHER INTERNATIONAL MATCHES – ROMANIA

Arwel Thomas sets up an attack against Romania at Wrexham in 1997 while Rob Appleyard and Allan Bateman await developments. Little Arwel scored ten tries for Wales from the outside-half position.

(© Huw Evans)

Wales K.A. Morgan (Pontypridd); W.T. Proctor (Llanelli), A.G. Bateman (Richmond), L.B. Davies (Cardiff), G. Thomas (Bridgend); A.C. Thomas (Swansea), P. John (Pontypridd); C.D. Loader (Swansea), B.H. Williams (Richmond), D. Young (Cardiff), S.J. Moore (Moseley), M.A. Rowley (Pontypridd), R.C. Appleyard (Swansea), N. Thomas (Bath), +R.G. Jones (Cardiff). Reps: N.K. Walker (Cardiff) for Proctor; *L. Jarvis (Cardiff) for A.C. Thomas; L. Mustoe (Cardiff) for Young; S.M. Williams (Cardiff) for Rowley.
T: Allan Bateman 2, Leigh Davies 2, Arwel Thomas 2, Nigel Walker, Steve Williams, Kevin Morgan, Barry Williams, Paul John.
C: Arwel Thomas 5, Lee Jarvis.
P: Arwel Thomas.

Romania V. Maftei; L. Colceriu, R. Gontineac, G. Solomie, I. Rotaru; S. Guranescu, M. Iacob; G. Vlad, M. Radoi, A. Salageanu, +T. Branza, V. Nedelcu, F. Corodeanu, C. Draguceanu, E. Septar. Reps: P. Mitu for Maftei; C. Stan for Salageanu; A. Ruxanda for Septar.
T: I. Rotaru, C. Draguceanu.
C: S. Guranescu.
P: S. Guranescu 3.
Referee: D. Iain Ramage (Scotland).

TONGA

Tonga 7 Wales 15

Teufaiva Stadium, Nuku'alofa. 12 June 1986

Wales won by 1 try, 1 con, 3 pens to 1 try, 1 pen.

Tonga literally went down fighting, with both Adrian Hadley and Phil Davies being laid out. Hadley was carried off and Glen Webbe came on to become the first black player to win a cap for Wales. It is noticeable that five of the Welsh team later turned professional: Hadley, Jonathan Davies, John Devereux, Stuart Evans and try-scorer Paul Moriarty.

Tonga T. Eteaki; L. Hopoate, P. Moala, F. Lavemai, S. Mohi; T. Lovo, T. Fifita; T. Bloomfield, A. Afu Fungavaka, M. Moala, +O. Vitelefi, M. Tu'ungafasi, E. Koloto, P. Tupou, P. Langi.
T: Talai Fifita.
P: Tomasi Lovo.

Wales M. Dacey; M.H. Titley (Swansea), J.A. Devereux (Bridgend/SG Inst), B. Bowen (South Wales Police), A.M. Hadley (Cardiff); J. Davies (Neath), R.N. Jones (Swansea); J. Whitefoot (Cardiff), W.J. James (Aberavon), S. Evans (Neath), R.L. Norster (Cardiff), +R.D. Moriarty, W.P. Moriarty (Swansea), P.T. Davies (Llanelli), M.A. Brown (Pontypool). Reps: *G.M.C. Webbe (Bridgend) for Hadley; *H.D. Richards (Neath) for Brown.
T: Paul Moriarty.
C: Malcolm Dacey.
P: Bleddyn Bowen 2, Dacey.
Referee: Brian Kinsey (Australia).

(NB: RWC 1987 Wales v Tonga)

Tonga 9 Wales 18

Teufaiva Stadium, Nuku'alofa. 22 June 1994

Wales won by 6 pens to 3 pens.

Four new caps were brought in, with Paul John partnering his boyhood pal and clubmate Neil Jenkins. North Wales rejoiced as Ian Buckett followed Robin McBryde into the team. On the wing, Gwilym Wilkins made his only appearance, to leave David Manley (Pontypridd) as the only uncapped player in the tour party. It was an error-strewn match, with Jenkins placing four penalty goals in the first half and two in the second. It was the fifth consecutive away win and the ninth in ten matches. Ieuan Evans skippered his 12th winning team to equal Billy Trew's performance in the early 1900s.

Tonga S. Tu'ipulotu; T. Va'enuku, F. Manukia, P. Latu, S. Taupeaafu; E. Vunipola, Manu Vunipola; T. Lutua, +Feao Vunipola, U. Fa, F. Mafi, V. Taumoepeau, T. Loto'ahea, T. Vikilani, K. Tu'ipulotu. Rep: F. Masila for Mafi (temp).
P: Sateki Tu'ipulotu 3.

Wales A. Clement (Swansea); +I.C. Evans (Llanelli), M.R. Hall (Cardiff), N. Boobyer (Llanelli), *G. Wilkins (Bridgend); N.R. Jenkins, *P. John (Pontypridd); *I.M. Buckett, G.R. Jenkins (Swansea), H. Williams-Jones, A.H. Copsey (Llanelli), G.O. Llewellyn (Neath), H.T. Taylor (Cardiff), *S.M. Williams (Neath), R.G. Collins (Pontypridd). Rep: N.G. Davies (Llanelli) for Hall.
P: Neil Jenkins 6.
Referee: Ephraim J. Sklar (Argentina).

Wales 46 Tonga 12

St Helen's, Swansea. 16 November 1997

Wales won by 6 tries, 2 cons, 4 pens to 2 tries, 1 con.

International rugby returned to Swansea for the first time since Wales defeated Scotland in 1954. There was also a return for Neil Jenkins, in his true position of outside-half. Unfortunately, the match was played in pouring rain in front of a crowd that was believed to be the smallest to watch Wales since the 1890s. Utility back Gareth Wyatt, aged 20, became the 955th player to be capped by Wales. He scored a try from full-back. Tonga included the Ebbw Vale club pair of Siua Taumalolo and Kuli Faletau, as well as David Tueti, who was soon to join Neath from Bristol and prop forward Ta'u who played for Pontypridd.

Wales *G. Wyatt (Pontypridd); G. Thomas (Bridgend), L.B. Davies (Cardiff), I.S. Gibbs (Swansea), N.K. Walker (Cardiff); N.R. Jenkins, P. John (Pontypridd); C.D. Loader (Swansea), B.H. Williams (Richmond), S.C. John (Cardiff), S.J. Moore (Moseley), M.J. Voyle (Llanelli), R.C. Appleyard (Swansea), N. Thomas (Bath), +R.G. Jones (Cardiff). Reps:

Derek Quinnell on the charge in a non-cap match against Tonga. The Llanelli utility forward was a Lion before winning his first Welsh cap and his sons Scott and Craig were to follow suit. (© Huw Evans)

D.R. James (Pontypridd) for G. Thomas; R. Howley (Cardiff) for P. John; J.M. Humphreys (Cardiff) for B.H. Williams; C.T. Anthony (Swansea) for S. John; S.M. Williams (Cardiff) for Moore.
T: Gareth Thomas 2, Leigh Davies, Nigel Walker, Gareth Wyatt, Chris Anthony.
C: Neil Jenkins 2.
P: Neil Jenkins 4.

Tonga G. Tonga; D. Tueti, F. Tatafu, P. Tanginoa, S. Faka'osi'folau; S. Taumalolo, S.M. Tu'ipulotu; +D. Briggs, V. Ma'asi, N. Ta'u, S. Latu, K. Faletau, H. Pohiva, K. Tu'ipulotu, T. Matakaiongo. Reps: S. Tai for Tatafu; H. Lavaka for Briggs; S. Hafoka for Pohiva; M. Molitika for Matakaiongo.
T: Fepi'kou Tatafu, Sione Tai.
C: Gustavo Tonga.
Referee: Santiago Borsani (Argentina).

WESTERN SAMOA

Western Samoa 14 Wales 32

Moamoa, Apia. 14 June 1986.

Wales won by 4 tries, 2 cons, 3 pens, 1 drop goal to 2 tries, 2 pens.

This was a fine performance by Wales, which they would have liked to repeat in later meetings with Western Samoa! Despite the heat, it was a satisfying result and a good end to an interesting tour, in which four matches were won and one lost by 29–13 to the Eastern Fijian side at Suva.

Western Samoa T. Aialupo; T. Vaega, L. Koko, N. Palamo, I. Tautua; T. Fong, T. Aleni; M. Jones, M. Patolo, +D. Tafua, F. Kelemete, P. Alalatoa, S. Toomalatai, A. Ma'atusi, L. Sasi.
T: D. Tafua, N. Palamo.
P: Tele'a Aialupo 2.

Wales M. Dacey; M.H. Titley (Swansea), J.A. Devereux (Bridgend/SG Inst), B. Bowen (South Wales Police), G.M.C. Webbe (Bridgend); J. Davies (Neath), R.N. Jones (Swansea); J. Whitefoot (Cardiff), W.J. James (Aberavon), S. Evans (Neath), R.L. Norster (Cardiff), +R.D. Moriarty, W.P. Moriarty (Swansea), P.T. Davies (Llanelli), M.A. Brown (Pontypool).
T: Bleddyn Bowen, John Devereux, Mark Titley, Richard Moriarty.
C: Malcolm Dacey 2.
P: Dacey 3.
DG: Jonathan Davies.
Referee: R.C. 'Bob' Francis (New Zealand).

Wales 28 Western Samoa 6

Arms Park, Cardiff. 12 November 1988

Wales won by 5 tries, 4 cons to 1 try, 1 con.

Out went Tony Gray and in came John Ryan as national coach. The new man was the first of the coaches not to have been capped as a player. One of his new caps was wing Carwyn Davies, a Llandovery farmer, who took his own life in February 1997. In this match, he scored a try before retiring injured. Another débutant, John Wakeford, also scored. The tourists, who held Wales to 12–6 in the first half, also lost in Wales to Bridgend and Aberavon.

Wales P.H. Thorburn (Neath); M.R. Hall (Bridgend), N.G. Davies (Llanelli), B. Bowen (Swansea), *C. Davies; +J. Davies (Llanelli), R.N. Jones (Swansea); *M. Griffiths, *W.H. Hall (Bridgend), D. Young (Cardiff), *J.D.M. Wakeford (South Wales Police), R.L. Norster (Cardiff), R.D. Phillips (Neath), P.T. Davies (Llanelli), D.J. Bryant (Bridgend). Reps: *R.V. Wintle (London Welsh) for C. Davies; A. Clement (Swansea) for Thorburn.
T: Nigel Davies 2, Jonathan Davies, Carwyn Davies, John Wakeford.
C: Paul Thorburn 4.

Western Samoa A. Aiolupo; +L. Koko, K. Sio, T. Faamasino, T. Ugapo; J. Ah Kuoi, V. Fepuleai; P. Fatialofa, S. Toomalatai, V. Alalatoa, S. Lemamea, D. Williams, L. Mano, S. Tupuola, M. Iupeli. Rep: V. Faasua for Iupeli.
T: Saini Lemamea.
C: Aanaterea Aiolupo.
Referee: Owen E. Doyle (Ireland).

(NB: RWC 1991 Wales v Western Samoa)

Western Samoa 34 Wales 9

Moamoa, Apia. 25 June 1994

Western Samoa won by 3 tries, 2 cons, 5 pens to 3 pens.

A combination of heat and a strong home side proved too much for Wales, who hung on for 40 minutes, changing ends only 9–14 down. The strong tackling, however, shattered Welsh hearts and it was a much more one-sided game than the one in the World Cup in Cardiff three years before. It looked like a match too far, as Pat Lam and Brian Lima ran in second-half tries. Phil Davies played for part of the match to become the most-capped forward for Wales.

Western Samoa A. Aiolupo; B. Lima, T.M. Vaega, F. Tuilagi, T. Samania; D.J. Kellett, V. Vitale; +P. Fatialofa, T. Leiasamaivao, G. Latu, M.L. Birtwistle, M. Keenan, S.L. Vaifale, P.R. Lam, M. Iupeli. Reps: S. Kaleta for Keenan; D. Mika for Lam.
T: Brian Lima 2, Pat Lam.
C: Darren Kellett 2.
P: Kellett 5.

Wales M.A. Rayer (Cardiff); +I.C. Evans (Llanelli), A. Clement (Swansea), N.G. Davies, W.T. Proctor (Llanelli); N.R. Jenkins (Pontypridd), R.H.StJ.B. Moon; R.L. Evans (Llanelli), G.R. Jenkins (Swansea), J.D. Davies (Neath), P.T. Davies (Llanelli), G.O. Llewellyn (Neath), E.W. Lewis, L.S. Quinnell (Llanelli), R.G. Collins (Pontypridd). Reps: H. Williams-Jones (Llanelli) for R.L. Evans; A.H. Copsey (Llanelli) for P.T. Davies; H.T. Taylor (Cardiff) for Quinnell.
P: Neil Jenkins 3.
Referee: Barry Leask (Australia)

(NB: RWC 1999. Wales v Samoa)

ZIMBABWE

Zimbabwe 14 Wales 35 – 1st Test

Bulawayo. 22 May 1993

Wales won by 4 tries, 3 cons, 2 pens, 1 drop goal to 1 try, 3 pens.

The public were not impressed by the fact that Wales were going back to Namibia and Zimbabwe on tour only three years after the last trip. This time there were two Tests with Zimbabwe and the tour brought victories in all six matches. The best performance came in the final match, when the South African Barbarians were defeated by 56–17. Neil Jenkins ended the tour with 89 points. Dental student Simon Hill started well in the 1st Test, with a début try after just seven minutes, and there was little danger of defeat after that. New caps Lyn Jones and Neil Boobyer ensured that Llanelli had eight representatives on the pitch.

Zimbabwe I. Noble; D. Nash, M. Letcher, +D. Walters, V. Olonga; C. Brown, S. Day; G. Snyder, B. Beattie, A. Garvey, R. Demblon, T. Tabvuma, S. Landman, R. Fargnoli, B. Dawson.
T: Victor Olonga.
P: Dave Walters 3.

Wales M.A. Rayer; *S.D. Hill (Cardiff), R.A. Bidgood (Newport), N.R. Jenkins (Pontypridd), W.T. Proctor (Llanelli); A. Davies (Cardiff), R.H.StJ.B. Moon (Llanelli); M. Griffiths (Cardiff), A.E. Lamerton (Llanelli), H. Williams-Jones (South Wales Police), P.T. Davies (Llanelli), +G.O. Llewellyn (Neath), M.A. Perego, E.W. Lewis, *R.L. Jones (Llanelli). Rep: *N. Boobyer (Llanelli) for Proctor; S. Davies (Swansea) for Lewis.
T: Phil Davies, Simon Hill, Rupert Moon, Wayne Proctor.
C: Neil Jenkins 3.
P: Jenkins 2.
DG: Adrian Davies.
Referee: Ian Rogers (South Africa).

Zimbabwe 13 Wales 42 – 2nd Test

The Police Grounds, Harare. 29 May 1993

Wales won by 6 tries, 3 cons, 2 pens to 1 try, 1 con, 2 pens.

Versatile Neil Jenkins had played at centre in the first Test but was now at full-back, as Michael Rayer was injured. It did not interfere with his goalkicking and he accumulated 17 more points, which included a try, while skipper Gareth Llewellyn twice crossed the Zimbabwe line.

Zimbabwe I. Noble; W. Schultz, M. Letcher, +D. Walters, V. Olonga; C. Brown, E. MacMillan; G. Snyder, B. Beattie, A. Garvey, R. Demblon, T. Tabvuma, S. Landman, D. Kirkman, B. Dawson. Reps: E. Chimbima for Schultz; B. Chivandire for Landman.
T: Victor Olonga.
C: Ian Noble.
P: Noble 2.

Wales N.R. Jenkins (Pontypridd); S.D. Hill (Cardiff), R.A. Bidgood (Newport), N. Boobyer, W.T. Proctor (Llanelli); A. Davies (Cardiff), R.H.StJ.B. Moon (Llanelli); M. Griffiths (Cardiff), A.E. Lamerton (Llanelli), J.D. Davies (Neath), P. Arnold (Swansea), +G.O. Llewellyn (Neath), S. Davies (Swansea), E.W. Lewis, R.L. Jones (Llanelli).
T: Gareth Llewellyn 2, Roger Bidgood, John Davies, Stuart Davies, Neil Jenkins.
C: Jenkins 3.
P: Jenkins 2.
Referee: Ian Anderson (South Africa).

Zimbabwe 11 Wales 49

National Sports Stadium, Harare. 6 June 1998

Wales won by 8 tries, 3 cons, 1 pen to 1 try, 2 pens.

Dennis John of Pontypridd became the 12th coach of the national team, albeit as a caretaker, as Wales 'scoured the world' for a permanent new man. The players were falling over themselves to miss out on a tour of southern Africa, which was not wanted by anyone, it seemed, except the WRU. It provided the most embarrassing moments in the history of Welsh rugby, bravely though the tour party tried. The Test against Zimbabwe proved to be the only victory on the six-match tour. It was played before a small audience, but at least showed that Byron Hayward was an international-class performer. He appeared after 33 minutes, when another débutant, David Weatherley, collapsed with a knee injury. Despite playing at full-back, Hayward ran in three tries, a feat only previously achieved by two other débutants, Willie Llewellyn (1899) and Gareth Thomas (1995). Scott Quinnell also broke down as quickly as he had done for the Lions a year earlier, and a total of six new caps were used. There was a brace of tries for the lively Richard Rees and 19 points for Arwel Thomas. The tour then moved to South Africa, with losses to the Emerging Springboks (13–35), Border (8–24), Natal (23–30) and Gauteng Falcons (37–39). Seven replacements were sent out, with one of them, flanker Dean Thomas of Swansea, receiving his marching orders in the Gauteng match.

Zimbabwe V. Olonga; R. Karimazondo, J. Ewing, B. French, C. Graham; K. Tsimba, R. Bekker; G. Snyder, W. Barratt, G. Stewart, B. Catterall, S. Landman, L. Greef, +B. Dawson, M. Mwerenga. Reps: D. Walters for Karimazondo; D. Trivella for Tsimba; C. McNab for Mwerenga; A. Nortse for Bekker; I. Nelson for Barratt.
T: Ryan Bekker.
P: Kenny Tsimba 2.

Wales *D.J. Weatherley; *R. Rees, M. Taylor (Swansea), D.R. James (Pontypridd), W.T. Proctor (Llanelli); A.C. Thomas (Swansea), +R. Howley (Cardiff); *D.R. Morris (Neath), G.R. Jenkins (Swansea), J.D. Davies (Richmond), Andrew P. Moore (Swansea), M.A. Jones (Ebbw Vale), N. Thomas (Bath), L.S. Quinnell (Richmond), M.E. Williams (Pontypridd). Reps: *B.I. Hayward (Ebbw Vale) for Weatherley; *J. Funnell (Ebbw Vale) for Taylor; P. John (Pontypridd) for Howley; B.H. Williams (Richmond) for Jenkins; *C.P. Wyatt (Llanelli) for Jones; C.L. Charvis (Swansea) for Quinnell.
T: Byron Hayward 3, Richard Rees 2, Arwel Thomas 2, Wayne Proctor.
C: Arwel Thomas 3.
P: Arwel Thomas.
Referee: Johann Meuwesen (South Africa).

BARBARIANS

Wales 24 Barbarians 31

Arms Park, Cardiff. 6 October 1990

Barbarians won by 4 tries, 3 cons, 3 pens to 1 try, 1 con, 5 pens, 1 drop goal.

The Welsh public found it astonishing that caps should be awarded, even if it did mark the Barbarians' centenary. After all, many Welsh clubs were having centenary seasons and they did not play Wales! It appeared to many that Wales were just determined to win a match. It did not work, however – they lost. From 21–21 at the interval, Wales led 24–21, but the Baa-baas hit back with tries by the uncapped Eric Rush and centre Jeremy Guscott. The Rush try was converted by former Wales Schools captain Stuart Barnes, who contributed 15 points. Statisticians noted begrudgingly that Paul Thorburn's 21 points was a Wales record and that eight Neath players began the match, with replacement Adrian Davies making it nine. Fred Howard was the referee for Wales's third successive match.

Wales +P.H. Thorburn (Neath); S.P. Ford, M.G. Ring (Cardiff), S.A. Parfitt (Swansea), D.A. Edmunds (Neath); D.W. Evans (Cardiff), C.J. Bridges; B.R. Williams, K.H. Phillips (Neath), M. Griffiths (Cardiff), Glyn D. Llewellyn (Neath), P. Arnold (Swansea), M.S. Morris, M.A. Jones (Neath), R.E. Webster (Swansea). Reps: *A. Davies (Neath/Cambridge U) for Ring; P. Knight (Pontypridd) for Williams.
T: Paul Thorburn.
C: Thorburn.

Powerful Swansea flanker Richard Webster shrugs off Australian Steve Cutler in the capped match against the Barbarians in 1990. Glyn Llewellyn, Paul Arnold and Mark Jones are up in support, while Dominique Erbani (France) and Nick Farr-Jones (Australia) are floored. (© Huw Evans)

P: Thorburn 5.
DG: David Evans.

Barbarians D.I. Campese (Australia); J.-B. Lafond (France), J.T. Stanley (NZ), J.C. Guscott (England), D. Charvet (France); S. Barnes (England), +N.C. Farr-Jones (Australia); P.A.G. Rendall (England), S.J. Smith (Ireland), R.W. Loe, I.D. Jones (NZ), S.A.G. Cutler (Australia), M.C. Teague (England), D. Erbani (France), E.J. Rush (Auckland). (NB: Rush was later capped for New Zealand.)
T: Joe Stanley, Nick Farr-Jones, Eric Rush, Jeremy Guscott.
C: Stuart Barnes 3.
P: Barnes 3.
Referee: Fred A. Howard (England).

Wales 31 Barbarians 10

Arms Park, Cardiff 24 August 1996.

Wales won by 5 tries, 3 cons to 2 tries.

Caps were again awarded against the Barbarians and, unlike in 1990, Wales were the winners. Nigel Walker and replacement Richie Collins had both been capped prior to the 1995 World Cup but now appeared against Wales. Walker was to reappear for Wales in 1997.

Wales W.T. Proctor; I.C. Evans (Llanelli), L.B. Davies (Cardiff), N.G. Davies (Llanelli), G. Thomas (Bridgend); N.R. Jenkins (Pontypridd), R. Howley (Cardiff); C.D. Loader (Swansea), +J.M. Humphreys (Cardiff), J.D. Davies (Neath), G.O. Llewellyn (Harlequins), D. Jones (Cardiff), *K.P. Jones (Ebbw Vale), S.M. Williams (Neath), *M.E. Williams (Pontypridd). Reps: W.J.L. Thomas (Cardiff) for N.G. Davies; P. John (Pontypridd) for Howley (temp); P. Arnold (Swansea) for D. Jones.
T: Nigel Davies 2, Wayne Proctor, Jonathan Humphreys, Robert Howley.
C: Neil Jenkins 3.

Barbarians D. Arrieta (Biarritz); A. Bose (Mana), R. Dourthe, S. Glas (France), N.K. Walker (Wales); P.W. Howard (Australia), A. Pichot (Argentina); A.G.J.Watt, J.A. Hay (Scotland), R.G.A. Snow (Canada), R.J. McCall (Australia), D. Sims (Gloucester), M. Gusuna (Mana), +A.R.B. Pene (NZ), D.S. Corkery (Ireland). Rep: R.G. Collins (Wales) for Gusuna.
(NB: Sims was later capped for England)
T: Arran Pene, David Corkery.
Referee: Jim M. Fleming (Scotland).

JAPAN

Wales 55 Japan 5

Arms Park, Cardiff, 16 October 1993

Wales won by 9 tries, 5 cons to 1 try.

For the first time in a full international match, Wales reached a half-century of points. It was a nine-try romp, begun by skipper Ieuan Evans after only 45 seconds of play. Centre Scott Gibbs scored his first points in what was his 19th match, while Japan's only score came from wing Ian Williams, who had already appeared 17 times for Australia.

Wales A. Clement (Swansea); +I.C. Evans (Llanelli), I.S. Gibbs (Swansea), N.R. Jenkins (Pontypridd), N.K. Walker; A. Davies (Cardiff), R.H.StJ.B. Moon (Llanelli); M. Griffiths (Cardiff), A.E. Lamerton (Llanelli), J.D. Davies (Neath), A.H. Copsey (Llanelli), G.O. Llewellyn (Neath), S. Davies (Swansea), E.W. Lewis, R.L. Jones (Llanelli). Reps: R.A. Bidgood (Newport) for Evans; M.A. Rayer (Cardiff) for Walker.
T: Ieuan Evans 2, Scott Gibbs 2, Neil Jenkins, Rupert Moon, Emyr Lewis, Mike Rayer, Tony Clement.
C: Jenkins 5.

Japan T. Matsuda; I. Williams, M. Fujikake, E. Kutsuki, Y. Yoshida; A. Aoki, Y. Nagatomo; O. Ota, +M. Kunda, T. Takahashi, Y. Sakuraba, B. Ferguson, S. Kaleta, S. Latu, H. Ouchi.
T: Ian Williams.
Referee: Ed F. Morrison (England).

(NB: Wales have also played Japan in RWC 1995 and 1999)

Skipper Eddie Butler on the burst in a non-test match against Japan in 1983. Nicknamed 'ET', he played on 16 occasions between 1980 and 1984. (© Huw Evans)

NZ MAORIS

Wales v NZ Maoris (native team)

St Helen's, Swansea. 22 December 1888
(No points were awarded until 1891)

Wales won by 1 goal, 2 tries to nil

Wales introduced eight new caps against the first tourists to visit Britain and one of those, Norman Biggs of Cardiff, was aged only 18 years and one month. Biggs is still the youngest player ever to appear for Wales. He played in eight matches before serving in the Boer War and then, at the age of 37, whilst in the role of Superintendent in the Nigerian Police, was killed by a poison arrow in a native ambush. With only two local players – Swansea dockers Bill Towers and Billy Bowen – playing, Wales were jeered by the small crowd. Among the new faces were Dickie Garrett from Penarth and Sid Nicholls, the elder brother of the great Gwyn Nicholls. Llanelli and Cardiff beat the Maoris, as did England, but the tourists defeated Ireland on a trip that contained 104 matches and lasted for 14 months. The visitors were not all Maoris, as they contained several colonists to bolster them.

Wales *J.E. Webb; *G. Thomas (Newport), *R.M. Garrett (Penarth), C.S. Arthur, *N.W. Biggs (Cardiff); C.J. Thomas (Newport), W.J. Stadden; +A.F. Hill, A.F. Bland, *S.H. Nicholls (Cardiff), *J. Hannan, *C.T. Harding (Newport), W.H. Towers, W.A. Bowen (Swansea), *D. Griffiths (Llanelli).
T: George Thomas, James Hannan, William Towers.
C: Jim Webb.

NZ Maoris W. Warbrick (Matata); E. McCausland (Gordon), W.T. Wynyard (North Shore), D.R. Gage (Poneke), W. Elliott (Grafton); P. Keogh (Kaikorai), F. Warbrick (Tauranga); T.R. Ellison (Poneke), G. Wynyard (North Shore), A. Webster (Hokianga), H.H. Lee (Riverton), G.A. Williams (Poneke), +J.A. Warbrick (Matata), D. Stewart (Thames), Wi Karauria (Nelson).
Referee: Spencer Mortimer (England).

NZ ARMY

Wales 3   NZ Army 6

St Helen's, Swansea. 21 April 1919

NZ Army won by 2 pens to 1 pen.

Centre 'Jack' Stohr, who had been capped for New Zealand in 1910, supplied the two penalty goals to defeat Wales in the first capped match after the First World War. It was against the New Zealand Services side, who played 39 matches in Britain and France, including several in the Kings Cup. Cardiff had drawn 0–0, but the New Zealanders were a strong side and Wales had only Walter Martin and skipper Glyn Stephens previously capped. Jerry Shea, a professional boxer and later a rugby league player, was playing out of position on the wing but scored the Welsh points. Evan Davies, Evan Rees, Ike Fowler, Trevor Nicholas, Aaron Rees and Bill Havard never appeared again, with Rees and Fowler turning to league.

Wales *E. Davies (Maesteg); *J. Shea (Pill Harriers), *B.M.G. Thomas (Bridgend), *E.B. Rees (Swansea), *T.J. Nicholas (Cardiff); W.J. Martin (Newport), *I.J. Fowler (Llanelli); +G. Stephens (Neath), *J. Jones (Aberavon), *Rev. W.T. Havard, *D.G. Francis (Llanelli), *J.J. Whitfield (Pill Harriers), *A. Rees (Maesteg), *W.G.H. Morris (Abertillery), *E.T. Parker (Swansea).
P: Jerry Shea.

NZ Army C.H. Capper; W.A. Ford, L.B. Stohr, P.W. Storey, +J. Ryan; W.R. Fea, C. Brown; M. Cain, E.W. Hasell, J. Kissick, J.E. Moffitt, A. Wilson, A.H. West, R. Fogarty, A.P. Singe.
P: Jack Stohr 2.
Referee: R. Charman (England).

WORLD CUP

The inaugural World Cup was held in Australia and New Zealand in 1987. Wales finished in third place, but in 1991 and 1995 they failed to pass the group stage. Though they progressed to the finals as hosts in 1999, they fell to Australia at Cardiff at the quarter-final stage.

1987 WORLD CUP

Wales 13 Ireland 6

Athletic Park, Wellington (New Zealand). 25 May 1987

Wales won by 1 try, 1 pen, 2 drop goals to 2 pens.

It was windy in Wellington and luckily Ireland, in this opening World Cup match, could not repeat their victory of eight weeks earlier. Jonathan Davies played a commanding role and Paul Thorburn helped create the try scored by Mark Ring. It was not a great start, but at least it was a winning one in this new competition.

Wales P.H. Thorburn (Neath); I.C. Evans (Llanelli), J.A. Devereux (Bridgend/SG Inst), M.G. Ring, A.M. Hadley (Cardiff); J. Davies (Neath), R.N. Jones (Swansea); J. Whitefoot (Cardiff), K.H. Phillips, S. Evans (Neath), +R.D. Moriarty (Swansea), R.L. Norster, G.J. Roberts (Cardiff), W.P. Moriarty (Swansea), R.G. Collins (South Wales Police).
T: Mark Ring.
P: Paul Thorburn.
DG: Jonathan Davies 2.

Ireland H.P. MacNeill (London Irish); T.M. Ringland (Ballymena), B.J. Mullin (Oxford U), M.J. Kiernan (Dolphin), K.D. Crossan (Instonians); P.M. Dean (St Mary's Coll), M.T. Bradley (Cork Const); P.A. Orr (Old Wesley), T. Kingston (Bective Rangers), D.C. Fitzgerald (Lansdowne), +D.G. Lenihan (Cork Const), W.A. Anderson (Dungannon), P.M. Matthews (Wanderers), B.J. Spillane (Bohemians), D.G. McGrath (Cork Const).   Rep: J.J. Glennon (Skerries) for Matthews.
P: Michael Kiernan 2.
Referee: Kerry J.V. Fitzgerald (Australia).

Wales 29 Tonga 16

Showgrounds Oval, Palmerston North (New Zealand). 29 May 1987

Wales won by 4 tries, 2 cons, 2 pens, 1 drop goal to 2 tries, 1 con, 2 pens.

Glen Webbe raced in for three tries, but was ruled to have concussion after a head-high Tongan tackle and was sent home, just when he was set to establish himself in the side. Webbe was understandably annoyed as he had finished the match on the field. Even worse news was that the strong prop forward, Stuart Evans, was injured and also departed the country. For the first time, Wales wore green jerseys.

Wales P.H. Thorburn (Neath); G.M.C. Webbe (Bridgend), K. Hopkins (Swansea), M.G. Ring, A.M. Hadley (Cardiff); M. Dacey, R.N. Jones (Swansea); *D.A. Buchanan (Llanelli), K.H. Phillips, S. Evans (Neath), +R.D. Moriarty (Swansea), H.D. Richards (Neath), W.P. Moriarty (Swansea), P.T. Davies (Llanelli), G.J. Roberts (Cardiff). Reps: J. Davies (Neath) for Dacey; S.W. Blackmore (Cardiff) for Evans.
T: Glen Webbe 3, Adrian Hadley.
C: Paul Thorburn 2.
P: Thorburn 2.
DG: Jonathan Davies.

Tonga T. Ete'aki; M. Vunipola, S. Mohi, T. Fukakitekei'aho, K. Fielea; A. 'Amone, T. Fifita; V. Lutua, A. Afu Fungavaka, H. Tupou, M. Tu'ungafasi, K. Fine, V.T. Kakato, M. Felise, +F. Valu. Reps: A. Liava'a for 'Amone; L. Va'eono for Tupou.
T: K. Fielea, Talai Fifita.
C: A Liava'a.
P: Liava'a, Asaeli 'Amone.
Referee: David J. Bishop (New Zealand).

Wales 40 Canada 9

Rugby Park, Invercargill (New Zealand). 3 June 1987

Wales won by 8 tries, 4 cons to 3 pens.

After being 9–6 down at the interval, Wales ran in seven second-half tries, as acting captain Jonathan Davies called the tune. Ieuan Evans scored four tries to equal the Welsh record and help his side top the group. Richard Moriarty, the elected World Cup captain, replaced his brother but Davies continued to lead the team.

Wales P.H. Thorburn (Neath); I.C. Evans (Llanelli), B. Bowen (South Wales Police), J.A. Devereux (Bridgend/SG Inst), A.M. Hadley (Cardiff); +J. Davies (Neath), R. Giles (Aberavon); J. Whitefoot, A.J. Phillips, S.W. Blackmore (Cardiff), S. Sutton (South Wales Police), R.L. Norster (Cardiff), W.P. Moriarty (Swansea), P.T.

Evans the bard: wing Ieuan Evans is feted at an Eisteddfod. The Llanelli speedster scored 33 tries in his 72 appearances for Wales. (© Huw Evans)

Davies (Llanelli), G.J. Roberts (Cardiff). Reps: K. Hopkins (Swansea) for Bowen; R.D. Moriarty (Swansea) for (W.P.) Moriarty.
T: Ieuan Evans 4, Adrian Hadley, Alan Phillips, John Devereux, Bleddyn Bowen.
C: Paul Thorburn 4.

Canada M. Wyatt; P. Palmer, T. Woods, J. Lecky, S.D. Gray; G.L. Rees, I. Stuart; R. McKellar, K. Svoboda, W. Handson, R. Hindson, +H. de Goede, B. Breen, G. Ennis, R. Frame. Rep: D. Tucker for Stuart.
P: Gareth Rees 3.
Referee: David J. Bishop (New Zealand).

Wales 16 England 3 – Quarter Final

Ballymore, Brisbane (Australia). 8 June 1987

Wales won by 3 tries, 2 cons to 1 pen.

This was not a classic, but Wales were deserved winners. It was confirmed by an interception and walk to the line by John Devereux that delighted the Welsh followers in the crowd. Robert Jones scored his first international try, catching the defence cold and following up his own kick. Injuries forced Wales to call up the 19-year-old David Young, who played so well that many wondered why they had hardly heard of him. He moved to rugby league in 1990, but was to return to union and to the Wales team.

Wales P.H. Thorburn (Neath); I.C. Evans (Llanelli), B. Bowen (South Wales Police), J.A. Devereux (Bridgend/SG Inst), A.M. Hadley (Cardiff); J. Davies (Neath), R.N. Jones (Swansea); D.A. Buchanan (Llanelli), A.J. Phillips (Cardiff), *D. Young (Swansea), +R.D. Moriarty (Swansea), R.L. Norster, G.J. Roberts (Cardiff), W.P. Moriarty (Swansea), R.G. Collins (South Wales Police). Rep: H.D. Richards (Neath) for Norster.
T: Gareth Roberts, Robert Jones, John Devereux.
C: Paul Thorburn 2.

England J. Webb (Bristol); +M.E. Harrison (Wakefield), K.G. Simms (Wasps), J.L.B. Salmon (Harlequins), R. Underwood (Leicester); P.N. Williams (Orrell), R.M. Harding (Bristol); P.A.G. Rendall (Wasps), B.C. Moore (Notts), G.S. Pearce (Northampton), W.A. Dooley (Fylde), N.C. Redman (Bath), G.W. Rees (Notts), D. Richards (Leicester), P.J. Winterbottom (Headingley). Rep: G.J. Chilcott (Bath) for Rendall.
P: Jon Webb.
Referee: René Hourquet (France).

Wales 6 New Zealand 49 – Semi Final

Ballymore, Brisbane (Australia). 14 June 1987

New Zealand won by 8 tries, 7 cons, 1 pen to 1 try, 1 con.

With Bob Norster out with injury, Huw Richards of Neath came in and was sent off in the second half for punching. It was a correct decision, but New Zealand skipper Wayne Shelford should also have been dismissed. The match was a non-contest, with Wales conceding eight tries in their biggest-ever beating – at that point! Strangely, it was centre John Devereux who scored the best try of the match. David Kirk's New Zealand went on to defeat France in the final.

Wales P.H. Thorburn (Neath); I.C. Evans (Llanelli), B. Bowen (South Wales Police), J.A. Devereux (Bridgend/SG Inst), A.M. Hadley (Cardiff); J. Davies (Neath), R.N. Jones (Swansea); D.A. Buchanan (Llanelli), K.H. Phillips (Neath), D. Young (Swansea), +R.D. Moriarty (Swansea), H.D. Richards (Neath), W.P. Moriarty (Swansea), P.T. Davies (Llanelli), R.G. Collins (South Wales Police). Rep: S. Sutton (South Wales Police) for Collins.
Sent off: Huw Richards.

Who wants it? Lock Gareth Llewellyn is supported in training by fellow forwards Emyr Lewis, Tony Copsey and Hugh Williams-Jones. (© Huw Evans)

T: John Devereux.
C: Paul Thorburn.

New Zealand J.A. Gallagher (Wellington); J.J. Kirwan, J.T. Stanley (Auckland), W.T. Taylor, C.I. Green (Canterbury); G.J. Fox, +D.E. Kirk; S.C. McDowell, S.B.T. Fitzpatrick, J.A. Drake (Auckland), M.J. Pierce (Wellington), G.W. Whetton, A.J. Whetton (Auckland), W.T. Shelford (North Harbour), M. Brooke-Cowden (Auckland). Rep: B.J. McCahill (Auckland) for Stanley.
T: John Kirwan 2, Wayne Shelford 2, Joe Stanley, John Drake, Alan Whetton, Marc Brooke-Cowden.
C: Grant Fox 7.
P: Fox.
Referee: Kerry J.V. Fitzgerald (Australia).

Wales 22 Australia 21 – 3rd Place Play Off

International Park, Rotorua (New Zealand). 18 June 1987

Wales won by 3 tries, 2 cons, 2 pens to 2 tries, 2 cons, 2 pens, 1 drop goal.

The third-place match was of little interest to Australian coach Alan Jones after losing to France in the match of the tournament. He even queried where Rotorua was, and his attitude got through to his players. Wales were probably never the third-best in the competition, but they deserved their win. Losing, in the final minute by 21–16, a good passing move sent Adrian Hadley in at the corner. Paul Thorburn put over a splendid conversion from the touchline to give his side victory. Australia had forward David Codey sent off in the fourth minute for stamping. Richard Webster, a month short of his 20th birthday, was playing club rugby in Australia and was called up for the injured Richie Collins. He proved a great success, though injury restricted his chances and he was to turn professional in 1993.

Wales P.H. Thorburn (Neath); I.C. Evans (Llanelli), J.A. Devereux (Bridgend/SG Inst), M.G. Ring, A.M. Hadley (Cardiff); J. Davies (Neath), R.N. Jones (Swansea); D.A. Buchanan (Llanelli), A.J. Phillips, S.W. Blackmore (Cardiff), +R.D. Moriarty (Swansea), S. Sutton (South Wales Police), G.J. Roberts (Cardiff), W.P. Moriarty, *R.E. Webster (Swansea).

T: Gareth Roberts, Paul Moriarty, Adrian Hadley
C: Paul Thorburn 2.
P: Thorburn 2.

Australia A. Leeds (NSW); P.C. Grigg, +A.G. Slack (Queensland), M.P. Burke, D.I. Campese (NSW); M.P. Lynagh, B.A. Smith; C.A. Lillicrap, T.A. Lawton, A.J. McIntyre (Queensland), S.A.G. Cutler (NSW), T. Coker, D. Codey (Queensland), S.N. Tuynman, S.P. Poidevin (NSW). Reps: N.C. Farr-Jones (NSW) for Grigg; E.E. Rodriguez (NSW) for Lillicrap.
Sent off: David Codey.

T: Matthew Burke, Peter Grigg.
C: Michael Lynagh 2.
P: Lynagh 2.
DG: Lynagh.
Referee: Fred A. Howard (England).

1991 WORLD CUP

Wales 13 Western Samoa 16

Arms Park, Cardiff. 6 October 1991

Western Samoa won by 2 tries, 1 con, 2 pens to 2 tries, 1 con, 1 pen.

Tremendous tackling, skilful play and a bit of luck saw Western Samoa win and Wales were effectively out of the World Cup after 80 minutes. Even a win over Argentina would be academic, as Australia were obviously going to defeat Wales. Phil May, aged 35, dislocated his shoulder, and when he came off was disconsolate on the touchline as Samoa swept on. Michael Rayer was a popular replacement, though many would have chosen him a lot earlier. There were protests at one of the Samoan tries, as Robert Jones claimed to have touched down first, but the match was already drifting away. Centre Frank Bunce and outside-half Steve Bachop soon appeared for New Zealand and Matt Keenan played for Pontypool.

Wales A. Clement (Swansea); +I.C. Evans (Llanelli), I.S. Gibbs (Neath), M.R. Hall, A. Emyr; M.G. Ring (Cardiff), R.N. Jones (Swansea); M. Griffiths (Cardiff), *K. Waters (Newbridge), L. Delaney, P.S. May (Llanelli), K. Moseley (Newport), E.W. Lewis, P.T. Davies (Llanelli), R.G. Collins (Cardiff). Reps: *M.A. Rayer (Cardiff) for Clement; M.S. Morris (Neath) for May; G.R. Jenkins (Pontypool) for Collins.
T: Arthur Emyr, Ieuan Evans.
C: Mark Ring.
P: Ring.

Western Samoa A. Aiolupo; B. Lima, T.M. Vaega, F.E. Bunce, T. Tagaloa; S.J. Bachop, M. Vaea; +P. Fatialofa, S. Toomalatai, V. Alalatoa, M.L. Birtwistle, M. Keenan, S. Vaifale, P.R. Lam, A. Perelini.
T: To'o Vaega, Sila Vaifale.
C: Matthew Vaea.
P: Vaea 2.
Referee: Patrick Robin (France).

Wales 16 Argentina 7

Arms Park, Cardiff. 9 October 1991

Wales won by 1 try, 4 pens to 1 try, 1 pen.

After seven defeats and one draw over a 19-month period, Wales had not won in Cardiff. When they did finally achieve it, they were neither exciting nor convincing. Mark Ring was not fully fit and fast wingers were wasted on a safety-first policy. The road ahead still looked bleak.

Wales M.A. Rayer (Cardiff); +I.C. Evans (Llanelli), I.S. Gibbs (Neath), M.R. Hall, A. Emyr; M.G. Ring (Cardiff), R.N. Jones (Swansea); M. Griffiths (Cardiff), G.R. Jenkins (Pontypool), L. Delaney (Llanelli), P. Arnold (Swansea), K. Moseley (Newport), E.W. Lewis, P.T. Davies (Llanelli), R.E. Webster (Swansea).
T: Paul Arnold.
P: Mark Ring 3, Mike Rayer.

Argentina G. del Castillo; M. Teran, E. Labòrde, H. García Simon, D. Cuesta Silva; I. Arbizu, G. Camardon; F. Mendez, R. le Fort, L. Molina, P. Sporleder, G. Llanes, +P. Garreton, M. Carreras, J. Santamarina.
T: Herman García Simon.
P: Guillermo del Castillo.
Referee: René Hourquet (France).

Wales 3 Australia 38

Arms Park, Cardiff. 12 October 1991

Australia won by 6 tries, 4 cons, 2 pens to 1 pen.

In some ways, a 38-point beating was seen as a victory, so low had standards fallen. John Eales cleaned out Wales in the lineout to such an extent that when Kevin Moseley was penalised in the second half, he shrugged his shoulders as if to say: 'What can I do to beat him?' It was the heaviest home defeat in Welsh history. Six tries had never been scored against Wales in a home Test. When Alan Davies met the media to announce his side, one pressman said: 'Don't bother, we just bought the programme on the way here.' Astonishingly, Tony Clement was at full-back and not Michael Rayer. At least Australia did go on to beat England 12–6 in the final at Twickenham.

Wales A. Clement (Swansea); +I.C. Evans (Llanelli), I.S. Gibbs (Neath), M.R. Hall, A. Emyr; M.G. Ring (Cardiff), R.N. Jones (Swansea); M. Griffiths (Cardiff), G.R. Jenkins (Pontypool), L. Delaney (Llanelli), P. Arnold (Swansea), K. Moseley (Newport), E.W. Lewis, P.T. Davies

(Llanelli), R.E. Webster (Swansea). Reps: M.A. Rayer (Cardiff) for Gibbs; D.W. Evans (Cardiff) for Emyr.
P: Mark Ring.

Australia M.C. Roebuck; D.I. Campese (NSW), J.S. Little, T.J. Horan (Queensland), R.H. Egerton (NSW); +M.P. Lynagh, P.J. Slattery (Queensland); A.J. Daly, P.N. Kearns, E.J.A. McKenzie (NSW), R.J. McCall, J.A. Eales (Queensland), S.P. Poidevin, V. Ofahengaue (NSW), J.S. Miller (Queensland).
T: Marty Roebuck 2, Peter Slattery, David Campese, Michael Lynagh, Tim Horan.
C: Lynagh 4.
P: Lynagh 2.
Referee: Keith H. Lawrence (New Zealand).

1995 WORLD CUP

Portugal 11 Wales 102 – Qualifier

The University Field, Lisbon. 17 May 1994.

Wales won by 16 tries, 11 cons to 1 try, 2 pens.

Ieuan Evans led Wales for the 19th time, to surpass the 18 by Arthur Gould, but the match was unworthy of Test status. It was played as a qualifier for the 3rd World Cup, with all the other home countries having gone through automatically to the final stage. Wales raced through to score 16 tries and just bring up a century of points in the closing minutes. Nigel Walker scored four and both Ieuan Evans and Mike Hall gained hat-tricks with Neil Jenkins contributing 22 points and reaching 209 points in 22 Tests. Even scrum-half Robert Jones scored – he had previously just one try in 47 matches. In a strong team, the only débutant was Hemi Taylor, the popular Cardiff and former Newbridge back-row forward, who became the first New Zealander to play for Wales.

Portugal J.M. Vilar-Gomez; P. Murinello, R. Perreira, N. Mourao, T. Morais; +J. Queimado, P. Netto Fernandes; S. Perreira, M. Batista, P. Domingos, A. Pecas, A. Andrade, P. Arsenio, J. Pires, P. Eusebio. Reps: E. Macedo for (S.) Perreira; A. Cunna for Pires.
T: Pedro Murinello.
P: Vilar-Gomez 2.

Wales M.A. Rayer (Cardiff); +I.C. Evans, N.G. Davies (Llanelli), M.R. Hall, N.K. Walker (Cardiff); N.R. Jenkins (Pontypridd), R.N. Jones (Swansea); R.L. Evans (Llanelli), G.R. Jenkins (Swansea), J.D. Davies (Neath), A.H. Copsey (Llanelli), G.O. Llewellyn (Neath), *H.T. Taylor (Cardiff), L.S. Quinnell, E.W. Lewis (Llanelli).
T: Nigel Walker 4, Ieuan Evans 3, Mike Hall 3, Robert Jones 2, Gareth Llewellyn, Hemi Taylor, Scott Quinnell.
C: Neil Jenkins 11.
Referee: David J. Bishop (New Zealand).

Wales prepare to meet Spain at Madrid in a 1994 World Cup qualifying match. It proved to be an easy 54–0 win in which Ieuan Evans scored three of the seven Welsh tries. *Back row*: A. Davies, G.R. Jenkins, R.L. Evans, J.D. Davies, R.C. McBryde. *Middle row*: A.H. Copsey, E.W. Lewis, L.S. Quinnell, G.O. Llewellyn, P. Arnold, M.A. Perego, N.G. Davies, H. Williams-Jones. *Front row*: M.A. Rayer, A. Clement, R.H.StJ.B. Moon, I.C. Evans (capt.), N.R. Jenkins, M.R. Hall, N.K. Walker, R.N. Jones. (© Huw Evans)

Spain 0 Wales 54 – Qualifier

Madrid University, Madrid. 21 May 1994

Wales won by 7 tries, 5 cons, 3 pens to nil.

Another meaningless one-sided match only proved that Spain were probably a bit stronger than Portugal. Another hat-trick of tries for Ieuan Evans took him to 19 in 43 matches, with Nigel Walker having scored eight in eight matches.

Spain J. Azkargorta; P. Martin, A. Mino, A. Enciso, J. Torres; F. Puertas, J. Hernandez-Gil; J. Alvarez, J. Aguiar, J. Diez, A. Malo, J. Villau, J. Etxebberia, J. López, +J. Gutiérrez. Reps: S. Espina for Alvarez; F. de la Calle for Etxebberia; I. de Lázaro for Diez; O. Solano for de Lázaro.

Wales A. Clement (Swansea); +I.C. Evans, N.G. Davies (Llanelli), M.R. Hall, N.K. Walker (Cardiff); N.R. Jenkins (Pontypridd), R.H.St J.B. Moon; R.L. Evans (Llanelli), G.R. Jenkins (Swansea), J.D. Davies, G.O. Llewellyn (Neath), P. Arnold (Swansea), E.W. Lewis, L.S. Quinnell, M.A. Perego (Llanelli). Rep: A.H. Copsey (Llanelli) for Lewis.
T: Ieuan Evans 3, Scott Quinnell, Nigel Walker, Garin Jenkins (pen try).
C: Neil Jenkins 5.
P: Neil Jenkins 3.
Referee: David J. Bishop (New Zealand).

Romania 9 Wales 16 – Euro-Seeding

The 23rd August Stadium, Bucharest. 17 September 1994

Wales won by 1 try, 1 con, 3 pens to 3 pens.

A superb try by Ieuan Evans enabled Wales to break their duck against Romania, having lost both of their previous encounters. A dull match, played in intense heat, saw Evans set a new Welsh best of 21 tries, with the remainder of the game best forgotten. Italy defeated Romania by 24–6 in Catania two weeks later and Wales needed to beat Italy to qualify for the supposedly easier Pool C in the finals.

Romania V. Brici; L. Colceriu, N. Racean, N. Fulina, G. Solomie; N. Nichitean, D. Neaga; G. Leonte, G. Ion, G. Vlad, S. Ciorascu, C. Cojocariu, T. Oroian, +T. Brinza, A. Guranescu. Reps: C. Gheorge for Leonte; C. Draguceanu for Brinza.
P: Neculai Nichitean 3.

Wales M.A. Rayer (Cardiff); +I.C. Evans (Llanelli), M.R. Hall (Cardiff), N.G. Davies, W.T. Proctor (Llanelli); N.R. Jenkins (Pontypridd), R.H.St J.B. Moon; R.L. Evans (Llanelli), G.R. Jenkins (Swansea), J.D. Davies (Neath), P.T. Davies (Llanelli), G.O. Llewellyn (Neath), H.T. Taylor, E.W. Lewis (Cardiff), R.G. Collins (Pontypridd).
T: Ieuan Evans.
C: Neil Jenkins.
P: Neil Jenkins 3.
Referee: David T.M. McHugh (Ireland).

Wales 29 Italy 19 – Euro-Seeding

Arms Park, Cardiff. 12 October 1994

Wales won by 1 try, 7 pens, 1 drop goal to 1 try, 1 con, 4 pens.

Neil Jenkins and Diego Domínguez, two of the most outstanding goalkickers in international rugby, duelled under the floodlights and 'Jenks' just came out on top with eight successful shots to equal the 24 points he had scored against Canada in 1993. Jenkins became the highest-ever scorer for Wales with an aggregate of 308 points, four more than Paul Thorburn had achieved. He'd also scored them in 28 Tests, compared with Thorburn's 37.

Wales M.A. Rayer (Cardiff); W.T. Proctor (Llanelli), M.R. Hall (Cardiff), N.G. Davies (Llanelli), A. Clement (Swansea); N.R. Jenkins (Pontypridd), R.H.St J.B. Moon; R.L. Evans (Llanelli), G.R. Jenkins (Swansea), J.D. Davies (Neath), P.T. Davies (Llanelli), +G.O. Llewellyn (Neath), H.T. Taylor, E.W. Lewis (Cardiff), R.G. Collins (Pontypridd). Rep: H. Williams-Jones (Llanelli) for (R.L.) Evans (temp).
T: Nigel Davies.
P: Neil Jenkins 7.
DG: Neil Jenkins.

Italy P. Vaccari (Milan); M. Gerosa (Piacenza), S. Bordon (Rovigo), M. Bonomi (Milan), I. Francescato (Treviso); D. Domínguez (Milan), A. Troncon (Treviso); +Massimo Cuttitta (Milan), C. Orlandi (Piacenza), G. Grespan, R. Favaro (Treviso), D. Scaglia (Tegola la Tarvisium), O. Arancio (Catania), C. Checchinato (Rovigo), A. Sgorlon (Lafert San Dona). Rep: M. dal Sie (Lafert San Dona) for Grespan.
T: Ivan Francescato.
C: Diego Domínguez.
P: Domínguez 4.
Referee: Ken W. McCartney (Scotland).

Wales 57 Japan 10

Springbok Park, Bloemfontein. 27 May 1995

Wales won by 7 tries, 5 cons, 4 pens to 2 tries.

If the Welsh win looked adequate, it was put into perspective by New Zealand's 145–17 beating of Japan eight days later. It was to be the only win by Wales in a World Cup that was as miserable for them as the 1991 tournament had been. Gareth Thomas, aged 20, became the first player this century to score three tries on his international début for Wales. Scrum-half Andy Moore impressed on his first appearance and Mike Hall led Wales for the first time, having been appointed ahead of Ieuan Evans by caretaker coach Alex Evans. While Ron Waldron had picked Neath players when he was coach, Evans turned to his Cardiff club and selected eight of them. Neil Jenkins was switched to centre and kicked 22 points.

Wales A. Clement (Swansea); I.C. Evans (Llanelli), +M.R. Hall (Cardiff), N.R. Jenkins (Pontypridd), *G. Thomas (Bridgend); A. Davies, *Andy P. Moore; M. Griffiths (Cardiff), G.R. Jenkins (Swansea), J.D. Davies (Neath), D. Jones (Cardiff), G.O. Llewellyn (Neath), S. Davies (Swansea), E.W. Lewis, H.T. Taylor (Cardiff). Reps: D.W. Evans (Treorchy) for (A.) Davies; *W.S.Roy (Cardiff) for Jones.
T: Gareth Thomas 3, Ieuan Evans 2, Hemi Taylor, Andy Moore.
C: Neil Jenkins 5.
P: Neil Jenkins 4.

Japan T. Matsuda; L. Oto, A. Yoshida, Y. Motoki, T. Masuho; S. Hirao, M. Horikoshi; O. Ota, +M. Kunda, K. Takahashi, Y. Sakuraba, B. Ferguson, H. Kajihara, Sione Latu, Sinali Latu.
T: Lopeti Oto 2.
Referee: Ephraim J. Sklar (Argentina).

Wales 9 New Zealand 34

Ellis Park, Johannesburg. 31 May 1995

New Zealand won by 3 tries, 2 cons, 4 pens, 1 drop goal to 2 pens, 1 drop goal.

Alex Evans dished out three new caps (two of them to Cardiff players) and switched lock Gareth Llewellyn to blind-side flanker. And that against the might of New Zealand! Good tackling frustrated the men in black and only three tries were conceded as Welshmen breathed a sigh of relief. Gareth Thomas and Neil Jenkins had positional switches after the win over Japan, while Wayne Proctor stuck to his task of halting the massive new sensation, Jonah Lomu. Durban-born Andrew Mehrtens was the latest in a long line of great New Zealand place-kickers.

Wales A. Clement (Swansea); I.C. Evans (Llanelli), +M.R. Hall (Cardiff), G. Thomas (Bridgend), W.T. Proctor (Llanelli); N.R. Jenkins (Pontypridd), R.N. Jones (Swansea); R.L. Evans (Llanelli), *J.M. Humphreys (Cardiff), J.D. Davies (Neath), D. Jones (Cardiff), *G. Prosser (Pontypridd), G.O. Llewellyn (Neath), H.T. Taylor, *A.M. Bennett (Cardiff).
P: Neil Jenkins 2.
DG: Jenkins.

New Zealand G.M. Osborne (North Harbour); J.T. Lomu (Counties), F.E. Bunce, W.K. Little (North Harbour), M.C.G. Ellis (Otago); A.P. Mehrtens, G.T.M. Bachop (Canterbury); C.W. Dowd, +S.B.T. Fitzpatrick, O.M. Brown (Auckland), I.D. Jones, B.P. Larsen (North Harbour), J.W. Joseph (Otago), M.R. Brewer (Canterbury), J.A. Kronfeld (Otago). Rep: E.J.Rush (North Harbour) for Lomu.
T: Walter Little, Marc Ellis, Josh Kronfeld.
C: Andrew Mehrtens 2.
P: Mehrtens 4.
DG: Mehrtens.
Referee: Ed F. Morrison (England).

Wales 23 Ireland 24

Ellis Park, Johannesburg. 4 June 1995

Ireland won by 3 tries, 3 cons, 1 pen to 2 tries, 2 cons, 2 pens, 1 drop goal.

Despite a last-minute try and conversion, Wales bowed out of the World Cup having been beaten by a more enthusiastic Ireland side who led 14–0 in the first 15 minutes of the match. Little could be said for Wales, who also appeared out of sorts off the field. Robert Jones became the most-capped Welsh scrum-half by making his 54th appearance. It was to be his last, along with Ricky Evans, who appeared on the field as Neil Jenkins kicked the final conversion with play not being restarted. Mike Hall and Adrian Davies did not reappear either.

Wales A. Clement (Swansea); I.C. Evans (Llanelli), +M.R. Hall (Cardiff), N.R. Jenkins (Pontypridd), G. Thomas (Bridgend); A. Davies (Cardiff), R.N. Jones (Swansea); M. Griffiths, J.M.Humphreys (Cardiff), J.D. Davies (Neath), D. Jones (Cardiff), G.O. Llewellyn (Neath), S. Davies (Swansea), E.W. Lewis, H.T. Taylor (Cardiff). Rep: R.L. Evans (Llanelli) for (J.D.) Davies.

Powerful centre Scott Gibbs on the charge against Ireland's outside-half Eric Elwood. Gibbs had played 45 times for Wales by the end of the 1999 World Cup, but his best performances came for the 1997 British Lions. (© Huw Evans)

T: Jonathan Humphreys, Hemi Taylor.
C: Neil Jenkins 2.
P: Jenkins 2.
DG: Adrian Davies.

Ireland C.M.P. O'Shea (Lansdowne); R.M. Wallace (Garryowen), B.J. Mullin (Blackrock Coll), J.C. Bell (Ballymena), S.P. Geoghegan (Bath); E.P. Elwood (Lansdowne), N.A. Hogan (Terenure Coll); N.J. Popplewell (Wasps), †T.J. Kingston (Dolphin), G.F. Halpin (London Irish), G.M. Fulcher (Cork Const), N.P.J. Francis (Old Belvedere), D. Corkery (Cork Const), P.S. Johns (Dungannon), W.D. McBride (Malone). Rep: E.O. Halvey (Shannon) for McBride (temp).

T: Nick Popplewell, Denis McBride, Eddie Halvey.
C: Eric Elwood 3.
P: Elwood.
Referee: Ian Rogers (South Africa).

1999 WORLD CUP

Wales 23 Argentina 18

The Millennium Stadium, Cardiff. 1 October 1999

Wales won by 2 tries, 2 cons, 3 pens to 6 pens.

Wales beat the United States by 53–24 in a non-cap match on 30 August and then waited 62 days before opening the fourth World Cup on a Friday afternoon in Cardiff. It was only a moderate beginning, but such was the change in fortunes that even a moderate performance brought a victory – the ninth in succession. Only two tries were scored – the first when flanker Colin Charvis charged through the defensive wall – the second from a delightful move by Dafydd James and Gareth Thomas that left Mark Taylor clear for the run-in. Charvis and prop Robert Grau received bans after being cited for violence; the former subsequently missed the Japan and Samoa matches. The match also saw the introduction of Jason Jones-Hughes after a tug-of-war between Wales and Australia for his services.

Wales S.P. Howarth (Newport); G. Thomas (Cardiff), M. Taylor, I.S. Gibbs (Swansea), D.R. James (Llanelli); N.R. Jenkins, +R. Howley (Cardiff); P.J.D. Rogers (Newport), G.R. Jenkins (Swansea), D. Young, J.C. Quinnell (Cardiff), C.P. Wyatt (Llanelli), C.L. Charvis (Swansea), L.S. Quinnell (Llanelli), B.D. Sinkinson (Neath). Rep: *J. Jones-Hughes (New South Wales) for Gibbs.
T: Colin Charvis, Mark Taylor.
C: Neil Jenkins 2.
P: Neil Jenkins 3.

Argentina M. Contepomi; O. Bartolucci, E. Simone, +L. Arbizu, D.L. Albanese; G. Quesada, A. Pichot; R. Grau, M. Ledesma, M. Reggiardo, I.F. Lobbe, A. Allub, S. Phelan, G. Longo, L. Ostiglia. Reps: G.F. Camardon for Bartolucci; O. Hasan-Jalil for Reggiardo; R.A. Martin for Ostiglia.
P: Gonzalo Quesada 6.
Referee: Paddy D. O'Brien (New Zealand).

No, he's not in pain – Colin Charvis is ecstatic at scoring the first Welsh try of the 1999 World Cup. It came in the first half of the match against Argentina. (© Huw Evans)

The golden boot of outside-half Neil Jenkins: by the end of 1999 he had scored 895 points for Wales, playing at outside-half, centre and full-back.
(© Huw Evans)

Wales 64 Japan 15

The Millennium Stadium, Cardiff. 9 October 1999

Wales won by 9 tries, 8 cons, 1 pen to 2 tries, 1 con, 1 pen.

More interest centred on Neil Jenkins than the final score. Wales won well enough after early scares, which included a splendid try by Daisuke Ohata. After that it remained to be seen whether Neil Jenkins could overtake Michael Lynagh of Australia as the leading points-scorer in international rugby. Including the 41 points Neil scored for the British Lions in South Africa, he had reached 911 by the end of the match and had equalled, but not passed, Lynagh's total.

Wales S.P. Howarth (Newport); J. Jones-Hughes (NSW), M. Taylor, I.S. Gibbs (Swansea), A.G. Bateman (Northampton); N.R. Jenkins, +R. Howley (Cardiff); P.J.D. Rogers (Newport), G.R. Jenkins (Swansea), D. Young, J.C. Quinnell (Cardiff), M.J. Voyle (Llanelli), M.E. Williams (Cardiff), G. Lewis (Pontypridd), B.D. Sinkinson (Neath). Reps: G. Thomas (Cardiff) for Bateman; D.S. Llewellyn (Newport) for Howley; A.L.P. Lewis (Cardiff) for Rogers; J.M. Humphreys (Cardiff) for (G.R.) Jenkins; B.R. Evans (Swansea) for Young; C.P. Wyatt (Llanelli) for Sinkinson.
T: Mark Taylor 2, Gareth Thomas, Robert Howley, Scott Gibbs, Shane Howarth, David Llewellyn, Allan Bateman (pen try).
C: Neil Jenkins 8.
P: Neil Jenkins.

Japan T. Hirao; D. Ohata, Y. Motoki, +A. McCormick, P. Tuidraki; K. Hirose, G.T.M. Bachop; S. Hasegawa, M. Kunda, N. Nakamura, R. Gordon, H. Tanuma, N. Okubo, J.W. Joseph, G. Smith. Reps: W. Murata for Bachop; T. Nakamichi for Hasegawa; M. Sakata for Kunda; Y. Sakuraba for Gordon; T. Ito for Okubo.
T: Daisuke Ohata, Patillai Tuidraki.
C: Keiji Hirose.
P: Hirose.
Referee: Joël Dumé (France).

Neil Jenkins wearing the old outside-half number 6 in training. He set a new Welsh record of 73 appearances when he played against Australia in the 1999 World Cup quarter-final. (© Huw Evans)

Wales 31 Samoa 38

The Millennium Stadium, Cardiff. 14 October 1999

Samoa won by 5 tries, 5 cons, 1 pen to 3 tries, 2 cons, 4 pens.

Western Samoa had beaten Wales in the 1991 World Cup and now, as Samoa, they completed an amazing double. Bad defensive play let Wales down and defeat came after ten successive victories. Hence they failed to equal the 11 wins between 1906 and 1910. At 31-all, Samoa broke away for full-back Silao Leaega to score in the corner and convert with a magnificent kick. Neil Jenkins had soon overtaken Michael Lynagh's international points record, but turned villain by passing to Samoan skipper Pat Lam, who raced three-quarters of the length of the pitch to score unopposed. Jenkins and Robert Howley were paired for the 25th time – a new Wales half-back record.

Wales S.P. Howarth (Newport); G. Thomas (Cardiff), M. Taylor, I.S. Gibbs (Swansea), D.R. James (Llanelli); N.R. Jenkins, +R. Howley (Cardiff); P.J.D. Rogers (Newport), G.R. Jenkins (Swansea), D. Young (Cardiff), G.O. Llewellyn (Harlequins), C.P. Wyatt (Llanelli), M.E. Williams (Cardiff), L.S. Quinnell (Llanelli), B.D. Sinkinson (Neath). Reps: A.L.P. Lewis (Cardiff) for Rogers; B.R. Evans (Swansea) for Young.
T: Gareth Thomas 2 (pen tries).
C: Neil Jenkins 2.
P: N.R. Jenkins 4.

Samoa S. Leaega; B. Lima, G.E. Leaupepe, T.M. Vaega, V.L. Tuigamala; S.J. Bachop, S. So'oialo; B. Reidy, T. Leota, R. Ale, L. Tone, L. Falaniko, P.J. Paramore, +P.R. Lam, C. Glendinning. Reps: T.L. Fanolua for Leaupepe; E. Va'a for Bachop; O. Mataulau for Leota; M. Mika for Ale; S. Ta'ala for Falaniko; S. Sititi for Paramore.
T: Stephen Bachop 2, Pat Lam, Silao Leaega, Lio Falaniko.
C: Leaega 5.
P: Leaega.
Referee: Ed F. Morrison (England).

Wing Dafydd James on the charge for Wales in the 1999 World Cup quarter-final against Australia. Scott Gibbs and Robert Howley are supporting with Australians Tim Horan, David Herbert, Stephen Larkham and Tiaan Strauss in defence. (© Huw Evans)

Wales 9 Australia 24 – Quarter Final

The Millennium Stadium, Cardiff. 23 October 1999

Australia won by 3 tries, 3 cons, 1 pen to 3 pens.

Garin Jenkins led Wales out for their second World Cup quarter-final. It was his 50th cap, while namesake Neil Jenkins made his 73rd appearance, passing Ieuan Evans as the most-capped Wales player of all time. The rains fell with the stadium roof wide open and both sides found handling difficult. Referee Colin Hawke came in for criticism after allowing the first and third Australian tries but, in truth, the Wallabies were the best side on the day, though the margin of 15 points was flattering.

Wales S.P. Howarth (Newport); G. Thomas (Cardiff), M. Taylor, I.S. Gibbs (Swansea), D.R. James (Llanelli); N.R. Jenkins, +R. Howley (Cardiff); P.J.D. Rogers (Newport), G.R. Jenkins (Swansea), D. Young, J.C. Quinnell (Cardiff), C.P. Wyatt (Llanelli), C.L. Charvis (Swansea), L.S. Quinnell (Llanelli), B.D. Sinkinson (Neath). Reps: A.G. Bateman (Northampton) for Thomas; A.L.P. Lewis (Cardiff) for Rogers; B.R. Evans (Swansea) for Young; M.J. Voyle (Llanelli) for (J.C.) Quinnell.
P: Neil Jenkins 3.

Australia M.C. Burke (NSW); B.N. Tune, D.J. Herbert, T.J. Horan (Queensland), J.W.C. Roff; S.J. Larkham, G.M. Gregan (ACT); R.L.L. Harry (NSW), M.A. Foley (Queensland), A.T. Blades (NSW), D. Giffin (ACT), +J.A. Eales, M.J. Cockbain (Queensland), C.P. Strauss (NSW), D.J. Wilson (Queensland). Reps: J.S. Little (NSW) for Tune; J.A. Paul (ACT) for Foley (temp); M. Connors (Queensland) for Eales; O.D.A. Finegan (ACT) for Cockbain.
T: George Gregan 2, Ben Tune.
C: Matt Burke 3.
P: Burke.
Referee: Colin J. Hawke (New Zealand).

STATISTICS

International Championship Winners
(– denotes uncompleted)

1883–84 England	1924–25 Scotland	1962–63 England
1884–85 –	1925–26 Ireland	1963–64 Scotland
1885–86 England	Scotland	Wales
Scotland	1926–27 Scotland	1964–65 Wales
1886–87 Scotland	Ireland	1965–66 Wales
1887–88 –	1927–28 England	1966–67 France
1888–89 –	1928–29 Scotland	1967–68 France
1889–90 England	1929–30 England	1968–69 Wales
Scotland	1930–31 Wales	1969–70 France
1890–91 Scotland	1931–32 England	Wales
1891–92 England	Wales	1970–71 Wales
1892–93 Wales	Ireland	1971–72 –
1893–94 Ireland	1932–33 Scotland	1972–73 *Five-way tie*
1894–95 Scotland	1933–34 England	1973–74 Ireland
1895–96 Ireland	1934–35 Ireland	1974–75 Wales
1896–97 –	1935–36 Wales	1975–76 Wales
1897–98 –	1936–37 England	1976–77 France
1898–99 Ireland	1937–38 Scotland	1977–78 Wales
1899–	1938–39 England	1978–79 Wales
1900 Wales	Wales	1979–80 England
1900–01 Scotland	Ireland	1980–81 France
1901–02 Wales	1946–47 Wales	1981–82 Ireland
1902–03 Scotland	England	1982–83 France
1903–04 Scotland	1947–48 Ireland	Ireland
1904–05 Wales	1948–49 Ireland	1983–84 Scotland
1905–06 Ireland	1949–50 Wales	1984–85 Ireland
Wales	1950–51 Ireland	1985–86 France
1906–07 Scotland	1951–52 Wales	Scotland
1907–08 Wales	1952–53 England	1986–87 France
1908–09 Wales	1953–54 England	1987–88 Wales
1909–10 England	France	France
1910–11 Wales	Wales	1988–89 France
1911–12 England	1954–55 Wales	1989–90 Scotland
Ireland	France	1990–91 England
1912–13 England	1955–56 Wales	1991–92 England
1913–14 England	1956–57 England	1992–93 France
1919–20 England	1957–58 England	1993–94 Wales
Scotland	1958–59 France	1994–95 England
Wales	1959–60 France	1995–96 England
1920–21 England	England	1996–97 France
1921–22 Wales	1960–61 France	1997–98 France
1922–23 England	1961–62 France	1998–99 Scotland
1923–24 England		

Welsh International Match Records

	PLAYED	WON	DRAWN	LOST
England	105	49	12	44
Scotland	103	56	2	45
Ireland	103	59	6	38
France	75	40	3	32
Australia	20	8	0	12**
New Zealand	17	3	0	14
South Africa	13	1	1	11
Argentina	5	5	0	0
Canada	5	4	0	1
Italy	5	5	0	0
Western Samoa	5	2	0	3
Fiji	4	4	0	0
Romania	4	2	0	2
Tonga	4	4	0	0
USA	4	4	0	0
Japan	3	3	0	0
Namibia	3	3	0	0
Zimbabwe	3	3	0	0
Barbarians	2	1	0	1
Portugal	1	1	0	0
Spain	1	1	0	0
New Zealand Army	1	0	0	1
New Zealand Native Team	1	1	0	0
TOTAL	**487**	**259**	**24**	**204**

(** includes match played against 1927–28 New South Wales side, which has now been granted full-cap status as Australia).

GRAND SLAM WINS

8 times   1908   1909   1911   1950   1952   1971   1976   1978

TRIPLE CROWN WINS

17 times   1893   1900   1902   1905   1908   1909   1911   1950   1952
          1965   1969   1971   1976   1977   1978   1979   1988

HOME MATCHES	WON	LOST	DRAWN	
Birkenhead	1	0	0	
Cardiff	110	64	7	
Swansea	33	17	1	
Newport	4	2	0	
Llanelli	4	0	1	
Wrexham	1	0	0	
Wembley	2	4	0	
Total	155	87	9	HOME TOTAL = 251

AWAY MATCHES	WON	LOST	DRAWN	TOTAL
	104	117	15	236
Total	259	204	24	487

Home and Away Results
(Wales wins, losses, draws v other countries)

v ENGLAND
Twickenham	(39)	11–21	D7	Cardiff	(35)	23–10	D2
Blackheath	(6)	1–5		Swansea	(13)	7–5	D1
Leeds	(1)	0–1		Newport	(2)	1–1	
Dewsbury	(1)	1–0		Llanelli	(1)	0–0	D1
Birkenhead	(1)	0-1		Wembley	(1)	1–0	
Gloucester	(1)	1–0		Total		32-16	D4
Bristol	(1)	1–0					
Richmond	(1)	1–0					
Leicester	(1)	0–0	D1				
Brisbane (Aust)	(1)	1–0					
Total		17–28	D8				

v SCOTLAND
Murrayfield	(34)	15–19		Cardiff	(35)	26–9	
Inverleith	(11)	4–6	D1	Swansea	(12)	7–5	
Raeburn Place	(6)	1–5		Newport	(3)	2–1	
Glasgow	(1)	0–0	D1	Wembley	(1)	1–0	
Total		20–30	D2	Total		36–15	

v IRELAND
Dublin	(32)	16–13	D3	Cardiff	(34)	20–12	D2
Belfast	(17)	7–9	D1	Swansea	(13)	11–2	
Limerick	(1)	1–0		Llanelli	(2)	2–0	
Wellington(NZ)	(1)	1–0		Wembley	(1)	0–1	
Johannesburg(SA)	(1)	0–1		Birkenhead	(1)	1–0	
Total		25–23	D4			34–15	D2

v FRANCE
Parc des Princes	(15)	3–12		Cardiff	(30)	18–10	D2
Stade Colombes	(21)	12–8	D1	Swansea	(7)	6–1	
Stade de France	(1)	1–0		Newport	(1)	1–0	
				Wembley	(1)	0–1	
Total		16–20	D1	Total		25–12	D2

v AUSTRALIA
Sydney	(3)	1–2		Cardiff	(13)	6–7*	
Brisbane	(3)	0–3		(*inc 1927–8 v NSW)			
Rotorua(NZ)	(1)	1–0					
Total		2–5					

v NEW ZEALAND
Christchurch	(2)	0–2		Cardiff	(9)	3–6	
Auckland	(2)	0–2		Swansea	(1)	0–1	
Brisbane(Aust)	(1)	0–1		Wembley	(1)	0–1	
Johannesburg(SA)	(1)	0–1					
Total		0–6				3–8	

v SOUTH AFRICA
Durban	(1)	0–1		Cardiff	(7)	1–5	D1
Johannesburg	(1)	0–1		Swansea	(2)	0–2	
Pretoria	(1)	0–1		Wembley	(1)	0–1	
Total		0–3		Total		1–8	D1

v ARGENTINA
Buenos Aires	(2)	2–0	Cardiff	(2)	2–0
			Llanelli	(1)	1–0

v CANADA
Toronto	(2)	2-0	Cardiff	(2)	1-1
Invercargill (NZ)	(1)	1-0			

v ITALY
Rome	(1)	1–0	Cardiff	(2)	2–0
Treviso	(1)	1-0	Llanelli	(1)	1–0

v (WESTERN) SAMOA
Apia	(2)	1–1	Cardiff	(3)	1–2

v FIJI
Suva	(2)	2–0	Cardiff	(2)	2–0

v ROMANIA
Bucharest	(2)	1–1	Cardiff	(1)	0–1
			Wrexham	(1)	1-0

v TONGA
Nuku'alofa	(2)	2–0	Swansea	(1)	1–0
Palmerston North (NZ)	(1)	1–0			

v USA
Wilmington	(1)	1–0	Cardiff	(2)	2–0
San Francisco	(1)	1–0			

v JAPAN
Bloemfontein (SA)	(1)	1–0	Cardiff	(2)	2–0

v NAMIBIA
Windhoek	(3)	3–0

v ZIMBABWE
Bulawayo	(1)	1–0
Harare	(2)	2–0

v BARBARIANS
		Cardiff	(2)	1–1

v PORTUGAL
Lisbon	(1)	1–0

v SPAIN
Madrid	(1)	1–0

v NEW ZEALAND ARMY
Swansea	(1)	0–1

v NEW ZEALAND NATIVE TEAM
Swansea	(1)	1–0

Individual Records

Leading Points Scorers in Tests

	CAPS	PTS	T	C	P	DG
Neil Jenkins	73	895	9	112	205	4
Paul Thorburn	37	304	2	43	70	0
Arwel Thomas	20	173	10	24	25	0
Phil Bennett	29	166	4	18	36	2
Ieuan Evans	72	157	33	0	0	0
Steve Fenwick	30	152	4	11	35	3
Gareth Thomas	40	105	21	0	0	0
Barry John	25	90	5	6	13	8
Gareth Edwards	53	88	20	2	1	3
Jack Bancroft	33	88	0	38	4	0
Jonathan Davies	32	81	5	2	6	13
Mark Wyatt	10	81	1	7	21	0
Gwyn Evans	10	74	0	4	22	0
Keith Jarrett	10	73	2	17	11	0
Gerald Davies	46	72	20	0	0	0

Top Try Scorers (caps in brackets)
- 33   Ieuan Evans (72)
- 21   Gareth Thomas (40)
- 20   Gareth Edwards (53), Gerald Davies (46)
- 17   Reggie Gibbs (16), Johnnie L. Williams (17), Ken J. Jones (44)
- 16   Willie Llewellyn (20)
- 14   Teddy Morgan (16)
- 12   J.J. Williams (30), Nigel Walker (17)

Most Conversions
- 112   Neil Jenkins (73)   43   Paul Thorburn (37)
- 38   Jack Bancroft (29)   24   Arwel Thomas (20)
- 20   W.J. Bancroft (33)

Most Penalty Goals
- 205   Neil Jenkins (73)   70   Paul Thorburn (37)
- 36   Phil Bennett (29)   35   Steve Fenwick (30)
- 25   Arwel Thomas (20)   22   Gwyn Evans (10)
- 21   Mark Wyatt (10)

Most Drop Goals
- 13   Jonathan Davies (32)
- 8   Barry John (25)
- 7   W. Gareth Davies (21)

Forwards Scoring Tries – Career
- 6   Jehoida Hodges*, Ivor Morgan, Dai Morris
- 5   Jack Whitfield, Phil Davies, Gareth Llewellyn, Scott Quinnell

(*Hodges scored 3 tries against England in 1903 after switching to the wing)

Match Records

Most tries in match	(Team)	16	Portugal 1994 (Lisbon) (RWC).
	(Ind)	4	Willie Llewellyn (début) v England 1899; Reg Gibbs v France 1908; Maurice Richards v England 1969; Ieuan Evans v Canada 1987 (RWC); Nigel Walker v Portugal 1994 (RWC); Gareth Thomas v Italy 1999.
Most cons in match	(Team)	11	Portugal 1994 (Lisbon) (RWC).
	(Ind)	11	Neil Jenkins v Portugal 1994 (RWC).
Most pens in match	(Team)	9	France (non-Champ) 1999 (Cardiff).
	(Ind)	9	Neil Jenkins v France (non-Champ) 1999 (Cardiff).
Most drop goals in match	(Team)	2	on several occasions.
	(Ind)	2	on several occasions.
Most points in match	(Team)	102	Portugal 1994 (Lisbon) (RWC).
	(Ind)	30	Neil Jenkins v Italy 1999.
Most points when only one scorer		24	Neil Jenkins v Canada 1993.

Three or More Tries in a Match
(* on début)

4	Willie Llewellyn (Llwynypia)	v England (Swansea)	1899*
4	Reggie Gibbs (Cardiff)	v France (Cardiff)	1908
4	Maurice Richards (Cardiff)	v England (Cardiff)	1969
4	Ieuan Evans (Llanelli)	v Canada (Invercargill) RWC	1987
4	Nigel Walker (Cardiff)	v Portugal (Lisbon) RWC	1994
4	Gareth Thomas (Cardiff)	v Italy (Treviso)	1999
3	Jehoida Hodges (Newport)	v England (Swansea)	1903
3	J.L. Williams (Cardiff)	v Ireland (Cardiff)	1907
3	Billy Trew (Swansea)	v France (Paris)	1909
3	Melville Baker (Newport)	v France (Paris)	1909
3	Reggie Gibbs (Cardiff)	v France (Swansea)	1910
3	J.L. Williams (Cardiff)	v Ireland (Dublin)	1910
3	Reggie Gibbs (Cardiff)	v Scotland (Inverleith)	1911
3	Bryn Williams (Llanelli)	v Ireland (Cardiff)	1920
3	J.J. Williams (Llanelli)	v Australia (Cardiff)	1975
3	Glen Webbe (Bridgend)	v Tonga (Palmerston North) RWC	1987
3	Ieuan Evans (Llanelli)	v Portugal (Lisbon) RWC	1994
3	Mike Hall (Cardiff)	v Portugal (Lisbon) RWC	1994
3	Ieuan Evans (Llanelli)	v Spain (Madrid) RWC	1994
3	Gareth Thomas (Bridgend)	v Japan (Bloemfontein) RWC	1995*
3	Wayne Proctor (Llanelli)	v USA(2) (San Francisco)	1997
3	Byron Hayward (Ebbw Vale)	v Zimbabwe (Harare)	1998 (rep)*

Most Points Scored by a Player in a Match

30	Neil Jenkins	(Pontypridd)	Italy	(Treviso)	1999
29	Neil Jenkins	(Cardiff)	France (n/c)	(Cardiff)	1999
28	Neil Jenkins	(Cardiff)	Canada	(Cardiff)	1999
24	Neil Jenkins	(Pontypridd)	Canada	(Cardiff)	1993
24	Neil Jenkins	(Pontypridd)	Italy	(Cardiff)	1994
23	Arwel Thomas	(Swansea)	Romania	(Wrexham)	1997
23	Neil Jenkins	(Pontypridd)	Argentina	(Llanelli)	1998
22	Neil Jenkins	(Pontypridd)	Portugal	(Lisbon)	1994
22	Neil Jenkins	(Pontypridd)	Japan	(Bloemfontein)	1995
22	Neil Jenkins	(Pontypridd)	England	(Wembley)	1999
21	Paul Thorburn	(Neath)	Barbarians	(Cardiff)	1990
20	Nigel Walker	(Cardiff)	Portugal	(Lisbon)	1994

20	Arwel Thomas	(Swansea)	USA	(Wilmington)	1997
20	Neil Jenkins	(Pontypridd)	Ireland	(Dublin)	1998
20	Gareth Thomas	(Cardiff)	Italy	(Treviso)	1999

Most Times as Captain

28	Ieuan Evans	(1991 – 1995)	(13 victories)
22	Robert Howley	(1998 – 1999)	(15 victories)
18	Arthur Gould	(1889 – 1897)	(8 victories)
17	Jonathan Humphreys	(1995 – 1997)	(6 victories)
14	Billy Trew	(1907 – 1913)	(12 victories)
14	Clive Rowlands	(1963 – 1965)	(6 victories)
13	John Gwilliam	(1950 – 1953)	(9 victories)
13	Gareth Edwards	(1968 – 1974)	(6 victories)
12	Haydn Tanner	(1947 – 1949)	(5 victories)
11	W.J. Bancroft	(1898 – 1901)	(7 victories)
10	Gwyn Nicholls	(1902 – 1906)	(7 victories)
10	Paul Thorburn	(1989 – 1991)	(1 victory)

Most Capped Players (30 caps or more)

N.R. Jenkins	73		A. Clement	37
I.C. Evans	72		D. Williams	36
G.O. Llewellyn	64		R.M. Owen	35
J.P.R. Williams	55		M. Griffiths	35
R.N. Jones	54		B.V. Meredith	34
G.O. Edwards	53		D.I.E. Bebb	34
G.R. Jenkins	50		W.D. Morris	34
T.G.R. Davies	46		A.J. Martin	34
P.T. Davies	46		R.L. Norster	34
I.S. Gibbs	45		John D. Davies	34
K.J. Jones	44		W.J. Bancroft	33
M.R. Hall	42		L.S. Quinnell	33
G. Price	41		B. Price	32
E.W. Lewis	41		J.R.G. Stephens	32
R. Howley	40		G.A.D. Wheel	32
G. Thomas	40		M.G. Ring	32
D. Young	39		J. Davies	32
T.M. Davies	38		J.M. Humphreys	32
W.T. Proctor	38		J.J. Williams	30
P.H. Thorburn	37		S.P. Fenwick	30

Tries on Début
Backs

Bill Evans	(Oxford U)	v Ireland	1882
James Bridie	(Newport)	v Ireland	1882
Charles Allen	(Oxford U & Llandovery)	v England	1884
Martyn Jordan	(Newport)	v England	1885 (2)
Tom 'Pryce' Jenkins	(London Welsh)	v Scotland	1888
George Thomas	(Newport)	v Maoris	1888
Tom Pearson	(Cardiff)	v England	1891
David Fitzgerald	(Cardiff)	v Scotland	1894
Dan Jones	(Aberavon)	v England	1897
Viv Huzzey	(Cardiff)	v Ireland	1898
Willie Llewellyn	(Llwynypia)	v England	1899 (4)
Billy Trew	(Swansea)	v England	1900

Wyndham Jones	(Mountain Ash)	v Ireland	1905
Hop Maddock	(London Welsh)	v England	1906
David 'Ponty' Jones	(Pontypool)	v Ireland	1907
Phil Hopkins	(Swansea)	v Australia	1908
Billy Spiller	(Cardiff)	v Scotland	1910
Louis Dyke	(Cardiff)	v Ireland	1910
George Hirst	(Newport)	v Scotland	1912
Reggie Plummer	(Newport)	v Scotland	1912
James 'Tuan' Jones	(Pontypool)	v Scotland	1913
Willie Watts	(Llanelli)	v England	1914
Ivor Davies	(Llanelli)	v Scotland	1914
Jack Wetter	(Newport)	v Scotland	1914
Wickham J. Powell	(Cardiff)	v England	1920
Johnny Ring	(Aberavon)	v England	1921
Bobby Delahay	(Bridgend)	v England	1922
Frank Palmer	(Swansea)	v England	1922
Cliff Richards	(Pontypool)	v England	1922
Islwyn Evans	(Swansea)	v England	1922
Albert Owen	(Swansea)	v England	1924
Vince Griffiths	(Newport)	v Scotland	1924
Ernie Finch	(Llanelli)	v France	1924
Cyril Thomas	(Bridgend)	v England	1925
Will James	(Aberavon)	v England	1925
Bernard Turnbull	(Cardiff)	v Ireland	1925
George Andrews	(Newport)	v England	1926
Guy Morgan	(Cambridge U)	v France	1927
Jack Morley	(Newport)	v England	1929
Tommy Jones-Davies	(London Welsh)	v England	1930
Graham Jones	(Cardiff)	v Scotland	1930
*Howie Jones	(Swansea)	v Ireland	1930
(*jointly with Harry Peacock)			
Raymond Ralph	(Newport)	v France	1931(2)
Mickie Davies	(Oxford U)	v Scotland	1939
Ray Williams	(Llanelli)	v Scotland	1954
Lynn Davies	(Cardiff)	v England	1956
John Collins	(Aberavon)	v Australia	1958
Cyril Roberts	(Neath)	v Ireland	1958
Dewi Bebb	(Swansea)	v England	1959
John Dawes	(London Welsh)	v Ireland	1964
Keith Jarrett	(Newport)	v England	1967
Laurie Daniel	(Newport)	v Scotland	1970
Ray Hopkins	(Maesteg)	v England	1970
John Bevan	(Cardiff)	v England	1971
Steve Fenwick	(Bridgend)	v France	1975
Brynmor Williams	(Newport)	v Australia (1)	1978
Terry Holmes	(Cardiff)	v Australia (2)	1978
Elgan Rees	(Neath)	v Scotland	1979
David Bishop	(Pontypool)	v Australia	1984
Jonathan Davies	(Neath)	v England	1985
Anthony Clement	(Swansea)	v USA	1987 (2)
Carwyn Davies	(Llanelli)	v W Samoa	1988
Steve Ford	(Cardiff)	v Ireland	1990
Chris Bridges	(Neath)	v Namibia (1)	1990
Simon Hill	(Cardiff)	v Zimbabwe (1)	1993
Gareth Thomas	(Bridgend)	v Japan	1995 (3)
Andy Moore	(Cardiff)	v Japan	1995
Robert Howley	(Bridgend)	v England	1996
Gareth Wyatt	(Pontypridd)	v Tonga	1997

Byron Hayward	(Ebbw Vale)	v Zimbabwe (rep)	1998 (3)
Richard Rees	(Swansea)	v Zimbabwe	1998 (2)

Forwards

Tom Baker Jones	(Newport)	v Ireland	1882
Tom Clapp	(Nantyglo)	v Ireland	1882
Jim Hannan	(Newport)	v Maoris	1888
David Samuel	(Swansea)	v Ireland	1891
William Elsey	(Cardiff)	v England	1895
Tom Dobson	(Cardiff)	v Ireland	1898
Will Osborne	(Mountain Ash)	v England	1902
Jack Brown	(Cardiff)	v England	1907
Ben Gronow	(Bridgend)	v France	1910
Dai Hiddlestone	(Neath)	v England	1922
Gwilym Michael	(Swansea)	v England	1923
Arnold Rickards	(Cardiff)	v France	1924
Harry Peacock	(Newport)	v Scotland	1929
Jim Lang	(Llanelli)	v France	1931
Will Davies	(Swansea)	v South Africa	1931
Allen McCarley	(Neath)	v England	1938
Rees Stephens	(Neath)	v England	1947
Gwyn Evans	(Cardiff)	v England	1947
Alun Meredith	(Devonport Services)	v England	1949
Robin Davies	(London Welsh)	v Scotland	1957
Alun Pask	(Abertillery)	v France	1961
Dai Hayward	(Cardiff)	v England	1963
Bobby Wanbon	(Aberavon)	v England	1968
Bobby Windsor	(Pontypool)	v Australia	1973
Terry Cobner	(Pontypool)	v Scotland	1974
Graham Price	(Pontypool)	v France	1975
Clive Burgess	(Ebbw Vale)	v Ireland	1977
Richard Moriarty	(Swansea)	v Australia	1981
Staff Jones	(Pontypool)	v Scotland	1983
Mark Jones	(Neath)	v Scotland	1987
John Wakeford	(South Wales Police)	v W Samoa	1988
Owain Williams	(Bridgend)	v Namibia (2)	1990
Stuart Davies	(Swansea)	v Ireland	1992
Hemi Taylor	(Cardiff)	v Portugal	1994
Barry Williams	(Neath)	v France (n/c)	1996

First Welsh Try Scorer of:

An International try	Tom Jones	v Ireland	1882
1 point try	Tom Pearson	v England	1891
2 point try	Jim Hannan	v Scotland	1892
3 point try	Fred Parfitt	v England	1894
4 point try	J.P.R. Williams	v England	1972
5 point try	Ieuan Evans	v England	1994

Players Sent Off:
For Wales

Geoff Wheel	(Swansea)	v Ireland	(Cardiff)	1977
Paul Ringer	(Llanelli)	v England	(Twickenham)	1980
Huw Richards	(Neath)	v New Zealand	(Brisbane)	1987
Kevin Moseley	(Pontypool)	v France	(Cardiff)	1990
John Davies	(Neath)	v England	(Cardiff)	1995
Garin Jenkins	(Swansea)	v South Africa	(Johannesburg)	1995

Against Wales

Willie Duggan	Ireland	(Cardiff)	1977
David Codey	Australia	(Rotorua)	1987
Andre Stoop	Namibia	(Windhoek)	1990

Half-back Pairings
- 26 Neil Jenkins & Robert Howley
- 24 Phil Bennett & Gareth Edwards
  (+ 1 match when Bennett played as a rep)
- 23 Barry John & Gareth Edwards
- 22 Jonathan Davies & Robert Jones
- 17 Gareth Davies & Terry Holmes
- 14 Cliff Morgan & Rex Willis, David Watkins & Clive Rowlands
- 13 R 'Bobby' Jones & Dickie Owen
- 12 Neil Jenkins & Rupert Moon, Neil Jenkins & Robert Jones

Welshmen on British Isles ('Lions') Tours

1888 **To Australia/New Zealand** 2
W.H. Thomas (London Welsh / Cambridge U); A.J. Stewart (Cardiff / Dewsbury)

1891 **To South Africa** 0

1896 **To South Africa** 0

1899 **To Australia** 1
E.G. Nicholls (Cardiff)

1903 **To South Africa** 1
R.T. Skrimshire (Newport / Blackheath)

1904 **To Australia/New Zealand** 8
R.T. Gabe, P.F. Bush (Cardiff); A.F. Harding (Cardiff / London Welsh); W. Llewellyn (Llwynypia / Newport); E. Morgan (London Welsh / Guy's Hosp.); T.H. Vile (Newport); T.S. Bevan, W.F. Jowett (Swansea)

1908 (Anglo-Welsh) **To Australia/New Zealand** 13
J.C.M. Dyke, R.A. Gibbs, J.L. Williams, W.L. Morgan (Cardiff); A.F. Harding (Cardiff / London Welsh, CAPT); R.B. Griffiths (Newport); L.S. Thomas (Penarth); J.F. Williams (London Welsh); R.K. Green (Neath); E. Morgan (Swansea); J.P. 'Tuan' Jones (Guy's Hosp.); J.P. 'Ponty' Jones (Pontypool / London Welsh); G.L. Williams (Liverpool)

1910: **To South Africa** 6
A.M. Baker, R.C.S. Plummer, P.D. Waller, H. Jarman (Newport); J.P. 'Ponty' Jones (Pontypool/Newport); A.J. Webb (Abertillery - rep) Joint manager: W.E. Rees
(S.H. Williams (Newport) was an England international and Dr T. Smyth (Newport) was an Ireland international)

1924: **To South Africa** 4
W.R. Harding (Swansea); H.J. Davies (rep), V.M. Griffiths (Newport); Marsden D. Jones (Cardiff / London Welsh) Manager: H. Packer
(Dr W.J. Roche (Newport / UC Cork) was an Ireland international and N.C. MacPherson (Newport) was a Scotland international)

1930: **To New Zealand/Australia** 7
J.A. Bassett (Penarth); J.C. Morley (Newport); H.M. Bowcott (Cambridge U/ Cardiff); T.E. Jones-Davies (London Welsh); H. Poole (Cardiff); D.S. Parker (Swansea); Ivor E. Jones (Llanelli)

1938: **To South Africa** 8
V.G.J. Jenkins (London Welsh); W.H. Clement, Elvet L. Jones (Llanelli); H. Tanner, M.E. Morgan (Swansea); W. Travers (Newport); A.R. Taylor (Cross Keys); I. Williams (Cardiff)

1950: **To New Zealand/Australia** 14
W.B. Cleaver, B.L. Williams, J. Matthews, Clifton Davies, W.R. Willis (Cardiff); B. Lewis Jones (Devonport Serv / Llanelli - rep); M.C. Thomas (Devonport Serv/ Newport); R.T. Evans, Ken J. Jones (Newport); J.R.G. Stephens, E.R. John (Neath); D.M. Davies (Somerset Police); Don J. Hayward (Newbridge); J.D. Robins (Birkenhead Park)

1955: **To South Africa** 11
Alun G. Thomas, R.H. Williams (Llanelli); H.T. Morris, G.M. Griffiths (rep), C.I. Morgan (Cardiff); C.C. Meredith (Neath); T. Lloyd (Maesteg); B.V. Meredith (Newport); W.O.G. Williams, R.C.C. Thomas (Swansea); R.J. Robins(Pontypridd) Asst Manager: D.E. Davies

1959: **To Australia/New Zealand** 9
T.J. Davies, R.H. Williams (Llanelli); M.J. Price, T.R. Prosser (Pontypool); M.C. Thomas, B.V. Meredith (Newport); W.R. Evans (Cardiff); H.J. Morgan (Abertillery); J. Faull (Swansea)

1962: **To South Africa** 10
D.I.E. Bebb (Swansea); D. Ken Jones (Llanelli); A. O'Connor (Aberavon); K.D. Jones, K.A. Rowlands (Cardiff); G.D. Davidge (rep), B.V. Meredith (Newport); A.E.I. Pask, H.J. Morgan (Abertillery); D. Nash (Ebbw Vale)

1966: **To Australia/New Zealand** 12
T.G. Price (rep), W. Delme Thomas (Llanelli); D.I.E. Bebb (Swansea); D.K. Jones, C.H. Norris (Cardiff); S.J. Watkins, D. Watkins, B. Price (Newport); R. Allan Lewis, A.E.I. Pask (Abertillery); G.J. Prothero (Bridgend); D. Williams (Ebbw Vale) Asst Manager: John D. Robins

1968: **To South Africa** 11
W. Keri Jones, M.C.R. Richards, T.G.R. Davies, B. John, G.O. Edwards, J.P. O'Shea (Cardiff); W.H. Raybould, J. Taylor (London Welsh); K.S. Jarrett (Newport); J. Young (Harrogate); W. Delme Thomas (Llanelli)

1971: **To Australia/New Zealand** 14
J.P.R. Williams, T.G.R. Davies, S.J. Dawes (CAPT), J. Taylor, T.G. Evans (rep), M.G. Roberts, T. Mervyn Davies (London Welsh); B. John, G.O. Edwards (Cardiff); J.C. Bevan (Cardiff Inst/Cardiff); A.J. Lewis (Ebbw Vale); R. Hopkins (Maesteg); D.L. Quinnell, W. Delme Thomas (Llanelli). Asst manager/coach: Carwyn R. James

1974: **To South Africa** 9
J.P.R. Williams, C.F.W. Rees (London Welsh); J.J. Williams, R.T.E. Bergiers, T.P. David, P. Bennett (Llanelli); G.O. Edwards (Cardiff); T. Mervyn Davies (Swansea); R.W. Windsor (Pontypool) Manager: Alun G. Thomas

1977: **To New Zealand/Fiji** 18
H. Elgan Rees (Neath); J.J. Williams, P. Bennett (CAPT), D.L. Quinnell (Llanelli); G.L. Evans, J. Squire (rep), D.H. Burcher (Newport); S.P. Fenwick (Bridgend); J.D. Bevan, A.J. Martin, C. Williams (Aberavon); D.B. Williams (Cardiff); T.J. Cobner, R.W. Windsor, A.G. Faulkner (rep), G. Price (Pontypool); Trevor P. Evans (Swansea); A.D. Lewis (Cambridge U / London Welsh - rep) Asst Manager / coach: S.J. Dawes

1980: **To South Africa** 15
A.J. Martin (Aberavon); P.J. Morgan, R.W.R. Gravell, D.L. Quinnell (Llanelli);D.S. Richards, C. Williams (Swansea); W. Gareth Davies, T.D. Holmes, S.M. Lane, A.J. Phillips (Cardiff); G. Price, J. Squire (Pontypool); H. Elgan Rees (rep) (Neath); I. Stephens (rep), Gareth P. Williams (rep) (Bridgend) Med officer: J. Matthews

1983: **To New Zealand** 8
G. Evans (Maesteg); R.A. Ackerman (London Welsh); T.D. Holmes, R.L. Norster (Cardiff); S.T. 'Staff' Jones, G. Price, E.T. Butler (rep), J.Squire (Pontypool)

1989: **To Australia** 8
I.C. Evans (Llanelli); M.R. Hall, J.A. Devereux, M. Griffiths (Bridgend); A. Clement (rep), R.N. Jones (Swansea); D. Young, R.L. Norster (Cardiff) Manager: D. Clive T. Rowlands

1993: **To New Zealand** 5
A. Clement, I.S. Gibbs, R.N. Jones, R. Webster (Swansea); I.C. Evans (Llanelli)

1997: **To South Africa** 8
N.R. Jenkins (Pontypridd); I.C. Evans (Llanelli); I.S. Gibbs (Swansea); A.G. Bateman, B.H. Williams, L.S. Quinnell (Richmond); R. Howley, D. Young (Cardiff) Physio: Mark Davies

Odds 'n' Ends

University Blues
CAMBRIDGE: E.P. Alexander; James Bevan; Harry Bowcott; Eddie Butler; William Cope; Adrian Davies; Glyn Davies; Haydn J. Davies; Gerald Davies; W. Gareth Davies; Roddy Evans; John Gwilliam; Mike R. Hall; Rowe Harding; D.N. Rocyn Jones; Raymond B. Jones; Cliff Jones; Brinley Lewis; Geoffrey Windsor Lewis; Clem Lewis; Windsor H. Lewis; Roger Michaelson; Harry Morgan; W. Guy Morgan; Charles H. Newman; Charles B. Nicholl; Billy Raybould; Arthur M. Rees; Brian I. Rees; T. Bryan Richards; John Roberts; Stuart Roy; Brian Thomas; Horace W. Thomas; Clem Thomas; Wm H. Thomas; Bernard Turnbull; Nick Walne; Wilf Wooller.

OXFORD: Charles Allen; Onllwyn Brace; Trevor Brewer; Ian Buckett; D. 'Bailey' Davies; Mickey J. Davies (war-time); Robin H. Davies; Gareth Davies; David Evans; Sir David Wyn Evans; Denis Evans; Walter Rice Evans; Gwyn Francis; Billy Geen; Viv Jenkins; G.R. Rees Jones; D. Ken Jones; Ian C. Jones; J. 'Strand' Jones; Ken W.J. Jones; Tony O'Connor; Mike Roberts; William Roberts; Wm L. Thomas; Leonard Watkins; C. Derek Williams; Richard Wintle.

Welsh Internationals who studied at Oxbridge and failed to win a Blue
Cambridge: Norman Biggs; Albert M. Jenkins; Tommy Jones-Davies; Edward J. Lewis.
Oxford: Alf Cattell; J. Alban Davies; Godfrey Darbishire; C.G. Harding; Hugh Ingledew; Tom Judson; Charles P. Lewis; Edward Peake; David E.A. Roberts.

Brothers Capped (27 pairs + 1 trio)

W.J. & Jack Bancroft	Jack & Arthur Bassett
Norman & Selwyn Biggs	Terry & Len Davies
George & Tom Dobson	John & Louis Dyke
David & William Gwynn	Bert & Tom Hollingdale
David & Evan James	J.P. 'Tuan', D.P. 'Ponty' & Jack P. Jones
Dick & Bobby Jones	Gareth & Glyn Llewellyn
Andrew Paul & Stephen Moore	Teddy & W.L. Morgan
Richard & Paul Moriarty	Charles & David Nicholl
Gwyn & Sid Nicholls	Jack & Wickham Powell
Dai & Glyn Prosser	Scott & Craig Quinnell
William & John Roberts	David & John Samuel
David L. & Harold W. Thomas	Bernard & Maurice Turnbull
Jack & Harry Wetter	Bleddyn & Lloyd Williams
Owain & Gareth Williams	Richard & Matthew Wintle

Fathers and Sons

Tom Baker Jones (1882–85)	Paul 'Baker' Jones (1921)
George Travers (1903–11)	W.H. 'Bunner' Travers (1937–49)
Howell Jones (1904)	Elwyn 'Howie' Jones (1930)
Glyn Stephens (1912–19)	Rees Stephens (1947–57)
Jack Gore (1924–25)	Bill Gore (1947)
Windsor H. Lewis (1926–28)	Geoffrey Windsor Lewis (1960)
D. Idwal Davies (1939)	D. Brian Davies (1962–63)
Len Blyth (1951–52)	Roger Blyth (1974–80)
Derek Quinnell (1972–80)	Scott Quinnell (1993–99)
	Craig Quinnell (1995–99)

(N.B: George Vickery was capped for England from Aberavon in 1905. His son, Walter Vickery, was capped for Wales from Aberavon in 1938–39)

Religion

John Bartlett	Curate and Royal Navy chaplain.
D. 'Bailey' Davies	Rector of Sutton and vicar of Eyeworth.
J. Alban Davies	Chaplain in the First World War and chaplain of Pretoria Prison.

Tom Graham		Minister of religion.
W.T. 'Bill' Havard		Bishop of St Asaph and Bishop of St David's.
Albert M. Jenkins		Army chaplain in the First World War and Archdeacon of Pretoria.
John 'Strand' Jones		Deacon; army chaplain in the First World War; chaplain of Karachi; chaplain of Shrewsbury Prison and rector of Great Hanwood.
Alfred A. Matthews		Vicar in Swansea whilst capped. Later vicar in Blaenavon.
John Roberts		Minister in Wales, Scotland and England.
John G. Stephens		RAF chaplain whilst still playing. vicar of Darlington and Bossall.
William L. Thomas		Vicar of Irton and Bootle.

Honours

Military Cross	Bill Clement; D. 'Bailey' Davies; Brinley S. Evans; Rev. Bill Havard; Frank Hawkins; J.P. 'Tuan' Jones; Barney McCall; Hop Maddock; Edgar Morgan; Frank Palmer.
Belgian Military Cross	Elvet Jones.
Knighted	William Cope (Baron Cope); David W. Evans; George Morris; Hugh Vincent.
British Empire Medal	Ron Evans; Delme Thomas.
Distinguished Conduct Medal	Mickey J. Davies.
Distinguished Service Order	Bernard Cowey.
Queen's Police Medal	Arthur Rees.

Welsh International Referees

Only includes games where a senior member country of the International Board awarded caps - or - the final stages of the Rugby World Cup.

(* denotes RWC +denotes also capped as a player 'Cent' denotes Centenary match)

(A- Australia; Arg- Argentina; C- Canada; E- England; F- France; G- Georgia; I- Ireland; It- Italy; J- Japan; NZ- New Zealand; Nam- Namibia; Pres- President's XV; R- Romania; S-Scotland; SA- South Africa; Sp- Spain; T- Tonga; W- Wales; WS- (Western) Samoa.)

42	W. Derek Bevan	1985 E/R; 1986 F/E, NZ/A(2); 1987 *NZ/Fiji, *F/Zim, A/NZ; 1988 I/WS; 1990 NZ/S; 1991 I/F, *F/Fiji, *S/WS, *E/A; 1992 S/E, E/I, NZ/World(2); 1993 F/S, NZ/A, C/A, Arg/SA(2); 1994 S/F, NZ/F(2); 1995 S/I, *SA/A, *NZ/S, *SA/F; 1996 S/E, SA/NZ, F/SA; 1997 NZ/SA; F/SA; 1998 E/I, NZ/A; 1999 S/I, NZ/A, I/Arg, *NZ/T, *F/Arg, *A/SA. (1991 England v Australia was the RWC final.)
25	Clive Norling	1978 I/NZ; 1979 E/S; 1980 F/E,; 1981 I/F, NZ/SA(2); F/NZ; 1982 I/S; 1983 A/Arg(2); 1984 F/I; 1985 E/S; 1986 E/I; 1987 I/F, *C/T, *F/Fiji; 1988 E/I, R/F; 1989 NZ/Arg(2); 1990 F/S, A/F(2); 1991 Nam/I(2)
23	D. Gwynne Walters	1959 F/S, I/E, E/S, I/F; 1960 S/F, E/I, I/S, F/I; 1961 F/SA, E/F; 1962 E/I, F/E; 1963 E/S, F/R; 1964 E/I, F/E, F/I, F/Fiji; 1965 I/F, S/.I, E/S, S/SA;1966 F/E
22	Meirion Joseph	1966 S/A; 1967 I/A; 1968 I/S, E/I, R/F; 1969 S/I, S/SA; 1970 S/E; 1971 I/E, S/E(Cent); 1972 S/F, S/E; 1973 I/NZ, S/Pres (Cent), F/J; 1974 E/I; 1975 F/Arg; 1976 E/A, F/A; 1977 E/S, S/I, F/S
18	Albert E Freethy	1923 F/E; 1924 E/F, I/NZ, F/USA; 1925 E/NZ, I/S, S/E, F/E; 1926 E/F; 1927 F/E; 1928 I/E, E/F; 1929 E/I, F/E; 1930 I/E, E/F; 1931 E/I, F/E (1924 France v USA- Olympic Games final).
16	Clayton Thomas	1995 S/C, I/F, *Arg/It; 1996 S/F, Arg/F; 1997 A/F(2); 1998 S/E, A/NZ, I/SA; 1999 F/S, WS/F, T/F, *I/A, *S/Sp, *E/Fiji.
14	Ivor David	1938 E/S; 1939 S/E; 1947 E/S; 1952 S/F, I/S, E/I; 1953 S/I; 1954 S/F, E/NZ, S/NZ, F/NZ, F/E; 1955 I/F; 1956 F/E

12	T.D. Schofield	1907 E/S; 1908 E/I; 1910 E/I; 1911 E/S; 1912 E/I, F/E; 1913 E/S; 1914 E/I, S/E; 1920 E/S; 1921 E/I; 1922 S/I
12+	Tommy H. Vile	1923 S/F, E/I, I/S, S/E; 1924 I/E, S/I, E/S; 1925 E/I; 1927 E/I; 1928 E/A, E/S; 1931 F/I
8	Ken Rowlands	1980 SA/SAmerica(2); 1981 F/S; 1982 S/E; 1986 SA/NZ Cavaliers (4)
7	Ron Lewis	1970 E/I; 1971 E/F; 1972 F/I; 1973 S/I, E/A; 1974 Arg/F(2)
6	Trevor Jones	1947 E/F; 1948 E/I, F/E; 1949 E/F; 1950 S/F; 1951 I/E
5	D.M. Hughes	1965 F/It; 1966 S/F, I/S; 1967 I/E, S/I
5	Gwilym J. Treharne	1960 I/SA; 1961 E/SA, I/E, I/F; 1963 S/I
4+	W.M. 'Billy' Douglas	1891 I/E; 1894 E/I; 1896 S/E; 1903 E/S
4	Winston Jones	1984 S/F, NZ/F(2); 1988 S/E
4	Jeff C. Kelleher	1973 E/S; 1974 F/E; 1976 R/F; 1977 E/F
4	Les J. Peard	1989 I/E; 1991 E/F, *F/R, *E/USA
4	Alun Richards	1980 R/F; 1981 A/F; 1982 E/A; 1983 F/S
4	Gareth Simmonds	1992 E/C; 1995 R/F; 1996 Arg/F. 1997 S/I
3	J. Wilfred Faull	1936 E/NZ, S/I; 1937 E/I
3	J. Games	1909 E/A; 1913 E/F; 1914 F/E
3	W. Ken M. Jones	1968 I/A; 1970 F/E; 1971 S/I
3	W.J. Llewellyn	1926 F/S, I/E; 1927 S/A
3	Cenydd G.P. Thomas	1977 F/NZ; 1978 S/F, F/I
3	W.H. Wilkins	1893 E/S; 1894 S/E; 1895 E/S
3	Robert G. Davies	1997 I/It; 1998 *I/G; 1999 S/It
2	W. Jack Evans	1958 I/A, F/E
2	Meirion S. Lewis	1975 F/S; 1976 I/S
2	Denzil M. Lloyd	1975 I/F; 1976 S/E
2	Vernon J. Parfitt	1953 E/F; 1954 I/S
2+	William D. Phillips	1887 I/E; 1889 I/S
2	Corris Thomas	1979 S/I; 1980 E/I
2	Robert Yeman	1993 I/R; 1994 NZ/SA
1+	D. Harry Bowen	1905 E/S
1	David R. Davies	1998 It/S
1	D. Herbert	1883 W/E
1	E.A. Johns	1911 E/F
1	D. Cyril Joynson	1955 E/S
1+	Charles P. Lewis	1885 W/E
1	Ernie M. Lewis	1971 F/A
1	A. Llewellyn	1906 E/I
1	Vernon S. Llewellyn	1951 E/F.
1+	Horace S. Lyne	1885 E/I
1	K. Morgan	1967 F/It
1	Richard Mullock	1886 I/E
1+	E. Gwyn Nicholls	1909 E/S
1	T.H. Phillips	1936 E/S
1	F.G. Price	1963 I/F
1	E. Roberts	1924 F/S
1+	Tom Williams	1904 E/I

Born Abroad

Argentina	John L. Morgan.
Australia	James A. Bevan; Jason Jones-Hughes; Max Wiltshire.
China	Dick Jones; Bobby Jones.
Egypt	Derrick Main; Graham Price.
Germany	Paul Thorburn.
India	John T. Hinton; Tom Pearson.
Kenya	Stuart Russell.
New Zealand	Dale McIntosh; Hemi Taylor; Shane Howarth; Brett Sinkinson.

Singapore	Clive Rees.
South Africa	Ian C. Jones.
Zambia	Dafydd James.

Welsh Players' Other Sporting Achievements

Baseball caps:	David Bishop H.V.P. Huzzey; Mark Ring; Jack Wetter.
Hockey caps:	Bert Dauncey; Tom Pearson; Maurice Turnbull.
Tennis cap:	Bert Dauncey.
Squash cap:	Maurice Turnbull.
England cricket cap:	Maurice Turnbull.
Angling cap:	Gareth Edwards.
Welsh Amateur Golf Champion:	Louis Phillips; Tom Barlow.
Professional Boxers:	Arthur 'Candy' Evans; Jerry Shea.
Welsh Amateur boxing champions:	Arthur 'Candy' Evans; George Oliver (Heavyweight); Byron Hayward (Light- Middleweight).
Billy Spiller:	First Glamorgan player to score a century in the county championship.
Ben Beynon:	Professional soccer player. Scored the goal that knocked Blackburn Rovers out of the FA Cup in 1915.
Ken J. Jones:	Won silver medal in Olympic 4x100m relay and captained GB at European Games (athletics).
Nigel Walker:	GB semi-finalist in 1984 Olympic hurdles. Bronze medals in 1987 World and European Indoor Championships.
H. Martyn Jordan:	(or his brother Charles) played for Ireland v Wales 1884.
Frank Hancock:	Brother P.F. Hancock capped by England.
Walter Vickery:	Father (George) capped for England.
David Weaver:	Also appeared for Zambia.
Charles B. Nicholl:	Played in 15 of 16 Welsh matches 1891-96, but he stood down from Wales team v Ireland 1894 for his brother, David, to win his only cap.
John Griffin:	Refereed the first-ever International match in South Africa – v British Isles 1891.
Billy McCutcheon:	Refereed rugby league Tests in 1908-09.
J.P.R. Williams	Junior Wimbledon Champion in 1966.

Oddities

Barney McCall	Given as dead in 1982 *Wisden* cricket obits, but died in 1991.
Syd Nicholls	Brother of Gwyn, was secretary of Hull RL club and chairman of the Welsh FA (Soccer).
Rex Richards	Known as 'Tarzan'. Appeared in *Wild Women of Wongo* (rated as one of the ten worst films ever made !). Stuntman and high diver in Florida.
Don Tarr	Broke his neck in his only international match (v NZ 1935).
John Davies	Died during a rugby league match for Dewsbury (aged 28)
Rev. Alfred Matthews	Daughter became Baroness Brooke.
Norman Biggs	Killed by a poisoned arrow in a native ambush in Nigeria.
Godfrey Darbishire	Died in a small hut in Florida, after suffering exposure at sea.
Alfred Brice	Suspended for 8 months after swearing at the referee (Wales v Ireland 1904).
BBC Wales Head of Sports	Cliff Morgan; Onllwyn Brace; Gareth Davies; Arthur Emyr.

Capped Pre- and Post-war
WW1   Tommy Vile; Clem Lewis; Glyn Stephens; Harry Uzzell; Walter Martin; Jack Wetter.
WW2   C. Howell Davies; Les Manfield; Haydn Tanner; Bill Travers.

Most Popular Surnames
60   JONES   (not inc Jones-Davies or Jones-Hughes);
56   DAVIES   (not inc Davis);
47   WILLIAMS   (not inc Williams-Jones);
47   EVANS
36   THOMAS
22   MORGAN
20   REES
19   LEWIS

Captains on Début
James Bevan; Charles P. Lewis; John R. Evans; Clive Rowlands; Mike Watkins.

Oldest and Youngest

Oldest to die	Ivor Thomas (b 1900; d 1995) aged 95.
Youngest to die	Tudor Williams (b 1899; d 1922) aged 23.
First to be born	Charles P. Lewis (b 20 August 1853).
First to die	Samuel Goldsworthy (d 28 September 1889).
Died in WW1	Richard Williams; Charles Taylor; Louis Phillips; Charlie Pritchard; Dai Westacott; Johnnie L. Williams; Dick Thomas; Phil Waller; Brinley Lewis; Billy Geen; David Watts.
Died in WW2	Maurice Turnbull; Cecil Davies; John R. Evans.

Teenage Caps
When Leigh Davies (Neath/Cardiff) was capped in 1966, he became the 47th player to make his début at the age of 19. However, the following ten players were even younger on début:

Norman Biggs	aged 18 yrs 50 days.	Début 22 Dec. 1888
Evan Williams	aged 18 yrs 214 days.	Début 17 Jan. 1925
Tom Pearson	aged 18 yrs 239 days.	Début 03 Jan. 1891
David Bowen	aged 18 yrs 8 mnths.	Début 16 Dec. 1882
Lewis Jones	aged 18 yrs 10 mnths.	Début 31 Dec. 1950
Wm Henry Thomas	aged 18 yrs 11 mnths.	Début 10 Jan. 1885
Keith Jarrett	aged 18 yrs 11 mnths.	Début 15 Apr. 1967
Haydn Tanner	aged 18 yrs 11 mnths.	Début 21 Dec. 1935
Algernon F. Hill	aged 18 yrs 362 days.	Début 10 Jan. 1885.
G. Llewellyn Lloyd	aged 18 yrs	Début 14 Mar. 1896

Wales Coaches Record

		P	W	D	L
David Nash	1967–68	5	1	1	3
Clive Rowlands	1968–74	29	18	4	7
John Dawes	1974–79	24	18	0	6
John Lloyd	1980–82	14	6	0	8
John Bevan	1982–85	15	7	1	7
Tony Gray	1985–88	24	15	0	9
John Ryan	1988–90	9	2	0	7
Ron Waldron	1990–91	10	2	1	7
Alan Davies	1991–95	35	18	0	17
Alex Evans*	1995	4	1	0	3
Kevin Bowring	1995–98	29	15	0	14
Dennis John*	1998	2	1	0	1
Graham Henry	1998–date	16	11	0	5
		216	115	7	94

(* Caretaker coach)

WALES INTERNATIONAL PLAYERS
– IN APPEARANCE ORDER

Positions
Fwd=Forward; Bck=Back; HB=Half-back; UtBk=Utility Back; FB=Full-Back; W=Wing; C=Centre; OH=Outside-half; SH=Scrum-half; P=Prop; H=Hooker; L=Lock; F=Flank; 8=Number 8; rep=replacement only. (* Died during world wars.)

CAP NO.	SURNAME	CHRISTIAN NAMES	KNOWN AS	TOTAL CAPS	FROM/TO	DATE OF BIRTH	DATE OF DEATH	POSITION
1	Newman	Charles Henry	Charlie	10	1881–87	28.2.1857	28.9.1922	FB/HB
2	Summers	Richard Henry Bowlas	Richard	1	1881	30.7.1860	22.12.1941	Back
3	Bevan	James Alfred	Jim	1	1881	15.4.1858	3.2.1938	Back
4	Peake	Edward	Edward	1	1881	29.3.1860	3.1.1945	Back
5	Watkins	Leonard	Leonard	1	1881	7.2.1859	7.2.1901	HB
6	Lewis	Edward John	E.J.	1	1881	5.12.1859	8.6.1925	HB
7	Williams	Richard Davies Gamons	Richard	1	1881	15.6.1856	27.9.1915*	HB
8	Rees	Theophilius Aneurin	Aneurin	1	1881	1858	11.9.1932	Fwd
9	Purdon	Frank T.	Frank	4	1881–83	c. 1857	unknown	Fwd
10	Harding	George Frederick	George	4	1881–83	1858	8.7.1927	FB/HB
11	Girling	Barry Edward	–	1	1881	1857	28.10.1905	Fwd
12	Mann	B.B.	–	1	1881	unknown	unknown	Fwd
13	Phillips	William David	William	5	1881–84	16.8.1855	15.10.1918	Fwd
14	Darbishire	Godfrey	Godfrey	1	1881	26.9.1853	29.10.1889	Fwd
15	Treharne	Edward	Edward	2	1881–82	1862	29.12.1904	Fwd
16	Lewis	Charles Prytherch	C.P.	5	1882–84	20.8.1853	28.5.1923	FB
17	Clark	Samuel Simmonds	Samuel	2	1882–87	1857	25.5.1947	Bk/FB
18	Norton	William Barron	–	6	1882–84	28.4.1862	17.12.1898	Back
19	Evans	William Frederick	Bill	2	1882–83	24.4.1857	c. 1935	Bk/HB
20	Bridie	James (or R.H.)	James	1	1882	c. 1857	unknown	HB
21	Jones	Thomas Baker	Tom	6	1882–85	16.9.1862	26.5.1959	Fwd
22	Gould	Robert	Bob	11	1882–87	1863	29.12.1931	Fwd
23	Clapp	Thomas John Sercombe	Tom	14	1882–88	1858	unknown	Fwd
24	Williams	Thomas	Tom	1	1882	1860	4.2.1913	Fwd
25	Morris	George Lockwood Bart (later Sir G.L.B. Morris)	George	5	1882–84	29.1.1859	23.11.1947	Fwd
26	Vincent	Hugh Corbett (later Sir H.C. Vincent)	Hugh	1	1882	27.4.1862	22.2.1931	Fwd
27	Bowen	David Harry	Harry	4	1882–87	4.5.1864	17.8.1913	FB
28	Clare	James Arthur	James	1	1882	1857	4.1.1930	Back
29	Gwynn (or Gwyn)	David	Dai	6	1882–91	1862	8.3.1910	Back
30	Judson	Thomas Haigh	Tom	2	1882–83	1857	4.9.1908	Fwd
31	Cattell	Alfred	Alfred	2	1882–83	27.4.1857	10.9.1933	Fwd
32	Lyne	Horace Sampson	Horace	5	1883–85	31.12.1860	1.5.1949	Fwd
33	Jones	John Arthur	Arthur	1	1883	1857	20.1.1919	Fwd
34	Griffin	John	John	1	1883	2.8.1859	13.7.1895	Fwd
35	Allen	Charles Peter	Charles	2	1884	2.12.1861	18.9.1930	Back
36	Taylor	Charles Gerald	Charles	9	1884–87	1863	24.1.1915*	Back
37	Gwynn	William Henry	Bill	5	1884–85	1856	1.4.1897	HB
38	Smith	J. Sidney	–	3	1884–85	c. 1858	unknown	Fwd
39	Simpson	Henry Joseph	Joe	3	1884	1856	22.3.1911	Fwd
40	Andrews	Frederick Graham	Fred	2	1884	15.9.1864	2.6.1929	Fwd
41	Margrave	Frederick Lofthouse	Fred	2	1884	25.12.1858	1.1.1946	Fwd

CAP NO.	SURNAME	CHRISTIAN NAMES	KNOWN AS	TOTAL CAPS	FROM/ TO	DATE OF BIRTH	DATE OF DEATH	POSITION
42	Barlow	Thomas Marriott	Tom	1	1884	1864	27.1.1942	FB
43	Hancock	Francis Escott	Frank	4	1884–86	7.12.1859	29.10.1943	Back
44	Stadden (Real name: Staddan)	William James Wood	'Buller'	8	1884–90	1861	30.12.1906	HB
45	Goldsworthy	Samuel James	Samuel	3	1884–85	1855	28.9.1889	Fwd
46	Hinton	John Thomas	John	1	1884	1860	4.2.1931	Fwd
47	Roderick	William Buckley	Buckley	1	1884	17.1.1862	1.2.1908	Fwd
48	Gould	Joseph Arthur	Arthur 'Monkey'	27	1885–97	10.10.1864	2.1.1919	FB/C
49	Jordan	Henry Martyn	Martyn	3	1885–89	7.3.1865	14.7.1902	Back
50	Richards	Evan Sloane	Evan	2	1885–87	1862	19.4.1931	Fwd
51	Thomas	Lewis Cobden	L.C.	2	1885	6.8.1865	14.4.1928	Fwd
52	Rowland	Ernest Melville	Ernest	1	1885	21.9.1864	unknown	Fwd
53	Alexander	Edward Perkins	E.P.	5	1885–87	7.8.1863	26.10.1931	Fwd
54	Hill	Algernon Frank	Frank	15	1885–94	13.1.1866	20.4.1927	Fwd
55	Thomas	William Henry	W.H.	11	1885–91	22.3.1866	11.10.1921	Fwd
56	Morgan	D.	–	7	1885–89	unknown	unknown	Fwd
57	Douglas	William M.	Billy	4	1886–87	2.7.1863	24.9.1943	Back
58	Lewis	David Henry	Dai	2	1886	4.12.1866	8.9.1943	Fwd
59	Young	George Avery	George	2	1886	1866	21.1.1900	Fwd
60	Bowen	William Arnold	–	13	1886–91	1864	26.9.1925	Fwd
61	Roberts	Evan	Evan	2	1886–87	19.9.1861	16.10.1927	Fwd
62	Mathews	Alfred Augustus	Alf	1	1886	7.2.1864	12.8.1946	HB
63	Evans	Owen James	Jem	4	1887–88	1867	14.10.1942	SH
64	Bland	Alexander Frederick	Alec	9	1887–90	24.11.1866	18.10.1947	Fwd
65	Hybart	Albert John	–	1	1887	1865	28.1.1945	Fwd
66	Lockwood	Thomas William	–	3	1887	1863	unknown	Fwd
67	Hughes	Hugh	Sawdust	2	1887–89	unknown	unknown	FB
68	Bowen	George Einon	George	4	1887–88	1863	13.1.1919	HB/Bk
69	Williams	William Edward Osbourne	–	5	1887–90	15.12.1866	22.6.1945	Fwd
70	Lewis	John Goulston	Johnny Bach	1	1887	25.12.1859	9.5.1935	HB
71	Towers	William Hunter	–	2	1887–88	1861	7.7.1904	Fwd
72	Roberts	Edward John	Ned	3	1888–89	1867	14.6.1940	FB
73	Jenkins	Thomas John Price (not Pryce-Jenkins)	Tom	2	1888	1.02.1864	6.8.1922	Back
74	Powell	Richard Whitcomb	Dick	2	1888	1864	11.1.1944	Fwd
75	Kedzlie	Quinton Dick	Dick	2	1888	1861	3.5.1920	Fwd
76	Meredith	John	John	4	1888–90	1863	30.11.1920	Fwd
77	Williams	T.	–	2	1888	unknown	unknown	Fwd
78	Howell (not Howells)	William Henry	–	2	1888	?.12.1863	unknown	Fwd
79	Arthur	Charles Suckling	Charlie	3	1888–91	1863	12.12.1925	Back
80	Thomas	Charles James	Charlie 'Moose'	9	1888–91	1864	8.3.1948	HB/W/C
81	Webb	James E.	Jim	2	1888–89	15.1.1863	8.3.1913	FB/Back
82	Thomas	George	George	3	1888–91	1857	14.6.1934	Back
83	Biggs	Notman Witchell	Norman	8	1888–94	3.11.1870	27.2.1908	Back/W
84	Garrett	Richard Marks	Dickie	8	1888–92	1865	17.2.1908	Back
85	Nicholls	Sydney Herbert	Syd	4	1888–91	1868	24.11.1946	Fwd
86	Hannan	James	Jim	19	1888–95	1864	22.6.1905	Fwd
87	Harding	Charles Theodore	Charles	3	1888–89	1860	13.7.1919	Fwd
88	Griffiths	Daniel	Dan	2	1888–89	20.6.1857	29.10.1936	Fwd
89	Bishop	Edward Hopkin	Teddy	1	1889	10.10.1864	24.2.1919	Back
90	Evans	George Rosser	Rosser	1	1889	6.10.1867	unknown	HB
91	Evans	David William (later Sir D.W. Evans)	David	5	1889–91	4.11.1866	17.8.1926	Fwd

CAP NO.	SURNAME	CHRISTIAN NAMES	KNOWN AS	TOTAL CAPS	FROM/TO	DATE OF BIRTH	DATE OF DEATH	POSITION
92	Thomas	Rowland Lewis	–	7	1889–92	11.7.1864	21.1.1949	Fwd
93	Davies	Abel Christmas	Abel	1	1889	25.12.1861	18.6.1914	W
94	Morgan	Thomas	Tom	1	1889	14.11.1866	22.3.1899	Back
95	Griffiths	Griffith	Gitto	1	1889	15.9.1864	22.7.1938	HB
96	Bancroft	William J.	Billy	33	1890–1901	2.3.1871	3.3.1959	FB
97	Lloyd	David Percy Marmaduke	Percy	4	1890–91	5.1.1871	10.3.1959	W
98	James	Evan	Evan	5	1890–92	1869	18.8.1901	HB
99	Evans	Walter Rice	Walter	3	1890–91	10.9.1863	9.6.1909	Fwd
100	Thomas	Stephen	Stephen	3	1890–91	22.8.1865	23.10.1937	Fwd
101	Ingledew	Hugh Murray	Hugh	3	1890–91	26.10.1865	1.2.1937	HB
102	Graham	Thomas Cooper	Tom	12	1890–95	1866	1.12.1945	Fwd
103	Pearson	Thomas William	Tom	13	1891–1903	10.5.1872	12.9.1957	W
104	Packer	Harry	Harry	7	1891–97	3.9.1868	25.5.1946	Fwd
105	Bennett	Percy	Percy	4	1891–92	unknown	unknown	Fwd
106	Pegge	Edward Vernon	Edward	1	1891	5.6.1864	21.3.1915	Fwd
107	McCutcheon	William Morgan	Billy	7	1891–94	1870	3.7.1949	W
108	Escott (known as Sweet-Escott)	Ralph Bond	Ralph	3	1891–95	11.1.1869	10.11.1907	HB
109	Daniel	David John	'Dai Sam'	8	1891–99	1871	30.4.1948	Fwd
110	James	David	David	4	1891–99	1866	2.1.1929	HB
111	Nicholl	Charles Bowen	'Boomer'	15	1891–96	19.6.1870	9.7.1939	Fwd
112	Samuel	John	John	1	1891	1868	23.12.1947	Fwd
113	Samuel	David	David	2	1891–93	1869	15.9.1943	Fwd
114	Deacon	J. Thomas	Tom	4	1891–92	1868	21.7.1921	Fwd
115	Phillips	Henry Percy	Percy 'Sparrow'	6	1892–94	1869	26.2.1947	Fwd
116	Rowles	George Albert	George	1	1892	1866	12.9.1922	HB
117	Mills	Frank Musgrove	Frank	13	1892–96	1871	17.2.1925	Fwd
118	Boucher	Arthur William	Arthur	13	1892–97	29.6.1870	25.4.1948	Fwd
119	Watts	Wallace Howard	Wallace	12	1892–96	25.3.1870	29.4.1950	Fwd
120	Rees (known as Conway-Rees)	John Conway	Conway	3	1892–94	13.1.1870	30.8.1932	Back
121	Gould	George Herbert	Bert	3	1892–93	1870	12.12.1913	C
122	Nicholls	F.E.	–	1	1892	unknown	unknown	C
123	Day	Henry Thomas	Harry	5	1892–94	?.9.1863	12.7.1911	Fwd
124	Parfitt	Frederick Charles	Fred	9	1893–96	12.8.1869	20.3.1953	HB
125	Fitzgerald	David	Dai	2	1894	1872	30.11.1951	C
126	Thomas	William Llewelyn	–	3	1894–95	6.5.1872	19.1.1943	W
127	Elliot (known as Elliott)	John E.	Jack	3	1894–95	1872	30.3.1938	C/SH
128	Nicholl	David Wilmot	David	1	1894	14.6.1871	11.3.1918	Fwd
129	Hutchinson	Frederick Osborne	Fred	3	1894–96	1867	?.05.1941	Fwd
130	Badger	Owen	Owen	4	1895–96	3.11.1871	17.3.1939	C
131	Biggs	Selwyn Hanam	Selwyn	9	1895–1900	1872	12.1.1943	OH
132	Davies	Benjamin	Ben	2	1895–96	5.6.1873	23.6.1930	HB
133	Jackson	Thomas Henry	Tom	1	1895	1870	1952	Fwd
134	Elsey	William John	–	1	1895	1871	13.6.1936	Fwd
135	Lloyd	Evan	Evan	1	1895	6.6.1871	28.2.1951	W
136	Pook	Thomas Richard	Tom	1	1895	1869	21.2.1948	Fwd
137	George	Ernest Edward	Ernie	3	1895–96	1871	28.11.1952	Fwd
138	Morgan	David	Dai	2	1895–96	14.7.1872	13.9.1933	HB
139	Jenkin	Albert Mortimer	Albert	2	1895–96	14.9.1872	3.7.1961	Fwd
140	Dauncey	Frederick Herbert	Bert	3	1896	1.12.1871	30.10.1955	W
141	Bowen	Clifford Albert	Cliff	4	1896–97	3.1.1875	30.4.1929	W
142	Ramsay (known as Ramsey)	Samuel H.	Sam	2	1896–1904	1873	14.1.1956	Fwd

WELSH INTERNATIONAL PLAYERS

CAP NO.	SURNAME	CHRISTIAN NAMES	KNOWN AS	TOTAL CAPS	FROM/ TO	DATE OF BIRTH	DATE OF DEATH	POSITION
143	Nicholls	Erith Gwynne	Gwyn	24	1896–1906	15.7.1874	24.3.1939	C
144	Evans	John	Jack	3	1896–97	23.2.1871	19.7.1924	Fwd
145	Morris	William	Bill	3	1896–97	29.10.1869	4.11.1946	Fwd
146	Cope	William (later Sir W. Cope)	William	1	1896	18.8.1870	15.7.1946	Fwd
147	Davies	W.	'Barry'	1	1896	unknown	unknown	Fwd
148	Evans	David	David	4	1896–98	1872	1.2.1912	Fwd
149	Lloyd	George Llewellyn	Llewellyn	12	1896–1903	1877	1.8.1957	HB
150	Millar (known as Miller)	William Henry	'Fred'	7	1896–1901	1873	unknown	Fwd
151	Jones	Daniel	Dan	1	1897	31.5.1875	1.1.1959	HB
152	Hellings	Richard	Dick	9	1897–1901	1.12.1873	9.2.1938	Fwd
153	Cornish	Frederick Henry	Fred	4	1897–99	1876	27.4.1940	Fwd
154	Rapps (known as Rhapps)	John	Jack	1	1897	?.7.1876	23.1.1950	Fwd
155	Jones	W.	'Pussy'	2	1898	1872	unknown	C
156	Huzzey	Henry Vivian Pugh	Viv	5	1898–99	24.7.1876	16.8.1929	W
157	Alexander	William H.	Billy	7	1898–1901	16.7.1874	1963	Fwd
158	Davies	Hopkin	Hopkin	4	1898–1901	unknown	unknown	Fwd
159	Boots	John George	George	16	1898–1904	2.7.1874	30.12.1928	Fwd
160	Dobson	Thomas	Tom	4	1898–99	1871	4.7.1937	Fwd
161	Booth	Joseph	Joe	1	1898	?.6.1873	28.4.1958	Fwd
162	Skrimshire	Reginald Truscott	Reg	3	1899	30.1.1878	20.9.1963	C
163	Llewellyn	Willie Morris	Willie	20	1899–1905	1.1.1878	22.3.1973	W
164	Blake	John	Jerry/Jere	9	1899–1901	1875	15.2.1933	Fwd
165	Scrine	Frederick George	Fred	3	1899–1901	25.3.1877	8.6.1962	Fwd
166	Brice	Alfred Bailey	Alfred 'Bobby'	19	1899–1904	23.9.1871	28.5.1938	Fwd
167	Hodges	Joseph Jehoida	Jehoida	23	1899–1906	15.7.1876	13.9.1930	Fwd
168	Parker	William James	Will	2	1899	1873	10.11.1955	Fwd
169	Rees	Daniel	Dan	5	1900–05	1876	unknown	C
170	Davies	George	George	9	1900–05	25.12.1875	23.7.1959	C/FB
171	Trew	William James	Billy	29	1900–13	1878	20.8.1926	W/OH/C
172	Phillips	Louis Augustus	Louis	4	1900–01	24.2.1878	14.3.1916*	HB
173	Williams	William Henry	'Buller'	4	1900–01	1873	9.1.1936	Fwd
174	Thomas	Robert	Bob	4	1900–01	1871	7.3.1910	Fwd
175	Dobson	George Alexander	George	1	1900	1873	8.6.1917	Fwd
176	Jones	John	'Bala'	1	1901	unknown	unknown	SH
177	Gape (known as Gabe)	Rees Thomas	Rhys 'Rusty'	24	1901–08	22.6.1880	15.9.1967	W/C
178	Jones	Richard Hughes	Dick	15	1901–10	27.11.1879	24.11.1958	HB
179	Owens	Richard Morgan (known as Owen)	Dicky	35	1901–12	17.11.1876	27.2.1932	SH
180	Jones	Robert	Bob	1	1901	3.6.1877	unknown	Fwd
181	Jones (known as Strand-Jones)	John	Strand	5	1902–03	2.12.1877	3.4.1958	FB
182	Morgan	Edward	Teddy	16	1902–08	22.5.1880	1.9.1949	W
183	Joseph	William	Will	16	1902–06	10.5.1877	1959	Fwd
184	Jones	David	Dai 'Tarw'	13	1902–06	1881	21.1.1933	Fwd
185	Osborne	William T.	Will	6	1902–03	1879	unknown	Fwd
186	Harding	Arthur Flowers	'Boxer'	20	1902–08	8.8.1878	15.5.1947	Fwd
187	Walters	Nathaniel	Danny	1	1902	23.5.1875	22.2.1956	Fwd
188	Jones	Harry	Harry	2	1902	1878	unknown	Fwd
189	Jowett	William Frederick	Fred	1	1903	1879	5.10.1939	W
190	Travers	George	George 'Twyber'	25	1903–11	9.6.1877	26.12.1945	H

CAP NO.	SURNAME	CHRISTIAN NAMES	KNOWN AS	TOTAL CAPS	FROM/TO	DATE OF BIRTH	DATE OF DEATH	POSITION
191	Arnold	William Richard	Willie	1	1903	7.7.1881	30.7.1957	W
192	Winfield	Herbert Ben	Bert	15	1903–08	1878	21.9.1919	FB
193	Thomas	David John	David	10	1904–11	15.3.1879	19.10.1925	Fwd
194	Evans	John William	Jack	1	1904	26.5.1875	5.7.1947	Fwd
195	Pritchard	Clifford Charles	Cliff	5	1904–06	1.10.1881	14.12.1954	C/Bk
196	Maynard	Edwin Thomas (known as Edwin Thomas)	'Beddoe'	6	1904–10	21.3.1878	20.11.1961	Fwd
197	O'Neil (known as O'Neill)	William	Billy	11	1904–08	5.6.1878	2.4.1955	Fwd
198	Davies	David Harris (or Horace)	–	1	1904	27.10.1877	30.9.1944	Fwd
199	Watkins	Harry Vaughan	Harry	6	1904–06	10.9.1875	16.5.1945	Fwd
200	Pritchard	Charles Meyrick	Charlie	14	1904–10	30.9.1882	14.8.1916*	Fwd
201	Bevan	Thomas Sidney	Sid	1	1904	2.5.1877	17.10.1933	Fwd
202	Jones	Howell	Howell	1	1904	5.4.1882	1.12.1908	Fwd
203	Jones	Anthony Windham	Wyndham	1	1905	1879	23.10.1959	HB
204	Williams	John Frederick	John 'Scethrog'	4	1905–06	18.11.1882	28.8.1911	Fwd
205	Bush	Percy Frank	Percy	8	1905–10	23.6.1879	19.5.1955	OH
206	Maddock	Hopkin Thomas	Hop	6	1906–10	1881	15.12.1921	W
207	Gibbs	Reginald Arthur	Reggie	16	1906–11	7.5.1882	28.11.1938	OH/W/B
208	Powell	John A.	Jack	1	1906	unknown	unknown	Fwd
209	Westacott	David	Dai	1	1906	1882	28.8.1917*	Fwd
210	Evans	Thomas Henry	Tom	18	1906–11	31.12.1882	19.3.1955	Fwd
211	Dyke	John Charles Meredith	John	1	1906	20.6.1884	9.7.1960	FB
212	Williams	John Lewis	Johnnie	17	1906–11	3.1.1882	12.7.1916*	W
213	Jenkins	John Charles	Jack	1	1906	19.4.1880	winter 1971	Fwd
214	Thomas	Edward John	Dick	4	1906–09	14.10.1883	7.7.1916*	Fwd
215	Davies	David	'Bailey'	1	1907	3.12.1884	24.8.1968	FB
216	Evans	John Hart	Jack	3	1907	9.4.1881	9.8.1959	C
217	Brown	John Alfred	John Alf	7	1907–09	?.10.1881	3.8.1936	Fwd
218	Watts	James	James	11	1907–09	?.3.1878	2.2.1933	Fwd
219	Dowell	William Henry	William	7	1907–08	21.5.1885	9.11.1949	Fwd
220	Webb	Alfred James	Jim	20	1907–12	1878	29.1.1955	Fwd
221	Jones	David Phillips	'Ponty'	1	1907	10.12.1881	9.1.1956	W
222	David	Richard Jenkin	Dickie	1	1907	1879	24.10.1936	SH
223	Vile	Thomas Henry	Tommy	8	1908–21	6.9.1882	30.11.1958	SH
224	Hayward	George	George	5	1908–09	1887	14.2.1948	Fwd
225	Hopkins	Philip	Phil	4	1909–10	31.1.1880	26.9.1966	W
226	Jones	John Phillips	Jack	14	1908–12	2.3.1886	19.3.1951	C/W
227	Waller	Phillip Dudley	Phil	6	1908–10	28.1.1889	14.12.1917*	Fwd
228	Morgan	William Ivor	Ivor	13	1908–12	?.8.1884	10.12.1943	Fwd
229	Bancroft	John	Jack	18	1909–14	1879	7.1.1942	FB
230	Blackmore	Joseph Henry (or Jacob W.)	Jake	1	1909	unknown	26.3.1964	Fwd
231	Baker	Albert Melville	Mel	3	1909–10	1885	unknown	W
232	Lloyd	Thomas John	'TC'	7	1909–14	1882	27.4.1938	Fwd
233	Thomas	Rees	Rees	8	1909–13	1882	15.6.1926	Fwd
234	Pullman	Joseph John	Joe	1	1910	19.6.1876	?.7.1955	Fwd
235	Gronow	Benjamin	Ben	4	1910	10.3.1887	24.11.1967	Fwd
236	Pugsley	Joseph	Joe	7	1910–11	10.5.1885	13.6.1976	Fwd
237	Jarman	Henry	Harry	4	1910–11	1883	13.12.1928	Fwd
238	Spiller	William John	Billy	10	1910–13	8.7.1886	9.6.1970	C
239	Morgan	William Llewellyn	–	1	1910	9.1.1884	11.4.1960	SH
240	Jenkins	Ernest	Ernie	2	1910	unknown	unknown	Fwd
241	Dyke	Louis Meredith	Louis	4	1910–11	1888	12.7.1961	C

CAP NO.	SURNAME	CHRISTIAN NAMES	KNOWN AS	TOTAL CAPS	FROM/TO	DATE OF BIRTH	DATE OF DEATH	POSITION
242	Birt	Frederick William	Fred	7	1911–13	10.11.1886	5.7.1956	C/FB
243	Coldrick	Albert Percival	Percy	6	1911–12	1888	26.12.1953	Fwd
244	Perry	William John	Bill	1	1911	22.9.1886	16.2.1970	Fwd
245	Birch	James	Jim	2	1911	30.12.1889	17.4.1968	Fwd
246	Evans	William George	William	1	1911	23.3.1886	1946 or '49	Fwd
247	Davies	David Evans George (or Ewan Gibson)	Ewan	2	1912	23.6.1887	2.9.1979	W
248	Lewis	John Morris Clement	Clem	11	1912–23	22.6.1890	25.10.1944	OH
249	Davies	Howell John	–	2	1912	unknown	unknown	Fwd
250	Stephens	Glyn	Glyn	10	1912–19	29.11.1891	22.4.1965	Fwd
251	Trump	Leonard Charles	Len	4	1912	23.4.1887	9.6.1948	Fwd
252	Uzzell	Henry	Harry	15	1912–20	6.1.1883	20.12.1960	Fwd
253	Plummer	Reginald Clifford Stanley	Reg	5	1912–13	29.12.1888	18.6.1953	W
254	Davies	William Avon	Willie	2	1912	27.12.1890	18.9.1967	C
255	Hirst	George Littlewood	George	6	1912–14	5.5.1890	30.7.1967	W
256	Lewis	Brinley Richard	Brinley	2	1912–13	4.1.1891	2.4.1917*	W
257	Martin	Walter John	Walter	3	1912–19	14.5.1883	30.4.1933	OH
258	Merry	James Augustus	Gus	2	1912	1888	14.12.1943	Fwd
259	Hiams	Harry	Harry	2	1912	1886	10.4.1954	Fwd
260	Williams	Thomas	Tom	6	1912–14	1887	13.8.1927	Fwd
261	Hawkins	Frank James	Frank	2	1912	1885	3.9.1960	Fwd
262	Jenkins	William Joseph	Billy	4	1912–13	1885	23.12.1956	Fwd
263	Thomas	Harold	Harold 'Drummer'	1	1912	unknown	unknown	FB
264	Williams	Robert Francis	Robbie	4	1912–14	1885	28.10.1967	FB
265	Geen	William Purdon	Billy	3	1912–13	14.3.1891	31.7.1915*	W/C
266	Thomas	Horace Wyndham	–	2	1912–13	28.7.1890	3.9.1916	OH
267	Perrett	Fred Leonard	Fred	5	1912–13	9.5.1891	1.12.1918	Fwd
268	Wetter	William Henry	Harry	2	1912–13	3.2.1882	4.2.1934	Fwd
269	Jones	Percy Llewellyn	Percy	8	1912–14	23.3.1887	31.3.1969	Fwd
270	Andrews	Frank	Frank	4	1912–13	1886	22.11.1944	Fwd
271	Hollingdale	Herbert George	Bert	2	1912–13	1889	11.2.1961	Fwd
272	Morgan	John Lewis	Johnnie	2	1912–13	23.10.1892	7.7.1947	Fwd
273	Jones	James Phillips	'Tuan'	1	1913	23.11.1883	4.12.1964	C
274	Lewis	Howell	Howell	4	1913–14	24.5.1888	29.5.1971	W
275	Lloyd	Robert A.	Bobby	7	1913–14	1888	18.1.1930	SH
276	Davies	Jenkin Alban	Rev. Alban	7	1913–14	5.9.1885	18.7.1976	Fwd
277	Richards	Rees	Rees	3	1913	1888	unknown	Fwd
278	Gething	Glyn Ivor	Glyn	1	1913	16.6.1892	20.3.1977	FB
279	Lewis	Mark	Mark	1	1913	?.3.1889	?.8.1968	W
280	Evans	William Henry	William	4	1914	9.2.1892	1979	C
281	Watts	William James	Willie	1	1914	16.5.1890	16.9.1950	C
282	Watts	David	David	4	1914	14.3.1886	14.7.1916*	Fwd
283	Jones	John L.	'Bedwellty'	4	1914	25.1.1890	unknown	Fwd
284	Morgan	Edgar	Edgar	4	1914	?.4.1882	?.4.1962	Fwd
285	Wetter	John James	Jack	10	1914–24	29.12.1897	29.7.1967	C/OH
286	Davies	Ivor Thomas	Ivor	3	1914	6.4.1892	2.7.1959	W
287	Davies	Evan	Ianto	1	1919	1892	1946	FB
288	Thomas	Beriah Melbourne Gwynne	Melbourne	6	1919–24	11.6.1896	23.6.1966	W
289	Rees	Evan B.	Evan	1	1919	unknown	unknown	C
290	Shea	Jeremiah	Jerry	4	1919–21	?.8.1892	30.6.1947	C
291	Nicholas	Trevor John	Trevor	1	1919	7.1.1894	13.3.1979	W
292	Fowler	Isaac John	Ike	1	1919	27.8.1894	17.6.1981	SH
293	Jones	James	Jim	6	1919–21	1893	unknown	Fwd
294	Havard	William Thomas	Rev. Bill	1	1919	23.10.1889	17.8.1956	Fwd

CAP NO.	SURNAME	CHRISTIAN NAMES	KNOWN AS	TOTAL CAPS	FROM/ TO	DATE OF BIRTH	DATE OF DEATH	POSITION
295	Francis	David Gwynn	Gwyn	2	1919–24	2.2.1896	7.5.1987	Fwd
296	Whitfield	John James	Jack	12	1919–24	23.3.1892	26.12.1927	Fwd
297	Rees	Aaron	Aaron	1	1919	unknown	unknown	Fwd
298	Morris	William George Henry	Bill	3	1919–21	1894	14.7.1967	Fwd
299	Parker	Edwin Thomas	Tom	15	1919–23	29.3.1891	25.11.1967	Fwd
300	Rees	Joseph	Joe	12	1920–24	3.6.1893	12.4.1950	FB
301	Powell	Wickham James	Wick	4	1920	13.9.1892	20.3.1961	W
302	Jenkins	Albert Edward	Albert	14	1920–28	11.3.1895	7.10.1953	C
303	Evans	Brinley Samuel	Brinley	5	1920–22	21.1.1894	28.6.1964	W/C
304	Beynon	Benjamin	Ben	2	1920	14.3.1894	21.5.1969	OH
305	Williams	John L.	Jack	7	1920–21	1891	6.12.1965	Fwd
306	Morris	Stephen	Steve	19	1920–25	1896	29.5.1965	Fwd
307	Oliver	George	George	4	1920	3.4.1891	21.7.1977	Fwd
308	Jones	Charles William	Charles	3	1920	18.6.1893	19.1.1960	Fwd
309	Williams	Brinley	Brinley	3	1920	3.4.1895	5.1.1987	W
310	Reeves	Frederick Charles	Fred	3	1920–21	12.6.1892	5.8.1976	SH
311	Huxtable	Richard	Dick	2	1920	13.10.1890	29.8.1970	Fwd
312	Morgan	David Edgar	Edgar	4	1920–21	17.5.1896	9.9.1983	Fwd
313	Ring	John	Johnny	1	1921	13.11.1900	10.11.1984	W
314	Johnson	Thomas Albert	W Tom 'Codger'	12	1921–25	1893	6.5.1948	W/FB
315	Attewell	Stephen Leonard	Len	3	1921	31.12.1895	26.2.1983	Fwd
316	Winmill	Stanley	Stan Docker	4	1921	5.5.1889	25.6.1940	Fwd
317	Edwards	David	Dai	1	1921	21.3.1896	24.8.1960	Fwd
318	Hodder	Wilfred	Wilf	3	1921	6.5.1896	12.11.1957	Fwd
319	Jones (not Marsden-Jones)	Marsden Douglas	Marsden	2	1921–24	1893	5.1.1955	Fwd
320	Evans	Frank	Frankie 'Dafen'	1	1921	3.4.1897	30.11.1972	W
321	Jones	Paul Esmond Russell	Paul 'Baker'	1	1921	27.12.1894	17.5.1934	C
322	Bowen	William E.	William	6	1921–22	6.12.1897	unknown	OH
323	Roberts	Thomas	Tom	9	1921–23	1897	28.9.1972	Fwd
324	Male	Benjamin Oswald	Ossie	11	1921–28	31.12.1893	23.2.1975	FB
325	Davies	Harry Graham	Harry	3	1921–25	19.4.1899	22.5.1989	C
326	Williams	Tudor	Tudor	1	1921	c. 1899	24.7.1922	SH
327	Davies	David Horace	Daph	2	1921–25	1898	22.9.1967	C
328	Brown	Archibald	Archie	1	1921	2.11.1894	unknown	SH
329	Prosser	Frederick John	Jack	1	1921	15.12.1892	15.6.1947	Fwd
330	Baker	Ambrose	Ambrose	5	1921–23	7.7.1897	24.11.1976	Fwd
331	Richards	William Clifford	Cliff 'Ginger'	5	1922	28.3.1901	13.2.1964	W
332	Evans	Haydn Islwyn	Islwyn	4	1922	25.12.1898	13.5.1974	C
333	Palmer	Frank Cyril	Frank	3	1922	26.6.1896	16.10.1925	W
334	Delahay	William James	Bobby	18	1922–27	2.9.1900	12.9.1978	O/C/SH
335	Jones	Thomas	Tom 'Cooking'	6	1922–24	13.12.1895	unknown	Fwd
336	Stephens	John Griffith	Rev. John	4	1922	30.10.1893	14.5.1956	Fwd
337	Cummins	William	Will	4	1922	20.3.1892	unknown	Fwd
338	Hiddlestone	David Daniel	Dai	5	1922–24	14.6.1890	16.11.1973	Fwd
339	Samuel	Thomas Frederick	Fred	3	1922	8.1.1897	c. 1941	FB
340	Cornish	Robert Arthur	Arthur	10	1923–26	30.6.1897	29.7.1948	C
341	Harding	W. Rowe	Rowe	17	1923–28	10.9.1901	10.2.1991	W
342	Davies	David G.	Dai	2	1923	c. 1897	unknown	Fwd
343	Thomas	Samuel Gethin	Gethin	4	1923	24.4.1897	1.2.1939	Fwd
344	Thompson	Joseph Francis	Joe	1	1923	22.12.1902	13.10.1983	Fwd
345	Michael	Gwilym Morgan	Gwilym	3	1923	1892	24.5.1941	Fwd
346	Jenkins	John Llewellyn	John	2	1923	12.3.1903	unknown	Fwd

CAP NO.	SURNAME	CHRISTIAN NAMES	KNOWN AS	TOTAL CAPS	FROM/TO	DATE OF BIRTH	DATE OF DEATH	POSITION
347	John	David Evan	Dai	5	1923–28	1.3.1902	20.11.1973	OH
348	Williams	Mapson Thomas	Mapson	1	1923	5.4.1891	15.7.1954	Fwd
349	Pascoe	Daniel	Dan	2	1923	7.7.1900	19.5.1971	Fwd
350	Collins	Thomas	Tom	1	1923	14.8.1895	8.4.1957	C
351	Powell	John	Jack	1	1923	12.8.1894	7.2.1968	W
352	Davies	Harry Stanley	Stan	1	1923	23.4.1895	14.2.1966	Fwd
353	Davies	John Henry	John	1	1923	c. 1897	unknown	Fwd
354	Richards	Thomas Lewis	Tom	1	1923	13.10.1895	25.5.1975	Fwd
355	Radford	William John	–	1	1923	8.4.1888	2.1.1924	Fwd
356	Davies	David Henry	Hunt	1	1924	11.11.1896	8.5.1979	C
357	Owen	Albert David	Albert	1	1924	31.7.1898	14.6.1964	OH
358	Watkins	Edward	Edward	4	1924	27.3.1899	12.10.1983	SH
359	Thomas	Ifor	Ivor	1	1924	30.4.1900	11.5.1995	Fwd
360	Ould	William John	Bill	2	1924	6.5.1899	19.10.1960	Fwd
361	Pugh	Charles Henry	Charlie	7	1924–25	7.3.1896	23.1.1951	Fwd
362	Evans	Arthur	'Candy'	3	1924	19.2.1904	7.1.1952	Fwd
363	Morris	Joseph Ivor Thomas	Ivor or Glyn	2	1924	4.8.1901	10.9.1964	Fwd
364	Jones	Ivor Egwad	Ivor	16	1924–30	10.12.1901	16.11.1982	Fwd
365	Davies	Harold Joseph	Harold	1	1924	5.12.1898	29.3.1976	W
366	Evans	John Elwyn	Jack Elwyn	1	1924	1897	15.7.1941	C
367	Rosser	Melvin Aaron	Mel	2	1924	18.4.1901	8.9.1988	C/FB
368	Griffiths	Vincent Morgan	Vince	3	1924	29.5.1901	7.1.1967	OH
369	Evans	Thomas David	Tommy 'Pete'	1	1924	8.5.1902	6.8.1969	C
370	Parker	David Stewart	Dai	10	1924–30	8.8.1904	16.6.1965	Fwd
371	Hathway	George Frederick	George	2	1924	23.1.1897	30.1.1971	Fwd
372	Randall	Robert John	Bob	2	1924	1891	7.7.1965	Fwd
373	Jones	William John	William	1	1924	4.2.1894	15.7.1978	Fwd
374	Gore	John Henry	Jack	4	1924–25	16.6.1899	18.3.1971	Fwd
375	Finch	Ernest	Ernie	7	1924–27	16.7.1899	1.10.1983	W
376	Stock	Albert	Bert	4	1924–26	21.4.1897	4.5.1969	C
377	Jones	Joseph	Joe	1	1924	15.3.1899	27.1.1960	C
378	Rickards	Arnold Robert	Arnold	1	1924	17.8.1901	18.6.1966	Fwd
379	Williams	Edwin	Eddie	2	1924–25	14.10.1898	31.1.1983	OH
380	Williams	Clifford	Cliff	2	1924–25	20.4.1898	28.5.1930	Fwd
381	James	William P.	Will	2	1925	c. 1902	unknown	W
382	Williams	Evan	Evan	2	1925	18.6.1906	18.11.1976	C
383	Thomas	Cyril Rhys	Cyril	2	1925	27.3.1902	5.12.1977	W
384	Hopkins	William John	Willie	2	1925	c. 1898	unknown	OH
385	Phillips	Brinley	Brinley	5	1925–26	11.10.1900	1980	Fwd
386	Richards	Evan Idris	Idris 'The Bank'	3	1925	1892	28.11.1962	Fwd
387	Jones	Walter Idris	Idris	4	1925	18.1.1900	5.7.1971	Fwd
388	Herrera	Ronald Cecil	Ron	8	1925–27	16.1.1905	16.3.1973	
389	Lawrence	Stephen David	Steve	6	1925–27	5.8.1899	13.2.1978	Fwd
390	Lewis	William	Will	1	1925	14.3.1899	26.1.1927	Fwd
391	Beynon	George Edward	Eddie	2	1925	1902	14.10.1957	Fwd
392	Jones (not Rocyn-Jones)	David Nathan Rocyn	Nathan	1	1925	17.7.1902	26.1.1984	FB
393	Turnbull	Bernard Ruel	Bernard 'Lou'	6	1925–30	16.10.1904	7.4.1984	C
394	John	David Arthur	Arthur	4	1925–28	1900	16.8.1929	SH
395	Brown	James	Jim	1	1925	22.3.1901	30.7.1976	Fwd
396	Hinam	Sydney	Syd	5	1925–26	29.8.1898	16.8.1982	Fwd
397	Evans	David Benjamin	'DB'	1	1926	3.9.1899	23.6.1977	FB
398	Andrews	George Edward	George	5	1926–27	24.8.1904	21.12.1989	W
399	Jones	Robert	Bobby 'Shanghai'	3	1926	?.10.1900	?.2.1970	OH

CAP NO.	SURNAME	CHRISTIAN NAMES	KNOWN AS	TOTAL CAPS	FROM/ TO	DATE OF BIRTH	DATE OF DEATH	POSITION
400	Lewis	Thomas William	Tom	3	1926–27	7.6.1902	31.5.1994	Fwd
401	John	John Howell	Howell	8	1926–27	31.8.1898	1977	Fwd
402	Hopkins	Thomas	Tom	4	1926	20.1.1903	26.1.1980	Fwd
403	Jenkins	David Morgan	David	4	1926	1901	22.4.1968	Fwd
404	Jones	David L.	Dai	5	1926–27	c. 1901	unknown	Fwd
405	Everson	William Aaron	Bill	1	1926	?.3.1905	26.3.1966	FB
406	Powell	William Charles	Wick	27	1926–35	c. 1905	c. 1973	SH/W
407	Watkins	Emlyn	Emlyn	3	1926	21.9.1904	15.5.1978	Fwd
408	Rees	Thomas Edgar	Tommy 'Guardsman'	4	1926–28	22.8. 1904	10.11.1968	FB
409	Rowlands	Charles Foster	Charles	1	1926	1899	10.11.1958	W
410	Lewis	Windsor Hopkin	Windsor	6	1926–28	11.11.1906	30.11.1982	OH
411	Roberts	john	John	13	1927–29	4.4.1906	31.10.1965	C/W
412	Phillips	Henry Thomas	Harry	9	1927–28	22.6.1903	16.12.1978	Fwd
413	Thomas	Watkin Gwyn	Watcyn	14	1927–33	16.1.1906	10.8.1977	Fwd
414	Williams	William Arthur	Billy	4	1927	27.12.1905	4.11.1973	Fwd
415	Bartlett	John Dudley	–	3	1927–28	6.8.1907	17.1.1967	W
416	Richards	Ernest Gwyn	Gwyn	1	1927	22.12.1905	17.12.1985	OH
417	Arthur	Thomas	Tom	18	1927–33	10.1.1906	1.11.1966	Fwd
418	Jenkins	Edward McDonald	Ned	21	1927–32	28.7.1904	8.11.1990	Fwd
419	Morgan	William Guy	Guy	8	1927–30	26.12.1907	29.7.1973	C
	(later changed name to W.G. Stewart-Morgan by deed poll)							
420	Burns	James Joseph	Jim 'Ocker'	2	1927	22.2.1899	1971	Fwd
421	Jones	William Roy	Ray	2	1927–28	22.2.1903	?.7.1973	C
422	Jones	Daniel	Dan	1	1927	2.3.1907	?.11.1988	W
423	Harris	Charles Albert	Tal	1	1927	4.2.1902	1.10.1963	SH
424	Bowdler	Frederick Arthur	Lonza	15	1927–33	4.1.1901	17.12.1962	H
425	Jenkins	David Rees	David	2	1927–29	12.4.1904	13.8.1951	Fwd
426	Broughton	Augustus Stephen	Gus	2	1927–29	29.4.1904	22.9.1981	Fwd
427	Hollingdale	Thomas Henry	Tom	6	1927–30	12.11.1900	14.4.1978	Fwd
428	Jones	Thomas Iorwerth	Iorwerth	5	1927–28	3.4.1903	31.8.1983	Fwd
429	Pritchard	Cecil Clifford	Cecil	8	1928–29	1.5.1902	27.8.1966	H
430	Skym	Archibald	Archie	20	1928–35	12.7.1906	15.6.1970	Fwd
431	Davies	Eiran Gwyne	Gwyn	3	1928–30	23.6.1908	21.7.1992	W
432	Bassett	John Archibald	Jack	15	1929–32	11.7.1905	19.2.1989	FB
433	Morley	John Cuthbert	Jack	14	1929–32	28.7.1909	7.3.1972	W
434	Roberts	William	Bill	1	1929	20.2.1909	7.12.1969	OH
435	Jones	Harold James	Harold	2	1929	22.12.1907	16.10.1955	Fwd
436	Jones	Richard	Dick 'Chink'	1	1929	5.11.1906	18.1.1986	Fwd
437	Bowcott	Henry Morgan	Harry	8	1929–33	30.4.1907		C/OH
438	Williams	Franklyn Lewis	Frank	14	1929–33	26.1.1910	7.7.1959	OH/C
439	Barrell	Robert John	Bob	4	1929–33	1.11.1905	13.1.1967	Fwd
440	Peacock	Harry	Harry	6	1929–30	14.2.1909	?.3.1996	Fwd
441	Lemon	Arthur Whitelock	Arthur	13	1929–33	15.4.1905	28.5.1982	Fwd
442	Jones–Davies	Thomas Ellis	Tommy	4	1930–31	4.3.1906	25.8.1960	C
443	Hickman	Arthur	Arthur	2	1930–33	6.8.1910		W
444	Roberts	David Edward Arfon	–	1	1930	23.1.1909	17.11.1995	SH
445	Thomas	William Trevor	Ocker	1	1930	c. 1909	unknown	Fwd
446	Jones	Glyn Graham	Graham 'Chick'	2	1930–31	24.11.1906	21.10.1987	C
447	Boon	Ronald Winston	Ronnie	12	1930–33	11.6.1909	3.8.1998	W
448	Day	Hubert Charles	Hubert	5	1930–31	8.5.1908	27.6.1977	Fwd
449	Thomas	David John	Dai	11	1930–35	30.3.1909		Fwd
450	Jones	Elwyn Howel	Howie	2	1930	8.9.1907	4.5.1983	W
451	Fender	Norman Henry	Norman	6	1930–31	2.9.1910	24.10.1983	Fwd
452	Scourfield	Thomas Brinley	Tommy	1	1930	1909	?.2.1976	FB

CAP NO.	SURNAME	CHRISTIAN NAMES	KNOWN AS	TOTAL CAPS	FROM/ TO	DATE OF BIRTH	DATE OF DEATH	POSITION
453	Davey	E. Claud	Claude	23	1930–38	14.12.1908		C
454	Jones	Edgar Lewis	Edgar	5	1930–35	4.5.1910	11.2.1986	Fwd
455	Day	Thomas Brynmor	Tom	13	1931–35	29.12.1907	18.9.1980	Fwd
456	Ralph	Albert Raymond	Dicky	6	1931–32	21.1.1908	5.10.1989	OH
457	James	David Rees	David	2	1931	7.10.1906	?.11.1984	Fwd
458	Lang	James	Jim	12	1931–37	1.10.1909	22.12.1991	Fwd
459	Davies	William	Will 'Sgili'	4	1931–32	14.2.1906	5.10.1975	Fwd
460	Jenkins	Vivian Gordon James	Viv	14	1933–39	2.11.1911		FB
461	Wooller	Wilfred	Wilf	19	1933–39	20.11.1912	10.3.1997	C/W
462	Jones	Arthur Hugh	Arthur	2	1933	2.10.1908	26.6.1964	W
463	Turnbull	Maurice Joseph Lawson	Maurice	2	1933	16.3.1906	5.8.1944*	SH
464	Evans	Brinley	Bryn	6	1933–37	21.7.1906	6.10.1978	Fwd
465	Jones	Raymond Bark	Raymond	2	1933	29.8.1911		Fwd
466	Isaacs	Iorwerth	Iorrie	2	1933	4.10.1910	25.4.1966	Fwd
467	Bayliss	Gwyn	Gwyn	1	1933	?.5.1907	10.3.1976	FB
468	Morris	Ronald Rhys	Ronnie	2	1933–37	13.6.1913	?.2.1983	OH
469	Evans	David Brinley	Bryn	1	1933	16.1.1902	27.4.1970	SH
470	Moore	William John	Billy	1	1933	17.2.1910	31.3.1976	Fwd
471	Rees	Lewis Morgan	Lewis	1	1933	17.1.1910	21.12.1976	Fwd
472	Howells	Brynmor	Bryn	1	1934	9.2.1911	6.6.1983	FB
473	Cowey	Bernard Turing Vionnee	Bernard 'Bun'	4	1934–35	20.11.1911	20.8.1997	W
474	Rees	John Idwal	Idwal	14	1934–38	25.7.1910	31.8.1991	W/C
475	Jones (known as Rees-Jones)	Geoffrey Rippon Rees	Geoffrey	5	1934–36	8.7.1914		W
476	Jones	William Clifford	Cliff	13	1934–38	12.3.1914	27.10.1990	OH
477	Evans	David Dan	David	1	1934	7.4.1909	?.9.1992	SH
478	Davies	Cecil Rhys	Cecil	1	1934	12.9.1909	25.12.1941*	P
479	Evans	John Raymond	John	1	1934	12.8.1911	8.3.1943*	H
480	Truman	William Henry	Harry	2	1934–35	11.12.1909	23.6.1984	Fwd
481	Hughes	Gomer	Gomer	3	1934	13.5.1910	14.11.1974	Fwd
482	Prosser	Idris Glyn	Glyn	4	1934–35	27.11.1907	13.11.1992	Fwd
483	Jones	Kenyon William James	Ken	1	1934	5.9.1911	16.12.1998	Fwd
484	Rees	Arthur Morgan	Arthur	13	1934–38	20.11.1912	13.5.1998	Fwd
485	Jones	William Herbert	Bert	2	1934	1.5.1906	31.7.1982	SH
486	Evans	Iorwerth	Iorrie	2	1934	1908	18.9.1985	Fwd
487	Prosser	David Rees	Dai	2	1934	13.10.1912	6.5.1973	Fwd
488	Ward	William Stanford	Bill	2	1934	6.1.1907	22.11.1973	Fwd
489	Fear	Albert George	Albert	4	1934–35	25.8.1907		Fwd
490	Bassett	Arthur	Arthur	6	1934–38	28.6.1914		W
491	Murphy	Cornelius Denis	Con	3	1935	3.9.1908	13.7.1964	Fwd
492	Rees	Thomas John	Tom	8	1935–37	8.5.1913	19.2.1990	Fwd
493	Williams	Trevor George	'Tabber'	8	1935–37	27.5.1907	27.8.1982	Fwd
494	James	Thomas Owen	Tommy	2	1935–37	6.10.1904	8.4.1984	FB
495	Tanner	Haydn	Haydn	25	1935–49	9.1.1917		SH
496	Payne	Harry	Harry	1	1935	10.12.1907		Fwd
497	Tarr	Donald James	Don	1	1935	11.3.1910	4.6.1980	H
498	Watkins	Edward Verdun	Eddie	8	1935–39	2.3.1916	28.6.1995	Fwd
499	McCall	Barney Ernest Wilford	Barney	3	1936	13.5.1913	31.3.1991	W
500	Thomas	Harold Watkin	Harold	6	1936–37	19.2.1914	10.12.1989	Fwd
501	Williams	Griffith Morgan	Griff	3	1936	30.6.1907	unknown	Fwd
502	Long	Edgar Cecil	Edgar	7	1936–39	1907	31.1.1958	Fwd
503	Davies	William Thomas Harcourt	Willie	6	1936–39	23.8.1916		OH/C

WELSH INTERNATIONAL MATCHES

CAP NO.	SURNAME	CHRISTIAN NAMES	KNOWN AS	TOTAL CAPS	FROM/TO	DATE OF BIRTH	DATE OF DEATH	POSITION
504	Clement	William Harries	Bill	6	1937–38	9.4.1915		W
505	Evans	Emrys	Emrys	3	1937–39	24.4.1911	23.6.1983	Fwd
506	Thomas	David Leyshon	David	1	1937	?.3.1909	28.5.1952	Fwd
507	Hopkin	William Henry	Bill	1	1937	1.7.1914		W
508	Travers	William	'Bunner'	12	1937–49	2.12.1913	4.6.1998	H
509	Rees	Henry Tudor	Harry	5	1937–38	9.5.1908	3.6.1978	Fwd
510	Legge	Walter Sydney George	Walter	2	1937–38	11.11.1911	1984	FB
511	Bennett	Ivor	Ivor	1	1937	16.6.1913	unknown	Fwd
512	Taylor	Albert Russell	Russell	3	1937–39	2.12.1914	9.10.1965	Fwd
513	Morgan	Morgan Edward	Eddie	4	1938–39	18.12.1913	1978	Fwd
514	Morgan	Frederick Luther	Fred	4	1938–39	11.2.1915	29.12.1988	Fwd
515	Vickery	Walter Elias	Walter	4	1938–39	25.10.1909		Fwd
516	McCarley	Allen	Allen	3	1938	5.12.1914	25.7.1963	Fwd
517	Ford	Frederick John Vivian	John	1	1939	13.10.1917		W
518	Davies	David Idwal	Idwal	1	1939	10.11.1915	7.7.1990	C
519	Williams	Sydney Arthur	Syd	3	1939	17.4.1918	28.8.1976	W
520	Davis	William Edward Norman	Wendy	3	1939	7.9.1913		Fwd
521	Challinor	Cyril	Cyril	1	1939	13.5.1912	29.11.1976	Fwd
522	Davies	Christian Howard	Howard	6	1939–47	25.12.1916	5.11.1987	FB
523	Jones	Elfed Lewis	Elvet	1	1939	29.4.1912	5.10.1989	W
524	Davies	Michael John	Mickey	2	1939	7.10.1918	8.7.1984	C
525	Davies	Leslie	Leslie 'Bychan'	2	1939	13.7.1913	4.9.1984	Fwd
526	Price	Edwin Ronald	Ron	2	1939	16.9.1915		Fwd
527	Manfield	Leslie	Les	7	1939–48	10.11.1915		Fwd
528	Matthews	Christopher Mansel	Chris	1	1939	1911	5.12.1965	W
529	Law	Vivian John	Viv	1	1939	11.6.1910	22.4.1989	Fwd
530	Jones	Kenneth Jeffrey	Ken	44	1947–57	30.12.1921		W
531	Matthews	Jack	Jack	17	1947–51	21.6.1920		C
532	Cleaver	William Benjamin	Billy	14	1947–50	15.9.1921		UtBk
533	Williams	William Leslie Thomas	Les	7	1947–49	10.5.1922		W/C
534	Williams	Bleddyn Llewellyn	Bleddyn	22	1947–55	22.2.1923		C/OH
535	Jones	David Charles Jenkin	Dai	7	1947–49	30.4.1916		P
536	Blakemore	Reginald Edward	Reg	1	1947	1.9.1924		H
537	Bevan	Griffith Wilfred	Griff	1	1947	15.8.1914		P
538	Williams	Stanley	Stan	6	1947–48	4.11.1914	21.11.1967	L
539	Parsons	George W.	George	1	1947	21.4.1926		L
540	Williams	Oswald	Ossie	7	1947–48	12.4.1921	23.3.1988	Fwd
541	Stephens	John Rees Glyn	Rees	32	1947–57	16.4.1922	4.2.1998	L/8
542	Evans	Gwynfor	Gwyn	12	1947–48	17.8.1918		F
543	Davies	Glyn	Glyn	11	1947–51	24.8.1927	7.11.1976	OH
544	Evans	Wilfred John	Wilf	1	1947	12.5.1914		P
545	Gore	William	Billy	3	1947	19.11.1919		H
546	Davies	Clifton	Cliff	16	1947–51	12.12.1919	28.1.1967	P
547	Tamplin	William Ewart	Bill	7	1947–48	10.5.1917	20.10.1989	L
548	Rees	Peter	Peter	2	1947	8.2.1925		W
549	Evans	Robert Thomas	Bob	10	1947–51	16.2.1921		F
550	Greville	Handel Glanffrwd	Handel	1	1947	13.9.1921		SH
551	Davies	Emlyn Price	Emlyn	2	1947–48	15.1.1922		P
552	James	David Maldwyn	Maldwyn	5	1947–48	28.6.1913		H
553	Gwilliam	John Albert	John	23	1947–54	28.2.1923		L/8
554	Trott	Richard Frank	Frank	8	1948–49	14.3.1915	28.3.1987	FB
555	Anthony	Leslie	Les	3	1948	21.11.1921		P
556	Jones	William Desmond	Des	1	1948	25.10.1925	15.8.1987	L
557	Coleman	Ernest Owain	Ernie	3	1949	3.11.1917		P

WELSH INTERNATIONAL PLAYERS

CAP NO.	SURNAME	CHRISTIAN NAMES	KNOWN AS	TOTAL CAPS	FROM/TO	DATE OF BIRTH	DATE OF DEATH	POSITION
558	Hayward	Donald James	Don	15	1949–52	30.6.1925	16.2.1999	L/P
559	Meredith	Alun	Alun	3	1949	9.11.1919		L
560	Cale	William Raymond	Ray	7	1949–50	18.7.1922		F
561	Cook	Terence J.	Terry	2	1949	27.6.1927		W
562	Thomas	Malcolm Campbell	Malcolm	27	1949–59	25.4.1929		C/W/OH
563	Major	Windsor Cynwyd	Windsor	2	1949–50	15.6.1927		W
564	Stone	Peter	Peter	1	1949	20.6.1924	10.7.1971	F
565	Thomas	Richard Clement Charles	Clem	26	1949–59	28.1.1929	5.9.1996	F
566	Jones	Benjamin Lewis	Lewis	10	1950–52	11.4.1931		UtBk
567	Brewer	Trevor John	Trevor	3	1950–55	16.8.1930		W
568	Willis	William Rex	Rex	21	1950–55	25.10.1924		SH
569	Robins	John Denning	John	11	1950–53	17.5.1926		P
570	Davies	David Maldwyn	Dai	17	1950–54	2.5.1925		H
571	John	Ernest Raymond	Roy	19	1950–54	3.12.1925	30.9.1981	L/F
572	Williams	Gerwyn	Gerwyn	13	1950–54	22.4.1924		FB
573	Evans	Peter Denzil	Peter	2	1951	20.6.1928		F
574	Forward	Allen	Allen	6	1951–52	4.6.1921	1.1.1994	F
575	Morgan	Clifford Issac	Cliff	29	1951–58	7.4.1930		OH
576	Edwards	Benjamin Oswald	Ben	1	1951	29.5.1923	2.9.1978	L
577	Morris	Haydn Thomas	Haydn	3	1951–55	14.7.1928		W
578	Williams	William Owen Gooding	Billy 'Stoker'	22	1951–56	19.11.1929		P
579	Blythe (known as Blyth)	Leonard Grist	Len	3	1951–52	20.11.1920	24.6.1995	F
580	Thomas	Alun Gruffydd	Alun	13	1952–55	3.2.1926	8.5.1991	UtBk
581	Williams	William Arthur	Billy	3	1952–53	9.9.1921		SH
582	Phillips	David Horace	Horace	1	1952	24.8.1928		W
583	Davies	Terence John	Terry	21	1953–61	24.9.1933		FB
584	Griffiths	Gareth Meredith	Gareth	12	1953–57	27.11.1931		W/C
585	Burnett	Roy	Roy	1	1953	6.10.1926	30.7.1998	OH
586	Beckingham	Geoffrey Thomas	Geoff	3	1953–58	29.7.1924		H
587	Judd	Sidney	Sid	10	1953–55	14.8.1928	24.2.1959	F/8
588	Johnson	William Dilwyn	Dill	1	1953	5.12.1923		F
589	Meredith	Courtenay Charles	Courtenay	14	1953–57	23.9.1926		P
590	Robins	Russell John	Russell	13	1953–57	21.2.1932		L/F/8
591	Lloyd	Trevor	Trevor	2	1953	5.9.1924		SH
592	Rowlands	Gwyn	Gwyn	4	1953–56	19.2.1928		W
593	John	D. Glyndwr	Glyn	2	1954	22.2.1932	7.6.1983	C/OH
594	Evans	Vivian	Viv	3	1954	14.7.1919		FB
595	Thomas	James Denzil	Denzil	1	1954	21.4.1929		C
596	Meredith	Brinley Victor	Bryn	34	1954–62	21.11.1930		H
597	Williams	Rhys Haydn	Rhys	23	1954–60	14.7.1930	27.1.1993	L
598	Jenkins	Leighton Hugh	Leighton	5	1954–56	1.7.1931		L/8
599	Sparks	Brian Anthonie	Brian	7	1954–57	23.6.1931		F
600	Davies	Leonard Morris	Len	3	1954–55	29.12.1930	23.9.1957	F
601	Williams	Henry Raymond	Ray	3	1954–58	13.11.1927		W
602	Edwards	Arthur Bernard	Arthur	2	1955	7.10.1927	19.9.1984	FB
603	Wells	Gordon Thomas	Gordon	7	1955–58	25.10.1928	?.4.1995	W/C
604	Davies	Neville Glyn	Glyn 'Shorty'	1	1955	29.11.1927		F
605	Owen	Garfield David	Garfield	6	1955–56	20.3.1932		FB
606	Williams	Charles Derek	Derek 'CD'	2	1955–56	28.11.1924		F
607	Morgan	Harry Perrott	Harry	4	1956	16.1.1930		C
608	Davies	Charles Lynn	'Cowboy'	3	1956	30.12.1929		W
609	Brace	David Onllwyn	Onllwyn 'Onkers'	9	1956–61	16.11.1932		SH

295

CAP NO.	SURNAME	CHRISTIAN NAMES	KNOWN AS	TOTAL CAPS	FROM/TO	DATE OF BIRTH	DATE OF DEATH	POSITION
610	Prosser	Thomas Raymond	Ray	22	1956–61	2.3.1927		P
611	Richards	Rex Clive	Rex 'Tarzan'	1	1956	4.2.1934	6.3.1989	P
612	Whitson	Geoffrey Keith	Geoff	3	1956–57	4.12.1930	18.5.1984	F
613	Howells	William Geoffrey	Geoff	4	1957	29.10.1929		W
614	Maddocks	Keith	Keith	1	1957	16.6.1927		W
615	O'Connor	Rory	Rory	1	1957	14.9.1932	7.3.1986	F
616	Williams	Lloyd Hugh	Lloyd	13	1957–62	19.10.1933		SH
617	Davies	Robin Harvard	Robin	6	1957–62	12.1.1934		F
618	Davies	Cyril Allan Harrard	Cyril	7	1957–61	21.11.1936		C
619	Powell	Graham	Graham	2	1957	17.11.1932		C
620	Morgan	Charles Henry	Henry	2	1957	22.12.1932		P
621	Faull	John	John	12	1957–60	30.6.1933		8/L
622	Collins	John Ernest	John	10	1958–61	16.1.1931		W
623	James	Carwyn Rees	Carwyn	2	1958	2.11.1929	10.1.1983	OH/C
624	Evans	Thomas Wynne	Wynne	1	1958	13.8.1926	8.5.1987	SH
625	Devereux	Donald Brian	Don	3	1958	18.10.1932	?.2.1995	P
626	Evans	William Roderick	Roddy	13	1958–62	19.12.1934		L
627	Morgan	Haydn John	Haydn	27	1958–66	30.7.1936		F
628	Priday	Alun James	Alun	2	1958–61	23.1.1933		FB
629	Roberts	Cyril Richard	Cyril	2	1958	19.12.1930		W
630	Nicholls	Howard Charles Warrender	Howard	1	1958	2.6.1931		W
631	Evans	John Davies	John 'JD'	2	1958	30.6.1926	25.3.1989	P
632	Davies	Haydn John	Haydn	2	1959	21.11.1936		C
633	Price	Malcolm John	Malcolm	9	1959–62	8.12.1937		C
634	Bebb	Dewi Iorwerth Ellis	Dewi	34	1959–67	7.8.1938	13.3.1996	W
635	Ashton	Clifford	Cliff	7	1959–60	17.12.1932		OH
636	Main	Derrick Roy	Derrick	4	1959	29.11.1931		P
637	Ford	Ian Reginald	Ian	2	1959	6.6.1929		L
638	Leleu	John	John	4	1959–60	13.3.1935		F
639	Harris	Daniel John Edward	Danny	8	1959–61	27.5.1937		L
640	Hurrell	Richard John	Jack	1	1959	17.8.1933		C
641	Watkins	William Raymond	Billy	1	1959	22.3.1933		SH
642	Davidge	Glyn David	Glyn	9	1959–62	31.12.1933		8/F
643	Lewis (known as Windsor-Lewis)	Geoffrey Windsor	Geoff	2	1960	7.4.1936		C
644	Evans	Colin	Colin	1	1960	20.11.1936	23.11.1982	SH
645	Cunningham	Leonard John	Len	14	1960–64	3.1.1931	20.7.1998	P
646	Payne	Gareth Webb	Gareth	3	1960	8.9.1935		L
647	Cresswell	Brian Robert	Brian	4	1960	9.11.1934		F
648	Morgan	Norman Henry	Norman	3	1960	26.3.1935		FB
649	Coles	Fenton Godfrey	Fenton	3	1960	14.9.1937		W
650	Jones	Brian James	Brian	2	1960	10.5.1935		C
651	Gale	Norman Reginald	Norman	25	1960–69	24.7.1939		H
652	Richards	Thomas Bryan	Bryan	1	1960	23.11.1932		OH
653	Evans	Denis Pritchard	Denis	1	1960	19.3.1936		W
654	Roberts	Hugh Meirion	Meirion	8	1960–63	11.9.1934		C
655	Richards	Kenneth Henry Llewellyn	Ken	5	1960–61	29.1.1934	8.1.1972	OH
656	O'Connor	Anthony	Tony	5	1960–62	24.4.1934		SH
657	Jones	Kingsley Daniel	Kingsley	10	1960–63	5.8.1935		P
658	Nash	David	David	6	1960–62	15.7.1939		L/8
659	Rees	Peter Maxwell	Peter	4	1961–64	14.10.1937		W
660	Morgan	Philip Edward John	Phil	3	1961	21.12.1937	9.4.1998	P
661	Britton	Gordon Richard	Gordon	1	1961	10.9.1939		C
662	Thomas	David Lynn	David	1	1961	29.4.1941		C

CAP NO.	SURNAME	CHRISTIAN NAMES	KNOWN AS	TOTAL CAPS	FROM/TO	DATE OF BIRTH	DATE OF DEATH	POSITION
663	Price	Brian	Brian	32	1961–69	30.10.1937		L
664	Mainwaring	Haydn James	Haydn	1	1961	10.6.1933		C
665	Thomas	William James	Billy	2	1961–63	1.9.1933		H
666	Pask	Alun Edward Islwyn	Alun	26	1961–67	10.9.1937	1.11.1995	8/F
667	Coslett	Thomas Kelvin	Kel	3	1962	14.1.1942		FB
668	Morgan	David Robert Ruskin	Robert	9	1962–63	29.8.1941	19.9.1999	W
669	Jones	David Kenneth	Ken	14	1962–66	7.8.1941		C/W
670	Rees	Alan Henry Morgan	Alan	3	1962	17.2.1938		OH
671	Greenslade	Desmond	Des	1	1962	11.1.1933		P
672	Rowlands	Keith Alun	Keith	5	1962–65	7.2.1936		L
673	Hodgson	Grahame Thornton Ridgway	Graham	15	1962–67	1.12.1936		FB
674	Davies	David Brian	Brian	3	1962–63	7.7.1941		C
675	Warlow	Douglas John	John	1	1962	13.2.1939		P
676	Davies	David John	John	1	1962	20.2.1941	16.4.1969	F
677	Watkins	David	David	21	1963–67	5.3.1942		OH
678	Rowlands	Daniel Clive Thomas	Clive 'Topcat'	14	1963–65	14.5.1938		SH
679	Williams	Denzel	Denzil	36	1963–71	17.10.1938		P
680	Thomas	Brian Edwin	Brian	21	1963–69	18.5.1940		L/P
681	Michaelson	Roger Carl Brandon	Roger	1	1963	31.3.1941		8
682	Hayward	David John	Dai	6	1963–64	1.3.1934		F
683	Evans	Ronald	Ron	3	1963	6.11.1941		C
684	Morris	William James Bunce	Bill	2	1963	21.5.1940		W
685	Jones	Graham	Graham	3	1963	24.11.1933		F
686	Norris	Charles Howard	Howie	2	1963–66	11.6.1934		P
687	Uzzell	John	Dick	5	1963–65	28.3.1942		C
688	Thomas	Alan	Alan	2	1963–64	16.4.1940		F
689	Weaver	David Samuel	David	1	1964	8.1.1942		W
690	Bradshaw	Keith	Keith	9	1964–66	7.4.1939		C
691	Mantle	John T.	John	2	1964	13.3.1942		F/8
692	Watkins	Stuart John	Stuart	26	1964–70	5.6.1941		W
693	Prothero	Gareth John	Gary	11	1964–66	7.12.1941		F
694	Dawes	Sydney John	John 'Sid'	22	1964–71	29.6.1940		C
695	Price	Terence Graham	Terry	8	1965–67	16.7.1945	7.4.1993	FB
696	Waldron	Ronald Gwyn	Ron	4	1965	14.12.1933		P
697	Morris	William John	Bill	2	1965–66	16.6.1941		L
698	Davies	Lyn	Lyn 'Tanky'	3	1966	2.2.1940		W
699	Lewis	Robert Allan	Allan	6	1966–67	7.10.1942		SH
700	Lloyd	David John	John	24	1966–73	29.3.1943		P
701	Davies	Thomas Gerald Reames	Gerald	46	1966–78	7.2.1945		W/C
702	John	Barry	Barry 'King'	25	1966–72	6.1.1945		OH
703	Thomas	William Delme	Delme	25	1966–74	12.9.1942		L
704	Braddock	Kenneth James	Ken	3	1966–67	28.8.1938		F
705	Raybould	William Henry	Billy	11	1967–70	6.3.1944		C
706	Hullin	William Gwyn	Billy	1	1967	2.1.1942		SH
707	Rees	Brian Idris	Brian	3	1967	28.8.1942		H
708	O'Shea	John Patrick	John 'Tessie'	5	1967–68	2.6.1940		P
709	Mainwaring	Gwilym Thomas	Billy	6	1967–68	24.1.1941		L
710	Taylor	John	John	26	1967–73	21.7.1945		F
711	Edwards	Gareth Owen	Gareth	53	1967–78	12.7.1947		SH
712	Jones	Ronald Elvet	Ron	5	1967–68	24.2.1943		F/8
713	Morris	William David	Dai 'Shadow'	34	1967–74	11.11.1941		F/8
714	Jarrett	Keith Stanley	Keith	10	1967–69	18.5.1948		FB/C
715	Wheeler	Paul James	Paul	2	1967–68	5.2.1947		FB
716	Hall	Ian	Ian	8	1967–74	4.11.1946		C/W

CAP NO.	SURNAME	CHRISTIAN NAMES	KNOWN AS	TOTAL CAPS	FROM/TO	DATE OF BIRTH	DATE OF DEATH	POSITION
717	Jones	William Keri	Keri	5	1967–69	13.1.1945		W
718	Wiltshire	Maxwell Lloyd	Max	4	1967–68	16.7.1938		L
719	Hughes	Dennis	Dennis	6	1967–70	3.7.1941		F
720	Jeffery	James John	John	1	1967	26.2.1945		8
721	James	John Boyo	Boyo	1	1968	4.9.1938		P
722	Wanbon	Robert	Bobby	1	1968	16.11.1943		8
723	Gray	Anthony John	Tony	2	1968	14.6.1942		F
724	Rees	Douglas	Doug	3	1968	15.1.1944		FB
725	Young	Jeffrey	Jeff	23	1968–73	16.9.1942		H
726	Richards	Maurice Charles Rees	Maurice	9	1968–69	2.2.1945		W
727	Jones	Ian Cronin	Ian	1	1968	2.3.1940		L
728	Williams	John Peter Rhys	John 'JPR'	55	1969–81	2.3.1949		FB/F
729	Davies	Thomas Mervyn	Mervyn 'The Swerve'	38	1969–76	9.12.1946		8
730	Bennett (1st replacement to be capped for Wales)	Philip	Phil	29	1969–79	24.10.1948		OH/FB/C/W
731	Perrins	Victor Charles	Vic	2	1970	3.9.1944		H
732	Llewelyn	Donald Barry	Barry	13	1970–72	6.1.1948		P
733	Evans	Thomas Geoffrey	Geoff	7	1970–72	1.5.1942		L
734	Daniel	Laurance Thomas David	Laurie	1	1970	5.3.1942		W
735	Hopkins	Raymond	Ray 'Chico'	1	1970	8.7.1946		SH(rep)
736	Hughes	Keith	Keith	3	1970–74	15.12.1949		W/C
737	Shanklin	James Llewellyn	Jim	4	1970–73	11.12.1948		W/C
738	Lewis	Arthur John Llewellyn	Arthur	11	1970–73	26.9.1941		C
739	Mathias	Roy	Roy	1	1970	2.9.1949		W
740	Gallacher	Ian Stuart	Stuart	1	1970	22.5.1946		L
741	Bevan	John Charles	John	10	1971–73	28.10.1950		W
742	Roberts	Michael Gordon	Mike	8	1971–79	20.2.1946		L
743	Bergiers	Roy Thomas Edmond	Roy	11	1972–75	11.11.1950		C
744	Quinnell	Derek Leslie	Derek	23	1972–79	22.5.1949		8/F/L
745	Shaw	Glyndwr	Glyn	12	1972–77	11.4.1951		P
746	Llewellyn	Philip David	Phil	5	1973	12.5.1947		P
747	David	Thomas P.	Tommy	4	1973	2.4.1948		F
748	Williams	John James	John 'JJ'	30	1973–79	1.4.1948		W
749	Windsor	Robert William	Bobby 'Duke'	28	1973–79	31.1.1946		H
750	Martin	Allan Jeffrey	Allan 'Panther'	34	1973–81	11.12.1948		L
751	Shell	Robert Clive	Clive	1	1973	9.9.1947		SH (rep)
752	Cobner	Terence John	Terry	19	1974–78	10.1.1946		F
753	Rees	Clive Frederick William	Clive 'Billy-Whiz'	13	1974–83	6.10.1951		W
754	Finlayson	Alexander Alfred James	Alex	3	1974	18.3.1948		C
755	Williams	Walter P. John	Walter	2	1974	14.12.1943	10.3.1985	P
756	Wheel	Geoffrey Arthur Derek	Geoff	32	1974–82	30.6.1951		L
757	Robinson	Ian Robert	Ian	2	1974	21.2.1944		L
758	Blyth	William Roger	Roger	6	1974–80	2.4.1950		FB
759	Fenwick	Steven Paul	Steve	30	1975–81	23.7.1951		C
760	Gravell (now changed to Gravel)	Raymond William Robert	Ray	23	1975–82	12.9.1951		C
761	Bevan	John David	John	4	1975	12.3.1948	5.6.1986	OH
762	Faulkner	Anthony George	Charlie	19	1975–79	27.2.1941		P
763	Price	Graham	Graham	41	1975–83	24.11.1951		P
764	Evans	Trefor Pryce	Trevor	10	1975–77	26.11.1947		F

CAP NO.	SURNAME	CHRISTIAN NAMES	KNOWN AS	TOTAL CAPS	FROM/TO	DATE OF BIRTH	DATE OF DEATH	POSITION
765	Knill	Franklyn Michael David	Mike	1	1976	22.12.1941		P (rep)
766	Burcher	David Howard	David	4	1977	26.10.1950		C
767	Squire	Jeffrey	Jeff	29	1977–83	23.9.1951		8/F
768	Burgess	Robert Clive	Clive	9	1977–82	25.11.1950		F
769	Evans	Gareth Lloyd	Gareth	3	1977–78	2.11.1952		W
770	Williams	Clive	Clive	8	1977–83	2.11.1948		P
771	Davies	William Gareth	Gareth 'Majid'	21	1978–85	29.9.1955		OH
772	Williams	David Brynmor	Brynmor	3	1978–81	29.10.1951		SH
773	Lane	Stuart Morris	Stuart	3	1978–80	12.11.1952		F
774	Donovan	Alun John	Alun	5	1978–82	5.10.1955		FB/C
775	Holmes	Terence David	Terry	25	1978–85	10.3.1957		SH
776	Davis	Clive Enoch	Clive	3	1978–81	17.9.1949		8/L
777	Richardson	Stanley John	John	2	1978	1.4.1947		P
778	Ringer	Paul	Paul	8	1978–80	28.1.1948		F
779	Rees	Harold Elgan	Elgan	13	1979–83	5.1.1954		W
780	Richards	David Stuart	David	17	1979–83	23.5.1954		C/W
781	Clegg	Barry George	Barry	1	1979	30.10.1951		L
782	Phillips	Allan John	Alan	15	1979–82	21.8.1954		H
783	Griffiths	Clive Ronald	Clive	1	1979	2.4.1954		FB (rep)
784	Keen	Leslie	Les	4	1980	13.11.1954		W
785	Butler	Edward Thomas	Eddie	16	1980–84	8.5.1957		8
786	Morgan	Peter John	Peter	4	1980–81	1.1.1959		C/OH
787	Ackerman	Robert Angus	Rob	22	1980–85	2.3.1961		W/C
788	Williams	Gareth Powell	Gareth	5	1980–82	6.11.1954		8/F
789	Nicholas	David Llewellyn	David	4	1981	3.3.1955		W
790	Stephens	Ian	Ian 'Ikey'	13	1981–87	25.5.1952		P
791	Lewis	John Rhodri	Rhodri	7	1981–82	25.2.1959		F
792	Evans	Gwyn	Gwyn	10	1981–83	6.9.1957		FB/C
793	Pearce	Peter Gareth	Gary	3	1981–82	11.11.1960		OH
794	Williams	Gerald	Gerald	4	1981–82	21.10.1954		SH
795	Daniels	Patrick Charles Thomas	Pat	2	1981–82	15.5.1957		C
796	Moriarty	Richard Daniel	Dick	22	1981–87	1.5.1957		L/8/F
797	Davies	Mark	Mark	3	1981	9.7.1958		F
798	Sutton	Stephen	Steve	9	1982–87	17.2.1958		L
799	Norster	Robert Leonard	Bob	34	1982–89	23.6.1957		L
800	Wyatt	Mark Anthony	Mark	10	1983–87	12.2.1957		FB
801	Ring	Mark Gerarde	Mark 'Ringo'	32	1983–91	15.10.1962		OH/C/FB
802	Dacey	Malcolm	Malcolm	15	1983–87	12.7.1960		OH/FB
803	James	William John	Billy	21	1983–87	18.7.1956		H
804	Pickering	David Francis	David	23	1983–87	16.12.1960		F
805	Jones	Stephen Thomas	Staff	10	1983–88	4.1.1959		P
806	Eidman	Ian Harold	Ian	13	1983–86	31.10.1957		P
807	Perkins	Sydney John	John 'Perky'	18	1983–86	27.2.1954		L
808	Donovan	Richard Evan	Richie	1	1983	20.1.1963		W (rep)
809	Titley	Mark Howard	Mark	15	1983–86	3.5.1959		W
810	Bowen	Bleddyn	Bleddyn	24	1983–89	16.7.1961		C/OH
811	Hadley	Adrian Michael	Adrian	27	1983–88	1.3.1963		W
812	Giles	Raymond	Ray	3	1983–87	15.1.1961		SH
813	Shaw	Terence Windsor	Terry	1	1983	9.8.1962		L
814	Brown	Mark Anthony	Mark 'Shaft'	6	1983–86	18.12.1958		F
815	Davies	Howell	Howell	4	1984	6.6.1959		FB
816	Douglas	Mark Henry James	Mark	3	1984	10.12.1960		SH
817	Morgan	Gerwyn Rhys	Rhys	1	1984	9.6.1954		P
818	Watkins	Michael John	Mike 'Spike'	4	1984	9.1.1952		H
819	Lewis	Philip Ivor	Phil	8	1984–86	6.1.1961		W

CAP NO.	SURNAME	CHRISTIAN NAMES	KNOWN AS	TOTAL CAPS	FROM/TO	DATE OF BIRTH	DATE OF DEATH	POSITION
820	Bishop	David Joseph	Dai 'Bish'	1	1984	31.10.1960		SH
821	Davies	Alun Eirian	Alun	1	1984	25.3.1956		F
822	Whitefoot	Jeffrey	Jeff	19	1984–87	18.4.1956		P
823	Morris	Martyn Stuart	Martyn	11	1985–92	23.8.1962		F
824	Thorburn	Paul Huw	Paul	37	1985–91	24.11.1962		FB
825	Evans	Stuart	Stuart	9	1985–87	14.6.1963		P
826	Roberts	Gareth John	Gareth	7	1985–87	15.1.1959		F
827	Hopkins	Kevin	Kevin	7	1985–87	29.9.1961		C
828	Davies	Jonathan	Jonathan	32	1985–97	24.10.1962		OH
829	Davies	Philip Thomas	Philip 'Tulip'	46	1985–95	19.10.1963		F/8/L
830	Devereux	John Anthony	John	21	1986–89	30.3.1966		C
831	Jones	Robert Nicholas	Robert	54	1986–95	10.11.1965		SH
832	Waters	David Ralph	David 'Muddy'	4	1986	4.6.1955		L
833	Moriarty	William Paul	Paul	20	1986–88	16.7.1964		F/8
834	Webbe	Glenfield Michael Charles	Glen	10	1986–88	21.1.1962		W
835	Richards	Huw David	Huw	4	1986–87	9.10.1960		L
836	Evans	Ieuan Cenydd	Ieuan	72	1987–98	21.3.1964		W
837	Phillips	Kevin Huw	Kevin	20	1987–91	15.6.1961		H
838	Collins	Richard Graham	Richie	28	1987–95	2.3.1962		F
839	Francis	Peter William	Peter	1	1987	9.7.1957		P
840	Jones	Mark Alun	Mark	15	1987–98	22.6.1965		8/L
841	Blackmore	Steven Walter	Steve	4	1987	3.3.1962		P
842	Buchanan	David Anthony	Anthony 'Buks'	5	1987–88	30.6.1955		P
843	Young	David	David	39	1987–99	26.7.1967		P
844	Webster	Richard Eward	Richard	13	1987–93	9.7.1967		F
845	Pugh	Jeremy David	Jeremy	3	1987–90	4.3.1960		P
846	Russell	Stuart	Stuart	1	1987	29.5.1963		L
847	Phillips	Rowland David	Rowland	10	1987–89	28.7.1965		F
848	Clement	Anthony	Tony	37	1987–95	8.2.1967		FB/OH/W
849	May	Phillip Stephen	Phil	7	1988–91	1.7.1956		L
850	Watkins	Ian John	Ian	10	1988–89	10.3.1963		H
851	Bryant	David John	David	8	1988–89	21.2.1967		F
852	Hall	Michael Robert	Mike	42	1988–91	13.10.1965		C/W
853	Fauvel	Timothy John	Tim	1	1988	9.6.1960		F (rep)
854	Davies	Nigel Gareth	Nigel	29	1988–97	29.3.1965		C
855	Griffiths	Jonathan Lynn	Jonathan	2	1988	23.8.1964		SH
856	Moseley	Kevin	Kevin	9	1988–91	2.7.1963		L
857	Jones	Gary	Gary	5	1988–90	17.7.1960		8/F
858	Mason	Jonathan Edward	Jonathan	1	1988	13.6.1965		FB (rep)
859	Davies	Carwyn	Carwyn	4	1988–89	17.4.1964	9.2.1997	W
860	Griffiths	Michael	Mike	35	1988–98	18.3.1962		P
861	Hall	Wayne Hopkin	Wayne	1	1988	29.1.1958		H
862	Wakeford	John Donald Marshall	John	2	1988	29.9.1966		L
863	Wintle	Richard Vivian	Richard	1	1988	11.12.1967		W (rep)
864	Diplock	Richard Sean	Richard	1	1988	7.5.1965		W
865	Williams-Jones	Hugh	Hugh	17	1989–95	10.1.1963		P
866	Delaney	Laurance	Laurance	11	1989–92	8.5.1956		P
867	Turner	Paul	Paul	3	1989	13.2.1959		OH
868	Evans	David Wyn	David	12	1989–95	1.11.1965		OH/C
869	Emyr	Arthur (born as Arthur Emyr Jones)	Arthur	13	1989–91	27.7.1962		W
870	Llewellyn	Gareth Owen	Gareth	64	1989–99	27.2.1969		L/F

WELSH INTERNATIONAL PLAYERS

CAP NO.	SURNAME	CHRISTIAN NAMES	KNOWN AS	TOTAL CAPS	FROM/TO	DATE OF BIRTH	DATE OF DEATH	POSITION
871	Pugh	Phillip	Phil	1	1989	8.10.1959		F
872	Allen	Andrew George	Andy	3	1990	5.4.1967		L
873	Bateman	Allan Glen	Allan	22	1990–99	6.3.1965		C/W
874	Williams	Brian Richard	Brian	5	1990–91	9.7.1960		P
875	Perego	Mark Angelo	Mark	9	1990–94	8.2.1964		F
876	Ford	Stephen Paul	Steve	8	1990–91	15.8.1965		W
877	Edmunds	David Alan	Alun	2	1990	8.10.1961		W
878	Bridges	Christopher Jeffrey	Chris	7	1990–91	31.8.1968		SH
879	Knight	Paul	Paul	5	1990–91	30.4.1959		P
880	Llewellyn	Glyn David	Glyn	9	1990–91	9.8.1965		L
881	Arnold	Paul	Paul	16	1990–96	28.4.1968		L/8
882	Reynolds	Alan David	Alan	3	1990–92	24.1.1966		F
883	Parfitt	Stuart Ashley	Stuart	2	1990	4.3.1966		C
884	Williams	Owain Llewellyn	Owain	1	1990	10.10.1964		F
885	Williams	David Aled	Aled	2	1990–95	26.1.1964		Bck (rep)
886	Davies	Adrian	Adrian	9	1990–95	9.2.1969		OH
887	Gibbs	Ian Scott	Scott	45	1991–99	23.1.1971		C
888	Jenkins	Neil Roger	Neil	73	1991–99	8.7.1971		OH/C/FB
889	Carter	Alun Jonathan	Alun	2	1991	13.12.1964		F
890	George	Glenn Maxwell	Glen	2	1991	30.9.1964		F
891	Davies	John David	John	32	1991–96	1.2.1969		P
892	Lewis	Emyr Wyn	Emyr 'Tarw'	41	1991–96	29.8.1968		F/8
893	Davis	Mark Edwin	Mark	1	1991	18.9.1970		P
894	Jenkins	Garin Richard	Garin	50	1991–99	18.8.1967		H
895	Evans	Iwan Luc	Luc	1	1991	13.6.1971		Bck (rep)
896	Waters	Kenneth	Ken	1	1991	9.10.1961		H
897	Rayer	Michael Anthony	Mike	21	1991–94	21.7.1965		FB
898	Stephens	Colin John	Colin	4	1992	29.11.1969		OH
899	Copsey	Anthony Hugh	Tony	16	1992–94	25.1.1965		L
900	Davies	Stuart	Stuart	17	1992–98	2.9.1965		8/F
901	Bidgood	Roger Anthony	Roger	5	1992–93	15.9.1965		C
902	Proctor	Wayne Thomas	Wayne	38	1992–98	12.6.1972		FB/W
903	Meek	Nigel	Nigel	3	1993	20.10.1964		H
904	Evans	Richard Lloyd	Ricky	19	1993–95	23.6.1961		P
905	Walker	Nigel Keith	Nigel	17	1993–98	15.6.1963		W
906	Moon	Rupert Henry St John Barker	Rupert	18	1993–95	1.2.1968		SH
907	Lamerton	Andrew Edwin	Andrew	5	1993	28.5.1970		H
908	Hill	Simon David	Simon	12	1993–97	27.5.1968		W/C
909	Jones	Richard Lyn	Lyn	5	1993	25.1.1968		F
910	Boobyer	Neil	Neil	7	1993–99	11.6.1972		C
911	Quinnell	Leon Scott	Scott	33	1993–99	20.8.1972		F/8
912	Taylor	Hemi Takatou	Hemi	24	1994–97	17.12.1964		F/8
913	McBryde	Robin Currie	Robbie	3	1994–97	3.7.1970		H
914	Wilkins	Gwilym	Gwilym	1	1994	4.5.1967		W
915	John	Paul	Paul	10	1994–98	25.1.1970		SH
916	Buckett	Ian Martin	Ian	1	1994	23.12.1967		P
917	Williams	Stephen Michael	Steve	20	1994–97	3.10.1970		F/8
918	Taylor	Mark	Mark	20	1994–99	27.2.1973		C
919	Jones	Derwyn	Derwyn	19	1994–96	14.11.1970		L
920	Back	Matthew J.	Matthew	4	1995	5.4.1970		FB
921	John	Spencer Courtney	Spender	5	1995–97	19.10.1973		P
922	Gibbs	Andrew	Andrew	6	1995–97	20.3.1972		F
923	Thomas	Gareth	Gareth	40	1995–99	25.7.1974		W/C
924	Moore	Andrew Philip	Andy	4	1995–96	6.9.1968		SH
925	Roy	William Stuart	Stuart	1	1995	25.12.1968		L (rep)

CAP NO.	SURNAME	CHRISTIAN NAMES	KNOWN AS	TOTAL CAPS	FROM/TO	DATE OF BIRTH	DATE OF DEATH	POSITION
926	Humphreys	Jonathan Matthews	Jonathan	33	1995–99	27.2.1969		H
927	Prosser	Greg	Greg	1	1995	21.5.1966		L
928	Bennett	Anthony Mark	Mark	3	1995	26.1.1968		F
929	Thomas	William Justin Lloyd	Justin	9	1995–97	1.11.1973		FB
930	Jones	Gareth H.	Gareth	1	1995	31.5.1975		C
931	Loader	Christian David	Christian	19	1995–97	26.10.1973		P
932	Moore	Andrew Paul	Andrew	8	1995–99	25.1.1974		L
933	Mustoe	Lyndon	Lyndon	10	1995–98	30.1.1969		P
934	Quinnell	Jonathan Craig	Craig	20	1995–99	9.7.1975		F/L
935	Wintle	Matthew Edward	Matthew	1	1996	12.2.1972		C
936	Davies	Leigh Barry	Leigh	19	1996–99	20.2.1976		C
937	Thomas	Arwel Camber	Arwel	20	1996–98	8.11.1974		OH
938	Lewis	Andrew Leighton Paul	Andrew 'Alp'	21	1996–99	13.6.1973		P
939	Jones	Rhodri Gwyn	Gwyn	13	1996–97	5.10.1972		F
940	Howley	Robert	Robert	40	1996–99	13.10.1970		SH
941	Voyle	Michael John	Mike	21	1996–99	3.1.1970		L
942	James	Dafydd Rhys	Dafydd	23	1996–99	24.7.1975		W/C
943	Jones	Kingsley Philip	Kingsley	10	1996–98	19.6.1969		F
944	Williams	Martyn Elwyn	Martyn	13	1996–99	1.9.1975		F
945	Williams	Barry Hugh	Barry	12	1996–99	6.1.1974		H
946	Charvis	Colin Lloyd	Colin	25	1996–99	27.12.1972		F/8
947	Rowley	Mark Andrew	Mark	6	1996–97	18.11.1964		L
948	McIntosh	Dale Lynsay Manawa	Dale 'Chief'	2	1996–97	23.11.1969		F
949	Thomas	Nathan	Nathan	8	1996–98	22.1.1976		F/8
950	Morgan	Kevin Andrew	Kevin	8	1997–98	23.2.1977		FB
951	Anthony	Christopher Thomas	Chris	7	1997–99	23.9.1976		P
952	Moore	Stephen John	Steve	3	1997	20.7.1972		L
953	Appleyard	Robert Charles	Rob	9	1997–98	9.12.1972		F
954	Jarvis	Lee	Lee	1	1997	30.9.1976		OH (rep)
955	Wyatt	Gareth	Gareth	1	1997	4.3.1977		FB
956	Stephens	Christopher	Chris	1	1998	27.3.1975		L (rep)
957	Weatherley	David Julian	David	1	1998	9.5.1972		FB
958	Rees	Richard	Richard	1	1998	21.9.1971		W
959	Morris	Darren Raymond	Darren	6	198–99	24.9.1974		P
960	Hayward	Byron Idris	Byron	2	1998	22.2.1969		FB
961	Funnell	John	John	2	1998	16.9.1975		C
962	Wyatt	Christopher Philip	Chris	18	1998–99	10.6.1973		L
963	Evans	Garan Rhys	Garan	1	1998	16.2.1973		W
964	Gough	Ian	Ian	2	1998–99	10.11.1976		L
965	Williams	Darril	Darril	1	1998	20.9.1975		FB (rep)
966	Jones	Stephen Michael	Stephen	3	1998–99	8.12.1977		C (rep)
967	Lewis	Geraint	Geraint P.	5	1998–99	12.1.1974		F
968	Llewellyn	David Stephen	David	4	1998–99	29.9.1970		SH (rep)
969	Howarth	Shane Paul	Shane	16	1998–99	8.7.1968		FB
970	Evans	Ben Ross	Ben	10	1998–99	31.7.1975		P
971	Robinson	Matthew Fitz David	Matthew	4	1999	2.4.1973		W
972	Rogers	Peter John Daniel	Peter	12	1999	20.1.1969		P
973	Sinkinson	Brett David	Brett	11	1999	30.12.1970		F
974	Walne	Nicholas John	Nick	3	1999	18.9.1975		W
975	Jones-Hughes	Jason	Jason	2	1999	13.9.1976		W/C

The uncredited photographs in this book have been reproduced by kind permission of Howard Evans, Tim Auty and Les Williams